ANGLO-CATHOLIC CLASSICS

Writings produced, re-published or edited by the Oxford fathers (or their disciples) that underwrite the Anglo-Catholic tradition.

NASHOTAH HOUSE PRESS

Nashotah House Theological Seminary
2777 Mission Road
Nashotah, WI 53058

www.nashotah.edu

Cover design by Ben Jefferies

Printed 2019

THE DOCTRINE

OF

THE REAL PRESENCE,

AS CONTAINED IN THE FATHERS

FROM THE DEATH

OF S. JOHN THE EVANGELIST TO THE FOURTH GENERAL COUNCIL,

VINDICATED, IN

NOTES ON A SERMON,

"THE PRESENCE OF CHRIST IN THE HOLY

EUCHARIST,"

PREACHED A.D. 1853, BEFORE THE UNIVERSITY OF OXFORD.

BY THE REV.

E. B. PUSEY, D.D.

REGIUS PROFESSOR OF HEBREW; CANON OF CHRIST CHURCH;
LATE FELLOW OF ORIEL COLLEGE.

PRINTED FOR

JOHN HENRY PARKER, OXFORD, & 377, STRAND, LONDON:
SOLD ALSO BY
F. & J. RIVINGTON, WATERLOO PLACE, LONDON.

MDCCCLV.

THE DOCTRINE

OF

THE REAL PRESENCE,

AS CONTAINED IN THE FATHERS

FROM THE DEATH

OF S. JOHN THE EVANGELIST TO THE FOURTH GENERAL COUNCIL,

VINDICATED, IN

NOTES ON A SERMON,

"THE PRESENCE OF CHRIST IN THE HOLY

EUCHARIST,"

PREACHED A.D. 1853, BEFORE THE UNIVERSITY OF OXFORD.

BY THE REV.

E. B. PUSEY, D.D.

REGIUS PROFESSOR OF HEBREW; CANON OF CHRIST CHURCH;
LATE FELLOW OF ORIEL COLLEGE.

PRINTED FOR

JOHN HENRY PARKER, OXFORD, & 377, STRAND, LONDON:
SOLD ALSO BY
F. & J. RIVINGTON, WATERLOO PLACE, LONDON.
MDCCCLV.

TABLE OF CONTENTS.

CONTENTS.

ERRATA ET ADDENDA.

Page 77, note ², *for* 20 *read* 40
— 132, note ¹, *for* 119—131 *read* 121—124
— 147, line 11, *for* acts *read* arts
— 178, *on* Victor of Antioch, *see further*, No. 64, p. 600

Page 467. To the passages quoted from S. Ambrose, this should have been added:

"Let the triumphant victims [the martyrs] enter the place where Christ is the Sacrifice. But He upon the Altar, Who suffered for all; they under the Altar, who were redeemed by His Passion. This place I had destined for myself. For it is meet that a Priest should rest *there* where he was wont to offer. But I yield up the right side to the holy victims: that place was due to Martyrs." S. Ambros. Ep. 22, ad Marcellin. soror.

Page 614. The lines in which Prudentius speaks of the Martyrs under the heavenly Altar are—

Hæc sub Altari sita *sempiterno*
Lapsibus nostris veniam precetur
Turba, quam servat procerum creatrix
         Purpureorum.
               Peristeph. Hymn. 4, fin.

THE DOCTRINE,

&c.

NOTE A.

On p. 6.

*The belief that the Elements remain after Consecration in their
natural substances was not supposed of old to involve any
tenet of Consubstantiation.*

THE term "Transubstantiation" was a term, altogether new, framed by those who believed the doctrine which it was intended to express, in order to
express what they believed. The term "Consubstantiation" was a term invented by persons to
stigmatize a doctrine which they rejected, and, as
mis-stating that doctrine, has never been accepted by
those whose belief it was meant to stigmatize, and
did misrepresent. Moreover, although a new form
of word, it still was necessarily connected with a
Theological term, of very defined and familiar, but
wholly distinct meaning, "Consubstantial." It could
not then fail, in popular usage, to partake of the
meaning of that term; and yet, as far as it was
understood to have a kindred meaning, it was, *ipso
facto*, misunderstood. But for this, "Consubstantiation" might perhaps have been taken simply to

signify " causing two substances to *co-exist*, or exist simultaneously." But since "Consubstantial" meant " of one and the same substance with," "Consubstantiality" "the being of one and the same substance," it could not but be that "Consubstantiation" would be taken to mean "making two substances to be blended into one." "Consubstantiate" is accordingly now too taken to mean, "to unite or co-exist in the *same* substance." Whereas the doctrine which it was in later times intended to impugn, was, "that the outward elements not being destroyed, the Body and Blood of Christ, by virtue of our Lord's words of consecration, came to be present *there*, where were the bread and wine in their natural substances." "Co-existence," the term which Occam uses, would have been the natural term to adopt, had people wished to express the truth, not to throw a slur upon a doctrine which they rejected. By employing the word "Consubstantiation," opponents have succeeded in raising an almost insurmountable prejudice, that to believe the presence of "the Body and Blood of our Lord under the forms of bread and wine" is, not simply to believe their simultaneous existence there, but to introduce some sort of confusion or admixture between our Lord's Presence and the earthly elements.

Guitmundus, writing against Berengarius, speaks against those who, allowing that "the substance of the Body of Christ is in the food of the Lord, yet, no ways believing that the bread and wine are, by the words of the Saviour, changed into His Body and Blood, but commingling Christ with bread and wine (*Christum pane et vino commiscentes*), framed another and subtler heresy[1]." These seem to have used *à priori* arguments. But it is not clear whether Guitmundus' statement expresses his own deduction only or their meaning. He says (p. 461), "That Christ should be incarnate, the ground of man's redemption demanded. The Prophets foretold that it should be. That it *was*, Christ showed, Apostles preached, the world believed. But that Christ should be impanate or invinate, no ground requireth, nor did Prophets foretel, nor Christ show, nor Apostles preach, nor the world (except those very few heretics) believe. The whole world sings in unison, 'as the reasonable soul and flesh is one man, so God and Man is One Christ.' No one dareth to say, so God and Man, and bread and wine is one Christ. Whence then have they this new companation?"

If such had been the meaning of those against whom Guitmundus wrote, their belief would be that which has been spoken of as "assumption," *i.e.* that by some sort of analogy with the Incarnation, our Lord took the bread and wine to be personally united with Himself. But Guitmundus shows in the sequel, that what he is really opposing is, the belief—not

---

[1] De Euch. Sacr. iii. Bibl. Patr. t. 18, p. 460. Quoted by Hospinian, Hist. Sacr., l. iv. p. 306, who says that Guitmundus took his language from Lanfranc, de Euch. cont. Berengarium. But there is no such language in that book.

that there was any Consubstantiation, or blending of substances, but "that the elements remain in their natural substances," unaltered as to that substance by the Presence of the Body and Blood of Christ. For in opposing authorities to those whom he condemns, this is the point which he specifies. Thus he quotes the author of the "de Sacramentis" as teaching, not that "the Body and Blood of Christ *lie hid* ('latere') in the bread and wine, but that the bread and wine are changed into the Body and Blood of the Lord¹." And again, "These His impanators the Lord Jesus slays with the word of His mouth, when, taking bread, and giving thanks, and blessing, He says, 'This is My Body.' He does not say, 'In this My Body lieth hid.' Nor did He say, 'In this wine is My Blood,' but 'This is My Blood.'" "Whence the Church of God too in the Canon of the Mass, itself from Apostolic tradition, prays—not that the Body and Blood should lie hid in it, nor that the Body and Blood should come into it, but that the oblation itself should become both the Body and Blood."

To the first argument from our Lord's words Durandus answers, that in whatever way the word "this" is explained, if the accidents only are supposed to remain, in that same way it may be explained, if the substance remains. The words of the

¹ The author of the De Sacramentis did believe that the natural substances remained. The passage will be considered below, in Note O.

prayer, "that this oblation may become to us the Body and Blood of thy most-beloved Son our Lord Jesus Christ" imply an objective Presence, not a physical change. But each several instance shows that what those to whom he imputes "impanation" and "invination" really held, was that the Body and Blood of Christ was present "under the form of bread and wine," these "remaining in their natural substances."

This same conception is imputed by Bellarmine to Rupertus Abbas, A.D. 1111. He says, "The [3] error of Rupertus lies in this, that he thought that when the Eucharist is consecrated, the bread is not converted into the Body of Christ but that it is assumed by the Divine Word as the Humanity was assumed." Baronius says, without any such inference, "He [4] fell incautiously into the error of asserting that the very entire Body and Blood of Christ were, in such wise, truly present in the most holy Sacrament of the Eucharist, that yet the substance itself of the bread and wine also remained entire." The passage to which Baronius refers is expressed in a very unguarded way. Yet we may fairly suppose that Rupertus was only illustrating, in such manner as he might, the sacramental Presence, not explaining his belief through that illustration. Else his words would express not a Presence *under* the elements, but (as Bellarmine ascribes to him) an

[3] De Scriptt. Eccles. in Ruperto.
[4] A.D. 1111, fin.

hypostatic union with the elements.   And yet it is incredible that he should have thought this; and similar language is used by a contemporary writer, Odo, Archbishop of Cambray, A.D. 1105, who believed the annihilation of the physical substance of the elements.   He paraphrases the words, " Fac, Domine, nostram oblationem ascriptam, *i. e.* scriptam verbo ascriptam,—that it may become the precious Body of Christ, united to the Word of God, and conjoined in unity of Person [5]."

The passage of Rupertus is, " ' But[6] ye shall eat it,' he saith, ' only roast with fire,' that is, ye shall attribute the whole to the operation of the Holy Spirit, the effect of which is not to destroy or corrupt the substance which He takes to His own use, but to the good of the substance, remaining what it was, to add in an invisible manner what it was not.   So He destroyed not human nature, when by His operation God conjoined it, from the Virgin's womb, to the Word in Unity of Person.   So the substance of bread and wine, subjected, as to the outward form, to the five senses, He doth not change or destroy, when He conjoins them to the same Word in the unity of the same Body which hung on the Cross, and of the same Blood which He shed from His Side.   So, again, as the Word sent down from above became Flesh, not

[5] Sacr. Can. Expos. B. P. xxi. p. 224.   He is quoted by Waterland, " The Sacramental Part of the Eucharist explained," vol. 8, p. 248.   Ed. Van Mild.

[6] In Exod. ii. 10, fin.

changed into flesh, but taking flesh : so both bread and wine, raised from beneath, become the Body and Blood of Christ, not changed into the taste of flesh, nor into the terrific form of blood, but assuming, invisibly, the truth of the immortal substance which is in Christ, both Human and Divine. Accordingly, as we truly, and as Catholics, confess that Man, Who, born of a virgin, hung on the cross, was God, so we truly assert that that which we receive from the holy altar is Christ, the Lamb of God."

Rupertus expresses himself in the like way as to the remaining of the elements in the De Div. Off. ii. 9. Yet, again, it does not seem that he thought of any Personal union of our Lord with inanimate matter, nor does his language imply more than that our Lord vouchsafes to use it, as an instrument, whereby He conveys His Presence.

"The matter or substance of the Sacrifice, which then was, and now is, in the hands of our High Priest, is not simple, as neither had our High Priest Himself only a Divine, or only a Human, Substance. For in the High Priest and in the Sacrifice alike there is a Divine and an earthly Substance. The earthly in each is that which can be seen corporally or locally; the Divine, in each, is the invisible Word, Who was in the beginning God with God. For when the great High Priest, holding the bread and wine, said, 'This is My Body,' 'This is My Blood,' it was the Voice of the Incarnate Word, the Voice of Him Who was from everlasting, the Voice of the Counsellor of old. The Word which had taken human nature abiding in the flesh, took the substance of bread and wine, [Himself, Who is] the Life intervening, joined bread with His Flesh, wine with His Blood. As in earthly thoughts, the tongue interveneth between the mind and the bodily air, and joining both, maketh one discourse, which, being transmitted into the ears, is soon consumed, and passes away, but the meaning of the discourse abides whole and unconsumed, both in him who speaketh and in him who heareth; so the Word of the Father, intervening between the Flesh and Blood which He had taken of the Virgin's womb, and the bread and wine which He took from the altar, maketh one sacrifice, which when the priest distributeth into the mouths of the faithful, the bread and wine is consumed, and passeth away; but That which was born of the Virgin, together with the Word of the Father united with It, abideth both in heaven and in men, whole and unconsumed. But into him, in whom faith is not, besides the visible species of the bread and wine, nothing of the sacrifice cometh.—He who eateth the visible bread of the sacrifice, and by not believing repelleth the invisible from his heart, slayeth Christ, because he separateth life from that which is enlivened, and with his teeth teareth the dead body of the sacrifice, and is thereby guilty of the Body and Blood of the Lord '."

' A third passage to the same effect, in Joh. L. 6, is quoted by Bellarmine (de Sacr. Euch. iii. 11). Rupertus is also attacked as Walerannus by Thom. Wald., (de Sacr. Euch. c. 47,) defended by Gerberon, Apol. pro Rup. et Blanciotti notæ fus. ad Th. Wald.

It is the more probable that Rupertus intended only the co-existence of the Body and Blood of Christ with the substance of the bread and wine, because his statement reappears afterwards.

Aquinas mentions and rejects the opinion of the co-existence of the bread and wine with the Body and Blood of Christ, yet without calling it heresy. "Some [*] have laid down that the consecrated bread and wine can be converted into something else, and so can nourish, because the substance of bread remains together with the substance of the Body and Blood of Christ." "This," he says, "is repugnant to the words of Scripture. For that which the Lord said, 'This is My Body,' would not be true; since 'this' which is so pointed to, is bread; but it ought rather to be said 'here,' *i.e.* in this place, is My Body." Yet when St. John Baptist pointed to our Lord, "Behold the Lamb of God which taketh away the sins of the world," he so pointed to Him, notwithstanding His dress. The outward raiment with which He was covered, formed no hindrance. The outward part of the elements no more interfere with the "inward part," the Body and Blood of Christ, than the raiment which He wore, with His Presence in the Flesh. His garment was the means of communicating the indwelling Virtue which went forth from Him, because He so willed. The outward sign of the Sacrament conveys, by His appointment, His

---

[*] In 1 Cor. c. xi.   Lect. v. p. 75.

Presence, which He has been pleased, by virtue of the consecration, to place there.

At the same time Card. Bonaventura[9] mentions different *opinions* on this subject. "It was the *opinion* of some (which yet the Master [P. Lombard] does not put down, because it is an *opinion* of moderns, or perhaps because it is not very probable), that the whole bread is not changed according to its substance, but some essential part remains. For it is plain that the accidents remain according to their being and operation. Because it appears that they remain according to their being, there have been who said that the matter also remains, which supports them, and the form passes away. But this is nought, for the matter is not formed to sustain the accidents nor to be in act, save in the form. Others, seeing that the accidents have their operation, and all operation has its origin from the substantial form, said that the matter passes away and the form remains. But this again is nought, because the form only acts in matter. Wherefore, although that Sacrament is full of miracles, yet since those miracles only are assumed, which relate to the truth of the Sacrament and its concealment, therefore doctors *commonly* lay down that the whole passes into the whole, the accidents only remaining as a necessary and useful cause. Wherefore, leaving the first *opinion*, which takes away the conversion of the mat-

[9] iv. dist. ii. p. i. art. i. q. 2 (quoted by Field, App. to B. iii. c. 17).

ter, and the other, which takes away the conversion
of the form, let us hold *the more Catholic* [opinion]
that the whole bread is converted into the Body of
Christ, and that conversion is best called transubstantiation."

Durandus, as is well known, even declares that
this supposition, viz. that the elements remain in their
natural substances, but that the Body and Blood of
Christ are present under them, has the fewest difficulties.

"The [19] first question is, whether the Body of Christ
be in this Sacrament through the conversion of the
substance of bread into It, or whether after the consecration the substance of the bread and wine remains. It is argued that the substance of the bread
and wine do remain, because that is the rather to be
chosen, whence fewest difficulties ensue. But if it
be supposed that the substance of the bread and
wine remains, there ensueth one only difficulty, and
that not very great, nor insoluble, viz. that two
bodies exist together. Whereas, if it be supposed
that the substances do not remain, many difficulties
follow, viz. how such accidents can nourish or be
corrupted, and how any thing can be generated from
them.

"Moreover, that only is effected in this Sacrament, which is expressed by the form of the words.
But by these words, 'This is My Body,' the exist-

[19] In iv. dist. xi. q. 1. He was made Bishop of Meaux by the
Pope A. 1326, and of Annecy, in 1327.

ence or presence of the Body of Christ in this Sacrament is alone expressed, and there is altogether no mention whatever of the ceasing of the substance of bread, and of its conversion into the Body of Christ. Therefore it is not to be laid down."

Durandus then sets down the three objections, the two philosophical difficulties, (1) That two bodies cannot be in the same place. (2) Aquinas' abstract argument, that a thing cannot, even through miracle, be where it was not before, except by change in itself, or of another into itself. (3) The argument from the words " *This* is My Body."

He himself held the doctrine of Transubstantiation, as being determined by the [Western] Church. Yet he says :—

" It is not to be denied, that another mode is possible to God, viz. that God could effect that the Body of Christ should be in the Sacrament, the substance of bread remaining. For all hold that God can do whatever does not imply a contradiction. But, that the Body of Christ should be in this Sacrament, without conversion of the substance of the bread into Itself, no more implies a contradiction, than that it should be in the Sacrament, the conversion having taken place. As then one is possible, so is the other."

For the only grounds, he says, are in one of the above arguments.

"But (1) in the first, the argument [that two

bodies cannot be in one place] destroys itself.   For the Body of Christ, which can exist together with a quantity foreign to Itself, can exist together with the substance subject to that quantity.   For there is no hindrance to the co-existence of two bodies, save by reason of the quantity, whose property it is to exclude another quantity from the same site. But the Body of Christ can co-exist with the quantity of bread.   For this is presupposed by every opinion which supposes that the true Body of Christ is in this Sacrament.   Therefore as easily can It co-exist with the substance of bread, remaining under its own quantity."

(2) Of Aquinas' abstract argument about a body being where it was not before, Durandus denies both premisses.   The major, because there can be change which is not conversion; the minor, because the Body of Christ, being anew in the Sacrament, is not *where* it was not before; because to be in the Sacrament is not to have a new *where* [i.e. locality]. He says, "It seemeth to derogate from the boundlessness of the Divine power to say that God could not cause His Body to be in the Sacrament in any other way, than by the conversion of the substance of the bread into itself; especially since, granting that the conversion does take place, it is most difficult to see, in what way this contributes to the presence of the Body of Christ in this Sacrament.   It is plain (he subjoins) that it is rash to say, that through the Divine power the Body of Christ cannot

be present in the Sacrament, save through the conversion of the bread into It."

(3) To the argument from the words, "This is My Body," he answers that the words "This is My Body" remain equally true, whether the substance or the accidents only be present; for the word "this" no more specifies the substance than the accidents, but may in either case equally apply to the Body of Christ then present.

He subjoins the remarkable avowal, "If this mode [the substance remaining] were true in fact, many doubts which occur as to this Sacrament, when it is held that the substance of bread does not remain, would be solved. For it is doubted how any thing can be nourished from this Sacrament, or the species can be corrupted, or any thing can be generated from them; all which would be saved according to nature in that other way, as they would be saved if the nature of bread and wine were not assumed to the nature of the Sacrament. For they are supposed to remain after the consecration."

Durandus concludes by submitting himself to the determination of the [Western] Church.

Shortly afterwards, Occam maintained the possibility of the co-existence of the substance of the elements with the Body and Blood of Christ, in language which was subsequently in great measure adopted by Cardinal d'Ailly. He made a distinction between the "substance" and the "primary substance," and so gave as one mode of explanation, "that the substance of the bread remains there, and therewith that the Body of Christ co-exists with the substance of the bread, so that the primary substance forsakes the accidents, not the secondary, but co-exists only [1]." "This explanation," he says, "is evident; since it can take place through the simple co-existence of the true Body of Christ with the substance of the bread, because quantity is no less repugnant to quantity, or substance to quantity, than substance to substance. But quantity can co-exist in the same place with other quantity, as is clear as to larger bodies existing in the same place. In like way substance can co-exist in the same place with another quantity. This is clear as to the Body of Christ. The other therefore is possible."

He then continues in language which will be given below, but slightly altered by Cardinal d'Ailly, and sums up, "Yet since there exists a determination of the Church to the contrary, as appears, 'Extra. de summa Trinitate et fide Cath. [2], et de celebr. miss. [3],' and commonly Doctors hold that the substance of bread does not remain there, therefore I too hold the same."

[1] In iv. q. 6, init.

[2] The decree of Innocent III. in the Fourth Lateran Council in Decr. Greg. I. 1. This was clearly no part of the Council itself. It does not occur in the Greek, and contains the doctrine of the double Procession, in the form which the Greeks would not have received. In the Decretals it is quoted "*Innocentius III. in Concilio generali.*"

[3] Innocent III. in Decr. Greg. III. 41. 6.

Occam speaks more clearly, in his "Centilogium Theologicum [1]:" "The third opinion is that which lays down that the bread of the Host is transubstantiated into the Body of Christ, not that it is in any way converted into the Body of Christ, as the first opinion supposes, nor that the bread ceases to be, as the second supposes. But, according to that way of understanding it, this transubstantiation into the Body of Christ is nothing else than that the Body of Christ, by virtue of the sacramental words, as a whole and with each part thereof, co-exists with each part of the bread; and then, according to that opinion, the accidents of the Host do not exist without any subject, after consecration, but they are in the bread as their subject, as before. And they who so think say, that it is not an article of faith to believe that the bread through transubstantiation ceases to be, but that it is so, to believe that the true Body of Christ through transubstantiation exists in the consecrated Host. And the Master [P. Lombard] touches on that opinion in the 4th book, and does not much disapprove it. And according to that opinion, all appearances would be easily solved, *i. e.* nourishment from the consecrated Host, and corruption of the Host from length of time, and so as to many others. But because that opinion is not commonly held, the conclusion has been laid down according to the second opinion, which by moderns chiefly is accounted contrary to the rest."

[1] Concl. 39.

Innocent III., whose decree at the Fourth Lateran Council contains the statement on Transubstantiation, subsequently appealed to, does, in his own work on the Holy Eucharist, speak of those as heretical who supposed the bread to be a mere figure [5], but does not in any way blame those who said that it remained.

"' He [6] brake.' Many inquire, few understand, what Christ then brake at the table, and what the Priest now breaketh at the altar. There were who said, that as the true accidents of bread remain after consecration, so also the true substance of bread. For as a subject cannot subsist without accidents, so accidents cannot exist without a subject; because the being of an accident is nothing but the being *in* another thing. But the substances of the bread and wine remaining, the Body and Blood of Christ do, at the utterance of those words, begin to be truly under them, so that under the same accidents Both are truly received, the bread and the Flesh, and the wine and the Blood, of which sense proves the one, faith believes the remainder. These say that the substance of the bread is broken and crushed, alleging to this end what the Apostle says, ' the bread which we break,' and Luke, ' on the first day of the week when we meet together to break bread.' These easily solve that question, ' What is eaten by a

---

[5] De Myst. Missæ, c. 7, noticed by Mr. Palmer, On the Church, b. iv. c. xi. s. 2.

[6] Ib. c. 9.

mouse, when the Sacrament is gnawed?' For according to them, that substance of bread is eaten, under which the Body of Christ forthwith ceases to be."

Scotus, nearly a century after the Council of Lateran, sets down strongly the principles in favour of the opinion that the substance of bread remains[1]. " In matters of faith, more things are not to be laid down, than can be evinced from the truth of what we believe; but the truth of the Eucharist can be maintained without that transubstantiation; therefore, etc. This last can be proved, because for the truth of the Eucharist there is required a sign and a thing signified, really contained. But the substance of bread, with its accidents, may be a sign as well as the accidents alone, nay more. For the substance of bread under the species is nourishment more than the mere accidents; therefore it represents the Body of Christ in regard to spiritual nourishment. That also which is contained, viz. the true Body of Christ, can equally be maintained with the substance of the bread as with the accidents; for it is no more inconsistent that substance should co-exist with substance, than with the quantity of that substance."

" 1. This is confirmed, in that the fewest miracles are to be assumed, which may be. But by supposing that bread remains together with its accidents, and that the Body of Christ is truly there, fewer mira-

[1] In iv. dist. xi. q. 3. n. 3.

cles are assumed, than by supposing that the bread is not there. For then an accident without a subject would not be assumed.

"2. (which comes to the same,) In matters of belief, handed down to us generally, a mode is not to be fixed upon, which is most difficult to understand, and which is attended by most inconveniences. But that the Body of Christ is delivered in the Holy Eucharist, is a truth delivered to us generally. But this way of understanding it, that the substance of the bread is not there, seems more difficult to maintain, and fewer inconveniences follow thereon, than if we suppose that the substance of the bread is there. Therefore, etc. The principle above stated is proved, because, since the faith has been given to us to be a way to salvation, it ought, as it seems, so to be determined and held by the Church, as most tends to salvation. But to lay down any way of understanding it, which is above measure difficult and which evidently involves inconveniences, becomes an occasion of repelling from the faith all philosophers, nay, almost all who follow natural reason. At least, it becomes an occasion of hindering them from being converted to the faith, if it be told them that such things belong to our faith. Nay, it would seem that a philosopher or any one who followed natural reason would regard what is here laid down, in denying the substance of the bread, a greater inconvenience than he would find in all the articles which relate to the Incarnation. And it seems strange, why in one article which is not a main article of faith, such a way of understanding it should be asserted, as lays faith open to the contempt of all who follow reason.

"3. Nothing is to be maintained as of the substance of faith, except what can be expressly derived from Scripture, or has been expressly declared by the Church, or which evidently follows from something plainly contained in Holy Scripture or plainly determined by the Church. This principle seems adequate. For a man would have no ground for exposing himself to death for any thing else ; while for all which belongs the substance of the faith, he would laudably expose himself to death. It would too seem to betray levity, to believe firmly what is in none of these ways certain. For if there be none of these grounds, there is no sufficient authority or reason. But it does not seem to be contained expressly, that the substance of bread does not exist there. For John 6, where the truth of the Eucharist is greatly set forth, is clear, where Christ saith, " I am the Bread of life; he that eateth of this bread," &c. ; and Paul says (1 Cor.), " The bread which we break, is it not the communion of the Body of Christ ?" nor is any place found, where the Church solemnly determines this truth, nor does it appear how it can be evidently inferred from any thing evidently believed.

" If you say, as one doctor saith [s], that 'when He saith, This is My Body, he expressly implies that the bread does not remain, for then the proposition would be false,' this has no constraining force. For, granting that the substance of bread remains, the substance of bread is not pointed out, but what is contained under the bread; as now the accidents are not pointed out, for then the proposition would be false. But the meaning is, 'This which is contained under this visible sign is My Body.'"

Also, in sacraments of truth, there ought to be nothing untrue. But those accidents naturally imply the substances which they assert. And if their substance be not there, this which they naturally designate will be false. This is an inconvenience. If you say that they signify the Body and Blood of Christ, and this signification is true, still, the natural signification is not changed on account of a signification annexed by the institution. So then those accidents naturally signify what they signified before. So then, on that side, there will be something false in the natural significancy, unless the things signified exist under the signs. But provided that they do so exist, then the natural signification of the accidents remains true.

Scotus answers at length the objections raised by Aquinas to the belief that the elements remain. To the argument from the words, "This is My

---

[s] Aquinas, hic. art. 1. q. 1, and 3 p. q. 75. n. 2.

Body," he answers, Both are true, '*this* is My Body,' and '*here* is My Body;' but then '*this*' is not *this* accident, but *this* which is contained under the accident. In the same way, if the bread *were*, not '*this* which is the substance of the bread' would be 'the Body,' but *this* which is contained under the bread is 'the Body.' But the Saviour willed to use this word *this*, rather than *here*, because the truth is more fully expressed, although either way of speaking would be true.

Scotus sums up, "it is *commonly* held, that neither does the bread remain (against the first opinion), nor is it annihilated or resolved into primary matter (against the second), but is converted into the Body of Christ." This he grounds chiefly on the decree of Pope Innocent in the Fourth Lateran Council. His arguments all turn on the supposition that nothing could be evidently proved from Holy Scripture (which he still held), or had been clearly laid down by the Church. They admitted then of a ready answer, on the supposition that the Church had decided, although the fact seems very questionable, whether the decree at the Council of Lateran was intended to assert any thing more than the Real Presence.

At the close of the same century, the celebrated Peter d'Ailly still speaks of the remaining of the elements as an open question, although he himself held the contrary, thinking that the Church leant that way. He became Bishop of Cambray A.D. 1396, and was made Cardinal A.D. 1411.   He was present at the Council of Pisa; and "President [9] at the 3rd session of the Council of Florence, and for three whole years a very influential member of it."

He says, then, in his work on the "Sentences [1]," " As to the third article, whether the bread is transubstantiated into the Body of Christ, you must know, that although Catholics are agreed herein that the Body of Christ is truly and principally in the sacrament under the forms of bread and wine, or where · the forms are visible, yet, as the Master recites [2], and the gloss ' de celebr. miss. *cum Marthæ*,' there were divers *opinions* as to the mode of supposing this.

" The first was, that the substance of the bread becomes the Body of Christ.   And some of those who hold this, said that although the bread becomes the Body of Christ, yet it is not to be granted that that substance is any way the flesh of Christ, because, as they say, the substance of the bread, after it is made the Flesh of Christ, is not the substance of bread but the substance of Flesh.

" But this opinion cannot be sustained.   And first as to the first part.   It is plain that it is not intelligible, unless it be laid down that the bread becomes part of the Body of Christ, as it is said, ' the farina becomes bread,' because it becomes part of it, &c.,

---

[9] Cave, A.D. 1396.

[1] Cameracensis in iv. sent. q. 6. art. 2. f. 265.

[2] Dist. xi.

which no one supposes. Secondly, as to the second part. This is simply intelligible, because if that which was bread is the Body of Christ, it follows that bread is the Body of Christ, which it implies. Whence against this opinion would be that rule, that every affirmative proposition, in which that term, 'the Body of Christ,' is predicated of that term 'bread,' is false, whether the copula be the verb *is*, or *can*, or *becomes*, as 'this bread is the Body of Christ,' or 'may be' or 'may become the Body of Christ,' or 'the bread becomes the Body of Christ.' And if any such be found in the sayings of the saints, they are false in matter of language, but are to be understood in a good sense, which will appear in the clearing up of the last opinion.

"The second opinion was, that the substance of bread does not remain bread, and yet does not simply cease to be, but is reduced into matter, subsisting by itself or receiving another form, and this whether in the same place or in another, and that the Body of Christ co-exists with the accidents of bread, and this opinion could not be disproved either by evident reason or by cogent authority of scripture, as is plain if we consider it.

"The third opinion was, that the substance of bread remains, and this may be imagined in two ways. In one way, as the Master rehearses, that it remains there where the Body of Christ begins to be, and thus the substance of the bread would be said to pass into the substance of the Body, because where this is, the Body beginneth to be. In another way, it might be imagined, that the substance of bread suddenly retires from its own place to another place, and the accidents would remain in the same place without a subject, and the Body of Christ would co-exist with them there.

" This opinion, as to the first mode, is possible; because it is exceeding (valde) possible that the substance of the Bread should co-exist with the substance of the body, nor is it more impossible that two substances should co-exist than two qualities. Wherefore, &c. But whether the Body of Christ could co-exist with the substance of the bread *by union,* is doubtful. And it might be said, that if it be possible that one creature should sustain another (as some say, and it is apparent that there is no repugnance, nor does it seem that it could be disproved by evident reason), then it is possible that the Body of Christ might assume the substance of bread by union. But, however this may be, it is plain that this mode is possible, nor is it repugnant to reason or *to the authority of the Bible.* Nay, *it is easier to understand, and more reasonable* than any of the others, because it supposes that the substance of bread conveyeth (*deferat*) the accidents, and not that the substance of the Body of Christ doth so. And thus it does not suppose accidents without a subject, which is one of the difficulties here supposed.

" But if it be said, that it seemeth a greater difficulty that two bodily substances should be together, I say no. For it is not more difficult than that two quantities or qualities should be together, or one substance and a quantity. And that species of the Host is not more compatible with (*compatitur*) another Host, than a substance with species is with another Host or substance; because that consecrated Host excludes (*repugnat*) another Host[3]. And so no inconvenience seemeth to follow from that first mode of supposing, if yet it would agree (*concordaret*) with the determination of the Church.

"But also the aforesaid opinion, as to the second mode, is possible, because it is not impossible to God that the substance of bread should suddenly be elsewhere, the species remaining in the same place and the Body of Christ co-existing with them. Yet this mode would not be so reasonable as the first; because it would suppose accidents without a subject, and a motion of the bread on a sudden, and the substance of bread without accidents, and that it suddenly had new accidents, which things are difficult. Wherefore, &c.

"4. The fourth *opinion* is *more common*, that the substance of bread doth not remain, but simply ceases to be. The possibility whereof is plain. For it is not impossible to God that that substance should suddenly cease to be, although it is not possible

---

[3] The argument seems to be, "on the supposition that the substance of the elements upon consecration ceases to exist, there would be in two Hosts only the accidents of the bread, and our Lord's Body in both." Therefore on this belief the accidents alone, without the substance, exclude the presence of each other.

through created power.   And although it *does not follow evidently from Scripture* that it is so, *nor* either, *as far as I can see, from the determination of the Church*, yet since the Church rather favours it, and the common opinion of saints [fathers] and doctors, therefore I hold it.   And according to this way, I say that the bread is transubstantiated into the Body of Christ in the meaning set forth in the description of transubstantiation."

Soon after this, Cardinal Caietan[4] distinguishes the two questions, one that the Body of Christ is under the consecrated Host; the other as to the conversion of the substance of the bread into the Substance of the Body of Christ.   Of the first he says, " we all confess that the Body of Christ, before not contained under this Host, is now truly contained, *although about the mode in which* it is contained there are (as will be said hereafter) various *opinions*.   On the second, he says, although all affirm in words a conversion *de novo*, yet in substance, many, not thinking that they do so, deny it.   And these are divided manifoldly, in that some understand by conversion identity of place, so that the bread should be said to become the Body of Christ, because where the bread is, there is the Body of Christ" (as P. Lombard[5] quotes and rejects).   Others understand by the name of conversion, an order of succession, as the Master [P. Lombard] mentions there, that the bread may

<hr>

[4] In p. 3. q. 75. art. 1.   [5] iv. dist. xi.

be said in that sense to be converted into the Body
of Christ, because after consecration the Body of
Christ is under the accidents under which the bread
was, which bread they said was annihilated or resolved into the fore-existing matter. This *opinion*
Scotus in the main follows, though more cautious in
opining, laying down that the bread is incidentally
reduced to nothing, and he calls the conversion adductive of Christ's Body thereto that It is present
to the accidents of bread. But as to the substance,
it comes to the same with the opinion mentioned
by the Master, because in reality the bread is not
converted into any thing, but parts into nothing,
and therefore in name only he lays down the conversion of the bread into the Body of Christ. But
some admit the conversion, both in name and substance, yet partially; of whom is Durandus, who lays
down that the matter of bread is turned into the
Body of Christ, because it begins to be informed
with the form of the Body of Christ, as nourishment is informed with the form of the person nourished, but the form of bread ceaseth to be (rejected
as erroneous by Pet. de Palude). Some, wholly admitting both name and substance of conversion, say
that the bread is converted into the Body of Christ,
not according to its substance, but according to its
sacramental being. This opinion Pet. de Pal. holds,
without however asserting it. "This," Caietan says,
" is alien from the truth, because it retains the word
transubstantiation in name only, because, in fact, the

substance of bread is turned into accident, and not into the substance of the Body of Christ. The *common* sentiment is, that the substance of the bread is converted into the substance of the Body of Christ, without any addition, without any increase in the substance of the Body of Christ."

Hurtado [6], early in the 17th century, (A.D. 1628,) sums up the question clearly, even on Roman ground. After mentioning briefly Bonaventura [7], Capreolus [8], Marsilius [9], and Ferrariensis [10], as taking the ground of Aquinas, he adds, "Scotus [11], however, Durandus [12], Richard [13], [à Media Villa,] Sotus [14], Caietan [15], Suarez [16], Vazquez [17], teach, that the Body of Christ, being in Heaven or in another place, and continuing there, could at least sacramentally be present under the species of bread, the proper substance of bread remaining under those species; because there is in this no contradiction nor repugnance. For if there were such, it would be either (1) that the Body of Christ, being and abiding circumscriptively in Heaven or in any other place, should be at the same time present in another; or (2) that two substances

[6] De Euch. Disp. 4. diff. xi.

[7] 4. dist. xi. p. 1.

[8] q. 1. art. 3.

[9] 4. q. 8.

[10] c. Gent. 4. 63.

[11] 4. d. 10.

[12] Dist. xi. q. 1.

[13] Art. 1. q. 1.

[14] Dist. 9. q. 2. art. 2.

[15] q. 75. art. 1.

[16] Disp. 49. 1. Suarez says that "this is the more common opinion of Theologians," on iv. d. 10, and adds the names of Gabriel, Major, and others, Ledesma, q. 16, art. 2, and claims also Ferrar. ad iv. Scoti cont. 2 dict. D. Thomæ.

[17] Disp. 182.

should be present in the same place; or (3), specially,
that a distinct substance should be present together
with accidents, whose own substance is and continues present.   But there is no repugnance (1) that
the Body of Christ, existing and continuing circumscriptively in Heaven or in another place, should
at the same time become present, at the least sacramentally in another; because, in fact, being and
continuing circumscriptively in Heaven, it becomes
sacramentally present with the quantity and other
accidents of bread existing in each.   Nor (2) that
two substances should be present together in the
same place; because that happened, even circumscriptively, in the Birth of Christ of a Virgin,
when the Body of Christ was penetrated together
with the Body of the Virgin, and in the Ascent of
Christ into the Heavens, wherein the Body of Christ
was penetrated together with them.   Nor (3) that a
distinct substance should become present to accidents, where one substance continues to be present;
because there is no solid ground for saying that God
cannot make a distinct bodily substance present to
accidents whose own substance continues to be
present, because the proper substance and one
distinct can be present together in the same place;
for the distinct substance, if it does not, by reason
of its accidents, remain cognizable by men, will be
hidden under the accidents of the other substance.

"I add, that the Body of Christ not only can
become present under the species of bread, the

substance of the bread abiding under them, but moreover while it abides, it can be united with them."

The remaining, then, of the "elements in their natural substances" was an open question at the beginning of the fifteenth century, and, so far from being supposed to involve any bad consequences, was rather held to remove difficulties. In all these discussions the term Consubstantiation was not used. Suarez even admits that the "old opinion was" (what he sets down as an error), that "the matter of bread remains[1]." The term was invented by the Zwinglians, who believed no sacred Presence at all, and was used as a term of reproach against any belief in an Objective Presence of "the Blessed Body and Blood of our Saviour Christ under the form of Bread and Wine," such as is recognized in our Book of Homilies.

[1] To be the subject of the accidents, and of the whole conversion. He refers for his statement to Bonavent. d. 11. art. 1. q. 2; and Scot. q. 3. art. 2; and says that "it is attributed to Ægidius, 'Theorem. 1 and 2."

NOTE B.

On p. 16.

Consubstantiation was not held by the Lutheran body; statement of the belief expressed in the Lutheran Articles and held by Luther.

THE doctrine of the Real Presence was stated in the first German Confession in words resembling those used in our Homilies. "Of the Supper of the Lord, it is taught that the very Body and Blood of Christ are verily present in the Lord's Supper under the form of bread and wine, and are distributed and taken in it." In the Confession of A.D. 1530, the important words "under the form of bread and wine" were omitted, but the Real Presence was still stated. "Of the Supper of the Lord, they teach that the Body and Blood of Christ are truly present, and are distributed to Communicants [vescentibus] in the Supper of the Lord, and they disapprove of those who teach otherwise."

The "Apology for the Confession" added the word "substantially," and defended the doctrine by Holy Scripture, and by the consent of the Latin and Greek Churches[1].

"The tenth Article is approved, in which we confess that we think, that in the Supper of the Lord, the Body and Blood of Christ are truly and substantially present, and are truly exhibited with

[1] Tittman, Libri Symbolici, p. 123.

those things which are visible, the bread and wine, to those who receive the sacrament.   This judgment we, having diligently considered and agitated the matter, steadfastly maintain.   For whereas Paul says, that the bread is the communion of the Body of Christ, it would follow that it is a communion, not of the Body, but only of the Spirit of Christ, unless the Body of the Lord were truly present.   And we learn that the Roman Church is not alone in affirming the corporal presence of Christ, inasmuch as the Greek Church both now so holdeth, and held so formerly. For the Canon of the Mass among them so attests, wherein the priest distinctly prays, that the bread being changed, it may become the Body of Christ. And the Bulgarian, [Theophylact,] no mean writer, (we think,) says plainly, that the bread is not a figure only, but is truly changed into flesh.   And S. Cyril teaches at length, on John, chap. 13, that Christ is exhibited to us corporally in the Supper.   For he saith, ‘We do not deny that we are spiritually united with Christ by faith and sincere love; but we deny altogether, that there is no union with Him according to the flesh.   This, we say, is altogether alien from the Divine Scriptures.   For who doubts but that Christ is thus also the vine, we the branches, who thence gain life to ourselves?   Hence Paul’s saying, that we are all one body in Christ, because, although many, we are yet one in Him.   For we are all partakers of that one bread.   Thinketh he that the virtue of the mystical blessing [Eucharist] is

D

unknown to us?   But this, coming to be in us, doth it not, by the communication of the Body of Christ, cause Christ to dwell in us, corporeally, too?'   And a little afterwards, 'Whence we ought to consider that Christ is in us, not only by that relation which is through love, but also by a natural participation.' These things we have recited, that whoever reads may clearly perceive that we maintain the doctrine received in the whole Church, that in the Supper of the Lord, the Body and Blood of Christ are truly and substantially present, and are truly exhibited together with the things which are seen, bread and wine.   We speak of the Presence of living Christ. For we know that death shall no more have dominion over Him."

In the Articles of Smalcald, A. D. 1537, it is said, "vi. Of the Sacrament of the Altar, we think that the bread and wine are the very Body and Blood, and are given and taken not only by pious, but also by impious Christians."   Communion under one kind is rejected, as not being "the whole ordination and institution, made, delivered, and commanded by Christ," although it is admitted that "it may perhaps be true that there may be as much under one kind as under both."   Transubstantiation is rejected, as stating that "bread and wine quit and lose their natural substance, and that only the appearance and colour of bread, and not true bread remains[2]."

In the Lesser Catechism, it is taught, "The Sacra-

<hr>

[2] Ib. p. 254.

ment of the Altar is the Very Body and Very Blood of our Lord Jesus Christ, under bread and wine, instituted by Christ Himself, for us Christians to eat and drink."

In the Larger Catechism, Luther varies his statement but little: "The Sacrament of the Altar is the very Body and Blood of our Lord Jesus, *in and* under bread and wine, through *the word of* Christ, instituted and commanded to us Christians to eat and drink."

Here again he maintains that the wicked really receive the Body and Blood of Christ. "Although the most abandoned profligate minister the Sacrament to others, or himself receive it, yet still he receives the Sacrament, *i. e.* the Body and Blood of Christ, no less than he who should receive and take it most reverently and worthily of all; for it depends not upon human holiness, but upon the word of God. And as no saint on earth nor angel in heaven can change the bread and wine into the Body and Blood of Christ, so no one can make it otherwise, although he abuse it most unworthily. For on account of the unworthiness and unbelief of the person, the word whereby the Sacrament was made or instituted does not become false nor void. For neither did He say, ' When ye believe and are worthy, then shall ye have My Body and Blood,' but 'Take, eat, drink, this is My Body and My Blood;' and again, ' This do ye,' *i. e.* what I am now doing, instituting, reaching to you to eat and drink. This is as if He had said, ' Whether thou be worthy or unworthy, thou hast here My Body and Blood, by virtue of these words, which are added to the bread and wine[3].' "Yet I would not deny, that despisers or brutish livers receive it only to their hurt and damnation[4]:"

The "Formula Concordiæ" enforced the same belief. VII. Aff. 6: "We believe, teach, and confess that the Body and Blood of Christ are received with the bread and wine, not only spiritually by faith, but by the mouth also; not, however, as the Capernaites, but in a supernatural and heavenly manner, by reason of the sacramental union.

"7. We believe, teach, and confess, that not those only who truly believe in Christ, and who approach worthily to the Lord's Supper, but the unworthy also and unbelieving receive the true Body and Blood of Christ; yet so, that they derive thence neither consolation nor life, but that rather that receiving turns to them to judgment and damnation, unless they are converted and repent. For although they repel from them Christ as a Saviour, yet, although most unwilling, they are compelled to admit Him as a severe Judge. But He, being present, no less exercises His judgment on those impenitent guests, than, being present, He worketh consolation and life in the hearts of true believers and worthy guests[5]."

In all these, the authorized statements of the Lutheran body, there is not a trace of a doctrine of Consubstantiation.

As expressing the belief of the Lutheran body,

[3] Pp. 424, 425.   [4] Ib. p. 433.   [5] Ib. p. 462.

these formulæ should be taken as a whole. For they collectively expressed the Lutheran belief, as long as it lasted. The words, "under the form of bread and wine," which are important as designating an Objective Presence in the Holy Eucharist, were retained through the two catechisms of Luther, even while they were dropped from the Confession of Augsburg. The Apology added the word "substantially." The belief that the wicked too receive that which is sacramentally the Body and Blood of Christ, even while they can in no wise be partakers of Christ, implied a firm belief in the Objective Presence of that Body and Blood. This was explicitly stated in the Smalcald Articles, the Larger Catechism of Luther, and the Formula Concordiæ. The belief in the Objective Presence may indeed be maintained without it, if it be held that God withdraws that Presence in such cases, as if through carelessness (as has often happened when the Sacrament has been reserved), the consecrated element be devoured by an animal.

The weak point in the Lutheran system is, that the only office assigned to the Sacrament is to kindle faith; so that according to them, if this language was pressed, God did not "work invisibly in us through the Sacrament," but rather on occasion of the Sacrament kindled faith, of which faith grace was the reward. According to the most natural interpretation of their words, they believed, not that God gave to faith through the Sacrament the gifts peculiar to the Sacrament, but through the Sacrament He awakened faith, which asked for and obtained the promises of God. Thus the Body and Blood of Christ were not according to them, the inward part of the Sacrament, or God's gift through it; but they were supposed to be given with a view to produce a further result, faith. The Body and Blood of Christ were, according to them, not gifts *to* faith, but gifts to excite faith. They were *only* means to an end beyond themselves.

The Zuinglians, then, rightly urged, "All[6] other places of the Confession wherein the Sacraments are treated of, confirm our opinion, and manifestly exclude that of the Lutherans or Ubiquitarians. For the thirteenth Article stands thus,—'Of the use of the Sacraments, they teach, that Sacraments were instituted, not only to be tokens of profession between men, but rather to be signs and witnesses of God's will towards us, set forth to excite and confirm faith in those who use them[7]. We must then in such wise use Sacraments, that faith should be added, which may believe in the promises which *are exhibited* and shown through them.'" And again, "Through[8] the word and Sacraments, as

[6] Hosp. ii. 157.

[7] The framers of our Articles, while using the words of this Article, in the hope of winning the foreign Protestants, supplied what was lacking in these words, " Sacraments—be certain sure witnesses and *effectual* [*efficacia*] signs of *grace* and God's good will towards us, *by the which He doth work invisibly in us.*" The statement thus filled up developes the meaning of the old saying, that " Sacraments are visible signs of invisible grace." It adds that they are signs of that sort, *by* which God works that grace.

[8] Art. 5.

through instruments, the Holy Spirit is given, Who produceth faith, where and when He wills." This faith, so to be produced through Sacraments, is not faith that God will give through His Sacrament, the gifts which He has promised through His Sacrament, but faith "that God through Christ justifies the sinner who believes that he is justified." So the faith worked through the Sacraments is explained to be " that God, not for our merits, but for Christ, justifies those who believe that they are received into grace for Christ's sake." Belief in our Lord is, of course, in those who are capable of that belief, required in order that Sacraments should be beneficial to us; it is not *the* fruit of the Sacraments. It is the condition of their efficacy; antecedent to their healthful operation in us; a grace in us, without which we cannot be " partakers of Christ." It, with all other graces, is strengthened through union with Christ by His Sacraments. But union with Christ is the end of Sacraments and the reward of faith; faith is not *the* object of Sacraments.

Again it is stated, as *the* benefit of Sacraments, that the recipient thereby remembers the benefits of Christ. "The[9] Mass was instituted, that in those who use the Sacraments, faith may recall to mind what benefits it receives through Christ, and may raise and comfort the timid conscience. For to remember Christ, is to remember His benefits, and to feel that they are really exhibited to us." "Remission of sins" is represented as the one end of the Sacraments. So

* De Abusu Missæ, ib. p. 25.

that the end of the reception of the Body and Blood of Christ is not (according to them) that "we may dwell in Christ and Christ in us, we may be one with Christ and Christ with us," but that our faith may more readily believe that our sins are forgiven to us. "Sacraments[1] are signs of promises. So then in their use, faith ought to be added. As, if any use the Lord's Supper, he should use it thus, 'Since this is a Sacrament of the New Testament, as Christ clearly says, let him be assured that the things promised in the N. T. are offered to him, *i. e.* free forgiveness of sins. And this thing let him receive with faith, raise the timid conscience, and feel that these testimonies are not fallacious; but as certain as if God by a new miracle from heaven were to promise that He would forgive.'" And "on the use of the Sacrament," it is laid down, "In the Sacrament, there are two things, the sign and the word. The *word* in the N. T. is the promise of grace added; the *promise* of the N. T. is the promise of forgiveness of sins, as the text here says, 'This is My Body which is given for you,' 'This is the Cup of the N. T. with My Blood, which will be shed for you for the remission of sins.' The *word* thus offers remission of sins. *The ceremony is as a picture of the word*, as Paul calls it, showing the promise."

The Lutheran doctrine then had two opposite elements; the one, the acceptance of the letter of our Lord's words, "This is My Body," the real Objective Presence; the other, the theory that the Sa-

---

[1] Apol. Conf. on Art. xiii. fin. p. 157.

crament had its efficacy as a picture to confirm faith. These two could not long co-exist. Christians could not long believe that they really received their Lord, His Body and Blood, and yet believe that the *only* end of this Great Gift was—not union with Himself, but a confirmation of their faith that He forgave them their sins.

Hence the importance of the seemingly slight variations in the *Confessio variata* of Melancthon, A.D. 1540. He[2] omitted the words "are present and distributed," and substituted the vague word "exhibited," of which it is difficult to know, whether it means "are given" by God, or "are set forth" only. "Of the Lord's Supper, they teach that with the bread and wine, the Body and Blood of Christ are verily exhibited to communicants in the Lord's Supper." The words, "They disapprove of those who teach otherwise," were omitted. The altered formula, at most, *need* express no more than an act of spiritual, as opposed to sacramental communion.

At best it expressed only the simultaneous Presence of the Body of Christ, as received by the communicant, but not as given to him in the distribution. The former word, "distributed," expressed not merely that the communicant becomes, by grace, a partaker of the Body and Blood of Christ, simultaneously with the reception of the consecrated elements; but that in the ancient language, those who administer the consecrated elements, "minister,

---

[2] Hosp. ii. 302.

distribute" the Body and Blood of Christ[3]. This statement corresponded with our own Article, "The Body of Christ is *given, taken,* and eaten in the Supper, only after an heavenly and spiritual manner[4]." It is given in a spiritual, not carnal, manner; as spiritual, not carnal, food. But it is *given* (as Mr. Knox remarked) by the Priest, *taken* by the people. It must be there, then, invisibly "under the form of bread and wine," to be *given* by the Priests, not simply communicated by God to the souls of the receivers.

The word "exhibited" had been substituted for "distributed" in the Concordia of Wittemberg, while the statement of the Real Presence had been strengthened. "They[5] confess, according to the words of Irenæus, that the Eucharist consists of two things, an earthly and a heavenly. They hold, then, and teach, that with the bread and wine, the Body and Blood of Christ are verily and substantially present, exhibited and received."

Luther's own statements vary considerably. He speaks positively of the Eucharistic presence. In this alone he was consistent. "We cleave simply to the words of Christ, willing to be ignorant what takes place there and content that the true Body of Christ, by virtue of the words, is present there[6]."

---

[3] See Sermon, p. 57, and the Fathers there quoted.

[4] *i. e.* not carnally, see below, Note P.

[5] In Hospin. ii. 243.

[6] De captiv. Babyl. quoted by Hospin. Hist. Sacr. P. 2. p. 5.

So believing, he set himself to show, not only that the Body of Christ was there, but that the Bread itself was the Body of Christ. "I, although I cannot attain to know how the bread is the Body of Christ, will yet take captive my understanding to the obedience of Christ, and, cleaving simply to His words, firmly believe, not only that the Body of Christ is in the bread, but that the bread is the Body of Christ." "In the Sacrament, in order that there be true Body and true Blood, it is not necessary that the bread and wine be transubstantiated, in order that Christ be held under both; but both remaining together, it is truly said, 'This bread is My Body, this wine is My Blood and conversely.'" This he held to be by virtue of the consecration. "If we pronounce these words over the bread, the Body of Christ is really present [7]." This Co-existence he defended, A.D. 1522, by the illustration, "The [8] Body of Christ is (the bread still existing) in the Sacrament, as fire is in iron, the substance of the iron existing, and God in man, the human nature existing,—the substances being in each case so united, that each retains its own operation and proper nature, and yet they constitute one thing."

It would not be fair to press such illustrations as these, more especially, when brought by such a rough, indefinite mind as Luther's. By both illustrations he probably meant only to show, how the

[7] Serm. cont. Swermer. A. 27. Ib.
[8] Cont. Henric. Reg. Ang. Ib. p. 8.

outward and inward parts of the Sacrament might co-exist in the same space. The likeness of the fire in iron he frequently repeated. In other places he uses the likeness of the sword in the scabbard, the liquid in a vessel, the "dove," "wherein," he says, "was the Holy Spirit[1]." Elsewhere, again, he adduces the instance of our Lord's passing through the closed tomb or the closed doors, or His birth *illæsa virginitate.* "As the stone of the tomb remained sealed, and the closed door unchanged, and yet the Body of Christ was together there where were the stone and wood; so also in the Sacrament the Body and Blood of Christ are, where the bread and wine are, which remain unchanged[3]." "Christum per clausum uterum virginis in lucem prodiisse. Nam hoc modo usus esse putatur, cum e virgine natus est[4]."

At another time, he explicitly puts aside the doctrine of the ubiquity of our Lord's Body by which he himself elsewhere defended this belief. "Here occurs the question. How can Christ be in the Sacrament corporally, since one body cannot be in several places at one and the same time? To this I answer, Christ said that He willed to be present there. Therefore He is truly in the Sacrament, and that corporally; and therefore He is truly there, nor ought any cause of that corporal presence to be sought than that only. For the words mean this; therefore what they mean, must be. But as to the Body Itself,

[1] Hosp. ii. 125.   [3] Ib. p. 89.   [4] Ib. p. 91.

Christ can be where He wills, every where and in all places, and therefore the case as to Him is other than as to our body.   Of ubiquity, or presence in all places, we ought not to dispute.   For in this case it is wholly different.   For the Schoolmen too say nothing of ubiquity, but retain the simple meaning of the corporal presence of the Body of Christ[5]." Then, again, he refers to the mere power of God. Thus, in the Conference of Marpurg, A.D. 1529: " I confess that the Body is in Heaven.   I confess also that it is in the Sacrament.   I care not that it is against nature, so that it be not against faith[6]." And again: " When he was asked, 'how the Lord was present and was eaten in the Eucharist,' he answered, 'That he knew well that the very Body and very Blood of the Lord was present and was eaten in the Sacrament, but in what way this took place, he commended to Christ, and should never scrutinize[7].'"   At other times, he states a doctrine of the Ubiquity of Christ's Body which nearly involves Eutychianism.   " The Body and Humanity of Christ are within and without all creatures, as God Himself is.   For since Christ is One Undivided Person, wheresoever He is according to His Divinity, there He also is at the same time according to His Humanity, or our faith is false[8]." And yet more offensively.   " He is present in all creatures, so that I could find Him in straw, fire,

---

[5] Opp. viii. f. 375 in Hospin. pp. 108, 109.
[6] Ib. p. 125.   [7] Ib. p. 217.   [8] Ib. p. 91.

water, or even a rope; for certainly He is there. Heaven and earth are His sack; as the corn fills the sack, so He fills all things[9]." In this way, while thinking that he was defending the doctrine of the Real Presence, he was really abandoning it. For he regarded the Holy Eucharist as an arbitrary symbol only, where He has told us that *He* is, Who is every where. "As if He said, 'Seek Me here; lay hold of Me here.' For this that He said, 'This is My Body,' is to be accounted as if He had said, Where the bread is, there is My Body[1]." Hence he says, "If God set a crab[2] before me, I would eat it spiritually. For wherever the Word of God is, there is spiritual eating. When then He added bodily eating, saying, 'This is My Body,' it must be believed. We eat by faith His Body, which is delivered for us. The mouth receives the Body of Christ. The soul believes the words, *because* it eats the Body[3]." Again, "To take up a piece of straw at God's command, is spiritual."

When he was asked, "For what end was Christ present and eaten," he answered, "As a pledge and testimony that He died to redeem us, and had sacrificed this His Body and Blood to the Father for us[4]." Thus, when he explained the doctrine which he believed, in the highest sense, it amounted to little more than that the Holy Eucharist was a sign to which remission of sins was attached. "In this

---

[9] Ib. p. 70. [1] Ib. [2] The sour apple, so called.
[3] Ib. p. 124. [4] Ib. p. 217.

Sacrament is remission of sins, and Christ has placed
the power and might of His Passion in the Sacrament, so that we should there fetch and find it[5]."
But it had this gift annexed, not through the
union of the communicant with Christ, but because
God had annexed the promise to the condition of
receiving it. It may be doubted, then, whether
there was any real change from the earlier time,
when his language was very little distinguishable from
the Zuinglian. Then he likened the Holy Eucharist
to the rainbow or Circumcision. "God," he says,
A.D. 1520, "in all His promises added to the word a
sign also for the greater certainty and confirmation
of faith. Thus to Noah He gave the rainbow, to
Abraham circumcision. Thus did Christ in this
Sacrament. For we poor men, since our life employs
the outward senses, need, at least, some outward *sign*,
annexed to the *words*; yet so that that sign should
be a Sacrament, *i. e.* that it be outward and yet have
and signify spiritual things[6]." And again: "'This is
My Body.' This is a sign and pledge of the promise.
Such is the counsel of Divine Goodness, to seal His
promises with some seal. So Circumcision was a seal
of a Covenant; so seals are appended to letters; stipu-
lations are made," &c.[7] In a yet fuller passage, A.D.
1519: "We all partake of that true Bread. This is the
spiritual and inward signification of the Sacrament.

[5] Ib. p. 54.
[6] Serm. de N. T., A.D. 1520. Ib. p. 11.
[7] De abrog. Miss. Priv., A.D. 1521. Ib.

And so to receive the Sacrament in bread and wine, is *nothing else, than to receive a certain sign* of this communion and incorporation with Christ and all His saints and faithful. As if a sign, handwriting, or some symbol were given to a citizen, whereby he was to be certainly persuaded, that he was received as a citizen, a member of the state, and was a sharer and partaker of all those things, which of right were his; whereof Paul speaketh to the Corinthians, ' We are all one bread and one body, who partake of the one bread.' This spiritual communion is, in the Sacrament of the Supper, promised, given, and made over to us, as in a sacred and certain sign. For it is expedient and necessary, that this communion with Christ and all saints should take place, secretly, invisibly, in Christ Himself, and that only a corporal, visible, and outward sign of it should be given to us [s]." In another place he separates the inward from the outward part, so as to make the gift previous to the reception of the Sacrament. " As in the Sacrament there are two things, the sign and the thing signified, so also communion is twofold, of which the first is inward, spiritual, unseen, which takes place and is received in the heart, when one by right faith, love, and hope is incorporated into the communion of Christ and His saints, such as is signified and exhibited in the Sacrament, and is the very virtue and operation of the Sacrament. But this communion

---

[s] Serm. de Sacram. Corp. Christi. Ib. p. 10.

must needs be distributed into the hearts of the faithful by God Himself only through the Holy Spirit, in the right faith of the Sacrament. The other and *subsequent communion* is outward, corporal, and visible, which takes place through the participation of the Sacrament, and this is the sign of that prior inward and spiritual communion [9]."

In another place, he mentions the outward elements and the promise as the only two parts of the Sacrament, and says that the promise is the essential part. "As in every Sacrament, two things ought to be considered, the word and the sacred signs, so also in the Sacrament of the Mass, or the Supper, there are words and bread and wine. The words are a Divine promise and Testament; the signs are Sacraments, i.e. sacred signs. As then much more lies in the Testament than in the Sacrament, so there is much more of moment in the word than in the signs. For the signs may even not be, and yet a man may sustain himself by the Word, and so may be saved without the Sacrament, but not without the Testament [10]."

Again, "The bread on the altar is only a sign, and promiseth nothing, unless the true Bread have been eaten within [11]." Again, "In the Sacrament of the Altar there are *only* two things, the word of promise, whereby the Body and Blood of Christ are promised, and the faith in the word which requireth nothing

[9] Serm. de Excomm. Ib.
[10] Serm. De Morte et præp. ad Euch. Ib. p. 13.
[11] Ib. p. 12.

E

save faith [1]."   Again; "Sacraments are *nothing else
than signs which confirm faith, and which invite us to
believe*, and without faith, profit nothing [2]. [Without
faith, where, by reason of age, there can be faith,
nothing, of course, profits; but this has simply no
connexion with what he had just said, that sacraments ' *only* confirm faith.'] Hospinian further quotes
Luther as saying that the words of consecration are
" words of promise and of faith, to which are annexed
the outward signs of the Sacrament;" and, " In the
Sacrament of the Eucharist, *nothing more is found
than a promise and faith* [3]."

He explains spiritual eating and drinking, of
belief only. "Of this faith, [of the Israelites,] that
corporeal Rock, from which they drank water corporeally, was a sign: as we, by taking corporeal
bread and wine on the Altar, eat and drink true
Christ spiritually, i.e. *by eating and drinking outwardly, we practise faith within* [4]."

And again :—

"He Himself [our Lord] saith afterwards, 'The
flesh profiteth nothing,' and again, ' *My* Flesh giveth
life to the world.' How shall we distinguish these
things? The Spirit distinguisheth this. Christ
meaneth, that the bodily eating of the Flesh of
Christ profiteth nothing; but to believe that the
Flesh is the Son of God, Who for us came down from

<hr>

1 De Abusu Missæ priv. Ib. p. 13.
2 Serm. De Morte et præp. ad Euch. Ib.
3 De Abrog. priv. Miss. c. 7, et alibi. Ib. p. 92.
4 Dom. Septuag. sup. i. Cor. 10. Ib. p. 11.

heaven, and shed His Blood for us. Wherefore to eat the flesh of the Son of God, and to drink His Blood, is *nothing else than* that I should *believe* that His Flesh was given for me, and His Blood shed for me, and therefore there ought to be this spiritual eating. But the Papists attempted to adapt this to the sign of the true Food, as though the sign ought to feed. But Christ did not deliver or say these things of outward food; but of that eating which takes place in the heart, that thus we may be fattened; else to receive without and not within is not truly to be fed[5]. And again, ' No eating quickens except of faith. For this is truly spiritual eating and life. For sacramental quickeneth not, since many eat unworthily, so that He cannot be understood to have spoken this of the Sacrament of bread [6].' "

This he afterwards retracted, confessing that by the words, " the flesh profiteth nothing," was meant not the Flesh of Christ, of which He had said, " My Flesh is meat indeed," but the fleshly mind, fleshly understanding[7].

There was scarcely a question upon the Sacrament in which he did not vary. In 1523, he said Anathema to those who held transubstantiation; before and after, he taught that it was indifferent whether it was held or no[8]. He contended that the wicked really ate the Body and Blood of Christ; and again he denied that those who disbelieved the

[5] In Joh. 6. Ib. p. 12.
[6] De Captiv. Bab. Ib.   [7] Ib. p. 54.   [8] Ib p. 9.

real Presence received it. "Whereas the fanatics believe that there is mere bread and wine only, assuredly so it is. As they believe, so they have it, and they eat there mere bread and wine: the Body of the Lord they have neither spiritually nor corporeally[9]."

He held communion in one kind to be unimportant, because he held all actual communion unimportant. "I should be glad, if a general Council should restore both kinds to the people; not that it has any need of both or that one did not suffice, *but for the fuller significancy. It has need of neither, but of faith only.* Both kinds are no more necessary than immersion in Baptism. One kind only signifies one part of the Sacrament, and therefore cannot *signify* the whole Communion of Saints[1]." "Christ enjoined neither one, nor both kinds, and therefore the faithful may abstain from both[2]." "They have taken away the 'kind' of wine altogether from the Church, *although it matters little, for more lies in the words than in the signs[3].*"

Again, he says, that, although needless, to forego it willingly, is to deny Christ. "I say, if any one knowingly omit, at least to desire the other part of the Sacrament, although neither is necessary, he is impious and denies Christ[4]." And "If any Council

---

[9] Quod Christi verba, &c.   Ib. p. 18.
[1] Serm. de Sacr. A.D. 1519.   Ib. p. 17.
[2] Serm. de Euch. A.D. 1520.   Ib.
[3] Serm. de N. T.   Ib.
[4] Assert. Artic. a Pap. damn. Art. 16.   Ib.

decreed or allowed both kinds, we would not use either, but in contempt of the Council and its decree, we would use one or neither or both, cursing all who used both on the authority or decree of the Council [5]."

In 1520 he said that "whole Christ was received under each kind;" afterwards he is said to have ridiculed and denied it [6].

The "elevation" of the Sacrament he taught, A.D. 1544, "to be piously retained, as a witness of the real and corporal Presence in the bread; as though, when the Priest made this elevation, he said by the very act, 'See, Christians, this is the Body of Christ which was given for you;'" he "opposed it only out of dislike to the Papists," and retained it out of dislike and contempt of Carlstadt (who held it to be idolatrous). Christian freedom, as he thought, required "that it should be retained where it was prohibited as impious, and abolished where it was enjoined as necessary [7]."

He held it not to be heretical either to adore or not to adore the Sacrament. He says, "Whoso believes not that Christ is present in the Sacrament by His Body and Blood, does rightly not to adore it either spiritually or carnally. But whoso believes this (as it has been shown more than enough that it ought to be believed), he cannot in any wise deny veneration to the Body and Blood of Christ without sin [8]."

---

[5] In Form. Miss. Ib.   [6] Ib. p. 18.
[7] Ib. p. 19.   [8] Lib. ad Wald. Ib.

The Lutheran doctrine, as it settled in that body, until faith as to Sacraments gave way, is fairly represented by Joh. Gerhard, a learned and pious Lutheran.

"On [*] account of the calumnies of the opposite party, we again call to mind that we lay down neither impanation, nor consubstantiation, nor any other physical or local presence, but we believe, teach, and confess, that according to the institution of Christ Himself, in a way known to God alone, but incomprehensible to us, the Body of Christ is truly, really, and substantially present to the Eucharistic bread as a medium appointed by God; and that in the same way the Blood of Christ, truly really and substantially present, is joined to the Eucharistic wine: so that, in transcendent mystery, we take, eat, and drink with that bread the real Body of Christ, and with that wine the real Blood of Christ. This Presence is called Sacramental, not in the sense in which the opponents use the word, for a relative ($\sigma\chi\epsilon\tau\iota\kappa\bar{\eta}$) presence, suggestive to the mind only, but because a heavenly thing is, in this mystery, given to and set before us in this mystery through the medium of outward sacramental symbols. The Presence is called 'true and real,' to exclude the fiction of a figurative, imaginary, and representative Presence ; it is called a 'substantial' Presence, to preclude the subterfuge of opponents,

[*] De S. Cœna, c. xi. n. 98.

as though there were nothing present in this mystery besides an ' efficacy ' of the Body and Blood of Christ. The Presence is called 'mystical, supernatural, and incomprehensible,' because the Body and Blood of Christ are not present in any manner of this world, but in that which is mystical, supernatural, and incomprehensible. Some of ours, following Cyril, [on John 13,] have called the Presence ' corporal,' respect being had to the object, but by no means to the mode. What they wished to say was, that not only the virtue and efficacy but the substance itself of the Body and Blood of Christ are present at the Holy Supper.—For they used this word in opposition to the spiritual Presence, as defined by opponents, but did not at all mean that the Body of Christ is present in a corporeal way by which a body exists in quantity. So Hilary [1] asserts that ' the Flesh of Christ remains in us *naturaliter*, in a way of nature;' which he there thus explains, ' That Christ is in us by the truth of nature, not only by the harmony of the will.'"

Gerhard's language as to the mode of the Presence, "being known to God alone," corresponds remarkably with the first statement of the Council of Trent, which declares only the Real Presence [2]: "In the sacred Sacrament of the holy Eucharist, after the consecration of the bread and wine, our Lord Jesus Christ, true God and Man, is truly, really, and substantially

[1] De Trin. l. 8.   [2] Sess. 13, c. 1.

contained under the species of those sensible things. For neither are these things mutually repugnant, that our Saviour Himself ever sitteth at the Right Hand of the Father in Heaven, according to the natural mode of existing, and that, nevertheless, He be in many other places sacramentally present unto us in His own substance, by that manner of existing which, though we can scarcely express it in words, we yet can, by the understanding illuminated by faith, suppose, and ought most faithfully to believe, to be possible unto God."

NOTE C.

On p. 23.

On the miracles of our Lord's passing through the closed tomb and the closed doors, after the resurrection, and His birth illæsa virginitate.

a) It is plain from S. Matt. 28. 2—6, that our Lord was risen, before the angel descended from Heaven to roll away the stone. For the angel descended when the women were there, to tell them that our Lord "*was* risen, as he said." So S. Chrysostom [1]. S. Jerome [2], "Let us not think that the angel came to open the tomb and roll back the stone for the Lord, rising again ; but, after the Lord

----

[1] On S. Joh. Hom. 85, § 4, p. 764, Oxf. Tr. and on S. Matt. Hom. 89, § 2, p. 1160, Oxf. Tr.

[2] Ep. ad Hedib. q. 6.

had risen, at the hour at which He willed, and which is known to no man, the angel pointed out what *had* been; and by the rolling away of the stone and his own presence, he showed the empty tomb." S. Fulgentius, "If[3] the angel descended not, would Christ not rise from the tomb? or did the stone hinder the Lord, unless it were removed by the angel? Yea, the Lord *was* risen, so that the angel was not needed. He was there in reverence, not to help." S. Fulgentius goes on to compare the two following miracles, as do Eusebius Gall.[4], and the author of Serm. 163, in App. S. Aug. S. Greg. of Nyssa[5], "The angel, having rolled away the stone, found the Lord risen, He having quitted, in a Divine manner, the tomb closed and made sure with seals and kept by the guard of soldiers, in like way as, entering the house while the doors were closed, He came to the disciples. Wherefore also the angel said, 'He is not here, He *hath* risen ($\dot{\eta}\gamma\acute{\epsilon}\rho\theta\eta$),' showing that the Saviour's wondrous Resurrection had taken place before his own coming, He having, as God, fulfilled it by His own power, executing the dispensation without need of angelic co-operation. For had this not been so, he would have said, 'Lo, He riseth ($\dot{\epsilon}\gamma\epsilon\acute{\iota}\rho\epsilon\tau\alpha\iota$),' pointing to what was then taking place. But since it had preceded, he said, using the past time, 'He is not here, He hath risen ($\dot{\eta}\gamma\acute{\epsilon}\rho\theta\eta$).'"

[3] Hom. 42 (de januis clausis), B. P. ix. 138.
[4] Hom. 9, de Pasch. B. P. vi. 642.
[5] In Christi Res. Orat. 2, t. iii. p. 401.

S. Chrysologus [1], " Him Whom closed virginity, had brought to this present life, the closed tomb gave back to life everlasting. It is a mark of Divinity ' clausam virginem reliquisse post partum ;' to have gone forth with the body from the closed tomb is a mark of Divinity [2]." The author of the Quæstt. et Resp. ad Orthod. q. 117, " Not for the sake of the Resurrection did the removal of the stone from the tomb take place, but that the Resurrection might be made known to the beholders." The author of the Christus Patiens in S. Greg. Naz. [3] speaks of it as a miracle.

b) The miracle of passing through the closed doors is dwelt upon or alluded to by S. Amphilochius [4], S. Epiphanius [5], S. Chrysostom [6], S. Ambrose [7], S. Cyril of Jerusalem [8], S. Augustine [9], S. Cyril of Alexandria [10], S. Jerome [11], Theodoret [12], S. Chrysologus [13], S. Leo [14]. The miracle is compared with our Lord's birth ' ex utero clauso' by S. Augus-

<hr>

[1] Serm. 75, B. P. vii. 904.
[2] Add Serm. 77, p. 906, col. 2, Serm. 80, p. 908.
[3] App. v. 2243-5.
[4] Ap. Theodoret. Dial. 2, T. iv. p. 152, 3, ed. Sch.
[5] Hær. 20, § 3 ; 64, § 64 ; 77, § 29.
[6] Hom. 87, in S. Joh.
[7] In S. Luc. c. ult. § 168.   [8] Lect. xiv. § 11, 12.
[9] Serm. 277, § 12, T. v. p. 1119.
[10] In S. Joh. L. xii. p. 1090-2, et 1107.
[11] Adv. Jovin. L. 1, c. 36, p. 295, ed. Vall.
[12] Dial. ii. p. 118.
[13] Serm. 81, B. P. vii. p. 909.
[14] Ep. 28, ad Flav. c. 5.

tine [1], S. Jerome [2] (perhaps with reference also to His rising from the closed tomb), S. Gaudentius [3], S. Fulgentius [4], Theodoret [5], S. Hilary [6] (somewhat obscurely, yet certainly, as to the Birth; at length, as to the closed doors), the author of the Christus Patiens in S. Gregory of Nazianzum [7], Theodotus of Ancyra [8], Eusebius Gall. [9], S. Gregory the Great [10]. It is remarkable that the same comparison is retained even in the Lutheran Formula Concordiæ [11].

A synod of Milan under S. Ambrose condemned Jovinian's denial of our Lord's Birth, 'utero clauso,' as heretical, contrary to the Apostles' Creed [12], as had Siricius generally in a Roman Presbytery [13]. S. Augustine mentions it among Jovinian's heresies [14]. The ancient belief is explicitly stated in the Formula Concordiæ [15], "The Son of God even in His Mother's womb showed His Divine Majesty, that He was born of a Virgin 'inviolatâ ipsius virginitate.' Whence also she was truly θεοτόκος, i. e. 'Dei genitrix,' and yet remained a virgin."

[1] In. S. Joh. Tr. 121, § 4, Epist. 137, § 8. Serm. 247, § 2, de Ag. Christ. c. 24.

[2] Ep. 48, ad Pammach. de err. Joh. fin.

[3] Tract. 9, B. P. v. 956. [4] l. c.

[5] Dial. 2. p. 118, ed. Sch.

[6] De Trin. iii. 19, 20. [7] v. 2495—2500.

[8] Hom. in Nat. Dom. in Conc. Eph. Act. 3, c. 9, p. 1512, ed. Col. [9] Serm. Dom. 1, post Pascha, B. P. vi. 759.

[10] Hom. 26 in Evang. § 1.

[11] c. 7 (Tittman, Libb. Symbol. p. 577).

[12] S. Ambr. Ep. 42, § 4, 5.

[13] Ib. Ep. 41. [14] Hær. 82. [15] P. 586.

NOTE D.

On p. 29.

It is a first principle of law, that in Testaments, the plain meaning of words is not to be departed from.

GERHARD (Loci 22, c. 10, § 73) quotes the following "imperial laws or responses of lawyers (l. Ille aut ille, 25, ff. de legatis 3), " When there is no ambiguity in the words, no question of will should be admitted." (l. Non aliter, 69, ff. de legatis et fidei commissis 3, in princip.), "It is not right to depart from the meaning of words, save when it is manifest that the testator meant something else." (l. Labeo 7, § 2, de supellect. legata), "Of what use are names, except to point out the will of the speaker? truly, I do not think any one will say what he does not think." (See Vigil. in § 1 inst. de pupill. et vulgari substitut. Tiraquell. in l. si unquam verb. Libertus, n. 17, Cod. de revoc. donat. Tilemann. p. ii. disp. 7, ff. th. 31, Godd. ad l. 219, de V. S. Stephan. de Phedericis tract. de interpr. legum, p. 155, and also the sayings of lawyers.) "If the testator meant the contrary, there was no difficulty in so disposing it." "The words of a testator are to be considered carefully, lest while we use over-much subtlety as to meanings of such sort, the intentions of the testators be defrauded." "In a dubious point, it is safer not to depart from the words, but to keep to them rigidly, without any foreign interpretation."

"Words should be weighed more than an imaginary and uncertain meaning." "The words of the testator must not be departed from, because the intention is presumed to have been such as the words properly mean." "It is not to be believed that the testator willed what he has not said." "We ought to be content with the limitations of the words, because no disposition goes farther than the words bear: the reader then of a deed has the solution of what he seeks." "What the testator does not say, he is presumed not to will." "When a thing is explained manifoldly, its meaning is unknown." "Many are deceived who do not weigh the words of testaments, which in themselves bear great weight in finding out what the meaning is." "Unless the contrary meaning be unquestionably evident, the proper signification of the words is not to be set aside."

NOTE E.

On p. 31.

Against the attempt to explain away the force of the words, " This is My Body," by the introduction of " a figure."

In a figurative sentence, the figure must lie either (1) in the thing spoken of, or (2) in that which is spoken of it, or (3) in the word by which these two are connected. Simple as this statement is, the neglect of it has introduced much confusion. People have seen that there is a figure somewhere in such a sentence as, " I am the Door," " I am the Good Shepherd," " I am the True Vine," and so have been open to the argument, " then there *may* be a figure in the words, 'This is My Body.'" If there had been, it must have lain in the word "This," or in the words "My Body," or in the word " is," which joins these together. The whole cannot be figurative, unless there be a figure somewhere in the parts.

I have pointed out in the sermon itself[1] that, most commonly, the figure lies in that which is affirmed of the subject spoken of; in logical language, the predicate. This is so in the words, " I am the Door," " I am the Good Shepherd," " I am the True Vine, and My Father is the Husbandman." The words " Door," " Good Shepherd," " True Vine," " Husbandman," &c., are metaphors, or figurative language. Our Lord means by them to picture to us, that when we would enter into the Church or the Kingdom of Heaven, it is through Him, that we are to find entrance. Wherein we need care, He is to us, as a shepherd is to his sheep. We have our life and strength from Him, as the branches derive their from the stock whence they issue. This sort of language must (as I have said) pervade Holy Scripture, whenever God would speak to us of His relations to us; because, as we know Him not yet "as He is," we can only understand Him through

---

[1] pp. 29—31.

things which we do know. But in all these cases the figure lies in the word spoken of our Lord, whether (as I said) it be Vine, Door, Shepherd, King, Judge, Merchant-Man, Priest, Prophet, Lamb, Light, Mountain, Corner Stone, Tower of Strength, Head, Captain of our Salvation, Physician, Bridegroom, Sun of Righteousness, Worm, the Way. This is obvious, as soon as it is stated. Such passages, then, as "I am the Door," "My Father is the Husband-man," in which the words Door and Husbandman are figurative, metaphorical, picture-words, form no plea for taking the words, "This is My Body which is given for you," figuratively. For the words, "My Body which is given for you," are not like the words "Door" and "Husbandman," figurative, but they speak of a true Body which for us was nailed upon the Cross.

As plainly there is no figure in the word This.

Neither does any figure ever lie in the word *is*. It simply serves to join the two parts of the sentence together, whether there be a figure or no. It simply expresses that the two ideas thus compared bear a certain relation to one another, that they agree together. If they do not agree, we insert the word "not." In Hebrew the simple word "is" is not expressed at all. "All flesh grass," "thou My servant," "I thy God," express in Hebrew without ambiguity what we express, with the insertion of the substantive verb, "All flesh *is* grass," "thou *art* My servant," "I *am* thy God." The metaphor cannot then lie in a word, which is not essential to the sentence, and which in Hebrew is not expressed at all. In the words, "all flesh is grass," "The Lord is the portion of mine inheritance and of my cup," "The Lord is King," "The Lord is my shepherd," the metaphor lies in the words "grass," "portion," "shepherd," "King," not in the word *is*. In the Psalm, "The Lord is my Rock, and my Fortress, and my Deliverer, my God, my strength, in whom I will trust, my buckler and the horn of my salvation, and my high tower," the word *is* joins alike the words rock, fortress, buckler, horn, tower, in which there is a figure, and those, "my God," "my Deliverer," in which there is none.

But, further, God does not leave us doubtful whether, in Holy Scripture, He is speaking to us plainly or figuratively. Where there is a figure, God shows plainly that there is one. In the passages commonly quoted by Calvinistic interpreters, to prove that the Holy Eucharist is a mere figure, Holy Scripture itself determines that there *is* a figure, wherever there is one. Thus, (1) Gen. xli. 26, "The seven good kine are seven years; and the seven good ears are seven years." It is the explanation of a dream, in which Joseph said, "God hath showed unto Pharaoh what He is about to do." (2) Ezek. xxxvii. 11, "These bones are the whole house of Israel," is the explanation of a vision.   (3) S. Matt. xiii. 38, 39, "The field is the world," is our

Lord's exposition of a parable: and (4) Rev. i. 20, "The seven stars are the angels of the seven Churches, and the seven candlesticks which thou sawest are the seven Churches," are our Lord's exposition of a vision. (5) 1 Cor. v. 7, "Christ our Passover, is sacrificed for us," refers to the types of the O. T., just as when S. John Baptist said, "Behold the Lamb of God." (6) S. Matt. xi. 14, "If ye will receive it, this was Elias which was for to come." S. John Baptist was no figure of Elias, but Elias of S. John. But the metaphorical meaning of Elias, *i. e.* a Prophet "in his spirit and power," had already been given in S. Luke i. 17.

In other places which these interpreters allege, they have simply misunderstood Holy Scripture. (7) Gen. ix. 9, The "bow" is not (as they say) called "the covenant" of God, but it *is* three times called "the *token* of the covenant" (ver. 12, 13, 17). The covenant itself (ver. 9) is, that God will no more destroy the earth with a flood. (8) Gen. xvii. 10, it is not said, "Circumcision is My covenant," whereas in ver. 11, "circumcision" is expressly called the "*token* of the covenant." In ver. 10 there is no figure of speech whatsoever. God says, "This is My covenant between Me and you, and thy seed after thee; every man child among you shall be circumcised." This *was* His covenant itself; not any figure of a covenant. (9) In like way, Ex. xxxi. 16, it is *not* said that "the sabbath is a covenant; but it *is* said (ver. 17) that it is "a *sign*." The words, "for an everlasting

F

covenant," are added (as in Gen. xvii. 7, Lev. xxiv. 8
also, or other equivalent words, "an ordinance for
ever," Ex. xii. 14, 17, xxvii. 21, xxviii. 43, xxx. 21.
Lev. iii. 17, vi. 18), declaring this to be a binding ob-
ligation, so long as the ritual system was in force.
This is said plainly, without any figure.   (10) Ex. xii.
11, "It is the Lord's Passover," does not mean, "it
is the sign of the Lord's passing over."   The "*blood*"
was a token, and is so called (ver. 12).   The whole
festival *was* a memorial, and is so called (ver. 14); or
a sign (Ib. xiii. 9, 16).   The lamb was not a sign,
and is not so called.   The Hebrew פסח is used in
different places for (1) the whole festival, (2) the
Paschal lamb; in both cases it is elliptical; in
neither figurative.   פסח in the one case stands for
חג הפסח, feast of the Passover (Ex. xxxiv. 25), in the
other, for זבח הפסח, "sacrifice of the Passover," which
occurs ver. 27.   Both idioms are common; to
"keep the Passover," "the statute of the Passover,"
of the feast; to "slay the Passover" (Ex. xii. 21);
"sacrifice the Passover" (Deut. xvi. 2, 5. 2 Chr.
xxx. 15, 17, &c.); "eat the Passover," 2 Chr. xxx.
18, of the victim.   Again, the idiom, "keep the
Passover to the Lord" (Ex. xii. 48), occurs of the
festival; to "sacrifice the Passover to the Lord," of
the Paschal lamb (Deut. xvi. 2); as there are also
the idioms, "a sabbath to the Lord" (Ex. xx. 10);
"a feast to the Lord."   Nor is this use of the name
of the feast, for the animal sacrificed at the feast, any
special or insulated idiom.   The common word for

"feast," חַג, is used for the sacrifice, in Ps. cxviii. 27. Ex. xxiii. 18. Mal. ii. 3.

There is, then, absolutely nothing remarkable in this idiom, which Zuingli relates to have come to him in a dream[1], as an illustration of our Lord's words, "This is my Body," and which others have copied from him.

(11) Exod. xxiv. 8, "Behold the blood of the covenant," has been mis-translated, "this blood is the covenant."

Two other passages are cited, in consequence of the rejection of true doctrine by those who cite them. Albertinus[2] says, "baptism is called the washing of regeneration (Tit. iii. 5) and burial with Christ" (Rom. vi. 4, and Col. ii. 12). But, according to the faith which came from the Apostles, baptism is called "the washing of regeneration," not as being a bare sign of it, but as the Sacrament, whereby Almighty God is pleased to work it. Nor, according to the same faith, is baptism any mere sign of "burial with Christ," but God's appointed means, whereby He conveys to the soul the inward spiritual grace, "a death unto sin, and a new birth unto righteousness." "As the Death of Christ in the flesh was real, so is one's to sin real," says S. Chrysostom[3].

---

[1] Coronis de Euch. Opp. ii. 249.

[2] De Sacr. Euch. 1. 11. p. 58.

[3] See further Scriptural Doctrine on Holy Baptism, pp. 93—109. 124—133.

It is quite true that the outward elements are a figure of the inward substance. They bear that same relation to the body, which the inward substance bears to the soul. They nourish and sustain the body, as union with Christ through the inward gift in the Holy Eucharist, the Body and Blood of Christ, sustains and gives life to the soul. The question as to the elements themselves is not whether they are a figure of His body broken, and of His Blood shed for us. The very action of the Holy Eucharist shows that they are. The question so far is, whether they are figures of what is present, although unseen, or of what is absent. But in these words of our Lord, "This is My Body," the question is, whether our Lord meant to express a spiritual reality, or whether, while He appeared to be speaking of a gift which He was bestowing, He meant that He gave to His Apostles and to us only a shadow, a rite as outward as any of the law, which He Himself came to fill up and to fulfil. He Himself was the substance of the shadows of the law. He did not come to give us fresh shadows, instead of realities.

The argument from language is conclusive. There would be endless confusion, and our whole faith might be turned into a figure, if men might assume as they pleased, that this or that, which they did not like to take literally, was a figure. The Docetæ might equally interpret, "The Word was made flesh" as a figure, and contend that S. John's words did not establish that our Lord had real flesh.

Nor has one who interprets as a figure, "This is
My Body," any answer to make to them. But to
save us from this uncertainty, all figures which occur
in Holy Scripture, are of two sorts. Either they
carry with them their own evidence, that they are
figures (as in what is plainly picture-language), or
Almighty God directly tells us that they are a figure.
Until some distinct case be adduced, in which
proper terms used to designate an actual subsisting
thing, are, without any hint or notice, to be understood unreally, we shall not be justified in so tam-
pering with the Word of God; and they who do
so tamper, prepare the way for the denial of truth,
which they themselves believe.

NOTE F.

On p. 34.

*The bearing of our Lord's words, " I will drink no more of this
fruit of the vine," on the doctrine of the Holy Eucharist.*

OUR Lord, according to S. Matthew, spoke the
words, "I will not drink henceforth of this fruit of
the vine, until that day when I drink it new with
you in My Father's kingdom," after the consecration
of the Cup. "Drink ye all of it, for this is My
Blood of the New Testament, which is shed for
many for the remission of sins. But I say unto you, I
will not drink henceforth, &c." (xxvi. 27—29.) Each
part of these words suggests an argument for our

belief. Our Lord as distinctly says, "this fruit of the vine," as He says, " This is My Body." He calls that which He had consecrated, and of which He had said, " This is My Blood of the New Testament," by the name of the natural element, " the fruit of the vine," as S. Paul calls the other element, after its consecration, by its natural name, " bread." All the Fathers, then, who believed these words to have been spoken by our Lord, in the place where S. Matthew and S. Mark distinctly place them, *i. e.* after the consecration of the Cup, believed certainly that our Lord gave to the consecrated element the name of its natural substance, " the fruit of the vine," as much as He called it His Blood.

Again, the words, " until I drink it new in the kingdom of God," are most naturally understood to include our Lord's condescending again to eat and drink after His Resurrection. The Apostles lay a stress on the fact, in proof of the reality of His Resurrection;—" who did eat and drink with Him after He rose from the dead" (Acts x. 41). Our Lord may have meant His words to embrace also that Feast of the Gospel, in which He drinks this fruit of the vine in His members who worthily communicate, as He is persecuted in those who suffer for His Name. He may speak, too, as do the Prophets, of Heaven as a feast, and of the torrent of pleasure in the richness of His House. All these may be meant by the words, and the same Father may interpret the

words of all. But if any Fathers hold that our Lord
did mean to speak of natural drinking of wine after
His Resurrection, then they must have understood
Him to speak of that which He had consecrated to
be His Blood, as being in its natural substance,
wine. When He said, " I will no more drink *this
fruit of the vine*, until I drink *it* new," &c., we
cannot suppose, that if He meant it of the
natural substance after His Resurrection, He meant
it of what was not a natural substance then. That
which is natural is the basis of that which is metaphorical. It is obvious, then, to pass from the
natural meaning of the word to the metaphorical; it
will not be intelligible, if one, after having cited a
word in a merely spiritual sense, were then to use
it, without explanation, of the physical object,
without marking that he was no longer speaking of
the same thing. It is very conceivable that our
Lord should pass from this mention of the natural
substance, or from Sacraments, to that Feast where
His saints shall behold Him with unveiled face, and
be satisfied with His contemplation, and be filled by
the indwelling of God. It is quite inconceivable
that, if our Lord meant in the second place to speak
of ordinary eating and drinking of natural food, He
should not also, in the first instance, have been
speaking of what was, in its natural substance, food.
Elsewhere, our Lord said, " Your fathers did eat
manna in the wilderness and are dead," and then went
on to speak of Himself as the " true Bread of life."

Or from the well of Samaria, He took occasion to speak of the "living water." But if that further drinking of which he speaks, be of the natural " fruit of the vine," *i. e.* wine, after the Resurrection, it is contrary to the analogy of His mode of speaking, to interpret the words, as He then used them, of what was not the natural substance. If by " the Kingdom of God," our Lord meant in part Heaven, then since our bodies there will not be supported by elements of this world, the feeding of which He speaks, must, by the very nature of the case, be wholly spiritual. There can be no ambiguity. But if by the Kingdom of God He means, at least in its beginning, that kingdom upon which He entered after His Resurrection, when He says, " All power is given to Me in Heaven and in earth," and by the drinking wine He means in part, the taking natural food with them in proof of His Resurrection, then it would be unnatural to understand Him, as not speaking of what was there before Him, as a natural substance. We could not paraphrase His words, " I will not drink of this, which was wine once, but is so no longer, until I drink it new in its natural substance after My Resurrection," although there is no difficulty in conceiving our Lord to go on from speaking even of Sacraments here, to that blessed state, when we shall need no veils nor sensible media, but eye to eye shall behold Him, and be satisfied with the unceasing influx of His love.

Roman controversialists show by the variety and contradictoriness of their answers, that they feel the difficulty. Thus some, and perhaps the most [1], allow that the words, "fruit of the vine," mean wine in its natural sense, but deny that it is used with reference to the Holy Eucharist at all; others allow it to have reference to the consecrated Cup, but say that it does not mean wine, but only the accidents of wine; one even says, that the fruit of the vine, or of this vine, means the Blood of our Lord, as being the True Vine, for which, however, he is blamed by others, as exposing the doctrine which he defends weakly.

The use of similar words in S. Luke cannot change the meaning of those in S. Matthew and S. Mark. The words in S. Matthew, "But I say unto you" ($\lambda \epsilon \gamma \omega \ \delta \epsilon$), *can* only be interpreted of that, in connexion with which they are said, the Eucharistic Cup. On the contrary, the words in S. Luke stand naturally, not as a mere anticipation, but in connexion with the earnest desire which our Lord had to celebrate that His last Feast with them, in which He was in a closer and more inward way, about to unite them to Himself for ever. He says, "Earnestly have I desired to celebrate this My parting Feast

---

[1] Albertinus, p. 109, quotes Maldonatus in Matt. 26. Lucas Brugensis, ad loc. p. 475 ; Stapleton, Antid. Ev. in Matt. 26. p. 118 ; Becanus, de Sacr. in Spec., a Lapide [in S. Matt. and] in 1 Cor. 11. So also Dion. Carthus., de Lira, Caietan, Sa, Sylveir. ad loc.

with you; the close of all before, the beginning of all to come; the source of salvation of the world. For verily I say unto you, I will no more eat or drink again with you, until in My new life after the Resurrection, I drink in a new way, in a Body which will need no renewal." And then He describes the Feast which He so desired, the Holy Eucharist. Any how, the plain meaning of the words in S. Matthew and S. Mark must stand.

Those Evangelists, recording the words as spoken after the consecration of the new Feast of the Gospel, and in direct connexion with the consecration of the Cup, cannot have meant them of the typical Passover, which has passed away. So to interpret would be to trifle with Inspiration and God's Word.

On the other hand, not only are the Fathers agreed in supposing the words to be used of the consecrated elements[2], but later writers also adduce the words in proof that wine is to be used in the Holy Eucharist[3]; or that our Lord Himself first tasted before He gave to His disciples[4].

[2] See Note M.

[3] Innocent iii. 27, Aq. ad loc, who also admits it to be a proof that our Lord ate and drank after His Resurrection, although it was to prove the truth of His Resurrection, not any need of Nature, c. Gentil. iv. 83; so in the East the Council in Trullo, c. 32, against the Armenians.

[4] Salmeron. T. 9, Tr. 15, p. 106, &c. Aquinas. 3, p. q. 81. Art. 1, fin. follows Eusebius in explaining Luke xxii. 15, of our Lord's sacramental eating.

NOTE G.

On p. 37.

*The Fathers speak of the continued existence of the elements in
their natural substances, most especially when they are speaking accurately in their controversies with heretics.*

ALL faith harmonizes together. Every portion of
the faith bears upon others. Hence heresies, seemingly unconnected, are brought in sudden contact
with each other. Or one heresy ramifies into others.
They have a secret sympathy with each other. A
heresy sends out its knotted roots underground,
and shoots up in another form, and in a distant spot,
which, looking along the surface, one should not
know how it reached. And so, it is even strange,
at first sight, how very distinct and various or opposite heresies are met by the true doctrine of the
Holy Eucharist.

But it has been, of old, observed that almost all heresies are, in some way, directed against the doctrine of
the Incarnation, the belief in our Lord Jesus Christ,
God, for us and for our salvation, become Man. It
is in harmony with this, that heresy should founder
on the true belief in the Holy Eucharist, through
which the fruits of the Incarnation especially accrue
to us, and by which He conveys to us, through His
Body and Blood, that union with Himself which it
was one object of His Holy Incarnation to impart.

S. Irenæus employs against the heretics who denied the resurrection of the body, the argument from the adaptation of the Holy Eucharist to our twofold nature.   He regards the Holy Eucharist (as do many other Fathers) as a means of immortality to the body also.   It nourishes the body by virtue of its earthly part ; but being the Body and Blood of Christ, It nourishes it to life immortal.   If the natural substance were not present, it could not nourish; whence some in later days have denied that It does strengthen and refresh the body.   "How[1] say they, that the flesh passeth to corruption and partaketh not of life, which is nourished from the Body of the Lord and His Blood?   Either let them change their mind, or abstain from offering the things above spoken of.   But our meaning is in harmony with the Eucharist, and the Eucharist again confirms our meaning.   And we offer to Him His own, carefully teaching the communication and union, and confessing the resurrection, of the flesh and spirit.   For as the bread from the earth, receiving the invocation of God, is no longer common bread, but the Eucharist, consisting of two things, an earthly and a heavenly, so also our bodies, receiving the Eucharist, are no longer perishable, having the hope of the Resurrection to life everlasting."

Tertullian again argues from the Holy Eucharist, against the Gnostics, that Christ had a real, not (as their phrensy was) a fantastic body, and that the

---

[1] iv. 18. 5.

God of the New Testament is the same as the God of the Old. " Having [2] declared, ' With desire have I desired to eat this Passover,' as His own (for it were unworthy that God should desire any thing not His own), He made the bread which He took and distributed to the disciples that His own Body, saying, 'This is My Body,' *i. e.* the figure of My Body. But it would not be a figure, unless His Body were a true Body. But an empty thing, as a phantom is, can admit of no figure of itself."

S. Ephrem uses the same argument against the Docetæ in his day. He argues from the real substance of the matter of the Sacrament, to the real substance of our Lord's Body which it figured and conveyed. " Sons [3] of truth, give praise. For your persecutors are your preachers, your haters are your guarantees. For they have guaranteed, and written, and set to their hands, that true and life-giving to all is the Body of the Christ. For a roll, on bread which they brake, have they written it; without ink, in wine have they marked it, to themselves, shame ; to you, a crown."

And more fully :—

" The brides [4] of the daughters of the Hebrews, their glory is in their veils. Lo in our veil is our

---

[2] Adv. Marcion. iv. 20.

[3] Adv. Hær. Rh. 45. init. ii. 539. Here, and throughout, the Syriac works of S. Ephrem are alone quoted, as being alone genuine.

[4] Adv. Hær. Rhythm 47. ii. 542, 3.

glory, the Blood of Christ, which is above all price.
The congregations of the infidels, in their veils there
is for them no true Blood of Christ.   They have [but]
a likeness of blood, who own not the Body of Christ.
Where is the true Body, there is also the true Blood.
If, because the body is defiled and hateful and
loathsome, the Lord abhorreth it, so is the cup of
redemption in the house of the infidels.   And how
did He loathe the body, and clothe Himself with
bread, whereas, lo! bread is the brother of weak
flesh !   And if dumb bread pleases Him, how much
more the speaking body!   Bread also the Lord used
as a likeness, Who accepted the shewbread at His
table.   The feast of Cana they have despised, that
far should it be from the Lord to approach unto it.
The Church they call the bride, and our Lord the
true Bridegroom ; and the figure of the wine of the
feast is in their cups; lo! a type of the feast is in
their festivals.   Teaching, divided against itself,
evermore reproveth one, though he doth not perceive.
For how infidel are their words, their deeds reprove
them.   The infidels, sons of hell, may they become,
O Lord, servants of thy tabernacle !

"And if then the Infidel should say, 'As a figure
we praise these things,' then in a figure and not in
truth does your teaching stand.   Let them then honour Satan a little !   But if there be one nature of
the Evil one and bread, why is the Evil one defiled
unto them, and bread, his brother, as a holy thing
to them ?   Praise be to Thee, O Lord, that, as

with a sword, the word of truth cut through, came forth.

"For that bread, the shewbread, they offered honey and milk, and since these things are all pure, not even thus have they found a way to confuse. For honey sufficeth not for an offering, nor milk for sprinkling and drink offerings; shewbread in a figure they offered, and blood and wine in type they sprinkled. The crucifiers and the teaching, the figure which Moses wrote, reproved.

"What then constrained our Redeemer, that He brake bread? Two things it was right that He should avoid, as a stranger to them: 1, He should teach that He had not clothed Himself with a defiled Body; 2, that He was like unto the Creator to whom the shewbread did not ascend [as an oblation], but was offered on His Table. To Thee be praise, that, as with a furnace, Thou hast revealed the brass of the foul doctrine!

"If the Lord put on a Body in appearance, it were right that they should break a shadow; and if He showed the likeness of blood, let them put into the Cup the shadow of wine. But if they break true bread, which they truly touch, and it is not in appearance, the sinful woman who approached our Lord touched a true Body. Do thou bless Him who bade Thomas touch a Body, not a shadow."

But both Tertullian and S. Ephrem would have exposed themselves to a terrible retort, had they held that the elements were as unsubstantial as the heretics feigned our Lord's Natural Body to be. I see no way in which they could have answered the retort; "True! real substances would be, as you say, an unnatural figure of that which we believe to have been unsubstantial; but a mere outward form without a substance is *the* natural figure of an unsubstantial body"

Tertullian's own indignant irony against the Marcionites shows that he was alive to that argument. "And[5] so his Christ was not what he seemed, and what he was, he averred falsely; flesh and yet not flesh; man and yet not man; and so Christ God and yet not God. For why should he not too have borne a phantom of God? Shall I believe him as to his inward substance who deceived as to the outward? How shall he be accounted true in what is hidden, being found so deceiving in what was open?"

Tertullian also, on this very subject, appeals to the outward senses as to the outward elements. "We[6] may not, we may not, call in question those senses, lest their truth should be questioned in Christ Himself, lest it should be said, perchance, that He saw untruly Satan cast down from heaven; or heard untruly the voice of the Father bearing witness of Him; or was deceived when He touched Peter's mother-in-law; or perceived, as other than it was, the breath of the ointment which He accepted

---

[5] Adv. Marcion. iii. 8.   [6] De Anima, c. 17.

for His burial; or afterwards, *the taste of the wine, which He consecrated to be a memorial of His Blood.* For so Marcion too preferred to believe Him a phantom, disdaining in Him the truth of the whole Body."

Again, against the Gnostics who rejected matter, he argues from our Lord's appointing the use of matter, as well in the two great Sacraments, as in other rites of the Church. This implies in a twofold way his belief in the continued existence of the elements.

1. The general argument implies that the matter continued. For if the matter had ceased to be, the Gnostics might have retorted the argument, and said, that it fell in with their view of matter, that matter was rejected in the Sacrament of the Holy Eucharist.

2. He refers naturally to the use of matter in both Sacraments, as being employed in both alike, as the instruments of the spiritual grace.

"He[1] hath not, until now, rejected either the water of the Creator, wherewith He cleanses His own; nor the oil, wherewith He anoints His own, nor the union of honey and milk, with which He nourishes His infants; nor bread, wherewith He maketh present[2] His own very Body, even in His

---

[1] Adv. Marcion. i. 14.

[2] The real question as to the meaning of " repræsento," as bearing on the doctrine of the Holy Eucharist, has been missed on both sides. The one adduces passages in which it signifies,

own Sacraments needing to be a mendicant to the Creator."

Adamantius (probably about the age of Constan-

"makes present to the mind," the other, passages where it means, "makes actually present." It always means "makes present," but this, either to the mind or in act, as the case may be. But in the one class of passages, the very subject itself implies that the object is present; in the other, that it is not. The nature of the " presence," whether it be in act, or to the mind only, is determined by the context, or the subject, not by the force of the word " repræsento." Tertullian uses the word "to make actually present," in the following passages: De res. carnis, c. 14, "de totius hominis repræsentatione;" c. 17, "carnem repræsentandam ipso judicio;" "non egeat repræsentatione carnis;" c. 23, "contemplatio est spei—per fidem, non repræsentatio;" c. ult. "ut ex illa repræsentetur Adam." Adv. Marc. iv. 9, "curationem statim repræsentasse;" iv. 16, "repræsentatione talionis quam repromissione ultionis;" iv. 22, "repræsentans eum—quem repromisi;" ib. 23, "repræsentat Creator ignium plagam;" v. 12, "corporum omnium repræsentationem." De Or. c. 5, "regni Dominici repræsentatio." De Pat. c. 3, "cœlestes ignes repræsentari oppido." Adv. Prax. c. 24, "non ex personæ repræsentatione," and "Filius repræsentator Patris." De Pudic. i. 6, "repræsentati judicii." On the other hand, it signifies "make present to the mind," or "represent," in the following,—Ad Nat. ii. 10, "ut sibi conlusorem repræsentaret." De pœnit. c. 3, "animus sibi repræsentat." Apol. c. 15, "Herculem repræsentat;" c. 16, "aliqua effigie repræsentat;" c. 23, "contemplatione et repræsentatione ignis illius." De spect. c. 17, "mimus repræsentat;" ib. fin. "per fidem, spiritu imaginante, repræsentata." De Præscr. n. 33, "repræsentantis faciem uniuscujusque." De jej. c. 13, "ipsa repræsentatio totius Christiani nominis," and "in spiritu invicem repræsentati." De Monog. 10, "omnia homini quæ non habet, imaginario fructu repræsentat." Adv. Prax. c. 14, "omnes pæne Psalmi Christum ad Deum verba facientem repræsentant." In every place in which the word signifies "make

tine [9]) uses the same argument against the Marcionites: "If [10], as these say, He was fleshless and bloodless, of what flesh, and of what body, and of what
blood did He, giving *the images,* enjoin upon the
disciples both the Bread and the Cup?"

S. Chrysostom in his letter to Cæsarius [1] employs

present to the mind," the very context makes it quite clear that
it is so. On the other hand, in all cases in which it is used
absolutely, without any limitation from the context, it signifies
" make actually present."

In another passage, Tertullian, in reference to the doctrine of
the Incarnation, employs the word while insisting that God makes
use of His creatures, material substances, in order to show His
nearness to man, " For why did He not come in some other more
worthy substance, and especially in His own, that He might not
seem to have been in need of what was unworthy and another's?
If my Creator, through means of the 'bush' and 'fire,' and again
afterwards, through the 'cloud' and 'pillar,' held converse with
man, and used the bodies of elements, in making Himself present,
these examples of Divine power show enough, that God did not
need the apparatus of false or even of real flesh. If we look to
certain truth, no substance is worthy that God should put it on.
Whatever He puts on, He makes worthy, but without untruth.
What a thing it were, that He should esteem true flesh, a greater
disgrace than lying flesh!" (Adv. Marc. iii. 10.) In this, Tertullian uses the word of God's becoming present in act, yet insists
upon its being with true matter, not the appearance of it.

[9] See Benedictin. Præf. ap. Orig. Opp. T. i. pp. 800-2.

[10] Dial. de recta Fide, s. iv. p. 853, ib.

[1] This Epistle to Cæsarius is quoted without doubt by Damascene (A.D. 730) and the later Greek writers. Nor has any valid
ground been brought against it. One can hardly think that its
genuineness would have been questioned, as it has been by Roman
Catholics, had there not been a previous bias against it, as expressing *our* belief that the natural substances remain in the
Holy Eucharist. When first the extract was produced, the very

the same truth, the twofold substances of the Holy
Eucharist, the earthly and the heavenly, against the

existence of the treatise was denied. When this could not be
denied, its genuineness was denied, on grounds whose validity
would not have been admitted in another case. Le Quien's
objection, that it is not quoted in the earlier writers, is not safe,
being simply negative. It might easily have escaped notice,
being a short Epistle to a private person, and (if the title be
true) written in exile. The argument for its antiquity, in that it
mentions no later heretics than Apollinarius, is urged by R. C.
critics, in behalf of other works. It is directed against the
Apollinarian, which in many things anticipated the Eutychian,
heresy, yet so as to use the terms which condemn the Nestorian.
It seems then strange that Le Quien should so groundlessly call
the writer a patron of the Nestorian heresy. (Diss. Damascen.
p. xlix.)   As for Le Quien's objection, that S. Chrysostom
could not have objected to the expression, "Deum pertulisse"
(p. 744, ed. Montf.), it is plain that he uses it in the sense of
θεότης (p. 743). It has been observed that S. Athanasius objects
to the phrase, "God suffered in the flesh," *i. e.* as used by the
Apollinarians, c. Apollin. ii. 13, fin. (Treatises against Arianism,
ii. 444, n. i. Oxf. Tr.), *i. e.* S. Athanasius objects to the very
same phrase, as used by the very heretics against whom the letter
is written, "How have ye written, that it was God who suffered
through the flesh, and rose again ? For if it was God who
suffered through the flesh, ye will say that the Father and the
Paraclete are liable to suffer, the Name being One, and One
Divine Nature."   Montfaucon shows (S. Chrys. Opp. iii. 738, 9)
that the language against which the author writes was that used
by Apollinarius, De Incarnat. (as quoted by Ephrem in Photius,
n. 229), but therewith he cuts away the imputation of Le Quien,
that it may have been directed against the language of S. Cyril.

The condemnation of the Epistle as a forgery was still more
hasty. For the Epistle is entitled "S. Chrysostom's" in the
heading and the subscription only, which form no part of the
Epistle. Even then, although it had not been S. Chrysostom's, it
might still have been a real Epistle written by a defender of the faith.

Apollinarian heresy: "For[2] as we call the bread, before it is sanctified, bread: but, when Divine grace has, through the intervention of the Priest, sanctified it, it is set free from the name, bread, and thought worthy to be called the Lord's Body, *although the nature of bread remains*, and we proclaim not two bodies, but the one Body of the Son; so here too, the Divine Nature having come to indwell in the Body, they have together formed one Son, one Person."

The same statement occurs in the Eutychian controversy in Theodoret. The Eutychian is supposed to urge the sacred mystery of the Holy Eucharist, as an illustration how the Humanity of our Lord is, according to him, absorbed in His Divinity. *Eran.* "I will[3] hence show then the change of the Lord's Body into another *Nature.*—How dost thou call these [the elements] after the consecration? *Orth.* The Body of Christ and the Blood of Christ. *Eran.* And dost thou believe that thou partakest of the Body and Blood of Christ? *Orth.* I do. *Eran.* As then the symbols of the Body and Blood of the Lord are one thing before the Priestly Invocation, and after the Invocation are changed and become others, so the Body of the Lord after the Ascension was absorbed into the Divine *Substance.* *Orth.* Thou art taken in the net which thou wovest. For neither after the consecration do the mystic symbols

<hr>

[2] Opp. T. iii. p. 744, ed. Ben.
[3] Dial. 2. Inconf. p. 125, ed. Sch.

depart from their own *nature*. For they remain in their former *substance* and figure and form, and can be seen and touched as before ; but in thought they are conceived and believed and adored, as being those things which are believed. Compare then the image with the Archetype, and thou wilt see the likeness. For that Body hath its former form and figure and circumference and, in a word, the *substance* of the Body. For It became Immortal after the Resurrection, and Incorruptible, and was exalted at the Right Hand, and is worshipped by all creation, as being entitled the Body of the Lord of Nature. *Eran.* But the mystical symbol changes its former name. For it is no longer called what it was before, but 'Body.' So then the Truth must be called 'God,' not 'Body.' *Orth.* Thou seemest to be ignorant. For it [the Eucharist] is called not only Body but Bread of life. So the Lord Himself called it. And His Very Body we call the Divine Body and lifegiving, and Body of the Lord, teaching that it is not common with any man, but is of our Lord Jesus Christ Who is God and Man."

The whole argument requires that the words should be retained in their special sense. Body is contrasted with Body, form with form, substance with substance. The heterodox argues, that as after consecration the consecrated elements are and are called the Body and Blood of our Lord, so after the glorification, the Body of our Lord is and is to be called God. Theodoret's answer is, that in both cases the natural substance remains, and the name also. The Bread is still called Bread, and, although mystically the Body and Blood of Christ, does "not depart from its own nature;" so neither does Christ. But had he thought of accidents without a substance, this would be analogous not to a real Body of Christ, but to a fantastic Body, such as the Gnostics fabled.

Theodoret uses the same argument in the first Dialogue:

" *Orth.* Thou' knowest that God hath called bread His own Body. *Eran.* I know it. *Orth.* And contrariwise He hath called the Flesh corn? *Eran.* I know this too (S. Joh. xii. 23, 24). *Orth.* But in instituting the mysteries He called the Bread 'Body,' and what is mingled, 'Blood.' *Eran.* He did so. *Orth.* But according to Nature, Body would be called body, and Blood, blood. *Eran.* Confessedly. *Orth.* But our Saviour interchanged the names; and to the Body gave the name of the symbol, and to the symbol that of the Body; so, having called Himself a Vine, He entitled the symbol Blood. *Eran.* Thou hast said truly. But I would know the cause of this change of names? *Orth.* The object is plain to those admitted to the Divine mysteries. For He willed that those who partake of the Divine Mysteries, should not attend to the *nature* of the things seen, but through the change of name, should believe in the change which takes place in this through grace. For He who called the *natural* (φύσει) Body

' T. iv. 25, ed. Sch.

corn and bread, and Himself again a Vine, honoured the symbols which are seen, with the title of bread and wine, *not changing the nature, but adding grace to the nature.*"

Towards the close of the same century, about A.D. 492, Pope Gelasius uses the same argument: "Certainly[4] the Sacrament of the Body and Blood of Christ which we receive is a divine thing, wherefore also we are by the Same made partakers of the Divine Nature, and yet *the substance and nature of bread and wine ceaseth not to be.*"

"And certainly the image and likeness of the Body and Blood of Christ are celebrated in the action of the mysteries. It is there shown us very clearly, that we must think of Christ the Lord Himself, the same which we profess, celebrate, and receive in His image, that as they [the elements] pass into this, *i. e.* the Divine substance, (the Holy Spirit perfecting this,) yet *abiding in their own proper nature*[5], so also

---

[4] " De duabus in Christo naturis adv. Eutychen et Nestorium," Bibl. Patr. viii 703. Four passages out of it are quoted, about 507, by S. Fulgentius (de 5 quæstt. ad Ferrand. c. 18, as written by " Pope Gelasius of blessed memory," Bibl. Patr. ix. 187); one is quoted by Pope John II. between A.D. 532-5. There can then be no question of its genuineness, and Labbe (in Bellarmin.) has admitted it, and " plerique," according to Spondanus, in Marg. Epitom. Baron. A.D. 496. (Baronius, Bellarmin., Suarez, Greg. de Valentia, and " orthodoxi una ferme sententia," according to Baronius, ad A.D. 496, n. 1, had denied it.)

[5] In the Bibl. Patr. ed. Lugd. 1677, it stands, " permanente tamen in suæ proprietate naturæ." For the construction we must read permanentes, or sua pr. natura. The sense is the same.

that that chief Mystery Itself, whose efficiency and virtue they truly represent to us, is out of those [two Natures] themselves continuing, whereof He is, One Christ, because they show that He abides perfectly and really."

Of the same character is the language of Facundus (A.D. 540), in the same church of which Gelasius was a native. "Christ[6] vouchsafed to take upon Him the Sacrament of adoption, both when He was circumcised and when He was baptized; and the Sacrament of adoption may be called adoption, as the Sacrament of His Body and Blood, which is *in* the consecrated Bread and Cup, we call His Body and Blood, not that the Bread is properly His Body, or the Cup His Blood, but because they contain *in* them the mystery of His Body and Blood. As then Christ's faithful, receiving the Sacrament of His Body and Blood, are rightly said to receive the Body and Blood of Christ, so also Christ Himself, when He had received the Sacrament of the adoption of sons, could be rightly said to have received the adoption of sons."

Ephrem, Patriarch of Antioch, A.D. 526 (who wrote against the Nestorians and Eutychians, and died in the year of the fifth general Council), uses the same argument as Theodoret. "S. John" [in his words, "That which was from the beginning, which we have seen and our hands have handled of the Word

---

[6] Pro defens. 3. Capp. L. 9, c. 5. Bibl. Patr. x. 79.

of Life"] " preaches that One and the Same has a tangible and Intangible substance. For in that he saith ' the Word,' he bare witness that the Intangible may be touched, and in that he said ' have seen,' he announces that the Invisible is seen. So then he makes known the One Christ, in substance both intangible and tangible, visible and invisible, and instructeth others to know this. For although each belong to one Person, yet no one in his right mind can say that the nature of the tangible and Intangible, visible and Invisible, is the same. Thus also the Body of Christ, which is received by the faithful, *departeth not from the sensible substance*, and remains inseparable from the invisible grace.   And Baptism, becoming wholly spiritual and being one, preserveth the property of the sensible substance (I mean, the water), and loseth not what it is become."

NOTE H.

On p. 39.

The consecrated elements are said by the Fathers not to be bare *elements.*

THE early Fathers quoted by Roman controversialists, in behalf of the physical change in the elements, say also that they are not "*bare* elements." But since they hold them not to be "*bare* elements," "*common* bread," and the like, it is plain that they must have held them to remain in some sense physically what they had been, bread and wine. No one would deny a substance to be *merely, barely,* that substance, who did not think it to be that substance at all. This is the more remarkable in S. Cyril of Jerusalem, because he so bids the communicants look away from the elements, that he has been quoted as denying their existence. Yet he bids his people not to look upon the elements as "*bare* elements," using the very same term which he uses of the water of Baptism or the oil of the Chrism. He says[1], that before consecration the bread and wine of the Eucharist were "*simple* (λιτὸς) bread and wine;" that, "after the Invocation of the Holy Ghost, it is no more *simple* (λιτὸς) bread." He bids the new communicant "contemplate the bread and wine not as *bare* elements"

---

[1] See the passages below in S. Cyril, Note S, No. 29.

(ὡς ψιλοῖς), but he says equally of the Chrism in Confirmation, "Beware[2] of supposing this to be *simple* (ψιλὸν) ointment;" "this ointment is no more *simple* [ψιλὸν] ointment, nor (so to say) *common* [κοινὸν], after the invocation, but the gift of Christ," and of the water of Baptism, he says, "Regard[3] the sacred laver," "not as *simple* [λιτῷ] water; regard rather the spiritual grace given with the water:—*plain* [λιτὸν] water, after the invocation of the Holy Ghost and of Christ, and of the Father, gains a sanctifying power;" and "Now then thou art to descend into the waters, consider not the *bare* element[4], look for its saving power by the operation of the Holy Ghost[5]."

In like way *S. Justin Martyr* says more briefly, "We[6] do not receive It as *common* [κοινὸν] bread or as *common* [κοινὸν] drink;" and *S. Irenæus*, "As[7] bread from the earth, receiving the invocation from God, is no longer *common* [κοινὸς] bread, but Eucharist, consisting of two things, an earthly and an heavenly;" and *S. Athanasius*, "As long as the prayers and supplications do not take place, it is *mere* [ψιλὸς] bread, and a *mere* [ψιλὸν] cup;" and again, "this bread and this cup, so long as the prayers and supplications have not taken

----

[2] Lect. Myst. 3, § 3, p. 268, Oxf. T.
[3] Lect. iii. 3, p. 26.
[4] τῷ ψιλῷ τοῦ ὕδατος.   [5] Ib. § 4.
[6] See the passage, Note S, No. 2.
[7] See ibid. No. 3.

place, are *bare* [ψιλὰ, bare elements[8]];" and at the close of the fourth century *Jerome of Jerusalem* says, " Whence[9]," *i. e.* from the spiritual effects of the Holy Eucharist, "the Christian is fully convinced that he doth not receive *mere* [ψιλὸν] bread and wine, but in truth the Body and Blood of the Son of God sanctified by the Holy Ghost." For he says, we experience no such effects " when we eat the *bare* [ψιλὸν] bread and wine on our table."

The force of the expression is illustrated by the contrast in the Homily on Penitence, inserted among the remains of S. Amphilochius. "Some[1] he [Satan] prepares to disbelieve and be troubled, and delay, as to the immortal, life-giving Communion, saying that this is *mere* [ψιλὸν] bread and *mere* [ψιλὸν] wine, *and nothing else.*" And S. Ambrose, in contrast with the invisible grace, denies that the water of Baptism is simple water. " Not[2] *simple* water then is the water of the heavenly mystery, whereby we attain to have our portion with Christ."

[8] See ib. No. 20.   [9] Ib. No. 55.
[1] Opp. S. Amphiloch. p. 92.
[2] De Sp. S. Præf. t. ii. p. 603.

NOTE I.

On p. 39.

*On the titles, types, antitypes, figures, symbols, images, as applied
to the Holy Eucharist.*

THE Sacrament of the Holy Eucharist having two
parts, an outward and an inward, and the outward
part having been instituted by our Blessed Lord
with a certain relation to the inward, and gifted
with a certain significance of it, nothing is more
natural than that the titles, type, antitype, symbol,
figure, image, should be given to the outward part.
S. Augustine says of Sacraments (in his well-known
words), " If [1] Sacraments had not some likeness to
the things whereof they are Sacraments, they would
not be Sacraments at all; but from this likeness
they for the most part also receive the names of the
things themselves."

There is, then, no even seeming difficulty in taking
these titles, as used by the Fathers, in their natural
and obvious sense.   The Calvinist party inferred
wrongly, that the Fathers who used these terms,
thought, with themselves, that the outward or visible
part was an emblem—not of the inward part or thing
signified, but of an absent thing.   Roman Catholic
controversialists denied that there was any outward
existing part, which was a symbol.   The Roman

[1] Epist. 98, ad Bonifac. § 9.

controversialists assumed that a thing which itself had no real substance, and so itself had no being, was the type, or representation of another. The Calvinists assumed that, itself existing, it was a type of something absent. Both, without real foundation, and against the natural meaning of the words. But with this exception, the words of Cardinal Perron correspond with those of our Catechism. "The[2] Sacrament of the altar has two natures, one outward, accidental, and visible; the other, inward, essential, invisible. According to the former, it is a sign, figure, antitype; according to the latter, it is verity, fulness, reality." Now, if by this, it was only intended to affirm that the outward part was in itself nothing, and that of which it was the vehicle was all, there would be nothing which we could not accept. It is alike an assumption to say that the outward symbol is the figure of an *absent* Body of our Lord, or that itself *is* not. Rather, the Eucharistic elements are an outward reality, figuring to us that hidden reality, which sacramentally they convey to us.

This class of title, figure, type, image, symbol, were used by minds of every character in the ancient Church freely, naturally. The writers use them, moreover, not as if they were saying any thing of their own, but as employing a current language. It is, so to speak, almost a technical, certainly a received language.

[2] De Euch. L. 2, Auth. i. ap. Albert. ii. p. 274.

Fathers use the words " symbols," "antitypes" in juxta-position with clear assertions of a real objective presence; *i. e.* they assert the actual presence both of the inward and the outward part; the Sacrament and the " res Sacramenti ;" the elements in their natural substance, and the Body and Blood of Christ.   There is no reason to question the genuineness of the fragment of S. Irenæus in which the expression occurs. Corresponding language is used by Tertullian; and the use of the term both in S. Basil's Liturgy and Apostolic Constitutions, makes it probable that it was a received expression.   The whole passage is,—" Wherefore [3] the oblations are not according to the law, the handwriting whereof the Lord having blotted out, took away, but according to the Spirit. For we must worship God in spirit and in truth. Wherefore also the oblation of the Eucharist is not fleshly but spiritual, and thereby clean. For we offer unto God the bread and the cup of blessing, giving thanks unto Him, that He has commanded the earth to send forth these fruits for our nourishment, and afterwards, having duly performed the oblation, we call forth the Holy Spirit that He would make this sacrifice and this Bread the Body of Christ, and the Cup the Blood of Christ, that they who receive these *antitypes* may obtain forgiveness of sins and eternal life."

The language and doctrine altogether correspond

---

[3] Pfaff. fragm. Anecdota S. Irenæi, pp. 26, 27.

with the well-known language of S. Irenæus, in which, with the same reference to the employment of the fruits of the earth, he distinguishes between the two parts of the Holy Eucharist, the earthly and the heavenly [4].

S. Clement of Alexandria says, "The mystic *symbol* then of the Holy Blood, the Scripture hath called wine [5]."

Tertullian uses the corresponding Latin expression, when he says, "He made it that His own Body, saying, 'This is My Body,' *i. e.* the *figure* of My Body [6]." The outward part *is* a figure of the inward. He had used nearly the same words before [7], —"For so God revealed in your Gospel too [8], calling bread His Body, that hence too thou mayest at once understand that He [9] gave to bread to be a *figure* of His Body, of which Body the Prophet aforetime spake figuratively as bread, the Lord Himself being about to explain this mystery afterwards."

Origen, having spoken of the bread as remaining,

[4] See below, Note S, No. 3.

[5] Paedag. ii. 2, p. 68.

[6] Adv. Marc. v. 40.

[7] Adv. Marc. iii. 19, p. 493-4, ed. Rig. In the adv. Jud. c. 10, p. 222 A, more briefly,—"For so Christ revealed, calling bread His Body, of whose Body afore the Prophet spake figuratively, as bread."

[8] S. Luke, which the Marcionites acknowledged.

[9] "Corporis sui figuram pani dedisse, cujus retro in corpus panem Prophetes figuravit."

says, " And [10] it is not the substance of the bread, but the word spoken over it, which benefits him who eateth it, not unworthily of the Lord;" and concludes, "and this may be said of the typical and symbolical Body."

Eusebius uses the words " image," "symbols" of the outward, though consecrated, elements.   In explaining the prophecy of Jacob, he says [1], " That ' his eyes are glad with wine,' and ' his teeth whiter than milk,' I think contain secretly the mysteries of the new covenant of our Saviour.   That ' his eyes were glad with wine,' seems to me to signify the gladness from the mystical wine which He gave to His disciples, saying, ' Take, drink, this is My Blood, shed for you for the remission of sins; do this in remembrance of Me."   And that ' his teeth are whiter than milk,' the brightness and purity of the mysterious food.   For again, He Himself delivered the *symbols* of the Divine dispensation to His own Disciples, bidding them make the *image* of His own Body.   For since He no longer admitted the bloody sacrifices, nor the slaughter of various animals, prescribed in the law of Moses, but ordained that they should use bread as the *symbol* of His own Body, well did He hint at the brightness and purity of the food by the words, ' his teeth are whiter than milk.' "

And again :—" Having received that we ought to

____

[10] In S. Matt. T. xi. n. 14 ; see in the passage in the context below, Note N.

[1] Dem. Evang. viii. 1, fin. p. 380, ed. Col.

celebrate the memory of this sacrifice [that of the Cross] on the table through the *symbols* of His Body and saving Blood, according to the laws of the new Covenant, we are again instructed by the Prophet David to say, ' Thou hast prepared a table before me, &c. [2] ' "

In like way, he uses the word " symbolize" (αἰνίττονται), "represent in a hidden manner:"—" Our Saviour Jesus, the Christ of God, in the manner of Melchizedek, does yet now too perform through His servants the office of the priesthood among men. For as he, being a priest of the nations, no where appeareth to have used bodily sacrifices, but blessed Abraham with bread and wine alone, in the same manner did our Saviour and Lord Himself first, then all the Priests from Him throughout all nations, performing the spiritual priestly act according to the laws of the Church, *symbolize* with bread and wine the mysteries both of His Body and saving Blood, Melchizedek having foreseen this by a Divine spirit, and having foreused the images of the things to come [3]."

Adamantius (about A.D. 320) uses the word " image [4] " of the Eucharistic elements.

Eustathius, A.D. 325 (quoted in the second Council of Nice as " the stable defender of the Orthodox faith, and destroyer of the Arian frenzy"), " Speaking by one and the same spirit " [he and S. Basil]

---

[2] Eus. Dem. Ev. i. 10, p. 39.

[3] Ib. v. 3.   [4] See above, Note G, p. 83.

" the one, Eustathius, explaining the words of Solomon in the Proverbs, 'Eat my bread and drink the wine which I have mingled for you,' says thus, ' by the bread and wine he preaches the *types* [ἀντίτυπα] of the bodily members of Christ [5]. The other (S. Basil) having drawn from the same fountain (as all know who are partakers of the sacred worship), says to this effect in the prayer of the Divine oblation [after the words of Consecration], ' We approach boldly to the sacred altar, and having placed there the *types* of the Holy Body and Blood of Thy Christ, we pray and beseech thee [6].' "

The Greek Scholiast, in answer to the statement in the Council that the elements were called types before consecration only, says, " the holy gifts are often found to be called types after consecration, as by Gregory of Nazianzum Theologus in his funeral oration and apology, in Cyril of Jerusalem, Cat. Myst. 5, and others [7]."

In the Clementine Constitutions there occur the words, " Moreover [8], we thank Thee, our Father, for the Precious Blood of Jesus Christ shed for us, and His Precious Body, whereof also we celebrate these *antitypes*, Himself commanding us to shew forth His Death ;" and, " offer [9] ye the acceptable Eucharist, the *antitype* of the Royal Body of Christ, both in your Churches and in the cemeteries ;" and,

[5] Conc. Nic. ii. Act. 6, tom. 3, fin. T. viii. p. 1100, ed. Col.
[6] Ibid.   [7] Ibid.
[8] vii. 25.   [9] vi. 30.

" when [1] He had delivered to us the Mysteries, *anti-typical* of His precious Body and Blood."

S. Cyril of Jerusalem says, " in [2] the *type* [τύπῳ] of bread is given to thee His Body, and in the *type* [τύπῳ] of wine His Blood."   In the very appeal, not to trust our senses as if they were *mere* bread and wine, he tells them, " trust [3] not the decision to thy bodily palate [which could only tell us of the earthly and outward part], for when we taste, we are bidden to taste, not bread and wine, but the *antitype* [ἀντιτύπου] of the Body and Blood of Christ."   In like way he had called " oil" in confirmation, " the antitype [4] [ἀντίτυπον] of the Holy Ghost," and said that Baptism was " the antitype [5] [ἀντίτυπον] of Christ's sufferings."

S. Epiphanius speaks of Melchizedek, as prefiguring by his oblation, the mysteries, *which* were the *antitypes* of our Lord, *antitypes* of His Blood. " When [6] Abraham was eighty or ninety years old, more or less, then Melchizedek met him, and brought forth bread and wine, prefiguring the mysteries of the Sacraments, the *antitypes* (ἀντίτυπα) of our Lord, Who said, ' I am the living Bread;' *antitypes* (ἀντίτυπα), too, of the Blood from His pierced Side, which flowed forth for the purification of those who communicate (κεκοινωμένων), and for the cleansing and salvation of our souls."

[1] v. 14.   [2] Lect. xxii. 3. See Note S, No. 29.
[3] Lect. xxiii. 20.   [4] Lect. xxi. 1.
[5] Lect. xx. 6.   [6] Hær. 55, n. 6, T. i. p. 472.

S. Ephrem speaks of the Holy Eucharist as "the Image of His Truth, and as shadowing forth Christ," "the Image of Christ," in a very remarkable passage in which he regards it as displacing heathen idolatry, and speaks of our Lord as invisibly present "*in* the Bread." The words are spoken by the Blessed Virgin to our Lord. "In' Thy visible Form I see Adam, and in Thy hidden Form I see Thy Father, Who is blended with Thee. Hast Thou then shewn me alone Thy Beauty in two Forms? Let Bread shadow forth Thee, and also the mind; dwell also *in* Bread and in the eaters thereof. In secret and openly too may Thy Church see Thee, as well as Thy Mother. He that hateth Thy Bread is like to him that hateth Thy Body. He that is far off that desireth Thy Bread, and he that is near that loveth *Thy Image*, are alike. *In* the bread and *in* the Body, the first and also the last have seen Thee. Yet Thy visible Bread is far more precious than Thy Body; for Thy Body even unbelievers have seen, but they have not seen Thy living Bread, Lo! *Thy Image* is shadowed forth in the blood of the grapes on the bread; and it is shadowed forth on the heart with the finger of love, with the colours of faith.

' On the Nativ. Rhythm xi. p. 50, 1. Oxf. Tr. t. ii. p. 420, Syr. Albertin. Art. Ephrem, p. 450, quotes from the " de natura Dei curiose non scrutanda." " Behold diligently, how, taking in His Hands the bread, He blessed and brake *as a figure* of His immaculate Body, and the Cup He blessed and gave to His Disciples *as a figure of* His Precious Blood."

Blessed be He that by the *Image of His Truth* caused the graven images to pass away."

S. Gregory of Nazianzum, relating the miraculous cure of his sister Gorgonia, says, " Whatsoever [8] of the *antitypes* [*i. e.* types] of the venerable Body or Blood her hand treasured," and even in the fervid appeal to the Magistrate for his people, " I offer [1] to thee Christ and His emptying of Himself for us, and the Passion of the Impassible, and the Cross and the Nails, by which I was loosed from sin, and the Blood, and the Burial, and the Resurrection and Ascension, yea and this Table, which we approach in common, *and the types of my salvation*, which I consecrate with the same mouth wherewith I intercede with thee, the holy Mystery which beareth us on high."

Again, in contrast with that unveiled fulness of fruition in heaven, he says, " We [2] shall partake of the Passover now indeed typically, even though more openly than the old Passover (for that of the law, I am

---

[8] Orat. 8, § 18, p. 229, ed. Ben. In Orat. 2, § 95, he uses the same word, of the Eucharistic sacrifice, as the type of the Sacrifice of the Cross. " I knowing these things, and that he is nowise worthy of the Great God and Sacrifice and Priest, who has not first offered up himself a holy living sacrifice to God, nor shewn the reasonable, acceptable service, nor sacrificed to God the sacrifice of praise and a broken heart, which sacrifice alone He who hath given all things demandeth back from us, how could I dare to offer to Him the visible [sacrifice], the *antitype* of the great Mysteries ? "

[1] Or. 17, § 12, p. 325.

[2] Or. 45, § 23, p. 863.

bold to say, was an obscure *type of a type*); but a little afterward, more perfectly and purely, when the Word drinketh it new with us in the kingdom of the Father, revealing and teaching what He hath shewn in less measures."

S. Macarius says of the ancient Fathers, "It³ had not come into their heart, that there shall be a baptism of fire and of the Holy Ghost, and that in the Church Bread and Wine are offered, an *antitype* (ἀντίτυπον) of His Flesh and Blood, and that they who partake of the visible⁴ bread spiritually eat the Flesh of the Lord."

S. Ambrose, and the author of De Sacramentis who imitated him, illustrate one another. Both affirm the Real Presence, but S. Ambrose speaks of the Body as *signified*, i. e. by the elements; the other writer speaks of the "oblation" as "a *figure* of the Body and Blood of our Lord."

S. Ambrose says, "Before the blessing of the heavenly words, another substance is named, after the consecration the Body is *signified*." He does not speak here of any change of the elements, but he says that, under the outward substance, *that* is *signified* which to the believer is his all, the Presence of Christ, of His Body and His Blood. "Before the

---

³ Hom. 27, p. 164.

⁴ φαινομένου, translated " visibili " by Joh. Picus. Turrianus interprets it wrongly, "apparent without the substance." See instances from S. Macarius in Suicer, v. φαίνομαι· and in Albertinus, Art. S. Cyril. Jer. p. 429, 30, and S. Macarius, p. 437.

consecration," he would say, "another substance is spoken of; after it, the Body is signified." He speaks of it as *signified*, i. e. denoted by the *sign*.

The author of the De Sacramentis, after stating, "Thou [5] hast learnt then, that of the bread there becometh the Body of Christ, and that wine and water are put into the Cup; but it becometh Blood by the consecration of the heavenly Word," still uses the words "likeness" and "figure." "But [6] perchance thou sayest, It has not the matter [7] of blood. But it hath a likeness. For as thou didst receive [in baptism] the likeness of death, so also thou drinkest the likeness of the precious Blood, that so there should be no horror at gore, and yet the price of our redemption should operate. Thou hast learnt then, that what thou receivest is the Body of Christ." "Wouldest [8] thou know that it is consecrated by heavenly words? Hear what the words are, The Priest says, ' Make to us this Oblation availing, valid, reasonable, acceptable, which [9] *is* the *figure* of the Body and Blood of our Lord Jesus

[5] iv. 4, § 19.   [6] Ib. 20.

[7] I have so translated " speciem," both on account of its use in S. Ambrose (de Myst. c. iv. § 25), whom this author imitates so closely, as on account of the contrast with " similitudo." Roman Catholics render it " outward appearance."

[8] iv. 5, § 21.

[9] " Quod figura est Corporis et Sanguinis Domini nostri Jesu Christi." This occupies the same place as the words " ut nobis Corpus et Sanguis fiat dilectissimi Filii Tu Domini Dei nostri Jesu Christi," in the old Roman Missal, Ass. Cod. Lit. iv. p. 160.

Christ,' " &c. In commenting on this prayer, he says, "Before [10] it is consecrated, it is bread ; but when the words of Christ are added, it is the Body of Christ ;" and again, " Before the words of Christ, it is a cup full of wine and water ; when the words of Christ have operated, then the Blood of Christ is produced who redeemed the world."

S. Jerome, in his translation of the 2nd Paschal Epistle of S. Theophilus of Alexandria, uses the word "ostenditur" in the same way, of the consecrated elements, as signs of the unseen Presence of our Lord's Body. "For [1] he [Origen] says that the Holy Ghost does not operate on things lifeless, nor come to things unendued with reason. In asserting this, he does not remember that the mystic waters in baptism are consecrated by the coming of the Holy Ghost: and that the Bread of the Lord, whereby the Body of the Saviour *is shewn*, and which we break to our sanctification, and the Sacred Cup, which are placed upon the Church's altar, are sanctified by the invocation and coming of the Holy Ghost."

S. Jerome accepts also without blame the statement of Jovinian [2], that " the Lord offered not water, but wine, in the *type* of His Blood."

---

[10] Ib. § 23.   [1] Ep. 98, i. 589, ed. Vall.

[2] Adv. Jovin. ii. 5, ii. 330, ed. Vall. S. Jerome, in his answer to Jovinian's argument, incidentally substitutes the words, "excepting the mystery which He depicted as a type of His Passion " (p. 352), but not as a correction of Jovinian's language.

S. Jerome himself uses the word "type" in explaining Jerem. xxxi. 12, "They shall flow together to the goodness of the Lord for wheat and for wine and for oil;" "of which [3]," he says, "the bread of the Lord is made, and the *type* of His Blood is fulfilled," &c.

S. Gregory of Nyssa :—

"But [4] we,—who have learned from the holy voice, that, 'except a man be born again of water and of the Spirit, he cannot enter into the kingdom of God;' and that 'he that eateth My Flesh, and drinketh My Blood, shall live for ever,' we believe that the mystery of godliness has its validity in the confession of the Holy Names; I mean of the Father, and of the Son, and of the Holy Ghost; and that our salvation is strengthened by participation in the mystical rites and *symbols*."

S. Augustine uses both the words "figure" and "sign" of the outward elements. "In [5] the history of the New Testament, by that so great and so marvellous patience of our Lord itself, that He bore so long with him [Judas] as if good, although not ignorant of his thoughts, when He brought him near to that feast in which He commended and delivered to His disciples the *figure* of His own Body and

The argument relates to the ordinary use of wine, not to the mystery of the Holy Eucharist. Either phrase is according to the received usage.

[3] Ad loc. t. iv. p. 1063, ed. Vall.

[4] Cont. Eunom. Orat. xi. T. 2, p. 704.

[5] In Ps. 3, §1.

Blood ;"—and, "The[6] Lord hesitated not to say, 'This is My Body,' when He gave a *sign* of His Body." And again, "These[7] things are therefore called Sacraments, because in them one thing is seen, another *understood*. What is seen hath a bodily form[8], what is understood hath a spiritual fruit." Again ; "This[9] Bread ['the Bread Which came down from Heaven'] the manna signified : this Bread the Altar of God doth *signify*. Those were Sacraments ; in signs they are diverse, in the thing signified they are alike."

S. Chrysostom says, "For[10] if Jesus did not die,

[6] c. Adimant. Man. c. 12, § 3.

[7] Serm. 272, ad Inf. p. 1104.

[8] "Speciem." Species is used by S. Augustine for the outward visible part, in Joann. Hom. xi. §. 4. p. 168. O. T. "If, then, the figure of the sea imported so much, what must the reality [species] of Baptism import ? If what was done in the figure was the means, that the people, being brought over, came to the manna ; what shall Christ make good in the verity of His Baptism, to His people through Him brought over?" And again, Hom. 26. § 12. p. 408, "'And did all drink the same spiritual drink.' They one thing ; we another ; but other, only in the visible object [specie visibili] which, however, should signify this same thing in its spiritual virtue." And from this very sermon, "that there may be the visible form [species] of bread, many grains are besprinkled into one." Albert. who quotes these (p. 518), adds from Arnob. in Psalm 104, "Rising from the dead, opening His storehouses, He succoureth there a thousand generations perishing with hunger, administering to them not only the kind [speciem] of corn but also of wine and oil." (Bibl. P. viii. 296.)

[9] Hom. 26 in S. John vi. 50. pp. 407, 408, O. T.

[10] On S. Matt. xxvi. 26, Hom. 82, § 1, p. 1084, Oxf. Tr.

of what are the rites the *symbols ?* " and " the [11] Priest only performs a symbol."

Palladius, A.D. 401, in his Life of S. Chrysostom, uses the word " symbols," where S. Chrysostom has spoken plainly of the " Blood [1] of Christ."   " He [2] (Acacius) rushed in shamelessly, like a wolf, parting the crowds with the flashing steel, and entering in, where are the holy waters, to hinder them that were being initiated into the resurrection of the Saviour: and having dashed with effrontery against the deacon, he overset the *symbols :* but the presbyters and other aged men, he having beaten about the head with clubs, sprinkles the font with blood."

He uses the word, as a received title of the consecrated elements.   " Not [3] finding them, he burns with faggots their cells, burning along with them all the Canonical Scriptures, and religious books, and a little boy (as eye-witnesses said), and the *symbols* of the mysteries."

And again : — " They [4] gave in the accusations, which himself had secretly dictated ; which had nothing true in them, except this, that he recommended all, after the Communion, to take a little water, or piece of bread, lest involuntarily with the spittle or phlegm, they should spit out ought of the *symbol.*"

[11] Twice.   Hom. 2, in 2 Tim. fin. p. 184, O. T.

[1] Ep. ad Innoc. iii. 519.   See below, Note S, No. 61.

[2] Dial. de Vit. S. Chrys. c. 9, Opp. S. Chrys. xiii. 34.

[3] Ib. c. 7, p. 23.   [4] Ib. c. 8, p. 26.

The reality both of the Symbols and of the Gift conveyed through them is expressed at once by the *Pseudo-Dionysius.* "The[5] venerable *symbols*, through which Christ is *signified* and partaken, being placed on the Divine Altar;" and then he has, "in presence of the most holy *symbols*[6]," which S. Maximus explains, "The Body[7] and Blood."

S. Hilary the Deacon; "As[8] a *type* whereof [of the Blood of Christ] we receive the mystical Cup of Blood for the defence of our body and soul."

S. Gaudentius uses the same word as Tertullian and S. Augustine, "figura." "The[9] toils of the Passion of Christ, both kings (the highest order of Priests), and each of lower degree, following them, whether of the Levitical order [Deacons], or the faithful of the people, we offer for the well-being of our common life, *in the figure* of His Body and Blood (in figura Corporis Ejus et Sanguinis)."

In harmony with this, he calls the Holy Eucharist "the pledge of our Lord's Presence." If Christ were not present, the Eucharist could be no "pledge of His Presence;" if there were not something distinct, it would not be a *pledge.* Thus far Bertram says truly, "a[1] pledge and image are of another thing, *i. e.* they look not to themselves but to some-

---

[5] τῶν σεβασμίων συμβόλων. De Eccl. Hier. c. 3, § 9.

[6] § 10.   [7] Ad loc. Ib. p. 311.

[8] In 1 Cor. xi. See the context, Note S, No. 32.

[9] Serm. xix. Bibl. P. iv. § 75.

[1] de Corp. et Sang. Dom. ap. Albert. p. 518.

thing else ; for a pledge is of that thing for which it is given." S. Gaudentius says, "This[2] (the Holy Eucharist) is truly the hereditary gift of His Testament, which on the night when He was delivered to be crucified, He left as *a pledge* of His Presence."

Victor of Antioch, about A.D. 400, uses the word "type," quoting an older Commentator, "Another[3] says, that Judas went out before [the mysteries]; for that the minister of the putting of Christ to death, would not have received the *type* [τύπον] of the saving Communion." Victor says also of that which our Lord blessed, that He "delivered to them these *symbols* [of the dispensation of His Passion] to celebrate."

S. Cyril of Alexandria. "That[4] the Communion of the mystical Eucharist is a sort of confession of the Resurrection of Christ, will very readily become clear to any one, by what He Himself said when He accomplished in His own Person the *type* of the mystery. For having broken the bread," &c.

Theodoret, in one and the same context, calls that which we receive, both the symbols of the Lord's Body, and His Body. "After[5] His Coming," he says, explaining 1 Cor. xi. 26, "we shall no more need the

---

[2] de Pasch. Tr. ii.   See more fully Note S, No. 56.

[3] In Cramer Cat. in Marc. xiv. 24, p. 422.   See more fully Note S, No. 64.

[4] In S. Joh. L. xii. p. 1104, 5.   See the context in Note S, No. 66.

[5] In 1 Cor. ad loc.

symbols of His Body, when His Body Itself appeareth.   Wherefore ‘ he saith, ‘ until He come ;’ ” and
then on v. 27, “ That ‘ he shall be guilty of the
Body and Blood,’ shews that, as Judas betrayed
Him and the Jews insulted Him, so they who
receive His all-holy Body in unclean hands, and
place It in a defiled mouth, dishonour Him.”   I
have already [6] quoted his words, where he says, “ He
gave to the *symbol* the name of the Body,” and
again, in the 2nd Dialogue [7]: “ *Orth*. The mystical
symbols offered to God by the priests, whereof are
they the *symbols?*   *Eran*. Of the Body and Blood
of the Lord.   *Orth*. Of that which is indeed a Body
or no?   *Eran*. Of that which is indeed.   *Orth*. If
then the Divine mysteries are *antitypes* of that
which is indeed a Body, then now too the Body
of the Lord is a body, and is not changed into the
nature of the Godhead, but is filled with Divine
Glory.”

And again in the 3rd Dialogue ; — “ *Eran*. A
Body [8] then hath obtained salvation for us.   *Orth*.
The Body of no mere man, but of our Lord Jesus
Christ, the Only Begotten Son of God.   But if this
appear to thee small and worthless, how dost thou
suppose that its *type* would be holy and saving? but
of that whose *type* is an object of worship and holy,
how could the archetype itself be despicable and
mean ? ”

[6] p. 87.   [7] p. 125, ed. Sch.
[8] Dial. iii. Impat. T. iv. p. 191.

And again : — " And [9] when He delivered the Divine mysteries, and had broken and distributed the *symbol*, He subjoined, 'This is My Body.' "

And, "The [1] Church offers the *symbols* of His Body and Blood, sanctifying the whole lump through the first fruits."

Pope *Gelasius* [2], when he states that the elements "abide in their own proper nature," speaks also of "the *image* and *likeness* of the Body and Blood of Christ in the action of the mysteries."

Procopius, A. D. 520, says, " No [3] longer admitting the bloody sacrifices of the law, He gave to His disciples the *image*, or *effigy*, or *type* of His Body."

Eutychius (A. D. 553), while asserting that our Lord gave Himself to His disciples in the Last Supper states carefully (for he does it more than once) that He did so in the "type" of bread. "He [4] sacrificed Himself then mystically, when, after supper, having taken the bread in His own Hands, having blessed, He presented [ἀνέδειξε] and brake it, having mixed Himself in the *antitype* [ἐκμίξας ἑαυτὸν τῷ ἀντιτύπῳ]. In like manner also, having mingled and blessed the cup of the fruit of the vine, and presented it to God the Father, He said, ' Take ye, eat ye,' and ' Take ye, drink ye,' ' This is My Body,' and ' This is My

---

[9] Ep. 145 ad Mon. Constant. p. 1251, ed. Sch.
[1] In Ps. 109 (110) 4, i. 1397, ed. Sch.
[2] See above, p. 88.
[3] In Gen. 49, p. 206.
[4] In Luc. ap. Mai Auctt. Class. x. 490, 1.

Blood.' So then every one receiveth whole the holy Body and the precious Blood of the Lord, although he only receive a portion of them. For He is divided indivisibly in all, on account of the immingling [ἔμμιξιν]. As also one seal imparts to the things which receive it, all its impressions [ἐκτυπώματα] and forms, and itself remains one, and even after the imparting is neither lessened nor changed toward the things which share it, although they be many : or as one voice, sent forth by any one and poured into the air, both remains whole in him who sent it forth, and, when in the air is wholly laid up [ἐναπετέθη] in the hearing of all, none of those hearing receiving more or less than the other, but it is whole, indivisible, and entire with all, although those hearing be ten thousand or more ; and yet it is a body, for a voice is nothing else than stricken air.   Let none then doubt that the Body and Blood of the Lord, incorruptible after the mystical Consecration and the holy Resurrection, and immortal and holy and life-giving, *inserted in the antitypes* [τοῖς ἀντιτύποις ἐντιθέμενον] through the consecration, impresses thereon [ἐναπομόργνυσθαι] its own powers, any less than in the aforesaid examples; but is found whole in the whole of them. For in the Lord's Body Itself 'dwelleth all the fulness of the Godhead,' of God the Word 'bodily,' *i. e.* essentially."

Andreas Cretensis, A. D. 635, unites the words " symbols" and "antitypes," meaning by "symbols" the sacred elements, imaging the sacrifice of the

Cross. "If then to-day, going to meet Christ, we submit ourselves to Him, we too shall be able to receive Him wholly in ourselves, continually immolated unimmolated for us (*for* He is immolated in the symbols *antitypal*, sacrificed for us), and we may bring Him under our roof substantially, being eaten as bread, conceived as a lamb [5];" and "make [6] thy heart the upper room furnished, that thou mayest receive Christ with thee to eat that supper; not that of Lazarus, but the mystical, which expresseth in a type the *image* [ἐκτυποῦν τὴν εἰκόνα] of that spiritual sacrifice."

The 338 Bishops of the Council of Constantinople (A. D. 754) alleged (as is well known) that "the [7] true image" [εἰκών] of our Lord is the Holy Eucharist, "which He Himself, our High Priest and God, having taken our substance wholly, did, at the time of His voluntary passion, deliver as a most evident *type* and memorial to His disciples. For when He was about to give Himself up voluntarily to that His memorable and life-giving Death, having taken Bread, He blessed, and having given thanks, He brake, and distributing, said, 'Take, eat, for the remission of sins, This is My Body.' In like way, having distributed the Cup also, He said, 'This is

---

[5] In Ramos Palm. p. 81.   [6] Ib. p. 90.

[7] Quoted in the Concil. Nic. 2, which rejected it, Act. 6. T. viii. p. 1097, ed. Col. It is said in the answer, p. 1100, that some of the Fathers used the word *types*, but before consecration; which is confessedly an entire mistake.

My Blood; do this in remembrance of Me;' as
though no other *form or type* [εἴδους ἢ τύπου] had
been chosen by Him under Heaven, which could
image [εἰκονίσαι] His Incarnation. . . So then this is
the *Image* of His Life-giving Body, formed pre-
ciously and honourably.   For what did the all-wise
God purpose in this?   No other than to show and
delineate plainly to us men the mystery worked in
His dispensation, that as what He took of us was
matter only of human substance, altogether perfect,
not expressing any distinct person, lest there should
be an addition of a Person in the Godhead, so also
He ordained that the *image*, chosen matter, viz. the
substance of bread, should be offered, not figuring
the form of man, lest idolatry should be introduced.
As then the natural Body of Christ is holy, as being
deified, so it is plain that that which is by institution
His Body, *i.e.* His *Image* (εἰκὼν), is holy, as being
deified by the grace of a certain sanctification.   For
this, as we said, the Lord Christ provided, that as
He deified the flesh which He took, by a holiness
belonging to It by Nature, from its very union, so
also He was pleased that the Bread of the Eucharist,
as being no untrue *image* of His natural Flesh, being
sanctified by the descent of the Holy Ghost, should
become a Divine Body, with the intervention of the
Priest, who makes the oblation, transferring what is
common to what is holy.   But the rational Flesh of
the Lord, having a soul and mind, was anointed by
the Holy Ghost with the Godhead.   In like way,

too, the God-given *image* of His Flesh, the Divine
Bread, was filled with the Holy Ghost, together
with the Cup of the Life-giving Blood of His Side.
This, then, is shewn to be no untrue *image* of the
Incarnation of Christ our God, as aforesaid, which
He Himself, the true Quickener and Maker of
nature, delivered with His own Voice[s]."

It is remarkable that a defender of image wor-
ship, Stephanus Stylites, still allows the same title of
Antitype, upon which the Council of Bishops had
raised their argument.   He addresses the Emperor
Constantine, "Wilt[9] thou also proscribe from the
Church the *antitypes* of the Body and Blood of
Christ, as having an *image* and true *figure* of them?"

In the Western Church the same language is
used, down to Bede, as faithfully imitating S. Augustine.   "The[1] solemnities of the old passover being
ended, which were observed in memory of the
ancient deliverance out of Egypt, He passed over to
the new, which the Church longeth to solemnize in
memory of her redemption; that is to say, that He,
giving in place of the flesh and blood of the lamb
the Sacrament of His own Flesh and Blood *in the
figure* of bread and wine, might show that He it is
to Whom 'the Lord sware and will not repent;

[s] In Concil. Nic. 2, Act. 6, Tom. iii. ; Conc. viii. 1096-8,
ed. Col.

[9] Vit. Steph. ap. Surium. Nov. 28, c. 36, quoted by Albertin. p. 913.

[1] In S. Luc. xxii. p. 331, ed. Gil.

Thou art a Priest for ever after the order of Melchizedek.'   But Himself breaketh the bread which He giveth, that He may show that the breaking of His Body would not be without His own free-will."

In the same general sense of a real substance shadowing what is unseen, I doubt not, the word "antitype" is to be taken, in the author of the Homily on our Lord's Resurrection, formerly ascribed to S. Epiphanius.   "Be[2] ye renewed this day, and renew ye a right spirit in your hearts, that ye may receive the mysteries of the new and true feast, and that ye may enjoy this day that indeed Heavenly delight, and may depart having been enlightened with the *antitypal* mysteries (μυστήρια ἀντίτυπα), which was not old, of the new Passover instead of the old."   The word must here be used of the Sacrament of Baptism[3], but its meaning is still "a type corresponding to the invisible grace typified by it."   The word, I doubt not, is not here used in our sense of antitype, "the substance corresponding to the type."   The contrast between "the old and the new Passover" has been already expressed;   the antitype, then, I cannot doubt, expresses something further, the relation of the outward part of the Sacrament to the inward unseen grace.

[2] Opp. S. Epiph. ii. 278.
[3] On account of the word " enlightened."

NOTE K.

On p. 28.

The coal in Isaiah's vision a type of the outward and inward part of the Holy Eucharist.

THE characteristic of the coal in Isaiah's vision [1], as a type of the Holy Eucharist, is that there is a bodily substance, whose virtue and power come wholly from that within, which penetrates and fills it. It is employed as a type also of the Divine and Human Nature of our Lord. For His Human Nature would have been the nature of a mere man, unless it had been hypostatically united with the Godhead. The point of comparison is not the union, but the Presence of that which is higher within that which is inferior, through which that which is higher operates and is effective. Our Lord worked that for which He became Man, through His Manhood, His Person being Divine. S. Cyril of Alexandria notices this characteristic of the comparison, although he applies it only to the Divine and Human Natures of our Lord. "As [2] the coal is wood by nature, but is wholly, throughout its whole self, filled with fire and hath its power and efficacy, in like way, I conceive, may our Lord Jesus Christ be rightly thought of. For the Word became flesh and tabernacled among us. But even though, according to the dispensation,

---

[1] Is. vi. 6.   [2] Ad loc. ii. 107, 108.

He was seen as Man among us, yet the whole
fulness of the Godhead dwelt in Him, in the way of
union.   In this way He is seen to have had, through
His own Flesh also, the most Divine powers of operation[3].   Thus He touched the bier, and raised the
dead son of the widow.   And having spat, He gave
sight to the blind, anointing the eyes with clay."

In his treatise against Nestorius, he places pro-
minently the same symbol, how although the Godhead and Manhood in our Lord, are, by nature,
essentially different, yet of both is One Christ, the
Godhead and Manhood meeting together by a true
union.   But in this very comparison, although
writing against Nestorius, he guards against opposite
heresy, insisting that the inferior substance, although
penetrated and influenced by the higher, still remained.   "But[4] He is likened to a coal, because He
is understood to be of two unlike substances, which,
however, so come together as to be in truth all but
bound together in oneness.   For fire, having entered
into wood, transelements it after a fashion into its
own glory and power, albeit retaining what it was."

The Fathers, then, were familiar with the thought
that the coal was a symbol of the union of two
unlike substances, as unlike as the Godhead and
the Manhood joined together by an union, whether
Personal as relates to our Lord's Divine and Human

---

[3] θεοπρεπεστάτας τὰς ἐνεργείας.

[4] εἰς οἰκείαν αὐτὸ μεταστοιχιεῖ τρόπον τινὰ δόξαν τε καὶ δύναμιν.
Adv. Nest. l. 2, vi. 32.

Natures, or Sacramental, but the lower nature also remaining in its natural substance and identity.

"Among the Syriac titles of the Eucharistic bread (Assemani[5] says), the most celebrated is *gmurto*, which signifies ' coal.' " " The coal[6]," says S. James of Sarug, " is a type of the Body of the Son of God. There was shown to him an image of what was to be on the earth, how the mercies should dawn, which should cleanse all sinners. Of the pearl which is here laid on the table, the coal which the Seraph gave to Isaiah was a figure. The prophet saw the whole type of things to come, how and by Whom the guilt of the world is purged. The Seraph took It not in his hands, that he might not burn; and the Prophet received It not in his mouth, that he might not perish. He took not, and he ate not that Glory. Because It was incorporeal, It was neither handled, nor eaten. Because this Coal was seen in a bodily form, lo! It is eaten from the table of the Deity."

S. Ephrem not only directly speaks of the living coal as a type, but that type is the groundwork of the expression by which he so commonly designates the Real Presence, as " Fire *in* the bread," " *in* the wine," " *in* the cup." By both he designates an inward spiritual Presence, beneath an outward substantial form.   In the following passage he combines both ;

---

[5] Bibl. Or. i. 79.
[6] Inserted in the Syriac of S. Ephrem, ad loc. ii. 30.

"*In* ' Thy visible vesture there dwelleth an hidden power. A little spittle from Thy mouth became also a great miracle of light in the midst of its clay. *In* Thy Bread is hidden the Spirit that cannot be eaten; *in* Thy Wine there dwelleth the Fire that cannot be drunk. Thy Spirit *in* Thy Bread and the Fire *in* Thy Cup are distinct miracles, which our lips receive. When the Lord came down to the earth unto mortal men, He created them a new creation, as in the Angels He mingled Fire and the Spirit, that they might be of Fire and Spirit in a hidden manner. The Seraph did not bring the living coal near with his fingers; it did not come close up to Isaiah's mouth; he did not himself lay hold of it or eat it; but unto us the Lord hath given both of them. To the Angels which are spiritual, Abraham brought bodily food, and they ate. A new miracle it is, that our mighty Lord giveth to bodily creatures Fire and the Spirit, as food and drink. Fire came down upon sinners in wrath, and consumed them. The Fire of the Merciful *in* bread cometh down and abideth. Instead of that fire which devoured men, ye eat a Fire *in* bread, and are quickened. As fire came down on the sacrifice of Elijah and consumed it, the Fire of Mercy hath become to us a Living Sacrifice. Fire ate up the oblations, and we, O Lord, have eaten Thy Fire *in* Thine oblation.

"'Who hath taken the Spirit in the hollow of

' Adv. Scrut. Rhythm 10, § 3. 5. 7, pp. 146, 147, Oxf. Tr. T. iii. p. 23, Syr.

his hand?' Come and see, O Solomon, what the Lord of thy father has done! Fire and Spirit against its nature, He hath mingled, and hath poured them into the hollow of the hands of His disciples. 'Who hath bound the waters in a garment?' he asked. Lo the fountain is in a garment, the skirts of Mary. From the Cup of life, the distilling of life, within the veil, do Thine handmaids take.

"Oh Might, hidden in the veil of the Sanctuary, Might which the mind never grasped, It hath His Love brought down; and It descended and lighted upon the veil of the altar of propitiation. Lo! Fire and Spirit in the bosom of her that bare Thee! Lo! Fire and Spirit in that river wherein Thou wert baptized; Fire and Spirit in our baptism! *In* the Bread and the Cup is Fire and the Holy Ghost. Thy Bread hath killed the greedy one who made us his bread; Thy Cup destroyeth death which swallowed us up. We have eaten Thee, O Lord, yea, we have drunken Thee, not that we shall make Thee fail, but that we might have life in Thee."

S. Ephrem interprets in the same way the coals of fire, in Ezekiel's vision, which the Cherub took and scattered over the city :—

"Those[s] 'coals,' again, and the man clothed in linen, who bringeth them forth and scattereth them upon the people, are a type of the priest of God, through whom the living coals of the life-giving

---

[s] On Ezek. x. 2, T. ii. p. 175.

Body of our Lord are given. But this, that another Cherub stretched out and placed them in his hand, this is a type that it is not the priest who can of bread make the Body, but Another, who is the Holy Spirit."

To give another instance of the mention of fire as a symbol of the Real Presence in the Holy Eucharist, "Thy[9] garment, seeing that it was the covering of Thy Human Nature, and Thy Body, seeing that It was the covering of Thy Divine Nature, coverings twain they were to Thee, Lord, the garment and the Body, that Bread, the Bread of life. Who would not marvel at Thy changes of garment? Lo! the Body covers Thy glorious fearful brightness; the garment covered Thy feebler nature; the bread covereth the Fire which dwells *therein.*"

Hence, also, in one of the many places in which he speaks of the Holy Eucharist, often and holily received in life, as a safeguard in death, he speaks of It as a Fire within us quenching the fire of hell. "Lo! Gehenna[10] looks to torment me, and yet Thy life-giving Body was mingled in me. I am clothed with the garment of the Holy Ghost, that I may not burn. When the stream of fire roareth for vengeance, may a fire from me extinguish it, when the smell of Thy Body and Blood striketh it."

S. Chrysostom compares the Holy Eucharist both

[9] Rhythm 19, init. p. 170, O. T. iii. 35, Syr.
[10] Paraenes. 23, T. iii. 458.

with the coal in Isaiah's vision, and with fire, in the same way as S. Ephrem; and the use of the image is too extensive both in Greek and Syriac, to allow of the supposition that it either originated with S. Ephrem, or was simply borrowed from him by S. Chrysostom. S. Chrysostom, in his Commentary [1], simply mentions the interpretation as that of others, himself keeping to the letter. "Some say that these things, the Altar, the Fire placed upon it, the ministering power, the being placed in the mouth, the cleansing of sins, are symbols of the Mysteries to come. But we, for the present, keep to the history, &c."

He himself expands it in his Homilies on the passage of Isaiah :—

"The [2] Seraphim cried the one to the other, Holy, holy, holy! Recognise ye this voice? Is it ours, or the Seraphim's? Both ours and the Seraphim's through 'Christ, Who took away the middle wall of partition, and reconciled the things in heaven and the things on the earth, even through Him Who made both one.' For before [His Incarnation] this hymn was sung in heaven alone; but since our Lord hath deigned to tread on the earth, He hath brought down this melody to us. Wherefore also this Great High Priest, when He standeth by this holy table, presenting the spiritual service, and offering the unbloody sacrifice, doth not only invite us to this holy minstrelsy, but having first spoken of

[1] Ad loc. § 4, T. vi. p. 69.
[2] In illud Vidi Dom. Hom. 5, § 3, T. vi. p. 141.

the Cherubim, and brought before our minds the
Seraphim, He so exhorts us to send up those most
awful words; bearing up our minds from earth
through memory of these our fellow-choristers, and
almost saying to each of us, with piercing voice,
'With the Seraphim thou singest, with the Seraphim take thy stand; with them stretch thy wings:
with them fly circling round the Royal throne.'
And what marvel, if thou standest with the Seraphim, since those things which the Seraphim
dared not touch, these God hath given thee with all
confidence! For he saith: 'There was sent to me
one of the Seraphim, having a coal of fire, which he
took with the tongs from the altar.' That altar is
an image and likeness of the altar; that fire, of this
spiritual fire: but the Seraphim dared not touch it
with the hand, but with the tongs, but thou receivest It in the hand. Were you indeed to regard
the dignity of what is there placed (τῶν προκειμένων),
it is far too great even for the touch of the Seraphim."

From this same likeness, he speaks both of the
Table as "full[3] of spiritual fire," of the Holy Eucharist as "making our mind gleam more than fire;"
of our returning from the Altar as "lions breathing
fire."

The writer of a Homily on Repentance[4] follows
the glowing language of S. Chrysostom, "Where-

<hr>

[3] See Note S, No. 61, S. Chrysostom.
[4] Hom. 9, De Pœnit. ap. S. Chrys. ii. 350.

fore also, when ye approach, think not that ye receive the Divine Body as from man; but as from the Seraphim themselves, with the tongs of fire which Isaiah saw, think that ye receive the Divine Body; and as touching with the lips the Divine and Unpolluted Side, so let us receive the Saving Blood."

He follows S. Chrysostom also in the image of " spiritual fire." " When [5] the mystical table is prepared, the Lamb of God slain for thee, the priests labouring for thee, spiritual fire bursting from the Undefiled Side, the Cherubim standing by, the Seraphim flying, the six-winged covering their faces, all the incorporeal powers, with the priest, praying for thee, the spiritual fire coming down, the Blood in the Cup for thy cleansing, emptied from the Undefiled Side, fearest thou not, art thou not ashamed, at that fearful hour too, to be found a liar?"

Theodoret says briefly, "The Seraphim [6], although having his name derived from fire, and accounted worthy of Divine ministry, not with bare hand, but with the tongs [λαβίδι], took the live coal, and having placed it on the mouth of the prophet, he indicated to him the remission of sin. But by these things is moreover described and fore-typified the participation of our blessings, the remission of sins through the Body and Blood of the Lord."

[5] Ib. p. 349.
[6] Ad loc. T. ii. p. 210, ed. Sch.

"Both[7] Greeks and Copts have a sacred vessel which they call ἀγία λαβίς, as being a type of the forceps, wherewith the Seraph took the coal from the altar and touched Isaiah's lips. For they call Christ a living Coal, full of the power of Divinity."

Another Syriac commentator says,—" The[8] coal which Isaiah saw, what does it pourtray? Isaiah saw in his mind the Divine revelation to come, and pictured it to himself in his thought, the Divine Nature and the Only Begotten Word, the Living immaterial Fire. But that it was with the forceps, is, that by the union with the Body, God the Word was apprehended and received. But that it was approached to the lips of the Prophet, this was, that He was united to our nature, and also became a hallowing food of our souls. The altar figured that which was to be, whereon was mystically ministered the mystery of the Body and Holy Blood, and the Seraphim was a type of the consecrating priest."

Mention is also made of this type in a prayer of the consecrating priest in the Liturgy of S. James, —" The[9] Lord bless us and make us worthy to take with the pure ' tongs' of our hands the fiery Coal, and to place it on the mouths of the faithful, for the cleansing and purifying of their souls and bodies, now and ever."

And more at length in the Liturgy of S. Cyril,—

[7] Renaudot. i. 195, ad Lit. Copt. S. Basil.
[8] Ad loc. ap. S. Ephr. ii. 31.
[9] Ass. Cod. Lit. T. v. p. 56.

"As [1] Thou didst cleanse the lips of Thy servant Isaiah the Prophet, when one of the Seraphim took with the forceps a live coal off the altar, and came to him, and said to him, 'Behold this hath touched thy lips, and thine iniquity shall be taken away, and all thy sins purged,' so also do to us poor sinners, Thy wretched servants. Vouchsafe to sanctify our souls, our bodies, our lips and hearts; and give us that true Coal, which giveth life to our souls, bodies, and spirits, that is, the holy Body and precious Blood of Thy Christ; not to our condemnation, nor that we should incur judgment."

Renaudot says generally, "That coal also whereby in the vision the lips of Isaiah were touched and purified, is commonly said, in the prayers of the Easterns, to have been a type of the Eucharist; and it is often said in their hymns which are sung at the distribution, that mortals receive fire in bread through the communion of the mysteries [2]."

The same interpretation occurs in the Quæstt. et responss. ad Orthod. (probably at the beginning of the fifth century). "Through [3] the vision according to the Prophet Isaiah, He showed the mystery of Christ, sitting on the throne of glory, and through the eating of His Holy Flesh, cleansing the sins of men [once] ungodly, who in the whole earth glorify the Holy and Coequal Trinity for the greatness of

---

[1] Renaudot. i. 49, 50. See also the Coptic, Ib. 54.

[2] Ib. i. p. 325.

[3] Resp. 44, ap. S. Justin M. App. pp. 457, 458.

the Divine gifts; in Whose Name being baptized they were justified, receiving the hope of the participation of the heavenly and eternal goods. For the coal which the Prophet saw brought to his unclean lips, for the purifying of iniquities and sins, indicated the Flesh of the Lord, cleansing from all ungodliness the conscience of those who eat Him."

And later, even in John Damascene,—" Wherefore [1] with all fear and a pure conscience and unwavering faith, let us approach; and it shall be to us in every respect, according as we believe, nothing doubting. Let us honour it with all purity, both of soul and body. For it is twofold. Let us approach it with a burning desire, and placing our hands in the form of a cross, let us receive the Body of the Crucified; and having signed eyes and lips and brow, let us receive the Divine Coal, that the fire of our longing, having received the enkindling of the Coal, may consume our sins, and enlighten our hearts, and that by the presence of that Divine fire, we may be enkindled and deified. Isaiah saw the coal; but coal is not *mere* wood, but wood united with fire; so, too, the bread of the communion is not *mere* bread, but united to the Divinity. But the Body being united with the Divinity, there is not one nature; but that of the Body is one, that of the Divinity united with It is another; so that they both are not one nature, but two."

[1] De Fide, iv. 13, pp. 271, 272.

And later yet, Euthymius, "Isaiah [5] saw the Coal. But a coal is not simply wood, but wood ignited in the fire. It enlightens the worthy; it burns the unworthy, according to the twofold energy of fire. It burns by punishing and consuming."

NOTE L.

On p. 40.

On the terms, "in, under, with, *the bread and wine,*" *as used by the Fathers.*

THE term "*in,*" as used by the Fathers, does not express any "local" inclusion of the Body and Blood of Christ; it denotes their presence there after the manner of a Sacrament. Gerhard observes that Holy Scripture says "Christ dwells in our hearts by faith," Eph. iii. 17. "God walketh in us," 2 Cor. vi. 16. "The Holy Spirit dwelleth in us," 1 Cor. xiii. 16. Holy Scripture does hereby tell us, that Father, Son, and Holy Ghost actually dwell *in* us. It does not, of course, imply local inclusion, nor any personal union with us, as our Lord, God and Man, was One Divine Person. Again, in some way, the Holy Ghost descended at our Lord's Baptism "in a bodily shape, like a dove," but there was no local inclusion of God the Holy Ghost in that bodily form. These are instances of the presence of God, as God. Yet the Presence of our Lord's Body and

On S. Matt. xxvi. 26, p. 1015, ed. Matth.

Blood in the Holy Eucharist is in a supernatural, Divine, ineffable way, not subject to the laws of natural bodies. The word *in*, like the word of our Book of Homilies, "*under* the form of Bread and Wine," only expresses a real Presence under that outward veil.

But the term *does* imply the existence of the elements, *in* which the Body and Blood of our Lord are said to be.

Passages from *Tertullian*, from *S. Ephrem*[1] repeatedly, from *S. Augustine, S. James of Sarug*, have already been given in the Sermon itself. In like way also S. Cyril of Jerusalem says, "*In* the type of bread is given to thee His Body, and *in* the type of wine His Blood." *S. Augustine* says again, "Receive ye that *in* the Bread, which hung on the Cross; receive ye that *in* the Cup which flowed from the Side." S. Augustine again, as quoted in the 'Sentences of Prosper,' "We drink His Blood *under* the form and flavour of wine." *S. Cyril of Alexandria*, "In the life-giving Eucharist, we receive *in* bread and wine His Holy Flesh and precious Blood[2]." And Theophylact, "In the Flesh and Blood of Christ the human mind receiveth nothing bloody, nothing corruptible, but a life-giving and saving substance *in* the bread and wine." *S. Hilary* says, "We truly receive the Word made flesh *through* the

---

[1] See these more at large in the context, above, Note K, pp. 119—131.

[2] Ep. ad Calosyr. Opp. vi. 365.

Food of the Lord" (vere verbum carnem factum cibo Dominico sumimus), " we receive truly *under* the mystery the flesh of His own Body;" and speaks of "the flesh to be communicated to us *under* the Sacrament." Tertullian again: "He[3] consecrated His Blood *in* wine."

S. Epiphanius says, "The[4] Bread indeed is food; but the might *in* it is for giving of life."

The "Cup," in the Fathers is altogether equivalent to the element of "wine," so that the "Cup" stands for the one element as much as the Bread for the other. It is in the same sense that *S. Chrysostome* says, "This[5] which is *in* the Cup is that which flowed from the Side, and thereof do we partake;" and "the Blood *in* the Cup is drawn for thy cleansing from the undefiled Side;" and S. Cyprian[6],— "Nor can His Blood whereby we have been redeemed and quickened, appear to be *in* the Cup, when the Cup is without that wine, whereby the Blood of Christ is *set forth*, as is declared by the mystical meaning and testimony of all the Scriptures."

Bede, following S. Augustine, says, "The[7] poor, *i.e.* those who despise the world, shall eat really, if this be referred to the Sacraments, and shall

---

[3] Adv. Marc. iv. 40, fin.
[4] Expos. Fid. c. 16 init. See Note N.
[5] In 1 Cor. 10, Hom. 24. § 3, p. 326, O. T.
[6] Ep. 63, ad Cæcil. § 1, p. 182, O. T.
[7] In Ps. 21, quoted by Albert. p. 910.

be satisfied eternally, because *in* the bread and wine visibly set before them, they shall understand another invisible thing, *i. e.* the very Body and Blood, which are true meat and drink, wherewith not the belly is distended, but the mind is enriched."

The same is expressed in a different idiom by Isychius. "That[8] mystery is at once Bread and Flesh."

Some old Scholia on S. Matthew employ "through" in the same sense.

"After[9] eating the Passover of the law, *i. e.* the lamb, He then delivers the Passover of grace *through* the bread (διὰ τοῦ ἄρτου)."

NOTE M.

On p. 41.

Our Lord's words, " I will drink no more of this fruit of the vine," were taken by the Fathers, from the first, to mean literally wine.

OUR Lord's words, "until I drink it new," were taken from the first in their literal sense, since they were, S. Jerome says, the groundwork of the belief that wine should be drunk, whether sacramentally or carnally, in the Millennium. "From[1] this place some

[8] In Lev. c. 8. The above passages are mostly quoted by Gerhard de S. Cœna, c. x. p. 76.

[9] Scholl. Vett. in Matth. 26, 27, in Maii Auctt. Class. vi. 483.

[1] Epist. 120, ad Hedib. q. 2, i. 817, ed. Vall.

build a fable of 1000 years, in which they contend
that Christ shall reign in the body, and shall drink
wine, which from that time unto the consummation
of the world He had not drunk." Among these
Millenarians he counts in different places "many[2]
of the ancients," "many of our people," and, in his
own time, "a very great multitude." Especially he
names Papias, Tertullian, Victorinus (whom he
praises highly), Lactantius, Severus, Nepos (whom S.
Dionysius of Alexandria much reverenced[3]), and these
as eminent only among others[4]. Both S. Justin
Martyr[5] and S. Irenæus[6] bear witness to its being a
very prevailing doctrine. Eusebius says that it had
been embraced by "far the greatest number of Church-
writers[7]." I have shown elsewhere[8] that S. Jerome
is historically wrong in attributing to S. Irenæus
and Tertullian, and probably to Nepos, the doctrine
of a carnal Millennium. But S. Justin and S.
Irenæus do, as he says, look upon a literal eating
and drinking as a fulfilment of our Lord's words.
S. Justin says, " He[9] said that He should come again

[2] " Multorum veterum," Præf. L. 18, in Is.   " Multi nos-
trorum," in Ezek. 36, init.   " Plurima multitudo," Id. in Is. l. c.

[3] In Euseb. H. E. vii. 24.

[4] On Ezek. l. c. he says, " Of the Greeks, to join the first
and last, Irenæus and Apollinarius." He omits S. Justin and,
seemingly, S. Melito.

[5] Dial. § 80.   [6] v. 31, 4. 35. 1.

[7] πλὴν καὶ τοῖς μετ' αὐτὸν [Papias] πλείστοις ὅσοις τῶν ἐκκλη-
σιαστικῶν. H. E. iii. 39.

[8] Note D, on Tertullian, pp. 120, sqq. Oxf. Tr.

[9] Dial. § 51.   See further on Tert., Note D, p. 124.

to Jerusalem, and there again eat and drink with the disciples." S. Irenæus, " He [1] promised to drink of the fruit of the vine with His disciples, showing forth both the inheritance of the earth, in which the new fruit of the vine is drunk, and the resurrection of His disciples in the flesh. For the new flesh which rises is the same as that which receiveth the new cup. For not above, in the place above the heavens, can He be understood as drinking the fruit of the vine with His disciples; nor, again, are they without flesh who drink it; for the drink which is received from the vine belongs to the flesh, not to the spirit." I cannot doubt that those Fathers meant, not ordinary, but Eucharistic, eating and drinking [2], yet still they meant such Eucharistic eating, as implied the reception of the natural substances of bread and wine.

And so S. Clement of Alexandria appeals to the passage as well as to the words of consecration, in proof that wine may be used, because our Lord used it. " How [3] think ye that our Lord drank, when for us He became Man? For know well, He too partook of wine; for He too was Man. And He blessed the wine, saying, 'Take ye, drink, this is

---

[1] v. 33, 1.

[2] Tert., Note D, p. 122. This is much confirmed by the discovery of the Clavis of Melito, who interprets in an Eucharistic sense, symbols used by S. Papias (see Spicileg. Solesmens. pp. v. vi.).

[3] Pædag. ii. 2, i. 186, ed. Pott.

My Blood,' [being] blood ⁴ of the grape. He alle-
gorically speaks of the Word, who was poured out
for many for the forgiveness of sins, the holy Fount
of joy. But that what was blessed was wine, He
showed again, saying to the disciples, 'I will not
drink of the fruit of this vine, &c.' But that what
was drunk by the Lord was wine, He Himself says
of Himself, upbraiding the Jews with hardness of
heart" (quoting S. Luke, vii. 34).

S. Cyprian employs the passage in proof that wine
must be used at the celebration, and as proving that
that was wine which He calls His Blood, teaching,
as our Church teaches after him, that it is both.
"Wherein ⁵ we find that the Cup which the Lord
offered was mixed, and that that was wine which
He called His Blood. Whence it is apparent that
the Blood of Christ is not offered, if there is no wine
in the Cup; nor the sacrifice of the Lord celebrated
by a legitimate consecration, unless our oblation and
sacrifice corresponds with His Passion. But how
shall we drink new wine of the fruit of the vine with
Christ in the kingdom of the Father, if in the sacrifice of God the Father and of Christ, we do not
offer wine, nor mingle the Cup of the Lord according to the Lord's institution?"

S. Hilary speaks of it as the Consecrated Cup,
and yet by its natural name. "Nor ⁶ could he

---

⁴ S. Clement adopts this construction to avoid separating our
Lord's words, else it is "This" blood of the grape " is My Blood."
⁵ *i. e.* in this passage. Ep. 63, § 6, p. 186, Oxf. Tr.
⁶ Ad loc. cap. 30, p. 740.

[Judas] drink with the Lord, who was not to drink in the kingdom, whereas He promised that all who then drank *of that fruit of the vine* should drink with Him afterwards."   S. Chrysostom regards our Lord's words, both as referring to the proof which He afterwards vouchsafed to give, that He arose in a real Body and as establishing the use of wine in the Holy Eucharist.   " Wherefore [1] did He drink, after He was risen again?   Lest the grosser sort might suppose that the Resurrection was an appearance. For the common sort made this an infallible test of His having risen again.   Wherefore also the Apostles, too, persuading them concerning the Resurrection, say this, ' *We who did eat and drink with Him.*' (Acts x. 41.)   To show therefore that they should see Him manifestly risen again, and that He should be with them once more, and that they themselves should be witnesses to the things that are done, both by sight and by act, He saith, ' *Until I drink it new with you,* you bearing witness.'   And wherefore did He not drink water, after He was risen again, but wine?   To pluck up by the roots another wicked heresy.   For since there are certain who use water in the mysteries; to show that both when He delivered the mysteries He had given wine, and that when He had risen and was setting before them a mere meal without mysteries, He used wine, ' *Of the fruit,*' He saith, ' *of the vine* '. But a vine produces wine, not water."

S. Victor of Antioch supposes in like way that

' Hom. 82, p. 1085, Oxf. Tr.

our Lord refers to this proof of His Resurrection.
" For [8]," he subjoins, " He was about to rise again,
and, having risen, to eat and drink with the disciples; so that a greater and truer belief in the
Resurrection might be implanted in them.   For
He called the Resurrection ' the kingdom of God '
the Father, because from it the kingdom came, and
the participation of it to other men.   When He
said then, ' I will not drink, &c. until,' He pointed
out, not the Resurrection only, but the nearness of
the Passion, in . that He should not have time any
more to partake with them of food and drink—
' Until I shall drink it new,' with you attesting.
For ye shall see Me, when risen.   But what means
' new?'   Unused, in that He had a body not liable
to suffering, but immortal and incorruptible and not
needing nourishment."

S. Epiphanius adduces the words against the
Encratites, as clearly [9] convicting them for not using
wine in the Mysteries.   S. Augustine says on them,
that our Lord, " through [1] the Sacrament of wine,
commends [to us] His Blood."   S. Eucherius, " The [2]
kingdom of God, as the learned interpret, is the
Church, in which, daily, Christ, through His saints,
drinketh His own Blood, as the Head in His members."   Juvencus [3] interprets it like S. Chrysostom,

[8] In Cat. ad Marc. 14. 26, p. 314.
[9] Hær. 47, § 3.   [1] Quæstt. Evang. L. i. q. 43.
[2] Quæstt. N. T. ad Matt. 26, 29. Bibl. Pat. vi. 848.
[3] L. 4. Bibl. Pat. iv. 75.

of drinking it after our Lord's Resurrection. The author of the Synopsis of Holy Scripture in S. Athanasius, speaks of it, in reference to the consecration of the Eucharist. "He[4] delivereth the Mystery; afterwards He says, 'I will not drink of the fruit of this vine.'" S. Basil alleges it in illustration against the heretic Eunomius, that inanimate[5] productions are called by this name (γέννημα), whereas animate are not so called, but sons; and S. Gregory of Nyssa, against the same heretic, that he would gain nothing by ascribing that title [γέννημα, 'product, offspring'] to the Son. "For[6] although wine is called by Scripture, 'fruit, product of the vine,' yet that neither so was sound doctrine injured. For that although, according to the language of the adversaries, the Son is called 'Produce' [γέννημα], we do not the less hereby, too, learn how His Essence is altogether the own Essence of the Father. For whereas wine is called 'the fruit of the vine,' in respect of humidity it is not found alien from that natural property inherent in the vine." S. Jerome himself understood the words of the Holy Eucharist[7].

[4] On S. Matt. T. 2, p. 180. The Benedictines, who question its being S. Athanasius', speak of it as " admirable, composed with the greatest care, wisdom, and learning," p. 125.

[5] C. Eunom. ii. 8, T. 1, p. 244.

[6] C. Eunom. iii. p. 518.

[7] Ep. 120, ad Hedib.

NOTE N.

On p. 41.

The belief of the early Fathers that the Holy Eucharist nourished implies that the natural substance remained.   Difficulties of the opposite theory.

HOLY Scripture itself has been understood to imply that our bodies are nourished by the consecrated elements, *i. e.* that the substance of the natural element is turned into the substance of our bodies. But the substance must be there, in order to be so turned.   The commencement of this change of the material substance, and its power of affecting the human body, is in the case of the one element instantaneous.   And it is precisely of this element, that Holy Scripture has been understood incidentally to speak.

Aquinas himself[1], in answer to the doubt whether the consecrated elements can nourish, appeals to Holy Scripture, where "the Apostle, speaking of this Sacrament, says 'the' one is hungry, the other is drunken.'" The "Glossa Ordinaria," to which Aquinas appeals, says, " He censures those who, after the sacrifice was finished, took back for themselves the gifts which they offered to the altars for making the sacrifice, and did not allow them to be imparted to others who had them not, so that they even

[1] P. 3, q. 77, art. 6.   [2] 1 Cor. xi. 21.

became drunk from them, while others were hungry." Aquinas adds, "which could not happen, unless the sacramental species nourished."

Alexander Alensis [2] quotes the beginning of the Gloss differently. "There the rich offered abundantly bread and wine, that they might be sanctified by the benediction and sanctification of the priest, and be made the Sacrament of the Body and Blood of the Lord. But after the celebration of the sacred mystery, and the consecration of the bread and wine, they claimed their oblations, and, not imparting to others, took them alone, so that they even became drunk," &c. Alensis adds, as an objection, "But accidents cannot inebriate or ingurgitate nor fatten. For accidents cannot pass into substance." He answers as Aquinas.

The earliest Fathers speak simply and naturally of the nourishment of the body through the Holy Eucharist. They knew well the philosophical statement, that substance is changed into substance, and that accidents without substance do not nourish. Substance, in material objects, according to that philosophy, included in it "matter." The early Fathers had exactly the same philosophical language as those in the middle ages. They and the later writers attached just the same ideas to "substance," "nature," "matter." They had the same philosophical theory and distinctions as to substance

---

[2] iv. q. 40, memb. i. art. 2.

and accidents. But the Fathers had no misgivings about the statement, that the Holy Eucharist nourished. Later writers at first denied it, and, when it could not be maintained against experience, they had to devise different theories to account for the fact. Both the earlier and later writers believed that the substance alone nourished, according to the laws which God had assigned to His creation. Later writers, who believed that the natural substances no longer remained, were obliged in consequence to resort to different and contradictory theories. The earlier Fathers had no such difficulties. Why, but that their belief was different? Had they believed that the substance no longer remained, they would have had the same philosophical difficulties as the moderns, and we should have had the same or similar solutions. We find, in fact, no such solutions, because they had no such difficulties.

As to the fact, that the early Fathers did believe that the Holy Eucharist nourished, S. Justin Martyr says, "The [4] bread and a cup of water and wine is brought to him who presideth over the brethren. And he, receiving them, sendeth up praise and glory to the Father of all, through the Name of the Son and the Holy Spirit, and maketh at much length an Eucharistic prayer for having had these things vouchsafed to him. He who presideth having made this prayer, and all the people having assented,

[4] Apol. i. § 65, 6.

those called among us 'deacons' give to each of those present to partake of the bread, and wine and water, over which thanksgiving has been made, and carry it to those not present. This food is by us called Eucharist." And having mentioned true faith, Baptism, and life according to Christ's commands, as prerequisites, he says, " For we do not receive these things as *common* bread and *common* drink; but in what way Jesus Christ our Saviour, incarnate through the Word of God, had both flesh and blood for our salvation, so we have been taught that the food over which thanksgiving has been made by prayer in His words [5], from which [food] through transmutation [6] our blood and flesh are nourished, are both the Flesh and Blood of Him the Incarnate Jesus."

I have quoted one passage from S. Irenæus [7]. He again employs this doctrine in proof of the immortality of the flesh. The body is nourished by that which is the Body of Christ. It is not nourished by the Body of Christ Itself, for that is spiritual and incorruptible; but our Lord gives through His Body that virtue to the consecrated elements that they impart to the body, the life which He Himself is. "Since [8] we are His members, and are nourished

[5] δι' εὐχῆς λόγου τοῦ παρ' αὐτοῦ, lit. " through the prayer of the word which is from Him."

[6] *i. e.* the material parts are changed into the substance of the human body. The Dublin Review, vol. xvi. p. 87, quotes this by mistake as an instance of the change of the elements into the Body and Blood of Christ.

[7] Above, Note G, p. 56.   [8] v. 2. 2 and 3.

through the creature, and He Himself gives us the creature, making His sun to rise, and raining, as He willeth, He owned the cup, which is from the creature, to be His own Blood, from which He bedeweth our blood, and the bread from the creature He affirmed to be His own Body, from which He increaseth our bodies. When then both the mingled Cup and the created bread receive the Word of God, and the Eucharist becometh the Body and Blood of Christ, and from these the substance of our flesh is increased and consisteth, how do they say that the flesh is not capable of receiving the gift of God, which is eternal life—it [the flesh] which is nourished by the Body and Blood of the Lord, and is His member, as the blessed Paul saith, that 'we are all members of His Body, of His Flesh, and of His Bones,' not speaking this of some spiritual and invisible man, (for spirit hath not bones nor flesh,) but of the constitution as to the very man, consisting of flesh and sinews and bones, which is nourished both from His Cup which is His Blood, and from the bread which is His Body. And as the wood of the vine laid in the earth bears fruit in its own season, and the corn of wheat, falling into the ground and dissolved, is raised manifold, through the Spirit of God, which holdeth all things together, and afterwards, through the wisdom of God, comes to the use of man, and receiving the Word of God becometh an Eucharist, which is the Body and Blood of Christ; so also our bodies, being nourished from it [the Eucharist], and placed in the ground, and dissolved in it, shall rise again in their due season, the Word of God granting them the Resurrection to the glory of God the Father."

S. Clement of Alex., explaining Gen. xlix. 11 (as do so many Fathers) in reference to the Holy Eucharist, says, " The vine[9] bears wine, as the Word blood; but both to meat and drink unto salvation; the wine, for the body, the Blood, for the spirit."   The same combination of the material element with the spiritual gift in the Holy Eucharist, occurs in a later chapter on the use of wine. " Twofold[1] is the Blood of the Lord. The one is His natural Blood, by which we have been redeemed from destruction; the other spiritual, *i. e.* wherewith we are anointed. And this is to drink the Blood of Jesus, to partake of the immortality of the Lord. But the virtue of the Word is the Spirit, as blood is of flesh. Analogously, then, the wine is mingled with the water, and the Spirit with the man. The one, the mingled drink feasteth unto faith; the other, the Spirit, leadeth to immortality. And the mingling of both, again, of the draught and the Word, is called Eucharist, an admi-

---

[9] Pædag. i. 5, p. 87, ed. Sylb.

[1] Pædag. ii. 2.   Potter observes, " He says that the Logos [Word] was admingled with the wine, as he had said before that the power of the Word was the Spirit, as blood is the strength of flesh.   Whence he adds a little after, that a man who worthily partakes of the Eucharist is a Divine mixture, in that God had united, and in a manner admingled him with the Spirit and the Word."

rable and beautiful grace, whereof they who partake, according to faith, are sanctified both as to body and soul, the Will of the Father mingling together mystically the Divine mixture, man, with the Spirit and the Word. For truly is the Spirit united with the soul, which is borne along by it, and the flesh with the Word, for which the Word became flesh."

The meaning must be the same, when the earthly substance is spoken of by the name of the heavenly. Then as J. Firmicus says, " We [2] know by what remedies the poisons of your acts are overcome. We drink the immortal Blood of Christ; the Blood of Christ is joined to our blood." Strictly speaking, it is the natural element which is "joined to our blood," but it has virtue from the Divine.

Origen has a statement [3] to the same effect, in commenting on our Lord's words, " Not that which entereth into a man defileth a man." The principles which he lays down broadly, are, that neither does any thing holy, in itself, without the holy action of the soul, hallow a man; nor doth any thing polluted, in itself, without any unholy action of the soul, defile the man. This principle he lays down, " Whoso well considereth this, will see then that it is possible that one who receiveth ill and with passion, what is accounted good, sinneth, and that it is possible that things called unclean, being used by us according to reason, are accounted clean." Origen

---

[2] De err. prof. rell. p. 44, ed. Wouw.
[3] In Matt. Tom. xi. n. 12, T. iii. p. 494, ed. de la Rue.

applies this first to circumcision and uncircumcision, and afterwards in part to the Holy Eucharist. "As[4] it is not the food, but the conscience of him who eateth with doubt, which defileth the eater; for he who doubteth, is damned if he eat, because he eateth not of faith ; and as to the defiled and unbelieving is nothing pure, not in itself, but through the defilement of the man, and his unbelief; so, that which is sanctified by the Word of God and by prayer, doth not sanctify the recipient of itself[5] ; for if so, it would sanctify even him who eateth unworthily the Bread of the Lord, and no one would, through that Food, become weak and sickly or sleep, for so hath Paul established in the words, ' For this cause many are weak and sickly among you, and many sleep.' And in this Bread of the Lord there is profit to the recipient, when with undefiled and pure conscience he receiveth that Bread. So too, neither by not eating, simply[6] from the not eating of the Bread which is sanctified by the Word of God and by prayer, do we lose any good, neither by eating do we gain any good ; for the cause of our loss is our wickedness and sin, and the cause of our gain is our righteousness and uprightness, for this is what is meant by Paul in the words, ' Neither if

---

[4] Ib. n. 14, pp. 498—500.

[5] *i e.* without any qualification on his part.

[6] *i e.* if this be without any fault of ours, as in one not old enough, or hindered, as in the case supposed in the rubric of our Communion of the Sick.

we eat are we the better, neither if we eat not are
we the worse.'   For if 'whatsoever entereth in at
the mouth goeth into the belly, and is cast out into
the draught,' and the food which is consecrated by the
Word of God and by prayer, doth, according to the
material part itself, 'go into the belly, and is cast out
into the draught,' but, according to the prayer which
cometh upon it according to the proportion of faith,
becomes beneficial, and the cause of the mind's perception, as it looks to that which benefiteth them
also, not *the matter* of the bread, but the words
spoken over it, is that which benefiteth him who
eateth it not unworthily of the Lord.   And this
may be said of the typical and symbolical body."

S. Epiphanius speaks of the bread as still remaining as our food, in the very same manner in which
he speaks of the remaining of the element of water
in Baptism.   "The[7] might of the bread and the
force of the water being here strengthened in Christ,
that not bread may be might to us, but that there
may be a might of Bread.   And the Bread indeed
is food; but the might *in* it, is for giving of life.
And not that the water should alone cleanse us, but
that in the force of water, through faith, and operation and hope, and accomplishment of the mysteries,
and the naming of the Consecration, it might be to
us to the perfecting of salvation."

Equally remarkable is the way in which another

---

[7] Expos. Fid. c. 16 init. i. 1098.

writer[8] meets what must be a painful question, if people *will* think about it, what becomes of that part of the material substances which do *not* turn to the nourishment of the body. This writer, the author of a homily on Repentance, formerly attributed to S. Chrysostome, meets the difficulty by affirming that the whole material substance is turned into the substance of the human body. His words are, "Behold[9] not, that it is bread, nor think

[8] De Pœnit. Hom. 9, t. ii. p. 350. The Benedictines say, "The style falls not a little short of the elegance of Chrysostome. So we leave these Homilies (de Pœnit. 7—9) among the genuine works of Chrysostome, not without some scruples. Yet we thought not good to separate them from the rest, since the style of the holy Doctor is not always equal." They speak of these Homilies as "at least suspected." Mr. Field, who has for some years been editing S. Chrysostome's works, has no doubt, on the ground of language, that the 9th Homily is not S. Chrysostome's.

[9] μὴ ὅτι ἄρτος ἐστίν, ἴδῃς. Albertinus (de Sacr. Euch. ii. 9, p. 576) gives the following instances of this idiom in S. Chrysostome : de B. Philogon., "Look not, that the time is short (μὴ ὅτι βραχὺς ὁ χρόνος, ἴδῃς), but consider this, that the Lord is loving to mankind." In tit. Ps. 50, "Look not, (μὴ ἴδῃς ὅτι) that I am little in form." De Cruc. et Latron. "Look not then, that (μὴ τοίνυν ἴδῃς, ὅτι) he was condemned below." In Gen. Hom. 29, "Consider not this then (μὴ τοίνυν τοῦτο ἴδῃς) that the just man was inebriated." De Anna Hom. 3, "For look not on this, that (μὴ γὰρ τοῦτο ἴδῃς, ὅτι) he did not slay [Isaac], but that he did the whole in will." In S. Matt. Hom. 48, § 6, "Look not at the poor, that (μὴ πρὸς τὸν πένητα ἴδῃς, ὅτι) he is dirty and ragged." For the meaning he refers to S. Chrys. in 1 Cor. Hom. 7, § 1, "For I do not judge what I see by the sight, but by the eyes of the mind ;" and the author of a Sermon on Baptism [S. Aug. T. vi. App. p. 289], "Ye ought not to estimate those waters by the sight, but by the mind" (both of Baptism). The three first instances are altogether the same idiom.

thereon[1] that it is wine. For not, as other foods, does it go into the draught. Perish the thought. Think not this. But as wax, brought near to fire, wastes nothing of its substance[2], leaves nothing over, so here, too, suppose that the mysteries are consumed together with[3] the substance of the body."

[1] Albertinus quotes S. Chrysostome in S. Matt. Hom. 19, fin. "Whereas we ought to stand in awe, nor think ($\mu\eta\delta\grave{\epsilon}$ $\nu o\mu\acute{\iota}\zeta\epsilon\iota\nu$) that we are on the earth."   De Bapt. Christi, " Who would not say it was a heart of stone, to think that he was then on the earth ? " ($\tau\grave{o}$ $\nu o\mu\acute{\iota}\zeta\epsilon\iota\nu$ $\grave{\epsilon}\pi\grave{\iota}$ $\gamma\tilde{\eta}\varsigma$ $\grave{\epsilon}\sigma\tau\acute{a}\nu a\iota$.)   In Col. Hom. 6 (of Baptism), " Since earth is subject to thee, think not that thou art on the earth ; thou art removed to heaven." De Sacerdot. L. iii. 4, p. 382, " Thinkest thou that thou art yet among men ($\ddot{a}\rho a$ $\ddot{\epsilon}\tau\iota$ $\mu\epsilon\tau\grave{a}$ $\dot{a}\nu\theta\rho\acute{\omega}\pi\omega\nu$ $\epsilon\tilde{\iota}\nu a\iota$ $\nu o\mu\acute{\iota}\zeta\epsilon\iota\varsigma$), and standing upon the earth ? " In S. Matt. Hom. 50, n. 3, " Think not that it is the Priest who doeth this ($\mu\grave{\eta}$ $\tau\grave{o}\nu$ $\acute{\iota}\epsilon\rho\acute{\epsilon}a$ $\nu\acute{o}\mu\iota\zeta\epsilon$ $\tau\grave{o}\nu$ $\tau o\tilde{\upsilon}\tau o$ $\pi o\iota o\tilde{\upsilon}\nu\tau a$), but that it is the Hand of Christ which is stretched out."   And in this Homily, " Think not that ye receive the Divine Body as from man ($\mu\grave{\eta}$ $\acute{\omega}\varsigma$ $\epsilon\xi$ $\dot{a}\nu\theta\rho\acute{\omega}\pi o\upsilon$ $\nu o\mu\acute{\iota}\sigma\eta\tau\epsilon$ $\mu\epsilon\tau a\lambda a\mu\beta\acute{a}\nu\epsilon\iota\nu$), but from the very Seraphim with tongs of fire."   [See above, p. 126.]

[2] $\dot{a}\pi o\upsilon\sigma\acute{\iota}a$ is used in Agatharcides ap. Phot. cod. 250, c. 11, of the loss undergone by gold in refining. $\dot{a}\pi o\upsilon\sigma\iota\acute{a}\zeta\omega$ is used of " parting with a person's very substance," in a very specific sense.

[3] Such is the only rendering of $\sigma\upsilon\nu a\nu a\lambda\acute{\iota}\sigma\kappa\epsilon\sigma\theta a\iota$ consistent with Greek idiom. "When construed with the dative, it can mean only " consumed, expended, together with."   See the instances in Albertinus l. c. and Steph. Thes. p. 2006, ed. Valpy. Dr. Gaisford, on my applying to him, kindly answered me,— " $\sigma\upsilon\nu a\nu a\lambda\acute{\iota}\sigma\kappa\epsilon\sigma\theta a\iota$] It appears to me that this word can only be explained by a periphrasis. The writer appears to me to mean that the elements are not thrown off like ordinary food, but that they become blended or assimilated to the body, and waste away as the body wastes away."   Mr. Field gives the same meaning.

The word " mysteries" here evidently (as through-out S. Chrysostome, and indeed in every writer on the Sacraments) means and can mean only that which is already consecrated, which is already " mys-terious." It cannot mean, by the very force of the word, the *un*consecrated elements, still less (if pos-sible) the natural substance of those unconsecrated elements, as distinct from their accidents, or their accidents as distinct from their substance. The writer moreover is speaking of that which happens to the "mysteries," not of that act whereby they *became* mysteries. He is speaking of a time pos-terior to consecration.

The question is exclusively, What becomes of the consecrated elements, the outward part, when they are received by communicants? The answer is, that they are taken into the substance of the body, and are consumed together with the body itself, wasting as the body itself does. The " body" here spoken of must be the body of the communicant, not the Body of Christ. For (1) the " mysteries " are, after and by consecration, spiritually, sacramentally, supernatu-rally (although not carnally), the Body of Christ. There remains no further change, according to the belief of any one, through which they could be brought into nearer connexion with the Body of Christ. (2) The Body of Christ, *i. e.* the inward part, is *not* consumed; but the process of which this writer speaks, is one in which the mysteries *are* con-sumed, and that *together with* the body. The words admit of no other sense. The point which the writer is anxious to secure is, that no disgrace should attach to the consecrated elements; that nothing employed in the Holy Eucharist should, after consecration, share what God had allotted to ordinary food. To this he gives an answer peculiar to himself, and un-philosophical; still it *is* an answer, on the supposition that the material part is wholly absorbed into the human body: it is *not* an answer, upon any other supposition, except that the elements after conse-cration were a mere phantom [4].

The same image of wax being absorbed in the fire, is used by Anastasius Sinaita of the bodily food which our Lord vouchsafed to take after His Resur-rection. " Nor did He sleep, or thirst, or hunger, but after the Resurrection ate in such wise as fire consumeth wax, and as the Angels ate, who were entertained by Abraham."

The same belief, without question, expressed by the same word (ἀναλίσκονται) re-appears in Euthy-mius, in the twelfth century. "They [5] [the elements] are neither corrupted nor pass into the draught, but are *consumed* into the essential substance of those who partake of them."

The interpretation of Bellarmin is inconsistent and unidiomatic. He gives as the meaning, " The [6]

---

[4] Hodeg. c. 23. B. P. ix. 856.

[5] εἰς σύστασιν ἀναλίσκονται οὐσιώδη τῶν μεταλαμβανόντων. (Euthym. in S. Matt. xxvi. 26, p. 1012, ed. Matth)

[6] De Euch. iii. 20.

whole substance of the mysteries, *i. e.* of the *consecrated bread,* is consumed by the coming of the Body of the Lord, as wax by fire, and yet there remains the external appearance of bread, as the senses themselves attest." In order to bear his meaning, it must have been "the unconsecrated bread." In regard to the mysteries, *i. e.* the consecrated elements, there could be no further approximation of the Body of the Lord, and (as was said) the word here used must signify "consumed together with," not "by," the body.

It may yet be remarked that the writer incidentally states, that when consecrated "it is bread." "Behold thou not, that it is bread," *i. e.* be not deceived by appearances, so as to look *only* on that which thou seest with the bodily eyes, that it is, as it is, bread, since it is also the Body of Christ.

In the early Church, then, we find it assumed or urged without misgiving, that the consecrated elements nourished; we find it even assumed that the whole material element was absorbed into the human body. In later times we find this denied altogether, or, when the fact that the elements *do* nourish, could not but be admitted, we find it accounted for in most discordant manners.

Two writers against Berengarius, A.D. 1035, *i. e.* Guitmundus, A. D. 1066, and Algerus, A. D. 1130, and in later times Thomas Waldensis, A. D. 1409, denied that the Holy Eucharist nourished at all [7]. Certain cases were excepted, in which it was supposed that the accidents nourished miraculously. This answer failing, different physical theories were devised, whose object it was to explain how, without having any substance, what seemed to be bread and wine could have the same physical effects as if the substance were there.

It was then assumed (1) that a person was not really nourished, but *comforted* by the scent or alteration of those accidents [8]; or (2) that the accidents alone nourished [9]; or (3) that by a supernatural virtue they were turned into substance [10]; or (4) that God gave miraculously to the accident of quantity the properties of substance [1]; or (5) that

[7] Guitmundus, de Verit. Euch. L. 2. (Bibl. P. T. 18, p. 449.) Algerus, de Sacr. Euch. Lib. 2, c. 1. (Ib. T. 21.) Thom. Waldensis (T. 2, de Sacram. c. 61) quoted by Suarez (Disp. 57. sect. 3).

[8] Mentioned and rejected by Alex. Al., Aq. Soto, Suarez.

[9] In Alex. Al. "Some say that as the species [accidents] are there without any subject, as though in the act of substance, so in nourishing they have the act of substance." (Alb. Mag. in iv. dist. 12, art. 16, ad 5, who allows of this equally with (10). It is held by Thom. de Argentin. ap. Major, who rejects it, as does Scotus.

[10] In Alex. Al. and Bonav.; argued against at length by Albertus, Mag. in iv. dist. 12, art. 16, n. 13.

[1] Alex. Al. "As God conferred on these accidents the same power as substance, that of being or abiding without a subject, so He bestowed upon them to effect that which the substance of bread and wine would effect, if they remained, viz. to inebriate, recruit, and the rest of this sort." Aq. q. 77, art. 5, ad 3. "The dimensive quantity retains the proper nature of bread and

the accidents exist after the manner of substance [2]; or (6) that at the moment of decay, quantity passes into matter [3]; or (7) that from it matter is produced, into which form is induced [4]; or (8) that the substantial form which remained, nourished [5]; or (9) that matter was produced "from the possibility of matter," which remained [6]; or (10) that the substance, which was there before, returned [7]; or (11) the same

wine, and receives miraculously the force and property of substance, and therefore can pass into both, *i. e.* substance and dimension,"—"the opinion of the older Thomists, as Ægidius, theorem. 44, 45." It is rejected by Soto, Suarez, and all the later writers. Suarez expresses it thus, "That the quantity alone suffices as a substratum to the substantial form supervening, whether educed from its potentiality or united through nutrition. This seems to be the opinion of S. Thom. here, which Ferrar. (c. gent. iv. 66) so explains and follows, and it is held by Henricus [de Gandavo], quodl. 8, q. 36. Vignerius Summa, v. 9, de Euch. Ruar. [Tapper] art. 14, § Accidentia." It was maintained by Greg. de Val. Disp. 6, qu. 5, de accident. reman. in Euch. punct. 4.

[2] Soto, dist. x. q. 2, art. 6, fin.

[3] Caietan.

[4] D. Soto, dist. 10, q. 2, art. 5, mod. 3.

[5] In Aq. q. 77, art. 6. Aq. denies that it remains, q. 75, art. 6, or that "form" nourishes.

[6] Richard, dist. 12, art. 2, q. 2, rejected by Suarez.

[7] Innocent III. de Myst. Miss. iv. c. 11. Alex. Al. iv. q. 70, memb. 2, art. 2, § 2, who says, "the act of [spiritual] feeding being ended, it ceases to be a sacrament, and feeds corporally," and that "the substance so returning, nourishes naturally." Bonav. accepts either this or 3 equally ; iv. dist. 12, p. i. art. 2, q. 1. Dom. Soto (dist. 10, q. 2, art. 5) says, "All others condemn it, as may be seen in Richard [Middleton] dist. 12, q. 2, art. 2, and in Scotus, q. ult. S. Tho. (q. 77, art. 5), explodes it on the ground that, (1) as the substances of

in kind, but not in number[8]; or (12) that the very
same substance of bread and wine was anew created,
on the decay of the accidents[9].

Thus, when it could not be denied that the consecrated elements did nourish, and that accidents in
themselves did not nourish, a further miracle was

bread and wine had been converted into the Body and Blood
of Christ, they could not return unless the Body and Blood were
again converted into the same substances, which is impossible; for
(2) that they could not return *while* the accidents are there, because
then the Body and Blood of Christ are there; nor *afterwards*,
because then there would be substance without its own accidents."

[8] In Aq. q. 77, art. 5.   Durand. dist. 12, q. 2, n. 10, says,
"matter must be made there anew by Divine power, in order to
nutrition."   Coninck says, "At the instant that the species
[accidents] are so altered, that the substance of bread and wine
could no lonzer naturally be preserved under them, the Body of
Christ ceases to be there, and God creates there matter, and unites
with it the quantity of bread and wine, together with the qualities which inhere in it at that instant, through which it is now
ultimately disposed to the reception of some substantial form,
which at the same instant the agent produces, which would
have produced it, if the substance of bread and wine had been
there before," qu. 77, art. 5.   Vazquez (Disp. 185, c. 3) sums
up, "The more probable opinion is, that the substance which is
produced after the change of the species, and seems to arise
from them, is not produced from them (1) as though from matter;
nor (2) from something holding the place of matter; nor (3) by
conversion of the species into its matter; nor (4) by conversion
into the substance itself; nor (5) generation by a created agent:
but (6) through creation by God Himself, the dispositions which
preceded in the quantity of the species in no way naturally
concurring thereto.

[9] Biel. (Expos. Can. Miss. Lect. 45) accepts alike this or
(10).   Lugo, de Sacr. Euch. Disp. 10, sect. 2, prefers this, and
Suarez, Disp. 57, § 4.

assumed to take place, to account for the consecrated elements having the physical efficacy of the natural substances. Of course (if God so willed and declared it) there would be no difficulty in believing that He annihilated the substance of bread and wine, while preserving every property of them to the senses, nor, again, that He should, if He so willed, re-create the substance of the bread and wine, so that they should nourish the Communicant. But of this last miracle nothing is claimed to be said either in Holy Scripture or in the tradition of the Church. There is no witness that God ever taught it.

It is an acknowledged principle, that miracles are not to be needlessly multiplied. Aquinas himself says, "It [10] doth not seem to be reasonably said, that any thing happens miraculously in this Sacrament, except from the Consecration itself, from which it does not follow that matter is created or returns."

But Greg. de Valentia answers fairly to this, that an ulterior miracle, beyond the immediate effect of the Consecration, is assumed by every Roman hypothesis. For the immediate effect of the Consecration is supposed to be, not the Presence only of the Body and Blood of Christ, but " the existence of the accidents of bread without a subject. When then from those accidents something is generated [either

---

[10] 3. p. q. 77, art. 5.

by nutrition or otherwise], then certainly, according to every opinion, something miraculous intervenes here above nature." "And therefore," he says, "a certain opinion of De Palude [1] who said most falsely, that the matter itself is produced here by the *natural* agent, from the passive power of quantity, is exploded by all [2]."

And yet all this mass of physical difficulties, involved in the belief that the substances cease to be, is, so to speak, gratuitously assumed.

It is allowed, that, in itself, there is no greater difficulty in believing that our Lord's Body is present with or under accidents which retain their substances, than with or under accidents whose substance is destroyed. But, in order to make way for a certain interpretation of Holy Scripture, it is assumed that, upon the words of Consecration, the substances of bread and wine by miracle cease to be, and by miracle are re-created as soon as the act of Communion is completed. The accidents, form, colour, quantity are supposed to decay without the substance, whereas they do decay through the decay of the substance; and when they so decay, the substance is supposed to return, not to be under the accidents, because they are decayed, and yet external to the human frame, into the substance of which it is to be converted. Certainly, it is much freer from difficulties to believe, what the words

---

[1] In iv. d. 10, q. 4.　　　　　　[2] l. c.

alone express, the existence or presence of the Body of Christ in this Sacrament, there being no mention whatsoever of the ceasing of the substance of bread, or of its [physical] conversion into the Body of Christ.

The Catechism of the Council of Trent appears to go back to the exploded opinion of De Palude, that accidents of bread have *naturally* the power of nourishing. For it says, "by[3] this name [bread] the Eucharist has been called, because it has the appearance, and still *retains* the quality, *natural* to bread, of supporting and nourishing."

If this be so, the statement of the change of substance would seem to become a name, since every thing would be supposed to remain, which the human mind can conceive of, as the "substance" of a physical object. And yet the belief that the substance of bread ceases to be, is required as an article of faith; while yet it would be hard to imagine what that substance is, since it is no longer what the Schoolmen, who did attach a definite notion to the word, supposed it to be.

In the mysteries of the Creed, we understand what is prescribed for our belief, although the subject of the mystery passes man's understanding. We know what we believe, when we confess that the Son is "of one substance with the Father," although, of course, we cannot understand the

[3] P. 2, c. iv. q. 38.

nature of the Divine essence.   But the question as to the substance of the bread belongs to our material world.   The Presence of the Body and Blood of Christ "under the form of bread and wine" is a miracle inscrutable to human reason.   The "substance" of the bread and wine is a term of human philosophy, as to created things, and therefore, since its meaning appears to have undergone a change, subsequently to the time when it was introduced into matters of belief in the Western Church, it may the rather be asked that that meaning should be defined.

NOTE O.

On pp. 42, 43.

The passages which it was intended to place together here, are perhaps better seen in relation to other passages.   They will be found then in other notes [1].

[1] The words of S. Hilary, "We receive the Word, made Flesh, through the Food of the Lord," have been given in connexion with similar expressions in Note L. p. 132.   A passage from Origen, in which he speaks of the matter of bread remaining, after consecration, has been given at length in Note N. p. 148, 9, as also one from S. Epiphanius, p. 149, that from S. Augustine on the bodily form, in Note I. p. 107.   The words of the author of the de Sacramentis, that the elements "both are what they were, and are changed into something else," will be considered better in Note R.

NOTE P.

On p. 42.

THE passages in which Fathers speak of the Holy Eucharist as "spiritual" food will be given under the names of those Fathers in Note S.

NOTE Q.

On p. 44.

On the words used by the Fathers, which Roman controversialists quote as implying the doctrine of Transubstantiation.

IT will perhaps be the best and plainest way, to place at the outset the argument of Roman Catholic controversialists in their own words, and then to show how that argument is neutralized, or rather turns against them.

For myself, it is perhaps the simplest way to select a statement directly bearing on my own sermon, "The Holy Eucharist a comfort to the Penitent."

A writer then in the Dublin Review[1] brought two classes of arguments from the Fathers, founded on (1) The use of certain words; (2) certain illustrations, which he gathered from four Fathers. Both

---

[1] Vol. xvi, 1844, on Dr. Mant's Romish Corruptions, p. 84, sqq. I did not see this article until some seven years after it was published.

of these, he held to prove, that the Fathers believed Transubstantiation in the sense of the modern Roman Divines, *i. e.* that, at the time of consecration, the material Substance of the elements ceases to be, and is replaced by the Substance of the Body and Blood of our Lord, which Substance sustains the outward appearances of bread and wine, of which the substance had ceased to be.

This language, he says, the writers of the English Church do not use, and therefore, he argues, our belief is different from that of the Fathers.

The illustrations referred to will be the subject of the next Note. I will only here observe, that if the mere disuse of certain words or illustrations were to imply a difference of belief, it might just as easily be shown that the Roman Divines have not the same belief as the Ancient Church, since they too would not use the same language. In whatsoever way they may explain it, they would not use the language of Pope Gelasius, that " the elements abide in their own proper nature ;" nor would they say with S. Irenæus, that the Eucharist " consists of two things, an earthly and a heavenly ;" nor with other Fathers, that they are " symbols, types, antitypes, figures, images, of our Lord's Body and Blood ;" nor with Theodoret, that " neither after Consecration do the mystic symbols depart from their own nature ; they remain in their former substance." " He doth not change the nature, but adds grace to the nature." They are obliged to explain, and in some

cases, to apologize for this language. Thorndike[2]
observes, as to Theodoret, " The preface to the
Roman edition of these Dialogues saith, that Theodoret uses this language, because the [Roman]
Church had as yet decreed nothing on this point."
He subjoins, " That which was not contrary to the
faith when Theodoret wrote it, can never be contrary to it."   As long as they could, Roman controversialists denied the genuineness of the work of
Pope Gelasius.

The Dublin Reviewer does not appeal to the
authority of the Roman Church, but to the Fathers.
The writer wishes to establish a presumption against
us, because we do not use certain language or illustrations of certain Fathers.   We may thus far simply answer, " Neither do they."

The writer proceeds,

" Remarkable[3] as this is in all the Anglican divines, it
never struck us so forcibly as on reading Dr. Pusey's sermon [that of 1843], and contrasting it with the ancient
originals from which it is mainly taken, and whose language, up to a certain point, it scrupulously adopts as its
own.   The sermon is, in truth, a string of quotations from
the Fathers, from the beginning to the end ; but, although
it is made up, text and notes, of an array of quotations, to
prove the *reality* of Christ's presence, and the completeness and intimacy of the *communicant's union* with Him,
yet there is a scrupulous avoidance (even when the same
discourse[4], nay the same page, and almost the same pas-

[2] On the Laws of the Church, c. 4, p. 35.   [3] p. 85.
[4] As S. Chrys. Hom. de Proditione Judæ, quoted in p. 20,
S. Ambr. de Mysteriis, in p. 6, S. Gregory Nyssen, p. 9, &c.

sage [a], which he cites, contains it) of every word, and sentence and illustration, which supposes or implies a *change of substance*, which would be construed into a sanction of the doctrine of Trent, or come into collision with the ill-omened twenty-eighth Article of England [b]."

I have already mentioned, in the Preface to my present sermon, why I did this, simply that the question of the *mode* of our Blessed Lord's Presence in the Holy Eucharist was wholly foreign to my subject. I was not writing or even preaching on the doctrine of the Holy Eucharist in itself; I was inculcating simply one aspect of it, that which is stated in the Dublin Review, "the completeness and intimacy of the communicant's union with Christ." *This* I wished to inculcate with all the depth and fervour and force which the glowing language of the Fathers enabled me. *This* I wished to live in the souls of those I preached to. In order to bring *this* home to people's minds and hearts, I avoided purposely every thing which might distract them from it. Explanation, controversy, argument, such as I was obliged to resort to in the present sermon, are an evil in the pulpit; nor could I have employed them even now, but as preparatory to what lay beyond them.

The writer of this article arrayed the words, used by different Fathers, with some rhetorical effect, forming a sort of climax in what he believed to express the doctrine of Transubstantiation. (1) The

---

[a] As in the Liturgy of S. John Chrysostom.   [b] p. 90.

Fathers say that the Eucharistic symbols *are* the Body and Blood of Christ; (2) that they are "*made*" or "*become*" so; (3) that the bread and wine are *changed* (μεταβάλλονται, mutantur, convertuntur) into the Body and Blood of Christ; (4) that they are *converted* into the same (μεθιστάσθαι, μετασκευαζέσθαι); (5) *transformed*, or *transfigured* (μεταρρυθμίζει, transfigurantur); (6) *transelemented* (μεταστοιχειοῦνται); (7) *transmade* (μεταποιοῦνται).

As the writer thinks these two last the most decisive, I will give his own words :—

" We[1] feel almost afraid of wearying and perplexing the reader by the copiousness and variety of the language employed by the Fathers to express the sacramental changes. Indeed it is not easy to follow in English the minute shades of varied meaning which the more delicate organization of the Greek language easily distinguishes from one another. Perhaps the phrase we are about to cite is less equivocal than any of those hitherto produced. It is one for which we have no English representative, but it will be equivalently expressed by saying that the sacred symbols are *transelemented* [μεταστοιχειοῦνται], that is, *their elements* [στοιχεῖα] *are changed* into the Body and Blood of Christ."

" There[2] remains yet another phrase, which we have reserved for the last place, to complete the climax of evidence. It is one which well displays the copiousness and strength of the Greek language, and which cannot be rendered faithfully but by the word now consecrated to Roman Catholic use, transubstantiation[3]. We have already seen

[1] p. 86.   [2] Ib.

[3] See the declaration of the Greek schismatical bishops on the subject of transubstantiation, appended to the " Perpétuité de la Foi," vol. i. p. 1199, and fol. Paris, 1841.

that the Fathers familiarly speak of the bread and wine *being made* the Body and Blood of Christ. They go still farther, and declare that they are *transmuted*, or—to coin a word, for we have none to supply its place—'trans-made' (μεταποιοῦνται), or *made into a new substance*, or transubstantiated. Perhaps there is none of the other forms of expression more common than this."

The writer recapitulates thus,

'To' recapitulate the singularly varied and expressive forms of language which they use, they declare, not only that the sacramental symbols *are* (class 1) the Body and Blood of Christ, and that what *was* bread *has been made* (class 2) His Body; but they further define the mode in which this has taken place, insisting (against all the apparent evidence of sense, on which, be it remembered, they never fail to dwell), and proving by illustrations and examples which have no meaning, except in the hypothesis of transubstantiation, that the symbols *are changed and converted* (classes 3, 4) into the Body and Blood; that by this change they are not only *transformed* (class 5), or *transfigured*, but that their *elements*, or *constituent parts* are (class 6) *changed;* and finally, to remove all possibility of doubt, that they are as it were (class 7), *transmade, made into a new thing*, or, in the apt language of the (Roman) Catholic dogma, *transubstantiated.*"

Now, in contrast with all this, an older writer, of acknowledged repute as a Scholastic Divine and Controversialist, Suarez, owns that none of these words *do* adequately express this modern Roman doctrine. He admits that even the word "trans-elementing" (which he supposes to have, in common use, its etymological meaning, *which it has not*) does

―――――――――
[1] p. 92.

not, of necessity, express the received Roman doctrine.   He allows that these words *are* inadequate;
that the new word, " transubstantiation," was coined,
on account of that inadequacy, and he apologizes for
its introduction at so late a period in the Church.

" As ' to the name, the reason is, that since in this
case the whole substance passes into the whole substance, which takes place in no other conversion,
there was no name signifying other conversions
which could indicate the special character of this
conversion; wherefore it was necessary to invent a
new name to explain it, both to enable us to speak
simply of this mystery, and to put a mark upon new
errors which were rising about this mystery. Wherefore, although the ancient Fathers used various
names, as we saw, in explaining this mystery, yet
they all are either general, as ' conversion,' ' change,'
' passing,' ' migrating ;' or are more adapted to a
change of accidents, as ' transfiguring,' or the like.
Only that name ' transelementing,' which Theophylact used, seems to approach nearer to explaining
the nature of the mystery; because it signifies
[etymologically, not in actual use] a change even to
the first elements, even to the primary matter; yet
that word is both somewhat harsh, and not altogether suitable.   For it may signify the conversion
of one element into another, or the resolving of a
mixed substance into its elements, but transubstan-

' In 3 p. T. 3. Disp. 50. Sect. i. p. 594.

tiation signifies most properly and suitably, transition or conversion of the whole substance into the whole substance."

Suarez adds, in defence, that it is no new thing in the Church to invent new names in order to confute heresies, as the words "Homoousios" and θεοτόκος; and blames those Schoolmen who said that the doctrine of transubstantiation was not very old. But the words, ὁμοούσιος and θεοτόκος *were* old words which had existed from the beginning, whereas the word "transubstantiation" does not occur, I believe, before the twelfth century.

So far, then, from this variety of words, used to express the change of the consecrated elements, being any argument in favour of the modern explanation of that change, it tells the other way. The very fact of this various use, shows that there was no one word appropriated to express that belief. The Fathers use words which do *not* express the doctrine now currently received; they use words which only in a vague way express change, without in the least implying of what sort that change is; still less implying any change of *substance.* They do NOT use the *one* word, now used universally in the Roman Church, which *does* express change of substance (μετουσίωσις), or "transubstantiation."

But further, all these various words, the use of which is alleged to show that the Fathers believed such a change, by which the fore-existing substance should cease to be, and they employ those terms as to other changes, which are not changes of substance, and in some of which to suppose a change of substance would be heresy. On the one side, many of the Fathers, as we have seen in the preceding notes, assert or imply that the natural substances remain. On the other, they do not use any one word which, in its received meaning or usage, expresses change of substance. They do not appropriate any one word to express the Sacramental change. They do not stamp an ecclesiastical sense upon any word, as if to express *that* one change in the Holy Eucharist. All the words which they use of the Holy Eucharist they use as freely, and more frequently, of changes, in which, as I said, to suppose a change of substance, would be heresy, or, in some cases, blasphemy.

But all arguments from words, implying *mere* change are, as Thorndike observes, and Bishop Pearson implies, beside the mark [3]. The whole

---

[3] " As it is by no means to be denied, that the elements are really changed, translated, turned, and converted into the Body and Blood of Christ (so that, whoso receiveth them with a living faith, is spiritually nourished by the same, he that with a dead faith, is guilty of crucifying Christ); yet is not this change destructive to the bodily substance of the elements, but cumulative of them, with the spiritual grace of Christ's Body and Blood ; so that the Body and Blood of Christ in the Sacrament turns to the nourishment of the body, whether the Body and Blood in the truth turn to the nourishment or damnation of the soul." (Thorndike, " Of the Laws of the Church," chap. iv. p. 33.)

" As therefore all the μεταστοιχείωσις of the sacramental elements maketh them not cease to be of the same nature which before they were ; so the Human Nature of Christ, joined to the

question is, not whether there be a change, but whether that change be one, through which the natural substances cease to be. Before consecration, the elements are, of course, *mere* natural substances. After consecration, they are not (in the language of S. Cyril and S. Athanasius) "bare, mere, bread and wine." It is the belief of the ancient Church, that after consecration, they are in a Divine, ineffable, supernatural way, the Body and Blood of Christ. They *are* then what they *were* not. And since they *are* what they were not, they *become* by consecration what they were not. It is but saying the same thing in different words. But it does not follow, that they are *in no sense* what they were. Even the Roman Divines admit that the form or accidents remain. Even the Roman Church has not defined (although this is commonly understood, and, I am told, that the contrary would be accounted heresy) that the physical substance is changed. The Roman Church has not defined its own word "substance," whether it be physical or metaphysical. Even according to certain Schoolmen who have not been condemned by that Church, it is a simpler statement and exposed to fewer difficulties, to believe that while our Lord's Blessed Body and Blood are present, the natural substances remain.

Roman Catholics assume that the " change" of a

Divine, loseth not the nature of humanity, but continueth with the Divinity as a substance in itself distinct." (Pearson on the Creed, Art. 3, note *p.*)

material object must necessarily be a material change, a total change of its very substance. The whole strength of their argument lies in this assumption. Wherever a word implying " change " is used of the consecrated elements, they assume that this change must be a total change of its physical substance or matter, and *that*, a change into another substance, or rather, an annihilation of the former.

The Fathers, on the contrary, at times are led to point out, that a change in a physical object does not imply any such alteration of substance. Tertullian does so with regard to three of the words selected by the Reviewer, "demutari, converti, transfigurari." He urges that words signifying change, cannot be bound down to mean change of substance, and that so to restrain them would involve an absurdity. Tertullian is vindicating our identity of substance after the Resurrection :—

" We⁴ will explain more fully the force and meaning of ' change⁵,' which almost yields a presumption of the resurrection of another flesh ; as though to be *changed* were to cease altogether, and wholly to perish. But *change* must be distinguished from every inference of destruction. For *change* is one thing, destruction another. Whereas, it were not another, if the flesh should be so changed as to perish. But, when changed, it will perish, if itself abide not in the change, which shall be shown forth in the Resurrection. For as it perisheth, if it riseth not, so even though it rise, if still it is withdrawn to change, equally it perishes. For

⁴ De res. carn. c. 55, 56, pp. 423, 424.
⁵ Demutationis, demutari, &c.

it will equally not *be*, as if it had not risen. And how absurd,
if it rise, to the end that it should not *be!* whereas it might
not have risen and so not have been ; because it had
already begun not to be. Things altogether diverse will
not be mixed, *change* and destruction, as being different in
their effects. The one destroys, the other changes. As,
therefore, what is destroyed is not changed, so what is
changed is not destroyed. For to perish is altogether not
to be what it had been ; to be changed, is to be in a different way. Further, when it *is* in a different way, it may
be the self-same thing ; for that which does not perish has
being. For it has undergone change, not destruction. And
therefore a thing can both be changed, and itself no whit the
less *be ;* so that both the whole man in this life is indeed
himself in substance, yet is manifoldly changed, both in
habit, and in bodily size itself, and in health and condition,
and dignity, and age ; in study, affairs, work, faculties,
abode, laws, manners ; nor yet doth he lose ought of a man ;
nor does he so become another, as to cease to be the same ;
yea rather, he becometh not another being, but another
thing. This kind of change divine proofs also attest. The
hand of Moses is *changed*, and, indeed, become bloodless,
as though dead, and from whitish, it became cold ; but, re-
covering heat again, and its glow poured anew through it,
it was the same flesh and blood. Afterwards his face too is
changed by brightness unbeholdable. But Moses, who was
not seen, continued to *be*. So too Stephen had already put
on angelic dignity ; but no other knees sunk under the
stoning. The Lord also in the retirement of the mount had
changed His very raiment with the light, but preserved fea-
tures recognizable by Peter. Where too, Moses and Elias,
the one in the image of flesh not yet restored, the other in
the truth of flesh not yet dead, taught that the same fashion
of body endured even in glory. By Whose example Paul
too instructed, said, ' who shall transfigure our vile body,
that it may be like unto His glorious Body.' But if you

maintain that both transfiguration and conversion are a *change* of any one's substance, then Saul too, *converted* into another man, departed from the body : and Satan himself, when he is *transfigured* into an angel of light, loses his quality.   I trow not.   So too at the coming of the resurrection one may be *changed, converted, re-formed, without loss of substance.* For how absurd, yea how unjust, and, in both, how unworthy of God, that one substance should work, another be recompensed by the reward ; that this flesh indeed be shredded by martyrdom, another be crowned : this flesh again should wallow in defilement, another be condemned !"

S. Cyril of Alexandria observes the same of a fourth word, ' became.' He says expressly (as indeed is evident), that it does not always mean a change of nature ;

" Having⁰ then ascribed to the Son so great glory, and having alleged of Him the very properties of the Nature of the Father, then he [S. Paul] saith, that ' He is made by so much better than the angels, as He hath a more excellent name than they,' as Son, and Heir, and Brightness, and Express Image, and Likeness, andCo-enthroned, and Creator.   But if, for these reasons, He be considered much better and more excellent than the angels, better therefore will be His Ministry than theirs.   But the word ' was made ' is very justly taken here, not to signify the process from not being to being.   (For ' the Word was in the beginning.')   Nor is the change from less to greater. For the Son was Perfect, of a Perfect Father.   But, as it were, in comparison of glory and dignity, the appearance was greater and better.   For as if a man should be compared with a horse, and should be said to be better than it by those who estimated it, as being a reasonable

⁰ Thes. App. xx. t. v. l, pp. 200, 201.

creature: for that '*becoming*' (γενέσθαι) does not wholly imply *a change of nature*, will be evident, for that one says to God, '*Become* Thou to me God my Shield.' And again, 'The Lord *became* to me a Refuge,' and, 'The Lord *became* my Salvation.' In point of ministry then, and glory, and not of nature, was the comparison of the Son with the angels."

To these must be added another idiom, in which S. Cyril and others speak of the change in the Eucharistic *elements*, not into the Body and Blood of Christ, but into the *energy* or *virtue* of that Body and Blood.

The passage is as follows;—

" He ' must needs then be in us through the Holy Ghost after a Divine sort; and also be mingled, as it were, with our bodies, through His Holy Flesh and His Precious Blood; Which we have also received for a Life-giving blessing, as in bread and wine; for, in order that we should not be horrified, seeing flesh and blood set out on the holy tables of our churches, God, condescending to our infirmities, *sendeth* [2] *forth a power of life into the elements, and transfers them into the efficacy of His own Flesh;* that we might have them for life-giving participation, and that the Body of life might be found in us a life-giving seed. And doubt not that is true, since He clearly saith; ' This is My Body,' and ' This is My Blood;' but rather receive in faith the Word of the Saviour; for being Truth, He doth not lie."

Now, accepting each of these ways of speaking as true, it remains to see how they are to be harmonized.

---

[1] On S. Luc. xxii. in Mai, Auctt. Class. x. 371-5.

[2] ἐνίησι τοῖς προκειμένοις δύναμιν ζωῆς καὶ μεθίστησιν αὐτὰ πρὸς ἐνέργειαν τῆς ἑαυτοῦ σαρκός.

They are plainly not the same. The "energy," "operation," "power," of an operative substance is not the same as that substance itself. Now the two idioms can be reconciled, if by the words "becoming the Body and Blood of Christ" we understand that, where, before the consecration, there was only "*common* bread," afterwards there is, "under the outward form of bread and wine," the Body and Blood of Christ. On the other hand, if the Eucharistic elements are "translated into the *virtue* of His Flesh," they are not, *as far as they are symbols*, translated *physically* into that very Body and Blood. The words express accurately *our* belief, not that of the modern Roman Divines. The Eucharistic symbols, as symbols, are by consecration, "translated into the *power* of" the Body and Blood of Christ, because they are outward parts, through and under which that Body and Blood are present and are conveyed. But the very words express, that the outward part is distinct from the inward.

The language corresponds with other language of S. Cyril, as when he says, "The [9] smallest Eucharist immingles our whole body with Itself and fills us with its own *efficacy* (ἐνεργείας); and thus Christ cometh to be in us, and we in Him."

Here, S. Cyril speaks of the outward part conveying the "efficacy" of the inward; elsewhere he speaks of the inward part, putting forth its efficacy

[9] In Joh. vi. 57, compared by Albert. p. 513.

through the outward. "The[1] very Body of the Lord was sanctified by the power of the united Word; and thus is made *efficacious* (ἐνεργὸν) towards the mystical Eucharist to us, so as to be able also to implant in us Its own sanctification."

The difference of the expression was felt by Aquinas, who both[2] in this passage of S. Cyril, and in one borrowed from it by Theophylact, substituted the word "*verity*" (veritatem), for "efficacy." S. Cyril's language does contain the doctrine of the real Presence. For the outward part could only be "changed into the *efficacy* of the Flesh of Christ," by conveying that Flesh to us; but S. Cyril distinguishes the outward part from the inward, in that he says, the "efficacy," not the "verity." He distinguishes between that which conveys the outward elements and That which is conveyed, the Body and Blood of Christ.

This appears to have been Ecclesiastical language before the end of the second century. For one cannot account for the language of S. Cyril being anticipated by the heretic Theodotus (A.D. 192), except on the supposition that Theodotus, after the wont of heretics, used studiously the language of the Church, in points which did not touch upon his heresy, or to veil it. He says,

---

[1] In S. Joh. xvii. 23, p. 979.

[2] Catena Aurea, from Theophylact on S. Marc. xiv. 22, and S. Cyril on S. Luc. xxii. 19. Theophylact's word is δύναμις, S. Cyril's is ἐνέργεια.

" And [3] the bread and the oil are sanctified by the power of the Name, not being, as they appear, the same as they were taken, but *by Power they are changed to spiritual power* [4]. In like manner the water too, which is exorcised and becometh Baptism, not only contains what is inferior, but also acquireth sanctifying."

S. Victor of Antioch (if the Catenæ are altogether to be trusted), in the lifetime of S. Cyril, incorporated the above passage of S. Cyril (although without his name), into his Commentary [5]. The phrases occur at a later period, A.D. 787, in Elias Cretensis [6], and, still later, S. Cyril is imitated by Theophylact [7].

With this language of S. Cyril, that an " energy "

[3] Excerpta Theod. n. 82, ad calc. S. Clem. Al. p. 988, ed. Pott.

[4] δυνάμει εἰς δύναμιν πνευματικὴν μεταβέβληνται.

[5] In the Commentary, as edited by Dr. Cramer in his Catena (t. i. p. 213),S. Cyril is quoted simply with the words, " Another says." The two first lines of the passage, as they stand in this Commentary, do not occur in S. Cyril on S. Luke, where the whole context fits together. The second and fuller publication of this Commentary by Card. Mai (Patr. Nova Biblioth. ii. 417, ed. Mai) herein agrees with the former (Auctt. Class. x.). The introduction has been dove-tailed in from some other source. The words are, " Another saith, He teaches us not to look to the nature of the things placed there, but to believe that through the blessing coming upon them, they are those very things " (ταῦτα ἐκεῖνα). The rest of the passage is made up of two quotations from S. Cyril on S. Luc. xxii. 19. The Commentary then is not S. Cyril's (as Dr. Cramer thought), nor has it come down quite free from interpolation. This passage of S. Cyril is quoted again, (with some variation in the turn of expressions,) as Origen, by Bulenger in Casaub. Diatr. 3, p. 178.

[6] In Naz. Orat. i. p. 201.   [7] On S. Marc. xiv. 22.

is imparted to the elements, agree two passages of S. Epiphanius, in the one of which he speaks of the " might [8] of Bread;" in the other, that the element is, as far as we see, "insensate as to power."   By both, he distinguishes the outward as really existing, from the inward part ; the outward being, to human eyes, " insensate as to power," but having that power as " strengthened in Christ " by His unseen Presence [9].

I will now give some of the evidence which has been collected, that all the words which any Fathers use of the change which follows upon consecration, they also use of changes which are *not* changes of substance.   I will take the words in an inverted order, putting first those which the Dublin Reviewer regards as the strongest.

Their strongest word, then, he accounts to be μεταποιεῖσθαι, which he renders " transmade," or " made into a new *substance*."   The question is, whether the use of this term implies a change in the physical substances, and that, such a change that those substances should cease to be.

Passages in which this word is used, are quoted from the Catechetical Oration of S. Gregory of Nyssa, and from Theodoret's Greek translation of a passage of S. Ambrose.   Yet it has been shown, not only that the word is used of changes not " substantial," but that in the very passage of S. Gregory and the very context, and over-against that other use,

[8] See above, p. 149.
[9] See below, in Note S. No. 36.

N 2

it is used of a change, which it would be blasphemy to think substantial.

S. Gregory is treating of the Holy Eucharist as a principle of life to the body, which, through the poison of the forbidden fruit, had become subject to death :—

" Since human nature," he says[1], " is twofold, commingled of soul and body, they who are saved must needs, by both, follow Him who leadeth unto life. Wherefore the soul, mingled with Him by faith, has thence the occasion of salvation. For union with the Life hath participation of the Life. But the body cometh, in another way, to the participation and commingling with that which saveth. For[2] as they who through evil design have received deadly poison, do by some other medicine allay its destructive power ; and as the destruction, so also the antidote, must be received within the bowels of man, that through them the power of that which cometh in stead, may be distributed to the whole body, so must we, who had tasted that which dissolved our nature, need that also which should bring together what had been dissolved ; that such an antidote, coming to be in us, might, through its contrary force, expel the injury of the poison which had before been infused into our body. What then is this ? No other than that Body which was shown to be mightier than death, and was the beginning of our life. For as ' a little leaven,' as the Apostle saith, assimilates to itself ' the whole lump,' so that Body, gifted with immortality by God, coming to be in ours, *transmakes and transfers* (μεταποιεῖ καὶ μετατίθησιν) the whole unto itself. For as, when the destructive is mingled with the sound, the whole which is commingled, is together spoiled, so also that immortal Body, coming to be in him who receiveth It,

[1] Orat. Catech. c. 37, t. iii. p. 102.

[2] The text of this part, as preserved in Theoriani Disp. cum Ners. (in Mai Scriptt. Vett. vi. 366 sqq.), is better than that in in S. Greg.'s works.

transmade also the whole into Its own Nature (πρὸς τὴν ἑαυτοῦ φύσιν καὶ τὸ πᾶν μετεποίησεν). But indeed nothing can come within the body, which is not through food and drink commingled with the bowels. So then it is necessary to receive, in a way possible to nature, the life-giving power of the Spirit. But since that Body which received God, alone received that grace, and since it hath been shown that our body cannot otherwise attain to immortality save through communion with the Immortal, we must consider how that One Body, being ever distributed among so many myriads of the faithful throughout the world, can be entire in each individual, and Itself remain in Itself entire."

Here, then, in the outset, S. Gregory twice uses the word, μεταποίησις, of the change of our bodies, even while yet in the flesh, from being subject to mortality, to being immortal, through their hidden conformity to the Body of our Lord which we receive in them. Yet whatever that is which they acquire, plainly they do not part with any thing of their own substance, although he says, "His Body, coming to be in ours, transmakes and transfers the whole to itself," "transmakes the whole [of us] into Its own nature."

After an explanation of the assimilating process in human digestion, S. Gregory resumes his question, "How the Body of Christ, in a man quickens the whole nature of man, in whom faith is, being distributed to all, and itself undiminished." He himself does not seem altogether confident as to his answer, as also it stands alone in all antiquity. He says, " Perchance then we are near a probable account." Then follows his statement.

" If the substance of every body comes from nourishment; and this is food and drink ; and among food is bread, and among drink water sweetened with wine ; and the Word of God (as explained at first), being both God and Word, was *commingled* with human nature, and coming to be in our body, did not devise any new condition for human nature, but perpetuated His own Body by the wonted and befitting means, holding together its being by meat and drink, but the food was bread. As then (as I have often said already), in one case, he who sees bread sees in a manner the human body, because, being in it, it becomes it [the human body] ; so, in that case too, the Body which received God, having received the nourishment of bread, in a manner became the same with it, the nourishment (as was said) passing into the substance of the body (for that which is proper to all is confessed to be as to this Body, that It too was maintained by bread); but that Body, through the indwelling of God the Word, was *transmade* into the Divine dignity (τὸ δὲ σῶμα τῇ ἐνοικήσει τοῦ Θεοῦ λόγου πρὸς τὴν θεϊκὴν ἀξίαν μετεποιήθη). Well then do I believe that now too, the bread, sanctified by the Word of God, is *transmade* (μεταποιεῖσθαι) into the Body of God the Word. For that Body [*i. e.* Christ's natural Body] was virtually bread [in that bread eaten passes into the natural Body]. But it was hallowed by the indwelling of the Word which tabernacled in the Flesh. Wherefore, whereby the bread being *transmade* (μεταποιηθεὶς) within that Body [our Lord's Natural Body] was *removed into* (μετέστη) a Divine power, thereby doth the like take place now. For both there [in our Lord's Natural Body] the grace of the Word hallowed that Body, Whose composition was from bread, and which Itself too was in a manner bread ; and here [in the Sacrament] in like way the Bread (as the Apostle says) is hallowed by the Word of God and prayer, not, through meat and drink, passing on into the Body of the Word, but *transmade* (μεταποιούμενος) straight into the Body of the Word, as was said by the Word, ' This is My Body.'

" But all flesh being nourished also through liquid (for our earthly parts would not, without the conjunction with this, abide in life), as through the firm and corresponding food, we support the firm part of the body, in the same manner do we make an accession to the moist also from the homogeneous nature, which, coming to be in us, is, through the alterative power, made blood, and especially through wine it receives power to the *transmaking* ($\mu\epsilon\tau\alpha\pi o i\eta\sigma\iota\nu$) into heat.   Since then His Flesh, which received God, received this part also to its own constitution ; but the Word, made manifest, did therefore mingle Itself with the mortal nature, that, by participation of the Godhead, humanity might, with It, be deified; therefore in all who believe the economy of grace, He inserts Himself through the Flesh, mingling Himself with the bodies of believers, which are composed of wine and bread, that through the inoneing with the Immortal, man too might become partaker of immortality.   But these things He giveth, *transelementing*, by the power of the blessing, the nature of the visible things unto that."

These last words will best be considered under their own (the next) head.   But here we have the same word used of every sort of change; (1) of our own bodies, while yet mortal and corruptible, so that they should, by union with our Lord's, have a principle of immortality; and of this he uses that strong language, " transmaking *the whole into* itself;" (2) of our Lord's Own Natural Body to a Divine Dignity: (3) the natural assimilation of food taken by our Lord, when in the Flesh, to His Human Body, (4) the Sacramental change of the elements.

All these changes are essentially of different sorts. None of them can be the same as the others.   Two

were certainly not physical; a third, that of the
assimilation of our Lord's Human Food into His
Human Body, was certainly physical; yet it was a
physical change wholly distinct from any change
which Roman Divines can believe of the Sacramental.   For the substance of the food, with which
our Lord vouchsafed to support His Bodily Frame,
did pass into the substance of His Body.   His
Human Body received growth and increase through
that food.   It ceased to be, as to outward form too,
what it was; it became what before was not, that
part of the Substance of our Lord's Human Frame,
to which it became an accession.   But it is confessed that our Lord's Human Body can *now*
receive no accession; and Roman Divines, when
they say that the substance of the bread is changed
into the Substance of our Lord's Body, do not mean
that it is changed at all, only that it ceases to be.

In a chapter following immediately, S. Gregory,
within a short paragraph, uses seven times this same
word, "transmaking," μεταποίησις, of the change in
man through Baptismal regeneration, saying distinctly that it was no change in human nature itself,
nor in the natural powers.   Clearly then, μεταποίησις,
"transmaking," has, in itself, no such meaning as
"change of substance."   With this word S. Gregory
combines others, which will be to be considered hereafter, in a sense purely spiritual.

  " The ' *transmaking* (μεταποίησις) of our life, which takes

  ' S. Greg. Nyss. Orat. Catech. c. 40, T. iii. p. 108, 9.

place through the regeneration, would be no *transmaking*, if we remained in the state in which we are. For I know not how we can think that he has become another man, who abides in the same state, in which no characteristic has been *transmade* (μετεποιήθη). For that the saving birth is received in order to the renovation and *change* of our nature (ἐπὶ ἀνακαινισμῷ καὶ τῇ μεταβολῇ τῆς φύσεως ἡμῶν), is evident to every one. But the *human nature* (ἀνθρωπότης) itself does not, itself in itself, admit of any *change* (μεταβολὴν) from Baptism ; nor doth the reasoning, or intelligent, or scientific power, or any other which properly characterizes human nature, undergo *transmaking* (ἐν μεταποιήσει γίνεται). For the *transmaking* (ἡ μεταποίησις) would be for the worse, if any of these properties of nature were exchanged away. If then the birth from above is a *re-formation* (ἀναστοιχείωσις) of the man, and these things do not admit of a *change*, we must consider, what being *transmade* (τίνος μεταποιηθέντος) the grace of regeneration is perfect. It is plain that when the evil characteristics of our nature have been effaced, the *translation* (μετάστασις) to what is better takes place. Wherefore, if, as the Prophet says, washed in this mystical bath, we become clean of purpose, washing away the wickednesses of our souls, we become better, and are *transmade* to what is better (μεταπεποιήμεθα)."

It has been shown long ago [3], that S. Gregory of Nyssa used this same word "transmade" of the glorious appearance of Moses' countenance, when he came from the Presence of God ; the change of the soul to good, or again to that which is more Divine, through the discipleship of Christ ; of the Christian character by the absence or the presence of love ; that to listen to the prayer of the angry would imply

---

[3] Albertin. de Euchar. Art. Greg. Nyss. p. 487.

a *change* of character in God; thrice it is used of the change of our Lord's Human Nature (after the Resurrection) "into the Divine Nature."

These are varied uses of the word, showing its idiomatic meaning in the living language, that it is simply an energetic word, used of any change, whether it be of quality, Human or Divine character, or of appearance, and that it does not in any way specially denote any *material* change.

I will first give instances from S. Gregory of Nyssa himself:—

"When[4] this [love] is not, the whole character of the image is *transmade* (μεταπεποίηται)."

"And[5] so the *transmaking* of Moses to a more glorious appearance (ἡ ἐπὶ τὸ ἐνδοξότερον μεταποίησις) was of such a kind and so great, that the manifestation of that glory could not be endured by the eyes of men."

"There[6] was one voice turned to God, 'He hath *transmade* all things to good' (πάντα πρὸς τὸ καλὸν μετεποίησεν)."

"The[7] goodness of Him Who cometh to him, *transmaking him into Itself* (πρὸς ἑαυτὴν τὸν δεξάμενον μεταποιούσης)."

"The[8] Divine gifts were amnesty of evils, removal of sin, *transelementing* of nature, *transmaking* of the corruptible to the incorruptible, delight of paradise, royal dignity, endless joy."

"May[9] the word teach us this one thing through the preface, that those who are led into the sacred recesses of the mysteries of this book are no longer men, but are *trans-*

---

[4] De Hom. Opif. c. 5, fin. p. 54.
[5] De Vita Mos. i. p. 234.
[6] In Ps. Inscript. L. i. c. 8, p. 280.
[7] Hom. viii. in Eccl. i. 457.
[8] In Cant. Hom. i. p. 479.   [9] Ib. p. 482.

made in nature (μεταποιηθῆναι τῇ φύσει) through the discipleship of Christ to that which is more Divine."

"The [1] Word having bidden the soul, now amended, to come undoubting to Himself, she being strengthened by the command, became such as the Bridegroom willed, having been *transmade* to that which is more Divine (μεταποιηθεῖσα πρὸς τὸ θειότερον), and from the glory in which she was, being by that good change *transformed* (μεταμορφωθεῖσα) to the higher glory."

"In [2] the Passion of the Human Nature His Divinity fulfilled the dispensation for us, having for a time disjoined His Soul from His Body, yet Itself separated from neither, with which It had been once commingled, and again joining together what had been parted, so that It gave to the whole human race the order and beginning of the resurrection from the dead; that all which is corruptible may be clothed with incorruption, and what is mortal with immortality. Our Firstfruits having been, through the blending with God, *transmade into the Divine Nature* (εἰς θείαν φύσιν μεταποιηθείσης), as Peter said, 'That Jesus whom ye have crucified, God hath made Lord and Christ."

"In [3] the one place, He is said in the same way to be made 'Priest and Apostle,' as, in the other, 'Lord and Christ.' 'Priest and Apostle,' with reference to the dispensation for us; 'Lord and Christ,' on account of the *change and transmaking* of the Human Nature to the Divine (τὴν πρὸς τὸ θεῖον τοῦ ἀνθρωπίνου μεταβολήν τε καὶ μεταποίησιν). For the Apostle expresses the *transmaking* (μεταποίησιν) by the word 'making' (ποίησιν)."

"For [4] we say, that the Body, in which He took on Him the Passion, being immingled with the Divine Nature, was *made* (πεποιῆσθαι) through the immingling that which the

---

[1] Ib. Hom. viii. p. 596.
[2] Id. cont. Eunom. Orat. ii. p. 484.
[3] Ib. Orat. v. p. 587.
[4] Ib. Or. iv. p. 581.

Nature which assumed it is. So far are we from any poor
thoughts of God the Only Begotten; that even though,
through the dispensation of loving-kindness towards man,
this lower nature was assumed, we believe that this was
transmade into the Divine and pure (μεταπεποιῆσθαι πρὸς
τὸ θεῖόν τε καὶ ἀκήρατον)."

" He[5] hath through His immingling of it with Himself,
transmade our mortality into a life-giving gift and power."

" God[6] is manifested in the Flesh. But the Flesh,
which exhibited God in Itself, after It had fulfilled through
Itself the great mystery of death, is *transmade* (μεταποιεῖται)
through the mingling, into the High and Divine, becoming
' Christ and Lord,' being *translated and changed* (μετατεθεῖσα
καὶ ἀλλαγεῖσα) into that which He was, Who manifested
Himself in that Flesh."

" As[7] He Who knew not sin, *becometh* (γίνεται) sin, that
He may take away the sin of the world, so again the Flesh
which received the Lord, *becometh* (γίνεται) Christ and
Lord, which It was not by nature, being *transmade* (μετα-
ποιουμένη) into It by the mingling. Whereby we learn, that
neither would God have been manifested in the Flesh, unless
the Word had *become* (ἐγένετο) flesh, nor would the flesh,
around Him, of the Manhood, have been *transmade* (μετεποιήθη πρὸς τὸ θεῖον) into the Divine Nature, unless what
was visible (τὸ φαινόμενον) had *become* (ἐγένετο) Christ and
Lord."

" This[8] [that God should listen to the prayer of the
angry] would involve, that the Deity should fall into passion
and be as man, and be *transmade* (μεταποιηθῆναι) from a
good nature into savage relentlessness."

" For[9] that which was by nature Incorruptible and Unchangeable, is always the same, not changed with our poor
nature, when It came to be in it according to the Dispensa-

[5] Id. p. 586.   [6] Ib. p. 594.   [7] Ib. p. 595.
[8] De Orat. Serm. i. T. i. p. 418.
[9] Ep. ad Eust. Ambr. et Basil. T. iii. p. 658.

tion, as the sun casting its ray into darkness dulled not the light of the ray, but through the ray *transmade* the darkness into light (τὸ σκότος διὰ τῆς ἀκτίνος εἰς φῶς μετεποίησεν); so also the true Light having shone in our darkness, was not Itself overshadowed by the darkness, but by Itself lightened the darkness. But let no one, not duly receiving the words of the Gospel, think that our nature in Christ was, by a certain advance and course, *transmade*, little by little, to that which is more Divine (κατ᾽ ὀλίγον πρὸς τὸ θειότερον μεταποιεῖσθαι). For 'the advancing in wisdom and knowledge and favour' (χάριτι) is related by Scripture in order to show that the Lord truly was in our substance (φυράματι)."

The same latitude of usage has been shown to occur in other Fathers, S. Cyril of Jerusalem, S. Basil, S. Gregory of Nazianzum, S. Chrysostom, and in a homily among his works. It also occurs in S. Asterius. S. Cyril of Jerusalem uses it of the change of the body at the Resurrection, but expressly stating that the body remains "the very same," and illustrates it by fire penetrating iron.

"This[1] body is raised again, not remaining only such a weak [body], but it is raised this very same thing (αὐτὸ τοῦτο), but being clothed upon with incorruption it is *transmade*, as iron when brought near to fire, *becomes* (γίνεται) fire, or rather as the Lord who raiseth it up knoweth."

S. Basil uses it of the changed appearance of the city and citizens in a religious festival.

"The[2] whole city is *transmade* (μεταπεποίηται) into a

<hr>

[1] Cat. 18, § 18.   [2] De S. Mamante, § 2, 3.

feast." "He whose feast we celebrate, for whom we are all thus bright, for whom life is *transmade*."

S. Gregory of Nazianzum employs it of change into good, or unchangeableness in good.

"He[3] who reverences and follows good for its own sake, since he loveth that which abideth, hath also an abiding desire for it. So, having in him the mind of God, he also may use the words of God, 'I am the same, and change not.' He then will not be *transmade* nor removed, &c. (μεταποιηθήσεται οὐδὲ μετατεθήσεται)."

"Apprehending[4] spiritually that ointment which was poured out for us, let us smell it, so made and *transmade* by it, that from us too may be smelled a sweet smelling savour."

In the same way, I doubt not, he uses it, in his glowing address to those recently baptized, of their union with Christ, and their power over their adversary.

"If[5] he [Satan] attack thee with covetousness, 'shewing thee all the kingdoms of the world in a moment of time,' as belonging to him, and demand worship of thee, despise him as having nothing : tell him, emboldened by your seal (of baptism), 'I also am the image of God, of the glory on high ; not as yet have I been cast down, like thee, for pride ; I am clothed with Christ, I am *changed*[6] by Baptism into Christ, worship thou me.' Well I know, he will depart

[3] S. Greg. Naz. Or. 36, § 9.
[4] Id. Orat. 40, § 38.   [5] Ib. § 10, p. 697, 8.
[6] Χριστὸν ἐνδέδυμαι· Χριστὸν μεταπεποίημαι. The Benedictines render, "I have laid claim to Christ by Baptism," but this would require a gen. not an acc. The single instance of an accus. alleged (Herod. ii. 178) is clearly an acc. absolute. "Bearing Christ (Χριστοφόρος) the baptized is, as to Satan, as Christ, Who 'bruises him under his feet.'"

defeated and ashamed, as from Christ, the First Light, so also from those who have been enlightened by Christ."

S. Chrysostom employs it of the working of leaven, in illustration of the working of the Gospel.

"As' the leaven is covered over, yet disappeareth not, but little by little *transmakes* all things to its own condition, in like way shall it come to pass in the preaching."

S. Asterius, against divorce, uses it of habit being *transmade* into nature.

"Where' is that lawful band, and the might of long habit which is both said proverbially and shown by experience to be *transmade* even *into nature ?*" (καὶ εἰς φύσιν μεταποιεῖσθαι.)"

In a homily on Repentance among those of S. Chrysostom, it is employed of "repentance *transmaking* sinners."

"Penitence," that writer says ', "is a medicine which taketh away sin ; it is a heavenly gift, a wondrous power, vanquishing by grace the course of laws. Wherefore it shaketh not off the fornicator; it repels not the adulterer ; it turns not aside the drunkard ; it abhors not the idolater ; it drives not away the reviler; it chases not away the blasphemer, nor the insolent, but *transmakes* (μεταποιεῖ) them all."

Such being the variety of meaning in which this word is employed among the Greek Fathers, there cannot be a shadow of ground for inferring that

---

' In S. Matt. Hom. xlvi. (al. xlvii.), § 2, p. 483. "It occurs again in S. Chrys. Hom ii. (al. i.) in S. Joh. viii. 15 D, but as a false reading for μεταπεσεῖν."—Field.

' Hom. an liceat dimitt. uxor.

' Hom. vii. de Pœnit. T. ii. p. 327, ed. Bened. The Benedictines and Mr. Field account it not to be S. Chrysostome's.

Theodoret intended to express that there is a *physical* change in the Holy Eucharist, when he translated the " transfigurandum " of S. Ambrose by μετα-ποίησιν. Theodoret's translation is, " Think [10] not then that the Body is in nature equal to the Godhead. For although thou believe that the Body of Christ is true, and bring to the altar *for transmaking* (πρὸς μεταποίησιν), but do not distinguish the nature of the Body and of the Godhead, we shall say to thee too, ' If thou rightly offer, but do not rightly divide, thou hast sinned, be still.'   Divide what is ours, and what is proper to the Word. I then had not what was His ; He had not what was mine ; and He took what was mine, in order to give me what was His own. And this He received, not to confusion, but to fill it."

On the contrary, the argument is more complete, on the supposition that there is no *physical* change of substance. S. Ambrose is arguing against those who did not " distinguish the nature of the Divinity and the Body."   Theodoret had already, in the Dialogue itself, argued against a like heresy from the twofold substance in the Holy Eucharist, the nature of the inferior substance remaining. Since the word μεταποίησις does not in itself signify " change of nature," the burden of proof lies upon those who assert that it does, and so set S. Ambrose, as quoted by Theodoret, at variance with Theodoret himself.

[10] Dial. 2, iv. 144, 5, ed. Sch.

Of the Greek Liturgies, it is even remarkable that this word is only found [1] in one attributed by the Copts to S. Gregory of Nazianzum, but which must have been interpolated, since it has a trace of the heresy of the Monophysites [2]. In another Liturgy, also called S. Gregory's, and in use among Syriac Christians, the word does not occur. The prayer for the descent of the Holy Spirit is in the simpler form.

" Have [3] mercy upon us, O God, have mercy upon us,

---

[1] Ass. Cod. Lit. vii. 106, " Do Thou, Lord, by Thy Voice, *transmake* the oblations ; Thyself, present, perfect this mystical service ; Thyself maintain for us the memory of Thy service ; Thyself send down Thine All-Holy Spirit, that, lighting down with Its holy and good and glorious Presence, It may sanctify and *transmake* the oblations, these precious and holy gifts to the very Body and Blood of our redemption." In what follows, there is a double reading : one is superfluous ; but it looks as if the Liturgy had been altered, καὶ ποιήσει τὸν μὲν ἄρτον τοῦτον γένηται εἰς τὸ ἅγιον σῶμά σου. The Coptic translation (if the Latin version of it is literal), for " Thyself present," substitutes " Thyself who art placed before us " (Ib. p. 143), *i. e.* our Lord present in the Eucharist, which would be altogether a new doctrine ; for it is acknowledged by all, that our Lord, as sacramentally present, does not exercise any office. He is received only. The word παρὼν is here plainly used, as συνὼν in the Liturgy of S. Chrysostom, fuller ; " Come to sanctify us, Thou who dwellest on high with the Father, and art with us here invisibly " (ὧδε ἡμῖν ἀοράτως συνών).

[2] Ib. p. 119. Assemani would give the expressions a good sense, but subjoins, " I cannot but own that this language is suspicious in the mouths of Copts " (p. 154, Præf. xviii.).

[3] Ass. vii. 190, 191, from Nitrian Syriac MSS. Except in the prayer of consecration and invocation, this Liturgy has scarcely any thing in common with that which the Copts ascribe to S. Gregory, and these two present only slight points of contact.

and send to us from the Throne of Thy kingdom the Holy
Ghost the Comforter, and Giver of holiness . . . . and,
coming down on this bread and this wine, may He fill us
also with His holiness, and make this Bread the quickening
Body, the life-giving Body, the saving Body, the Body of
our very God and Saviour Jesus Christ, for the remission
of debts, and forgiveness of sins, and life eternal.   And, in
like way, may He make this wine also Blood of the New
Testament," &c.

No other writer of the six or seven first centuries, I believe, uses the word μεταποιέω of the Holy
Eucharist, so that when the Dublin Reviewer says,
" Perhaps [4] there is none of the other forms of expression more common than this," and, " it would
be very easy to have multiplied the examples both in
this and the other classes," he must, I suppose, have
used the word " Fathers " in that wider sense, according to which Bellarmin [5] comprehends twelve
centuries as the period of the Fathers, and even
counts among them some of the early Schoolmen.

In so saying, I knowingly pass over the passage
alleged in controversy from the Arian Theodorus
Heracleotes [6].   For the compilers of the Catena in
which this supposed extract is given, were confessedly
inaccurate, both as to the names of the authors, and

[4] p. 91.

[5] De Euch. ii. 37. iii. 20.

[6] Quoted even in Klee's Dogmatik (together with a passage
attributed by the same careless compilers to Theodore of Mopsuestia), iii. 209, from the Catena on S. Matt. xxvi. 26, edited
by Possini.

the words of their extracts; e. g. they ascribe to S. Chrysostome in the fourth century passages from Theophylact in the twelfth; and do not give accurately the words of authors cited [7]. The mere fact then that the compilers of this Catena ascribe the passage to Theodorus Heracleotes, is no evidence that it belongs to him rather than any other out of the very numerous [8] Theodori, or to any Theodorus at all; nor is there any ground to trust to the words as being correctly quoted. The passage is in fact contracted from one *interpolated* into a genuine passage of S. Cyril [9].

ii. The next word is μετασοιχειοῦσθαι, which the Dublin Reviewer translates by "transelementing," and which he supposes to express, by force of its very etymology, "a physical change of the ele-

[7] See even Possini's Preface. "The very many passages which the author of this compilation, whoever he be, attributes to Chrysostom, are mostly, *in substance,* found in Theophylact; *the words,* as far as I have observed, *are always different.*" (Præf. ad T. i.)

[8] See Leo Allat. de Theodoris, Mai Patrum Bibl. Nov. vi. 95, &c.

[9] The genuine passage of S. Cyril will be given below, Note S. No. 66, from his Commentary, edited by Card. Mai. The passage, as interpolated, is given in the 2nd vol. of Possini, p. 754, and thence in Albertin. p. 769. It may save repetition, to say that the passage quoted in the same Catena from Theodorus of Mopsuestia is derived from another interpolation in S. Cyril. This is cited for the word μεταβάλλεσθαι.

ments " into the Body and Blood of Christ.   Whoever has been ever so little conversant with the study of language, knows how utterly unsafe it is, to argue, as to the actual meaning of a word in a living language, from the idea originally contained in its root. "Truth " is, in one aspect, what a man " troweth ;" for in matter of honesty, " truth " is to speak what one thinks to be true. But it was a play on etymology, to infer that all truth is matter of opinion. For truth, as uttered by man, is certain or uncertain, as his knowledge is.   "Truth " from God must be as certain as Himself. It is, again, a familiar instance, how the same word, in different languages, signified "martial valour," Christian virtue, or elegance of taste.

I will, for the sake of identifying the word to an English reader, retain, in passages of S. Gregory and other Fathers, the word " transelementing," the use of which by S. Gregory is supposed to show that he believed Transubstantiation. The very use will show how little the idea of " change of the elements " was attached to the word.

Indeed, as to this word, it is almost superfluous to give proofs, since S. Cyril of Alexandria, in a passage already quoted, uses it of a physical substance of which he expressly says that the substance remains. The Dublin critic, pressing the etymology, says, " The sacred symbols are *transelemented* (μετα-στοιχειοῦνται), *i.e.* their *elements* (στοιχεῖα) are *changed*." S. Cyril uses the word of the Coal in Isaiah's vision, as a symbol of the union of our Lord's Divine and Human Natures, and also of His Presence in the Holy Eucharist, and expressly remarks that in it the elements are not changed. "Fire [1] having entered into wood *transelements* it after a fashion into its own glory and power, albeit *retaining what it was.*"

The word μεταστοιχειόω, as applied to the Holy Eucharist, occurs (as far as I am aware) in S. Gregory of Nyssa alone of the Fathers [2], in the *one* passage already quoted, "These things He gives, *transelementing,* by the power of the blessing, to It the nature of the visible elements." So far is it from being an ecclesiastical word, that, besides this place, it is, I believe, used of the Holy Eucharist only in a later writer, of the 11th century, Theophylact. And this, notwithstanding its frequent use of other changes.

The only question, then, is, whether S. Gregory of Nyssa meant, in this place, to speak of such a change, by which the substance or element of bread should cease to be.

Albertinus [3] states that, "besides this place, S. Gregory uses this word in nineteen other places

[1] See above, p. 120.

[2] It occurs in a prayer of the above-mentioned interpolated Liturgy attributed by the Copts to S. Gregory of Nazianzum (Ass. vii. 117), which prayer, however, does not occur even in the Coptic translation, which has a different "preface," (Ib. 150,) nor of course in the Syriac.

[3] Art. Greg. Nyss. p. 488.

only, and in all, without any exception, to designate change of condition or virtue, *not of substance.*"

S. Gregory employs the word of our Lord's making His own Nature Impassible, after the Resurrection; the religious change of nature in us; of our life to that which is more Divine; of the body to incorruption; of ourselves into a spiritual nature; and that, by regeneration through Baptism; of the union of our Lord's Human Nature with His Divine, and of our very nature in Him.

"He[4] did not alter His Impassible Nature into passivity, but He *transelemented* our changeable and passible nature, by the communion with the unchangeable, into Impassibility (τὸ τρεπτόν τε καὶ ἐμπαθὲς εἰς ἀπάθειαν μετεστοιχείωσεν)."

"For[5] when this fluctuating and transitory time shall come to an end, wherein one is ever being born, and another going to corruption, and the necessity of birth shall have passed away, and there shall no longer be any thing subject to corruption, the expected resurrection *transelementing* (μεταστοιχειούσης) our nature into some other condition (κατάστασιν)."

"But[6] when the Kingdom which is above all has come upon them too, they who before were without a Master now become heirs of God through faith in Him that was born this day; Him I mean Who is set up as King over them, who are themselves too born and made kings; in whom the rod of iron, that is, the immutable power, having crushed that which was of earth and clay, hath *transelemented* them

---

[4] De Vit. Mos. (myst. interp.) i. 192.
[5] Tract. alter in Ps. c. 5, i. 301
[6] Ib. c. 8, i. 308.

(μετεστοιχείωσεν) into the incorruptible nature, showing that faith in Him is alone blessed."

"But[7] thou understandest certainly by the Stone which cuts away that which is impure, the Stone Itself, which is Christ, that is, the Word of Truth ; and that then ceaseth the defiling stream of the affairs of life, the human life being *transelemented* to that which is more divine (μετα-στοιχειωθείσης πρὸς τὸ θειότερον)."

"For[8] as, after the Resurrection, the body, *transelemented into incorruption* (μεταστοιχειωθὲν πρὸς τὸ ἄφθαρ-τον), is conjoined to the soul of man. To the dowry of the bride in the Canticles belongs '*transelementation*'[9] of nature (μεταστοιχείωσις φύσεως)."

"What[10] is it then which we say? The human race was once frozen with the chill of idolatry, the moveable nature of man being *changed* (μεταβληθείσης) into the nature of their immoveable objects of worship. For 'may[1] they,' he says, 'be like them that make them, and all they that put their trust in them.' And reasonable was it that so it should be. For as they who gaze on the true Divinity receive within themselves the properties (ἰδιώματα) of the Divine Nature, so he that gave heed to the vanity of idols was *transelemented* (μετεστοιχειοῦτο) into that which he saw, becoming from a man a stone."

"Let[2] us hear then the heavenly words by which Scripture describes the beauty of the immaculate virgin. Let us hear however as those who are out of flesh and blood, and have been *transelemented* (μεταστοιχειωθέντες) *into the spiritual nature.*"

"It[3] will be well, on this day, not only to bring to God, through the grace of the laver, those who have been *trans-*

---

[7] In Ps. 6, i. 368.

[8] Hom. i. in Cant. p. 479. See above in *transmaking*, p. 186.

[9] Ib. p. 482. [10] Ib. Hom. 5, i. 542.

[1] Ps. cxxxiv. 18, LXX. [2] Ib. Hom. 9, init. i. 601.

[3] Ep. Canon. ad Letoium, init. ii. 114.

elemented by regeneration, &c. (τοὺς ἐκ παλιγγενεσίας μεταστοιχειουμένους)."

"For[4] our reasoning doth not advocate a number of Christs (as Eunomius accuseth), but the union of the man with the Divine; of the mortal with the Immortal; of the slave with the Lord; of sin with righteousness; of the curse with the blessing, and the *transelementation* of the man *to Christ* (τὴν τοῦ ἀνθρώπου πρὸς τὸν Χριστὸν μεταστοιχείωσιν), designating it by the word 'making'" (ποίησιν ὀνομάζων)."

"For[5] Paul saith, that having made Himself a little lower than the angels for the suffering of death, those who were before changed into the nature of a thorn He made a crown to Himself through the dispensation according to death, *transelementing* the thorn [*i. e.* our human nature] through the Passion to honour and glory."

"The[6] kingdom of life is come, and the power of death broken. And there hath become another birth, a different life, another kind of life, a *transelementing* of our very nature itself (αὐτῆς τῆς φύσεως ἡμῶν μεταστοιχείωσις). The birth of Him, is 'not of blood, nor of the will of man, nor of the will of flesh, but of God.' How is this? I will set before thee the grace through the Word. This birth is conceived by faith: through the regeneration of Baptism it is brought to life."

"Let[7] none then of the inconsiderate accuse the body, with which, having been through the regeneration *transelemented* to that which is more Divine (μεταστοιχειωθέντι πρὸς τὸ Θειότερον), the soul shall be adorned, when death shall

---

[4] Cont. Eunom. Or. iv. fin. p. 591.

[5] Acts ii. 36, "God hath *made* Jesus, both Lord and Christ."

[6] De perf. Christiani forma, iii. 293.

[7] In Christi Res. Orat. i. Ib. 384. See also cont. Eunom. Orat. ii. p. 431, below, in μετασκευάζω.

[8] De mortuis. Ib. 638.

have cleansed away what is superfluous and useless for the enjoyment of the life to come."

" He [a] then Who *transelemented* our nature to the Divine Virtue (ὁ τὴν φύσιν ἡμῶν πρὸς τὴν θείαν δύναμιν μεταστοιχειώσας), preserved it unmaimed and diseaseless in Himself, not admitting the maiming which comes from sin to the will."

Of other Fathers, Eusebius of Thessalonica and S. Chrysostome use the words of our Lord's Body. Eusebius notices that it was *transelemented*, and yet the very same Body.

" He [1] did this [ate and drank after the Resurrection] supernaturally (ὑπερφυῶς) by a dispensation, that He might assure the disciples, and through them all believers, that that very Body which suffered and was crucified, rose again, and no other than It, although It was *transelemented* into incorruption and impassibility [πρὸς ἀφθαρσίαν καὶ ἀπάθειαν μετεστοιχειώθη]."

" Being [2] the first, not according to the Deity (God for-

[a] Ep. ad Eust. Ambr. et Basil. Ib. 658. Besides the above, there are others, less evident, that " the universe shall be *transelemented* into some other condition " (de Hom. Opif. c. 24), and (de Virgin. c. iv. t. iii. 127.) " All things necessarily expect the *transelementing.*" (The matter of the universe, it was supposed, would remain.) De inscr. Ps. c. 8, p. 308, " The rod of iron, *i. e.* His immutable power crushing what was of earth and clay, *transelemented* it into an incorrupt nature, teaching that to trust in Him is the only bliss" (where there is a metaphor, as also in Hom. vii. in Cant. p. 573), " We were in the hands of the workman, and He made us a ' chariot ' for Himself, *transelementing* the nature of wood through regeneration into gold and silver and bright purple and the lustre of precious stones."

[1] Euseb. Thessal. ap. Phot. cod. 162, fin.

[2] S. Chrys. de Incarnat. ap. Phot. cod. 277, and thence Opp. t. xiii. p. 268, ed. Ben.

bid !   For it were an indignity to God to be called first of creatures, Who in an ineffable way and inconceivable eminence is raised and set aloft above all nature), but He is first according to His Humanity, being the Foregoer of our Resurrection, and of the *transelementing* from corruption to incorruption."

And another of a moral change : —

" For [3] this cause I [our Lord] allowed shrinking to the flesh, that I may *transelement* it to good courage."

S. Gregory of Nazianzum employs the word, of the change in our nature through Christ.

" He [4] [Apollinaris] affirms that the Flesh, which in the dispensation was taken to Him by the Only Begotten Son for the *transelementing* of our nature (ἐπὶ μεταστοιχειώσει τῆς φύσεως ἡμῶν) was not taken from without," &c.

From S. Cyril of Alexandria, Albertinus quotes thirty instances in which the word is used of changes in which there is no *material* alteration ; of changing our flesh into life, all things to newness ; of man's being changed to his primæval state ; by the Holy Spirit into all kind of virtue ; of the Gospel changing body, soul, and spirit, into its own quality ; the water of Baptism being changed into a Divine and ineffable power ; Israel into a new people ; our minds ; and even of our union with our Lord ; and our Lord's transelementing His own Human Body to glory.

---

[3] Quoted as S. Chrys. on S. Joh. xii. 27, in Cat. Cord. p. 311.

[4] Epist. 202, ad Nect. ii. 168, ed. Ben.

" Christ [5] the First Born from the dead, to us the way of the Resurrection, Who *transelementeth* to newness (πρὸς καινότητα μεταστοιχειῶν) and removeth decay."

" The [6] Saviour likens to leaven, the excellent and beneficial power of the Divine and Evangelic instruction, because its life-giving in-working, entering into the mind and heart, *transelementeth* soul and body and spirit into, as it were, its own quality (ψυχήν τε καὶ σῶμα καὶ πνεῦμα πρὸς ἰδίαν ὥσπερ ποιότητα μεταστοιχειοῖ)."

"The new moon [7] may be a type of the world to come, having, as a beginning, the Resurrection of Christ, through which we have passed to newness, enriched with the Spirit in the earnest of grace and with an unfailing hope of life immortal, *transelemented* into our primæval state (μεταστοιχειούμενοι πρὸς τὸ ἐν ἀρχαῖς), and going backwards as it were, conformed to the world to come."

" Of [8] His own free will too did the Only Begotten Word of God come among us . . . . in order that, having appeared in a form subject to death, He might *transelement* it unto life."

" They [9] of Israel too have become children of the Church through faith in Christ, no longer reckoned to that old people, but rather *transelemented* (μεταστοιχειούμενοι εἰς νέον) into the new, blended with those from the Gentiles."

"But [1] when our Lord Jesus Christ returned to life, and as a sheaf [2], presented Himself, the first fruits of our humanity, to God and the Father, then were we *transelemented* as it were to a new life (εἰς νέαν ὥσπερ ζωὴν μεταστοιχειούμεθα).   For we live an Evangelic life, &c."

[5] De Adorat. L. xvii. p. 611, and in the same sense μεταστοιχίζω, L. xi. p. 405, " according to His great mercy, we have been lightened of corruption, and been *transelemented* into newness of life in Christ, God pitying us."

[6] Ib. p. 614.   [7] Ib. p. 625.
[8] Id. Glaph. in Gen. p. 11.   [9] Glaph. in Gen. L. iv. p. 113.
[1] Glaph. in Num. fin. p. 399.   [2] Lev. xxiii. 10.

"He[3] took our nature, not that He might seem evil with us, but to make us good, *transelementing* (μεταστοιχειώσας) us by the Holy Spirit to all manner of virtue."

"The[4] words 'Thy Maker' are for 'He Who createth thee,' and *transformeth* (μεταμορφῶν) to another mode of life and to a becoming conversation. For we are *transelemented* in Christ to newness of a holy and Evangelic life, ascending to a beauty of form through the Spirit, so that for the future we are evidently different beings."

"I[5] create thee, He saith, not as a smith making vessels out of matter with tools and fire, but rather by an ineffable and invisible *transelementing* and re-formation (μεταστοιχειώσει καὶ ἀναπλασμῷ), and, as it were, spiritual regeneration, which the Saviour Himself formerly laid open to Nicodemus."

"For[6] that He might win over the whole world and bring to God the Father mankind under the whole Heaven, *transelementing* (μεταστοιχειώσας) all things to a better state, and as it were renewing the face of the earth."

"Things[7] in Him are a new creation, as it is written, 'old things have passed away, and new have come,' through Him *transelementing* the things of man, and renewing them ; so that, again, all should be good (μεταστοιχειοῦντος τὰ ἀνθρώπινα)."

"But[8] the spirit of man is formed in Him, not called to the beginning of His being, although made by Him, but as it were *transformed* (μεταμορφούμενον) from weakness to strength, from cowardice to endurance, and altogether spiritually *transelemented* (μεταστοιχειούμενον) from a foul to a better state."

"The[9] Creator, having long had patience, pities at last the corrupted world, and in His goodness hasted to unite

---

[3] Glaph. in Num. fin. p. 409.
[4] Ib. p. 770, 1.
[5] In Mich. v. init. iii. 434.
[6] In Joh. 2, c. 1, iv. p. 122.
[7] In Is. L. v. p. 760.
[8] Ib. p. 854.
[9] In Zech. xii. init. p. 773.

the renegade band on earth to those above, and decreed to *transelement* (μεταστοιχειοῦν) again human nature to the ancient image, through the Spirit."

"I[1] nothing wrong any, *re-ordering* (μεταρρυθμίζων) Mine own laws, and *transelementing* things which were spoken darkly to those of old, from the grossness of the letter, to spiritual contemplation."

"As[2] then I, although I became Flesh (for this is the meaning of being 'sent'), live through the Living Father, *i.e.* preserving in myself the qualities of the Father, so he, who through participation of My Flesh receiveth Me, shall have life in himself, altogether *wholly transelemented* (μεταστοιχειούμενος) *into Me*, Who have power to impart life, being from the Life-giving Root, *i.e.* from God the Father."

"Yet[3] profitably were the human feelings troubled in Christ, without sin, not that the emotions should prevail, and go forward, as in us, but that having begun they might be cut short, by the power of reason [or 'the Word'], nature in Christ first being *transelemented* into some better and Diviner change (πρὸς ἀμείνω τινὰ καὶ θειοτέραν μετάστασιν μεταστοιχειουμένης)."

"It[4] was then altogether fitting, that we should be sharers and partakers of the Divine Nature of the Word, or that having left our own life, we should be *transformed* (μετα-σκιναζέσθαι) into another, and *be transelemented* to the new-ness of citizenship, in friendship with God (πρὸς καινότητα πολιτείας μεταστοιχειοῦσθαι τῆς θεοφιλοῦς), and this we could only attain through the communication and participa-tion of the Holy Spirit."

"For[5] when (saith He) My Spirit hath made you dif-ferent men, and *transelementeth* your mind (μεταστοιχειώσῃ νοῦν) to will and to be able henceforth to despise the types

---

[1] Ib. L. iii. p. 253.　　　[2] Ib. L. iv. c. 3, init. p. 366.
[3] Ib. 703.　　　[4] Ib. p. 919.
[5] Ib. L. x. p. 923.

of the law, and to choose rather the beauty of worship in spirit, and to prefer the truth to shadows."

" Our[6] Lord Jesus Christ, having not as yet *transelemented* (μεταστοιχειώσας) His Own temple [His Body] into the glory due and befitting it."

" Again[7] did He send forth into him that Divine and Holy Spirit which had once entirely left him, *transelementing* him well after the most fair image (μεταστοιχειοῦν), and able and willing, by means of His Own Essence, to *re-order* (μεταρρυθμίζειν) us after His Likeness."

" The[8] Holy Tabernacle being revealed to us in the fit time, in which we are *transelemented* to newness of life (εἰς καινότητα ζωῆς μεταστοιχειώμεθα)."

" For[9] since the Word of God is Life by Nature, He made that which was liable to corruption His own Body, in order that, having broken the force of death that was in it, He might *transelement it to incorruption* (μεταστοιχειώσῃ πρὸς ἀφθαρσίαν)."

" It[1] was *transelemented* (μετεστοιχειοῦτο) as it were into a Divine and unspeakable purity, sin being dead in it."

" He[2] rose again the third day, having, as God, quickened His Own Temple, and become the Firstfruits of them that slept, and the First Born from the dead, that He might make the nature of man superior to death and corruption, and *transelement* (εἰς μακραίωνα ζωὴν μεταστοιχειώσῃ) him to immortal life."

" He[3] indeed is new, who is *transelemented* into the newness of life which is in Christ (εἰς καινότητα ζωῆς τῆς ἐν Χριστῷ μεταστοιχειούμενος)."

[6] Ib. L. xii. p. 1092.
[7] De S. Trin. Dial. vii. T. v. 1, p. 653.
[8] De Fest. Pasch. Hom. xvi. T. v. 2, p. 216.
[9] Ib. Hom. xvii. p. 233.   [1] Ib. Hom. xix. p. 252.
[2] Ib. Hom. xx. p. 265.   The phrase occurs again Hom. xxiv. p. 295.
[3] Ib. Hom. xxiii. p. 281.

" That ' He may bring us to the Father, having freed us from the charges of our old sins, and having *transelemented* us to newness of life in the Spirit (εἰς καινότητα ζωῆς μεταστοιχειώσας ἐν πνεύματι)."

" The ' Word from God the Father was born among us according to the flesh, that we too might gain the birth of God through the Spirit, no longer being called children of the flesh, but rather *transelemented* to that which is above nature (μεταστοιχειούμενοι εἰς τὰ ὑπὲρ φύσιν), and called sons of God according to grace."

" For ' so is Christ formed in us, the Holy Spirit as it were *transelementing* us from human things to His own (μεταστοιχειοῦντος ὥσπερ ἡμᾶς ἐκ τῶν ἀνθρωπίνων εἰς τὰ αὑτοῦ)."

" But ' we say that He suffered death by a dispensation in His Own Flesh, in order that, having trodden it under foot, and being raised again, as being by nature Life and quickening, He might *transelement to incorruption* (μετα-στοιχειώσῃ πρὸς ἀφθαρσίαν) that which was tyrannized over by death, to wit, the body."

" That ' Christ arose more glorious and more wonderful than in His Transfiguration on the mount; and that, on rising again, He did not *transelement* His Body into the glory fitting to It (οὐ μετεστοιχείωσεν ἀναστὰς τὸ σῶμα πρὸς δόξαν τὴν αὐτῷ κεχρεωστημένην), but manifested It such as It also was before death, and this Cyril saith."

St. Cyril uses the word ἀναστοιχειοῦται, or μετα-στοιχειοῦται, of the water of Baptism :—

" For ' by the Spirit the spirit of man is sanctified ; the body again by the sanctified water. For as water poured

<hr>

' De recta fide, p. 167.

' Adv. Nest. L. iii. c. 2, T. vi. p. 70.   ' Ib. p 72.

' Ib. L. v. p. 122.

' Phot. Cod. 232. Steph. Gob. c. 50.

' In S. Joh. iii. 5, iv. p. 147.

forth in cauldrons, meeting with the points of fire, derives into itself its [the fire's] power, so through the inworking of the Spirit, the tangible[1] water is *transelemented* [ἀναστοι-χειοῦται, *v. l.* μεταστοιχειοῦται] into a certain divine and unspeakable power, and afterward sanctifieth, for the time to come, them to whom it is."

Indeed the word ἀναστοιχειόω illustrates, in this respect, the use of μεταστοιχειόω, that in neither is there any reference to the "elements" of which any thing is composed. ἀναστοιχειόω is to "re-form," μεταστοιχειόω, to "transform;" the one, to "restore to a previous condition;" the other, to change into another; but neither, by the mere force of the word, has reference to any physical change. S. Cyril uses ἀναστοιχειόω of "re-formation" through Christ, when to render it "re-element," and to suppose a physical change, would involve heresy.

"For[2] since Christ is a new creation, according to the Scriptures, we too therefore receive Him in ourselves, through His Holy Flesh and Blood, that being re-formed (ἀναστοιχειούμενοι) through Him and in Him, we may put off the old man, which is corrupt according to the deceitful lusts."

Since Theophylact has been cited, it may be well to give instances, that Theophylact also employs the word "transelement" of changes, in which the matter or substance does not cease to be. He uses it three

---

[1] This last sentence, "The tangible water," &c. is, in Corderius's Catena, quoted as Ammonius's. There is added, "the water in conception only is diverse from the Spirit, since it is the same in operation" (ad loc. p. 89).

[2] De Adorat. L. xii. p. 419.

times of our Resurrection, once of union with our
Lord, once of religious confusion.

" We [3] cast down countless who stand, that we may set
up our own will (when it were worthy not to be set up, but
to be buried), and we *transelement* (μεταστοιχειοῦμεν) all
things, and transpose all things," &c.

" He [4] who eateth Me shall live by Me, as it were immingled and *transelemented into Me*, Who am able to give
life."

" The [5] body, which we now have, is ensouled, *i. e.* ruled
by the soul, and vivified by qualities and powers of nature
and the soul.   But that after the Resurrection, Paul called
spiritual, *i. e.* vivified and ruled by a Divine Spirit and not
by the soul, in an ineffable and spiritual manner *transelemented* to incorruption, and preserved in it."

" Believe [6] that what now is corruptible, and in a worser
state, shall be *transelemented* to what is incorruptible and
better."

" Lest [7] any, hearing that ' flesh and blood shall not inherit the kingdom,' and again, that ' the dead shall be raised
incorruptible,' should think that the bodies are not raised,
because they now consist of flesh and blood, he subjoins, that
the bodies are raised, but not being flesh and blood, but
transelemented to incorruption.   Mark that saying against
those who say that not the same, but other bodies arise.
For he saith, ' *this* corruptible,' and ' *this* mortal ;' not
another, but ' *this*,' pointing to it.   So then the body remains the same (for it is this which is clothed upon), but
mortality and corruption disappear, incorruption and immortality encompassing it."

[3] De err. Latin. c. 16, Opp. t. ii. p. 525.
[4] In S. Joh. vi. 57, i. 595.
[5] In S. Luc. xxiv. 39, p. 496.
[6] In 1 Cor. xv. 46, iii. 228.
[7] On ver. 53, p. 230.

The substance then of the "transelemented" body Theophylact holds to be the same, its condition different.

iii.—vi. As next in importance to these, the Dublin Reviewer alleges, that S. Chrysostom (*and he alone*) *once* [s] employs the word (iii.) μεταρρυθμίζω, which may be rendered "*re-order*, or *remodel*," and *once* the word (iv.) μετασκευάζω, "*transfashion;*" that S. Ambrose *twice* uses the word (v.) "transfiguro," *transfigure*, and that S. Gregory of Nyssa and S. Cyril of Alexandria employ, each once, the word (vi.) μεθίστημι, "translate," not of a change of

---

[s] The word is repeated in what even Montfaucon calls a *Second* Homily "on the betrayal by Judas." Yet it is evidently a different report of the same homily, with a different beginning, consisting of a few lines, prefixed to it. That very beginning contradicts the homily itself. For in the body of the homily S. Chrysostom says, "For this cause I am now *for the fourth day* discoursing with you about prayer for enemies, that through the continuous peal of my exhortation the word of teaching may become abiding, that it may be rooted in your minds" (p. 387, E). But the new heading of six lines, prefixed to this second homily, says, "I would again touch on the subject of the Patriarch, and thence set before you the spiritual feast, but the ingratitude of the traitor draws our speech to the subject of himself, and the occasion of the day calls on us to speak of the madness of his presumption." This implies that the course was just broken off, as, in fact, S. Chrysostom did break off his course of homilies on Abraham on the day of the betrayal of our Lord (Hom. 33 in Gen. init. quoted by Montfaucon, Monitum, ii. 375). The six lines then of preface are probably the beginning of a sermon of S. Chrysostom, but have been wrongly prefixed to this edition of his sermon on Judas, which they contradict.

the elements into the Body and Blood of Christ, but of a translation, as Greg. Nyss. says, "into Divine *power;*" as S. Cyril says, into the *energy of* His Flesh, *i. e.* the elements have conferred upon them the power of conveying the unseen Presence of the Body and Blood of Christ.

The facts then which these, the ivth and vth classes of the Dublin Reviewer, really contain, are, that S. Chrysostom *once* employs, of the elements of the Holy Eucharist, the word "*re-order,*" and *once* uses "transfashion;" and S. Ambrose *twice* "transfigure."

Now in all this discussion it is safest to repeat, even again and again, that the only question is, whether there be such a change, that the *substance* of the elements *ceases to be.* Neither μεταρρυθμίζω, "*re-order,*" nor μετασκευάζω, "*re-fashion,*" either in their etymology or their usage, imply any change of substance, but the contrary. To "re-order," "re-fashion," expresses a re-arrangement of that which *is;* an ordering for some other end, which is exactly our belief of the consecrated elements, as the outward and visible sign of the inward substance.

iii. μεταρρυθμίζω, "re-order." The single passage in which S. Chrysostom uses this word of the Holy Eucharist is;

"Christ[1] is present now too. The same who adorned that Table, adorneth this too now. For it is

[1] Hom. 1, de Prod. Jud. § 6, T. ii. p. 384.

not man who maketh what lieth there to become the Body and Blood of Christ, but Christ Himself Who was crucified for us. The priest standeth, filling up a figure, speaking these words, the power and grace are of God. 'This is My Body,' He saith. This word *re-ordereth* what lieth there, and as that voice, 'increase and multiply and replenish the earth,' was spoken once, but throughout all time, in effect giveth power to our race to the procreation of children, so also that voice, once spoken, doth on every Table in the Churches from that time even till now, and unto His coming, complete the sacrifice."

The object of S. Chrysostom's illustration is to show the power of God, either in strengthening the laws of nature, or above nature.   He does not speak any thing of any *physical* change, but of the power of the Word of God in ordering or re-ordering as He wills.

This is illustrated by the very instances in which he uses the word of a change in a physical subject, when God stopped the lions' mouths or restrained the violence of fire.   In the lions there was no physical change; the fire retained its own burning nature, for it slew the mighty men who came near its mouth.   But God changed the will of the lions, and withheld the effects of the fire from passing upon the three children.   Yet for both S. Chrysostom uses this same word, " *re-order.*"

" What[1] wonder if they have mastered enemies, when

[1] Exp. in Ps. 10, init. T. v. p. 113.

they have overcome the world itself? For the elements, forgetting their own nature, were *changed* ($\mu\epsilon\tau\epsilon\beta\dot{\alpha}\lambda\lambda o\nu\tau o$) into what was profitable for them; and the wild beasts were no longer beasts, nor the furnace, a furnace. For hope in God *remodels* all things ($\dot{\eta}$ $\gamma\dot{\alpha}\rho$ $\epsilon\dot{\iota}\varsigma$ $\tau\dot{o}\nu$ $\Theta\epsilon\dot{o}\nu$ $\dot{\epsilon}\lambda\pi\dot{\iota}\varsigma$ $\pi\dot{\alpha}\nu\tau a$ $\mu\epsilon\tau a\rho\rho\nu\theta\mu\dot{\iota}\zeta\epsilon\iota$). For there were sharpened teeth and a narrow prison, fierceness of nature, and hunger arming nature, and a fence no where, and mouths near the body of the prophet; but hope in God, mightier than any bridle, falling upon their mouths, drew them backwards."

In like way, in another place, in which S. Chrysostom speaks of God's *re-ordering* nature, it relates not to any physical change in nature, but to a suspension of its laws; and this, in answer to those who deified nature. Nature, he argues, cannot be God, because there is One who overruleth and *re-ordereth* nature.

" Not [2] only do they [the powers of nature] accomplish those things for which they are prepared, but even if He enjoin the contrary, here too there is great obedience. He commanded the sea, and not only did it not overwhelm, which was its office, but lulling its waves, it transmitted the Jewish people more safely than a rock. The furnace not only burnt not, but yielded a whistling dew. The wild beasts not only devoured not, but held the place of a body-guard to Daniel. The whale not only devoured not, but preserved its deposit safe. The earth not only bare not, but overwhelmed more grievously than the sea itself, when it opened and swallowed up Dathan, and covered the congre-

---

[2] In Ps. 110, n. 2, T. v. p. 267. In the same reference S. Chrys. says, " God it is Who maketh and *re-fashioneth* all things, and *re-ordereth* all things at His Will " ($\dot{o}$ $\pi\dot{\alpha}\nu\tau a$ $\pi o\iota\tilde{\omega}\nu$ $\kappa a\dot{\iota}$ $\mu\epsilon\tau a\sigma\kappa\epsilon\nu\dot{\alpha}\zeta\omega\nu$ $\kappa a\dot{\iota}$ $\mu\epsilon\tau a\rho\rho\nu\theta\mu\dot{\iota}\zeta\omega\nu$). (In Gen. Hom. ii. 2, iv. 10, A.)

gation of Abiram, and many other marvellous works might any one observe; that those who are exceeding senseless, and deify nature, may learn that things are not hurried along by a tyranny of nature, but that all things give way and yield to the Will of God. For this is the Creator of nature, and at Its good pleasure It *re-orders* all the things which are, at one time retaining their bounds immoveable, and again when It wills, easily removing them, and changing to the contrary."

On another Psalm [3] he gives nearly the same instances in correction of the same errors.

"He bringeth forth substances which are not, and when produced He transposeth them (μετατίθησι), and *re-ordereth* whereto He wills."

He distinguishes.

"Sometimes He changes the substances themselves, sometimes He transposes them, *abiding*, into *another energy* (εἰς ἐτέραν μετατίθησιν ἐνέργειαν)."

And so he even insists on the abiding of the natural substances,

"It *was* fire, and it burned not; there *was* sea; there *was* earth. There *were* lions in the case of Daniel, and they displayed the gentleness of sheep, *their nature not being destroyed, but its operation changed*."

Elsewhere [4], while using the word "re-order," he expressly denies any change of substance. Speaking of our Lord's coming to judgment, he says,

"How doth He come? The very creation being then *transfigured* (μετασχηματιζομένης), for 'the sun shall be darkened,' *not destroyed*, but overcome by the light of His Presence. 'And the stars shall fall.' For what need of

---

[3] In Ps. 147, n. 1, pp. 483, 4.
[4] Hom. 76, in S. Matt. xxiv. 29, p. 1013, O. T.

them any more, there being no night! 'and the powers of Heaven shall be shaken,' very naturally, seeing so great a change coming to pass. For if when the stars were made, they trembled and marvelled [5], much more seeing all things *remodelled*, and their fellow-servants giving account,— how shall they but tremble and shake!"

Elsewhere, S. Chrysostom uses it of moral or spiritual changes. Thus, of man's re-formation in Baptism, the re-harmonizing of his being, the restoration of that state in which he was in harmony with God and with himself.

" When [6] he confessed (his belief) in the life everlasting, he confessed a second creation. He took dust from the earth, and formed man; yet now, dust no longer, but the Holy Spirit; with This he is formed, with This *harmonized* ($\rho\nu\theta\mu\iota\zeta\epsilon\tau\alpha\iota$), even as Himself was in the womb of the Virgin. He said not 'in Paradise,' but 'in Heaven.' For deem not that, because the subject is earth, it is done on earth; he is removed thither, to Heaven; there these things are transacted, in the midst of angels; God taketh up thy soul above; above, He *harmonizeth it anew*, He placeth thee near to the kingly throne. He is formed in the water, he receiveth spirit instead of a soul."

And of Christ's transforming power:

" What [7] sayest thou! If I give mine enemy drink, do I then punish him? if I let go my goods, do I then have them! if I humble myself, shall I then be exalted? Yea, saith He. For such is My power. By means of contraries, contraries are effected. I am wealthy and full of resources; fear not. The nature of things followeth My own will, I

[5] Job xxxviii. 7, LXX.
[6] Hom. 6, in Col. n. 4, p. 253, O. T.
[7] Hom. 25, in Ep. ad Heb. T. 12, p. 230.

follow not nature.   Therefore I can transmould and *remodel* these things (διὸ καὶ μεταπλάττειν καὶ μεταρρυθμίζειν αὐτὰ δύναμαι).

And again of Baptism :—

"Great[8] indeed is the might of Baptism.   It makes them that partake of that gift quite other men.   It suffereth not men to be men.   Make the Heathen believe that great is the power of the Spirit, that it hath re-formed, that it hath *remodelled* [ὅτι μετέπλασε, ὅτι μετερρύθμισε]."

"He[9] loathed not her deformity [of that which He made the Church], but He changed, remoulded, *remodelled* (μετέβαλε, μετέπλασε, μετερρύθμισεν) what was unpleasing, and forgave her sins."

And of love :—

"Him[1] do thou imitate; *remodel* her [an ill-mannered wife] by goodness and tenderness, as Christ also did the Church."

"Love[2] is a great teacher; and able both to withdraw men from error, and to *remodel* the character (τρόπον μεταρρυθμίσαι)."

And of the fruits of our Lord's passion :—

"On[3] the Parasccue when thy Lord was crucified for the world, and such a Sacrifice was offered, and Paradise was opened, and the Robber brought back to the ancient home, the curse was dissolved, and sin was destroyed, and the long war was taken away, and God was reconciled with man, and all things were '*re-ordered*' (restored to their ancient order and harmony, πάντα μετερρύθμιζετο)."

Of the hymns of Paul and Silas :—

[8] Hom. 23, in Act. n. 3, p. 336, O. T.
[9] Quales ducend. sunt uxores, § 2, iii. 214.   [1] Ibid.
[2] In 1 Cor. Hom. 33, n. 6, p. 468, O. T.
[3] Cont. Lud. et Theatr. vi. 273.

" The ' voice of those sacred hymns entering the soul of each of the prisoners, remoulded it, so to say, and *re-ordered* it (μετέπλαττεν αὐτὴν, ὡς εἰπεῖν, καὶ μετερρύθμιζεν)."

Lastly, of the amending of laws:

" But ' if some of them were dissolved, they were *re-modelled,* not for the worse, but for the better."

So again S. Clement of Alexandria:

" Democritus ' says well, that nature and teaching are very near alike.   And we have briefly added the cause. For instruction *re-orders* (μεταρρυθμίζει) the man ; and, *re-ordering* (μεταρρυθμοῦσα), imparts a nature (φυσιοποιεῖ). And it differeth nothing that he should be formed such by nature, or recast (μετατυπωθῆναι) by time and learning. But the Lord gave both : the one by creation : the other according to the re-creation and renewal (ἀνάκτισίν τε καὶ ἀνανέωσιν) from the covenant."

And Theodoret:

" The ' nature of fire obeyeth thee not, nor doth it depart from its native operation (for it is thy fellow-servant); but, obeying the will of its Creator, it is *re-ordered* (μεταρρυθμίζεται), and the nature bearing upwards becomes down-bearing."

And S. Cyril of Alexandria:

" They ' [man's natural powers] are *remodelled* to the use of virtue, and to the ministry of holiness (μεταρρυθμίζεται εἰς ἀρετῆς χρείαν), as, surely, the golden and silver vessels of Egypt are pointed out as being useful for the furnishing and completion of the holy tabernacle.

' In illud Diligentib. Deum, c. 3, t. 3, p. 154.
' In Ps. 110, T. v. 274.
' Strom. iv. 23, ed. Pott.
' De Provid. Orat. i. p. 491, ed. Sch.
' De Adorat. L. i. T. 1, p. 46.

" Moved [9] by the spirit of the prophecy, and through it foreknowing things to come, the blessed prophet understood that the human race could no otherwise be saved, except only by the Epiphany of the Son of God, Who, without difficulty, can *re-order* whereto He will (ἐφ᾽ ὅπερ ἂν βούλοιτο μεταῤῥυθμίζειν ἰσχύοντος).

" Wherein [1] most of all, we should admire alike the forbearance of our Saviour, and the power of Him who easily *remodels* even untutored understandings to an admirable frame.

" Having [2] once received this healing through faith, and having been *remodelled* [3] into newness of life, it was necessary that the oldness of the letter of the law should become of no effect.

" All things [4] He transposed (μετετίθει) for the better, and, *remodelling* [5] the corrupted nature of man to newness of life, as being loosed from chains, He presented us free to the Father.

" Having *remodelled* [6] all things in us to a better order and firm condition.

" It [7] seemed good to Him, Who is good by nature, the Maker of all things, to *transmould* (μεταπλάττειν) the living creature to incorruption ; and by re-formations [8] to godliness, well to *re-element* them into that incorrupt beauty which was in the beginning.

[9] In Joh. L. i. c. 3, p. 18.

[1] τὰς ἀπαιδεύτους διανοίας εἰς ἀξιάγαστον ἕξιν εὐκόλως μεταῤῥυθμίζοντος.   Ib. L. ii. c. 4, p. 184.

[2] Ib. c. 5, p. 209.

[3] εἰς καινότητα μεταῤῥυθμισθέντας ζωῆς.

[4] De Fest. Pasch. vi. T. v. 2, p. 79.

[5] τὴν κατεφθαρμένην τοῦ ἀνθρώπου φύσιν εἰς καινότητα μεταῤῥυθμίζων ζωῆς.

[6] πάντα μεταῤῥυθμήσας τὰ ἐν ἡμῖν.   Ib. vii. p. 91.

[7] Ib. xiv. p. 197.

[8] ταῖς εἰς εὐσέβειαν ἀναμορφώσεσι ἀναστοιχειοῦν εὖ μάλα πρὸς τὸ ἐν ἀρχαῖς ἀκήρατον κάλλος.

" He remained then what He was, even with the Flesh, and having vouchsafed to empty Himself according to the Dispensation, as it is written, He appeared upon earth, and was conversant among men; *remodelling*[9] unto holiness, justifying by faith whoso cometh to Him."

And S. Gregory of Nyssa;

" For"[10] this indeed was a proof of his great wisdom, that *re-modelling* his whole generation collectively *to a new life*, &c.

" What"[11] shall we do, not employing rods? Shall we leave him unregarded? Not so. But we will *remodel* him by reason to another fashion, as the case requires."

iv.—μετασκευάζω, "transform," "transfashion." The single place in which this word is used of the Holy Eucharist is in S. Chrysostom, " What[1] lieth there is no work of human power. He who then did all things at that feast, He now also worketh there. *We* have the rank of servants; He who sanctifieth them and *transformeth* them, is Himself."

Now the very context (as has been already pointed out) relates not to any *mode* of change, but to the power of God, put forth in the Sacraments; that, whereas they were before *bare* elements of this world, now, through the operation of Christ, they are His Body and Blood. The same appeal as to Divine power, S. Chrysostom makes as to Baptism also. " The[2] Spirit is the chief agent, through

---

[9] μεταῤῥυθμίζων εἰς ἁγιασμόν.

[10] Vit. S. Greg. Thaum. iii. 574.

[11] De Castigat. iii. 316.

[1] In S. Matth. Hom. 82, n. 5, vii. 789.

[2] In Act. Hom. 1, 5, p. 18, O. T. Alb. p. 483.

Whom the water also operateth." "The[3] Lord of the Angels worketh all." "The[4] whole is of the Spirit." And of both Sacraments together, "Man[5] introduceth nothing into the things which lie before us[6] [the Eucharistic elements], but the whole is of the power of God, and He it is Who initiates you into the Mysteries." And with reference also to the Holy Eucharist, "It[7] is God who worketh all ; all is of God's doing."

But apart from this, S. Chrysostom himself uses the word of changes which are not changes of substance.

"Noah," he says[8], "endured nobly, knowing that all was easy to the Lord, and that being the Creator of nature, He maketh and *transformeth* all things as He will."

And of the barren Sarah,

"Do[9] not I make and *transform* all things?"

And further of moral or spiritual changes :—

"Here[1] [in the Gospel] He hath *transformed* ($\tau\grave{\eta}\nu$ $\iota\epsilon\rho o\nu\rho\gamma\iota a\nu$ $\mu\epsilon\tau\epsilon\sigma\kappa\epsilon\acute{\nu}a\sigma\epsilon$) the sacerdotal office to that which is far more awful and glorious, changing the very sacrifice itself." And, "The[2] gifts are diverse, the one befitting one,

---

[3] In S. Joh. Hom. 36, i. p. 302, O. T.
[4] In Ep. ad Rom. Hom. 16, p. 287, O. T.
[5] In 1 Cor. Hom. 8, n. 2, p. 102, O. T.
[6] $\tau\grave{a}$ $\pi\rho o\kappa\epsilon\acute{\iota}\mu\epsilon\nu a$.
[7] In 2 Tim. Hom. 2, p. 184, O. T.
[8] In Gen. Hom. 25, 6, p. 241.
[9] Ib. Hom. 41, 6, p. 421.
[1] Hom. 24, in 1 Cor. n. 2, p. 327, O. T.
[2] Hom. 34, in Act. init. p. 468, O. T.

the other another set of characters, and if they be *interchanged* (μετασκευάσωνται), harm results instead of good." And, " This[3] tablet [Paul's soul] was lately lying covered with soot, full of spiders' webs (for nothing can be worse than blasphemy); but when He came who *transformeth* all things, &c."

S. Clement of Alexandria says that,

" The[4] devil by his enticements *transformed* (μετεσκεύασε) women into harlots."

S. Gregory of Nyssa,

" We[5] conceive that not the friends of the Bridegroom, but the enemies, are signified, whom, being sons of darkness, and children of wrath, He, by the participation of the fruit, *transformeth* into children of the light and children of the day (εἰς υἱοὺς φωτὸς καὶ υἱοὺς ἡμέρας μετασκευάζει)."

And again,

" When[6] He saith to the sea, ' Peace, be still,' all things *were transformed* (μετασκευάσθη) into a calm and stillness."

And,

" It[7] is asked how the Lord was at the same time in Hades and in Paradise? In that God had, through the immingling with Himself, *transformed*[8] the whole Man to the Divine Nature, that which had once been immingled did not, at the time of the dispensation after the Passion, depart from either part."

S. Gregory, in his contrast between the first birth

---

[3] Hom. 13, in 1 Cor. p. 172.
[4] Pædag. iii. 2.
[5] Hom. 4, in Cant. p. 527.
[6] Hom. 5, p. 545.
[7] De Res. Christi Orat. i. T. iii. 392.
[8] ὅλον τὸν ἄνθρωπον—εἰς τὴν θείαν φύσιν μετασκευάσαντος.

and the second, speaks in both cases of a *superadded*, supernatural gift, not of change, while he uses the word signifying change.

"The[2] original element of man's natural birth has as little visible relation to his intellectual being, as the water to his spiritual existence. Whatever answer then might probably be given to us by those who were asked, 'how is it credible that man should be composed of this!' this we will answer, when asked of the re-birth which takes place through the water. For there too the first thing for any one to say, when questioned, is, that by the Divine power does that man come into being, which power if it be not present, that (basis of his being) is immoveable and inoperative. If then in this case too, the substratum maketh not the man, but the Divine Power *transmakes* the visible substance (μεταποιεῖ τὸ φαινόμενον) it would be the extremest folly, after having attested in that case so great power of God, to think that in this [the re-birth], the Deity is powerless to the fulfilment of His will. 'What,' he saith, 'have water and life in common?' 'What,' we will ask him, 'have moisture and the image of God in common?' But in that case it is nothing marvellous, if, at the will of God, that moisture passeth over to a most noble being. The like we say in this case, that there is nothing wonderful, if the presence of Divine Power *transformeth* what is born in a corruptible nature to incorruption[1]."

And again of Baptism :—

"This[3] is the word of the Mystery [Baptism] in which, through the birth from above, our *nature* is *transformed*[3]

Catechet. Orat. c. 33, iii. 95, 6.
πρὸς ἀφθαρσίαν μετασκευάζει τὸ ἐν τῇ φθαρτῇ φύσει γειόμενον.
[2] Orat. ii. c. Eunom. init. ii. 430, 1.
[3] μετασκευάζεται ἡμῶν ἡ φύσις ἀπὸ τοῦ φθαρτοῦ πρὸς τὸ ἄφθαρτον.

from corruptible to incorruption, being, from the old man, renewed according to the image of Him Who in the beginning created the Divine likeness."

And then having spoken of heresy as being "a denial of the Godhead revealed in this doctrine [of the Trinity]," he says,—

" For we have once learnt from the Lord to what we ought to look, through what the *transelementation* (μετα-στοιχείωσις) of our nature from mortal to immortal takes place ; and this is the Father and the Son and the Holy Ghost."

S. Gregory of Nazianzum :—

" Approach ‘ to the truth ; be ye at least thus late *trans-formed*‘, honour God ;" and " O ‘ Lord of life and death : Guardian and Benefactor of our souls, Who makest all things and *transformest* (μετασκευάζων) them in due season by the disposing Word, and as Thou knowest in the depth of Thy Wisdom and Providence, now too receive Cæsarius."

St. Cyril of Alexandria uses the word of the re-formation of our whole nature in the Person of Christ :—

" The ’ Only Begotten receiveth the Holy Spirit, not for Himself, for the Spirit is His and in Him and through Him, but because, having become Man, He had the whole [human] nature in Himself, that He might restore it all, *transforming*‘ it to its ancient condition.

" Incorruption ’ again is a good, proper to the Divine Nature. For the dead shall be changed, and the corruptible

‘ Orat. 22, fin. p. 767.
‘ Or. 7, p. 215.
‘ μετασκευάσας εἰς τὸ ἀρχαῖον.
’ De recta fide ad Imp. T. v. P. ii. p. 92.
‘ μετασκευάζεσθε ὀψὲ γοῦν.
’ In S. Joh. vii. 39, p. 472.

shall put on incorruption, the Only Begotten having become as we, and having *removed* (μεθιστάντος) *mortality into immortality*, and *transforming* (μετασκευάζοντος) the corruptible to incorruption first in Himself. For thus He became a way to life to ourselves also.

" When [1] the life-giving Word of God dwelt in the flesh, He *transformed* (μετεσκεύασεν) it into His Own proper good, *i. e.* life.

" Transforming [2] (μετασκευάζοντι) His own nature into its original state, and renewing it to incorruption."

Or of the re-formation in ourselves personally :—

" We [3] were to become partakers of the Divine Nature of the Word, and quitting our own life to be *transformed* (μετασκευάζεσθαι) to another, and to be *transelemented* (μεταστοιχειοῦσθαι) to a newness of God-loving conversation.

" We [4] have been *transformed* (μετεσκευάσμεθα) to the newness of Evangelic life, and have been filled with the Divine learning.

" Why [5], then, does the Prophet attempt to *transform* them (μετασκευάζειν) by good admonitions? "

S. Cyril uses it again of fragrance imparting its own qualities where it is present :

" For [6] if the fragrance of perfumes impresses its own power on dress, and in a manner *transforms* (μετασκευάζει) the things in which it is, to itself, how could not the Holy

---

[1] In S. Joh. vi. 51, l. iv. c. 2, p. 354.
[2] Cont. Nestor. L. iv. p. 107.
[3] In S. Joh. xvi. 7, p. 919.   [4] C. Julian. x. p. 346.
[5] In Is. L. i. Orat. 1, p. 12.
[6] In S. Joh. xvi. 15. L. xi. c. 2, p. 932. S. Cyril uses the same expression of honey imparting its sweetness. Ib. L. iv. p. 376.

Spirit, being by Nature from God, make those in whom it is, partakers of the Divine Nature, through Itself?"

v. The passages alleged for the use of $\mu\epsilon\theta\iota\sigma\tau\eta\mu\iota$, "transfer," speak, as was said [7], of transference into Divine power. They do, as has been already shown, imply the continued presence of the consecrated elements, not their annihilation. For translation into a " Divine *power*," or "into the energy of His Flesh," implies that, in some way, the visible substances are endued with that power and energy, not that they are physically converted into those very substances.

I will subjoin however two passages illustrating the use of the word. That from S. Chrysostom will show how the Fathers speak of change of nature, when they mean only change of operation. S. Chrysostom supposes that the words, " Who laid out the earth above the waters," meant that the whole mass of the earth rested on water. He infers, " The [8] Creator of all maketh all things contrariwise to human nature, that thence too thou mayest learn His unspeakable power, and that, when He wills, the very elements themselves, obeying the command of the Creator, display effects the very contrary to their proper efficacity." He then instances, as before [9], the fiery furnace, into which the three children were cast, and the Red Sea.

[7] Above, p. 175.   [8] In Gen. ii. Hom. xii. 2, t. iv. p. 94.
[9] See above, p. 214.

"The [10] *substance* of the fire, as it were, fulfilling obedience, and serving the command of the Lord, guarded, unscathed, and untouched, those wondrous children, and, walking as in a meadow or garden, they abode so securely in the furnace.   And that no one should think that what was seen was not the efficacity of fire, therefore the loving Lord did not fetter its efficacity, but, having allowed its power of burning to remain in it, made His own servants superior to injury from it.   But that they too who cast them in might learn, how great is the power of the God of all, the fire displayed against them its own efficacity: and that self-same (fire) surrounded those within it, but those who stood without, it burnt up and consumed.   Seest thou, how, when the Lord willeth, He *transformeth* [1] each of the elements into the contrary *substance?* for He is Creator and Lord, and dispenseth all things after His Own Will.   Would you again this same thing take place in water?   As here the fire abstained from those within it, and forgot its own *efficacity* (ἐνεργείας), but fulfilled its own office towards those without, so also we shall see the waters drowning the one, and giving way to others, that so they should pass through safely.   So well did the elements know how to respect the Lord's servants, and to hold in their own impetuosity."   And in the application to man's angry tempers, "What is more,

[10] Ib. n. 3.

[1] ἕκαστον τῶν στοιχείων πρὸς τὴν ἐναντίαν μεθίστησιν οὐσίαν.

fire having this *substance* (οὐσίαν), I mean, burning, did not display its own *efficacity* (ἐνέργειαν)!" Again, in his summary: "See² how 'He founded the earth upon the waters,' which, apart from faith, human reasoning cannot receive, and prepares all *substances* (οὐσίας) when He wills, to perform what is contrary to their own *efficacity* (ἐνεργείᾳ)."

S. Chrysostom strengthens the force of the word μεθίστημι by adding, "into the contrary substance." The very fact that he so strengthens it, implies that it did not, in itself, signify a substantial change. And yet the whole context shows that S. Chrysostom did not mean, in any technical or physical way, to speak of a substantial change. Indeed, he says the very contrary, that the *substance* of the fire retained its own *efficacity*, and held it in, and put it forth, at one and the same time, towards different persons, as God willed.

The other passage is one, in which S. Cyril of Alexandria applies this term also to our Lord's uniting with Himself our human nature.

"In² an unspeakable manner, and passing man's understanding, the Word being united to His Own Flesh, and having *translated*, as it were, *It all into Himself* (ὅλην ὥσπερ εἰς ἑαυτὸν μεταστήσας), according to that efficacious power, whereby He can quicken things which need life, He expelled corruption from our nature, and took out of the way death, which of old prevailed through sin."

¹ Ib. p. 96.   ² In Joh. vi. 55, t. iv. p. 363.

Q 2

The converse of this expression occurs in a Gallican Sacramentary, and in the writer called Eusebius Gallicanus. The prayer in the Gallican Sacramentary, is, "We[4] pray Thee, Almighty Father, that Thou wouldest infuse into these creatures placed upon Thy Altar the Spirit of sanctification, that through the transfusion of the heavenly and invisible Sacrament, this bread changed into Flesh, and the Cup *translated* into Blood, may be grace to all, and medicine to those who receive."

This word, too, is used by Cassian in an idiom, so strongly expressing change of substance, that we must have understood him to mean entire change of substance, but that it would have been heresy.

" This[5] is to say, We have known Christ after the Flesh: as long as there was what could be known after the Flesh; now we have known Him no longer, since it hath *ceased to be.* For the *nature[6] of the flesh is translated into a spiritual substance,* and that *which was once of man, is now* become *wholly of God.* And therefore we know not Christ after the flesh ; because bodily infirmity being absorbed by the Divine Majesty, nought remained in His Holy Body, whence the infirmity of the flesh could be known therein. And thereby, whatsoever before was of double substance, was made of one virtue. Since in truth it is not doubtful that Christ, who was crucified through our weakness, wholly liveth by the Power of God."

The words " the nature of the flesh is translated

---

[4] Mone Messen. p. 21.   [5] De Incarn. iii. 3, p. 700.
[6] Natura enim carnis in spiritualem est translata substantiam: et illud quod fuerat quondam hominis, factum est totum Dei.

into a spiritual substance," are said so strongly, that the Benedictine editor is obliged to add, " Not that it ceases to be true and corporeal flesh in itself, but that it is made spiritual, that is, incorruptible, and glorious, and free from all infirmity: as saith the Apostle, ' It is sown a natural body, it is raised a spiritual body.' ' For the resurrection of the Lord,' saith S. Leo[7], ' was not the end of flesh, but its *change* [commutatio] *nor was the substance consumed by the increase of its virtue* [nec virtutis augmento consumpta substantia est]. The quality passed away, the nature failed not; and the Body, Which could be crucified, became impassible : It became immortal, Which could be killed : It became incorruptible, Which could be wounded. And rightly is the Flesh of Christ said not to be known in that state, in which It had been known, because there remained in It nothing passible, nothing weak, so that It is Itself by essence, not Itself through glory. But what marvel, if he (the Apostle) professes this of the Body of Christ, which he says of all spiritual Christians : ' Therefore henceforth know we no man after the Flesh.' "

vi. On the meaning of the word " transfigure," which S. Ambrose employs, Tertullian, cited above[8], will be a competent authority. S. Ambrose's words are :

[7] Serm. i. de Res. Dom.   [8] p. 172, sqq.

"So [9] often as we receive the Sacraments, which, by the mystery of the sacred prayer, are *transfigured* into Body and Blood, we show forth the Death of the Lord."

And,

"For [10] although thou believe, that true Flesh was taken by Christ, and offer the body to the altars to be *transfigured*, but dost not rightly distinguish the nature of the Divinity and the Body, to thee too it is said, ' if thou rightly offerest, but dividest not rightly, thou hast sinned.' "

The word "transfigure [11]" was already a well-known title to Christians, when S. Ambrose thus used it. It was the term appropriated to the manifestation of our Lord's hidden glory, in His "transfiguration." In the old Latin translation, it represented two words of Holy Scripture, which relate to changes which are not changes of substance. The readers of S. Ambrose were accustomed to hear of the "transfiguration" of our Lord. It was used contrariwise of Satan being "*transfigured* into an Angel of light,"

---

[9] De Fide, iv. 10, n. 124, t. ii. 544.

[10] De Incarn. Dom. Sacr. c. iv. n. 23, p. 709.

[11] It stands for (1) $\mu\epsilon\tau\alpha\sigma\chi\eta\mu\alpha\tau i\zeta\omega$ in all five places, 1 Cor. iv. 6; 2 Cor. xi. 13—15; Phil. iii. 21 ; in S. Irenæus' old Latin Translation ; Tertullian and S. Hilary. See in Sabatier, ad loc. (2) $\mu\epsilon\tau\alpha\mu\rho\phi\delta\rho\mu\alpha\iota$, S. Matt. xvii. 2 ; S. Marc. ix. 2 ; and by Tertullian in 2 Cor. iii. 18. In Phil. iii. 21, the Vulgate uses "reformavit" for "transfigurabit," but then contrariwise, it substitutes "configuratum" for "conformatum."

false Apostles "*transfiguring* themselves into Apostles of Christ," "the ministers of Satan being *transfigured* as ministers of righteousness." In the oldest translation, it was used of that change in the resurrection, "when our Lord Jesus Christ shall *transfigure* our vile body, conformed to His glorious Body." Tertullian uses it of our being "transfigured from glory to glory."

Now, in the transfiguration of our Lord, the inward glory of the Godhead shone forth in that earthly form, which for us He vouchsafed to take. In the "transfiguration of our bodies" after the resurrection, the substances will be the same, but there shall be a glory from the Indwelling of the Spirit. In those false transfigurings of Satan and his ministers, there was an assumed glory, although not theirs. When then S. Ambrose employed the word "transfigured" of the Holy Eucharist, Christians were familiar with it, as expressing the presence of a hidden glory, although indeed manifested without, also. The force of the word expressed, in no way, a change of substance, but the contrary. Its use in Holy Scripture forbad, as Tertullian had pointed out, that it should be used of "change of substance." So far then from the use of this word being an argument that S. Ambrose believed in a change of substance, it may rather be inferred that, had he meant to express a change of substance, he would have avoided the use of a term, which described a change not substantial.

vii. viii. The two remaining expressions are, that the elements (vii.) are "changed into," (viii.) "become" the Body and Blood of Christ.

Now, of course, since the elements *were* before Consecration *mere* bread and wine, and after Consecration they are *mere* bread and wine no longer, but are, as I said, "not in any physical or carnal way, but really, spiritually, sacramentally, Divinely, mystically, ineffably, the Body and Blood of Christ," plainly they *become* what they *were* not. There is a change of some sort. The question is not, whether there be any change, but whether it be a change by which they cease to *be*. It is confessed on all hands, that the phrases "*become*," "to be changed into," are not to be taken strictly. For, strictly speaking (as was said), one thing *becomes* another by being changed into that thing, *which before was not.* The water *became* wine, not only ceasing to be water, but becoming wine which *before was not.* It is a contradiction, that a thing should *become* a pre-existing thing[1]. "I say," says Scotus[2], "that, properly speaking, transubstantiation is *not change;*" and another[3], "in transubstantiation, there is no change, properly so called, in respect of the bread."

---

[1] "Every thing, whatsoever is transfigured into another thing, ceases to be what it had been, and begins to be what it was not." Tert. adv. Prax. c. 27.

[2] Ad iv. Dist. xi. q. 1, n. 10.

[3] Gamach. ad q. 75, c. 6, both quoted by Alb. i. 22, p. 136.

Suarez[4] and Gregory de Valentia[5], speak of "a quasi-change," on this same ground, that all change implies, not only that "what is changed, so far as it is changed, does not abide," but that also, positively, "it, in some manner, becomes or passes into a new being." But it is confessed by all, that the bread does not pass into the Body of Christ. Therefore, it is not, properly, change or conversion, in any physical way. Whence, consistently, some Schoolmen[6], as Gab. Biel, Major, Occam, Angelus, Scotus, in fact, Durandus, and Albertus Magnus, scrupled not to say, that the elements were annihilated.

The Fathers were familiar with this. But they were familiar also with a more popular use of the word " change," in which that word was used to express, that the object spoken of took to itself or acquired something which it was not, without ceasing to be what it was.

Thus "the[7] Word *became* Flesh," *i. e.* clothed Himself with Flesh, without ceasing to be the Unchangeable God. On the other hand, God shall "*transfashion*[8] (μετασχηματίσει) our vile bodies, to be made like unto His Glorious Body;" but, although filled with light, and incorruptible and spiritual, they shall be the same substance still. Our Lord was *transfigured*[9]

---

[4] Disp. 50, sect. 2, § Tertio, p. 596, quoted Ib.

[5] Disp. 6, q 3, punct. 3.

[6] Quoted by Suarez, Ib. sect. 7.   [7] S. Joh. i. 14.

[8] Phil. iii. 21.   [9] S. Matt. xvii. 2.

(μετεμορφώθη), but the same Flesh suffered, which He took in the Virgin's womb. "We [1] all," says S. Paul, "beholding, as in a glass, with unveiled face, the glory of the Lord, are *transformed* into the same image (τὴν αὐτὴν εἰκόνα μεταμορφούμεθα) from glory to glory," "*transformed*," not essentially, as some mystics have inferred, into the Divine Essence, but by partaking of the glory and brightness and holiness of God through Christ.

But, this being so, why should the Fathers hesitate to use words in this less rigid sense, since they were compelled by the Faith itself to use them in that same sense in Holy Scripture? The Fathers had often to insist that "the Word *became* Flesh," "not by conversion of the Godhead into flesh, but by taking of the manhood into God." S. Athanasius urged this against the Arians;

" As [2] when S. John says, 'the Word was made Flesh,' we do not conceive the whole Word Himself to be Flesh, but to have put on Flesh and become Man; and on hearing, 'Christ hath become a curse for us,' and 'He hath made Him sin for us Who knew no sin,' we do not simply conceive this, that whole Christ has become curse and sin, but that He has taken on Him the curse which lay against us, as the Apostle has said, 'has redeemed us from the curse,' and has 'carried,' as Esaias has said, 'our sins,' and as Peter has written, 'has borne them in the Body on the wood;' so, if it is said in the Proverbs, 'He created,' we must not conceive that the whole Word is in nature a creature, but that He put on the created Body, and that God created Him for our sakes, preparing for Him the

[1] 2 Cor. iii. 18.   [2] Orat. ii. § 47, p. 347, O. T.

created Body, as it is written, 'for us,' that in Him we might be capable of being renewed and made gods."

And again :

" If [a] the Son be in the number of the Angels, then let the word *become* apply to Him as to them, and let Him not differ at all from them in nature; but be they either sons with Him, or He an angel with them; sit they one and all together on the right Hand of the Father, or be the Son standing with them all as a ministering Spirit, sent forth to minister Himself as they are.   But if, on the other hand, Paul distinguishes the Son from things generate, saying, 'to which of the Angels said He at any time, Thou art My Son?' and the One frames Heaven and earth, but *they* are made by Him; and He sitteth with the Father, but they stand by ministering; who does not see that he has not used the word '*become*' of the *substance* of the Word, but of the ministration come through Him? For as, being the Word, He became Flesh, so when become Man, He became by so much better in His ministry than the ministry which came by the Angels, as Son excels servants, and Framer things framed.   Let them cease therefore to take the word *become* of the substance of the Son, for He is not one of generated things; and let them acknowledge that it is indicative of His ministry, and the economy which came to pass. . . . . . If they carry on the contest, it will be proper, upon their rash daring, to close with them, and to oppose to them those similar expressions which are used concerning the Father Himself. . . . . . Now it is written, '*Become* my strong rock and house of defence, that Thou mayest save me.'   And again, ' The Lord *became* a defence for the oppressed,' and the like, which are found in Divine Scripture.   If, then, they apply these passages to the Son, which perhaps is nearest the truth, then let them acknowledge that the sacred

[a] Orat. i. § 62, p. 268, O. T.

writers ask Him, as not being generate, to *become* to them a strong rock and house of defence ; and for the future let them understand *become*, and He *made*, and He *created*, of His Incarnate Presence.   For then did He *become* a strong rock and house of defence, when He bore our sins in His own Body upon the tree, and said, ' Come unto Me, all ye that labour and are heavy laden, and I will give you rest.' "

And then having instanced human benefactors, he adds,

" As [4] then, should one and the other of these benefited persons say, ' Such a one became an assistance to me,' and another, 'and to me a refuge,' and ' to another, a supply,' yet in so saying he would not be speaking of the original becoming or the *substance* of their benefactors, but of the beneficence coming to themselves from them, so also when the sacred writers say concerning God, ' He *became*,' and ' *Become* Thou,' they do not denote any original *becoming*, (for God is unoriginate, and not generate,) but the salvation which is made to be unto men from Him.

" This being so understood, it is parallel also respecting the Son, that whatever, and however often, is said, such as, ' He became,' and ' become,' should ever have the same sense ; so that, as when we hear the words in question, ' become better than the Angels,' and ' He became,' we should not conceive any original *becoming* of the Word, nor in any way fancy from such terms that He is generate ; but should understand Paul's words of His ministry and economy when He became Man.   For when the Word *became* Flesh and dwelt among us, and came to minister and to grant salvation to all, then He *became* to us salvation, and *became* life, and *became* propitiation ; then His economy in our behalf *became* much better than the Angels,

[4] Ib. §§ 63, 64, pp. 270, 271, O. T.

and He *became* the Way, and *became* the Resurrection. And as the words, ' Become my strong rock ' do not denote that the *substance* of God Himself *became*, but His loving-kindness, as has been said, so also here the having *become* ' better than the Angels,' and ' He became,' and ' by so much is Jesus become a better Surety,' do not signify that the *substance* of the Word is generate (perish the thought!), but the beneficence which towards us came to be through His Incarnation."

Since then S. Athanasius had so often impressed upon others, that the word " became " did not neces-sarily imply "a change of substance," we have no ground to infer from his merely using the word " became," that he meant to speak of any *such* change. Roman Catholic controversialists argue from the mere fact of his using this word, that he meant not a sacramental, but a physical, change ; not merely that our Lord's Holy Body and Blood should be, where before They were not, but that the bread and wine should cease to be. The very context implies the contrary. For since (as I have said) S. Athanasius says this in contrast with what they were before, " *mere* bread and a *common* Cup," this implies that he believed them to be in some sense bread and cup still.

" Thou ' wilt see the Levites [Deacons] bearing bread and a Cup of wine, and placing them on the table ; and so long as the supplications and prayers have not yet taken place, *bare* (ψιλός) is the bread and the Cup ; but when the

---

' Sermo ad Baptizat. Quoted by Eutych. de Pasch. in Card. Mai Biblioth. Nov. iv. 62 ; also in Scriptt. Vett. Vat. Coll. ix. 623.

great and wonderful prayers have been completed over it; then the bread becometh the Body, the Cup, the Blood of our Lord Jesus Christ."

And again,

" Let us come to the consecration of the mysteries. This bread and this Cup, so long as the prayers and supplications have not yet taken place, are *bare* elements, but when the great prayers and holy supplications have been sent up, the Word cometh down into the bread and Cup, and His Body is produced ($\gamma \acute{\iota} \nu \epsilon \tau \alpha \iota$)."

S. Gregory of Nyssa says in the same way as S. Athanasius, "The[6] bread again is thus far *common* bread, but when the mystery consecrates it, it is called, and it *becomes*, the Body of Christ."

But S. Gregory of Nyssa, in the same way as S. Athanasius, urged against the heretic Eunomius, that our Lord *became* Man without being changed.

" The[7] Only Begotten God, He Who is in the Bosom of the Father, being Word and King and Lord, and every high Name and Thought, lacketh not *to become* any good thing, being Himself the Fulness of all good. Into what can He be changed ($\dot{o}$ $\delta \grave{\epsilon}$ $\epsilon \grave{\iota} \varsigma$ $\tau \grave{\iota}$ $\mu \epsilon \tau \alpha \beta \alpha \lambda \lambda \acute{o} \mu \epsilon \nu o \varsigma$) that He should *become* that which He was not before? As then He Who knew no sin, *becomes* sin, that He may take away the sin of the world, so again the Flesh that received the Lord, *becometh* Christ and Lord, *transmade* into that which it was not *by nature*, through the commingling (δ $\mu \grave{\eta}$ $\mathring{\eta} \nu$ $\tau \tilde{\eta}$ $\phi \acute{\upsilon} \sigma \epsilon \iota$ $\epsilon \grave{\iota} \varsigma$ $\tau o \tilde{\upsilon} \tau o$ $\mu \epsilon \tau \alpha \pi o \iota o \upsilon \mu \acute{\epsilon} \nu \eta$ $\delta \iota \grave{\alpha}$ $\tau \tilde{\eta} \varsigma$ $\dot{\alpha} \nu \alpha \kappa \rho \acute{\alpha} \sigma \epsilon \omega \varsigma$). Hence we learn, that neither would God have appeared in the flesh, unless the Word *had become* Flesh ; nor would the Human Flesh around Him have been *transmade* into Divinity

---

[6] De Bapt. Christi, iii. 370.
[7] Cont. Eunom. Or. v. T. ii. p. 595.

(οὔτ᾽ ἂν μετεποιήθη πρὸς τὸ θεῖον), had not the Visible Nature (τὸ φαινόμενον) *become* Christ and Lord."

Both these Fathers, S. Athanasius and S. Gregory, contrast the change in the Holy Eucharist, not with the substance, but with the *qualities* of the elements; not with their being bread and wine at all, but with their being any longer *mere* bread and *mere* wine, *bare* elements of this world. A change then there has been; yet the very context leads us to think that it is not a change of their own physical substance, but an accession to it. S. Ambrose's disciple [a], in answer to the question, "How can that which *is* bread be the Body of Christ?" says the same in other words, "How much more is the word of the Lord Jesus operative, that things which were should *be*, and should be changed into something else?" They are what they were, in that, physically, they are bread and wine still; they are "changed into something else," in that they are no longer common bread and wine, but "under the form of bread and wine, the Body and Blood of Christ."

S. Athanasius urged, that when "the Word became flesh," His unchangeable Godhead did not change. He became flesh, without ceasing to be God. He veiled His Godhead under His Manhood, His Godhead being unchanged. And now He veils both Godhead and Manhood under those poor outward forms, the forms of Bread and Wine. Yet those forms do not therefore cease to be. The Word *became*

---

[a] The author of the De Sacramentis. See Note R.

Flesh, yet was the Word still; so now the lower substance, the earthly part, *the bread and wine become,* in the language of S. Ambrose, S. Chrysostom, S. Athanasius, S. Gregory of Nyssa, "the Body and Blood of Christ," without therefore ceasing to be, as to the outward part, bread and wine still.

The same principle is maintained by Tertullian as to the word "changed," speaking of a physical substance, our own bodies. There will not, he contends as a matter of faith, be at the Resurrection such a change, that the substance of the human body should cease to be[9]. But then, this is decisive, that such is not of necessity the force of the word. And since the word does not, in itself, convey the idea of change of substance, such substantial or physical change cannot (it is obvious) be inferred from the mere use of the word.

Tertullian himself says, "Changed[1] in a moment into the *substance* of Angels (*demutati* in Angelicam substantiam), through that clothing-upon of incorruption we shall be removed into the heavenly kingdom."

I have already[2] mentioned, under the word "re-order," instances which show how S. Chrysostom speaks of God's "re-ordering nature," without thereby meaning that He in any way changed its physical structure. In exactly the same way, and of one of the same great miracles, he says, "nature

---

[9] See above, pp. 172—174.   [1] Adv. Marcion, iii. ult.

[2] pp. 212—214.

being changed," when he meant only that God partially suspended its operation. He is speaking of "the three children."

" The[2] fire became a wall unto them, and the flame a robe; and the furnace was a fountain; and whereas it received them bound, it rendered them free. It received bodies that were mortal, but abstained from them as if they had been immortal! It knew their nature, yet it reverenced their piety! The tyrant bound their feet, and their feet bound the operation of the fire! O marvellous thing! The flame loosed those who were bound, and was itself afterwards bound by those who had been in bonds; for the piety of the youths *changed the nature of things* (μετέβαλε τῶν πραγμάτων τὴν φύσιν). Yea, rather did not change nature, but what was far more marvellous, stayed the operation, while the nature remained. For it did not quench the fire, but though burning made it powerless. . . . . The force of the fire was both quenched, and not quenched: for whilst it came in contact with the bodies of these saints, it was quenched; but when it was necessary to burst their bonds, it was not quenched; wherefore it broke their bonds, but touched not their ancles. Do you see how near? Yet the fire was not deceived, and dared not penetrate within the bonds. The tyrant bound, and the flame set loose; that thou mightest learn at once the fierceness of the barbarian, and the submissiveness of the element. For what reason did he bind, when he was about to cast into the fire? In order that the miracle might be the greater; that the sign might be more unaccountable; that thou mayest not suppose that what was seen was but an illusion of the sight. For if that fire had been no fire, it would not have consumed the bands; and what is much more, it would not have seized

---

[2] Ad Pop. Ant. Hom. iv. § 3, T. ii. p. 53. On the Statues pp. 83, 84, O. T.

upon the soldiers who were placed without the furnace; but as the case was, it showed its power upon those without; but towards those within, its submissiveness."

And again;

"The ⁴ word of Elisha *changed* the waters, and made them bear iron on their surface."

Again, in one passage quoted to prove Transubstantiation ⁵, S. Cyril assigns as the ground of the Eucharistic change, "*Whatsoever* ⁶ the Holy Ghost has touched, is *sanctified and changed.*" Now no Roman Catholic would, any more than ourselves, believe this to be true in any other sense than of a sacramental change. The word " whatsoever" necessarily includes other things besides the immediate subject. S. Cyril makes here a general statement, of which the change in the Holy Eucharist is one particular instance. He argues, that God the Holy Ghost changes the bread and wine, because He sanctifies and changes *all* which He touches. It is a statement of the widest kind. It is true of the human soul, in one way, and S. Cyril himself includes under it, His sanctifying the water of Baptism, and the chrism which was used in Confirmation. But what he says of all must be true of each. It *is* true, if we believe him to speak of a *sacramental change;* it would not be true on any hypothesis if we supposed

---

⁴ Ib. Hom. 8, § 2, ii. 93. On the Statues, p. 150, O. T.
⁵ Dublin Review, xvi. p. 88.
⁶ Lect. 23, § 5, p. 275, O. T.

him to mean a change in which the substance ceases
to be. For no one supposes it to be true of all;
that God the Holy Ghost *in this way* changes whatsoever He has touched. Therefore S. Cyril cannot
mean to affirm it of all. But since he does not affirm
it of all, he does affirm it of none. For the same
general assertion cannot affirm different things of
the several objects included under it. There may
be different *degrees* comprehended under it. But it
cannot by the mere force of the term express any one
of these more than another. Holy Scripture says "we
shall all be changed;" " all have come short of the
glory of God;" "of His fulness have we all received;"
" to every one that hath shall be given ;" " Godliness
is profitable to all things;" "all things work together for good to those who love God." All these and
the like sayings do not *exclude* a certain difference as
to the individuals who make up each whole. But
they do not *express*, as to any, what they do not
express as to all. Men, in a state of nature, fall short
in different degrees of the Glory of God. We shall
be changed into different degrees of glory, degrees so
different, that there shall be evident unlikeness as
well as likeness. " Star differeth from star in glory."
·We *all* receive of the fulness of our Lord, but
unequally. "*All* things work together for good
to those who love God," but some in ways the
most opposite ; and "godliness is profitable to all
things," yet, in very different ways, to temporal and
eternal peace. As, then, in these sayings, that only

is affirmed of any, which is affirmed of all, so when S. Cyril says, " *Whatsoever* the Holy Ghost hath touched is sanctified and changed," he affirms, *in these words*, only that degree of change which is common to any other matter used in Sacraments. He must speak here of a sacramental, not of a physical change. For his words would not be true, in any other sense. So far then from showing that S. Cyril by this word "change" necessarily means a physical change, the passage shows that the word need only mean a sacramental change. The word here *can* only signify a sacramental change. Something more then beyond the mere use of the word, is needed elsewhere also, to show that it means any thing more. Not only is the word used of every sort of change, but even, in direct reference to the Holy Eucharist itself, it is used so that it cannot mean more than a sacramental change.

There can then be no doubt whatever, that the word " change " does not describe or limit the nature of the change, whether it be physical, moral, spiritual, or sacramental. I will therefore under this head limit myself to the mention of some instances, in which the Fathers speak even of change of nature or substance, when they intend, not the abolition of that which is, but the addition of that which is not.

S. Chrysologus and the author known as Eusebius Gallicanus, use " converted " in the sense in which Holy Scripture employs " became," of our " Lord becoming Man."

If the phrase were pressed, as Roman controversialists press it as to the Holy Eucharist, it
would be the very term of the heresy condemned in
the Athanasian Creed, "not by *conversion* of the
Godhead into Flesh."

"Be' Thou *turned*, O Lord. Whence? Whither?
From God *into man* ; from the Lord into a servant; from
the Judge into a Father (convertere—de Deo in hominem)."

The writer called Eusebius[8] used the word "commutatus" even in a dogmatic statement opposed to
heretics.

"But[9] for us, let us, by a solid confession, hold Christ
our Lord to be God and Man ; that He, the Son of God,
was in the last times, begotten of an unwedded Mother,
faith being her husband ; was humbled of His Own Will,
not lowered by necessity ; was, through the Holy Ghost
coming down upon the Virgin, Man marvellously filled by
God, and God mercifully *changed into* Man (Deum in hominem mirabiliter commutatum)."

Again he says,

"When[1] Moses contended with the magicians, first the

---

[7] Serm. 45 in Ps. vi. B. P. viii. 881.

[8] The Homilies which bear the title of Eusebius have been
variously attributed to Faustus, Hilary of Arles, Eucherius,
Cæsarius. Richter, on the Decretals, says, that the sermon on the
Holy Eucharist, quoted de Cons. D. ii. c. 35, has also been given
to Rabanus Maurus or Bede. Cave says that they have been
given to Bruno Astensis, A. D. 1087, and others more recent, and
that " the difference of style evidently shows that they are from
different authors."

[9] De Deo trino et uno, B. P. vi. 668.

[1] De Pasch. Hom. iii. Ib. p. 635.

rod was turned into a serpent, then the serpent back again into a rod.   What, is the rod changed into a serpent!   It is, *God changed into Man*[2].   What, the serpent turned into a rod! that is, man received into God."

And of the light which shall be the robe of immortality of our bodies;

" Where[3] for the robe of holy bodies eternal light shall shine forth, there the raiment, never for endless ages to be put off, shall be *changed into the body*[4]; there that angelic robe shall no longer be clothing, no longer be a habit, but nature."

Again S. Hilary,

" That[5] the wings are referred to the *change* (demutationem) of earthly bodies into a spiritual and eternal nature, there is prophetic authority (quoting Prov. xxiii. 5)."

" When[6] then we are renewed by the laver of Baptism through the virtue of the Word, we are separated from the sins and authors of our being,—we must needs hate the wont of our inborn and old habits of action.   And because the body itself, deadened by faith, *passeth into the nature of the soul* (in naturam animæ evadat), which cometh from the inbreathing of God, because communion is established between them from the Word; therefore now it beginneth to will to be made one and the same with the soul, *i. e.* as it is spiritual, &c."

And even more strongly :—

[2] Deus in hominem commutatus.

[3] Ad Monach. Hom. x.   Ib. 665 fin.

[4] Vestitus convertetur in corpus.   This is no mere metaphor. The idea is, that the glory which in Heaven shall be for raiment, shall enter into and become, as it were, part of the glorified body.

[5] In Ps. cxxxviii. § 24, p. 515.

[6] Id. in S. Matt. c. 10, § 24.

" But ' as, if they flew upward, they would be one, that is,
the body would *have passed*' *into the nature of the soul*, and
that heaviness of earthly matter would be *abolished*' *into*
the progress and *substance of the soul*, and the body would
rather become spiritual ; so in them who are sold for the
price of their sins, the subtlety of the soul gravitates into
the nature of the body, and contracts earthy matter from
the filth of vices, and becomes one of those which is delivered
into earth."

S. Chrysologus again of our human nature;

" Let ' Him come, let Him come, to repair the soul,
renew the mind, *change nature itself into a heavenly substance*
(ipsam naturam in cœlestem commutet substantiam)."

S. Ambrose, in the same way as S. Chrysostom,
speaks of nature being changed by miracles, when he
does not mean any change of substance;

" Let ' them learn that nature can be changed, when the
rock flowed forth waters, and iron swam on the water,
which Elisha obtained by praying, not by commanding."

Again of a moral change;

" She ' [Theola] changed even the nature of the wild
beasts, through veneration of virginity. The beast forgetting its own nature, had put on the nature which men
had lost. Thou mightest see, by a sort of transfusion of
nature, men, clad with savageness, enjoining savageness on
the beast, the beast kissing the feet of the virgin, teaching
what men should do."

' Ib. n. 19, p. 658.
' In naturam animæ transisset.
' In profectum et substantiam animæ *aboleretur.*
' S. Chrysol. Serm. 45, in Ps. vi. B. P. vii. 881.
' Hexaem. iii. 2, § 9.
' De Virgin. ii. 3. 19, 20.

I have quoted already [4] the language of Cassian, in which he speaks of the nature of our Lord's Human Flesh being changed.

I will subjoin a few instances, from Albertinus, in which Greek Fathers use their word μεταβάλλω of a change of nature, which is not a change of the *substance* of nature.

" It [5] is mystical, connected with the *change* of the saints into Angels (τῆς περὶ τῶν ἁγίων εἰς ἀγγέλους μεταβολῆς)."

" Wherefore [6] our souls must be altered and *changed* (ἀλλαγῆναι καὶ μεταβληθῆναι) from the present condition into another condition and divine *Nature* (φύσιν), and become new for old, *i. e.* good and kind and faithful, instead of bitter and infidel, and so, having been made meet, to be removed to the heavenly kingdom. For the blessed Paul so speaks of his *change* (μεταβολῆς), and the apprehension whereby he was apprehended of the Lord."

" For [7] all are *changed* (εἰς θεϊκὴν γὰρ φύσιν ἅπαντες μεταβάλλονται) into the Divine Nature, having become good and gods and children of God."

" He [8] [S. Paul] most accurately of all both observed the character of Christ, and by his acts showed what manner of person one named from Him ought to be. Imitating Him so visibly, as to exhibit his Master figured in himself through most exact copying, the form of his own soul being *changed* (μεταβληθέντος) to its Prototype, so that it seemed no longer to be Paul who lived and spake, but that Christ Himself lived in him."

And now, to recapitulate, in part, the result of

---

[4] Above, p. 228.

[5] Origen in Joh. T. 10, § 18, p. 191.

[6] S. Macarius, Hom. 44, p. 218.

[7] Id. Hom. 34, p. 190.

[8] S. Greg. Nyss. de perf. Christian. forma, T. iii. p. 276.

this discussion, two questions are generally assumed on the Roman side, in this controversy. (1) That five of the above words, those rendered "transelement," "transmake," "transfashion," "remodel," "transfigure," do, by the very force of the terms, express a physical change. Else, although they make a show, they furnish no induction whatever. Of the two words which the Dublin Reviewer selects as the strongest, "*transelement*" and "*transmake,*" the one, "*transmake*" is, I believe, during the first seven centuries, used by *one* Father only, S. Gregory of Nyssa, as his own, in *one* passage, and by another, in translating a Latin Father. The second, "*transelement,*" is used *once* only, in that *same* passage of the same Father, S. Gregory of Nyssa. Two other of these words, "*transfashion*" and "*re-order,*" occur, each *once* only, in that Father who writes so copiously and so fervently on the Holy Eucharist, S. Chrysostom. The fifth, "*transfigure,*" occurs twice in the Latin S. Ambrose. I have repeated the proof, already given by Albertinus, that these words do not in themselves express "change of nature." They are (as has been pointed out) used familiarly by the very same Fathers, to express every sort of change, and, in some cases, where to believe a change, would involve heresy. The Dublin Reviewer dwells much on "the copiousness and variety of the language used by the Greek Fathers." S. Cyril of Alexandria and S. Chrysostom write very fully upon the Holy Eucharist. Since they were both such wonderful masters of language, it is even remarkable that these strong words occur so seldom. In the period before the Fourth General Council, the middle of the fifth century, some eighty authorities may be adduced, who mention or dwell upon (and some very fully) the doctrine of the Real Presence. I do not believe that during that period more than three Fathers, S. Gregory of Nyssa, S. Chrysostom, and S. Ambrose, use, as their own, the five words which the Dublin Reviewer selects as expressing best the Roman doctrine, and these, in all, only in six passages. Two of these words are favourites of S. Cyril of Alexandria, and S. Gregory of Nyssa, but of the sacramental change they are used only in one passage by the latter. Let any one contrast the frequency with which Roman Catholics now use the word transubstantiation.

(2) The other point commonly assumed in Roman controversy, is that any word, which in any way expresses "change," must mean that special change whereby the substance of the bread ceases to be. This is, of course, to assume the whole point at issue. Since the words *can* express either a substantial or a sacramental change, the mere occurrence of the words will not determine which change is intended. Since the consecrated elements *are*, as we believe, by virtue of the consecration, sacramentally, the Body and Blood of Christ, and were not so before, then they *become* such by consecration; and since they *become* such, they are *changed* sacramentally

from what they were before, and God only can so *change* or *make* them. The simple words belong to us as much as to the Roman writers; and when the Fathers do express any change at all, these are the words by which they mostly express it.

But further, it will appear hereafter[2], that the Fathers do, in the most varied way, express the doctrine of the Real Objective Presence of the Body and Blood of Christ. They assume every where that the Body and Blood of Christ are actually present there, and that, being present, we receive them. Comparatively, they speak but seldom of the elements *becoming* the Body and Blood of Christ, and when they do so speak, they speak in the simplest way.

It is remarkable how, in almost all the Liturgies, the simplest words are used. The Roman and Ambrosian[1] use the word " become." The Old Gallican Liturgy, in its earliest form, was probably the same as the Ambrosian[2]. The word " trans-

---

[1] Note S.

[2] In the Ambrosian Canon there is the expression " transformed the · bread and wine, which Melchizedek, as a priest, had offered, prefiguring the future mystery, *into the Sacrament* of His Body and Blood" (Muratori de Reb. Lit. p. 131); but this relates to the institution of the *Sacrament*, in lieu of the *type* of Melchizedek, not to this effect of consecration. It speaks of the *change into the Sacrament* only; and so rather illustrates how the word " transformation " was used of simple change. The consecration is expressed afterwards in the Ambrosian Canon by the simple word " fiat "

[2] The Canon, as preserved for Maundy Thursday (Mabillon Miss. Gall. p. 349), is taken from the Ambrosian.

formation" occurs only in insulated festival services [3].

The earlier Greek Liturgies, ascribed to S. James
and S. Mark, used in Palestine and Alexandria,
employ only the simpler words, " sanctify," " consecrate," or " perfect," " appoint," and " make [4]."

[3] In the feast of the Circumcision (Mabillon, p. 202, and the Cathedra S. Petri, p. 228) the word fiat is retained. " Vouch-safe to receive bless and sanctify this sacrifice, that it may become to us a lawful Eucharist in Thy Name and of Thy Son and of the Holy Spirit, into the transformation of the Body and Blood of our Lord God Jesus Christ Thine Only Begotten." In the service of S. Leodegar (which could not have been earlier than the close of the 7th century, since he was martyred A.D. 678) there occurs, " That Thy blessing may descend upon this bread and cup in the transformation of thy Holy Spirit." (Ib. 285.)   In one on the Assumption [*i e.* the decease] of the B. V., " The bread being translated into the Body, the cup into the Blood." (Ib. 214.)   In the 6th of some services for the Lord's Day, " With devoted mind we pray Thee, O Eternal Majesty, that Thy Virtue operating, the bread changed into Flesh, the wine turned into blood, we may receive that in the Cup, which flowed from Thee on the Cross from the Side" (p. 300).

[4] The Liturgy of S. James has " hallow and make," ἁγιάσῃ καὶ ποιήσῃ (Ass. v. 40), in the Syriac only a word corresponding to ἀναδείξῃ, " appoint or consecrate " (Ib. p. 139).   That attributed to S. Cyril has only a word corresponding to τελειώσῃ, "perfect" (Ib. p. 164).   S. Cyril himself, in his account, only uses the word " make " (Lect. Myst. v. 7).   The Liturgy of S. Mark has the words ἁγιάσῃ καὶ τελειώσῃ καὶ ποιήσῃ (Ib. vii. 34, 35). That of S. Basil, ἁγιάσαι καὶ ἀναδείξαι ἅγια ἁγίων, " That Thy Holy Spirit may come upon us Thy servants, and upon these Thy gifts lying here, and sanctify and consecrate [or appoint] them holy of holies," καὶ ποιήσῃ (Ib. 59, 60).   The Coptic of S. Basil has the same (Ib. P. ii. p. 57), as also the Æthiopic from Dioscorus (Ib. vii. 203).   The Syriac, translated by Masius,

Renaudot, in his second volume, exhibits thirty-nine Liturgies which have the corresponding Syriac words. On the other hand, words signifying "change," only occur in certain Jacobite Liturgies [5], and those which are translated from the Liturgy of S. Chrysostom. S. Chrysostom appears to have retained the ancient formula, and to have added at the end, "changing by Thy Spirit." The prayer in his Liturgy is,

omits "consecrate" (Ib. 220). A form used in the Monastery of S. Macarius uses no other word (Ib. 183). A Coptic Liturgy, which is inscribed S. Basil's, has no invocation of the Holy Spirit, but ends a prayer to our Lord, abridged from one in S. Mark's, with a form of its own; "Bless them, sanctify them, purify them, change them, that this Bread may become Thy Holy Body, and this mixture which is in this Cup may become Thy Precious Blood" (Ib. P. ii. p. 13). The beginning of the prayer thus ended, has some resemblance to a Prayer *to* the Son, in the Liturgy of S. Mark, which ends, "Through the loving-kindness of *Thine* Only Begotten Son" (Renaud. i. 143. Ass. vii. 17), so here too there must have been confusion. The words, "change them," belong to the later Coptic compiler.

[5] See above, p. 194. There are also (1) a Liturgy which the Jacobites attributed to S. Maruthas, but which is clearly Jacobite. (Ren. ii. 270. Mr. Neale supposes it to be later than A. D. 1100. Holy East. Church, i. 330.) (2) One by Dionysius Barsalibi, A. D. 1154-71. (Neale. Ib.) (3) One by Dioscorus, Bishop of Cardou, A. D. 1285. Of these, the Liturgies of Pseudo-Maruthas and Barsalibi agree in praying for the descent of the Holy Ghost, "who perfects ('essentially,' *Mar.*) all the mysteries of the Church" ('by His coming,' *Bars.*). Ren. ii. 264, 450. This allusion to the operation of the Holy Ghost in "perfecting *all* the mysteries of the Church," is rather opposed to the belief of transubstantiation, since the other mysteries are "perfected" without any change of substance. But all these liturgies are very late.

"Send[6] down Thy Holy Spirit upon us, and upon these gifts lying here, and make this bread the Precious Body of Thy Christ, and that which is in this cup the Blood of Thy Christ, *changing* ($\mu\epsilon\tau\alpha\beta\alpha\lambda\grave{\omega}\nu$) by Thy Holy Spirit."

The word "change" does not, in itself, describe the nature of the change. A sacramental change satisfies the meaning of the term. Still the addition to the older forms appears to have been his. The Liturgy of his fellow-pupil, Theodorus of Mopsuestia, has only the words, "May[7] the grace of the Holy Spirit bless, sanctify, and seal this bread and this cup, and may the bread become, &c." That of Nestorius inserts the words, "Thou changing," exactly where S. Chrysostom inserted them, and was probably brought by Nestorius from Constantinople[8], where he had been Patriarch.

The modern Armenian also follows S. Chrysostom with one remarkable addition[9]. The Priest "blesses" each element separately; and prays that God would "send down His Holy Consubstantial Spirit, and bless the bread and make it the Body of our Lord and Saviour Jesus Christ;" then, "that He would bless that which is in the Cup, so as to make it truly the Blood of our Lord and Saviour Jesus Christ." Then, he repeats the prayer for both together, "Bless this bread and wine, so as to make them truly the Body and Blood of our Lord and Saviour Jesus Christ," and on this second blessing

[6] In Renaudot, ii. 621.   [7] Ib. 633.   [8] Ib. 510.

[9] Liturgia Armena, trasportata in Italiano per cura del P. Gabr. Avedichian.

he adds, "changing them by the Holy Ghost[1]." This repetition shows that the Armenians at least, did not ascribe to the Invocation of the Holy Ghost, *the* Consecration of the sacred elements. Else, having prayed, that God would make them the Body and Blood of Christ, they would not have repeated the prayer.

The Æthiopic has a form, as far as I have observed, peculiar to itself, yet of the earlier and simpler character.

"Now[2] then, O Lord, commemorating Thy Death and Resurrection, we offer to Thee this Bread and this Cup, rendering thanks unto Thee, that thereby Thou hast made us worthy to stand before Thee, and to exercise the priestly office before Thee. We pray and entreat Thee, O Lord, that Thou wouldest send the Holy Spirit and virtue upon this bread and upon this cup, and that It may make both, the Body and Blood of our Lord and Saviour Jesus Christ for ever and ever. Grant that to all who receive them, they may be to sanctification and fulness of the Holy Spirit, and to strengthening of faith, that they may glorify Thee through our Lord and Saviour Jesus Christ, with the Holy Ghost for ever and ever."

This prayer for the Descent of the Holy Ghost stands in the usual place, after the Consecration, and connected with it. The Liturgy has been largely corrupted by the Copts, and prayers from the Liturgy to which they gave the name of S. Basil's, have almost displaced the original prayers. Among these they inserted at the very beginning of the

---

[1] Neale on Lit. pp. 570-571.
[2] Ren. i. 517.

Liturgy the prayer to our Lord that He would Himself change the elements. The Æthiopians, probably, hold their original prayer of consecration sacred; and so, while other parts of the service underwent alterations, this part remained unchanged. This older prayer, in which the word "change" does not occur, agrees herein with another fragment of an Æthiopic Liturgy[3] which has been preserved, and which contains a form of consecration and invocation.

Other prayers rather imply the belief that the substances remain; as one ascribed to S. Gregory,

" As[4] Thou hast vouchsafed to fill with all holiness these Thy most holy and precious gifts through the illapse of Thy Holy Spirit, so vouchsafe also to sanctify the souls, bodies, spirits of thy sinful servants."

This prayer implies an unseen Presence in the elements, rather than a change or cessation of the material substance of the elements themselves.

The Liturgies, then, bring us to the same result as other works of the Fathers. There is nothing in them which should lead us to think of more than a sacramental change. They use the simplest words, " become," " make." Their earliest form is the simplest. No word, in any way designating change, occurs until S. Chrysostom introduced one. The terms upon which the Dublin Reviewer relics, are not

---

[3] Published from a MS. of Pococke by Wansleb at the end of Ludolf Lexic. Æthiop. ed. 1.

[4] Ass. vii. 120 and 152.

introduced at all, except in one late heretical Liturgy.

The Fathers, however, not only say that the bread *becomes* the Body of Christ, but that it *is* the Body of Christ. Yet Roman controversialists allege that this is inconsistent with conversion, as they believe it, or transubstantiation. Thus Vazquez;

"If⁵ the pronoun 'this' in those words, 'This is My Body,' pointed to the bread, we too confess that it would follow, that there could be no conversion, by virtue of those words, because the bread, of which they are enunciated, ought to remain."

Suarez, in like way,

"The⁶ first opinion is, that the pronoun 'this' means the bread, which is variously explained, in so far as the bread still remains in its own substance; yet so that the whole proposition should be understood, not as actually, but transitively; 'This is My Body,' *i. e.* passes into the body, or from this becomes the body. But this opinion is in no way to be endured by Catholics. For it destroys the proper meaning of the word 'is,' which, if it be once allowed, there is no force in these words to prove the Real Presence of the Body of Christ. Moreover, it cannot then be proved, that the substance of bread does not remain here; for as these explain, 'This bread passes into the Body,' so a heretic may explain 'this bread retains' or 'represents the Body.'"

And Fisher,

"If⁷ the substance of bread remains, although then Christ ought to have spoken otherwise, yet by the addition

⁵ Disp. 170, c. 9, n. 91. Alb. p. 107.
⁶ Disp. 58, Art. i. sect. vii. p. 712.
⁷ Cont. Luth. Bab. Capt. c. 4, n. 12. Ib.

of one little word, He could have removed this discord. For if He had said, ' This bread is My Body,' ' This wine is My Blood,' all controversy would have been wholly taken away."

The proposition, " This bread is My Body," could have no other meaning than that it was in some way, both. "This, which is in its natural substance, bread, is sacramentally My Body, through the Presence of My Body under its form."

Yet the Fathers say this, or what is equivalent to it. To give instances [1] which have been brought together [2]. S. Irenæus, "The Lord affirmed that that bread which is from the creature is His Body." Tatian, " Taking bread, then the cup of wine, attesting that they are His own Body and Blood, He commanded them to eat and drink." Tertullian, "Calling bread His own Body." The author of the Carm. adv. Marcion, "Taking bread, and the juice of the vine, He says, ' My Body and My Blood which is shed, this is.' " Origen, "The bread which God owns to be His own Body." S. Cyprian, " The Lord calls bread His own Body." S. Cyril of Jerusalem, " The Lord says of bread, ' This is My Body.' " S. Chrysostom, " What is bread ? The Body of Christ." S. Augustine, " Bread is the Body of Christ." S. Jerome, " Let us hear that the bread which the Lord brake and gave to the disciples, is the Body of the Saviour." Theodoret, " In the delivery of the mysteries, the Lord called bread His own

---

[1] See the passages at full below, in Note S.
[2] Alb. p. 47, 8.

Body, and wine His Blood." The author of the De Promiss. "Establishing that the sanctified bread, on His table, was His own consecrated Body." Facundus [3], "The Lord Himself called the blessed bread and cup which He delivered to His disciples, His own Body and Blood." The Malabar Christians in their Liturgy, "He [4] gave to His disciples, and said, Take and eat, all ye, of this bread, This is My Body.'" And the Æthiopic in the very words of consecration, "This bread is My Body."

But whereas the words which the Fathers use of the sacramental change, are undefined, not, in any way, leading to a belief in any change of substance, there is, on the other hand, positive evidence that they believed that the natural substances remained. Several of them say so in express terms. They plainly so understand our Lord Himself, when He speaks of the consecrated element as "the fruit of the vine" (Notes F. and M.); they say most explicitly that the natural substance remains, when arguing accurately against heretics (Note G.); they say that the outward elements are not *bare* elements, *common*, *mere* bread and wine, thereby implying that they are, in some sense, such (Note H.); they speak of the outward elements, as *figures* or *types*, *i. e.* of that which is the inward substance (Note I.); they speak of the Body and Blood of Christ as given *in* or *under* bread and wine (Notes K. and L.); and

[3] L. ix. c. ult.   [4] B. P. xxvii. 675.

of Isaiah's coal as a type of it, in that it had both an outward and inward substance. (Note K.) The earliest Fathers, who speak of the bread and wine *becoming* the Body and Blood of Christ, speak also of the natural power of nourishing, as still existing in the consecrated elements, which power of nourishing they believed to lie in the natural substance or matter. (Note N.)   I have said already that I mention this, not as a question of philosophy, but as an index of their belief. They supposed that (in the language of Aristotle) " nourishment ' appertaineth to matter." Since then they believed that the Holy Eucharist nourished, they must have supposed that the matter remained.   With the same physical system as those in the middle ages, if they had also had the same belief as to the cessation of the substance of bread and wine, we must have had the same or corresponding explanations, whereby to reconcile their physical theory and their religious belief. The question is not as to the philosophical opinion itself, but how that opinion would affect the expression of their belief. If a person holds a philosophical opinion, apparently conflicting with his belief, he will not, if he is a religious man, state it broadly, without any explanation. Faith is sensitive, and will not allow a person even to seem to contradict what he believes.

Thus, had S. Augustine believed that the natural qualities or accidents remain in the Holy Eucharist

---

' De gen. et corrupt. ii. 8, quoted by Albert. p. 121.

without the substance, he, possessed of so accurate a
mind, could not have used the language which he
does so often and so broadly.   He could not have
said,

"If[*] the subject be changed, *in no way can* that which
exists inseparably in it, not be changed."
"The[*] subject *cannot* be changed, unless that which exists
in the subject be changed also."

He speaks of it as a fundamental principle,

"If[*] the subject is changed, *all* which is in the subject
is of necessity changed.
"There *can* be some change of those things which exist
in the subject, while yet the subject itself, according to that
which it is, and is called, is not changed.   But if the change
of those things which exist in the subject be so great,
that that which was said to be the substance, can no longer
be spoken of as existing (as when, through the heat of fire,
wax is dissolved into the air, and undergoes such changes
that the subject which *was* wax, may rightly be understood
to be changed, and *is* wax no longer) then *in no way*, or on
any understanding, *could aught of those things*, which was
therefore in that subject, because it was that subject, be
thought to remain."
"That[*] which does not exist of itself, if it be deprived of
that whereby it is, forthwith will not *be*."
"*In no way*[*] can form or colour, or that very tempera-
ment of the body, which is a sort of commixture of those
four substances of which that body subsists, detach itself
from that, in which subject it exists inseparably."

[*] Opp. i. p. 388.   De Imm. Anim. c. 2, quoted by Albert.
p. 742.

[*] Ib. c. 5, p. 390.   [*] Ib.
[*] Ib. c. 8, p. 393.   [*] Ib. c. 10, p. 391.

"Dost[2] thou not grant, that that which exists inseparably in the subject, if the subject does not abide, it also cannot abide? Who would grant, or to whom would it seem to be possible, that that which exists in the subject, should remain, when the subject itself perishes? For it is monstrous and most alien from truth, that what would not *be*, unless it were in that other, could *be*, even if that other were not."

"If[3] whatever is in a subject abideth ever, the subject itself must abide ever."

"But[4] perchance it may be, that, the subject perishing, that which is in the subject may remain. What shall ever persuade me of this?"

And in answer to Julian, who had misapplied the principle:

"Nor[5] doth that logic tell thee falsely, but thou understandest it not. For it is true which thou learnedst there. Those things which exist in a subject, such as qualities, *cannot be* without the subject in which they are, as colour or form are in the subject."

And S. Irenæus;

"The[6] one *cannot* be conceived without the other, as neither can water without moisture, nor fire without heat, nor a stone without hardness, for these are universally united, and one *cannot* be separated from the other, but ever co-exists with it."

S. Methodius;

"The[7] quality cannot be separated from the matter, so as to exist."

[2] Solil. ii. 12, 13.　　　[3] c. 13, p. 379.
[4] c. 19, p. 393.　　　[5] cont. Julian, v. 14, T. 10, p. 653.
[6] 2, 12, 2.
[7] De Resurr. Opp. p. 331, from Photius cod. 234, p. 915, ed. Hoesch.

Still earlier (about A. D. 196 [8],) Maximus;

" It [9] may not be said of any substance whatever, that it is without qualities."

S. Cyril of Alexandria illustrates even the relation of the Father and the Son, through the inseparableness of the subject and its qualities. Sweetness is inherent in honey; warmth in fire; " divisible [1] in idea," he says, " but one in nature, and one proceeding from the other by an indivisible and continuous procession, so as to seem to be separated from that in which it is; yet although they may be so conceived, yet they both appear in the other, and are in essence the same."

Albertinus further quotes Titus Bostrensis, " Qualities [2] are inseparable." S. Athanasius, " Every [3] quality is in a substance." Isidore Hispalensis, "Quantity [4], *quality* and *situation, cannot* be without substance." And even Damascene, " Accident [5] is that which *cannot* exist in itself, but is contemplated in the essence."

It is no answer to this, that Bellarmine says [6], " S.

[8] Cave sub tit.

[9] Quoted by Eus. Præp. Ev. vii. 22.

[1] In Joann. L. i. c. 3, fin. pp. 28, 9 (quoted by Alb. p. 746), comp. c. 5, p. 48. Alb. quotes many other passages from S. Cyril.

[2] C. Manich. L. i. in Alb. p. 126.

[3] Orat. iv. c. Arian. § 2, p. 515, O. T.

[4] Orig. ii. 26.   [5] Dialect. c. 4.

[6] De Euch. iii. 24, ad 5, 6.

Augustine speaks of that which can be in the way of nature." This answer might suffice, if any one limited the power of God ; but it is not an answer to the argument, that S. Augustine's cautious and accurate mind would not have laid down so broadly, what, taken literally, would contradict his belief. No Roman Catholic now would think of saying, "Qualities *cannot* exist without the subject in which they are." Had S. Augustine then explained the Real Presence in the same way as modern Roman Catholics, neither could he. He could not have used language, which would have contradicted his faith, as embodied in his daily devotions.

NOTE R.

On p. 45.

The illustrations employed by the Fathers in reference to the consecration of the Holy Eucharist imply supernatural operation, not a physical change of the elements.

THE writer in the Dublin Review, already quoted, here too states his case with rhetorical skill. He marshals what are in fact three or four Fathers, writing under circumstances different from ours, so that they should seem a large array.

" Before[1] we proceed to the critical examination of their [the Fathers'] language, we would beg our readers to com-

----

[1] p. 84.

pare the very strongest phraseology employed by the modern Anglicans—by Dr. Pusey, in his Sermon, or by any of the older divines quoted by him in the Appendix,—with any single discourse of the early Fathers,—of Justin, or Gregory, or Cyril, or Chrysostom, or Ambrose. We defy any man, after a calm and dispassionate comparison of both, to persuade himself into the belief that they are speaking of the *same sort* of presence, or that they are considering it under the same light. We find in the former none of those appeals to the omnipotence of God (as an evidence of His power to effect what faith teaches regarding the Eucharist) with which the latter abound [2]; none of those cautionary admonitions against the evidence of the senses [3]; none of those illustrations from supernatural, and even from natural changes, which they employ to facilitate the belief of what they preach regarding the Sacramental change; no reference to the conversion of water into wine at Cana, as in S. Cyril's lectures [4]; no allusion to the transformation of Moses' rod into a serpent, and its restoration to its natural condition [5]; to the change of the water of the Nile into blood, and back again into water [6]; or to the sweetening of the waters of Marah, as in S. Ambrose [7]; no appeal to the natural conversion of the food we eat into the substance of our body, as in S. Justin [8] and S. Gregory of Nyssa [9]; to the liquefaction of wax before the fire [10], or the change of the rain and dew of Heaven into the substance of the plants which they fertilize and support, as in S. John Chrysostom."

[2] "As S. Ambros. ii. 337, Ben. ed. See also Damascene, de Fide Orth. lib. iv. p. 317, and Chrys. ii. 394."

[3] "S. Chrys. tom. v. 269. Also S. Cyril, Jer. pp. 271—278."

[4] S. Cyril, Jer. Ibid.

[5] S. Ambrose, de Mysteriis, ix. ii. 337.

[6] S. Ambrose. Ibid.   [7] Ibid.

[8] Opera, p. 98. Ed. Cologne, 1686.

[9] Tom. ii. p. 337.   [10] Tom. v. p. 269.

Of these five Fathers, the passage from *S. Justin* has already been given [11]. He simply states the fact that our "blood and flesh are nourished" through the consecrated elements. There is no explicit comparison between the nourishment of our bodies and that of our souls. If there were a tacit one, it would correspond to that in our Catechism, "The strengthening and refreshing of our souls through the Body and Blood of Christ, as our bodies are by the bread and wine."

What statements of *S. Chrysostom* [12] are intended, I cannot say. The only passage, in which the likeness of "wax" is used, is in a homily *not* by S. Chrysostom; and so far from implying the doctrine of Transubstantiation, it implies on the contrary that the elements remain in their natural substances, nourishing the body, and wholly absorbed into the human system. It has been already considered above [13], and shown to express that meaning.

The remaining passages are taken from Fathers who are explaining the truth of the Holy Eucharist, for the first time, to those who previously knew nothing of it. The passages are taken from *Cate-*

---

[11] Above, p. 144.

[12] The Reviewer's reference, Note 2, to S. Chrys. ii. 394, is to the Benedictine Edition. As to S. Chrys. v. 269, (quoted in Notes 3 and 10) there is, in the ed. Bened. v. 268, 269, reference to the moral teaching of the creation, but none to the Holy Eucharist. In v. 269, ed. Mor. there is reference to the two Sacraments, but not to the illustrations alluded to.

[1] pp. 150—154.

chetical Lectures of S. Cyril of Jerusalem on the Sacraments; a Catechetical instruction, and a sermon on baptism, with reference to the unbaptized, by S. Gregory of Nyssa; and a treatise of S. Ambrose, for those who were then "initiated," *i. e.* made acquainted with and partakers of the Christian " mysteries," or sacraments.

The Ancient Church had to take care that the Christian Sacraments should not be profaned, or turned into sport and jest by the Heathen. We know from the story told of S. Athanasius' childhood, how natural it is for children to imitate in their play sacred rites which they have seen. We have heard of such things ourselves. The well-authenticated history of the player Genesius shows that the caution of the early Christians was not misplaced. The Sacrament of Baptism, as administered to the sick, was represented publicly on the stage, with coarse buffoonery, exciting the laughter of the spectators; and then the new-made Christian was taken to the persecuting Emperor Diocletian, to represent an apostacy. In the case of Genesius [1] God interposed, kindled "a [2] sudden piety," gave him grace to believe the truth, and strength to maintain it to death. It was a jest to the heathen to represent the Christians, as first initiated by their sacred rites, and then denying Christ. The Christians, in those days, knew

[1] Ruinart, Acta Martyr. p. 282.
[2] S. Aug. c. Don. vii. 52.

better than we can, to what profaneness our " Holy Things " might be then exposed.·

But the early Church saw that *knowledge* of the Sacraments might be dangerous even to Catechumens, so long as they did not will to become partakers of them.   When the Catechumen was ready to become wholly a Christian, and to renounce the world and its lusts, then it was laid open to him what gifts God had for him in His Sacraments.   S. Athanasius, whose wonderful practical wisdom no one who knows him can doubt, says, "We[3] ought not then to parade the holy mysteries before the uninitiated, lest the heathen in their ignorance deride them, and the Catechumens, being over-curious, be offended."

S. Cyril of Jerusalem says in like way; the Catechumen, "if[4] he should hear from the believer, is made delirious; for, not understanding what he has heard, he finds fault with it, and scoffs at it."

S. Ambrose, another of the Fathers quoted, also speaks of the danger of communicating this knowledge to those unfit to receive it.   "There[5] is peril, not in saying things false only, but even things true; if any one convey them to those to whom they ought not."

Such was the deliberate judgment and practice of the ancient Church; and we may trust them to have judged well for *their* day, as the Church now judges

[3] Apol. ag. Ar. § 11, p. 28, O. T.
[4] Procat. § 7, p. 6, O. T.
[5] In Ps. 118, Serm. 2, § 25, p. 990, comp. de Myst. init.

what is best for our day. However such *was* their practice, and the language adduced by the Dublin Reviewer, corresponds with it. But the argument proves too much. The persons addressed knew beforehand, that there *were* mysteries, the knowledge of which had been withheld from them. They had not, as we, been instructed in them from childhood. They were brought suddenly to the knowledge of the actual sacraments, when they were made partakers of them. Yet they saw only some of the simplest outward substances of this world, water in the one Sacrament, bread and wine in the other. Those who taught them, had to teach them *as to both Sacraments* alike, that they were not to judge by their bodily senses, but to believe the power of God.

" In truth," says Tertullian [f], " there is nothing which so hardeneth the minds of men, as the simplicity of the Divine works as visible in the act, and their greatness promised in the effect ; so that in this case also, because a man going down into the water, and being with few words washed therein, with so much simplicity, without pomp, without any novel preparation, and finally without expense, riseth again not much or not a whit the cleaner, therefore his gaining eternity is thought incredible. I am much mistaken if the rites and mysteries pertaining to idols, on the contrary, build not their credit and authority on their equipments and their outward show and their sumptuousness. O wretched unbelief! who deniest to God His own proper qualities, simplicity and power ! What then ? Is it not wonderful that death should be washed away by a mere bath ? Yea, but if, because it is wonderful, it be therefore not believed, it ought on that account the rather to be believed.

[f] De Bapt. c. 2, p. 256, O. T.

For what else should the works of God be, but above all wonder? We ourselves also wonder, but because we believe; while unbelief wondereth and believeth not, for it wondereth at simple things, as foolish, and at great things, as impossible."

These Fathers, then, *do*, as is alleged, appeal to the Omnipotence of God; they *do* bid their hearers not to trust to their senses alone; they *do* appeal to the miracles of old time. But they make all these appeals in the case of Baptism as well as of the Holy Eucharist. It would, of course, be utterly mistaken to infer from this, that the Fathers believed no more of the Holy Eucharist than they do of Baptism. But it *is* true, that *these* appeals to the power of God, and the wonders of old time, *prove* no more as to the one than the other, because they are used in reference to both. Since they are alleged for both Sacraments, they cannot specifically prove of one, what they do not prove as to both.

This will, perhaps, appear most naturally in considering the several passages. Without, then, anticipating further, I will again, for precaution and distinctness, state that the one change, denied by our Articles and Rubric, and affirmed by modern Roman divines, relates to the physical substance of the elements; our formularies affirming that the "natural substance" remains, Roman divines, that it ceases to be. Had Almighty God indeed made any such revelation as to the natural substances, there would, of course, have been no difficulty in believing this, any more than in believing any other mystery of faith. But it has been confessed by grave writers who believed the doctrine, that it is not proved, of necessity, by Holy Scripture.

The question here is, " Do the illustrations employed by the Fathers, imply that they believed any change *of this sort?*"   Roman controversialists commonly assume, that, if any change is implied at all, it is *this;* that the things not only *become* what they were not, but *altogether* cease to be, *in their natural substances,* what they were.   Thus the writer in the Dublin Review above quoted, says :

" In the natural use of language, one thing cannot be said to *become,* or to *be made, another,* without *ceasing to be what it was.*   The water of Cana did not become wine, without ceasing to be water ; Moses' rod did not become a serpent, till it ceased to be a rod ; a layman does not become a priest, without ceasing to be a layman."

This is true of physical changes.   But the analogies thus pressed, contradict one another and the doctrine itself.   In the change of Moses' rod, vegetable substance was changed into animal structure. To the water of Cana God superadded at once all those qualities which it would have gained, had it passed through the vine, been ripened in the grape, been expressed and fermented[7].   These *were* physical changes, although of different sorts, the one being an addition only.   But in the third, there is no physical change at all.   "*Layman*" is a mere

[7] In a sermon (118. 3) published as S. Augustine's by Card. Mai, (Bibl. Patr. Nov. i. Serm. 249,) the writer says, among other things of the same sort, " Christ did that in the water, which at a certain season, He doth in the vine."

negative title, meaning one who is not a priest; and, plainly, a person cannot be at once a priest and not a priest, at the same time. But "lay" is a mere epithet. He remains physically a man, as he was before, and could not, of course, be a priest, unless he were so. An office, and, if he be worthy, grace is superadded; nature is not changed. So (in the Fathers' language) it is inconsistent that the elements should be "*mere* bread" and yet the Body of Christ; as it is that a person should be a "*lay*man" and yet a priest. But there is no inconsistency, that it should be bread in its natural substance and qualities, and ineffably and Divinely the Body of Christ, *i. e.* that there should be no physical change; any more than it is inconsistent that a person should be physically a man, and by office and grace a priest. I do not use this as any explanation. All earthly types can be but imperfect illustrations of things Divine. Each can illustrate, and that imperfectly, one side only of any Divine truth. Each needs to be corrected and limited by others. And the evil of this application of the illustrations of the Fathers, is that when their object was to illustrate the Divine Power, or the superiority of grace to nature, or the supernatural workings of the Divine Word, this mode of explanation limits them, to what only a portion of them will bear at all, a physical change in the natural substances.

The whole passage quoted from *S. Gregory of Nyssa* is in illustration, not of the Holy Eucharist, but of the other great Sacrament, Baptism. The sermon, in which it occurs, was preached at one of the solemn seasons of Baptism, the Epiphany of our Lord, when His Baptism for us was commemorated. Those present consisted of the baptized, and the unbaptized, who were brought for Baptism. He addresses them;

"Ye[8], who have made trial of the good things of our faith, have come in crowds, and, as good fathers, ye have brought those, as yet inexperienced therein, with care and tenderness, guiding the uninitiated to the perfect reception of godliness. But I joy with both; with those initiated, that ye have been enriched with a great gift; with those uninitiated, that ye hope for a good expectation, forgiveness of guiltiness, loosing of chains, to be of the family of God, freedom of intercourse [with God] and for slavish degradation to rank equal with the angels. For these things, and whatsoever is involved in them, the grace of Baptism pledges and gives."

The whole sequel of his sermon is on the greatness of Baptism; all his illustrations centre in this point, how God makes use of things, outwardly of no account, to work, by them, miracles of His grace and power. The Holy Eucharist is mentioned only as one instance out of many, which illustrate this principle of God's dealing, as shown in Baptism. He continues;

"Baptism[9] is the cleansing of sins, the remission of offences, the cause of renewal and regeneration. Regeneration, not seen with the eyes, but beheld by the mind. For

[8] De Bapt. Christi, iii. 367.
[9] Ib. 368—371.

T

not indeed, as was the grosser conception of the Hebrew Nicodemus, shall we change the old man into a boy ; nor shall we transform the wrinkled and hoary man into a tender youth, nor bring a man back to his mother's womb ; but him who is spotted with sins and inveterate in evil prac- tices, we, by royal grace, bring back to the guiltlessness of a child.   For as the new-born child is free from accusa- tions and punishments, so also the son of the regeneration hath not for what to answer, being, by a royal gift, freed from all charges.   This benefit the water conferreth not, (for the gift is higher than all creatures), but the command of God, and the descent of the Spirit, coming sacramentally to our deliverance.   But the water serveth to indicate the cleansing.   For since we are wont, washing with water a body fouled with filth and mire, to make it clean, therefore in the sacramental act also, we employ the same, showing the incorporeal brightness by things subject to the senses. Nay, let us continue to inquire more narrowly about Baptism, beginning, as from a fountain-head, from the command of Holy Scripture, ' Except a man be born of water and of the Spirit, he cannot enter into the kingdom of God.'   Why are these two and not the Spirit alone thought all-sufficient for the completion of Baptism ?   Man is compound, and not simple, as we well know.   And therefore for the two-fold and blended being, kindred and like remedies were allotted for his healing ; for the visible body the sensible water, and for the in- visible soul the viewless Spirit, called by faith, coming ineffably.   ' For the Spirit bloweth where It listeth, and thou hearest the sound thereof, but canst not tell whence It cometh or whither It goeth.'   It blesses the baptized body, and the water which baptizeth.   Wherefore despise not the Divine laver, nor hold it cheap as a common thing, on account of the use of water.   For That which worketh is mighty, and from It wonderful are the things accomplished. For this holy altar too, by which we stand, is, as to its

nature, common stone, nothing differing from other slabs
which build up our walls and adorn the pavements.   But
after it was hallowed to the service of God, and received
the blessing, it is a holy table, an undefiled altar, no more
touched by all, but by the priests only, and by these too,
reverently.   The Bread again is, up to a certain time, *common* bread, but when the Mystery shall consecrate it, it is
called and becomes the Body of Christ.   So the Mystical
oil, so the wine, worth but little before the blessing ; after
the sanctification of the Spirit, each worketh differently.
But the same power of the Word maketh the priest too
honourable and venerable, when separated by the newness
of the blessing from what he has in common with the
many.   For having been, yesterday and afore, one of the
multitude and of the people, he is at once made a guide,
president, teacher of piety, instructor in hidden mysteries.
And this he does, nothing changed in body or form ; but
being, in outward appearance [1], the same which he was, by
some invisible power and grace *transformed* [2] in the invisible
to something better.   In like way, as thou appliest thy
mind to many other things, thou wilt see the outward appearances [3] contemptible, but the things accomplished by
them, great ;   and especially when you select out of the
ancient history what is like and akin to what we are en-
quiring about.   The rod of Moses was of hazel.   What else
than common wood, which any hand cuts and carries, *frames* [4]
to what seems to him good, and puts in the fire at will ?
But when God willed to accomplish through it mighty
miracles, above all words, He changed the wood into a serpent.   And again elsewhere, smiting the waters, at one
time He made the water blood, at another sent forth the
countless progeny of frogs.   And again, He divided the
sea, cut through to its very depths, and not flowing together
again.   So the goatskin mantle of one of the prophets made

[1] τὸ φαινόμενον.   [2] μεταμορφωθείς.
[3] τὰ φαινόμενα.   [4] ῥυθμίζει.

Elisha the talk of the world. The wood of the Cross is saving to all men, being, as I hear, a portion of some contemptible tree, less esteemed than most others. And the bramble-bush showed to Moses the manifestation of God; and the remains of Elisha raised a dead man; and clay enlightened the man born blind. And all these, being lifeless and insensate substances, ministered to great miracles, having received the power of God. But by a like train of reasoning, the water also, being nothing else than other water, renews the man to the spiritual regeneration, the grace from above blessing it. But if any further trouble me, doubting and wavering, and persevere in questioning, '*How* water regenerates and the mystery is accomplished in it!' most justly shall I say to him, tell me the mode of the birth after the flesh, and I will describe to thee the power of the new birth in the soul."

Passages from S. Chrysostom have already been adduced, in which he speaks freely of "change of nature," or of God's power over nature, even while asserting that the natural substances remain. That very appeal as to the senses, that they would mislead us, if we trusted them, he employs as to Baptism. He illustrates the change in the Holy Eucharist by the operation of grace, through the water of Baptism. I do not, of course, mean that he regards the Presence as the same in both. But he lays down the same principle as to Baptism, that the senses may report amiss; but that God's Word, which the ear hears, must be true.

"Let' us obey God every where, and contradict in nothing, although what is said may seem contrary to our

---

' Hom. 82, in S. Matth., § 4, p. 787 ed. Montf. 468, ed. Field.

reasonings and to appearances. But let His word be mightier than reasonings or appearances. So also let us do as to the mysteries, not looking only on what lieth before us, but holding to His words. For His word is infallible, but our senses are easily deceived. That never failed; this, often. Since, then, the Lord says, ' This is My Body,' let us both obey and believe, and see It with spiritual eyes. For It gives us nothing to be perceived by sense ; but *in* things of sense, all spiritual. So also in Baptism, the gift takes place through a matter of sense, *i. e.* the water; but what is wrought is spiritual, the regeneration and renewal. For if thou wert incorporeal, He would have given thee nakedly the incorporeal gifts; but, since the soul is united with the body, He giveth thee the things spiritual *in things sensible.*"

Theophilus of Alexandria compares the elements of the two Sacraments in the same way, in answer to a statement of Origen, that "The Holy Spirit doth not operate on things inanimate, nor come to things unintelligent."

" Asserting [6] this, he thinks not that the mystical waters in Baptism are consecrated by the coming of the Holy Spirit ; and that the Bread of the Lord, whereby the Body of the Lord *is set forth* [7] and which we break to our sanctification, and the sacred Cup, which are placed on the altars of the Church, and yet are inanimate, are sanctified by the invocation and coming of the Holy Spirit."

2. In like way S. Cyril of Jerusalem, in one place, in order to illustrate the power of God, as shown in the Holy Eucharist, compares it to the change of the water into wine at the marriage feast ; in another,

[6] Ep. Pasch. i. Bibl. Pat. T. 5, p. 846.
[7] "Ostenditur."

like S. Gregory of Nyssa, to the Chrism, *which undergoes no physical change.*   He says,

" Beware [a] of supposing this to be *plain* ointment. For as
the Bread of the Eucharist, after the invocation of the Holy
Ghost, is *mere* bread no longer, but the Body of Christ, so
also this holy ointment is no more *simple* ointment, nor (so
to say) *common*, after the invocation, but the gift of Christ ;
and by the presence of His Godhead, it causes in us the
Holy Ghost.   It is symbolically applied to thy forehead and
thy other senses; and while thy body is anointed with visible
ointment, thy soul is sanctified by the Holy and life-giving
Spirit."

There is, *thus far*, the same contrast between the
two outward symbols.   S. Cyril had, *thus far*, the
same error to guard against, lest people should under-
value God's gifts on account of the poorness of the
outward symbols through which He bestowed it.
" Beware," he says, " of supposing this to be *mere*
ointment."   *Before* consecration, it was *simple* ointment ; so also the "bread of the Eucharist" was *mere*
bread.   *After* consecration, " the bread is *mere* bread
no longer ;" and " this holy ointment," he says, " is no
more *simple* ointment," but " the bread is the Body
of Christ," and " the Chrism is Christ's gift of grace."
Yet it was not the Chrism *itself* which was Christ's
gift of grace.   It was but the instrument and vehicle
of it.   He calls the Chrism by the name of the grace
which it conveys.   So then the parallel fits in best
with the belief, that the elements remain, but are

____

[a] Lect. xxi. 3, p. 268, O. T.

called the Body and Blood of Christ, because they contain Them "under the form of bread and wine," and the consecrated elements convey the spiritual Substance which they contain.

Roman divines assume that S. Cyril, in making the parallel between God's miracles of old and the miracles of His grace and love in the Holy Eucharist, means that they are miracles of exactly the same sort. This, plainly, they are not. For the miracles of old, although tokens of God's favour, were but *outward signs.* The Holy Eucharist is a spiritual miracle of His love, whereby He gives His Body and Blood to His people. In the miracles of old, that which was miraculous was *wholly outward;* no inward grace accompanied them. In the Sacraments of the Church, that which is miraculous is *wholly inward;* there is nothing outward or visible. But besides this, S. Cyril himself employs God's material miracles, as an argument that we should believe the spiritual, in cases where there is no change of substance.

"Shall[*] not He, O man, who woke Lazarus, a corpse of four days, which stank, shall not He much more easily raise up thee, a living man?"

And again, of our restoration after the Resurrection, when our substance shall be the same, only glorified.

"The[1] rod of Moses was by the counsel of God changed into the dissimilar *nature* of a serpent: and shall not man, who has fallen into death, be again restored to himself?"

[*] Ib. ii. 5, p. 16, O. T.   [1] Ib. iv. 30, p. 47.

The parallel, then, does not in itself establish that S. Cyril conceived the change to affect the physical substance of the elements; while the context rather contrasts things physical with things spiritual. He contrasts the natural gifts in an earthly marriage with the spiritual gifts to the "children of His Bridechamber."

"He ª once in Cana of Galilee turned water into wine, which is akin to blood, and is it incredible that He should have turned wine into Blood? That wonderful work He miraculously wrought, when called to an earthly marriage; and should He not much rather be acknowledged to have *bestowed the fruition of His Body and Blood* upon 'the children of the Bridechamber?'"

But S. Cyril does not *therefore* imply that it has lost the physical substance of bread, (although no longer *mere* bread,) for he goes on to speak of the Body and Blood of Christ being given *in* the Bread and wine, the *types* of them ª. The " type " (τύπος) was the visible emblem or picture of that which was invisible, whether present or absent. But the type itself was some visible substance. When, then, S. Cyril speaks of "the type of Bread," *i. e.* bread which was a type of His Body, and "the type of wine," *i. e.* wine which was a type of His Blood, and that that Body and Blood were given *in* these things, which were the types of them, it is too much to assume that S. Cyril thought that those visible symbols of the In-

---

ª Ib. xxii. (Myst. iv.) § 2, p. 270, O. T.

ª See above, Note I. p. 94 sqq. and Note L. p. 132.

visible had no longer any real existence.   S. Cyril's words are,

"Therefore[4] let us, with fullest assurance, partake as of the Body and Blood of Christ; for *in* the type of Bread is given to thee His Body, and *in* the type of wine His Blood; that thou, by partaking of the Body and Blood of Christ, mightest be made of the same body and the same blood with Him."

3. The author of the " de Sacramentis" had to meet the difficulty of the Catechumen, that the Jewish Sacrament had that which ours have not, in that the Manna came down from Heaven.

"13. Who[5] then is the Author of sacraments but the Lord Jesus?   Those Sacraments came from Heaven; for all counsel [of God] is from Heaven.   But truly it was a great and Divine Miracle that God rained down to the people Manna from Heaven, and the people laboured not, and ate.

"14. You say, perhaps, 'my bread is common bread.'   But that bread is bread before the words of the Sacraments; when the consecration is added, from bread it becomes the Flesh of Christ.   How can that which *is* bread, *be* the Body of Christ?   By Consecration.   And the Consecration, in whose words is it?   The Lord Jesus'.   For all the rest which had been said before is said by the priest; praises are offered to God; prayer is made for the people, for kings, for the rest. When the venerable Sacrament is to be consecrated, the priest now no longer uses his own words, but he uses the words of Christ.   So, then, the word of Christ consecrates the Sacrament.

"15. What is the word of Christ?   That by which all things were made.   The Lord commanded, and the Heaven

[4] § 3.
[5] L iv. c. 4, ap. S. Ambr. T. ii. p. 368 sqq.

was made; the Lord commanded, and the earth was made; the Lord commanded, and the seas were made; the Lord commanded, and all creatures were brought forth.   Thou seest, then, how powerful in working is the word of Christ. If, then, there is such power in the word of the Lord Jesus, that those things which were not should begin to be, how much more is it operative, that the things which *were*, *should still be*[6], *and be changed into something else?*   The

[6] "Ut sint quæ erant, et in aliud commutentur."   Algerus (de Sacram. i. 7, Bibl. P. xxi. 257) paraphrases the words, "that the bread and wine should be what they were, and be changed into what is better," and admits, that "the passage seems to establish that they are *substantially* what they were, and are changed into something else."   I have translated the words as Card. Perron, because the bread and wine are not the immediate antecedents, and the contrast is between 'inciperent esse quæ non erant,' and 'sint quæ erant.'   But according to the later Roman doctrine, the things themselves cease to *be*.   As one says, "the consecration being completed, nothing whatever of the substance of bread remains; nor *is* it actually, any more than if it had never been, or was before the creation of the world." (Gamach. T. 3, q. 74, c. 4, quoted by Albertin. p. 510.)   Nor is that any real answer which is made in the Perpetuité de la Foi (T. iii. l. vi. c, 6, 7, quoted by the Bened. in S. Ambr. ii. 369), that air and river-water are continually changed, and yet are spoken of as the same.   We may say, "the air of the room is corrupted," "the air is fresh," yet we do not mean the same air, but that portion of the air of which we are at the time speaking. We imply by our very way of speaking that we mean different air. We give the name of a whole to its parts, and might say, "this crowd," when thinking, immediately, now of this, now of that, part of the crowd; but if we were speaking of parts of it, we should not mean that the individuals were the same.   But here the author of the De Sacram. is speaking of the same individual substances, the bread and the wine, and says that after consecration they "*are and* are changed."   Modern writers say "they *are not*, but are replaced, and cease to be, as if they had never been."

Heaven was not; the sea was not; the earth was not; but hear David saying, 'He spake, and they were made; He commanded and they were created.'

"16. So then, that I may answer thee, it was not the Body of Christ before the consecration; but after the consecration I say to thee that now it is the Body of Christ. 'He spake, and it was made; He commanded, and it was created.' Thou thyself *wert*, but thou wert an old creature; after thou *wert* consecrated, thou begannest to be a new creature. Wouldest thou hear, how a new creature? 'Every one,' he saith, 'in Christ is a new creature.'

"17. Hear, then, how the word of Christ is wont to *change* all creation, and *changes*, when it wills, the appointments of nature. Askest thou, how? Hear; and first of all, take an instance from its generation. It is the wont that a man should not be born, save of man and woman, and the use of marriage; but because the Lord willed, because He chose this sacrament, Christ was born of the Holy Ghost and the Virgin, *i. e.* the Mediator between God and man, Christ Jesus. Seest thou how against its appointments and order He was born, a Man was born of a Virgin?

"18. Take another. The Jewish people was pressed upon by the Egyptian; it was intercepted by the sea. At the Divine command, Moses touched the waters with the rod, and the waves divided, not according to the wont of its nature, but according to the grace of the heavenly command. Take another. The people thirsted, came to the fountain; the fountain was bitter; holy Moses cast wood into the fountain, and the fountain which was bitter was made sweet, *i. e.* it changed the wont of its nature; it received the sweetness of grace. Take again a fourth example. The iron of the axe had fallen into the waters; as being iron, after its wont, it sunk. Elisha cast wood; forthwith the iron was raised, and swam upon the waters; of a truth against the wont of iron, for it is a heavier matter than is the element of water.

"19. From all these things, dost thou not understand how much the heavenly word operateth? If it operated in the earthly fountain, if the heavenly word operated in other things, doth it not operate in heavenly sacraments? Thou hast learnt, then, that of bread there becometh the Body of Christ, and that wine and water are poured into the chalice, but it becometh Blood by the consecration of the Heavenly Word.

"20. But haply thou sayest, ' I see not the appearance of Blood.' But it hath a likeness. For as thou hast received a likeness of death, so also thou drinkest a likeness of the Precious Blood, that there may be no horror at gore, and yet the price of redemption taketh effect. Thou hast learned that what thou receivest is the Body of Christ.

"21. Wouldest thou know by what heavenly words it is consecrated? Hear what the words are. The priest saith, ' Let this oblation be ascribed [to us], valid, reasonable, acceptable, because it is a figure of the Body and Blood of our Lord Jesus Christ, Who, the day before He suffered, took bread in His Holy Hands, looked up to Heaven to Thee, Holy Father, Almighty Everlasting God, giving thanks, blessed, brake, and when broken, He gave it to His Apostles and His disciples, saying, Take and eat ye all of this, for this is My Body, which shall be broken for many.'

"22. Likewise also, after He had supped, the day before He suffered, He took the Cup, looked to Heaven to Thee, Holy Father, Almighty Everlasting God, giving thanks, He blessed, gave to His Apostles and His disciples, saying, ' Take and drink ye all of this, for this is My Blood.' Look at this altogether. All those are the words of the Evangelist unto ' take,' whether the Body or Blood. Thence they are words of Christ. ' Take and drink ye all of this, for this is My Blood.' And consider it in detail.

"23. ' Who,' he saith, ' the day before He suffered, took bread in His Holy Hands.' Before it is consecrated, it is bread ; when the words of Christ are added, it is the Body of Christ.   Then hear Himself saying, 'Take and eat ye all of this, for this is My Body.'   And before the words of Christ, it is a cup, full of wine and water; when the words of Christ have operated, the Blood of Christ is caused to be there', which redeemed His people.   See, then, in what ways the word of Christ is powerful to change all things.   Thus the Lord Jesus Himself testifies to us, that we receive His own Body and Blood.   Ought we to doubt of His faithfulness and attestation ?

"24. Now return with me to my proposition.   Great, indeed, and venerable is it, that He rained to the Jews manna from heaven.   But understand.   Which is greater, manna from heaven or the Body of Christ?   The Body of Christ, Who is the Author of Heaven.   Then, he who ate manna, died; he who eateth this Body, shall have remission of sins, and shall not die for ever.

"25. So then not idly dost thou say Amen, already thereby confessing in spirit that thou receivest the Body of Christ.   The Priest saith to thee, 'The Body of Christ,' and thou sayest Amen, *i. e.* true.   What thy tongue confesseth, let thy affections retain."

To this extract should be added another summary from the same writer, in which he refers back to this.

" 1. As * our Lord Jesus Christ is the very Son of God, not as men, by grace, but as the Son from the Substance of the Father; so (as He Himself said) that which we receive is true Flesh, and His true drink.

" 2. But haply thou mayest say, (what the very disciples of Christ then said, when they heard Him saying, ' Except a man eat My Flesh and drink My Blood, He shall not abide in Me nor have eternal life ;) haply thou mayest say, ' How, true ? I, who see the likeness', see not the truth of blood ?'

<hr>

' " Ibi sanguis Christi efficitur."   * vi. init.
* " Similitudinem video."

"3. First of all, I spake to you of the word of Christ which operateth, that it can change and convert the appointed orders of nature.   Then, when the disciples of Christ endured not His words, hearing that He would give them His Flesh to eat and His Blood to drink, they went back : but Peter alone said, ' Thou hast the words of eternal life, and shall I go back from Thee?'   Lest men now should say this, as though there were a certain horror of blood, and yet that the grace of the Redemption might remain, therefore as a likeness [1] thou receivest the Sacrament, but truly thou obtainest the grace [2] and virtue of the Nature."

The author of the De Sacramentis teaches the Catechumen to believe a change, in that before it was " *common* bread," after the consecration it is the Body of Christ."   He does not tie himself to this form of words, but says equally, " the Blood of Christ is caused to be *there;*" or "thou drinkest *the likeness of* the precious Blood ;" or, "*as a likeness* thou receivest the Sacraments, but truly thou obtainest *the grace and virtue of the Nature*," where certainly he seems to express that the outward or visible part is the physical substance; the inward, although real, is not physical, but spiritual.   The words, " that the things which were should *be, and* be changed into something else," assert the continued *being* of the outward elements.

But his illustrations also are directed to show a power of God over nature, not a change of natural substance.   His very first instance,—man before

---

[1] " In similitudinem."
[2] " Naturæ gratiam virtutemque consequeris."

and after regeneration, relates to superadded grace. The man is physically what he was before. The Holy Spirit dwells in him, whereas, before, He did not. Again, in our Lord's Birth of a Virgin, He took real Flesh, of the substance of His Mother, the same Flesh as ours, although not in the same way. There was no change of substance, although there was a production of our Lord's Human Nature, above the order of nature. As He took Flesh of His Mother, by the overshadowing of the Holy Ghost, without an earthly Father, so He causes His Body and Blood to be, in a way above nature, present in the Sacrament. The analogy leads to a mode of presence above nature, not to a physical change in the natural substances. Nor was there any such change at the dividing of the Red Sea; nor when the axe's iron head was raised. He, at Whose will and through Whose power the waters of the sea roll in restless motion, and the iron sinks to the bottom, willed to suspend His usual laws; but there was no change in the physical structure. Lastly, in the sweetening of the bitter water, He who willed that that water should hold in solution that which imparted to it its bitter taste, willed that when the tree was cast into it, it should lose its bitter taste, but the substance of the water was as before. All were instances of Almighty Power, working that which is above nature; but none of those operations illustrate the particular physical change in the elements, by which the natural substance is supposed to cease to be.

4. The instances of miraculous working which occur in S. Ambrose, have been already considered in the passage from the De Sacramentis, which is in some cases a comment upon them. All illustrate one great truth, which belongs to both Sacraments, that the grace of God is more powerful than nature, that through His grace He effects what is above and beyond the course of nature.

Had S. Ambrose intended by the illustrations to prove a physical change in the Holy Eucharist, he would not have used the same illustrations of the grace in Baptism. Yet he not only appeals to the miracle at Marah in regard to Baptism also, but still more largely, he contrasts the outward working and the invisible power.

"Marah[3] was a most bitter fountain. Moses cast wood into it, and it became sweet. For water, without the preaching of the Cross of the Lord, is of no use to our future salvation; but when it has been consecrated by the mystery of the saving Cross, then it is tempered for the use of the spiritual laver and the saving Cup. As then Moses, *i.e.* the prophet, cast wood into that fountain, so also into this font the priest casts the preaching of the Lord, and the water becomes sweet for grace."

And then he makes use of the same sort of appeal as he does with regard to the Holy Eucharist;

"Believe[4] not then the eyes of thy body alone. More seen is what is not seen. For that is temporal; this, the

---

[3] De Myst. c. 3, § 14.   Of the Holy Eucharist, c. 9, § 51.
[4] c. 3, § 15.

eternal, is gazed on, which is not grasped by the eyes, but is discerned by the mind and understanding."

And after giving the history of Naaman;

" Therefore[5] was this predicted for thee, that thou shouldest not believe that only which thou sawest, lest perchance thou too shouldest say, 'Is this that great mystery, which eye hath not seen, nor ear heard, nor hath it entered into the heart of man?' I see waters, which I have been seeing daily. Can these cleanse me, into which I have often gone down and never was cleansed? Know hence, that water cleanseth not without the Spirit."

" For[6] what is water without the Cross of Christ? A common element without any sacramental efficacy. Nor yet again without water is the mystery of regeneration. 'For except a man be born again of water and the Spirit, he cannot enter into the kingdom of God.'"

" As[7] though buried with [Christ] in that element of the world, dead to sin, thou art raised again to life eternal. Believe then that the waters are not void."

And again on the miracle of the pool of Siloam :—

" To[8] them there was a sign, to thee faith; to them the Angel descended, to thee the Holy Spirit; to them the creature was moved, to thee Christ operateth, the Lord of the creature."

" To[9] them that pool was a figure, that thou mightest believe, that into this font a Divine power descended."

On the Holy Eucharist itself, S. Ambrose has to answer the difficulty, that what there lies in sight is a mere substance of this world. " Haply[1] thou mayest say, I see something else; how dost thou assert to me, that I shall *receive* the Body of Christ?"

[5] c. 4, § 19.   [6] § 20.   [7] § 21.
[8] § 22.   [9] § 23.   [1] c. 9, § 50.

U

His answer is, " Let us prove that not *that* is, which nature formed, but what the blessing has consecrated, and that greater is the force of blessing than of nature, because, by blessing, nature itself is changed." He then [2] instances miracles of the Old Testament, in some of which there was a physical change, as Moses' rod being turned into a serpent, and the waters of Egypt into blood, and back again, and the sweetening of the waters of Marah, as he had before with regard to baptism. In as many others, the division of the Red Sea, the Jordan, and the raising of the axe's head by Elisha (elsewhere spoken of as a type of Baptism), there is no physical change of one thing into another, but Almighty God suspended the laws, which He imposes on His creation. In the remaining case, there was no change at all, only a miraculous eliciting of water out of the rock. Yet of the Red Sea and the Jordan, he uses precisely the same words, as of the rod and the waters made blood, that " their nature [3] was changed." Of the rock, and the iron-axe, he says, that "grace operated contrary to nature," " this we know was done contrary to nature." It would, then, be to stretch these illustrations of S. Ambrose beyond the object for which they were adduced, to infer that he adduced them to prove a *physical* change in the natural elements employed in the Holy Eucharist, not a super-

[2] § 51.
[3] Mutatam esse naturam et serpentis et virgæ—naturam vel maritimorum fluctuum vel fluvialis cursus esse mutatam.

natural change, in that they become really, but sacramentally, the Body and Blood of Christ.

But it will be more satisfactory to give the whole passage, premising that there are indications in the passage itself, that S. Ambrose believed the substance of the elements to remain.

" 47. In truth, wonderful is it, that God rained manna upon the fathers, and even fed them daily with the daily food of Heaven. Whence it is said, ' Man did eat Angels' food.' Yet all they who did eat that bread, died in the wilderness. But that Food which thou receivest, that living Bread which came down from Heaven, ministers the substance of eternal life; and whosoever shall eat this, shall never die; and it is the Body of Christ.

" 48. Consider now, whether the ' bread of Angels' be greater, or the Flesh of Christ, which is the Body of life. That Manna, is from Heaven, this is above the Heaven; that is of Heaven, this of the Lord of the Heavens. That was liable to corruption, if it was kept till the next day. *This* is alien from all corruption, which whosoever tastes religiously, cannot feel corruption. To them waters flowed from the rock; to thee Blood from Christ: those waters satisfied for an hour; thee Blood washeth for ever. The Jew drinks and thirsteth; thou, when thou drinkest, canst not thirst; that was in shadow, this in truth.

" 49. If that which thou admirest is a shadow, how great is that whose very shadow thou admirest! Hear that what took place among the fathers was a shadow. ' They drank,' he saith, ' of that rock which followed them; but that rock was Christ. But with many of them God was not well pleased. For they were overthrown in the wilderness. But all these things were done in a figure of us.' Thou knowest which is best. For light is better than shade; truth than a shadow; the Body of the Author than manna from Heaven.

U 2

"50. Haply thou mayest say, ' I see something else; how dost thou assert to me that I shall *receive* the Body of Christ?' We have to prove this also. What examples use we then? Let us prove that it is not that which nature formed, but what the blessing consecrated; and that greater is the power of the blessing than of nature; for by the blessing nature itself is changed.

"51. Moses held a rod; he cast it down and it became a serpent. Again he took the tail of the serpent, and it returned into the nature of a rod. Seest thou therefore that the nature both of serpent and rod was twice changed by prophetic grace? The rivers of Egypt ran with a free course of waters; suddenly from the pores of the fountains blood began to burst forth, and there was nothing to drink in the rivers. Again at the prophet's prayer, the gore of the rivers ceased; the nature of waters flowed anew. The Hebrew people were closed in on all sides; walled in on this side by the Egyptians, on the other shut in by the sea. Moses lifted his rod, the water divided, and stood congealed as walls; and amid the waves a foot-path appeared. Jordan, turned backwards against nature, returned towards its own source. Is it not clear that the nature, whether of the waves of the sea or of the course of the river, was changed? The people of our forefathers thirsted, Moses touched the rock, and water flowed from the rock. Did not, against nature, grace operate, that a rock should pour out water, which nature had not. Marah was a most bitter stream, so that the thirsting people could not drink. Moses cast wood into the water, and the nature of the waters, tempered by grace suddenly infused, laid aside its bitterness. In the time of Elisha the prophet, iron was struck off from the axe of one of the sons of the prophets, and forthwith it was sunk. He who had lost the iron, prayed Elisha; Elisha cast wood into the water, and the iron swam. This too we know to have been done against nature; for heavier is the nature of iron, than the moisture of water.

"52. We see therefore that grace is of greater virtue

than nature, and as yet we are only rehearsing the grace of prophetic blessing. But if human blessing was of such avail as to change nature, what say we of the Divine consecration itself, wherein the very words of our Lord and Saviour operate? For that Sacrament which thou receivest is consecrated by the word of Christ. But if the word of Elijah was of so great power, as to bring down fire from Heaven, shall not the word of Christ avail to change the nature of the elements? Of the works of the whole world thou hast read, ' He spake, and they were made; He commanded, and they were created.' The word of Christ then which could make of nothing what (as yet) was not, cannot it change the things which are, into that which they were not? For it is not a less thing to give new natures to things, than to change natures.

" 53. But why use we arguments? Let us use His own example, and build up the truth of the mystery by the example of the Incarnation. Did the wont of nature precede, when the Lord Jesus was born of a Virgin? If we inquire for the order of nature, woman united with man was wont to bear. And this Body which we consecrate, is from the Virgin. Why inquirest thou here for the order of nature in the Body of Christ, when, against nature, the Lord Jesus Himself was born of a Virgin? True is the Flesh of Christ, which was crucified, which was buried; true therefore is the Sacrament of that Flesh.

" 54. The Lord Jesus Himself declares, ' This is My Body.' Before the blessing of the heavenly words, another kind is named; after the consecration the Body is *signified*. He Himself saith, it is His Blood. Before consecration it is called other; after the consecration, it is named Blood. And thou sayest, Amen, *i. e.* it is true; what the mouth speaketh, let the inward mind confess; what the speech uttereth, let the affection feel."

It is a miracle, the very greatest miracle, which S. Ambrose has to illustrate. The question is not as to the greatness of the miracle, but as to its nature. Of the miracles which S. Ambrose cites, Roman divines are wont to press just one side of one class only, and that a small class. They observe in some of those miracles a physical change of the natural substances, and that change being prominent in their own minds, they assume it to have been so in the mind of S. Ambrose. It seems, in itself, a ground against pressing these analogies, that when there was a physical change in the substance, there was a change in the appearance also. But, beyond this, *this* very portion of the illustrations employed by S. Ambrose would, if pressed, be contrary to the doctrine itself; the rest would be irrelevant. On no principle of interpretation, can the illustration be pressed on the one side without being taken strictly on the other also. The two are inseparable. The rod of Moses did not become a serpent without ceasing to be a rod also; true: but the rod of Moses became a serpent, which serpent had no being, until the rod became that serpent. The illustration, if pressed in one way, would imply a physical change; but it would imply a physical change which it would be heresy to believe.

But those other illustrations, the Red Sea, the Jordan, the raising of the axe-head, would not simply be irrelevant; they would, on the contrary, be opposed to the doctrine. The Red Sea, the Jordan, the axe-head, remained identically the same natural substances which they were before; the waters of

Marah parted with a noxious ingredient which they had absorbed into them; they retained all their natural substance, as water.   When the water gushed from the rock, there was no parting with any natural substance, but either the creation of a new substance, or a passage given in a way above nature, to the waters which lay below.   Yet these, S. Ambrose urges, were lesser miracles, the fruits only of prophetic blessing.   *The* instance (as we have seen) upon which he lays especial stress, is our Lord's Birth of the Virgin.   But in that Birth, there was, again, no change of nature, but a Production not in the way of nature.   He, through the overshadowing of the Holy Ghost, formed in her that Human Nature, which "for us men and for our salvation" He vouchsafed to take.   With that Human Nature which He then took, He, in the very act of giving being to It, united His Divine Nature.   God and Man, He "abhorred not the Virgin's womb."   As He lay hid in the Virgin's womb, so we believe that (in the words of the Homilies), "under the form of bread and wine" we "receive the Body and Blood of Christ," and, therewith, Himself.

But all the analogies of S. Ambrose harmonize and blend in one, if, without pressing them as to physical changes of substance, we dwell upon them all as signal instances of the mighty power of God, and so look not to what is seen, but to what is not seen; and believe that He Who hath said, "This is My Body," "This is My Blood," worketh what He saith, not by any order of nature, but in a way above nature, as in the miracles of old, or in the mystery of His own Incarnation.

With this agree two expressions of S. Ambrose, in which he applies his own instances, "True⁴ is the Flesh of Christ which was crucified, which was buried; truly therefore is it the Sacrament of that Flesh." That which he desires to establish is "the Presence of the true Body and Blood of Christ;" yet he does not identify that Presence with the outward sign, but says, "it is the Sacrament of His Flesh." And then, "Before⁵ the blessing of the Heavenly words, another *kind* is named; after consecration a Body *is signified*."

S. Ambrose closes his book with the same argument from the mystery of the Incarnation, as above nature and superseding nature, but in this place he applies it to Baptism :—

" Wherefore⁶ having received all these things [both Sacraments] let us know that we have been regenerated ; and let us not say ' *How* have we been regenerated ! Have we entered into our mother's womb and been re-born? I recognize not the wont of nature.' But here there is no order of nature, where there is the excellency of grace. Then too birth doth not always come from the use of nature. We confess that the Lord Christ was born of the Virgin, and we deny the order of nature. For Mary conceived not of man ; but received in her womb from the Holy Spirit, as Matthew says, ' That she was found having in the womb from the Holy Ghost.' If then the Holy Ghost

⁴ § 53.   ⁵ § 54.   ⁶ § 59.

coming upon the Virgin, operated the Conception, and fulfilled the office of generation, it is not to be doubted, that
coming upon the Font, or upon those who obtain Baptism,
He operates the truth of regeneration."

The like argument from the miracle of Cana is
used by a writer who in one sentence imitates S.
Ambrose, in illustration of the Resurrection of our
own bodies.

" Let[7] us enquire then what sign He worked, in order to
declare His Divinity to the people.   He is related, as His
first miracle, to have changed the water into wine.   A great
miracle, and enough for us to believe the Majesty of God.
For who would not marvel that the elements were translated into other than they were.   For no one can change
nature, but the Lord of nature.   It must be believed that
mortal man can be changed into immortality, in that the vile
substance was changed into the precious substance.   For
this sign contains the whole mystery of the Resurrection.
For water, worthless, pale, cold, changed into wine, precious,
red, fiery, signifies that the substance of man, mortal in condition, worthless through weakness, pale through death, shall,
in the Resurrection, be changed into glory, which is precious through eternity, glowing with glory, kindled with the
spirit of immortality.   If it is wonderful to have supplied
to guests wine which was lacking, how much more to have
repaired life which was exhausted !   And if it is glorious to
change water into wine, how much more glorious to change
sins into righteousness, and to temper manners rather than
wine ! "

The writer of another sermon in the same collection, comparing the miracles of the Exodus with
Baptism, says :—

[7] Serm. 8, de Epiph. i.   App. S. Ambr. ii. p. 401.

"To[s] them water is made solid, to us the flames are cooled, and *against* the wont of nature the sea is dried up by heat; by the fountain of Baptism, Hell is softened."

S. Ephrem compares the miracle of the Holy Eucharist with the miracles of the loaves, and of Cana; yet not as to any physical change, but as to the duration. Our Lord's word, then, produced natural food which satisfied men's wants, and passed away. By His word of consecration, He produced a Food which lasts through all times, in all lands, to all people, unto immortality. "The[v] bread which the First-born brake in the wilderness failed and passed away, though very good. He returned again and broke the New Bread, which ages and generations shall not waste away! The seven loaves, also, that He brake, failed; and the five loaves, too, that He multiplied, were consumed. The bread that He brake exceeded the world's needs; for the more it was divided, the more it multiplied exceedingly. With much wine also He filled the waterpots. They drew it out, yet it failed, though it was abundant. Though of the Cup that He gave the draught was small, very great was its strength, so that there is no stint thereto. A Cup is He that containeth all strong wines, and also a Mystery, in the midst of which He Himself is! The one Bread that He brake hath no bound, and the one Cup that He mingled hath no stint! The wheat that was sown, on the third day came up, and filled the

[s] Ib. Serm. 19, p. 415.
[v] On the Nativ. Rhythm 3, p. 19, Oxf. Tr., T. ii. p. 409, Syr.

Garner of Life.   The Spiritual Bread, as the Giver of it, quickeneth the spiritual spiritually, and he that receiveth it carnally receiveth it rashly to no profit. This Bread of grace let the spirit receive discerningly, as the medicine of life."

S. Augustine employs the same likeness of the change of the water into wine, to strengthen the hope of the Resurrection.

" What[1] is that flesh ? We ought not to despise it.   For what is it ? 'Grass;' but it will be gold.   Despise not the grass; it shall be changed into gold. For He who had power to change water into wine hath power to change grass into gold, man into an angel.   If He made man out of filth, shall He not of man make an Angel?   As mortal flesh is *changed into the body of an An gel*, so also lamentation shall be changed into praises."

An unknown writer of a sermon, once wrongly attributed to S. Augustine, speaks of the change of nature in the restoration of Lazarus to life :

" Whom[2] [Lazarus] Christ therefore raised to the life of nature, that He might *change nature*, and alter the course of life."

There is no question that the Sacraments are great miracles of the Grace of God.   His Almighty Spirit, through the poor element of water, worketh in us that good thing " which by nature we cannot have," our new birth of Him.   His Almighty Word makes present, under the form of every-day food, bread and wine, the Body and Blood of Christ.   His operation

[1] Serm. 45, fin. T. v. p. 225, Ben.
[2] S. Aug. App. Serm. 96, § 2, p. 171.

is above nature. He changes nature, by giving us,
through and under the form of visible creatures, the
Invisible Substance of the Sacrament, the Body and
Blood of Christ. We believe a change, but Sacramental, not physical; a superadded gift, not a destruction of the bodily element. We do not hesitate
to receive and believe God's miracles of Grace. We
demur only to a miracle, of which we believe that
God has not spoken in His Word as interpreted by
His Church.

I have already quoted Durandus [3], Scotus [4], Cardinal d'Ailly [5], as stating that our belief agrees with
Holy Scripture as well as the modern Roman : that
the words, "This is My Body," do not imply their
belief more than ours. I have also mentioned writers
who speak of this question as matter of "opinion."
Occam [6] implies that what is our belief is rejected
"by moderns chiefly." Suarez [7] even admits it to
have been " the old opinion."

Now what is once matter of opinion cannot but
remain matter of opinion ; even as what is matter of
faith must remain matter of faith. The Church de-
fines what is already matter of faith. It does not
make it so. Before it is so defined, individuals are
the less to blame, if they express themselves unguard-
edly. They would probably have explained themselves accurately, had they been asked. But, in this
case, divines deliberately declared that the Real

---

[3] Above, pp. 12—14.　　　　　　[4] pp. 21, 22.
[5] pp. 25—27.　　　[6] p. 16.　　　[7] p. 31.

Presence being a matter of faith, there were various *opinions* as to the remaining of the natural substances. They distinguished between what was matter of faith, and what was matter of opinion; and allowed that the belief, expressed by the English formula, contained all which was matter of faith.

Thus Cardinal Henri de Segusio, Bishop of Ostia (Hostiensis), A.D. 1262, mentions three opinions as lawful, and distinguishes from them the fourth as heretical. His authority is well known, and was frequently alleged. He lived after the fourth Lateran Council, at which Pope Innocent III. had published his decree.

"Concerning[*] the Body of Christ there are four opinions. One says that that substance which before was bread and wine, afterwards becomes the Body and Blood of Christ[*]. The second holds that the substance of bread and wine ceases to be, and yet that their accidents remain, *i.e.* taste and colour and weight, and that under these accidents is the Body of Christ, according to Vincentius; so that the bread should cease to be, and the Body of Christ take its place. If it is inquired what becomes of the substance of bread and wine, they say that it is resolved into its pre-existing matter, or is reduced to nothing, which He can do Who made all things of nothing. Some, however, find fault with this, saying, that if any one is clothed in another's garments, he is not therefore said to be changed or to pass into him whose garments he puts on. Yet this seems to be approved of[*]. The third says that the sub-

---

[*] In Decr. T. ii. f. 174, v. de celebr. missa, § ex eo autem.

[*] De consecr. Dist. ii. Panis est in altari [c. 55]. Quia corpus [c. 35].

[*] De summâ Trinitate et fide Cath. in Decr. Greg. I. 1, fin.

stance of bread and wine remains, and that the Body of
Christ is in the same place and under the same form[1]; and
any one of these opinions confesses that the true Body of
Christ is on the Altar, according to John[3]. The fourth says
that not the truth of the Body and Blood, but a shadow
only, form and figure are on the altar; and this is wholly
heretical; whence also it is rejected here, and again § in
quadam[4], and de consecr. § ego[5]."

Occam insists that the Real Presence *is* taught in
Holy Scripture, but not that the natural substances
do not remain, and repeats the tradition of difference
of " opinions."

" It[6] is to be observed, that although it is found expressed in the New Testament, that the Body of Christ,
under the form of bread, is to be taken by the faithful for a
memorial of the Passion of the Lord and for the remission
of their sins, yet it is not expressed there that the substance
of bread does not remain.   Whence also there were, of old,
different *opinions* on this. As the Master of the Sentences[7]
recites, and Hostiensis[8].   Whence they say that, concerning the conversion of the bread into the Body of Christ,
there were three *opinions*.   The third holds that the substance of the bread and wine remains there, and in the same
place, under the same form, is the Body of Christ."

Canus mentions among those things which appertain to Christian doctrine, but are not expressed in

[1] De consecr. Dist. ii. c. 42. Ego Berengarius.
[3] The author of the old gloss on the decretals.
[4] Decr. Greg. iii. 41. 8.
[5] De cons. Dist. ii. c. 42.
[6] De sacr. alt. c. 5.   [7] iv. d. xi.
[8] In summa extra de conse. et glo. de con. di. ii.   In sacra-
mentorum [de consecr. d. ii. c. 1] et glo. extra de celebr. miss.
cum Marthæ.

the sacred Scriptures, "the [9] conversion of the bread and wine into the Body and Blood of Christ."

G. Biel, adopting what was ruled by "the Roman Church," equally attests what was commonly held before : —

"The [1] bodily presence of the Body of Christ under the form of bread, on the enunciating of the sacramental form, has been shown. We must accordingly inquire by what change the Body of Christ begins to be in the Sacrament. In respect of which we must note, that although it is expressly delivered in Scripture that the Body of Christ is really contained under the form of bread and is received by the faithful (as was evident in the preceding lecture) ; yet how the Body of Christ is there, whether by conversion of ought into It, or whether, without conversion, the Body of Christ begins to exist along with the bread, the substance and accidents of the bread remaining, is not found expressed in the Canon of Scripture. Whence concerning this there have been from old time *diverse opinions*, as the Master rehearseth. Whence they enumerate three opinions which are mentioned in the gloss [2] ; and Innocent III. [3] rehearseth the same. One, that the substance of the bread remains together with the Body of Christ ; and that nothing, which pre-exists there before consecration, ceases to be."

Bassolis, a favourite pupil of Scotus (A.D. 1322), states clearly the grounds for the remaining of the natural substances, although adhering to the decision of the Roman Church, *i.e.* Innocent III.

[9] De trad. Ap. iii. 3, fund. 2.
[1] Expos. Can. Missæ Lect. 40, init.
[2] Decr. Greg. IX. iii. 41. 6.
[3] De Officio Miss. p. iii. cap. xviii.

" As[4] to the first, there is *one opinion* which *was common to many* : that the substance of bread remains in this Sacrament in very truth, and in that which it *is*; and that it is not changed, or transubstantiated, so as not to remain. For this is more consonant to the words of the Gospel. which calls that Sacrament or Eucharist ' Bread;' ' The[5] Bread which I will give is My Flesh for the life of the world,' and many other like words. Secondly, because, whereas the Gospel does force us to lay down, that in or under the Sacrament is the Body of Christ, our faith, whether as it is written in the Gospel or as it is unfolded in creeds, does not compel us to determine that the substance of bread does not remain. But then, as one following reason must not lay down things without necessity of reason[6], so one following faith must not lay down things without necessity of faith, and unless faith require it. Thirdly, since the authorities of the Fathers do not seem to limit to that belief, but rather to this, viz. that the substance of bread remains according to a mode which shall be mentioned hereafter. For both Dionysius and Damascene seem to say that this is a Sacrament of assumption, and that in this Sacrament the bread and wine are assumed by the Word; and consequently remain. Yet that is not common to all who hold that common conclusion ; as shall be said below. Fourthly, because when any thing is delivered to be believed absolutely, which may hold in many ways, and may in many ways be maintained, it ought not to be tied to the more difficult way of understanding it, without constraining cause, or reason, or authority. But now, the most difficult way of understanding, and the least intelligible way of maintaining that the Body of Christ is in or under the Sacrament, is the way which lays down that the substance of bread does not remain. For if the substance of bread does

[4] In iv. Dist. xi.　　　　[5] John vi.

[6] Phys. L. i.

not remain, it follows that the accident is there without the subject, and thereon follow innumerable difficulties. It also follows, that thus the Sacrament has not so properly the character of nourishment, as if the substance of bread remained. Similarly, too, it follows that the Sacrament has not so truly and properly the character of a sign, as if the substance of bread remained. For the *substance* of bread would signify more truly the *substance* of Christ's Body, than accidents [would signify] substance. Similarly, too, the thing contained, *i.e.* the true Body of Christ, can just as well be present there, together with the substance of bread remaining (as was said above). Since, then, all can be held, and more easily, with the substance of bread remaining than not remaining: and neither faith, nor the authority of the Church, nor the authority of the Fathers compels us to lay down that the substance of bread does not remain (as will appear more clearly below, in a more subtle mode of statement, under that common conclusion), we must lay down, and it is more convenient, that the substance of bread should remain, than that it should not remain. But under this conclusion are or were three distinct ways of laying it down. First, that the substance of bread remains, and is not changed in any way, but that the Body of Christ comes to be under the dimensions of bread, together with the substance of the bread, in fact, remaining in that way, in which two bodies can be in the same place at once: so does bread actually exist with the Body of Christ (as hath been said above), because this (speaking absolutely) is possible to God."

Cusanus, also, admits that some of the ancient theologians held, as we do, the accession of that which before was not present there, the Body and Blood of Christ, not the destruction of that which was there, the natural substance of the bread and wine.

" If' any one understand that bread is not transubstantiated, but is clothed upon with a nobler substance, as we
look to be clothed upon by the light of glory, while retaining
our substance (as certain old theologians are found to have
understood it, who said that not only bread, but also the
Body of Christ also is in the Sacrament), he must attend to
the force of the word."

It is even admitted by some, that the Fathers say
little of the Roman doctrine. Alph. de Castro
pleads in behalf of Indulgences, that

" Many* things are known to those who come after, of
which those old writers were wholly ignorant. For of the
Transubstantiation of bread into the Body of Christ, there
is *rare* mention in ancient writers."

To sum up this section, the grounds against pressing the physical character of any miracles to which
those Fathers appeal,—as if *this* physical character
of some of them, rather than the miraculous character generally, were the ground of the comparison,—
arise both out of the things compared, and the
things with which they are compared.

i. *The things with which they are compared*, for
they are compared with Baptism and regeneration, in
which there is no physical change; and yet the point
of comparison must apply to all; ii. *the things compared*, because the likenesses used are not by any
means exclusively derived from physical changes;
and yet, obviously, the argument must be drawn from
that which is common to all, *i. e.* their miraculous

' Excitat. L. vi. p. 522, e Serm. 4.
' Voc. Indulgentiæ quoted (with the above) Alb. p. 102.

supernatural character, not from that which belongs to a part only, whether physical or non-physical.

And yet it is clear, as has been urged by Roman divines themselves, that the Fathers themselves *did* mean to insist upon a change. Ysambert[9] contends against some who would make Transubstantiation a mere succession of our Lord's Body in the place of the bread and wine, that had the Fathers meant this, they would not have been so diligent in bringing instances of real changes.

Since, then, the Fathers intended to speak of a real change, and the instances which they adduce do not agree in any physical change, and there is, further, properly no physical *change* of one thing into another in the Holy Eucharist, the passages alleged from them do not harmonize with the Roman doctrine, but they do with ours. For all their instances harmonize in this one point—a power above nature put forth in things of nature; and there is a real, sacramental change, whereby what was before a mere element of this world becomes sacramentally the Body and Blood of Christ.

For although Roman writers adopted the teaching of the decree of Innocent III., first as most probable, then as certain, they were perplexed how to reconcile this belief with the meaning of the word "Transubstantiation." For, taking the words in their plain meaning, it was contrary to the truth which they themselves believed. For whereas, while our

[9] Ad q. 75, Disp. 8, art. 2.

Lord was in the flesh, His Human Body did receive accession from His bodily food, and the *substance* of the bread with which He condescended to be nourished, *was* changed into the *substance* of His Body, they believed and knew that, in that sense, "the substance of the bread is" *not* now "turned into His Body," nor "the substance of wine into His Blood." For His Body can receive no accession.

Hence arose a number of conflicting interpretations of Transubstantiation, the authors of the one interpretation rejecting and censuring the explanations of the others.

These explanations have been thus classified;

1. That Transubstantiation is "*no change*, *nor* the *production* of any thing, but only a sort of relation of order between the substance which cometh to an end, and that into which it is said to end."

This explanation is given by, at least, one very eminent among them, Vazquez, on the remarkable ground, that "*it* was [1] in no way opposed to true Philosophy, nor had, like the preceding explanations, any difficulties on this ground." He speaks of the explanations of others, as "needlessly [2] and incautiously exposing the mysteries of the faith to the ridicule of heretics, as bringing them into straits and difficulties, which can hardly be overcome in accordance with true philosophy."

---

[1] Disp. 181, c. xi. n. 116, which he claims to be, "without controversy, the opinion of the older Schoolmen."

[2] Ib. c. xii. 141.

Yet his explanation, too, is rejected by others[3] of no less name, (among them, Suarez and de Lugo), and one even says, "there[4] are not wanting those who think this opinion not only rash, but even unsafe as to matters of faith."

" 2. Transubstantiation[5] is the very action of consecration whereby the Body and Blood of Christ are *preserved* in their ancient being."

This explanation of Gabriel Biel (Vazquez says) "marvellously[6] pleased moderns;" and yet it is even strange that any one could ever think that a statement as to our Lord's Body and Blood, which would apply equally to their being in Heaven, was an explanation of the change in the Sacrament, or that a "*preservation* in their ancient being " could be represented as equivalent to Transubstantiation, *i. e.* the *change* of one substance into another.

It too was refuted by others[7].

" 3. Transubstantiation[8] is an action, whereby the Body and Blood of Christ detach from the bread or wine the accidents of the bread or wine, and maintain them apart from any subject, and are in a manner united with them, and so

[3] Albertin. (i. 23, p. 141) quotes Suarez (Disp. 50, sect. 3), Gamachæus (q. 75, c. 5), Mærat. (Disp. 12, sect. 1), de Lugo (Disp. 7, sect. 5), Ysambert (ad q. 75, Disp. 8, art. 1).

[4] Ysambert, l. c.

[5] G. Biel, Expos. Can. Miss. Lect. 40, and in iv. dist. xi. q. 1, art. 3, dub. i.

[6] l. c. c. v. n. 47.

[7] Alb. mentions Vazquez, Greg. de Valentia, Gamach., De Lugo, Ysambert.

[8] Henriquez de Euch. viii. 22, 25, and others.

may be said to be converted into the substances of bread and wine."

It was answered to this [9], that in this way it might be said that a thing could be transubstantiated into God.

" 4. Transubstantiation [1] is an action, whereby the Body of Christ is brought to be [adducitur] under the species of bread."

Suarez [2] says that the moderns, writing against heretics, readily embraced this opinion, as having a certain appearance of easiness.

Ysambert answers that this [as it does] destroys transubstantiation; that "a [3] thing may be brought into another, without any real change of any substance into it."

" 5. Transubstantiation is an action so efficacious [4] that it could produce the Body and Blood of Christ the Lord, which, however, it in fact does not produce, because they already exist."

To this it was answered that it contradicted the very idea of an action, and that the result of such Transubstantiation would be, not that the Body and Blood of Christ *would* be present, but that they *could* be present.

[9] By Mærat. disp. 13, s. 1.

[1] The opinion of " Scotus and many of the old Schoolmen, and subsequently of Alanus, Bellarmin, Becanus, a::d many others." (Alb. p. 142.)   " It was opposed by Suarez, Coninck (ad q. 75, art. 4, dub. 4). Gamachæus (ib. c. 5). Ysambert, l. c." (Id.)

[2] Disp. 50, s. 4, p. 601.   [3] l. c. art. 2.

[4] Dom. a Soto, answered by Suarez, Vazquez, De Valentia, Gamach., Ysamb.

" 6. Transubstantiation[5] is a real action, by which the Body of Christ is *produced* or *reproduced* under the species of bread."

De Valentia speaks of this as " foolish and altogether false." It was answered at great length by De Lugo[6]. A thing already existing cannot, in this sense, be *produced ;* else it would be the same as the " adduced " of Scotus. " *Reproduced* " is in fact the same as "produced ;" for, in its obvious sense of being " produced anew " after it had ceased to be, it is obvious that no one would use it of the Body of Christ.

7, 8. The seventh and eighth can hardly be made intelligible without a philosophical discussion. The 7th, held by De Palude, laid down that "Transubstantiation is an action which ends in the mode of Christ's Presence under the species;" to which Vazquez and Bellarmin objected that it was an accidental, not a substantial, change.

The 8th, that " Transubstantiation was not an action by which the Body of Christ was produced, but only an action whereby there was produced a certain substantial relation of the Body of Christ to the accidents of the bread. The opponents of the theory denied[7] (1) that there was any such, (2) that if there was, it would be any substantial change, *i. e.* any Transubstantiation.

---

[5] Held by Suarez, Coninck, Gamach., Ysamb.
[6] Disp. vii. s. 3, 4, also by Mæerat.
[7] See in Albert , p. 146.

9. "Transubstantiation is *not* [s] any *production* or any new *conservation* of the Body of Christ, but only a new introduction of the Body of Christ under these species;" and this introduction, it is said, "is *not* an action bringing (*adductive of*) the Body of Christ, *nor* simply *unitive*, but an action, constituting the Body of Christ under the species, implying at the same time the ending of the substance of the bread."

This explanation varies but slightly, in words, from those which preceded it. For, as was urged against de Lugo, an action which should "constitute" one object *in* another, is, in fact, no other than either to adduce or produce it there, both of which De Lugo himself rejects.

Now, all these explanations fail just in this one point, which it is the object of them all to reconcile. It is not a mere question of difficulty in explaining mysteries. For it is not in regard to the mystery itself,—the Presence of our Lord's Body and Blood, —that they fail. There is no difficulty in believing that our Lord, by a supernatural act of His Power and Love, causes His Body and Blood to be present under the sacramental symbols. And whether it be said, that the Body and Blood of Christ were present there as "preserved in their former way of being" (No. 2), or were brought to be present there (No.

---

[s] Maintained by De Lugo, " answered by Suarez and Vazquez, and at great length by Ysambert."

4); or (which is the same) were produced or re-produced there (*i. e.* came anew to be there, not having been there before) (No. 6); or were constituted there, or [sacramentally] united with it (No. 9); these would be only so many different ways of affirming that it *comes* to be present under the consecrated symbols, which before were but bare elements of this world.

But it is obvious, on the very surface, that none of those are any explanation whatever of Transubstantiation, *i. e.* of the conversion of one substance into another. They assume, by the way, the Roman statement, that the elements, in their natural substances, cease to be. This they assume to be contemporaneous with that which they speak of. But their positive statement, viz. that the Body and Blood of Christ come to be present there, and their negative statement, viz. that the substance of the bread and wine cease to be, have simply no connexion with one another. What they have to explain, is the passing or conversion or change of the natural substances of the bread and wine *into* the substances of the Body and Blood of Christ. What they *do* state, is the coming of the Body and Blood of Christ to be there. But, as they state, the one against the other, this is not "conversion." Roman Controversialists press against *us* the literal meaning of the word "conversion," that it is the turning or changing one thing into another, which thing has then a new being, and which new being is a new mode of existence to that which has been changed into it. But the same writers, when employed in explaining their own doctrine among themselves, abandon altogether *this* idea of conversion or change, and introduce one wholly different, about which they satisfy, each his own section, and none besides.

Now, as bearing on these passages of the Fathers, it is clear that the words which they press against us do not express their belief; for while they urge against us the words " conversion," and the like, they themselves, when explaining their meaning, speak of nothing less than " conversion." " Adduction," " production," " re-production," " conservation," " constitution," " unition " are *not* Transubstantiation, but are, on the contrary, opposed to it.

Had the Fathers meant the same as Pope Innocent III. they would have felt the difficulties which embarrass the recent explanations; and the very absence of any mention of those difficulties shows that they did not hold the belief which involves those difficulties. On the other hand, *our* belief of a sacramental change, by reason of the real Objective Presence, does satisfy the language of the Fathers, and corresponds with the whole of their teaching, that the elements remain, but that under them are present the Body and Blood of Christ.

NOTE S.

On pp. 47—66.

List of Ancient authorities from the Apostles' time to A. D. 451
*(the 4th General Council) on the Real Objective Presence
in the Holy Eucharist.*

THE following list has been made as full as I was
enabled to make it. Some passages, which would
otherwise find place in it, have been the subjects of
discussion in the previous pages. These will be
simply referred to, unless it should be expedient to
exhibit them in connexion with a larger context,
which might rather have distracted the attention
from the points for which they were quoted. On a
doctrine of such a primary importance as the Holy
Eucharist, the main passages of the Fathers must
long have been the common property of students of
the Fathers. Some have been supplied from the
originals recently published by Dom Pitra and Card.
Mai. It is remarkable that the single volume of
Dom Pitra should furnish three new early authorities.
So deeply impressed was the Christian faith, that evidence is furnished in all sorts of ways; from an inscription on a font, or a discussion on images. The
Festal Epistles of S. Athanasius, recovered by means
of the Syriac Translation, give large accession to the
evidence of the teaching of that great Father, whose
life was consecrated to maintain the true faith in
Trinity. His practical teaching, thus made known

to us, gave him more occasion to speak of the Holy Eucharist. Much additional evidence might probably yet be furnished from the Syriac and the Armenian. And although there is much confusion in some Catenæ, much may be gained from those which are carefully compiled. The Catena on S. John furnished the evidence of the Arian, Theodorus Heracliotes, and S. Didymus of Alexandria; that published by Dr. Cramer supplies those of Titus of Bostra and Apollinarius. Card. Mai intended, out of one Catena on the Proverbs, to supply additional evidence as to Origen, S. Didymus, and S. Hippolytus [1]. The testimony of Pope Damasus is derived from an epitaph on a martyr [2].

Asseman supplied witnesses almost unknown in the West, S. Isaac the Great and S. Maruthas. S. Maruthas' History of the Martyrs furnishes the earlier testimony of the martyrs under Sapor.

But additional evidence (however interesting, either from the character of the individuals or as an earnest of a boundless amount of testimony, if we had all the works which God has allowed to perish) is in fact superfluous. The following evidence that the belief in the Real Presence was part of the faith of Christians from the first, is more than enough to convince one who is willing to be convinced. If this convince not, neither would any other. There is no flaw, no doubt, I might almost say, no loophole, ex-

[1] Bibl. Patr. Nov. vi. 498, note.
[2] Baron. A.D. 384, n. 21.

cept that man always finds one, to escape what he is unwilling to accept.

The English Church certainly believed that there is a definite testimony to the faith, plainly recognizable in Christian antiquity, so that no one who wished to know the facts could fail to discern them. Once more, I may prefix to this evidence, the rule which that Convocation which gave us the Articles, recognized as its guide.

"They [3] (preachers) shall in the first place be careful never to teach any thing from the pulpit to be religiously held and believed by the people, but what is agreeable to the doctrine of the Old or New Testament, and *collected out of that very Doctrine by the Catholic Fathers and ancient Bishops.*"

1. S. IGNATIUS.

Consecrated Bp. of Antioch by S. Peter (Theod. Dial. i.), and so A.D. 43; martyr about A.D. 107.

"They [4] [the Docetæ, who denied that our Lord had a true Body] abstain from Eucharist and prayer, because they confess not that the Eucharist is the Flesh of our Saviour Jesus Christ, Which suffered for our sins, Which the Father in His mercy raised again. They, then, who speak against the Gifts, perish while disputing; good had it been for them to love It, that they might rise again!"

"Haste [5] ye then to partake of One Eucharist. For there is one Flesh of our Lord Jesus Christ, and one Cup for the uniting of His Blood, one Altar."

[3] Canon of the Convocation of 1571.
[4] Ep. ad Smyrn. n. 7.   [5] Ep. ad Phil. n. 4.

"Breaking[6] one bread, which is the medicine of immortality, the antidote that we should not die, but live in Jesus Christ for ever."

2. S. Justin Martyr.

Converted A.D. 133, Martyr A.D. 165. "A disciple of Apostles" (Ep. ad Diogn.); "A man not far from the Apostles, either in time or in virtue" (S. Method. in Phot. Cod. 247).

S. Justin speaks of the consecrated elements, as not being common *bread or* common *drink* (above, pp. 92; 144); *he believed that our Lord by " the fruit of the vine" meant real wine* (above, pp. 134—136); *and that the consecrated elements nourished* (p. 144).

"We[7], after we have thus washed him who is persuaded and has assented to our belief, lead him to those called brethren, where they are assembled, that we may with earnestness make common prayers for ourselves and the enlightened [baptized] person, and all others every where, that it may be vouchsafed to us, having learned the truth, to be found, in deeds good administrators and guardians of the commandments, that so we may be saved by an everlasting salvation. Having ceased from the prayers, we greet one another with a kiss; then bread and a cup of water and wine are brought to him who presideth over the brethren, and he, receiving them, sendeth up praise and glory to the Father of all, through the Name of the Son and the Holy Spirit, and maketh at much length an Eucharistic prayer

---

[6] Ep. ad Eph. n. 20.   [7] Apol. i. 65—67.

for having had these things vouchsafed to him. When he hath ended the prayer and thanksgiving, the whole people present join in with one voice, saying, Amen (but Amen is in Hebrew, 'so be it'). He who presideth, having made this prayer, and all the people having assented, those called among us 'deacons' give to each of those present to partake of the bread, and wine and water, over which thanksgiving has been made, and carry it to those not present.

"This Food is amongst us called Eucharist, whereof no one may partake, save he who believeth that what is taught by us is true, and hath been washed in that laver which is for the remission of sins and to regeneration, and liveth as Christ hath delivered; for we do not receive It as *common* bread or as *common* drink, but, in what way Jesus Christ our Saviour, being through the Word of God Incarnate, had both flesh and blood for our salvation, so also have we been taught that the Food, over which thanksgiving has been made by the prayer of the word which is from Him (from which [food] our blood and flesh are by transmutation nourished), is the Flesh and Blood of Him, the Incarnate Jesus. For the Apostles, in their records which are called the Gospels, have delivered that Jesus so commanded them, that He, having taken bread and given thanks, said, 'Do this in remembrance of Me. This is My Body;' and likewise, having taken the Cup and given thanks, He said, 'This is My Blood,' and gave it to them alone. Which also, wicked devils imitating, delivered to be observed in the mysteries of Mithra. For that bread and a cup of water are placed in the rites of the initiated, with certain words subjoined, ye either know, or can learn.

"Henceforward we ever remind one another of these things; and we, who have means, succour all who are needy, and are ever united to one another. And over all our oblations we bless the Creator of all things through His Son Jesus Christ, and through the Holy Ghost. And on the day called Sunday all who live in city or country meet together, and the memoirs of the Apostles or the writings of Prophets are read, as the time permits. Then, when the reader has closed, he who presides admonishes and exhorts in a sermon to the imitation of these noble deeds. Then we all rise together, and send up prayers: and, as we said before, when we have done prayer, bread is brought, and wine, and water: and he who presides utters prayers and thanksgivings to the best of his power, and the people join in with one voice, saying, Amen: and those things over which the Eucharistic prayer has been said, are distributed and received by each, and are sent to the absent by the Deacons."

3. S. Irenæus, Martyr.

"Lived near the time of the Apostles." (S. Basil de Sp. S. c. 29.) "I remember [*]," S. Irenæus himself says, "the

---

[*] Fragm. Ep. ad Florin. in Eus. H. E. v. 20, and Opp. p. 339, 40, ed. Ben.

things of that time [his youth with Polycarp] better than
recent things (for those which we learn from boyhood,
growing up with the soul, are in-oned with it); so that I
can even name the place, where the blessed Polycarp sat
and conversed, and his goings out, and his comings in, and
the character of his life, and the appearance of his body,
and his discourse with the multitude, and his familiar intercourse with John, which he used to tell us of, and with the
rest who had seen the Lord, and how he used to recall their
sayings, and concerning the Lord, what things he had heard
from them, and concerning His mighty works, and His
Teaching, as Polycarp, having received them from the eye-
witnesses of the Word of life, used to relate them, consonant in all things to the Scriptures. These things at that
time also, through the mercy of God towards me, I diligently heard, noting them down not on paper, but in my
heart, and ever through the grace of God I truly ruminate on them."

*S. Irenæus regarded the outward elements as sym-
bols* (see the passage above, p. 96), *understood our
Lord's words "the fruit of the vine," to mean real
wine, adapted to real flesh* (see above, p. 136), *believed
that the consecrated elements nourished* (see the passages, pp. 76 and 144).

Immediately before the passage quoted, p. 76,
S. Irenæus says :—

"This[9] oblation the Church alone offers pure to the
Creator, offering it to Him with thanksgiving from
His creation. But the Jews do not offer; for their
hands are full of blood; for they have not received
the Word, Which is offered to God. But neither

---

[9] iv. 18, 4.

do all the synagogues of the heretics. For some, saying that there is another Father besides the Creator, offering to Him the things of our creation, imply that He is covetous of what is another's, and greedy of what is not His. But they who say that our creation is the result of defection, ignorance and passion [1], offering the fruits of ignorance, passion and defection, sin against their Father, dishonouring Him rather than giving Him thanks. But how shall they know certainly that that bread, over which thanks are given, is the Body of their Lord, and that the Cup is the Cup of His Blood, if they do not acknowledge Him as the Son of the Creator of the world, *i. e.* His Word, through Which wood yields fruit, and fountains flow, and the earth yieldeth first the blade, then the ear, then the full corn in the ear [2]?

"But [3] counselling also His disciples, to offer to God firstfruits from His creatures, not as though He needed ought, but that they might not be unfruitful nor ungrateful, He took that which of His creation is bread, and gave thanks, saying, 'This is My Body.' And likewise the Cup, which is of that our creation, He confessed to be His Blood, and taught that it is the new Oblation of the New Testament, of which among the twelve Prophets, Malachi thus presignified: 'I have no pleasure in you, saith the Lord of

---

[1] Gnostic speculations.

[2] From which we have severally the wine, water, bread of the Holy Eucharist.

[3] iv. 17, 5.

Hosts, neither will I receive an offering at your hands. For from the rising of the sun unto the going down thereof My Name shall be great among the heathen, and in every place incense shall be offered unto My Name, and a pure offering; for My Name shall be great among the heathen, saith the Lord of Hosts;' most clearly signifying by these words, that the former people indeed shall cease to offer to God; but in every place sacrifice shall be offered to Him, and that pure ; and His Name shall be glorified among the heathen."

" If [4] the Lord belonged to another Father, how was it just that taking bread, of this our creation, He confessed that it was His Own Body [5], and He affirmed that the mingled drink [6] of the cup was His own Blood."

" They [7] [the Ebionites] reject the commixture of the heavenly cup, and will that there should only be water of this world [8]; not receiving God to their commixture, but persevering in Adam who was overcome, and cast out of Paradise; not contemplating that, as from the beginning of our formation in Adam, that which was from God, the breath of life, united to the clay, animated the man, and made

[4] iv. 33, 2. [5] See above, p. 258.

[6] " Temperamentum calicis," as, in another place, " mixtum calicem," " mingled cup," (v. 11, 3,) *i. e.* wine mingled with water.

[7] v. 1, 3, p. 293.

[8] The Ebionites used water only in their Eucharist. S. Epiph. Hær. 21, n. 6.

Y 2

him a rational animal; so, at the end, the Word of the Father, and the Spirit of God, united to the ancient substance of the formation of Adam, made him a living and perfect man, with the capacity of receiving the perfect Father; that as in the father of our flesh we all die, so in the spiritual Father we may all be made alive."

"But [9] altogether vain are they, who despise the whole dispensation of God, and deny the salvation of the flesh, and despise its regeneration, saying that it is not capable of incorruption. But if it will not be saved, in truth the Lord hath not redeemed us by His Blood; nor is the cup of the Eucharist the communication of His Blood, nor the bread which we break the communication of His Body. For blood is not, save of veins and flesh and of the rest of human substance, in which the Word of God was truly made. By His Blood He redeemed us, as also His Apostle saith: 'In Whom we have redemption through His Blood, even the remission of sins.'"

"For [1] the Greeks seizing the slaves of Christian Catechumens, then torturing them that so they might learn from them some secret thing respecting the Christians, these slaves, not being able to speak what should please those who were torturing them, except as far as they had heard from their masters, that the Divine Communion is the Body and Blood

[9] v. 2, 2.

[1] Fragm. ap. Œcumen. ad i. Pet. iii. p. 498. Massuet. p. 343.

of Christ—they, supposing that it was really flesh and blood, told this to those who inquired. But they, immediately on learning that this was a sacred rite of the Christians, both sent word of this to the other Greeks, and tried to compel by torture the martyrs Sanctus and Blandina to confess it. To whom Blandina well and courageously answered, 'How,' said she, 'could they endure such things, who for religious discipline abstain even from lawful meats?'"

Heretics earlier than S. Irenæus.—Marcus, about A. D. 160, in his wild and blasphemous parody of the Holy Eucharist, strangely attests the doctrine which he mimicked.

"He[1] pretending to consecrate, as an Eucharist, a drink mingled with wine, and prolonging at great length the words of invocation, makes it appear purple and red, so that it might be thought that the Grace from those above the universe through his Invocation, distils Its own blood into that Chalice, and that those present may have an exceeding desire to taste of that drink, that on them too the Grace, extolled by this magician, may shower down. Again, having given mixed drink to the women, he commands them to consecrate, himself standing by them. And this being done, he, bringing another cup, much larger than that which the deceived woman had consecrated, and having emptied from the smaller

[1] S. Iren. i. 13, 2.

one, which was consecrated by the woman, into that prepared by himself, at the same time saying thus, 'The Grace which is before all things, incomprehensible and unspeakable, fulfil thine inner man, and make to abound in thee knowledge of herself, sowing the grain of mustard seed in good ground;' and having said thus, and having maddened the miserable woman, he appeared a worker of miracles, the great cup being filled from the small one, so as even to run over."

By his rude and coarse copy, he attests the prevailing belief of the real Presence of our Lord's Blood in the Cup, and that, by virtue of the consecration.

Heracleon, again, says, of the Passover, "This[3] is the great feast. For it was a type of the Passion of the Saviour, when not only was the Lamb slain, but, being eaten, gave rest."

Even the Ophites, who worshipped the serpent as Christ, "introduced[4] him to bless their Eucharist."

4. S. MELITO [presented his defence of the Christians to Antoninus, A.D. 170].

The Evidence of this great man (of whom it is said that "his[5] whole conversation was in the Holy Ghost," and who in his own times was accounted a Prophet[6]), is in his Clavis, in which he explains the

---

[3] Ap. Orig. in Jo. T. x. § 14, iv. 179, 180, ed. de la Rue.

[4] Adv. omn. Hær. App. Tertull. de Præscript. c. 47, p. 250, ed. Rig.   [5] Polycr. in Eus. H. E. v. 24.

[6] Tertullian in S. Jerome de Scriptt. c. 24.

spiritual meaning of words used in Holy Scripture, and the Eucharistic parable mentioned by Papias, which so many, following Eusebius, have misinterpreted. S. Melito understood the 6th Chapter of S. John of the Holy Eucharist. He says, " WINE ', the Blood of Christ, in the Gospel. 'He who eateth My Flesh and drinketh My Blood.'"

The only ground on which "wine" could be interpreted of the Blood of Christ is, that in the Holy Eucharist, by virtue of the consecration, we "receive, under the form of wine, the Blood of Christ" (Homilies). The passage of S. John, in which "wine" is not named, can only prove that "wine" stands for "the Blood of Christ," if it is assumed as certain that our Lord in that place was speaking, by anticipation, of the Sacrament which He purposed to ordain.

5. TATIAN, A.D. 172; or if AMMONIUS, A.D. 220.

" And [8] then, having taken bread, and afterwards the cup of wine, He bare witness that it was His Body and Blood, and bade them eat and drink, for that it was a memorial of His coming Suffering and Death."

6. S. CLEMENT OF ALEXANDRIA, A.D. 192.

He had learnt of those who had themselves learnt of the Apostles. See in Eus. H. E. v. 12, comp. vi. 13.

---

[7] This extract is published in the Spicil. Solesm. p. vi. ed. Pitra.

[8] Harmon. iv. Evang. Bibl. Patr. ii. P. 2, p. 210.

On the Real Presence and on the nourishment of the body through the natural elements, and on the two-fold nature of the Holy Eucharist, see above, pp. 146, 147. *S. Clement calls wine the symbol of the Blood of Christ* (see p. 97), *calls the consecrated elements "blood of the grape," and uses the words "this fruit of the vine" in proof that our Lord, as Man, drank wine* (see pp. 136, 137).

"One [9] is the Father of all. One also the Word of all; and the Holy Spirit, One and the Same every where. And one only virgin mother is formed. I would call her, Church. This mother alone had not milk, because she alone never became a woman; but she is at once a virgin and a mother; undefiled, as a virgin; full of love, as a mother; and calling her children to her, she nurses them with holy milk, the Infant Word. Therefore she had not milk; because this her own beautiful Child was milk, the Body of Christ, nourishing for the Word that new progeny, with whom the Lord Himself travailed with bodily pang, whom the Lord Himself swaddled with Precious Blood. O holy Birth! O holy swaddling bands! The Word is all to the infant, Father and Mother, Instructor and Nourisher. 'Eat ye,' He saith, ' My Flesh, and drink My Blood.' This Food from Himself the Lord provideth for us, and offereth Flesh and poureth out Blood, and nothing is wanting to the children's growth. O marvellous Mystery! He bids us put off from us the old corruption of the

[9] Pædag. i. 6, p. 123.

flesh, as also the old food, and partaking of another new nourishment, that of Christ, receiving Him as far as possible [1], to lay Him up in ourselves and place the Saviour in our breast, that we may correct the passions of our flesh."

" But [2] that rich and fat and abundant and all-sufficing Food and delight of the Blessed, ' the fatted Calf,' is sacrificed, Who again is also called a Lamb; not simply, lest any one should think it little, but the great and the very greatest. For not little is that Lamb of God Who taketh away the sins of the world, Who was led as a lamb to the slaughter; that Sacrifice full of marrow, of which, according to the gracious law, all the fat was the Lord's (for [3] every sacrifice which is dedicated is offered wholly unto the Lord), so well nourished and exceedingly enlarged, as to suffice for all things, and be distributed, and fill those who eat Him and are satiated with Him; Who is both Bread and Flesh, and giveth Himself, being both, to us to eat. To the sons then

[1] I have rendered εἰ δυνατὸν, " as far as possible;" the meaning being, apparently, that we receive Christ in ourselves, Who, as God, filleth heaven and earth, and therefore cannot be received wholly.

[2] Fragm. S. Clem. Alex. e Macarii Chrysoceph. orat. xi. in Luc. fin. p. 1018, ed. Pott.

[3] The text in the Barocci MS. ccxi. fol. 145, b. (from which Grabe transcribed the fragment) is, (as the Rev. H. O. Coxe, of the Bodleian, has kindly ascertained for me,) πᾶς γὰρ ὁ ἀνακείμενος καὶ ἀναθυόμενος [not, as in Potter, ἀνατεθειμένος] τῷ Κυρίῳ. Above it ought, probably, to be κατὰ τὸν ἱερὸν νόμον, " according to the sacred law," but the text has ἱλαρόν.

who approach, the Father giveth the Calf and slayeth It, and It is eaten; but those who approach not, He chaseth away and disinheriteth. But those who eat are so instrengthened, and are strong with such might from the life-giving Food within them, that through It they are valiant against the enemy, and armed, as it were, with the horns of a bull."

" Hear[4] on the other hand the Saviour: 'I regenerated thee, who wast miserably born by the world unto death. I freed, I healed, I redeemed thee; I will show thee the Face of thy good Father God; call no man thy father upon the earth; let the dead bury their dead, but do thou follow Me; for I will lead thee back to the rest of unspeakable and unceasing good things, 'which eye hath not seen, nor ear heard, neither hath entered into the heart of man,' 'into which the angels desire to look,' and see what 'good things God hath prepared for' His Saints and the children 'who love Him.' I am thy Nourisher, Who give thee Myself as Bread, of Which whoso tasteth, no more tasteth death, and Who daily give thee the drink of immortality. I am thy Teacher in heavenly instruction; for thy sake I suffered unto death, and for thee I paid to the uttermost the penalty of death, which thou owedst for thy previous sins and unbelief against God.'

" Of[5] these wounds Jesus is the only healer, wholly

---

[4] Quis dives salvetur, § 23, tom. ii. p. 948. Ed. Potter.
[5] Ib. § 29, p. 952.

and utterly uprooting the passions; not, as the law, removing the bare offshoots, the fruits of the evil plants, but laying the axe of Himself to the roots of evil.   He it is, Who, having poured out the wine and Blood of the vine of David upon our wounded souls, bringeth to them oil from the bowels of the Spirit, and giveth it freely."

6 b. *Heretic contemporary with S. Clement of Alexandria—Theodotus.*   See his testimony above, pp. 177, 178.

7. TERTULLIAN.

His earliest treatise is probably the de Pallio, A.D. 196, written upon his conversion; his lapse into Montanism probably A.D. 201.   See Pref. to his Treatises, p. ii. Oxf. Tr. I know not on what ground Cave (sub tit. A.D. 192) places his conversion A.D. 185; his ordination, A.D. 192.

Passages have already been quoted from him in which he argues from the Holy Eucharist, as a real material substance, to the truth of our Lord's human nature (above, p. 77); *appeals thereon to the senses* (pp. 80, 81); *speaks of the outward elements as a figure* (p. 97); *and of the Blood of Christ being consecrated in wine* (Sermon, p. 40, and above, p. 133).

" We [6] feel pained if any of the wine, or even of our bread, be spilled upon the ground."

" To [7] give thy testimony for the gladiator out of the mouth with which thou hast uttered Amen to *That Holy Thing?* "

[6] De Cor. § 3, p. 164, O. T.
[7] De Spect. § 25, p. 214.

"The [8] zeal of Faith might speak on this head all the day long, mourning that the Christian should come from the idols into the Church, from the work-shop of the enemy into the house of God; that he should raise to God the Father hands that are the mothers of idols; should worship Him with those hands which are themselves worshipped out of the Church in enmity to God; that he should approach those hands to the Body of the Lord, which bestowed bodies on dæmons. Nor is this enough. It were a small matter that they should receive from other hands That Which they defile, but they themselves also deliver to others That Which they have defiled. Makers of idols are chosen into the ministry of the Church. Horrid sin! The Jews laid violent hands but once upon Christ; these every day assault His Body. O, hands worthy of being cut off! Let them now consider whether it were said only in a figure, 'If thine hand offend thee, cut it off.' What hands ought more to be cut off than those by which the Body of the Lord is offended?"

"We [9] may rather understand spiritually, GIVE US THIS DAY OUR DAILY BREAD. For Christ is our Bread, because Christ is life, and bread is life. 'I am,' saith He, 'the Bread of life,' and a little above, 'The Bread is the Word of the living God, which cometh down from Heaven.' Then again, because *in* the Bread is understood His Body: 'This is My Body.'

[8] De Idol. § 8, p. 228, O. T.
[9] De Orat. § 6, pp. 303, 304.

Wherefore, in praying for 'daily bread,' we pray to be perpetually in Christ, and undivided from His Body."

"In[1] like manner, also, most think that on the days of stations they ought not to attend the prayers at the sacrifices, because, when the Body of the Lord hath been received, the station must be broken up. Doth, then, the Eucharist break up a service devoted to God? Doth it not the more bind to God? Will not thy station be the more solemn, if thou standest also at the altar of God? When the Body of the Lord hath been received and reserved, both are saved, both the partaking of the sacrifice and the fulfilment of the service."

"The[2] flesh is washed, that the soul may be cleansed. The flesh is anointed, that the soul may be consecrated. The flesh is sealed, that the soul too may be fortified. The flesh is overshadowed by the laying on of hands, that the soul too may be illumined by the Spirit. The flesh feeds on the Body and Blood of Christ, that the soul, too, may be fattened from God. They cannot then be separated in reward, whom labour has joined together."

"He[3] [the Heathen convert] remembers God His Father; he returns to Him, being appeased; he recovers his former raiment, that state which Adam, by transgression, had lost. He receives also, then, first,

---

[1] Ib. § 19, p. 312, O. T.
[2] De Res. Carn. c. 8, pp. 384, 5, Rig.
[3] De Pudic. c. 9, p. 725, Rig.

the ring, wherewith he, having been interrogated [4], seals his covenant of faith, and so, henceforth, is fed with the fatness of the Lord's Body, even the Eucharist [5]."

" Will [6] not thy husband know what thou tastest in secret before all food? and if he knoweth it to be bread, will he not believe it to be that which is reported [7]?"

I have stated already [8] how Tertullian's argument against the Gnostics [9] might have been retorted against him, had he not believed the outward substance to remain. The sequel will be clearer if the passage already quoted is prefixed.

" Having declared, 'With desire have I desired to eat this Passover,' as His own (for it were unworthy that God should desire any thing not His own), He made the bread which He took and distributed to His disciples that His own Body, saying, 'This is My Body,' *i.e.* the figure of My Body. But it would not be a figure, unless His Body were a true Body. But an empty thing, as a phantom is, can admit of no figure of itself. Or if He pretended that bread was His Body, because He had in truth no Body, He ought then to have given Bread for us. It belonged to the vanity of Marcion, that bread should

---

[4] *i. e.* in the Baptismal interrogations.

[5] Opimitate Dominici Corporis vescitur, Eucharistia scilicet.

[6] Ad Ux. ii. 5, p. 427, O. T.

[7] An allusion to the calumnies against Christians. See note on Tert. Apol. c. 2, p. 5, and Note g, and c. 7.

[8] P. 77 sqq.   [9] Adv. Marc. iv. 40.

be crucified. But why doth He call His Body bread, and not rather a pompion, which Marcion had instead of a heart? not understanding that that was an ancient figure of the Body of Christ, saying through Jeremiah, 'They have devised devices against Me, saying, Let us cast wood to His bread,' that is, the cross on His Body. Therefore the Enlightener of the things of old hath plainly shown what He meant bread to signify, calling His Body bread. So too in the mention of the Cup, He, when establishing the testament sealed with His Blood, confirmed the substantiality of His Body. For there cannot be blood of any body, save flesh. For if some unfleshly quality of a body be opposed to us, surely, unless fleshly, it will not have blood. Thus the proof of a body consisteth in the testimony as to flesh; the proof of flesh in the testimony as to blood. But that you may recognize the ancient figure of blood in wine, Esaias will aid. 'Who is This,' saith he, 'that cometh from Edom, with dyed garments from Bozrah? He that is glorious in apparel, wine-stained, with might. Wherefore art Thou red in Thine apparel, and Thy garments like him that treadeth in the winefat?' For the Spirit of Prophecy, already, as it were, contemplating the Lord coming to His Passion (*i. e.* clothed in flesh, in that He suffered in it), describes, under the redness of His apparel, the raiment of His Flesh all bloody, by the force of His Passion trodden down and squeezed out, as in a winepress; because from the redness of the wine men go down thence as though blood-stained. Much more clearly did Genesis, in the Blessing of Judah, from whose tribe the descent of Christ, after the Flesh, was to proceed, delineate Christ even then in Judah. 'He shall wash,' saith he, 'His Garments in wine, and His Clothes in the blood of grapes.' So now too He *hath consecrated His Blood in wine*, Who then figured forth wine in Blood."

7 b. I may place here the ancient *author of the Carmina adversus Marcionem.* He too, following Tertullian, is arguing from the Holy Eucharist for the truth of Christ's Body.

"Deeds [1] will prove that He was blended God and Man, nor will the world supply few seals thereof [of this faith]. Was not then faith made manifest? were not all things fixed? Celebrating the Passover the day before He suffered, He, delivering to His disciples the Memorial of that deed, said of the bread received, and juice of the vine also, 'This is My Body and My Blood, which is shed for you,' which He bade ever after to be done. From what creation suppose ye the Bread and Wine are, and must be confessed to be, His Body and Blood? Proved not He Himself the Maker of the world by deeds? And at the same time that He bare a Body of Flesh and Blood?"

[1] L. 5, ap. Tertull. p. 806, col. 2, ed. Rig.

8. *Inscription at Autun*, close of second century.

The inscription of Autun was brought together in 1839, from the fragments of a decayed wall in an ancient and abandoned cemetery. The inscription, being Greek, belongs to the Greek period of the Church at Autun. The character on the stone is said to be Asiatic; the flow of the verses is certainly very elegant, though, of course, $\theta \acute{a} \lambda \pi \epsilon \breve{o} \ \psi \upsilon \chi \grave{\eta} \nu$ would not be classical. The Greek period of the Gallican Church falls apparently in the latter part of the second century, between the coming of Pothinus and S. Irenæus, and the desolation of the Church, A.D. 202.

The six first lines of the inscription are nearly perfect. The words which are broken off do not affect the tenour of the meaning. The inscription, thus far, is—

ΙΧΘΥΟC.Ο . . . . ΙΟΝ . ΓΕΝΟC.ΗΤΟΡΙCΕΜΝ̇
ΧΡΗCΕ.ΛΑΒѠ . . . . . . Ν.ΑΜΒΡΟΤΟΝΕΝΒΡΟΤΕΟΙs
ΘΕCΠΕCΙѠΝ ΥΔΑΤѠΝ ΤΗΝ CΗΝΦΙΛΕΘΑλΠΕΟΨΥΧην
ΥΔΑCΙΝΑΕΝΑΟΙC ΠΛΟΥΤΟΔΟΤΟΥCΟΦΙΗC
CѠΤΗΡΟC ΑΓΙѠΝ ΜεΛΙΗΔΕΑΛαΜΒαΝ . . . .
ΕCΘΙΕΠΙΝ . . . . ΝΙΧΘΥΝ ΕΧѠΝΠΑΛΑΜΑΙC.

Of six Greek critics, all, in the first verse, agree in restoring OYPANIOY, of which the O still remains; then, two supply AΓION, four, more probably, ΘEION (the ION still remaining). In the second line, two supply ZΩHN, three, more probably, ΠHΓHN. In the fifth line, there seems no doubt that BPΩΣIN is to be supplied; in the sixth, ΔYOIN or TEAIN. I have given the doubtful readings.

There are also slight variations as to the construction. I have rendered the whole, without doubt, as addressed to the Christian.

"Divine race of the Heavenly ΙΧΘΥΣ', a holy heart

Put forth, receiving among mortals immortal $\dfrac{\text{life}}{\text{fount}}$

Of divine waters: nourish, beloved, thy soul
With the ever-flowing waters of enriching wisdom:
Receive the honey-sweet Food of the holy things of the Saviour;

Eat, drink; having ΙΧΘΥΣ in $\dfrac{\text{thy}}{\text{two}}$ hands."

In the fifth verse, I have taken ἀγίων in its liturgical use, as in the well-known formula ἅγια τοῖς ἁγίοις, "sancta sanctis," whereas others have rendered it (there can be no question, wrongly) "the Saviour of the holy."

9. S. Hippolytus,

Bp. of Portus, and a disciple of S. Irenæus (Photius, Cod. 121), about A.D. 220.

' The well-known anagram, for ΙΗΣΟΥΣ ΧΡΙΣΤΟΣ ΘΕΟΥ ΥΙΟΣ ΣΩΤΙΙΡ "Jesus Christ, Son of God, Saviour:" see Tertullian, de Bapt. i. p. 256, O.T.; and S. Aug. Conf. xiii. 21, p. 296, O.T., and note. It occurs in a hymn ascribed to S. Clement of Alexandria, Ἰχθῦς ἀγνούς; T. i. p. 312. Ed. Pot. Vallars on S. Jerome, Ep. 7, ad Chrom. (T. i. p. 18), mentions a very choice gem where our Lord is represented as a fisherman, with this inscription. S. Clement mentions a dove, a *fish*, a ship at full sail, a lyre, or an anchor, as legitimate emblems for Christian rings. Pædag. iii. 11, p. 106. Ed. Sylb. See also S. Aug. de Civ. Dei 18, 23. S. Paulinus, Ep. 13, ad Pamm.

Since the above has been in type, Dr. Scott, the Master of Balliol, has suggested to me in the second line, χρή σε λαβεῖν, ΕΙ for Ω, and ΑΜΦΟΙΝ in the sixth line.

"She [3] [Divine Wisdom] mingled her wine in the cup, *i. e.* the Saviour, uniting His Own Godhead with the flesh, as pure wine, in the Virgin, was born of her without confusion, God and Man. 'And she prepared her Table;' the Knowledge of the Holy Trinity promised, and His precious and pure Body and Blood, which daily at the Mystical and Divine Table are consecrated, being sacrificed in remembrance of that ever-to-be-remembered and first Table of the Divine and Mystical Supper. 'She sent forth her servants.' Wisdom, that is, Christ, calling with a sublime preaching, 'Whoso is simple, let him turn to Me,' *i. e.* sending forth the holy Apostles, who traversed the whole world and called the nations to the Knowledge of Him by their truly sublime and Divine preaching. But she said, 'those who want understanding,' *i. e.* those who had not yet obtained the power of the Holy Ghost, 'Come, eat of My Bread, and drink of the wine which I have mingled for you,' *i. e.* He gave us His Divine Flesh and His Precious Blood to eat and to drink for the remission of sins."

"'His [4] Bread is rich, and He will give dainties to Kings;' we understand this as a type of our calling, for 'rich' means excellent. And whose Bread is more excellent than ours? for the Lord Himself is our

---

[3] In Prov. ix. 1, i. 282, ed. Fabric.
[4] Id. Fragm. in Gen. ed. Fabr. ii. 28.

Bread, as He Himself too saith: 'I am the Bread of Life.' But who else shall give food to Kings than our Lord Jesus Christ, not only to those who believe of the Gentiles, but to those of the circumcision also, who have the empire of faith, *i.e.* Fathers and Patriarchs and Prophets, and all who believe in His Name and in His Passion."

10. ORIGEN, A.D. 230.

For Origen's belief that the natural substance remains and nourishes, see the passage above, pp. 147 —149, *and the term* " *symbolical body,*" p. 149. *He should have been added also to those who understood our Lord, after the consecration of the Cup, to speak of what He had consecrated, as being in its natural substance, wine. For Origen uses our Lord's words, as they occur in S. Matthew and S. Mark, in proof that, whereas our Lord had heretofore drank wine, now He should cease to do so.*

" We [5] inquire then how our Lord and Saviour, Who is the true High Priest, with His disciples, who are true priests, before He approacheth the Altar of God, drinketh wine, but when He had begun to approach, He drinketh not. The Saviour had come into this world that, for our sins, He might offer His Flesh a Sacrifice to God. Before He offered this, He drank wine, in the interval of the dispensations. In short, He was called 'a Man gluttonous, and a winebibber, a Friend of publicans

[5] In Lev. Hom. vii. T. ii. p. 220.

and sinners.' But when the time of His Cross came, and He was about to approach to the Altar, to offer there the Sacrifice of His Flesh, 'He took the Cup, and blessed and gave to His disciples, saying, Take, drink ye of it.' Drink ye, saith He, who are not now about to approach the Altar. But Himself, as being about to approach the Altar, says of Himself, 'Verily I say unto you, I will no more drink of this fruit of the vine, until I drink it new with you in the kingdom of My Father.'"

"He[6] who keepeth in mind that Christ our Passover hath been sacrificed for us, and that we must feast, eating the Flesh of the Word, at all times keepeth the Passover, passing ever in thought and in every word and deed from the things of this life to God, and hastening to His City."

"Let[7] Celsus, as being ignorant of God, render his thank-offerings to devils; but we, rendering thanks (εὐχαριστοῦντες) to the Creator of the universe, eat the Bread, offered with thanksgiving (εὐχαριστίας) and prayer over the things offered, which (bread) becometh, for the prayer's sake, a certain Holy Body, which halloweth those who use the same with a sound purpose."

"Ye[8] who are wont to be present at the Divine Mysteries, know how, when ye receive the Body of the Lord, ye keep It with all care and veneration,

[6] Cont. Cels 8, 22, p. 759, ed. De la Rue.
[7] Ib. c. 33, p. 766.   [8] In Exod. Hom. xiii. § 3, p. 176.

lest any particle of It should fall, lest any of the consecrated Gift should escape you. For ye believe yourselves guilty (and ye believe rightly) if any thereof fall through negligence; but if ye use so great caution, and rightly use it, in preserving His Body, how do ye think it a less guilt to have neglected the word of God than His Body?"

"But[9] thou, who hast come to Christ, the true High Priest, Who, by His own Blood, hath made God propitious to thee, and reconciled thee to the Father, stop not at the Blood of the Flesh, but learn rather the Blood of the Word, and hear Himself saying to thee, 'This is My Blood which is shed for you for the remission of sins.' He who is imbued with the mysteries knoweth the Flesh and Blood of the Word of God."

"When[1] thou receivest the mystical bread, eat it in a clean place; *i.e.* receive not the Sacraments of the Lord's Body in a soul defiled and polluted by sins. 'For whosoever eateth this bread and drinketh this cup unworthily, shall be guilty of the Body and Blood of the Lord.'"

"Aforetime[9] in similitude was a Baptism in the cloud and in the sea; now, in reality, is regeneration in water and the Holy Spirit. Then, in similitude, was manna food; now, in reality, is the Flesh of the Word of God true Food, as He Himself also saith,

[9] Id. in Levit. Hom. ix. § 10.
[1] Ib. Hom. xiii. § 5 fin. T. ii. p. 257.
[9] Id. in Num. Hom. vii. § 2, p. 290.

'My Flesh is meat indeed, and My Blood is drink indeed.'"

"Who[3] is that people who are accustomed to drink blood? These were the things, which when in the Gospel also, those of the Jews who followed the Lord heard, they were offended, and said: 'Who can eat flesh and drink blood?' But the Christian people, the faithful people, heareth these things and embraceth them, and followeth Him Who saith: 'Except ye eat My Flesh and drink My Blood, ye have no life in you: for My Flesh is Meat indeed, and My Blood is Drink indeed.' And in truth He Who said these things was wounded for men; for 'He was wounded for our sins,' as Esaias saith. But we are said to drink the Blood of Christ not only[4] in the way of Sacraments, but also when we receive His Word, in which is life, as also Himself saith: 'The words which I speak unto you, they are spirit and they are life.'"

"But[5] that thou mayest more clearly understand that these things are written of our people, who are confederated in the Sacraments of Christ, hear how in other places also Moses declares the like, saying: 'Butter of kine, and milk of sheep, with fat of lambs, and rams of the breed of Bashan, and goats, with the fat of kidneys of wheat; and wine they shall drink,

---

[3] Hom. xvi. in Num. § 8, T. ii. p. 334.

[4] As we say, not only sacramentally but spiritually.

[5] Ibid.

the blood of the grape.' And this then which is called 'the blood of the grape,' is Blood of that grape which springs of that Vine, whereof the Saviour saith: 'I am the true Vine,' the disciples 'the branches,' the Father 'the Husbandman,' Who purgeth them, that they may bring forth very much fruit. Thou, then, art the true people of Israel, which canst drink blood, and canst eat the Flesh of the Word of God and drink His Blood, and canst suck up the Blood of that grape which is of the true vine, and of those branches which the Father purgeth."

"But[6] when thou seest Gentiles coming in to the faith, Churches built, Altars, not sprinkled with blood of cattle, but consecrated with the precious Blood of Christ: when thou seest Priests and Levites ministering, not the blood of bulls and of goats, but the Word of God through the grace of the Holy Ghost, then say that Jesus succeeded Moses and obtained the princedom, not Jesus the son of Nun, but Jesus the Son of God."

"Therefore[7] further on in the Psalm, hinting at the mystical food, as it seems, he said: 'Taste, and see that the Lord is good.' Perchance exhorting to taste Christ Himself, he hinted by these words at

[6] In Jos. Hom. xi. T. ii. p. 400.
[7] Id. Sel. in Psalm. T. ii. p. 520.

His Body, whereof there was a symbol in the Law; the Eucharistic Body of Christ succeeding to the shewbread."

" When [8] thy soul is sick, and is oppressed with the disease of sins, art thou at ease, despisest thou hell, disregardest and mockest thou at the punishment of eternal fire? holdest thou cheap the judgment of God, and despisest thou the Church warning thee? fearest thou not, approaching the Eucharist to communicate of the Body of Christ, as though clean and pure, and there were nothing in thee unworthy? and in all these things thinkest thou to escape the judgment of God?   Remember ye not what is written, ' Therefore are many weak and sickly among you, and many sleep?'   Why are many weak? because they judge not their own selves, nor examine themselves, nor understand what it is to communicate with the Church, or what it is to approach such great and wonderful sacraments."

" For [9] no one who keepeth the Passover as Jesus willeth is below the upper chamber: but if any one feasteth with Jesus, he is above in the great upper chamber, in an upper chamber swept, in an upper chamber adorned and ready.   But if thou go up with Him to keep the Paschal Feast, He both giveth

[8] Id. Hom. ii. in Ps. 37, § 6, T. ii. p. 688.
[9] Id. in Jerem. Hom. 18, § 13, T. iii. p. 256.

thee the Bread of Blessing, His own Body, and bestoweth on thee His own Blood."

" But[1] if thou canst understand the spiritual Table, and spiritual Food, and the Supper of the Lord, with all of which he [Judas] had been honoured by Christ, thou wilt see more abundantly the multitude of his malice whereby he betrayed his Master the Saviour, together with the Food of the Divine Table and of the Cup, not remembering either as to temporal goods the love of his Master, or in spiritual His doctrine, ever communicated without stint. Such are all in the Church who plot against their brethren with whom they have been together frequently at the same Table of the Body of Christ and at the same draught of His Blood[2]."

[1] Id. in S. Matth. Tract. 35, § 82, T. iii. p. 897.

[2] In the sequel is a passage of great difficulty (§ 85), in which Origen seems to be contrasting the outward element, as considered by itself, and the Inward Presence of our Lord. " That Bread which God the Word owneth to be His Body, is the Word which nourisheth souls; the Word coming from God the Word, and Bread from the heavenly Bread which is placed on the table, of which it is written: 'Thou hast prepared a table before me against them which trouble me.' And that drink which God the Word owneth to be His Blood, is the Word which bedeweth and inebriateth the hearts of those who drink, which is in that Cup of which it is written: ' And Thy inebriating Cup, how excellent is it.' And the drink is that fruit of the True Vine, which saith, ' I am the True Vine.' And it is the blood of that grape which, cast into the wine-press of the Passion, brought forth this drink. So also the bread is the Word of Christ, made of that seed-corn which falling into the ground yieldeth much fruit. For not that

" Scripture [3] marvels that the Queen of Sheba came from the ends of the earth to hear the wisdom of Solomon; and when she had seen his feasting, and furniture, and the ministering of his house, she fainted, and was wholly astonished. We, if we do not gladly embrace so great riches of our Lord, so great furniture of speech, and richness of doctrines, if we do not eat the Bread of life, if we do not feed on the Flesh of Christ, and drink His Blood, if we despise the Feast of our Saviour, must know that God hath both goodness and severity."

"And [4] so not unpersuasively might it be said on this passage, that 'he that eateth the Bread of the Lord or drinketh His Cup unworthily, eateth and drinketh damnation to himself;' one and the same excellent Power in the Bread and in the Cup, inworking good in a good disposition which receives It, and implanting damnation in the evil. So the sop from Jesus was of a like nature [5] with that which was given to the rest of the Apostles, with the words, 'Take, eat,' but to the one for salvation, to Judas for dam-

visible bread which He held in His Hands did God the Word call His Body, but the Word, in the mystery of whom that bread was to be broken. Nor did He call that visible drink His Blood, but the Word, in whose mystery that drink was to be poured out. For the Body of God the Word, or His Blood, what else can it be than the Word which nourisheth, and the Word which gladdeneth the heart?"

[3] In Luke Hom. xxxviii. T. 3, p. 977.
[4] In John, Tom. x. 32, § 16, V. iv. p. 444.
[5] In its material substance, and its effects.

nation, since after the sop Satan entered into him. Let the bread and the cup be considered by the more simple, according to the more common interpretation of the Eucharist; by those who have learnt to hear deeper meanings, according to the more divine promise also, concerning the nourishing word of truth; as if I should say, for example, that the most nourishing bread for the body increases the state of fever, but restores to health one of a good habit of body."

Card. Mai purposed also to publish a further doctrinal statement on the Holy Eucharist, on Prov. ix.[6]

11. S. Firmilian.

Eminent as a Bishop a.d. 231, and counted by S. Dionysius the Great, one of the most illustrious Bishops of his time (Eus. H. E. vi. 26, vii. 5. See further, S. Cyprian's Ep. 75, p. 288, note, O. T.).

"How[7] great is the sin, whether of those who admit, or of those admitted, that, their defilements unwashed by the laver of the Church, their sins not laid aside, they, in communion rashly granted, touch the Body and Blood of the Lord, whereas it is written, 'Whosoever shall eat the Bread or drink the Cup of the Lord unworthily, shall be guilty of the Body and Blood of the Lord.'"

12. S. Dionysius the Great, of Alexandria.

Rector of the Catechetical School of Alexandria, a.d. 232; Archbishop of Alexandria, a.d. 247; chief in the

[6] See above, p. 316.
[7] Ap. S. Cyprian, Ep. lxxv. 21, p. 282, Oxf. Tr.

East in checking the heresies of Novatian, and those of
Sabellius and Paul of Samosata; consulted in well-nigh all
important matters of his time.

"His [s] (S. Dionysius') fifth letter was written to
Xystus, Bishop of the Romans, wherein, having said
many things against the heretics, he sets forth something of this sort, which happened in his time, saying,
'And in very deed, brother, I need advice, and I
ask an opinion of thee, fearing lest I mistake in a
matter of such moment as was brought to me. For
one of the brethren, a communicant, who is accounted
an ancient believer, and who even before my ordination, and I think even before the appointment of
Heraclas, of blessed memory, formed part of the congregation, happening to be present lately when some
were baptized, and hearing the questions and answers,
came to me weeping and bewailing himself, and falling
at my feet, confessing and affirming by oath, that the
Baptism wherewith he was baptized among the
heretics was nothing of this sort, nor in fact had any
thing in common with it; for it was full of impiety and
blasphemies. He said, moreover, that his soul was
now pierced through, and that he did not feel free to
lift up his eyes to God, taking his beginning from
those unholy words and deeds. Wherefore he besought to be admitted to that most holy cleansing
and reception and grace [*i. e.* Baptism]. This I did
not venture to do, saying that the Communion for

[s] Euseb. H. E. vii. 9.

so long time in itself sufficed thereto.   For I could not venture to renew from the beginning one who had heard the Eucharist, and joined in answering the Amen; and stood by the Table, and stretched forth his hands to receive the Holy Food, and had received It; and for a long while had partaken of the Body and Blood of our Lord Jesus Christ.   But I bade him be of good cheer, and with firm faith and a good conscience approach to partake of the Holy Things.   But he does not cease lamenting, and trembles to approach to the Table, and scarcely, when encouraged, ventures to stand with us at the prayers."

"For [9] I do not think that women who are faithful and devout would venture, in such a state, either to approach the Holy Table, or to touch the Body and Blood of Christ."   "But into the Holy of holies, he that is not altogether pure, both in soul and body, will be forbidden to enter."

I quote the Epistle to Paul of Samosata, no sufficient ground having been alleged against its genuineness.   This writer speaks in the person of Dionysius, and of the overthrow of the heretics, whom Dionysius had opposed, and of heathenism as not yet extinct [1].

Paul of Samosata had asked,

---

[9] Ep. ad Basilid. Can. 2, p. 114.
[1] See Præf. of Roman Editor, p. xxii. sqq.

"It' is written in the Gospel; 'And He took the cup and gave thanks, and said, Take this, and divide it among yourselves: This Cup is the New Testament in My Blood, which is shed for you.' How then is the Blood incorruptible, if it is divided and poured out?"

Both Paul's heretical inference from the truth, and S. Dionysius' answer, presuppose alike the doctrine of the Real Presence as the acknowledged truth, from which inferences might be made. S. Dionysius, in his answer, assumes, equally with Paul, that the Blood of Christ is "divided and poured out" in the Holy Eucharist, but disproves the inferences.

"He' of Samosata rose up first, uttering unrighteous words, saying that the Blood of Jesus is corruptible, even Jesus the God of Israel; and the Redemption from all corruption and suffering and death, our Ransom from the bondage of corruption, he calls the Blood of a mortal, and of a passible Man: because the Lord of glory said to His Disciples: 'Take this and divide it among yourselves; this is the New Testament in My Blood; do this:' and because He said, 'Which is shed for you.'"

"That' he might please Satan, that army-enlister, the Samosatan hath risen up against the life-giving Blood and the Holy Ghost, trampling upon them, for if the Holy Blood be corruptible through Its being divided and poured out, so too will be found the

' Q. 4, p. 225, ed. Rom.   ' Ep. p. 233.   ' p. 234.

Holy Ghost, as much as the Blood of life." [He quotes in proof, Acts ii. 1. 14; xxi. 9.] "No[5] one would say that because the Holy Ghost is poured forth He is therefore corruptible: God forbid: nor yet because He is divided: and it is the same also as to the life-giving Blood, as it is written: 'The water, the blood, and the Spirit, these three are one.'"

"As[6] Noah sent forth from the ark the dove, and himself received her back, after that image we must understand, that His is the Coeternal Spirit, Which was His, and Which He hath freely imparted to us, and hath poured forth on all flesh of the faithful, because He is God and Lord, Who hath imparted to us His Blood and the Spirit." "Lo, in all things have we shown to the torrent of iniquity [Paul of Samosata], that the Holy Blood of our God Jesus Christ is not corruptible, nor that of a mortal man like us, but is [the Blood] of Very God, Who is the Torrent of pleasure to them that partake of Him."

And against Paul's cavil on the words "He emptied Himself;"

"Himself[7] testifieth, Who is ever truly with the Father, saying, 'I am the Light of the world,' that is, the Lord of the world, having in Himself the Father, and the Spirit, life-giving and Lord; but 'He emptied Himself.' Wherefore also the ineffable mystery, His giving Himself to us in the Mystical Supper, is thus called by God Himself, the New

<hr>

[5] Ep. p. 235.   [6] p. 236.   [7] Ad q. 7, p. 254.

Testament; not as they under the law of Aaron's priesthood used of old to place the flesh of brute animals upon the altar. And Moses writes, saying, 'That the holy flesh shall be upon the altar, and both the people shall eat, and whoever, being unclean, shall touch it, shall be utterly destroyed.' But now not so. But the Lord Himself and God of Israel, our Saviour, saith, ' Whoso eateth Me, even he shall live by Me.' It is God then, Who dwelleth in us according to the Covenant, which He covenanted with us, saying, 'Take this, and divide it among yourselves; this is the New Testament; this do.' This is the emptying of God to us, that it might be vouchsafed to us to contain Him. For of this fearful Mystery the Apostle saith, 'He emptied Himself;' not leaving His Father (God forbid), He was contained in us. But I will set before thee the words of God Himself, saying, 'I and the Father will come, and will make our abode with him (He says) who believes on Me.' See, how great accuracy the teacher of the mysteries of truth used, the chosen vessel : ' He took upon Him the form of a servant, and was made in the likeness of men.' The Apostle (as I said before) thus explains a little afterwards the emptying, that the Mystery of life came to us through His pure and incorruptible and Divine Hands, that we, the faithful, may be able to contain Him, and to become the abode of God, receiving Him Whole." "Christ Jesus, Who emptied Himself, having in Himself the Head, even the Father, 'for the Head of Christ is God,' 'showed strength with His Arm, and exalted the lowly,' that the Most High might be contained in them, and might dwell in us through His Lovingkindness, and the Goodness, wherewith He loved us. This is the emptying of the Right Hand of the Most High. So then the emptying signifieth not change in Him (God forbid), but our renewal through His emptying, which He Who emptied Himself hath freely given us. The Holy Ghost, poured forth upon all flesh, remaineth full; and the holy and life-giving Blood, poured forth from the depth of the Divine Side, remaineth full, even Jesus Christ, Who emptied Himself, having poured forth into us His Incorruptible and Living and life-giving Blood[8]."

13. S. CYPRIAN.

In one place, together with 41 African Bishops.

Converted A.D. 246, consecrated A.D. 248, martyred A.D. 258, favoured with divine revelations throughout his whole Episcopate. Instances of this are given in the remarks on his life prefixed to his Epistles, pp. xxi. xxii. Oxf. Tr. See also life by Pontius, c. 13, prefixed to his treatises, Oxf. Tr.

He speaks of "the Blood in *the Cup,"* i. e. *in the wine, and as being "*set *forth by the wine"* (see above, p. 133). *He employs our Lord's words, "this fruit of the vine," in proof that wine is to be used in Holy Eucharist* (see above, p. 137).

---

[8] The text is slightly corrupt. I have only read καὶ ζῶν καὶ ζωῆς χορηγὸν for καὶ ζῶν ὃς ζωῆς χορηγόν.

"The[1] Father both chastises and protects us, yet only while we in tribulation and distress, are steadfast in the faith clinging fast to His Christ, as it is written, ' Who shall separate us from the love of Christ? shall tribulation, or distress, or persecution, or famine, or nakedness, or peril, or sword ?' None of these can separate believers, none can rend off those that cleave on to His Body and Blood."

"They[2], contrary to the law of the Gospel, contrary also to your respectful petition, before penance undergone, before confession made of their most grievous and extreme sin, before imposition of hands by the Bishops and Clergy in token of their repentance, dare to make oblations for them, and to give them the Eucharist, that is, to profane the sacred Body of the Lord ; though it is written, ' Whoever shall eat the bread and drink the cup of the Lord unworthily, shall be guilty of the Body and Blood of the Lord.' "

Synodical letter with forty-one other Bishops.

" We[3] perceive that you have, with befitting severity, and deservedly, reproved both those who, unmindful of their sins, in your absence, with hasty and precipitate eagerness, had extorted peace from the Presbyters, and those who, without heed to the Gospel, had, with sacrilegious readiness, given the holy of the Lord unto dogs."

[1] Ep. xi. 6, p. 27, O. T.
[2] Ep. xv. ad Mart. n. 1, p. 38.
[3] Ep. 31, § 7, p. 72.

A a 2

"Peace[1] is to be granted to those who have not departed from the Church of the Lord, but from the first day of their fall have not ceased to do penance and to lament and entreat the Lord, and they must be armed and accoutred for the impending battle.

"Now peace is necessary not for the sick, but for the strong; not to the dying, but the living must we grant communion; so as not to leave unarmed and naked, whom we rouse and exhort to battle, but fortify them with the protection of the Body and Blood of Christ; and since the Eucharist is ordained for this, that It may be a safeguard to them that receive It, those whom we would have safe against the adversary, we must arm with the defence of the fulness of the Lord. For how do we teach or provoke them to shed their blood in confession of the Name, if, when about to engage, we deny them the Blood of Christ?"

"A[5] more severe and fiercer struggle now hangs over us, to which the soldiers of Christ must prepare themselves by faith untainted, and by sturdy courage; considering that they therefore daily drink the Cup of the Blood of Christ, that they too may be able to shed their blood for Christ."

"Let[6] us also arm the right hand with the 'sword of the Spirit,' that we may boldly reject the deadly sacrifices, and mindful of the Eucharist, the hand

---

[1] Ep. lvii. ad Cornel. 1, p. 138.
[5] Ep. lviii. ad Thibarit. § 1, p. 142.
[6] Ib. § 10, p. 149.

which has received the Lord's Body, may embrace the Lord Himself, from Him to receive hereafter the reward of heavenly crowns."

"Nor[7] can His Blood, whereby we have been redeemed and quickened, appear to be in the Cup, when the Cup is without that wine, whereby the Blood of Christ is set forth, as is declared by the mystical meaning and testimony of all the Scriptures."

"Who[8] is more a priest of the most High God, than our Lord Jesus Christ, Who offered a Sacrifice to God the Father, and offered that same which Melchizedech had offered, that is, bread and wine, namely, His own Body and Blood."

"When[9] the blood of grapes is mentioned, what else is shown than the wine of the Cup of the Blood of the Lord?"

"Mention[1] is therefore made of wine, that the Blood of the Lord may be understood; and what was afterwards manifested in the Cup of the Lord, might be foreshown in the predictions of the Prophets. The treading and pressure of the wine-vat is also dwelt upon; because as men cannot come to the drinking of wine unless the cluster be first trodden and pressed, so neither could we drink the Blood of Christ, unless Christ had been first trodden and pressed, and first drank of the Cup, in which He should give believers to drink."

[7] Ep. 73, § 1, p. 182.   [8] Ib. § 3, p. 183.
[9] Ib. § 4, p. 184.   [1] Ib. p. 185.

"Those [2] mouths sanctified by heavenly food, after the Body and Blood of the Lord, loathed the profane contagion and the relics of idol-feasts."

"Men [3] turn from the altars of Satan to the Holy Thing of the Lord, with foul and tainted hands; still over-charged with the poisonous idol-feasts, their jaws breathing their crime, and fresh from the deadly infection, they invade the Body of the Lord, in despite of Holy Scripture, its resisting voice and word: 'They that be clean shall eat of the flesh; but the soul that eateth of the flesh of the sacrifices of the peace-offerings, that pertain unto the Lord, having his uncleanness upon him, even that soul shall be cut off from his people;' while the Apostle likewise bears witness, saying, 'Ye cannot drink the cup of the Lord and the cup of Devils; ye cannot be partakers of the Lord's table, and of the table of Devils;' and he further threatens and denounces the stubborn and perverse, saying, 'Whosoever eateth the bread or drinketh the cup of the Lord unworthily, is guilty of the Body and Blood of the Lord.' In scorn and dishonour of all this, a violence is offered to His Body and Blood and they sin more now against the Lord, with hand and mouth, than when they were denying Him."

"The [4] fallen threatens the upright, the wounded, the sound; and is impiously wrathful against the Priests, because he is not permitted at once to take

[2] De lapsis, § 2, p. 154, Oxf. Tr.
[3] Ib. 11, p. 163.   [4] Ib. 14, p. 167.

the Lord's Body in his defiled hands, and drink the Lord's Blood with his polluted mouth."

" Listen [5] to an event that took place in my own presence, and on my own testimony. Some parents who made their escape, in the thoughtlessness of terror left behind them at nurse an infant daughter, whom the nurse finding in her hands gave over to the magistrates. Unable, through its tender years, to eat flesh, they gave it, before an Idol to which the crowd assembled, bread mingled with some wine, which however was remains of that which had been used in the soul-slaughter of perishing Christians. The Mother afterwards got back her child; but the infant was as unable to express and make known the acts that had been committed, as she had before been to understand or to prevent it. Through ignorance therefore it arose, that, when we were sacrificing, the mother brought it in with her. The child however, mixed with the holy congregation, could not bear our prayers and worship; it was at one moment convulsed with weeping, then became tossed like a wave by throbs of feeling, and the babe's soul, while yet in the tender days, confessed a consciousness of what had happened with what signs it could, as if forced to do so by a torturer. When, however, after the solemnities were complete, the Deacon began to offer the Cup to those who were there, and in the course of their receiving, its turn came,

---

[5] Ib. 16, pp. 168—170.

the little child turned its face away, under the instinct of God's majesty, compressed its lips in resistance, and refused the Cup. The Deacon however persevered, and forced upon her, against her will, of the Sacrament of the Cup. There followed a sobbing and vomiting. The Eucharist was not able to remain in a body and mouth that had been polluted. The draught which had been consecrated in the Blood of the Lord, made its way from a body which had been desecrated. So great is the power of the Lord, so great the majesty." "Another advanced in life, and of maturer years, who secretly introduced herself while we were sacrificing, seeking bread found a sword, and as if she had admitted some deadly poison into the mouth and body, was presently seized with a fit of agony and frenzy: smitten no more by persecution, but by her guilt, quivering and trembling she fell to the ground. The offence, secreted in her conscience, was not long unpunished or concealed; though she had deceived man, the retribution of God found her. When another person endeavoured with desecrated hands to open her ark, in which was the Holy Thing of the Lord, by fire rising from within was she frighted off from daring to touch it. Another person also, who adventured secretly, after having defiled himself, when the Sacrifice was celebrated by the Priest, to accept his portion with the rest, was disabled from eating or handling the Holy Thing of the Lord, on opening his hands, he found that they contained a cinder.   Thus, by the instance of one, it was shown that the Lord withdraws when He is denied, and that what unfit persons receive cannot profit them unto salvation, since the saving grace turns into ashes, when holiness departs."

" ' Give [6] us this day our daily bread.'   This may be understood, both in the spiritual and in the simple meaning, seeing that either purport contains a divine aid for the advancing of our salvation.   For Christ is the Bread of life, and this Bread belongs not to all men, but to us; and as we say Our Father, because the Father of the understanding and believing, so we speak of our Bread, because Christ is the Bread of us, who appertain to His body.   This Bread we pray that it be given us day by day, lest we who are in Christ, and who daily receive the Eucharist for food of salvation, should, by the admission of any grievous crime, and our being therefore shut out from Communion, and forbidden the heavenly Bread, be separated from the Body of Christ, according as Himself preaches and forewarns; ' I am the Bread of Life, which came down from heaven.   If any man eat of My Bread, he shall live for ever.   But the Bread that I will give is My Flesh, for the life of the world.'   Seeing, therefore, He says, that if any man eat of His Bread, he shall live for ever, it follows, that while it is manifest that those do thus live, who appertain to His Body and receive the Eucharist by right of

[6] De Orat. n. 13, p. 187.

communication, so also is it matter both for our fears and prayers, that none of us by being forbidden Communion be separated from the Body of Christ, and so remain far from salvation as Himself threatens and declares, 'Unless ye eat the flesh of the Son of Man, and drink His Blood, ye shall have no life in you.' Hence, then, we pray that our Bread, that is, Christ, may be given to us day by day; that we who abide in Christ, and live in Him, may not draw back from His sanctification and His Body."

It appears from his "Testimonies" that S. Cyprian believed the practice of Infant Communion to rest on S. John vi. 53. He combines the same two texts, so often combined by S. Augustine.

13 b. S. Cornelius.
Bishop of Rome, A.D. 251, Martyr, A.D. 252.

"When[7] he [Novatian] had made the oblations, and was distributing to each his share, when he gave it, he compels the hapless men to swear instead of blessing, holding with both his hands the hands of the receiver, and not letting them go until they swear, saying (I will use his own words) 'Swear to me by the Body and Blood of our Lord Jesus Christ[8], that thou wilt never leave me and return to Cornelius.' And the miserable man tasteth not, until he have first cursed himself. And instead of saying 'Amen,'

[7] Ep. ad Fabium in Eus. H. E. vi. 43, p. 315, ed. Read.

[8] S. Jerome mentions an instance in which this was done as a religious act, by Bishops. See below, No. 52, adv. Jov. ii. 25.

when he receiveth that Bread, he saith, 'I will never return to Cornelius.'"

14. S. LAURENCE THE MARTYR, A.D. 257.

"Let[9] us not either pass by holy Laurence, who, when he saw Xystus, his bishop, led to martyrdom, began to weep, not *his* suffering, but his own remaining behind. So then he began to call to him in these words, 'Whither goest thou forth, father, without thy son? whither hastenest thou, holy priest, without thy deacon? Never wert thou wont to offer sacrifice without thy minister. What, then, in me has displeased thee, father? Try, at least, whether thou hast chosen a befitting minister. To whom thou hast committed the consecrated[1] Blood of Christ, the fellowship in the completion of the sacraments, dost thou refuse to him the fellowship of thy blood?'" ·

15. MAGNES.

A. D. 265. A late authority, Nicephorus, Patriarch of Constantinople, A.D. 806 (died 828), places Magnes at the beginning of the fourth century; another, Germanus, also Patriarch there A.D. 715, says that he was at the Council of Antioch held against Paul of Samosata [A.D. 265]. (Cave, tit. Magnes.) Nicephorus mentions, that in the title of his book, he was designated as Bishop, and that in a very old MS. he was depicted in an episcopal dress. (Spicil. Solesm. i. 307.) Of Magnes' date, he says, "We learn that he flourished above 300 years after the Apostolic and Divine preaching shone out." (Ib.) Much of the pas-

---

[9] In S. Ambr. de Offic. i. 41, n. 214.
See Serm. p. 57, n. 12.

sage on the Holy Eucharist was quoted in the twelfth century, by John, Patriarch of Antioch, in his work " On the Sacred Mysteries."   (Spicil. Sol. p. 548.)

" For[2] it is not a type of the Body, nor a type of the Blood, as some have blindly and idly said, but is in truth the Body and Blood of Christ."

" Through[3] that union whereby I am united, the Holy with the earthly, I give bread and wine, commanding them to be My Body and Blood."

" For[4] if Abraham, or any other just and holy man, had said, ' My Flesh is meat and My Blood drink,' he would have dared a great lie; or if he had said, ' This is My Body,' and ' This is My Blood.'   For it would not be his own substance, but that of another: nor, when eaten, would they give life to the eaters. Forasmuch as what hath not the living Word united with a body which was of earth would not bring the eaters thereof to eternal life.   Christ then gave to believers His own Body and Blood, infusing into them the life-giving medicine of Divinity."

" Common[5] bread from the culture of the earth, although it is a sort of flesh of the earth, yet promiseth not to give eternal Life, but giveth only a brief solace, to those who partake[6] of it, since soon does it come to an end without the Divine Spirit.

[2] Frag. ap. Gall. iii. 541.
[3] Ib. § 2.   [4] Ib. § 3.   [5] Ib. § 4.
[6] The text has " præbentibus" which is corrupt.   " Præbentibus " has probably come in by an oversight from " præbere " in the previous line.

But the Bread, which, in the blessed Earth of Christ, is formed by the virtue of the united Divinity, by its taste alone bringeth Immortality to man. For the mystical Bread, when it hath the inseparable blessing of the Father, that blessing, I say, which is given in His Body and Blood, uniteth him that eateth the Body of Christ, and maketh him a member of Christ."
— " That Body which is that mystical Bread, and the Blood which is that Wine, give from themselves to him who partaketh, the Immortality of the undefiled Divinity, and, through it, bring him back to the incorruptible abiding of the Creator. For neither is the Flesh of the Saviour corrupted when eaten, nor is this Blood, when drunk, consumed. But he who eateth is uplifted to an increase of Divine powers; and that which is eaten is unexpended, since in a manner It is kindred to, and inseparable from, that inexhaustible Nature."

16. S. Peter of Alexandria.

Archbishop of Alexandria A.D. 300, Martyr A.D. 311. " A divine and wondrous Bishop, for life and virtue, and study of Holy Scripture." Eus. H. E. ix. 6.

" Those[1] who were betrayed and fell, and those who of themselves approached the conflict, confessing that they were Christians, and were cast into prison with tortures, it is reasonable to strengthen yet more in gladness of heart, and communicate with them in all things, both in prayers, and in the parti-

---

[1] Can. 8, Routh Reliq. iv. 31.

cipation of the Body and Blood, and the exhortation of the word; that they, too, wound up to strive more steadfastly, may be made worthy of the prize of their high calling. 'For,' he saith, 'the righteous shall fall seven times and rise again.' Which if all who fall had done, they would have shown the most perfect and whole-hearted repentance."

17. EUSEBIUS OF CÆSAREA.

Historian and Arian; Bishop of Cæsarea, A.D. 315.

He speaks repeatedly of the Eucharistic elements, as symbols. See above, pp. 98, 99.

"But[s] when the poor shall eat and be satisfied, then shall they who seek the Lord praise Him, eating the Food given to them by Him; and, seeking Him, they shall have great fruit, for 'their heart shall live for ever.' For the Bread of Life supplied to them by Him shall be to them a cause of immortality and life eternal, as He Himself taught, 'I am the Bread of Life[9],' &c.

"On every day of the Lord's Resurrection, which is called the Lord's Day, you may see those who partake of the holy Food and the Saviour's Body receive It, and, after eating, worship Him Who giveth and provideth the Life-giving Food, and marvel at the completion of the words fulfilled in deed to the very letter."

" When[1] then he [David], having partaken of the

[s] In Ps. xxi. 26. 31, in Montf. Nova Coll. i. 84, 85.
[9] John vi. 35. 39.   [1] In Ps. xxxiii. 6, p. 132.

shewbread, 'altered his taste;' then he perceived by the taste the Divine Power which was supplied to him. So then according to the words, 'Without guile I have received, liberally do I communicate,' he exhorts others, too, to hasten to the like taste with himself, and to pray that they might be nourished with the Bread of life; of which the shewbread, ordained through Moses, was a type and image. Wherefore David, understanding of what the shewbread was the image, exhorts us to hasten, not after the bodily bread, but after that which is understood through it. We, then, who are upon earth partake of the Bread which came down from Heaven, and the Word Which emptied Itself and made Itself small. But they who are in the kingdom of Heaven partake of It Full and Perfect, nourished by Its Divinity, and enjoying the contemplation of Wisdom. Whereof we, too, should hope one day to partake."

"He[2] will be able to delight himself in the Lord that hath the senses of his soul purified, so as to be able to eat the living Bread, and His Life-giving Flesh, and to drink His saving Blood. By these do thou, nourished and made fat, and enjoying the Divine inebriation, 'delight thee in the Lord, and He shall give thee thy heart's desire.'"

"Analogously[3] to those who eat the Flesh of the saving Word."

"For[4] being of the household of the Saviour, he

---

[2] In Ps. xxxvi. 4, p. 149.   [3] In Ps. lxxiii. 15, p. 441.
[4] Id. in Ps. xl. 10, p. 171.

[Judas] did not eat with Him only common bread, but was admitted to partake of that also which nourisheth the soul, of which the Saviour said; 'I am the Bread of Life, Who came down from Heaven and give life to men.'"

"Accordingly [5], He filled them, vouchsafing to them food from Himself; not the bodily only, but the heavenly and spiritual also, when the Christ of God sojourned with them first. He gave them for food the heavenly Bread. Himself (gave) Himself (αὐτὸς ἑαυτόν)."

"We [6] offer the shewbread, rekindling the saving remembrance, and [we offer] the Blood of sprinkling of the Lamb of God, Which taketh away the sin of the world, the cleansing of our souls."

"In [7] another way, we say that from the Jewish synagogue was taken away 'the staff of bread and the staff of water:' and this relateth to the mysteries. For we, indeed, who through faith have been called to holiness, have Bread from heaven, that is, Christ, or, indeed, His Body. But if any ask of what kind Its strength is, we say that It is life-giving, for It giveth life unto the world. . . . But the Jews are deprived of such goods; for with them there is no staff of bread, that is, quickening in Christ, nor have they the staff of water."

"For [8] He saveth freely all who will to serve Him.

[5] In Ps. lxxx. 17, p. 504.

[6] In Ps. xci. p. 608, A.

[7] In Is. iii. 2. Montf. ii. 368.

[8] In Is. lxv. 11. 586.

He will receive them, and will give them the heavenly
Food, the saving Word which says, 'I am the Bread
which came down from heaven.'   These then will be
nourished and filled by the Bread which has been
spoken of: but ' ye,' says He, ' who do not receive My
grace, shall hunger for want of the spiritual food ;' and
again, they who serve Me shall be filled with the immortal drink of life, of which it is said, ' Whosoever
drinketh of the water which I shall give him, it shall
be in him a well of water, welling up unto everlasting
life.' "

18. COUNCIL OF NICE, 318 Bishops from the whole
world, A. D. 325.

" It [9] hath come before the holy and great Synod,
that, in certain places and cities, the Deacons give
the Eucharist to the Presbyters, which neither the
Canon nor usage has handed down, that those who
have no power to offer, should give to those who offer,
the Body of Christ.   It also came to our knowledge,
that some of the deacons take the Eucharist even
before the Bishops.   Let all this be done away."

ADAMANTIUS (*about the same time*) *and* EUSTA-
THIUS, *who was present at the Council of Nice ("a
confessor, pious in faith, and of great zeal for the
truth." S. Ath. Ep. ad. Mon. § 4, p. 222, O. T.)
spoke of the Eucharistic elements as symbols* (above,
pp. 83. 99, 100).

19. S. JAMES OF NISIBIS.

Present, as Bishop, at the Council of Nice, " to combat

[9] Can. 18.

B b

for the right faith, as a chief, in the forefront of the whole army." Theodoret, Hist. Relig. c. 1, (T. 3, p. 1108 sqq. ed. Sch.) who (there and H. E. ii. 31,) speaks of great and public miracles wrought by him, and of his gift of prophecy.

"One[10] door thou hast to thine house, and thy house is the Temple of God. It is then shocking and altogether unfit, O man, that through the door whereby the King entereth, thou shouldest bring out filth and other defilements. But abstain thou from all uncleanness, and then receive the Body and Blood of Christ, and carefully guard thy mouth through which the King hath entered; nor mayest thou, O man, any more bring forth through thy mouth words of uncleanness. Attend to what the Lord, our Life, hath said, 'That which entereth into a man, &c.'"

"They[1] will not be cleansed, unless they be washed in the water of the laver of Baptism, and receive the Body and Blood of Christ. Blood is expiated by Blood, and the body is cleansed by the Body, and the sins are washed away by water."

"They[2] keep His watch, and bark against thieves, like dogs, and love our Lord, and lick His wounds when they receive His Body, and place It on their eyes, and lick It with their tongue as a dog licketh his master."

---

[10] Serm. iii. § 2, p. 46, ed. Rom. Not being acquainted with Armenian, I have been obliged to translate from the Latin translation of Antonelli.

[1] Serm. iv. de Orat. fin. p. 77.

[2] Serm. vii. de Pœnit. § 8, p. 248.

"Our[3] Saviour ate the Passover with His disciples on that 14th night, when He was taken and gave His disciples the Sacrament of the true Passover; for after Judas was gone out from them, He took bread and blessed and brake and gave to His disciples, saying, 'This is my Body, take and eat ye all of It,' and the wine He thus blessed and said to them, 'This is My Blood of the New Testament which is shed for many for the remission of sins; this ye shall do in remembrance of Me, when ye shall be gathered together.' This our Lord did, before He was taken. And from that place where He kept the Passover, and gave His Body that they should eat, and His Blood that they should drink, He went away and departed thither with His disciples where they took Him. When then His Body was eaten and His Blood drunk, He was 'counted among the dead.' For our Lord with His own Hands gave His Body for food, and when He was not yet crucified, He gave His Blood for drink." "In that night which dawned into the Lord's day, at the same hour at which He gave to His disciples His own Body and Blood, He rose again from the dead." "Night[4] was that hour when Judas departed from them, and the eleven disciples ate the Flesh and drank the Blood of the Saviour."

"To them[5] [the Jews] was given manna for food, and our Lord brought forth for us His own Flesh for food."

[3] Serm. xiv. de Pasch. § 4, p. 341.
[4] § 5, p. 344.   [5] § 6, p. 345.

B b 2

" He [6] who eateth of Christ, the true Lamb, girdeth up his reins with faith, and is shod with the might of the Gospel, and hath in his hand the sword of the Spirit, which is the Word of God itself.   Then also He commanded, ' a bone of Him shall not be broken.' This was fulfilled on the Cross, when they ' broke not His legs.'   He addeth, ' a servant bought with money, when ye have circumcised him, then shall he eat the Passover.' ' A servant bought with money ' is a sinner, who, when he repenteth, is bought with the Blood of Christ; and circumcising his heart from evil works, cometh to the laver of Baptism, which is the perfection and complement of the true circumcision, and cometh and is made partaker of the mysteries of God, and communicates of the Body and Blood of Christ."

" When [7] He had washed His disciples' feet, He sat down at the table, and then gave them His Body and Blood."

20. S. Athanasius the Great.

Defender of the faith, as Deacon at the Council of Nice. Archbishop of Alexandria, A.D. 326.   Five times banished for the faith.   " His life and manners were the rule of the Episcopate, his doctrines the law of orthodoxy." (S. Greg. Naz. Orat. 21, fin. p. 411, ed. Ben.)   Ob. A.D. 373.

On his words that the consecrated elements are not " mere *bread*," " mere *Cup*," " bare *elements*," see above, p. 92; *that they " become the Body and Blood of Christ,"* see pp. 237, 238.

<hr>

[6] p. 346.   [7] p. 347.

" Now[8], however, that the devil is slain, that tyrant against the whole world, we do not approach the feast, my beloved, as a temporal feast, but as being eternal and heavenly. For we proclaim it not as it were in shadows, but we come to it in the truth. They indeed, when filled with the flesh of an irrational lamb, accomplished the feast, and having anointed their door-posts with the blood, deprecated the destroyer. But now we, eating of the Word of the Father, and having the lintels of our hearts sealed with the Blood of the New Testament, acknowledge the grace given us from the Saviour, Who said, ' Behold, I have given unto you to tread upon serpents and scorpions, and over all the power of the enemy.'"

" We[9], my beloved, the shadow having received its fulfilment, and the types being accomplished, should no longer consider the feast a figurative feast; neither should we go up to Jerusalem, which is beneath, to sacrifice the Passover, according to the unseasonable observance of the Jews, lest, while the season passes away, we should be regarded as acting unseasonably; but, in accordance with the injunction of the Apostles, let us go beyond the types, and sing the new song of praise. For this they also observed; and as being assembled together with the Truth, they drew near, and said unto our Saviour, ' Where wilt Thou that we should make ready for Thee the

---

[8] Pasch. Ep. iv. p. 33, Oxf. Tr.   [9] Ib. p. 34.

Passover?' For no longer were these things done
at Jerusalem which is beneath; neither was it considered that the feast should be celebrated there
alone, but wherever God willed it to be. Now He
willed it to be in every place, so that 'in every place
incense and a sacrifice might be offered to Him.' For
although, as in the historical account, they were
commanded not to introduce the feast of the Passover any where, but only in Jerusalem, yet when
the things pertaining to that time were fulfilled,
and those which belonged to shadows had passed
away, and the preaching of the Gospel was to be
extended every where; when, indeed, the disciples
were spreading the feast in all places, they asked
our Saviour, 'Where wilt Thou that we shall make
ready?' Our Saviour also, since He was changing
the typical for the spiritual, promised them that
they should no longer eat the flesh of a lamb, but
His own, saying, 'Take, eat and drink; this is My
Body and My Blood.' When we are, then, nourished
by these things, we shall also, my beloved, properly
keep the feast of the Passover."

"Again[1] the time has arrived which brings to us
a new beginning, even the announcement of the
blessed Passover, in which our Lord was sacrificed.
We eat, as it were, the food of life; and, thirsting
continually, are at all times delighted, as it were
from a fountain, by His precious Blood. For we, on

[1] Ep. v. p. 36.

the one hand, are always eagerly desirous; He, on the other, stands ready for those who thirst; and for those who thirst there is the word of our Saviour, which, according to His loving-kindness, He vouchsafed in the day of the feast, 'If any man thirst, let him come to Me and drink.'"

"" For[2] even God is not ashamed to be called the God of those who truly mortify their members which are upon the earth, but live in Christ; for He is the God of the living, not of the dead. And He, by His living Word, quickeneth all men, and gives Him to be Food and life to the saints, as also the Lord exclaims, 'I am the Bread of life.'"

"Let[3] us also now keep the feast, my beloved, not as introducing a day of suffering, but of joy in Christ, by Whom we are fed every day."

"Those[4] words, 'Sit Thou on My Right Hand,' were said of the Lord's Body. For if, as Jeremiah saith, 'I fill heaven and earth, saith the Lord,' and God containeth all things, and is contained by nothing; on what throne doth He sit? It is the Body, then, to which He saith, 'Sit on My Right Hand,' of which Body, also, the Devil with the evil powers, and the Jews and the Greeks, were enemies. Through that same Body also did He become and was called our High Priest and Apostle, through that Mystery

[2] Ep. vii. pp. 58, 59.
[3] Ep. xiii. pp. 109, 110.
[4] Major Orat. de Fide ap. Theod. Dial. ii. T. iv. p. 137, ed. Sch.

which He delivered to us, saying, 'This is My Body Which was given for you,' and 'The Blood of the New Testament,' not of the Old, ' Which was shed for you.' Yet Godhead hath neither Body nor Blood, but the Man Whom He bore, born from Mary, was the cause of these things, of whom the Apostles said, ' Jesus of Nazareth, a Man approved of God among you.'" -

" 'Give[5] not that which is holy to dogs, neither cast ye your pearls before swine,' saith Christ. . . . . Let us not, then, cast the pearls of our undefiled mysteries before men of swinish habits. 'But,'saith one, ' they desire to partake of the holy things;' and they are shameless dogs, and swine wallowing in pleasure. But thou, give them not. For the sick, too, desire water, yet the physicians permit it not; and usurpers desire the royal purple; but they who keep it, suspecting the danger, give it not. See, then, thou too, O deacon, that thou give not to the unworthy the purple of the sinless Body."

"And[6] again, whereas the Lord saith of Himself, ' I am the living Bread, Which came down from Heaven;' in another place, He calls the Holy Ghost ' Bread from Heaven,' saying: 'Give us this day our daily bread.' For He taught us in our prayer in this present life to ask for bread ἐπιούσιον, *i. e.* future, whereof we receive the firstfruits in the present life, partaking of the Flesh of the Lord, as Himself said.

[5] Serm. in S. Matt. De incontam. myst. in Montf. Nov. Coll. ii. 35.

[6] De Incarn. et cont. Ar. § 18, T. i. P. 2, p. 883.

'The Bread which I will give is My Flesh, for the life of the world.' For the Lord's Flesh is Life-giving Spirit, because He was conceived of the Life-giving Spirit. But 'that which is born of the Spirit is spirit.'"

"And' here (S. Joh. vi. 62) He affirms both of Himself, Flesh and Spirit, and He distinguished the Spirit from the flesh, in order that, believing not only what was seen of Him (τὸ φαινόμενον), but what was invisible, they might understand that the things which He speaketh are not fleshly but spiritual. For to how many would His Body have sufficed for food, that it should become the food of the whole world? And therefore did He make mention of the Ascension of the Son of Man into Heaven, that He might draw them off from corporeal thoughts, and that they might for the future understand that the flesh whereof He spake was Heavenly Food from above. For, He saith, 'The words which I have spoken unto you are spirit and life;' as though He said, 'That which is visible and is given for the salvation of the world, is the Flesh which I bear, and Its Blood shall be given by Me spiritually as Food, so that it may be distributed spiritually in each, and may become to all a protection, to the resurrection of life eternal."

I have quoted in the Sermon [8], some words of the larger exposition of the Psalms, published as S.

---

[7] Epist. iv. ad Serapion. § 19, p. 710, ed Ben.

[8] p. 58.

Athanasius'.   Some of this work is certainly his[9]; some extracts I have identified formerly in other Fathers[1].

The following passage is, any how, ancient—

"The[2] Divine Word owneth the spiritual Food. The Word Himself saith that He is bread. 'I am the Bread of life Who came down from heaven.' He saith also, 'He that eateth My Flesh hath life in himself.' Eating Him, then, we burst forth into a hymn."

21. ANONYMOUS AUTHOR—*De Solemnitatibus*.
Soon after the Council of Nice[3].

"Some[4] things the Evangelist relates that He

[9] See Bened. Pref. S. Ath. Opp. T. i. P. 2, pp. 1004, 5. Passages quoted by ancient writers as Athanasius' occur in this fuller Commentary ; and not in the de tit. Psalm. Rom. 1746.

[1] The Benedictines have noted some from Theodoret. Antonelli (de tit. Psalm. Præf. p. xvii.) quotes Tillemont (Mém. Eccl. viii 257) as saying the same.

[2] In Ps. cxviii. v. 171, p. 1219.

[3] The writer says (c. 7), immediately after the passage here quoted, " Whence the elect and beloved spouse of Christ, the *Universal Church*, anathematizes those who, with the Jews, pronounce that, in the Paschal festival, the 14th of the month is to be waited for."   But the "Universal Church" did not excommunicate Quarto-decimans, until after the Council of Nice. The Council of Nice itself did not annex any such penalty ; but since after the decision of a general Council, disobedience was a schismatic act, excommunication followed, as was ruled by the Council of Antioch (Can. i.). The Council of Constantinople states that it had been the custom to receive such, on acknowledging their heresies (see further Bingham, 20, 5. 3). The writer speaks, in addition, of this uniformity of observation having taken place recently, " quod nunc maxime Ecclesia observat," c. 7.

[4] c. 5, 6, in Spicil. Solesm. p. 11, ed. Pitra.

[our Lord] did contrary to the figure [of the Passover]. For when He was delivered by Judas to the Jews, He was not taken on the 10th day of the first month. And when He vouchsafed to give to His disciples, in His own lifetime, the sacrament of His Body and Blood, He is shown to have done this contrary to the figure. For that lamb, which was commanded to be slain on the Passover, as a type of Christ, was directed to be consumed by the people, after it was slain, being roasted with fire, with the head and legs, and purtenance thereof. But this, as it seems to me, the Lord is known to have done for two reasonable causes, lest, seeing that He had eaten the Passover with the disciples, unless He had subsequently changed the sacrifice, saying, 'This is My Body,' it should be believed that it was subsequently to be observed in that same way.

"But the other cause, as I think, is this; that when, before the Passover, they saw the Body of Christ whole, and containing Its Blood within It, they might believe that they were in the body spiritually refreshed. And this we also ought now to believe. We ought to consider this, too; that not on the 14th day, at even, as the law commandeth, was that Lamb of God Who taketh away the sins of the world, and our Passover, Christ, slain; but on the 15th day, wherein it is plain that the Feast of the Jews, with its sacrifice, was abolished by the Lord. But what ought we to understand in this, that He first ate the flesh of the lamb, which was a figure, and afterwards refreshed

His Apostles with the Food of His own Body; and, after the typical sacrifice of the Jews, Christ, our Sacrifice was slain? This, I deem; that the figure preceded the truth, not the truth, the figure. For that was not first which was spiritual, but that which was natural, and afterwards that which was spiritual."

22. JUVENCUS, A.D. 330.
A Spanish Poet.

"When [5] He said these things, He brake the Bread with His Hands, and being broken, He gave It to them, and having holily prayed, He taught His disciples that He gave them His own Body.

"Then the Lord taketh the Cup, and It being filled with wine, He sanctifieth It with mighty words, and giveth It to them to drink, and taught them that He had divided His own Blood. And He saith: 'This Blood will remit the sins of the people, This My Blood drink ye: for (believe ye the truth) henceforth will I no more taste juice of the vine, until, with gift of better life, the kingdoms of My Father allow Me again to arise to [drink] new wine.'"

23. THEODORUS HERACLEOTES, A.D. 334.

Distinguished for learning, but, as an Arian, deposed by the Council of Sardica.

"When [6] he saith, 'approach,' he exhorteth to 'taste' also, *i. e.* to make trial of the goodness of God. But

[5] Hist. Evang. L. iv. B P. iv. 74.
[6] In Ps. 33. 9. in Cord.r. Cat. i. 596. On the spuriousness o
a passage attributed to him in Possini's Catena, see above, p. 195.

it harmonizeth, according to the deep hidden meaning, that the grace of the Divine mysteries should be shadowed hereby. For through Holy Baptism enlightening accrues to those who approach thereto, and the taste of the life-giving Food shows clearly the goodness of God. For through His death for us, He hath become both Food and fountain to believers. Since also the Lord is 'true Bread,' and His Flesh is mystical Food, the sweetness of the Bread must needs come to be in us through spiritual taste."

24. S. JULIUS, Bishop of Rome, A.D. 337—352.

An energetic practical defender of the faith against Arianism. Two letters only of his are extant.

" I have [7] also thought it necessary to point out to you this circumstance, viz. that Athanasius positively asserted that Macarius was kept at Tyre under a guard of soldiers, while only his accuser accompanied those who went to the Mareotis; and that the Presbyters who desired to attend the inquiry were not permitted, while the said inquiry respecting the chalice and the Table was carried on before the Prefect and his band, and in the presence of Heathens and Jews. This at first seemed incredible; but it was proved to have been so from the reports; which caused great astonishment to us, as I suppose, dearly beloved, it does to you also. Presbyters, who are the ministers of the mysteries, are not permitted

---

[7] Ep. ad Euseb. in S. Ath. Apol. ag. Ar. § 31, pp. 51, 52, Oxf. Tr.

to attend, but an inquiry concerning Christ's Blood and Christ's Body is carried on before an external judge, in the presence of Catechumens, nay, worse than that, before Heathens and Jews, who have so bad a name in regard to Christianity."

25. Council of Alexandria, a.d. 339.

Of nearly 100 Bishops, out of Egypt, the Thebais, Libya, and Pentapolis, in behalf of S. Athanasius.

" No [8] one did Athanasius commit into the hands of the executioner ; and the prison, so far as he was concerned, was never disturbed. Our sanctuaries are now, as they have always been, pure and honoured only with the Blood of Christ and His pious worship."

"The [9] chalice, which belongs to the mysteries, and which, if it be broken intentionally, makes the perpetrator of the deed an impious person, is found only among those who are lawfully appointed to preside over the Church. This is the only description that can be given of this kind of chalice ; there is none other; of this you drink prior to the people; this you have received according to the canon of the Church ; this belongs only to those who preside over the Catholic Church; for to you only it appertains to have the first taste of the Blood of Christ, and to none besides. But as he who breaks a sacred cup is an impious person, much more impious is he who insults the Blood of Christ."

[8] S. Ath. Apol. c. Arian. init. p. 14, O. T.
[9] In S. Ath. Apol. ag. Ar. § 6, p. 20, O. T.

26. JULIUS FIRMICUS, about A.D. 342.
Learned Christian Apologist.

" Other [1] is that Bread which giveth salvation and life ; other is that Food which both commends and restores man to the Most High God. There is a Food which recruiteth the sick, recalleth the erring, raiseth up the fallen, which to the dying gives the pledge of Immortality. Seek the Bread of Christ, the Cup of Christ, that, despising earthly frailty, the substance of man may be enriched by Immortal Food."

" But [2] that that Divine Bread is bestowed by God upon men consecrated, the Holy Ghost saith by Isaiah : 'Thus saith the Lord, Behold, My servants shall eat, but ye shall be hungry ; Behold, My servants shall rejoice, but ye shall be ashamed : for the Lord God shall slay you.'

" The Holy Ghost saith by David : 'Taste and see that the Lord is good,' sweet is the heavenly Food, sweet the Food of God ; It admitteth not in itself the sad torment of miserable hunger, and forth from the very marrow of men It casts the venom of the preceding poison. . . . . . These things the following words of the oracle declare : 'Fear the Lord, all ye His Saints ; for they that fear Him, lack nothing. The rich have lacked and hungered ; but they that seek the Lord, shall want no manner of thing that is good.'"

[1] De err. Prof. relig. p. 36, ed. Ouz.   [2] p. 37.

"But [3] to say more plainly what is that Bread, whereby the destructiveness of miserable death is overcome, the Lord Himself with His holy and venerable mouth hath shown, lest through diverse handlings the hopes of men should be deceived by wrong interpretations. For He saith in the Gospel of S. John: 'I am the Bread of Life: he that cometh to Me shall not hunger ; and he that believeth on Me shall never thirst.'

"Also in the following verses He shows the same in like manner, for He saith : 'If any man thirst, let him come unto Me and drink.'   And again Himself, that He might deliver the substance of His Majesty to believers, says: 'Except ye eat the Flesh of the Son of Man, and drink His Blood, ye have no life in you.'   Wherefore have nothing to do with timbrels [4], the hateful food, O wretched mortals; seek the grace of the health-giving food, and drink the Immortal Cup. Christ by His Feast recals you to the light, and quickens your limbs putrefying with the deadly poison, and your torpid members. With heavenly Food renew ye the lost man, that, whatever in you is dead, by the Divine benefits may be reborn. Ye have learnt what is fit for you to do ; choose what ye will. From the one, death has its birth ; from the other, immortal life is given."

"We [5] have learnt the ways of thy death ; we

---

[3] p. 38.   [4] An allusion to the heathen mysteries.
[5] Ib. p. 44. See above, p. 147.

know by what remedies the poisons of thy wiles are subdued.   We drink the Immortal Blood of Christ; to our blood is the Blood of Christ united; this is the healthful remedy for thy wickedness; this, which expels from the people of God the deadly venom."

27. S. THEODORE.

Successor to S. Pachomius in his Monastery in the Thebais, A. D. 344.

"But[6] let the catechumens too, who are in the monasteries, and look for the awful remission of sins, and the grace of the spiritual mystery, hear through you, that they ought to weep and bewail their former sins, and prepare themselves for the sanctifying of their souls and bodies, that they may be able to endure the Blood and the Body of the Lord, the Saviour, to think even whereof is awful[1]."

28. S. THECLA, MARIA, MARTHA, MARIA, AMI.

Martyrs under Sapor in the 7th year of his persecution, *i. e.* A.D. 337 [Assem. Bibl. Or. i. 191].

"Is[7] this that Holy propitiatory Thing which we received from thy hands?   Is this the life-giving Blood, which thou usedst to bring near to our mouths?"

---

[6] Epist. ad omn. monasteria de Pascha, Gall. iv. p. 734.

[7] The words were said to Paulus, an apostate priest, on his inviting them to apostatize, adore the sun, and eat.   They are recorded by S. Maruthas, the friend of S. Chrysostom (published in Assem. Acta Mart. i. 125).

29. S. CYRIL OF JERUSALEM.

Bishop of Jerusalem, A.D. 349 or 350 to A.D. 386. See further, Preface to his Lectures, pp. iii.—vi. O. T.

On his assertions that the consecrated elements are not "bare elements," which he makes alike of the water of Baptism, the oil of confirmation, and the elements of the Holy Eucharist, see above, pp. 91, 92. *On his calling the consecrated elements the "type" or "antitype of the Body and Blood of Christ,"* see p. 101. *On his speaking of the Body and Blood of Christ being "given in the type of bread and wine,"* see p. 132. *On his words "Whatsoever the Holy Ghost hath touched is changed,"* see pp. 242—244. *On his use of the word "changed,"* see p. 232, sqq. *On his comparison of the change of the water into wine,* see pp. 277—280.

"2. He once, in Cana of Galilee, turned water into wine, which is akin to blood; and is it incredible that He should have turned wine into Blood? That wonderful work He miraculously wrought, when called to an earthly marriage: and shall He not much rather be acknowledged to have bestowed the fruition of His Body and Blood on the children of the bride-chamber?"

"For[s] as the bread and wine of the Eucharist before the holy invocation of the Adorable Trinity was *simple* (λιτὸς) bread and wine, while after the

[s] Lect. xix. Myst. i. § 7, pp. 260, 261, Oxf. Tr.

invocation the Bread becomes the Body of Christ, and the Wine the Blood of Christ; so in like manner, such meats belonging to the pomp of Satan, though in their own nature *plain* and *simple*, become profane by the invocation of the evil spirit."

" But [9] beware of supposing this to be *plain* [ψιλὸν] ointment. For as the Bread of the Eucharist, after the invocation of the Holy Ghost, is *mere* [λιτὸς] bread no longer, but the Body of Christ ; *so also* this holy ointment is no more *simple* [ψιλὸν] ointment, nor (so to say) *common* [κοινὸν] after the invocation, but the gift of Christ; and by the presence of His Godhead, it causes in us the Holy Ghost. It is symbolically applied to thy forehead and thy other senses; and while thy body is anointed with visible ointment, thy soul is sanctified by the Holy and life-giving Spirit."

"This [1] teaching of the blessed Paul is alone sufficient to give you a full assurance concerning those Divine mysteries, which when ye are vouchsafed, ye are of the same body and blood with Christ. For he has just distinctly said, 'That our Lord Jesus Christ the same night in which He was betrayed, took bread, and when He had given thanks He brake it, and said, Take, eat, this is My Body, and having taken the cup and given thanks, He said, Take, drink, this is my Blood.' Since then He Himself has

---

[9] Lect. xxi. Myst. iii. § 3, p. 268.
[1] Lect. xxii. Myst. v. init. p. 270.

c c 2

declared and said of the Bread, 'This is My Body,' who shall dare to doubt any longer? And since He has affirmed and said, 'This is My Blood,' who shall ever hesitate, saying, that it is not His blood?"

" 4. Therefore with fullest assurance let us partake as of the Body and Blood of Christ: for *in* the figure of Bread is given to thee His Body, and *in* the figure of Wine His Blood, that thou by partaking of the Body and Blood of Christ, mightest be made of the same body and the same blood with Him. For thus we come to bear Christ in us, because His Body and Blood are diffused through our members; thus it is that, according to the blessed Peter, 'we become partakers of the Divine nature.'"

" 5. Even under the Old Testament there was shewbread, but this, as it belonged to the Old Testament, came to an end ; but in the New Testament there is the Bread of heaven, and the Cup of salvation, sanctifying soul and body ; for as the Bread has respect to our body, so is the word appropriate to our soul."

" 6. Contemplate, therefore, the Bread and Wine not *as bare* (ὡς ψιλοῖς) elements ; for they are, according to the Lord's declaration, the Body and Blood of Christ ; for, though sense suggest this to thee, let faith stablish thee.   Judge not the matter from taste, but from faith be fully assured without misgiving, that thou hast been vouchsafed the Body and Blood of Christ."

"9. These [2] things having learnt, and being fully persuaded that what seems bread is not bread, though bread by taste, but the Body of Christ; and that what seems wine is not wine, though the taste will have it so, but the Blood of Christ; and that of this David sang of old, saying, 'And bread which strengtheneth man's heart, and oil to make his face to shine,' 'strengthen thine heart,' partaking thereof as spiritual, and 'make the face of thy soul to shine.'"

"Then [3], having sanctified ourselves by these spiritual Hymns, we call upon the merciful God to send forth His Holy Spirit upon the gifts lying before Him, that He may make the Bread the Body of Christ, and the Wine the Blood of Christ; for whatsoever the Holy Ghost has touched is sanctified and changed."

"15. 'Give [4] us this day our super-substantial bread.' This common bread is not super-substantial bread, but this Holy Bread is super-substantial; that is, appointed for the substance of the soul. For this Bread 'goeth *not* into the belly, and is cast out into the draught,' but is diffused through all thou art, for the benefit of body and soul."

"20. After [5] this ye hear the chanter, with a sacred melody inviting you to the communion of the Holy Mysteries, and saying 'O taste, and see that the Lord is good.' Trust not the decision to thy bodily palate, no, but to faith unfaltering; for when we

---

[2] p. 272.   [3] Lect. xxiii. Myst. v. § 7, p. 275.
[4] p. 277.   [5] p. 278.

taste we are bidden to taste, not bread and wine, but the *antitype* of the Body and Blood of Christ."

" 21. Approaching[6], therefore, come not with thy wrists extended, or thy fingers open, but make thy left hand as if a throne for thy right, which is on the eve of receiving the King. And having hollowed thy palm, receive the Body of Christ, saying, after it, Amen. Then, after thou hast with carefulness hallowed thine eyes by the touch of the Holy Body, partake thereof; giving heed lest thou lose any of It, for what thou losest is a loss to thee, as it were from one of thine own members. For tell me, if any one gave thee gold dust, wouldest thou not with all precaution keep it fast, being on thy guard against losing any of it, and suffering loss. How much more cautiously, then, wilt thou observe that not a crumb falls from thee, of what is more precious than gold and precious stones ?

" 22. Then after having partaken of the Body of Christ, approach also to the Cup of His Blood ; not stretching forth thine hands, but bending and saying in the way of worship and reverence, Amen, be thou hallowed by partaking also of the Blood of Christ."

30. S. GREGORY[7],

Illuminator of Armenia, A. D. 350. He extended the Gospel both in Greater and Lesser Armenia. He converted the King Tiridates, and was consecrated Bishop by Leon-

---

[6] p. 279.

[7] The passage here quoted is from his Acts, and was accounted his by Nicephorus, Patriarch of Constantinople, A.D. 806.

tius of Cæsaria in Cappadocia.   His success is thought to
have been the cause of the hostility and desolating war of
Maximin.

"2. As [s] a witness, shall the great martyr stand
forth, Gregory, who shed forth the light of the knowledge of God among the Armenians, and preached
the Divine word. He, when in the very extremity of
perils, and at the very issue of the conflict, and
bedewed with the streams of martyrdom, addressing
a prayer at once of thanksgiving and supplication
to the God of all, goes through topics of this sort on
this subject.

"'Since men loved to worship images of the human
form, carved in wood by the skill of the artificer, He
Himself became the true image of man, that He
might subdue image-makers, and image-carvers, and
image-worshippers, to the true Image of the Godhead. And since men were wont to worship dead
lifeless idols, He Himself became, on the Cross, a
dead Image, and died, and became lifeless, that He
might the more readily, through their wont, subdue
them to the true Image; and that using the Cross as
the hook, He might make His own Body Food to the
world, that in this He might catch all unto the Royal
Table of His Godhead. And instead of carved wood,
He fixed the Cross in the centre of the world, that
many who were wont to worship wood, might through

* Nicephorus Antioch, cont. Euseb. c. 75. Spicil. Solesm. pp.
499—501.

such wont have faith to worship His Cross, and the Image in Human Form upon it.'"

And afterwards;

"And since men were wont, at the temples of their idols, to rejoice in the oblations which they offered to the inanimate, therefore Thou too didst call the world to the sacrifice of Thy Son, and saidst, 'My Calf is slain, and My Feast is prepared.' And Thou madest full the joy from the Cross of Thy Son, and didst *satisfy all the ends of the earth with His Life-giving Body.*"

And a little after,

"And since men drank the blood of the sacrifices, when they worshipped devils, therefore He emptied forth His own Blood upon the Cross, that the wood might be instead of the graven image, and that very Image in the Human Form, for the detestable image; and IIis Blood, instead of the blood of the sacrifice, might become the renewal of bodies, to the restoration of human nature."

31. LIBERIUS, Bishop of Rome.

A. D. 352—365.

He recovered his fall, in signing, after two years of banishment, an heretical creed, acknowledging the Arians, and separating from the communion of S. Athanasius, A. D. 357. Hence S. Ambrose speaks of him here in terms of respect. S. Basil calls him "Liberius of most blessed memory," even when speaking of a case in which he had been imposed upon. (Ep. 263, § 3, ad Occident. iii. 406.)   S.

Epiphanius also calls him " Liberius of blessed memory." Hær. 75, § 2, p. 906, quoted by the Benedictines, ad loc.

S. Ambrose thus introduces Liberius' address to his own [S. Ambrose's] sister, Marcellina.

" It [9] is time, holy sister, to revolve the precepts of Liberius of blessed memory, on which you used to confer with me : since the holier the man, the pleasanter the discourse. For when at S. Peter's, on the birthday of the Saviour, you marked the profession of virginity by the change of habit also, (and on what day better than that on which a virgin gained an offspring?) many daughters of God too standing there emulous of your fellowship, he said to you, 'A good Bridal, daughter, hast thou longed for. Seest thou how large a multitude has assembled on the birthday of thy Espoused, and no one departeth unfed? He it is who, when bidden to the marriage, turned water into wine. On thee too will He confer the pure sacrament of virginity, who before wast subject to the poor elements of our material nature . . . This is He Who with five loaves and two fishes fed four thousand of the people in the wilderness. More He could have fed, if then there had been more to be fed. More has IIe called to thy espousals; but now not bread from barley, but a Body is ministered from heaven.'"

32. S. HILARY,

Bishop of Poictiers, probably about A.D. 349 [Vita S.

[9] S. Ambr. de Virgin. iii. 1.

Hil. c. 3, 4, n. 29, ed. Ben.] ; banished for the faith A.D. 356, died about A.D. 367.

On his use of the words " through *the Food of the Lord* " " under *the Sacrament,*" *as implying that the substance remains,* see above, pp. 132-3.   *On his applying our Lord's words, " fruit of the vine," to the consecrated Cup,* see above, pp. 137-8.

" 13. If[1] the Word was truly made Flesh, and we, through the Food of the Lord, truly receive the Word made Flesh, how must He not be thought to abide in us by the way of nature, Who, being born Man, took to Himself the nature of our flesh, now inseparable from Him, and *under the Sacrament* of the Flesh to be communicated to us, hath mingled the Nature of His own Flesh with His eternal Nature?   Whoso then will deny that the Father is by Nature in Christ, let him first deny that either he is by way of nature in Christ or Christ in him ; because the Father in Christ and Christ in us make us to be one in them . . . If then Christ truly took the Nature of our body, and that Man, Who was born of Mary, is truly Christ, and we truly under a mystery receive the Flesh of His Body (and thereby shall be One thing [unum] because the Father is in Him and He in us), how is it asserted that the Unity is of will only, whereas the natural property (conveyed) through the Sacrament is the Sacrament of a perfect Unity?

" 14. We must not, in the things of God, speak

[1] De Trin. viii. 13—17.

after the way of men or of the world; nor may the perverseness of an alien and ungodly meaning be, by a strained and reckless teaching, extorted from the soundness of the heavenly words. What is written let us read, and what we have read let us understand, and then we shall discharge the duty of a perfect faith. For what we say of the truth of Christ in us by nature, unless we have learnt from Him, we say foolishly and impiously. For He Himself saith: 'He that eateth My Flesh and drinketh My Blood dwelleth in Me and I in him. As the Living Father hath sent Me and I live by the Father, so he that eateth Me, even he shall live by Me.' Of the truth of the Flesh and Blood there is no room left for doubt. For now according both to the declaration of the Lord Himself and our faith, it is truly Flesh and truly Blood. And these received and drunk into us, cause, that both we are in Christ and Christ is in us. Is not this truth? Be it not truth to those who deny that Christ Jesus is true God. He Himself then is in us through the flesh, and we are in Him, since this, which we are, is with Him in God.

" 15. But how much we are in Him through the Sacrament of His communicated Body and Blood, He Himself beareth witness, saying, 'The world seeth Me no more, but ye shall see Me; because I live, ye shall live also. For I am in the Father, and ye in Me, and I in you.' If He willed only that an unity of *will* be understood, why did He set forth a certain gradation and order in perfecting that unity, save that, since He is in the Father by the Nature of Divinity, and we again in Him by His bodily Birth, and He again is believed to be in us by the mystery of the Sacraments, there would be thus taught a perfect unity through the Mediator; since He, in whom we abide, abideth in the Father, and, abiding in the Father, He abideth in us, and thus we advance to the Unity of the Father, in that in Him Who is the Father by way of Nature, according to His [Eternal] Nativity, we also are, by way of nature, since He Himself, by way of nature, abideth in us.

"16. But how this Unity is in us, after the way of nature, Himself thus beareth witness: 'Whoso eateth My Flesh and drinketh My Blood, dwelleth in Me, and I in him.' For no one will be in Him, save He in whom Himself is; and He hath *his* flesh only taken into Himself, who hath received His own. But the Sacrament of this perfect Unity He had explained above, saying, 'As the Living Father hath sent Me, and I live by the Father, even so he that eateth Me shall live by Me.' He then liveth by the Father; and in like way as He liveth by the Father, in that same way we live by His Flesh. . . . This then is the cause of our life, that in ourselves who are in the flesh, we have Christ abiding through the flesh; in that we shall live through Him under the same condition as He liveth by the Father. If then we live through Him by way of nature according to the flesh, *i. e.* having obtained the nature of His Flesh, how hath He not the Father in Himself by Nature, according to His Divine Spirit, since He Himself liveth by the Father?

"17. These things we have therefore mentioned, because the heretics alleging falsely an unity of will only between the Father and the Son, made use of the example of our unity with God, as though we were united to the Son, and through the Son to the Father, only by obedience and religious will, and no proper and natural communion were bestowed upon us through the Sacrament of the Flesh and Blood; whereas, both through the honour of the Son given to us, and through the Son abiding in us through the flesh, and through our being united corporeally and inseparably in Him, the mystery of a true unity by way of nature is to be taught."

"Having[2] taken the bread and the fish, the Lord looked up to Heaven, blessed and brake, giving thanks to the Eternal Father, that He was changed into the food of the Gospel."

"Was[3] He unwilling to suffer? but, before, He had consecrated the Blood of His Own Body to be shed for the remission of sins."

"'Give[4] us this day our daily bread,' for what doth God so will, as that Christ should daily dwell in us, Who is the Bread of Life and the Bread from Heaven? And because it is a daily prayer, daily also is it prayed that that Bread be given."

---

[2] In Matt. c. 14, § 11, p. 681.
[3] Ib. c. 31, § 7, p. 743.   [4] Fragm. p. 1368.

" And [5] what is this Food ?   That wherein we are prepared for the fellowship of God, to be by the Communion of the Holy Body, placed henceforth in the Communion of the Holy Body."

" In [6] this bodily life our soul is to be nourished, obtaining through the food of these toils, the Living Bread, the Heavenly Bread, from Him Who said, ' I am the Living Bread from Heaven,' which whoso, according to the Apostle's law, 'receiveth unworthily, bringeth judgment on himself.' "

" The [7] Table of the Lord is that from which we take the Food of the Living Bread, of which the virtue is this : that, Himself living, He quickens those who receive Him."

" Thy [8] tribunes came to the holy of holies, and, with all cruelty, opening a way for themselves through the people, dragged forth the priests from the Altar. Thinkest thou, thou wicked one, that thy sin was lighter than the impiety of the Jews ?   They, indeed, shed the blood of Zacharias ; but thou, as much as in thee lay, didst sever from Christ [9] those incorporated into Christ."

" What frenzy didst thou exercise against the Church of Thoulouse !   The Clergy were beaten with clubs ; the Deacons were crushed with boxing-gloves

---

[5] In Ps. lxiv. § 14, p 169.

[6] In Ps. cxxvii. § 6, p. 425.   [7] § 10, p. 428.

[8] c. Const. Imp. § 11, pp. 1246-7.

[9] As he had said " from the altar," where the Body of Christ was.

armed with lead [1]; and on Himself, as the holy will understand, on Christ Himself hands were laid."

Arian Council, at Philippolis, A.D. 347.

Of Paul, the Orthodox and banished Bishop of Constantinople, they say: "Presbyters [2] were dragged naked by him to the market-place, and (what must be said with tears and grief) he openly and publicly profaned the consecrated Body of the Lord, hung to the necks of the priests."

Of S. Athanasius,

"Sinning [3] profanely and atrociously against the Body of the Lord and His mysteries."

33. HILARY, the Deacon, A.D. 354.

Banished A.D. 355, for not condemning S. Athanasius: afterwards he joined the schism of Lucifer of Cagliari.

"He [4] shows them (1 Cor. xi. 23—25) that the mystery of the Eucharist was celebrated in the course of the supper. It was not the supper itself. For it is the spiritual medicine, which, eaten with reverence, purifies for itself the devout. For it is the Memorial of our Redemption; that we, being mindful of the Redeemer, may deserve to obtain greater things from Him.

"'As often as ye eat this Bread, and drink this Cup, ye shall shew forth the Lord's death till He come.' (1 Cor. xi. 26.) For since by the Lord's

---

[1] "plumbo elisi," lit. with lead.
[2] Preserved by S. Hilary, Fragm. iii. 9, p. 1313.
[3] Ib. § 23.
[4] In 1 Cor. xi. 23. App. S. Ambros. ii. 149.

Death we were made free, in memory of this, by eating and drinking the Flesh and the Blood which have been offered for us, we signify that we have obtained in these the New Testament, which is the new law that conveys into the kingdom of heaven him who obeys its commands.   For Moses, too, when he had taken in a bason the blood of a heifer, sprinkled the children of Israel, saying, 'This is the enjoined Covenant, which God hath made with you.' (Exod. xxiv. 8.) This was a figure of the Testament, which God by the prophets hath called New; so that that which Moses delivered is Old. The Testament, therefore, was confirmed by blood, because blood is the attester of the Divine benefit.   In type whereof we receive the mystic cup of Blood to the preservation of our bodies and souls; because the Blood of the Lord hath redeemed our blood, that is, hath saved the whole man. For the Flesh of the Saviour was given for the salvation of the body, but the Blood was shed for our souls, as had been formerly prefigured by Moses; for thus he saith : 'The flesh is offered for your bodies, but the blood for your souls' (Exod. xii. 11, Vulg.), and that therefore the blood was not to be eaten. If there was among those of old the image of the Truth, which hath now appeared and hath been made manifest in the coming of the Saviour, how does the Old seem to heretics to be contrary to the New, whereas they are a mutual testimony one to the other?

" He teaches (vv. 28, 29) that with devout mind

and with fear we must approach to the Communion; that the mind may know that it owes reverence to Him Whose Body it approaches to receive. For this he ought to judge within himself: that it is the Lord, Whose Blood he drinks in a mystery, which Blood is a witness of the good deed of God. This if we receive, amid self-discipline, we shall not be unworthy of the Body and Blood of the Lord; for we shall be seen to render thanks to our Redeemer.

"'For this cause many are weak and sickly among you, and many sleep.' That he may prove it to be true, that there will be a trial of those who receive the Body of the Lord, he already shows here the semblance of judgment upon them, who had received carelessly the Body of the Lord, in that they were seized by fevers and sicknesses, and many died: that by them the rest might learn, and, terrified by the example of a few, might amend, knowing that the negligent reception of the Body of the Lord is not unavenged: and that he whose punishment shall have been delayed here, shall be dealt with more severely, because he hath despised example.

"'But if we would judge ourselves we should not be judged. For when we are judged, we are corrected of the Lord, that we be not condemned with the world.' He says that if we ourselves would correct our faults, we should not be judged of the Lord. And since we are corrected, yet is it for our sakes, that by the very fear we may be amended. For in few is there entire amendment. 'That we be not con-

demned with the world,' that is, with unbelievers.
For he who approaches carelessly to the Table of the
Lord, in nothing differs from an infidel."

34. Marius Victorinus, a.d. 362.

An African rhetorician (to whom, for his eloquence, a
statue was raised in the Roman Forum), converted in his
old age (see S. Aug. Conf. viii. 2, p. 135 sqq., O. T., and
note *d*); he gave up his chair when Julian forbad Christians
to teach.   Ib. c. 5, pp. 140-1.

" Whence[5] is ἐπιούσιον derived but from substance?   Give us our bread ἐπιούσιον this day.   Since
Jesus is Life, and His Body is Life, but His Body
is bread, as is said, ' Give us bread from heaven:'
ἐπιούσιον signifies *from* or *in* the substance itself, *i.e.*
the Bread of Life.

" We[6] Christians, *i.e.* who believe in Christ, are
taught in the Gospel how we ought to pray God the
Father; in which prayer, among many other petitions, we ask for bread, which bread is Life, as it is
written, 'This is the Bread which came down from
Heaven.'   This Life both of Christ and God, *i.e.*
eternal, which He Himself calls by the name of
ἐπιούσιον ἄρτον, ' bread from the same οὐσία ' (essence),
i.e. from the life of God.   For whence shall we be
sons of God, save by the participation of eternal life,
which Christ gave us, bringing it from the Father.
This then is δὸς ἡμῖν ἐπιούσιον ἄρτον [give us bread
ἐπιούσιον], *i.e.* life *from the same substance;* for if

---

[5] Advers. Arium. i. 30. Gall. viii. 163.
[6] Ib. ii. c. 8, p. 177.

what we receive is the Body of Christ, but Christ is Life, we seek for ἄρτον ἐπιούσιον. For Riches dwelt in Christ bodily.

" 'As' the Living Father sent Me.' And lest any one should think that that Christ in the Flesh [only] said this, He straightway subjoined, 'This is the Bread which came down from Heaven.' Then, that He is 'Life' and 'Life Eternal,' He thus attests, thus teaches; 'Unless ye receive the Body of the Son of Man' as the Bread of life, 'and drink His Blood, ye have no Life in you; but whoso eateth His Flesh and drinketh His Blood hath eternal life.' All then which Christ is, is eternal life, whether spirit, or soul, or flesh. For of all these He Himself is the Logos (Word). But the Logos is primæval Life; therefore those things too which He puts on are life. Whence those same things in us too will obtain eternal life, they too being made spiritual through the Spirit which Christ giveth unto us. And lest any one should think that Christ saith this of Christ according to the flesh only, and not of His whole self, Who is Spirit, Soul, and Flesh, what saith He? 'What and if ye see the Son of Man ascending?' Who is the Son of Man? Spirit, Soul, Flesh. For these He had when He ascended, and with these He ascended."

35. TITUS, Bishop of Bostra, A.D. 362.

Julian endeavoured in vain to inflame the people against

' Ib. iv. 7, pp. 188-9.

him. He was present at the Council of Antioch, A.D. 363;
died A.D. 371.

"'But[8] I will not eat this Passover, until it be
fulfilled in the kingdom of God.' It was His custom
to call justification by faith, the calling through Holy
Baptism, and the participation in Holy Baptism, and
the power of worshipping in spirit, 'the kingdom of
Heaven.' Therefore I will not look, saith He, on
ought of such a Passover, *i. e.* that which was typically pointed out by Moses, until it be fulfilled in
the kingdom of God; that is, the time declared,
when the kingdom of Heaven is manifested. For
the true Passover is fulfilled in us who honour the
'passing over' which is above the law; and not a lamb
from the flock sanctifieth us who are in Christ, but
rather Himself holily ministered through the mystic
Eucharist, through which we are blessed and quickened. For He hath become to us the living Bread
Which came down from Heaven, and giveth life to
the world."

35 b. S. DAMASUS, Bishop of Rome, A.D. 366—384.

"A distinguished man, and learned in the Scriptures"
(S. Jerome, Ep. 48, ad Pammach, § 17, p. 228, ed. Vall.);
"chosen by the judgment of God" (S. Ambr. Ep. 17 ad
Valentin. § 10); "adorned with all kinds of virtue and
praiseworthy life, prepared both to speak and act in behalf
of Apostolic doctrine." (Theod. H. E. ii. 22, and v. 2.)

 "Holy[9] Tarsicius, bearing in his hand
  Christ's sacred Mysteries, when a ruffian band

---

[8] On S. Luke xxii. 14 in Cramer Catena, ii. 154.
[9] Carm. 18, de S. Tarsicio, published from the Antiq. Inscript.

Assail'd him, bent those mysteries to expose
To eyes profane, beneath their murderous blows
His very soul was fain to yield away,
Nor to rude dogs the heavenly Body to betray."

36. S. Epiphanius, Bishop of Salamis, in Cyprus, A. D. 368.

A passage in which he speaks of the consecrated elements as " Antitypes," has been given above, p. 101 (a term which he also used of Baptism, p. 118). In pp. 133. 149, one has been quoted, in which he speaks of " the might in bread," the "bread" being bodily " food." He interprets " the fruit of the vine " of the natural element of wine, p. 139.

In the following passage, while he avoids the mention of the sacred words, on the principle already mentioned[1], he shows clearly that he takes the words, "This is My Body," literally, in the sense that that which outwardly is wholly unlike His Body, is inwardly that Body.

"All[2] have this, that they are in the Image of God, but not by nature. For men have not that Image by any equality with God. For God is incomprehensible, inconceivable, being a Spirit and above all spirits, and Light above all lights. But

in App. p. 1174, n. 2. The history is, that he was an Acolyth, was carrying home the Sacrament (as was done, dating perhaps from times of persecution, when it was difficult to meet daily in public, to receive it) and refusing to give It up to the Heathen rabble, was beaten with clubs and stones, till he died. (Baronius Martyrol. Rom. Aug. 15, p. 314.)

[1] Above, pp. 267—269.   [2] Ancorat. 57. T. ii. p. 60.

what He decreed, we disown not. True is He Who, with grace, gave to man to be in His Image, and whatever else is of the like sort. For we see that the Saviour took into His hands, as it is in the Gospel, that He arose at supper and took these things, and having given thanks He said, 'This is *that* of Me.' And we see that it is not equal, nor like, either to the Incarnate Image, or the Invisible Godhead, or the characters of the limbs; for that is somewhat cubical, and insensate as to power. And He willed by grace to say, 'This is *that* of Me,' and no one disbelieveth His Word. For whoso believeth not that it is true, as He said, falleth from grace and salvation. But whatsoever we may hear [affirmed of it], we believe that it is His. But we know that our Lord is wholly perception, wholly perceptible, wholly God, wholly giveth motion, wholly operating, wholly light, wholly incomprehensible, but with grace giveth us this thing."

S. Epiphanius uses the same form of words, when showing, against Marcion, that our Lord kept the Jewish Passover before He instituted the Holy Eucharist. "And[1] after supper, taking this and that, He saith, 'This is that and that.'" On the one side, S. Epiphanius contrasts the Holy Eucharist with the old Passover, which he says "was *nothing but* the sacrifice of a lamb, and eating of flesh, and participation of an animal and unleavened bread." On the

---

[1] Hær. xlii. Schol. 61. T. i. p. 344.

other side, in both places, he shows by the form of words that he supposes that it was the bread, of which our Lord says, "This is My Body," which yet Roman Divines say[4] is opposed to the doctrine of Transubstantiation.

In another place, he speaks of our really receiving the Blood of Christ: "For[5] the Only-Begotten hath come, hath come! and so declares our Mother Church, the quiet harbour of peace, the sweetness that 'breathes of the bloom of the vine,' and gives to us the Cluster of Blessing, and that offers to us day by day the draught which lightens toil, the Blood of Christ, unmixed and true."

The strange heresy of the Ophites still lasted in S. Epiphanius' time. They worshipped the serpent as Christ. The debased character of their Eucharist was in keeping with the heresy itself; but it could hardly have been devised, except in the midst of a belief that our Lord Himself consecrates the Eucharist, and is present there[6].

---

[4] See above, pp. 257—259.

[5] Expos. Fid. Cath. n. 14. T. i. p. 1096.

[6] S. Epiphanius' account, in his own time, is : " They have a real serpent which they keep in a chest."   " At the time of the mysteries, heaping up bread about the hole of the box, they invite it out ; then 'when it had curled around the bread,' they said that *this was a perfect sacrifice ;* whence S. Epiphanius says, ' that he had heard, they not only brake the bread amid which the serpent had curled and distributed to the recipients, but each kissed the mouth of the serpent,' it having first been charmed." (Hær. 37, § 5, p. 272.)

37. S. Optatus, Bishop of Milevis, in Africa,
A.D. 368.

"And[7] what seems a light thing to you, an
unheard-of offence was committed, in that your
Bishops, above-mentioned, violated all the most Holy
Things. They ordered the Eucharist to be thrown
to the dogs, not without marks of Divine judgment;
for those same dogs, kindled with madness, with
avenging tooth, tore their very masters, as though
they were robbers, strangers, and foes, being guilty
of the Holy Body."

" For[8] what is so sacrilegious as to break, scrape,
take away the Altars of God, on which yourselves
also have some time made your offering? whereon
have been borne both the prayers of the people and
the members of Christ; where Almighty God hath
been invoked; where the Holy Spirit, when besought, hath come down; whence have been received
by many both the pledge of eternal salvation, and
the guard of faith, and the hope of the resurrection.
Altars, I say, on which the Saviour commanded that
the offerings of the brotherhood should not be laid,
unless such as had been seasoned with peace. 'Leave
there,' He saith, 'thy gift before the altar, and go
thy way, first be reconciled to thy brother, that the
priest may be able to offer for thee[9].' For what is
the Altar, but the throne of the Body and Blood of

---

[7] De Schism. Donat. ii. 19, p. 42, ed. Dupin.
[8] Ib. vi. 1, p. 90.
[9] Matt. v. 24.

Christ? all these your madness hath either scraped, or broken, or removed."

" If[1], in the judgment of many, we seemed to you defiled, what had God done to you, Who was wont to be called on here? wherein had Christ offended you, Whose Body and Blood dwelt here at stated times? wherein had ye yourselves offended yourselves, that ye should break these Altars, where, for long periods of time before us, ye offered, as ye suppose, holily? While ye impiously persecute our hands, there where the Body of Christ was wont to dwell, ye have pierced your own also. In this way ye have imitated the Jews; they lay their hands on Christ on the Cross; by you IIe was smitten on the Altar."

" This[2] great crime has been doubled by you, in that ye brake the Chalices too, which bear the Blood of Christ."

38. S. Pacian, Bishop of Barcelona, A.D. 368.

" Died, in extreme old age," before A.D. 392. S. Jerome, see further, Pref. to S. Cyprian and S. Pacian, p. xxii. Oxf. Tr.

" Then[3] I shall speak of those faithful who, ashamed of their remedy, use an ill-timed bashfulness, and communicate with body defiled and mind polluted. In the sight of men most timid, before the Lord most shameless, they contaminate with

---

[1] Ib. p. 91.   [2] c. 2, p. 92.
[3] Par. ad Pæn. § 6, p. 365, O. T.

profane hands and polluted mouth the Altar, to be dreaded even by Saints and Angels."

" You [4] then I first call on, brethren, who, having committed crimes, refuse penance; you, I say, timid after being shameless, modest after sinning; who blush not to sin, yet blush to confess; who with evil conscience touch the Holy Things of God, and fear not the Altar of the Lord; who come to the hands of the priest, who come in the sight of angels with the confidence of innocence; who insult the Divine patience; who bring to God, as if because silent He knew not, a polluted soul and a profane body."

" But [5] grant that it is a thing of old, that the unclean were not permitted to approach the table of God! Open the writings of the Apostles, and learn what is of later date. In the first Epistle to the Corinthians, Paul hath inserted these words, ' Whosoever,' he saith, ' shall eat this Bread, and drink this Cup of the Lord unworthily, shall be guilty of the Body and Blood of the Lord.' So likewise below, ' For he that eateth and drinketh unworthily, eateth and drinketh damnation to himself, not discerning the Lord's Body. For this cause many are weak and sickly among you, and many sleep. For if we would judge ourselves, we should not be judged. But when we are judged we are chastened of the Lord, that we should not be condemned with the

---

[4] Ib. n. 12, pp. 368-9.   [5] Ib. § 12, 13, pp. 369-70.

world.' Do ye tremble or not? 'Shall be guilty,' he saith, 'of the Body and Blood of the Lord.' One guilty as to human life could not be absolved; doth he escape who violates 'the Body of the Lord?' 'He that eateth and drinketh unworthily,' he saith, 'eateth and drinketh damnation to himself.' Awake, O sinner! Fear judgment present within thee, if thou hast done any such thing. 'For this cause,' he saith, 'many are weak and sickly among you, and many sleep.' If then any one fears not the future, let him now, at least, dread present sickness and present death. 'But when we are judged,' he saith, 'we are chastened of the Lord, that we should not be condemned with the world.' Rejoice, O sinner, if in this life thou art either cut off by death, or wasted by sickness, that thou be not punished in the life to come. See how great wickedness he committeth, who cometh when unworthy to the Altar, to whom it is reckoned as a remedy if he either labours under sickness or is destroyed by death."

39. S. Ephrem of Edessa.

Son of an idolatrous priest: baptized by S. James of Nisibis: ordained Deacon by S. Basil (afterwards Priest, Pref. to select works, p. xiii. Oxf. Tr.). He is said to have been present at the Council of Nice. Theodoret and Sozomen certainly imply that he knew no Greek. Theodoret calls him " the best author among the Syrians" (ii. 30) ; and says, " Ephrem, *using the language of the Syrians*, sent forth the rays of spiritual grace. For *not* having *tasted Greek instruction*, he refuted the manifold errors of the Greeks " (iv. 29). He adds, that S. Ephrem took from Bardesanes (the

Gnostic), "the harmony of measure, and mingled with it piety, and so brought to his hearers a most sweet and healthful antidote." So, then, his entire ignorance of Greek education stands between a statement, that he wrote in Syriac, and an account of his Syriac hymns. Sozomen (iii. 16) relates how, unexpectedly, amid his "Monastic philosophy," he, in Syriac, advanced to such a degree of instruction, as to surpass the most distinguished Greek *writers.* For his works did not lose by translation : " For in his lifetime, and until now, they *translate into Greek what he wrote,* and they do not fall much short of their original excellence. But read in Greek, he is admired as much as in Syriac." S. Jerome (de Vir. Ill. c. 115) mentions having read a Greek volume of his on the Holy Spirit, which some had translated from Syriac, and that he perceived the acumen of his lofty genius, even in the translation. These clearly knew S. Ephrem only as a Syriac writer. S. Jerome adds, " He attained such celebrity, that in some Churches his writings are read publicly, after the reading of Holy Scripture."

S. Ephrem argues from the substance of the matter of the Sacrament to the real substance of our Lord's Body (see in pp. 77, 78); *he speaks of it as " an image of Christ"* (pp. 102, 103); *of our Lord's dwelling* in *the Bread* (in the same passage, and in pp. 122—124); *of the live coal, full of fire, as an emblem of the Holy Eucharist* (pp. 123, 124).

These passages strongly and fully affirm the doctrine of the Real Presence; but since they have been given at full length, it is needless to repeat them. In the remaining extracts, I confine myself to the Syriac works.

The following are comments on Holy Scripture :—

" ' Standing [6] on their feet,' because one sitting may not receive the living Body; ' and no stranger shall eat thereof,' because no one unbaptized eateth of the Body."

" ' Blessed [7] shall be thy barns:' he mentioneth the holy Table and the Body upon it."

" ' Out [8] of the eater came forth meat; and from the bitter, the sweet.' This is, from death, the devourer, which ate the Body of our Lord like the rest, when He tasted death through His own will. 'There came forth meat,' when He conquered death and rose in glory. His Body became to us Food for life and for redemption. 'And from the bitter, the sweet.' From death, which is very bitter, there gushed forth to us the sweetness of the life-giving Food, which sweeteneth the bitterness of our nature. And again ' from the eater came forth meat,' *i.e.* from death came forth the Body, which the Church eateth.

" The [9] Table of gold is the Christ in truth, which the Wisdom of God prepared, and set thereon bread, which nourishes the souls of the righteous to life everlasting. The shewbread figures the mystery of our sacrifices which are offered through Christ by the Ministers of the Church. Two crowns encircle the Table, because two natures, a higher and a lower, Angelic and human, stand around Emmanuel."

[6] On Exod. xii. T. i. p. 213.
[7] On Deut. xxviii. 4, ib. p. 283.
[8] On Jud. xiii. 14, p. 324.
[9] In 1 Reg. vii. 28, p. 461.

"This[1], that the prophet bade the widow's son to live on the horn and the cruise, which were multiplied by the power of God, this figures to us the type of the sons of the Holy Church at the Table of Emmanuel, if under the meal which was increased we understand the living Food through the Body, and under the oil which was multiplied, we understand the gift of the Holy Anointing."

"The[2] righteous, with sinners, fill themselves with the Living Body which is on the Altar."

"Although[3] it was in Jerusalem that in this day of their deliverance they feasted and praised, yet this was fulfilled in our Lord, when in the Mount of Jerusalem He brake His Body and divided His Blood, and said, 'This ye shall do for a remembrance of Me.' This is a heavenly and spiritual feast, 'a feast laid up and rich,' which giveth us life, 'and strong,' *i.e.* which strengtheneth us; and this it is which all people drink."

"'I[4] will set in the wilderness cedars and planes,' *i.e.* in the nations priests and chief priests and Levites, who consecrate the Body and Blood, and break it, for the forgiveness of souls."

"Mystically[5] this was fulfilled through Christ, Who gave to His people whom He had redeemed, *i.e.* His Church, mystical corn and wine and oil;

[1] In 1 Reg. xvii. 21, p. 493.
[2] Explanation of Isa. xi. 6, T. ii. p. 40.
[3] In Isa. xxv. 26. Ib. p. 61.
[4] In Isa. xli. 19, p. 89.   [5] In Joel ii. 24, p. 252.

corn, which figures His Holy Body, and wine, His Atoning Blood; and, again, oil for the fragrant ointment, wherewith the baptized are sealed and put on the armour of the Holy Spirit."

He explains Zech. ix. 17: "Souls[6], which are barren to the seed of the Accuser, and which corrupted not their fair nature, for *their* feast is reserved the wine of the Cluster[7] which hung upon the Cross."

In his Rhythms on the Nativity;

" His[8] Body became bread, to quicken our deadness."

" Blessed[9] the Branch that did become the Cup of our Redemption! Blessed also be the Cluster, Fount of medicine of life!

In his Rhythms on the Faith;

" For[10] *in* bread the Strong One that cannot be eaten, is eaten. *In* strong wine also is drunk the Power which cannot be drunk. We also anoint ourselves in oil with the Power which cannot be used as ointment. And as He hath softened Himself for the mouth in pleasant meats, and it eateth Him, so He hath made the sight of Himself soft to the eye. He hath softened His might in words, so that the ear may also hear Him. Amongst those conceived Thou art marvellous; amongst those born Thou art glorious; amongst the baptized Thou art

---

[6] p. 300. [7] See S. Greg. Nyss. below, p. 431.

[8] Rhythm 2, on the Nativity, p. 12, O. T. p. 402, Syr.

[9] Ib. p. 13. [10] De Scrut. Rhythm vi. 2, p. 127, O. T.

approved; amongst the redeemed Thou art desirable; amongst the sacrificed Thou art slain; amongst pleasant meats Thou art eaten; among the Prophets Thou art mingled; in the Apostles Thou art mixed; the Whole of Thee, Lord, is in all; in the deep Thou art buried; in the height Thou art worshipped."

S. Ephrem dwells upon the Holy Eucharist far more frequently in his Ecclesiastical Hymns, and these again have the more weight, because they were received throughout the Syriac Churches, and were continued in those bodies, which were broken off by heresy [1]. They were composed, partly as funeral hymns for the departed of every age, sex, office, partly as hortatory hymns. In both, there is frequent mention of the Day of Judgment, which was ever before S. Ephrem's eyes; and with the mention of the Day of Judgment, there is very frequent appeal to our Lord, to spare those on whom He had bestowed His Body and Blood. The frequency of these appeals shows, what place the doctrine of the Real Presence held in S. Ephrem's mind and in that of the Church, which received many of these hymns into its worship.

" Spare [2] the body and the soul. Thou who didst mingle Thy Body with our body, and didst blend Thy Spirit with our spirit. Lo! in our body is Thy

---

[1] Assem. Bibl. Or. Art. S. Ephr. viii. ix. T. i. pp. 133. 138.
[2] Can. 12, T. iii. p. 246.

Baptism, and in our persons Thy living Body. In us, Lord, there is a portion from Thee; let us not be a portion for the fire."

"Thou[3] wilt not burn the hand which received a portion of Thy Holy Body, together with the hand which smote Thee on Thy Cheek, Thee, the Creator. The mouth which ate Thee will not howl, together with the mouth which spat on Thee, on Thy Face."

"Whom[4] Thou hast made meet to administer in the Sanctuary, and to distribute Thy Body and Thy Blood to Thy flock, may his pasture be with Thy lambs."

"The[5] armour of the Cross is with thee; and Baptism and the Body and Blood of Christ are a great shield."

"Lo[6]! with thee descendeth into the tomb, He Who divided the sea before Moses, and on thee there maketh its light to arise in darkness, the pillar that led Israel; for there is hidden in thy limbs the Body that raiseth all, and in the blood of thy spirit is there mingled the Cup of Salvation which leaveth not thy body in destruction. Take Baptism and the Body and Blood of Christ with thee as a passport."

"We[7] implore Thy goodness, O Christ (our) king, that Thou wilt not remember follies against Thy

---

[3] Ibid.   [4] Can. 13, p. 247.
[5] Can. 20, p. 268, and 54, § 3, p. 316.
[6] Can. 23, p. 272.   [7] Can. 66, p. 334.

servants, who have received the Sacrament of Thy Body."

"Blessed [8] be Christ, Who humbled Himself, and tasted death, and gave us His Body and Blood, and restored life to Adam and his sons, and redeemed them by His Cross."

" As [9] provision for a journey, Thee have I taken unto me, Thou Son of God, and when an hungered, of Thee have I eaten, O Redeemer of the world! Far be the fire from my limbs. And when the scent of Thy Body and Blood striketh from me, may Baptism be to me a ship that foundereth not."

" No [1], O Lord! No, O Lord! loose not Thy hold on us, whom Thou hast fed with Thy Body and Blood."

" Lo [2]! Lord, I have kissed Thy Body, Whose Feet she kissed."

"I have [3] with me the token of Thy Blood, a weapon whereat the vast mouth of Hell, which hungers and thirsts for the wicked, will shrink back affrighted. Through the blood of the lamb, Death shrank back from the Hebrews. Through Thy Precious Blood, O Lord, how shall Hell shrink back!"

" O [4] fatted Calf that wert killed to be a Sacrifice

[8] Can. 76, p. 348.   [9] Can. 81, init. p. 355.
[1] Can. 85, p. 358.
[2] Paræn. 3, p. 383, alluding apparently to the title "kiss" given to Holy Communion in allusion to Cant. i. 2. See on S. Cypr. Ep. vi. § 3, p. 15, O. T.
[3] Ib. p. 386.   [4] Paræn. 5, p. 414.

for sinners, blot not out me, wretched man, O Lord, from the number of those redeemed by Thy Blood! Thy Body have I eaten, and Thy Blood have I drunken, and by Thy Death have I believed that I should live."

"Thy[5] Right Hand was fastened with nails, for mine, which stretched to the fruit.   For the sake of Thy Body, forgive me what I have sinned."

"Because[6] Thou hast given me Thy Body to eat, and Thy living Blood to drink, by Thy Body may I be pardoned, and by Thy Blood have my sins forgiven, and rise to praise Thee among the assemblies of Thy saints."

"That[7] sea of fire disturbeth me and terrifieth me, and I am in fear by reason of the iniquity I have done.   May Thy Cross, O Son of the Living God, be to me a bridge, and from Thy Body and Thy Blood may Gehenna go away ashamed, and I by Thy mercies be redeemed!"

"Better[8] is Thy love than wine, and than thousands of the upright Thy tender mercy.   Through Thy wine are we blessed, and through the Cup of Thy Blood have we received new life; and the upright praise Thy tender mercy."

"He[9] brake His Body before thee, and mingled His Blood and gave it thee."

"Leave[1] me not in the hands of the enemy, and

---

[5] P. 8, p. 421.
[6] Paræn. 11, p. 429.
[7] Paræn. 13, p. 432.
[8] P. 14, pp. 437, 438.
[9] P. 16, p. 439.
[1] Paræn. 21, pp. 452, 453.

give him not hold on me, Who hast mingled Thy Body and Blood in me, and Whose Cross is stamped between my eyes." " Let what is hateful in us be made white by Thy hyssop; and our stains be effaced by Thy Blood; and the secret motions of our thoughts be sanctified by Thy Body."

" For [2] the ointment which the sinner then brought, lo! Thy Body and Blood are mingled in my limbs."

" The [3] fire threateneth my limbs, O Lord, and Thine atoning Blood, O my Redeemer, is hidden in me.   Lo! Gehenna, &c.," as above, p. 124.

" There [4] are three things which I fear, O Lord, the fire, and Gehenna, and the worm which dieth not. Let the fire and the burning be extinguished, yea, let Thy Body and Blood deliver me."

" The [5] departed, who were clothed with Thee, Lord, in Baptism, and ate of Thy Body and drank Thy living Blood, may they rise, Lord, on the Right Hand, and with the Angels be filled with joy in Eden."

" From [6] hateful desires free me, through Thy living Body which I have eaten; and may I lie down and sleep in quiet, and Thy Blood be to me a guardian."

" Thy [7] living Body and Thine atoning Blood,

<hr>

[2] P. 23, p. 457. [3] Ib. p. 458.
[4] Ib. p. 459. [5] P. 29, p. 480.
[6] P. 30, Ib. [7] P. 31, p. 482.

Which I have received from the hands of the priests—through these, O Lord, may I be forgiven."

"Spare [8] us, and spare our departed, and all the departed who have confessed and believed in Thee, and have eaten of Thy Body and drank Thy living Blood."

" And [9] let Thy Body wherewith Thou hast fed us, and Thy Baptism wherewith Thou hast clothed us, rise for us in the Judgment, and deliver us from the torments of Hell."

" And [1] if we have sinned against Thee with our deeds, do Thou turn us to repentance, Who hast fed us with Thy Body, and given us Thy living Blood to drink, and hast commingled Thyself with us, and us with Thee, for Thy Mercy's sake, and forgive our folly."

"Spare [2] us through the tender mercy of Thy goodness; and for Thy Body's sake, wherewith Thou hast fed us, have mercy upon us."

" And [3] although I am not meet for forgiveness, spare me for the sake of Thy Body and Blood which are hidden in me. Thee have I loved, and Thy Cross have I adored, and in Thy Body and Blood hath my delight been. Through these may I be restored to favour, and pardon Thou me my guilt and my sins."

[8] P. 34, p. 487.　　　　[9] P. 35, p. 488.
[1] Ib. fin. p. 490.　　　　[2] P. 38, p. 493.
[3] Ib. p. 494.

> " Call [4] with Thy voice commandingly ;
> And let us rise lightly ;
> Who eat Thy Body gloriously,
> And drink Thy Blood purely ;
> And when Thou comest swiftly,
> In the glory of the Angels terribly,
> We will enter with Thee collectively,
> To dwell with Thee joyously."

" Let [5] Thy Body and Blood be to me a companion, and thereby may I be saved from the burning ; let Thy Cross be a bridge to us all, that we may pass the pit full of terror."

" Let [6] the hands which bore Thy Body and Blood receive from Thee pardon of sins."

" Thy [7] Body and Blood, as a pledge of life, are hidden in their members, and they will offer praise to Thee, Lord, and to the Father, and to the Holy Ghost for ever."

" It [8] were a reproach, Lord, that we should ask of Thee bread, Who hast fed me with the atoning Body."

" Lo [9], Thou art sacrificed upon our Table ; And Thou art sprinkled upon our lips ; By Thee be our prayer accepted ; Blessed be Thou of all, Who pitiest all."

" Holy [1] One, we praise Thee ; may we be hallowed by Thy Body and Blood, and from the

[4] P. 54, p. 519.
[5] P. 64, p. 535.
[6] P. 70, p. 541.
[7] P. 73, p. 545.
[8] P. 74, p. 551.
[9] Ib. fin. p. 555.
[1] Serm. 13, p. 638.

redeemed who have eaten Thy Body and drunk
Thy precious Blood, to Thee be praise."

40. S. Basil the Great, Bishop of Cæsarea,

Born about A.D. 329 ; imbued in all secular learning at
Cæsarea, Constantinople, Athens, till about A.D. 355 ; embraced monastic life, A.D. 357 ; ordained Presbyter, A.D.
364 ; Bishop of Cæsarea, A.D. 370 ; passed his episcopate
in labours for the restoration of the Church, died A.D. 378,
three years before its accomplishment at the Second General
Council. "The by-doings of this man were far more precious and illustrious than the laboured doings of others."
(S. Greg. Orat. 43, § 77, p. 830.)

He spoke of the consecrated elements as " types,"
(see p. 100,) *and interpreted " this fruit of the vine "*
of the natural substance of wine (p. 140).

"Dost thou [2] know, then, Who He is Whom thou
art about to receive? He Who promised us, 'I and
the Father will come and make Our abode with him.'
Why then dost thou anticipate by drunkenness, and
close the entrance against thy Lord? Why dost
thou encourage thine enemy to be beforehand in
gaining possession of thy fortresses? Drunkenness
receives not the Lord : drunkenness drives away the
Holy Ghost."

" He [Israel] [3] would not have drunk of the spiritual Rock, unless he had been typically baptized ; nor
will any one give thee the true Drink, unless thou
art truly baptized. He ate angels' food, after that

---

[2] De Jejunio, Hom. 1, § 11, T. ii. p. 10.
[3] In S. Bapt. § 2, T. ii. p. 115.

baptism ; thou, how wilt thou eat the living Bread, unless thou first receivest baptism ?"

In the following "Rules," S. Basil lays down certain theses, which he supports by Holy Scripture. His own words then, and the passages of Scripture by which he supports them, together express his full meaning. Thus in the first, he lays down that the Holy Eucharist is a mystery above our reason.

"That[4] we ought not to dispute and doubt as to things which the Lord has said, but be fully assured that every word of God is true and possible, even if nature oppose it. For here, too, is the fight of faith."

S. Basil gives as instances, S. Peter's fear when walking on the water (S. Matt. xiv. 25); the Jews disputing "How can this man give us His Flesh to eat?" (S. Joh. vi. 55); the doubt of Zachariah (S. Luke i. 13. 18); and the opposed instance of Abraham's faith (Rom. iv. 29).

Rule 21, c. 1. "That[5] the participation of the Body and Blood of Christ is necessary, even to everlasting life itself" (S. Joh. vi. 53 sqq.).

C. 2. "That he is nothing benefited, who, without considering the ground according to which the participation of the Body and Blood of Christ is given, approacheth to the Communion. But he who partaketh unworthily is condemned" (S. Joh. ibid. and v. 61—63. 1 Cor. xi. 27—29).

---

[4] Moralia Reg. 8, c. 1, T. ii. pp. 240, 1.
[5] pp. 253, 4.

C. 3. " In what way we should eat the Body and drink the Blood of the Lord, to the commemoration of the Lord's obedience unto death, that they who live may no longer live unto themselves, but to Him Who died for them and rose again" (S. Luke xxii. 19, 20. 1 Cor. xi. 23—26. 2 Cor. v. 14, 15. Rom. xii. 5. ·1 Cor. x. 16, 17).

Last rule, last chapter, end :

" What* is the characteristic of a Christian ? Faith, which worketh by love, &c.—What is the characteristic of a Christian? To be born from above, by Baptism from water and the Spirit, &c.—What is the characteristic of a Christian? To be cleansed from all defilement of flesh and spirit in the Blood of Christ; to perfect holiness in the fear of God, and the love of Christ; and not to have spot, or wrinkle, or any such thing, and so to eat the Body of Christ and drink His Blood. 'For whoso eateth and drinketh unworthily, eateth and drinketh damnation to himself.' "

In his shorter rules:

" With' what fear, or what conviction, or what disposition, should we partake of the Body and the Blood of Christ?

" The Apostle teacheth us the 'fear,' saying, 'He that eateth and drinketh unworthily, eateth and drinketh damnation to himself.' But the 'conviction'

---

* pp. 317, 18.
' Reg. Brev. Tract. Int. 172, p. 472.

is infused by the faith of the words of Christ, Who saith, 'This is My Body, which is given for you, this do in remembrance of Me;' and (by the faith) too of the witness of John, who, having first related the glory of the Word, subjoins the mode of the Incarnation, when he said that 'the Word became Flesh, and dwelt among us, and we beheld His glory, the glory as of the Only Begotten of the Father, full of grace and truth, &c.' "

"To [8] approach in uncleanness to holy things, we have learnt, even from the Old Testament, to be a fearful thing.   But since *here* is That which is greater than the temple (πλεῖον τοῦ ἱεροῦ) the Apostle will teach us something more fearful: 'He who eateth and drinketh unworthily, eateth and drinketh damnation to himself.' "

"Thou [9] introducest higgling into spiritual things and the Church, where we are entrusted with the Body and Blood of Christ."

"To [1] communicate daily, and to partake of the Holy Body and Blood of Christ, is right and most useful; since Himself saith plainly, 'He who eateth My Flesh and drinketh My Blood hath everlasting life.' For who doubteth that to partake frequently of life, is nothing else than manifold life?"

"Concerning [2] a priest who, through ignorance, has

[8] Ib. Interr. 309, p. 525.
[9] Ep. 53, Chorepisc. § 1, iii. 147.
[1] Id. Epist. 93, ad Cæsariam. p. 186.
[2] Ep. 199 (Canon. 2), can. 27, p. 294.

been entangled in an unlawful marriage, I have decided what is to be done: that he should retain his seat [as presbyter] but abstain from all acts of his office. For pardon is sufficient for such an one. But for him to bless another, who ought to heed his own wounds, is unreasonable. For blessing is an imparting of holiness. But he who, through the fall in ignorance, has not this, how can he impart it to another? Let him not bless either publicly or privately, nor distribute the Body of Christ to others, nor perform any liturgical office; but, satisfied with his rank, let him weep before the Lord, that his sin of ignorance may be forgiven him."

I add here extracts from the two books on Baptism in S. Basil's works, on the ground of the later editor, that the writer refers naturally to other works of S. Basil, as his own. If not S. Basil's then, they must have been a deliberate forgery, which there is no ground to suspect. The books must then be a work of S. Basil, which in some way did not receive his finishing hand. In doctrine they agree with and dilate upon, what S. Basil elsewhere wrote.

" But [3] all we who believe are redeemed from such condemnation for our sins, by the grace of God which is through His Only Begotten Son our Lord Jesus Christ, Who says: 'This is My Blood of the New Testament, Which is shed for many for the remission of sins.'"

" Such [4] an one adds against himself the judgment of the Apostle, who saith, ' He that eateth and drinketh unworthily, eateth and drinketh judgment unto himself, not discerning the Lord's Body.' For not only hath *he* a fearful judgment, who approacheth holy things unworthily in defile-

---

[3] De Bapt. 1, c. 1, § 3, p. 626.   [4] c. 3, § 3, p. 651.

ment of flesh and spirit (for so approaching, he becomes guilty of the Body and Blood of the Lord), but he too who idly and uselessly 'eateth and drinketh;' in that he doth not, through the memory of our Lord Jesus Christ, Who for us died and rose again, keep the saying, 'The love of Christ constraineth us, because we thus judge, that if one died for all, then were all dead,' and the rest. For in that, unconscientiously and unprofitably, he bringeth to nought such and so great a good, and in that he approacheth thanklessly to such a mystery, he bringeth on him the judgment of slothfulness. For the Lord doth not leave unjudged even those who utter 'an idle word,' but putteth forth yet more severely the judgment against slothfulness, in the case of him who kept the talent unimpaired in slothfulness. The Apostle too hath delivered to us, that even he who uttereth good words, yet dispenseth not for the edification of faith, grieveth the Holy Ghost. So then ought we to consider the judgment of him who eateth and drinketh unworthily. But if he that grieveth his brother for the sake of meat, hath fallen from love, without which the fruits of great gifts of graces, and of works of righteousness profit nothing, what can one say of him who dares idly and unprofitably eat the Body and drink the Blood of our Lord Jesus Christ, and hereby to grieve exceedingly the Holy Ghost, and who dares to eat and drink without that constraining love, which judgeth that he should 'not live to himself, but to our Lord Jesus Christ Who died for us.' It behoves then him who approacheth the Body and Blood of Christ, in remembrance of Him 'Who died and rose again for us,' not only 'to purify himself from all defilement of flesh and spirit,' lest 'he eat and drink judgment,' but also to show his remembrance of Him, 'Who died and rose again for us,' by dying to sin and the world and himself, and living to God and Christ Jesus our Lord."

"When[3] the Lord says, 'Lo, here is one greater than

[3] L. ii. Resp. 2, p. 653.

the temple,' He teacheth us that whoso [being defiled] dares to consecrate the Body of the Lord, Who 'gave Himself for us an Offering and a Sacrifice to God for a sweet-smelling savour,' is by so much the more impious as the Body of the Only Begotten Son of God surpasses that of bulls and of goats."

" *Q.* Is⁶ it safe for a man who purifieth not himself 'from all defilement of flesh and spirit,' to eat the Body of the Lord, and to drink His Blood?

" *A.* God, in the law, having ordained the severest punishment against him who in defilement dared to touch holy things (for it was written typically for them, but for our admonition'), if such a threat lay against those who merely approached things consecrated by men, what would one say against him who dared the same against such and so great a mystery? For by how much there is here That which is 'greater than the temple,' according to the Lord's words, by so much the more dreadful and fearful is it, in defilement of soul to dare to touch the Body of Christ, than to touch rams or bulls, as the Apostle says, 'Whosoever shall eat this Bread, or drink this Cup of the Lord unworthily, shall be guilty of the Body and Blood of the Lord.' Enforcing yet more vehemently and fearfully the judgment on such receiving, he says: 'Let a man examine himself, and so let him eat of that Bread, and drink of that Cup. For he that eateth and drinketh unworthily, eateth and drinketh judgment to himself, not considering the Lord's Body.' But if he who is merely unclean (the characteristic of uncleanness we learn typically from the law) has so fearful a judgment, how much more will he, who is in sin, and dareth upon the Body of the Lord, draw upon himself a more dreadful punishment! Let us then purify ourselves from all defilement (for the distinction between defilement and uncleanness is plain to those of understand-

⁶ Qu. et Resp. 3, p. 654.

⁷ Lev. xxii. 1—3.

ing), and so let us approach the holy things, that we may escape the judgment of them who slew the Lord, since ' he that eateth the bread or drinketh the Cup of the Lord unworthily, shall be guilty of the Body and Blood of the Lord.' So shall we have everlasting life, as our Lord and God Jesus Christ, Who cannot lie, hath promised ; if we, eating and drinking, remember Him Who died for us, and keep the judgment of the Apostle who saith : ' The Love of Christ constraineth us, because we thus judge, that if one die for all, then were all dead, and that He died for all, that they which live should no more live to themselves, but to Him Who died for them and rose again,' as we covenanted in our Baptism."

41. S. GREGORY OF NYSSA.

Younger brother of S. Basil; Bishop of Nyssa, A.D. 370 ; banished for the faith until A.D. 378 ; said to have been employed to complete the Nicene Creed at the Second General Council ; selected there to preach the Funeral Oration over S. Meletius ; lived to be present at the Council of Constantinople, held A.D. 394.

He spoke of the consecrated elements as symbols (see above, p. 107), *and understood our Lord's words, " This fruit of the vine," of the natural substance of wine* (see p. 140). *The context of the passage, in which he uses the words " transmake," " transelement," has been given already above* (pp. 180—183), *and considered there* (pp. 183—191. 196—210). *The whole passage, in which he compares the miracle of Baptism with others in the Old and New Testament, and, among them, the Holy Eucharist, has been given and considered above* (p. 271 sqq., and Sermon, pp. 45, 46).

" What [8] do we learn [from the history of the Manna]? With what cleansings, with what purifyings is it meet that any should cleanse himself from the Egyptian and alien life, so as to cleanse the sack of his soul from all food of vices, and thus to receive in himself, with a pure soul, the Food which cometh down from Heaven, which no sowing hath produced to us by husbandry, but the Bread is ready, unsown and untilled, coming down from above, yet found on earth! For thou perceivest this the true Bread under the type in the history [of the Manna], that the Bread which cometh down from Heaven is not an unembodied thing. For how could the unembodied become food for the body? But what is not unembodied is body. But the body of this bread neither ploughing nor sowing hath yielded to us; yet the earth, abiding as it is, is found full of this Divine Food, whereof they who hunger partake, having first been instructed, through this marvellous work, in the mystery relating to the Virgin. This untilled Bread then is also the Word, Who through the manifoldness of His qualities changeth His virtue according to the qualifications of those who eat It."

" For [9] that cluster hanging on the wood, what else is it than the Cluster Which in these last days hung upon the wood, Whose Blood becometh a saving Drink for the faithful? Moses, foretelling

---

[8] De Vita Mos. T. i. p. 214.   [9] Ib. p. 244.

this, saith to us darkly, 'He drank the Blood of the grape,' whereby His saving Passion is pointed out."

"Since[1] then all defilement of sin is ill-savoured, and, contrariwise, virtue is a good savour of Christ, and the power of love worketh by nature an immingling with that which is loved, then what we love through friendship, *that* we become, the good savour of Christ, or an ill savour. For he who loveth good, becometh also himself good, the goodness of Him Who cometh to be in him, transmaking (μεταποιού-σης) the receiver into Itself. Wherefore also He Who ever *is*, sets Himself before us as Food, that we, receiving Him in ourselves, may become that which He is. 'For,' He saith, 'My Flesh is meat indeed, and My Blood is drink indeed.' He then who loveth this Flesh, is not a friend to his own flesh, and he who is well disposed to this Blood, will be pure from the natural blood. For the Flesh of the Word and the Blood which is in that Flesh hath not one grace only, but is both sweet to those that taste, and desirable to those who long, and lovely to those who love."

"He[2] Himself is the true Cluster, Who showed Himself upon the beams of wood, Whose Blood to them who are saved, and delight themselves therein,

---

[1] In Eccles. iii. 8, Hom. viii. T. i. pp. 456, 457.
[2] In Cant. Hom. iii. fin. p. 517.

becometh a saving Drink,—in Christ Jesus our Lord, to Whom be Glory and Power for ever and ever.   Amen."

"But[*] if any one, looking to the mystery, say that the Lord is properly called Meat and Drink, neither does this depart from the Lord's declaration. 'For His Flesh is meat indeed, and His Blood drink indeed.' But in the meaning above-mentioned, it is in the power of all to partake of the Word, Who becometh meat and drink, set before all indiscriminately, being received by those who seek Him.   But in the other meaning, the participation of such food and drink is not without sifting and discrimination, the Apostle having so ruled, 'Let a man examine himself, and so let him eat of that Bread, and drink of that Cup. For he that eateth and drinketh unworthily, eateth and drinketh damnation to himself.' Looking to this, the Evangelist seems to me assuredly to have suggested something of this sort. For at the time of the mystic Passion, that honourable counsellor, having received the Body of the Lord in spotless and pure fine linen, laid It in a new and clean tomb. So that both the precept of the Apostle and the remark of the Evangelist are a law to us all, to receive the Holy Body with a pure conscience, and should there be any where any spot of sin, first to wash it away with the water of our tears."

[*] De Perf. Christiani forma, iii. 286.

F f

" He [4] Who disposeth all things according to His supreme Will, awaiteth not the compulsion from the Betrayal, and the violent assault of the Jews, and the lawless judgment of Pilate, so that their malice should be the beginning and the cause of the common salvation of man; but by this dispensation He anticipateth their assault according to the mode of His priestly act, ineffable and invisible to man, and offered Himself as an Offering and Sacrifice for us, Priest at once and 'the Lamb of God, Who taketh away the sins of the world.' When was this? When He gave His own Body to be eaten for food, and His Blood to be drunk by those who were with Him. For it is plain to every one, that a sheep would not be eaten by man, unless it were first killed for food. He therefore Who gave His Body for Food to His disciples clearly showeth, under the form of a Lamb, that the Sacrifice was now perfected. For the body of the victim would not have been fit for food, if it had been alive. When therefore He gave His Body for Food, and His Blood for Drink to His disciples, He had already, after an unspeakable and invisible manner, in will, sacrificed His Body by His Power as Dispenser of the mysteries. And the soul, which sojourneth in that region in the heart, was in those things, in which the power of the Dispenser laid it up, together with the Divine power intermingled

[4] In Christ. Resur. Or. 1, iii. 389, 390.

with it. Whoever therefore reckoneth the time, from that moment when the Sacrifice was offered to God by the Great High Priest, Who ineffably and invisibly offered Himself a Lamb for the common sin of man, will not err from the truth."

" Pass [5] we not over in silence, brethren, either that honourable counsellor, Joseph of Arimathæa, who, having received as a gift that undefiled and Holy Body, wrappeth it in pure fine linen, and layeth it up in a new tomb. Be the deed of that honourable counsellor a law to us, that we too take the like counsel, when we receive that gift of the Body, not to receive It in defiled linen of our conscience, nor to lay It in the tomb of our heart, while stinking from dead bones and all uncleanness. But, as the Apostle saith, ' Let a man examine himself,' that the grace be not condemnation to him who receiveth the grace unworthily."

42. S. GREGORY OF NAZIANZUM, the Theologian.

Consecrated Bishop to assist his father about A.D. 371, invited to Constantinople to uphold the faith A.D. 378, presided, as Patriarch, over the Second General Council after the death of Meletius, A.D. 381, resigned, died about A.D. 389. " It is a plain indication that a man is not of the right faith, who does not agree with the faith of Gregory." (Rufin. Prolog. in libb. S. Greg.)

" With [6] unholy blood he [Julian] obliterates the Laver [of Baptism], opposing to our initiation the initiation of defilement, 'a sow wallowing in the mire,'

---

[5] Ib. p. 398.   [6] Orat. iv. c. 52, p. 101, ed. Ben.

according to the proverb; and he unhallows his hands, cleansing them from the unbloody Sacrifice, whereby we communicate with Christ, and partake of His Sufferings and Divinity."

"Despairing[7] of all besides, she [Gorgonia, his sister] betakes herself to the Physician of all, and having waited for the dead of night, her disease giving way a little, she falls in faith before the altar, and calling upon Him Who is honoured thereupon, with a great cry, and by every Name, and calling to His Remembrance all His mighty Works at any time (for she was instructed 'in things old and new'), at last, unabashed with a holy and noble shamelessness, she imitates her who stanched her issue of blood with the hem of Christ's garment. And what does she? Leaning her head against the altar with as loud a cry, and with tears rich herein (as one of old bedewed the Feet of Christ), and declaring she would not desist till she obtained a healing; then anointing her whole body with the ointment which she had and whatever of the antitypes of the Precious Body or Blood her hand treasured, mingling with it her tears (wonderful!), she departed straightway, feeling health, light in body and soul and mind, having, as the reward of hope, received what she hoped for, and with strong health of soul having recovered that of body also. Great is this, but true."

"Thus[8] brought up and instructed (as even now

---

[7] Orat. viii. c. 18, p. 229.   [8] Orat. xxi. c. 7, p. 389.

those should be, who are to be over the people, and to handle the mighty Body of Christ), he [S. Athanasius] (according to the mighty will and foreknowledge of God, Which from afar layeth the foundations of great things) is enrolled in this great rank, and becomes one of those who approach to the approaching God, and is accounted worthy of the holy station and order."

" Fare thee well [9], O seat, thou envied and perilous height, council of Bishops, honoured through the reverence and age of priests, and whoever besides ministers about the holy Table of God, and approaches to the approaching God ! "

" In [1] respect of the staff [2] and of its mystical meaning, I thus understand it. I know that one staff is for support, another belongs to the pastoral office, whereby the rational sheep are turned back into the way. Here then the law commends to thee the staff for support, lest thy reason founder, when thou hearest of the Blood of God, and His Passion and Death, lest thou be carried away in ungodliness, while espousing the cause of God. But, unashamed, undoubting, eat thou the Body, drink the Blood, if thou desirest life, neither disbelieving what is told thee as to His Flesh, nor taking harm at the circumstances of His Passion."

" But [3], O most devout, be not slack in praying

---

[9] Orat. xlii. c. 26, p. 767.

[1] Orat. xliv. c. 19, p. 860.   [2] Exod. xii. 11.

[3] Ep. clxxi. ad Amphiloch. T. ii. p. 140, ed. Ben.

and pleading for us, when by the word you draw
down the Word, when with bloodless cutting you
divide the Body and Blood of the Lord, having
your voice as a knife."

S. Gregory wrote verses, because Julian prohibited Christian teachers from using the classics.

> " Happy [4] he who, ruling the people, by pure
>   And mighty sacrifices brings Christ to mortals."

> " Our [5] offerings are, of the Flesh of God
>   And of the Passion of God the Communion."

> " But [6] the other with trembling and holy hands
>   Brings the Gift, restored to favour by the Flesh of Christ
>   And by the mighty sufferings, which God here endured,
>   A ransom for our primæval sufferings."

> " And [7] thou, wretched man, wilt thou boldly receive
>   In thy palms the Mystic Food, or God embrace
>   With hands, wherewith thou hast dug up my grave."

43. Cæsarius.

The youngest brother of S. Gregory of Nazianzum, a
physician and officer at the imperial court; died before he
was forty, A.D. 368. The genuineness of this work was
questioned by Tillemont (Mém. Eccl. T. ix. p. 702, n. 41,
sur S. Greg. de Naz.), whose objection was answered by
Gallandi (Bibl. Pat. T. vi. and c. 1 de Cæsario). The
treatise agrees with what S. Gregory says of his varied
learning, and of his disputing in defence of the faith. It has

---

[4] Carm. L. i. s. 2, n. 17, l. 14, p. 488.
[5] Ib. n. 34, l. 238, p. 622.
[6] L. ii. s. 1, n. 17, l. 21, p. 880, ed. Ben.
[7] L. ii. s. 2, Epigr. 69, p. 1192. Each age has its own trials.
The violators of graves, in S. Gregory's time, while searching for
gold, pleaded that they were searching for remains of martyrs.
The number of S. Gregory's inscriptions on the subject, evinces
the extent of the practice.

also the defects of a youthful style.   Nor was there any
temptation to forge the name of Cæsarius.   Photius' account of the " Ecclesiastical Chapters " of Cæsarius, brother
of S. Gregory of Nazianzum, agrees well with the book
now extant, Cod. 210, Cæsarius, p. 539, ed. Hoesch.

" He[8] trampleth under foot God the Word, the
Son of God, who, in covetous hands lifted up against
his neighbour, receiveth fearlessly the Sacramental
Elements[9], accounting them like *common* bread and
wine, which, in the eyes of the faithful mind, are
contemplated, God.

" I[1] did not say that He [God] *is* by nature, but
that He *comes to be,* united with our souls and
bodies; since the same Holy Word coming to be
with us, and living with us, being what He was, and
being beheld as what He was not, saith to the band
of the Apostles, distributing bread, ' Take, eat of it
all [of you], This is My Body,' when as yet He was
not made a sacrifice in the flesh, and ' Take, drink,
This is My Blood,' when He was not yet pierced in
the Side upon the Cross by the lance.   And we see
that holy Bread at this day on the unbloody Altar,
at the time of the Divine and Mystical Office, placed
on the undefiled Table, not like to the Image of the
saving Body of God the Word, and the Cup of Wine,
which is placed together with the Bread, not like

[8] Interrog. 140, Dial. 3. Gall. vi. 98.

[9] I have substituted the more general word for κράματα in the
original, which properly denotes the Cup only, whereas both
elements must be intended.

[1] Ib. 169, p. 127.

the Blood mingled in it. [They are like,] neither to the articulation of limbs, nor to the qualities of flesh and blood, nor to the unseen, invisibly united Deity Who is without all form. For the one hath blood, soul, nerves, is red, articulate, with various arteries and veins, wherewith the creating Word is interwoven to the very hair and nails; for I call the hair of Christ the hair of God, and likewise the feet and nails and blood and water. For, for my sake is the Word united to what is mine. And the one [our Lord's Human Form] is upright, articulate, can walk and act; but the other [the Bread] is round, unarticulate, inanimate, bloodless, motionless, like to neither [the Godhead or the Manhood], unlike to that which is visible of Him Who is, in His Godhead, Invisible. And yet we believe the Divine Revelation, that not as being equal or like, yet that still properly and fitly, It is the Divine Body Which is consecrated on the holy Table, and is indivisibly distributed to the whole sacred band, and partaken of without ceasing to be."

44. S. Amphilochius.

Bishop of Iconium, A.D. 370; the friend and correspondent of S. Basil and S. Gregory of Nazianzum, consulted by them; present at the Second General Council; survived the Council of Constantinople, A.D. 394.

"To[2] speak briefly, He, the Father, is both greater and equal, greater than He Who slept in

[2] Serm. adv. Arian. in Conc. Const. Act. 1, ap. Mai, Scriptt. Vett. iv. p. 10.

the stern, equal to Him Who rebuked the sea; greater than He Who was judged before Pilate, equal to Him Who delivers the world from judgment; greater than He Who was buffeted, Who was crucified with the thieves, equal to Him Who justified the robber freely; greater than He Who was stripped of His raiment, equal to Him Who arrayeth the soul; greater than He Who received vinegar to drink, equal to Him Who poureth out as wine His own proper Blood (τοῦ τὸ οἰκεῖον οἰνοχοοῦντος αἷμα); greater than the Temple which was dissolved; equal to Him Who, even after the dissolution, raised again His own proper Temple; greater than this one, equal to That."

45. *Apollinarius.*

Bishop of Laodicea, A.D. 370; author of the heresy named from him.

" This [3] is true Food that succoureth not this temporal and perishable life, but prepareth the eternal. This too is the true Drink, not sufficing for a little while against thirst, but ever giving sufficiency to him that is filled therewith, as He said to the woman of Samaria. But His saying, 'He that eateth My Flesh, and drinketh My Blood, dwelleth in Me, and I in him,' showeth that He is immingled in him."

46. S. Didymus of Alexandria.

Head of the Catechetical School at Alexandria, preceptor of S. Jerome and Rufinus. " Blind from childhood, so as

---

[3] In S. Joh. vi. 52. Cramer, Catena, T. ii. p. 255.

not to have learnt his letters," but "a wonderful and eloquent man" (Socr. H. E. iv. 25); "taught of God" (S. Jerom. de Vir. Ill. c. 109); "being blind, had eyes, wherewith he clearly contemplated God and beheld the light of true knowledge" (S. Antony). Died A. D. 399, aged 90. See Gallandi, T. vi. c. 3, de Did. Alex.

Card. Mai purposed to publish fragments on the Holy Eucharist from Didymus' Commentary on Proverbs (see above, p. 316).

"What[1] sacrifice would be not? Plainly that of the law of Moses, whereof God speaks by Malachi also, 'I have no pleasure in you, and I will not receive an offering at your hands; wherefore from the rising of the sun to the going down thereof My Name is glorified among the heathen;' and by Isaiah, 'What is the multitude of your oblations to Me? Who hath required them at your hands?' Having thus utterly banished all Jewish sacrifices, so that even incense offered by them was accounted abomination by God, He brings in, in place thereof, the bloodless and reasonable sacrifice of the Body and Blood of the Lord, in the new song through the New Testament, of which [Body and Blood] He said, 'Whoso eateth My Flesh and drinketh My Blood hath eternal life.' 'Wherefore,' He said, 'sacrifice and offering Thou wouldest not; but a Body Thou hast prepared for me.' But Christ Himself prepared for the Church a Body, the Lord's. And that He did, not vaguely, but at the time of the

---

[1] In Corder. Cat. in Ps. 39 (40), 7, i. 748.

mystical supper, when He said, 'Take and eat.' This Body, then, He prepared for our participation."

47. Esaias Abbas, a.d. 471.

It is uncertain whether the Ascetics so named were the same, and, if not, to which the works now extant belong. The most celebrated was known to Ammon, before the death of S. Athanasius. It seems most probable that he was the author of the works. See Tillemont, T. vii. 430; viii. 447. 789. Gall. T. vii. p. vii.

" Woe[5] to us who, when the Apostle saith, ' he who eateth and drinketh unworthily, eateth and drinketh damnation to himself, not discerning the Lord's Body,' defiled by our uncleannesses, approach to the awful and fearful mysteries of God, ourselves forgiving ourselves the things which ' nocturnis imaginationibus cogitando fecimus.' For he who hath neither pure thoughts, nor chaste eyes, nor undefiled body, nor clean soul, and sits down by God (assidet Deo), exposes himself to many sufferings of body and sicknesses of the mind, and afterwards will incur eternal torments and boundless shame."

"If[6] thou shouldest be at Mass, guard diligently thy thoughts and senses, and stand before the most high God with fear; that thou mayest be worthy to receive the Body and Blood of Christ, and to heal thy passions."

" If[7] thou willest to take the Body of Christ, take

---

[5] Orat. 29, § 6. Gall. vii. 320.
[6] Reg. ad Monach. 37. Ib. p. 323.
[7] Ib. Reg. 50. Ib.

heed that there be no anger or hatred in thy heart against any one; and if thou know of any one displeased with thee, ask forgiveness first of him, as our Lord hath commanded."

48. S. MACARIUS of Egypt, called "The Great." A. D. 300—391.

In his youth he was called by the Monks "the boy-old-man" (παιδαριογέρων) from his proficiency (Soz. iii. 14); ordained priest at 40; died at 90, A. D. 391, having passed sixty years in the desert (Ib.). " He performed so many cures, and expelled from dæmoniacs so many devils, that to relate what, by the grace of God, he did, would require a distinct work" (Socr. iv. 23, p. 239). "Both (he and S. Macarius of Alexandria) were wonderful for divine foreknowledge and wisdom, and a terror to dæmons, and workers of many wonderful works and cures. It is *said* of the Egyptian, that he made a dead man to live, in order to convince one heterodox that there would be a resurrection of the dead" (Soz. iii. 14). He was contemporary with S. Athanasius, acquainted with S. Antony (Cotel. Mon. Eccl. Gr. i. 530 sq.). His homilies have been loved by all classes of minds."

He calls the consecrated elements " an antitype of the Flesh and Blood of Christ," saying that "they who partake of the visible bread, spiritually eat the Flesh of the Lord" (above, p. 104).

"For[s] as God, having made this body not from His own Nature, neither did He give it to have life and food and drink and clothing and sandals, from

<hr>

[s] Hom. i. p. 8, ed. Paris.

the body itself; but having made the body, itself for itself, naked, gave it to have, from without, the whole economy of its life; and it is impossible for the body to live without the things external to the body, *i. e.* without food and drink and clothing, and if it stand to its own nature alone, taking to it nothing from without, it wastes and perishes; in the same manner the soul, too, which hath not a Divine light, although it was created in the Image of God (for so did He dispose and will, that it should have eternal life) hath, not from its own nature, but from His own Godhead, from His own Spirit, from His own Light, spiritual food and drink and heavenly raiment, which are indeed the life of the soul.   As, then, the life of the body (as I said) is not from itself, but from without, *i. e.* from the earth, and without the things external to itself it cannot live, so also the soul, unless it be borne from this present being to that land of the living, and be thence spiritually nourished and thence spiritually grow, advancing to the Lord, and be clothed from the Godhead with hidden raiment of heavenly beauty, cannot live from itself in joy and rest, without that Food.   For the Divine Nature hath also a Bread of Life, Him who saith, ' I am the Bread of Life,' and a living water, and wine gladdening the heart of man, and oil of exultation, and varied nourishment of the heavenly spirit, and heavenly raiment of light, which come from God.   In these is the eternal life of the soul."

" The [9] Spirit of the Lord cometh to the refreshment of worthy souls, to their exultation and delight and life everlasting.   For the Lord embodieth [1] Him-

[9] Hom. iv. p. 22.

[1] There is no especial stress, in this passage, on the word σωματοποιεῖ, "embodies," as though it expressed the *mode* of the Presence of our Lord in the Holy Eucharist. It does express an in-dwelling, so to speak, a Presence within the consecrated elements, but no relation to them, (such as Consubstantiation has been used to express,) nor any analogy to the Incarnation. For S. Macarius uses this same word, in this very context, to express the in-dwelling of the Godhead in faithful souls. I give the whole context, omitting, for briefness, some sentences not bearing on the main thought of S. Macarius.

"The Infinite and Unapproachable and Uncreated God, for His infinite and inconceivable goodness, embodied Himself, and (so to speak) contracted Himself from His unapproachable Glory, that He might be able to be united with His visible creatures (as the souls of saints and angels), that they might be able to partake of the Life of the Godhead. . . . The Infinite and Inconceivable God, through His goodness, contracted Himself, and put on the limbs of this body, and gathered Himself from His unapproachable Glory, and, for His tenderness and love for man, being transformed, embodies Himself and immingles Himself, and takes holy and well-pleasing souls, and ' becomes one spirit ' with them (according to the Divine saying of Paul), soul (so to speak) to soul, and substance to substance, that the soul may be able to live in newness, and feel the immortal life, and may become partaker of incorruptible glory, the soul which is worthy of Him and acceptable. . . . In what way the Infinite and Inexpressible skill of the manifold wisdom of God created, of the things which were not, bodies denser and more subtle and tender, to subsist by His Will, how much more doth He Himself, being as He wills and what He wills, through His unutterable bounty and inconceivable goodness, change and contract and assimilate Himself,

self even into meat and drink, (as it is written in the Gospel: 'he that eateth this Bread shall live for ever,') that He may ineffably rest the soul, and fill it with spiritual joy; for He saith, 'I am the Bread of Life.'   In like way, also, [He embodieth Himself] into drink of a heavenly fountain, as He saith, ' he who drinketh of this water, which I shall give him, it shall be in him a fountain of living water,

embodying Himself, according to their capacities, with holy, worthy, and faithful souls, that so the Invisible may be seen by them, and the Intangible may be touched according to the subtle nature of the soul, and they may perceive His sweetness, and enjoy, by the very trial, the goodness of the light of the Ineffable fruition!   When He willeth, He becometh fire, bur..ing up every bad and alien passion of the soul, ' for our God,' he saith, ' is a consuming fire.'   When He willeth, He is ineffable and unutterable rest, that the soul may rest in the rest of the Godhead. When He willeth, He is joy and peace, cherishing and tending it; but if He will to liken Himself to one of His creatures, for the exultation and gladness of His intelligent creatures, (such as the City of Light, Jerusalem, or the Heavenly Mount Zion,) He can do all things as He wills, as was said, 'But ye have come to Mount Zion and to the City of the Living God, the Heavenly Jerusalem.'   All things are easy and ready to Him, changing Himself to what He willeth for souls faithful and worthy of Him. Only let any one strive to be a friend, and well-pleasing to Him, and by the very trial and perception, he shall see heavenly goods and delight unutterable and boundless riches of the Godhead. Truly, ' what eye hath not seen, nor ear heard, neither hath entered into the heart of man,' " &c., as in the text.   The whole passage nearly recurs in the ' De Elevatione Mentis,' where the words relating to the Holy Eucharist are, " For He embodieth Himself, as into spiritual Food, so also into array and unspeakable beauty, that so He might fill it with spiritual joy, For I, He saith, am the Bread of life," &c.

springing up unto eternal life.'   And 'they all drink of the same drink.'"

"For[2] as one who hath large possessions and slaves and children, giveth one sort of food to the slaves, and another to his own children, because the children are heirs of the father and eat with him, being likened to their father, so also Christ, the true Lord, Himself created all things and nourisheth the evil and ungrateful; but the children whom He hath Himself begotten, and to whom He hath imparted of His grace, in whom the Lord is formed, He nourisheth up with a special refreshment and food and meat and drink, and giveth Himself to them, who are living with their Father, as the Lord Himself saith, 'he who eateth My Flesh and drinketh My Blood dwelleth in Me and I in him, and shall not see death.'"

"The[3] children of Israel remove, having celebrated the Passover. The soul advanceth, having received the life of the Holy Ghost, and having tasted the Lamb and being anointed with His Blood, and eating the true Bread, the Living Word."

"Consider[4] that these visible things are types and shadows of the things hidden; the visible temple, of the temple of the heart; the priest, of the true priest of the grace of God; and so on. As then, in this visible Church, unless first the readings and

[2] Hom. 14, p. 76.   [3] Hom. 47, p. 231.
[4] De Caritate, § 29. Gall. vii. 207.

psalmody, and the rest of the prescribed order, were to precede, it would not be in order, that the priest should celebrate the Divine mystery itself of the Body and Blood of Christ; or again, although even the whole ecclesiastical canon were added, but the mystic Eucharist of the Oblation by the priest, and the communion of the Body of Christ did not take place, the ecclesiastical ordinances would not be fulfilled, and the Divine service of the mystery would be defective; so think thou as to the state of the Christian, &c."

49 (more probably 78). EUSEBIUS OF ALEXANDRIA, perhaps A. D. 444.

In placing Eusebius of Alexandria at A.D. 373, I followed the authority of the Cod. Vindob. ccxlix. This contains an ascetic work of Nico, where are mentioned "questions of Macarius of Alexandria to the great Eusebius of Alexandria." (Mai, Spicileg. Rom. T. ix. p. 5.) S. Macarius of Alexandria was a younger contemporary of S. Macarius of Egypt. But Nico lived far too late to be of any authority, probably about A.D. 1060. (Fabr. v. 426, T. x. p. 284.) If Eusebius had been at all contemporary with S. Macarius, it must have been as a much younger contemporary. For S. Macarius died in very advanced age, A.D. 404. But Eusebius of Alexandria survived S. Melania (as Card. Mai pointed out, Patr. Nov. Biblioth. ii. 500). For he instances her as one " rich, and richer in almsgiving" and speaks of her as deceased ($\mathring{\eta}\nu$, ib. § 21, p. 520). But even the elder Melania survived Valens 37 years, and so died A.D. 415. (Pallad. Hist. Laus. Opp. Meurs. viii. 117. 120, quoted Ib.) This Eusebius then must have lived at some time after A.D. 415 (for he refers to her as one who " *was*," not as if her decease was recent). On the other

G g

hand, he must have lived some time before the close of the sixth century. For he is quoted as an authority by John the Monk, a compiler of Sacra Parallela, who lived under the younger Heraclius, after the Cross had been taken by the Persians, and before Heraclius recovered it ; consequently between A.D. 614 and 628. (Le Quien in Joh. Damascen. ii. 275, 276.)

He is called again and again in MSS. an Alexandrian and a Bishop. Yet there is no known place for him among the Patriarchs of Alexandria. The choice then lies between the conjecture of Le Quien, that 1) he was a Bishop without a see, as other Greek Ascetics are recorded to have been. (Le Quien, l. c. Tit. 29, pp. 66, 67, note). Or, 2) if the life of Eusebius published by Mai (Spicil. Rom. ix. 703) be authentic (it professes to be by a contemporary), he was consecrated a Bishop by S. Cyril in his life time. This would agree with the statement that he was Pope [Bishop] of Alexandria. Yet it is inconceivable that in all the troubles occasioned by S. Cyril's heretical successor, Dioscorus, there should have been no question as to the claim of the see itself. It was also forbidden at that time for a Bishop to appoint, and consecrate his successor.

" After [5] the dismissal of the Church on the holy Lord's day, when the blessed Eusebius, the Bishop, was sitting, Alexander came and said to him, 'Tell me, my lord, I pray you, why it is necessary for us to keep the Lord's day, and not to work, and what gain we have in not working?' The blessed man began to say, ' Hear, my son, and I will tell you why it has been delivered to us that we should keep the Lord's day and not work. When the Lord delivered the Mystery to the disciples, having taken bread, He blessed,

---

[5] Orat. de Die Dom. init. Gall. viii. 252, 253.

and having broken, He gave to His disciples, saying, ' Take, eat, this is My Body which is broken for you for the remission of sins ;' in like way also, He gave them the Cup, saying, ' Drink ye all of it, .this is My Blood of the New Testament which is shed for you and for many for the remission of sins ; this do in remembrance of Me.'   The holy Lord's day is then the commemoration of the Lord. Wherefore also it is called the Lord's day, as being the Lord of days ; for before the Passion of the Lord, it was not called the Lord's day, but the first day.   In this day the Lord began the first-fruit of the Resurrection, *i.e.* of the creation of the world, and in this day the Lord bestowed the first-fruit of the Resurrection ; in this day, as we said, He also commanded the consecration of the Holy Mysteries.   Such a day then became to us the beginning of all goodness, the beginning of the creation of the world, the beginning of the week. —The week then having seven days, God hath given us the six to work in, and the one He hath given us for prayer and rest and the remission of sins, and that if in the six days we have committed any sins, we may, in the Lord's day, propitiate God for them. Be early then in the Church of God, approach the Lord, confess to Him thy sins, repent with prayer and a broken heart, abide during the Divine and Holy Eucharistic service, complete thy prayer, on no account leaving before the dismissal.   Behold thy Lord, divided in pieces and distributed and not expended ; and if thou hast thy conscience clean,

G g 2

approach and communicate of the Body and Blood. But if thy conscience condemn thee in evil and foul deeds, decline the Communion until thou have amended by repentance. But continue during the prayer, and go not out of the Church until thou be dismissed. Remember Judas the traitor. For the beginning of his destruction was his not abiding with them all in the prayer. Having taken, it is said, the bread, he, first of all, went out and hastened to betray the Lord. . . . If then thou goest out before the dismissal, thou imitatest Judas."

" Many [6] Presbyters, being sinners, offer the gifts, and God turneth not away, but by the Holy Ghost hallows the gifts placed there; and the Bread becometh the Body, and the Cup becometh the Blood of our Lord Jesus Christ; and there are some who, thinking that they do well, do not communicate with the Presbyters, as knowing of some evil in the Presbyter, and they know not, that they sin more, wishing to do well."

" The [7] Lord was born of a Virgin, that the Manhood might come to perfection. He vouchsafed, being swaddled, to be laid in a manger, that we approaching the manger, as a table, might, instead of the food of animals, partake of rational food; for Christ is the Food of rational beings, for He is the Bread which came down from Heaven."

---

[6] Serm. v. in Maii Spicil. Rom. ix. p. 660.
[7] Serm. x. de Nativ. Dom. in Maii Spicil. Rom. ix. 675.

"I [8] know many who come to the memories of the saints, and add to their sins and so depart, for they come, not for prayer, but for pleasure. Some seek the first seats, lofty places, make tumults, stir up fights and unpleasantnesses; others sit down and stop their ears like adders, and hear neither scripture nor psalmody, nor prayer, but sharpen their tongues like serpents, and cease not chattering, looking about them and laughing, and deriding their neighbour. These are their vigils, and thus they employ themselves. And when sleep overpowers them, they go out and give themselves to sleep, and lie as dead till mid-day. And when they are aroused, they begin to prepare shows and disturb those who wish to stay for the prayer, and amuse themselves to their destruction; for they make noises as in a wrestling-match. Within, the Priest offers the supplication for the people, setting forth the Body and Blood of our Lord Jesus Christ for the salvation of the world, and without there are jestings."

"All [9] those who do such things God remembereth not, nor accepteth, but rather chaseth from Him, saying, 'Depart from Me.' For 'come,' is for the merciful; but 'depart' for those who know Me not; for I know you not, nor do 'I know whence ye are,' that I should call you also into My Kingdom: 'Depart from Me, I know you not.' Why do ye

[8] Ib. Serm. viii. Maii, p. 671, also in Latin. Bib. P. xxvii. p. 480.

[9] Serm. de Elcem. § 14. Maii, Biblioth. Nov. Pat. ii. 513.

call upon Me, saying, 'Lord, why dost Thou send us from Thee? have we not the seal of Thy Body? &c.'"

50. S. AMBROSE.

Born A.D. 333.   Bishop of Milan A.D. 374.   President of the Council of Aquileia A.D. 382.   Persecution against him checked by miracle A.D. 386 (S. Aug. Conf. ix. § 16, p. 167, O. T. and notes).   The converter and teacher of S. Augustine ; foretold his own death four years before. Died A.D. 397.

On S. Ambrose's use of the word " transfigure," for the sacramental change in the Holy Eucharist, see above, pp. 229—232, compare with pp. 172—174. On his comparison of other miracles of the Old and New Testaments with those of the Sacraments, see pp. 291 —293.   S. Ambrose, on the other hand, speaks of the Body of Christ as " signified " by the consecrated elements, and still more plainly in the well-known comparison of the " shadow in the law, the image in the Gospel, the truth in the heavens."   Unless there were a Real Presence, the Sacrament of the Gospel would be a less expressive shadow, than the Paschal Lamb.   Yet it is different, he says, from the truth.   The sacrament of the Gospel stands between the shadow in the law and the truth in the heavens, in that it has, like the law, a visible image, yet an image of the truth, not absent, as in the law, but invisibly present with us.

" First [1], then, the shadow went before, the image followed, the truth *will* be.   The shadow in the

---

[1] In Ps. xxxviii. § 25, p. 852.

Law; the image in the Gospel; the truth in the heavenly places. The shadow of the Gospel and of the congregation of the Church in the Law; the image of the truth to come, in the Gospel; the truth in the judgment of God. Therefore of those things which are now celebrated in the Church, the shadow was in the discourses of the Prophets, the shadow in the deluge, the shadow in the Red Sea, since our fathers were baptized in the cloud, and in the sea; the shadow in the rock, which brought forth water, and followed the people. Was not that Sacrament a shadow of this all-holy Mystery? Was not the water from the rock a shadow? the water, as it were Blood from Christ, which followed the people, while fleeing, that they might drink, and not thirst, might be redeemed, and not perish? But now hath the shade of night and of the darkness of the Jews departed; the day of the Church hath drawn nigh. We have seen the High Priest coming to us, we have seen and heard Him offering for us His Blood: we priests follow, as we can; that we may offer sacrifice for the people: although weak in deserts, yet honourable in sacrifice: since though Christ is not now seen to offer, yet Himself is offered on earth, when the Body of Christ is offered: yea Himself is plainly seen to offer in us, Whose Word sanctifieth the Sacrifice which is offered. And Himself indeed standeth by us, as an Advocate with the Father: but now we see Him not: then shall we see Him, when the image shall have passed away, the truth come. Then at length not in a glass, but face to face, shall be seen that which is perfect."

And again;

"Those [2] things then we must desire, wherein is perfection, wherein is truth. Here is the shadow; here the image; there the Truth. The shadow in the Law, the image in the Gospel, Truth in the heavenly places. Before, a lamb was offered; a calf too was offered; now Christ is offered. But He is offered as a Man, as capable of suffering; and He offers Himself as a Priest, to forgive our sins; here in image, there in truth, where He intercedeth for us as an Advocate with the Father. Here then we walk in an image, we see in an image; there face to face, where is full perfection, since all perfection is in the Truth."

"What [3] more noble than Christ, Who in the Feast of the Church both ministers and is ministered? Join thyself to the side of that Guest, and unite thyself with God; despise not the Table which Christ hath chosen."

"Rich [4] indeed is that Bread which whoso eateth, cannot hunger. This Bread He gave to the Apostles to divide to the believing people; and at this day, He giveth It to us, seeing He Himself daily,

[2] De Off. i. 48, § 248, ii. 63.
[3] De Cain and Abel i. 5, § 19.
[4] De Bened. Patr. c. 9, § 38.

the Priest, consecrates It with His own words. This Bread then is become the Food of saints."

" We[5] too may understand the Lord Himself Who giveth His own Flesh to us, as He Himself said, ' I am the Bread of life.   Your fathers did eat manna in the wilderness and are dead.   This is the Bread which cometh down from Heaven, that a man may eat thereof and not die.'   And lest any should think that He says this of the death which takes place through the severance of soul and body, and rightly stand in doubt, knowing that the holy Apostles did die this death, He added, ' I am the Living Bread which came down from Heaven : if any man eat of this Bread, he shall live for ever;' *i. e.* I spoke above, not of a temporal death, nor of the death of this life, of which if any were even dead, yet if he have received of My Bread, he shall live for ever.   For he receiveth who proveth himself; but whoso receiveth shall not die the sinner's death, for this Bread is the remission of sins."

" Blessed[6] wood of the Lord which hath crucified the sins of all! blessed Flesh of the Lord which hath ministered food to all !"

" No[7] otherwise can men come to the kingdom of Heaven, since the Lord Himself said, ' Except ye eat My Flesh and drink My Blood, ye shall not have eternal life.'   It is shown then that the Lord

[5] Ib. § 39.

[6] In Ps. 35, Præf. § 3.

[7] In Ps. 43, § 36, p. 902.

is our Food, is our Feast, or the sustenance of those who eat; as He Himself said, 'I am the Living Bread which came down from Heaven.'"

"Then[8] assist prepared, that thou mayest receive to thee a defence, that thou mayest eat the Body of the Lord Jesus, in which is the remission of sins, the entreaty of the Divine reconciliation and eternal protection. Receive first the Lord Jesus in the hostelry of thy mind; where His Body is, there is Christ. When the adversary shall see thy hostelry occupied by the brightness of the Heavenly Presence, he, understanding that all avenue for his temptations is intercepted by Christ, will flee and depart; and thou shalt pass midnight without offence. For the evening sacrifice admonishes thee never to forget Christ. Thou canst not forget, when thou climbest up into thy bed, that Lord to Whom at the close of day thou pouredst out thy prayer, Who filled thee an hungered with the Feast of His Body. For what thou shalt have thought of in the evening, thou wilt soon review when thou awakest. The Lord Jesus Himself will awake thee, will admonish thee to arise, and to take the arms of prayer at what time the tempter is wont to assault."

"He[9] Himself feeds and refreshes us. The 'good' pastures' are the Divine Sacraments. Thou gatherest there the new flower which giveth forth the sweet

---

[8] In Ps. 119, Serm. viii. § 48, pp. 1073, 1074.
[9] Ib. Serm. xiv. § 2, p. 1140.   [1] Ps. xxiii. 2.

smell of the Resurrection; thou gatherest the lily, that is, the brightness of eternity; thou gatherest the rose, that is, the Blood of the Lord's Body."

"Thou [2] hast apostolic food: eat it, and thou wilt not fail. Eat this first, that thou mayest come to the Food of Christ, the Food of the Lord's Body, the Feast of the Sacrament, that Cup whereby the affections of the faithful are inebriated, so that they are clad with joy for the remission of sins, and lay aside the cares of this world, the fear of death and all anxiety. Through this inebriation the body stumbleth not, but riseth again; the mind is not confounded, but consecrated."

"I [3], aforetime a despised people of sinners, am admitted to the venerable and heavenly sacraments. I am now received to the honour of the Heavenly Table. Rain doth not stream down for my feasts, nor doth the earth travail for me, nor fruits of trees. Rivers and fountains are not to be sought for my drink. Christ is Food to me; Christ is Drink to me. The Flesh of God is Food to me; the Blood of God is Drink to me. I wait not now for the annual harvest to satisfy me; Christ is daily ministered to me. . . . My food is that, which if a man eat, he shall not hunger. My food is that which doth not fatten the body, but strengtheneth the heart of man. Formerly I had wonderful food from

---

[2] Ib. Serm. xv § 28, p. 1166.
[3] Ib. Serm. 18. § 26—28, pp. 1202, 1203.

Heaven; for it is written, 'He gave them bread from Heaven.' Yet that was not the true Bread, but the shadow of that which was to come; that true Bread from Heaven, the Father reserved for me; to me that Bread of God came down from Heaven which giveth life to this world.

"Why askest thou, O Jew, that He should give thee Bread, which He giveth to all, giveth daily, giveth ever? it is with thee to receive this Bread. Approach to this Bread, and thou wilt receive it. Of this Bread it is said, 'They that are far from Thee shall perish.' If thou go far from Him, thou shalt perish; if thou approach Him, thou shalt live. This is the Bread of Life: whoso then eateth Life cannot die. For how should *he* die whose food is Life? how shall *he* fail who hath a Living substance? Approach to Him, and be satisfied, because He is Bread; approach to Him, and drink, because He is a Fountain; approach to Him, and be enlightened, because He is Light; approach to Him, and be set free, because 'where the Spirit of the Lord is, there is liberty;' approach to Him, and be absolved, because He is the remission·of sins. Ask ye Who He is? Hear Himself saying. 'I am the Bread of Life: whoso cometh unto Me shall not hunger; whoso believeth in Me shall never thirst.'"

"But ‘ he [the Angel] appeared [to Zechariah]

‘ In S. Luc. L. i. § 28, p. 1275.

on the right hand of the altar of incense, because he brought a token of the Divine mercy. For 'the Lord is on my right hand, therefore I shall not be moved.' And elsewhere, 'The Lord is thy protection upon thy right hand.' And would that, to us too, burning incense at the Altars, and offering Sacrifice, the Angel would stand by; yea, rather, would permit himself to be seen! For thou canst not doubt that the Angel stands by, when Christ standeth by, when Christ is offered."

"Every where[5] then the order of the Mystery is preserved, that first, by remission of sins, medicine is given to the wounds; afterwards, the nourishment of the Heavenly Table overflows; although this crowd is not yet nourished with stronger food, and the hearts, unnourished by a more solid faith, are not fed with the Body and Blood of Christ. The five loaves are as it were milk; but the more solid food is the Body of Christ, the stronger drink is the Blood of the Lord."

"That[6] also hath a mystical meaning, that the people 'eat and are satisfied,' and the Apostles minister. For by their very satiety it is hinted that hunger shall be banished for ever. For he who has received the Food of Christ shall never hunger; and in the ministering of the Apostles is set forth the future distribution of the Body and Blood of the Lord."

[5] Ib. L. vi. § 71, p. 1400.
[6] Ib. § 84, p. 1404.

"There [7] is then a food of refreshment, there is a food of Blood. For as the Flesh of the Lord is truly food, so the Blood is truly our drink."

"The [8] just man is after the image of God, if, in order to imitate the likeness of the Divine conversation, he contemn this world through the knowledge of God, and despise earthly pleasures through the reception of the Word of God, whereby we are nourished to life, whence also we eat the Body of Christ that we may be able to be partakers of life eternal."

"After [9] death, the blood curdles in our bodies; but from that Body, incorrupted, though dead, the Life of all did flow. For water and blood went forth: the one to wash, the other to redeem. Let us therefore drink our Ransom, that, by drinking, we may be redeemed."

"In [1] our own memory, a maiden, long noble in the world, now more noble to God, when she was pressed by her parents and relations to marry, flees to the all-holy Altar. For where is a virgin better, than where the sacrifice of virginity is offered? Nor did her boldness end here. She was standing at the Altar of God, a sacrifice of modesty, an offering of chastity; now placing upon her head the Bishop's right hand, asking for the prayer, now impatient of

[7] Ib. L. viii. § 51, p. 1483.
[8] Ib. L. x. § 49, p. 1514.
[9] Ib. § 135, p. 1533.
[1] De Virg. i. 11, § 65, ii. 162.

the due delay, and placing her head beneath the Altar. Will any veil cover me better than the Altar, which sanctifies the veils themselves? Rather such a veil befits me, where Christ, the Head of all, is daily consecrated."

" At[2] the same time, it is shown what sort of person he ought to be, who ministereth to Christ. For, first of all, he must be free from the allurements of various pleasures, shun inward drowsiness of mind and body, that he may administer the Body and Blood of Christ. For one who is sick with his own sins, and unsound, cannot minister the remedies of immortal health. See what thou doest, O priest, and touch not with feverish hand the Body of Christ. First be cured, that thou mayest be able to minister."

"Thee[3] now, O Lord, I entreat, that upon this Thine house, upon these Altars which this day are dedicated, upon these spiritual stones, in each of which a spiritual temple is consecrated to Thee, daily Thou wouldst in Thy Divine mercy look down, and receive the prayers of Thy servants, which are poured forth in this place. Be every sacrifice for a sweet-smelling savour unto Thee, which in this temple is offered to Thee, with pure faith, with pious zeal. And when thou lookest on that saving Sacrifice, whereby the sin of this world is blotted out, look also on these sacrifices of pious chastity, and defend

---

[2] De Vid. c. x. § 65, p. 203.

[3] Exh. Virg. § ult. p. 302.

them by Thy daily help, that they may be to Thee sacrifices acceptable, for an odour of sweetness, pleasing Christ the Lord, and vouchsafe to ' preserve their whole spirit and soul and body unblameable,' unto the Day of Thy Son, our Lord Jesus Christ."

S. Ambrose sums up the passage already quoted from his treatise on the mysteries;

" With[4] these Sacraments, then, Christ feedeth His Church, with which the substance of the soul is strengthened, and seeing her continuous progress in grace, says to her, ' How fair,' " &c. (Cant. iv. 10 sq.)

" Why[5] He speaks of meat and drink (Cant. v. 1) understand, O faithful.   There is no doubt that in us He Himself eateth and drinketh, as thou hast read that in us, He saith, He is in prison.

" Whence the Church, too, seeing so great grace, exhorteth her sons ; exhorteth her neighbours to flock to the Sacraments, saying, ' Eat, O my neighbours, and be inebriated, O my brethren.' What we eat, what we drink, the Holy Ghost hath in another place told thee by the Prophet, saying, ' Taste and see that the Lord is good ; blessed is the man that trusteth in Him.'   In that Sacrament Christ is : because it is the Body of Christ ; it is not therefore bodily Food, but spiritual. Whence, too, the Apostle saith of its type: 'our fathers did eat spiritual meat, and did drink spiritual drink.'   For the Body of God is a spiritual Body: the Body of Christ is the Body of the Divine Spirit:

[4] § 55, p. 340.   [5] §§ 57, 58. ib.

since Christ is Spirit, as we read, 'The Spirit before our face is Christ the Lord.'   And in the Epistle of Peter we have, 'Christ died for us.'   Lastly, that Food strengtheneth our heart, and that Drink 'maketh glad the heart of man,' as the Prophet recorded."

"Let[6] us see, however, whether the Prophet does not say that *that* Earth is to be adored, which the Lord Jesus, by assuming flesh, took upon Him.   So, then, by the footstool is understood the earth : but by the earth the Flesh of Christ, Which now too, we in Mysteries adore[7], and Which the Apostles, as we said above, adored in the Lord Jesus.   For Christ is not divided, but is One.   Nor, when He is adored as Son of God, is His Birth of a Virgin denied.   Since then the Sacrament of the Incarnation is to be adored, but the Incarnation is the work of the Spirit, as it is written : 'The Holy Ghost shall come upon thee, and the power of the Most High shall overshadow thee: wherefore also that Holy Thing which shall be born

[6] De Sp. S. iii. 11, § 79, ii. 604.

[7] *i. e.* Christ, Man as well as God.   "We," Bishop Andrewes comments (Resp. ad Apol. Bell. p. 195), " ' adore the Flesh of Christ in the Mysteries,' with Ambrose ; not It, but Him, Who is worshipped on the Altar.   Nor do we eat the Flesh, but, with Augustine, we first worship.   And yet we in no wise adore the Sacrament."   He had just said, " Christ Himself, the Substance [res] of the Sacrament, in and with the Sacrament, out of and without the Sacrament, is, wherever He is, to be adored.   But the king [James, whom he was defending] laid down that Christ truly present in the Eucharist, is truly to be adored, *i. e.* the Substance of the Sacrament, but not the Sacrament, *i. e.* the earthly part, as Irenæus ; the visible, as Augustine."

of thee shall be called the Son of God;' doubtless the Holy Ghost also is to be adored, since He is adored, who, according to the Flesh, was born of the Holy Ghost."

"It[8] [the measure of wine] is understood more fully of the Blood of Christ, of the grace whereof nothing is diminished, nothing added. Whether thou take little or much, it is to all the perfect measure of redemption."

"On[9] learning that calamity, so full of woe [the massacre at Thessalonica] that Ambrose, whom I have often mentioned, having met the king (who had arrived at Milan, and purposed, as usual, to enter the holy temple) outside the vestibule, in these words forbade him to enter the holy threshold: 'Thou knowest not, I think, O King, the enormity of that blood-guiltiness. . . . Thou, O king, rulest men of one nature with thyself; yea, thy fellow-servants. With what eyes, then, wilt thou behold the temple of our common Lord? with what feet wilt thou tread that holy floor? how wilt thou stretch forth hands still reeking with the blood of this unjust murder? how in such hands wilt thou receive the all-holy Body of the Lord? how wilt thou bear to thy mouth the Precious Blood, having in thine anger unlawfully shed so much blood?   Retire, then, and attempt not to increase thy former transgression by a second, but accept the bond [of excommunication] which

[8] Ep. vii. ad Just. § 8, p. 779.
[9] Theodoret, Eccl. Hist. l. v. c. xvii. T. iii. p. 1047.

God the Lord of all, from above, sanctioneth. It is healing, and a pledge of health."

51. *The Author of the De Sacramentis, among S. Ambrose's works.*

The Benedictines have shown that he was a Bishop who was instructing the newly-baptized, and the people entrusted to his care; that he lived before Infant Baptism had become the entire rule of the Church; that there were yet many heathens in his diocese (vi. 4 and 5). He mentions no heretics, except the Arians, and those who denied the Divinity of our Lord. After Pelagius' time, *his* heresy would naturally come to be noticed in connexion with baptism, in like way as S. Augustine is so full of it. The Vulgate also was not yet received.

The writer lived also in a place where the practices of the Church of Rome were looked up to, not altogether followed. The well-known passage occurs here, " In all things I desire to follow the Roman Church; yet we, too, are gifted with understanding, so, then, what is observed rightly elsewhere, we, too, observe rightly " (iii. 5). He lived in times when negligent Christians, "as Greeks in the East have been wont to do, communicated once in the year only" (v. 25). He imitates S. Ambrose closely, yet neither as a mere copyist, nor a compiler.

The work looks to me like the work of a disciple, reproducing the thoughts of his master. The six books are, in fact, six sermons, which their author delivered from Easter Tuesday to the following Sunday, and in which he freely used the language and thoughts of his " Master." The indications observed by the Benedictines make me suppose that these sermons were composed, not much after the time of S. Ambrose.

The chief part of this Bishop's Sermon on the Holy Eucharist has been already given above (pp. 281

—287). *He speaks of the oblation as a "figure of the Body and Blood of our Lord (p. 105)." I will add here what remains on the doctrine of the Real Presence, or its effects.*

"Hear[1] David saying, 'Thy youth shall be renewed as the eagle's.' Good eagles about the Altar. For 'where the body is, there too the eagles.' The Altar is a figure of the Body, and the Body of Christ is on the Altar; ye are the eagles, renewed by the washing away of sin."

"Thy[2] mind, or human nature, or the Church, seeing itself purified from all sin, and worthy to approach to the Altar of Christ (for what is the Altar, save a figure of Christ's Body), saw marvellous Sacraments, and said, 'Let Him kiss[3] me with the kisses of His mouth.'"

"Thou[4] hast come to the Altar; thou hast received the Body of Christ. Hear again what sacraments thou hast attained unto."

"Ye[5] have come then to the Altar, ye have received the grace of Christ, ye have attained unto the heavenly sacraments. The Church rejoices in the redemption of many, and rejoices with spiritual exultation that her family stand by her, purified."

"Dost[6] thou see that the joy is of a sort, not polluted by the defilements of any sin? For as oft as

[1] L. iv. c. 2, § 7, p. 366.
[2] L. v. c. 2, § 7, p. 374.
[3] See above.
[4] Ib. c. 3, § 12.
[5] Ib. § 14.
[6] Ib. § 17.

thou drinkest, thou receivest remission of sins, and art inebriated in spirit. Whence also the Apostle saith, 'Be not inebriated with wine, but be ye filled with the Holy Ghost.' For he who is inebriated with wine totters and reels; he who is inebriated with the Spirit, is rooted in Christ. And therefore it is a noble inebriation, which worketh sobriety of mind."

"'Give' us this day our daily Bread.' I remember my sermon, when I treated of the Sacraments. I told you, that, before the words of Christ, what is offered is called bread: when the words of Christ have been uttered, it is no longer called bread, but a Body. Why then in the Lord's prayer, which follows, does he say, 'our Bread?' He said indeed Bread, but ἐπιούσιον, that is, 'supersubstantial.' It is not that bread which passes into the body; but that Bread of eternal life, which fortifies the substance of our souls. Therefore in Greek it is called ἐπιούσιος: but the Latins call this Bread 'daily,' which the Greeks call 'coming,' because the Greeks call τὴν ἐπιοῦσαν ἡμέραν, 'the coming day.' Therefore what the Latin says, and what the Greek says, are each useful: the Greek comprehends both in one word, the Latin says 'daily.'"

"If the 'Bread' is 'daily,' why dost thou receive it after a year, as the Greeks in the East are wont to do? Receive daily what may daily profit thee.

^r Ib. c. 4, §§ 24, 25.

So live, that thou mayest be worthy to receive daily. He who is not worthy to receive daily, is not worthy to receive after a year."

"'I [8] am,' He says, 'the Living Bread which came down from Heaven.' But flesh came not down from Heaven, that is, He took Flesh on earth of the Virgin. How then did Bread come down from Heaven, and Living Bread? Because the same our Lord Jesus Christ partaketh both of Divinity and a Body; and thou who receivest Flesh, dost in that Food partake of His Divine Substance."

52. S. JEROME, PRESBYTER and DOCTOR.

Born A.D. 329; studied under S. Gregory of Nazianzum, Apollinarius, Paulinus of Antioch, and in later times Didymus of Alexandria. Ordained Presbyter A.D. 370. Secretary to Damasus Bishop of Rome A.D. 382—385. Died, A.D. 420, entitled " Doctor Maximus."

He speaks of the consecrated elements as "types" (pp. 106, 107), and believed that our Lord, when speaking of the "fruit of the vine," meant to speak of His members receiving the Holy Eucharist. I will prefix those passages which themselves show at the same time how S. Jerome united with this, the belief in the Real Presence.

"This [9] is the wheat, and this the wine, of which none shall eat, save those who praise the Lord, and none shall drink save in His holy Courts, of which the Lord said in His Passion, ' Verily, verily, I say

---

[8] L. vi. c. 1, § 4.
[9] In Is. 62, 9, L. 17, T. iv. p. 743.

unto you, I will no more drink of this fruit of the vine, until I drink it new in the kingdom of My Father:' which words are partly fulfilled in the Church, when our Lord says to His disciples, ' Drink, O friends, and be inebriated, my brethren, with the wine that maketh glad the heart of man;' and more fully shall they be fulfilled, when the ' earth shall be overflowed [1] with the blessings of the Lord.' Wheat also, whereof heavenly bread is made, that is, whereof the Lord speaketh, ' My Flesh is Meat indeed.' And again of wine, ' And My Blood is Drink indeed.' "

' Himself [2] is ' the Prince,' and ' High Priest after the order of Melchisedec,' and Sacrifice, and Priest, Who, in the Presence of His Father, with us eateth the heavenly Bread, and drinketh the Wine, whereof He saith in the Gospel : ' I will not drink of the fruit of this vine, until I drink it new in the kingdom of My Father:' to wit, in that kingdom, whereof He Himself saith in another place : ' The kingdom of God is within you.' ' And the gate shall be shut.' For no one can understand the Sacraments of the Passion of the Lord, and of His Body and Blood, suitably to their real Majesty."

" They [3] too shall plant vineyards with Noah, and shall drink of the wine thereof and be inebriated, and shall hear from the Lord the Saviour: ' Drink,

---

[1] Lit. " inebriated."

[2] In Ezech. 44, 2, T. v. p. 537.

[3] In Amos 9, 14, L. 3, T. vi. pp. 357, 358.

O my friends, and be inebriated!' But they shall drink the wine which He promised that He would drink new with His Apostles in the kingdom of His Father. This is the vine of Sorec, whereof we daily drink in the Mysteries."

And in direct explanation of the passage, in contrast with those whom he supposed to have interpreted it of a mere carnal drinking of wine in the Millennium [4]:

"But [5] let us hear that the Bread which the Lord brake and gave to His disciples was the Body of the Lord our Saviour, since He Himself said to them, 'Take, eat: This is My Body;' and that the Cup was That of which He said again, 'Drink ye all of this: for this is My Blood of the New Testament, which is shed for many.' That is the Cup of which we read in the Prophet, 'I will receive the Cup of Salvation.' And in another place: 'Thine inebriating Cup, how good is it!' If then 'the bread which came down from Heaven' is the Lord's Body; and 'the wine which He gave to His disciples is the Blood of the New Testament, which was shed for many for the remission of sins,' let us reject Jewish fables, and go up with the Lord into the large upper room, furnished and prepared, and let us receive from Him on high the Cup of the New Testament, and keeping there with Him the Passover, let us be inebriated with that wine of soberness.

[4] See above, pp. 134, 135.
[5] Ep. 120, ad Hedib. q. 2, T. i. ed. Vallars, p. 818.

'For the kingdom of God is not meat and drink, but righteousness, and joy, and peace in the Holy Ghost.' Nor hath Moses given us the True Bread, but the Lord Jesus: Himself Guest and Banquet; Himself eating with us, and He Who is eaten. His Blood we drink, and without Him we cannot drink; and daily, in His Sacrifices, we tread out from the fruit of the True Vine and of the Vineyard of Sorec, which is interpreted 'chosen,' the red juice, and therefrom we drink new wine from the kingdom of the Father, not in the oldness of the letter, but in the newness of the Spirit: singing the new song which no man can sing, but in the kingdom of the Church, which is the kingdom of the Father. This Bread too the Patriarch Jacob desired to eat, saying, 'If the Lord God will be with me, and will give me bread to eat, and raiment to put on.' For ' as many of us as are baptized in Christ, have put on Christ,' and eat ' the Bread of Angels,' and hear the Lord saying, ' My meat is to do the will of the Father Who hath sent Me, that I may finish His work.' Let us then do the will of Him the Father, Who hath sent us, and finish His work, and Christ shall drink His own Blood with us in the kingdom of the Church."

Hence, conversely, some consecrated virgins pleaded for their wine-drinking, that it was the element used in the Sacrament.

" And⁶ if they wish to seem witty and sportive,

⁶ Ep. 22, ad Eustoch. § 13, p. 96.

when they have drenched themselves with wine, adding sacrilege to ebriety, they say, 'Forbid that I should abstain from the Blood of Christ.'"   "And if they see any one pale and sad, they call her a miserable Solitary, and a Manichæan."

There is no reason to doubt (as Albertinus urges), that they "were speaking according to the common faith of the Church."   For S. Jerome does not blame their language; only the profaneness of their application of it.   But as their language proved, on the one hand, what Albertinus urges, that the Church believed of old that the consecrated element remained in its natural substance, wine, so it does equally, that they believed the Sacrament to be "the Blood of Christ."

"God[7] forbid that I should speak any thing unfavourable of these; for, succeeding to the Apostolic rank, with holy mouth they make[8] Christ's Body; through whom also we are Christians."

"The[9] fatted Calf, sacrificed for the salvation of the penitent, is the Saviour Himself, by Whose Flesh we are daily fed, Whose Blood we drink."

"If[10] any handmaidens share thy purpose, be not

[7] Ep. 14, ad Heliod. § 8, p. 33.

[8] Comp. Hooker, v. 77. 2.   "To whom Christ hath imparted power both over that mystical body which is the society of souls, and over that natural which is Himself for the knitting of both in one (a work which antiquity doth call the *making of Christ's Body*)."

[9] Ep. 21, ad Damas, § 26, p. 79.

[10] Ep. 22, ad Eustoch. § 29, p. 111.

proud towards them, be not puffed up as their mistress. Ye have begun to have one Spouse; together ye sing; together ye receive the Body of Christ; why should ye have a different table?"

"Turn [1] back to Genesis, and thou shalt find Melchisedec, King of Salem, to be the Prince of this city, who even then in type of Christ offered Bread and Wine, and consecrated the Christian Mystery in the Body and Blood of the Saviour."

"Whether [2] is greater? to pray, or to receive the Body of Christ? Certainly, to receive the Body of Christ. I know that at Rome there is this custom, that the faithful at all times receive the Body of Christ, which thing I neither censure nor approve. ' Let every one be fully persuaded in his own mind.' But I put it to their own consciences: why do they not dare to visit the Martyrs? Why do they not enter the Churches? Is there one Christ in public, another at home? What is not lawful in the Church, neither is it lawful at home. No place is closed to God; even the darkness is light with God. Let each one prove himself, and so let him approach the Body of Christ."

"If [3] she wills to receive the Body of Christ, let her do penance."

"How [4] much more a Chief Priest and a Bishop,

---

[1] Ep. 46, Paul. et Eustoch. ad Marc. § 2, p. 198.
[2] Ep. 48, ad Pamm. § 15, p. 225.
[3] Ep. 55, ad Amand. § 4, p. 296.
[4] Ep. 64, ad Fabiol. § 5, p. 356.

who ought to be blameless; and of such virtue, as ever to live in holy things: and to be ready to offer sacrifice for the people, a mediator between men and God, and making [5] with holy mouth the Flesh of the Lamb: 'for the holy oil of Christ his God is upon him.'"

" We [6] have marvelled at the great benefit of thy work to all the Churches, that they who are ignorant may learn, being instructed by the testimony of the Scriptures, with how great reverence they ought to regard Holy things, and to serve the ministry of Christ's Altar; and not to account the Sacred Chalices and the Sacred veils, and the other things pertaining to the Service of the Lord's Passion, as useless and senseless things, which possess no sanctity; but as being for the association with the Body and Blood of Christ, to be reverenced with the same Majesty as His Body and Blood."

" S. Exuperius [7], Bishop of Toulouse, an imitator of the widow of Sarepta, hungry himself, feedeth others, and, with face pale with fasts, is tortured by others' hunger; and his whole substance hath he laid out on the bowels of Christ. Nought richer than he who carries the Body of the Lord in a wicker basket, His Blood in a glass."

" What [8] ails the minister of tables and of widows [the Deacon], that he swells and lifts himself up

[5] "Conficiens."   [6] Ep. 114, ad Theoph. § 2, p. 753.
[7] Ep. 125, § 20, p. 941.
[8] Ep. 146, § 1, p. 1075.

above those [Bishops and Priests] at whose prayers the Body and Blood of Christ is made [9]?"

"Knowest [1] thou not that both Laics and Clerks have one Christ, and that there is not one God for the neophytes, another for Bishops? Why then doth not he who receives penitent Laics, receive the Clergy also? *Lucif.* It is not the same thing to shed tears for sins, and to handle the Body of the Lord. It is not the same thing to fall at the feet of the brethren, and from on high to administer the Eucharist to the people."

"The [2] Bishops met together, who, entrapped in the toils of Ariminum, were reputed to be heretics, but unconscious of heresy, protesting by the Body of the Lord, and whatever is holy in the Church, that they had suspected nothing amiss in their faith."

"As [3] though we too did not equally receive the Body of Christ! In the Mysteries one is the sanctification of lord and servant, noble and ignoble, king and soldier: although, according to the deserts of the recipients, that becometh diverse which is One. 'For whosoever shall eat and drink unworthily, shall be guilty of the Body and Blood of Christ.' Or because even Judas drank of the same Cup as the other Apostles, were his deserts therefore the same as theirs?"

---

[9] "Conficitur."

[2] Ib. § 19, p. 191.

[1] Adv. Lucif. § 3, T. ii. p. 173.

[3] Adv. Jov. L. 2, § 25, p. 364.

"He[4] so taught His Apostles, that believers should, at the Sacrifice of that Body, venture to say, 'Our Father,'" &c.

"In[5] that he says, 'Thou art a Priest for ever after the order of Melchisedec,' our mystery is signified under the word 'order,' not in sacrificing irrational animals through [the order of] Aaron, but by the offering bread and wine, that is, the Body and Blood of the Lord Jesus."

In the same volume, S. Jerome unites sacramental and spiritual communion.

"Since[6] the Flesh of the Lord is true Food, and His Blood is true Drink, the spiritual meaning [of Eccl. 3, 13] is, that in this present life we have one only good, to feed on His Flesh and drink His Blood, not only in the Mystery [the Eucharist] but also in the reading of Scriptures. For the true food and drink which is derived from the Word of God, is knowledge of the Scriptures."

"We[7] may say figuratively: All lovers of pleasure more than lovers of God, 'sanctify themselves in gardens' and doorways, because they cannot enter the Mysteries of truth, and 'eat the abomination,' since they are not holy in body and spirit; they neither eat the Flesh of Jesus, nor drink His Blood, whereof Himself saith, 'Whoso eateth My Flesh

---

[4] C. Pelag. iii. 15, p. 786.
[5] Quæstt. Heb. in Gen. 14, 18, T. iii. 329.
[6] In Eccl. 3, 13, p. 413.
[7] In Is. 66, 17, T. iv. p. 816.

and drinketh My Blood hath eternal life.'　'For
even Christ our Passover is sacrificed for us,' Who is
not eaten without, but in one house and within."

On Ezek. xliii. S. Jerome so identifies "the Bread
and the Cup" with the Body and Blood of Christ, as
even to substitute the words the "Body and Blood,"
when quoting the Apostle:

"Whence[8] the Apostle too says, 'Let a man examine himself, and so let him approach the Body and
Blood of the Lord.'"

"'And[9] ye offer My Bread,' to wit, the shewbread, in all Churches and the whole world, which
springs from one Bread [that consecrated by our Lord
at the last Supper], and not bread only, but the fat
also whereof it is written, 'He satisfied them with
the marrow of wheat,' and the Blood Which was
shed in Christ's Passion."

"And[1] the Priest, he saith, shall take of His
Blood, what shall be for the sin of all: [His] Who, in
other words, is called a 'lamb,' in Exodus and in
the Gospel, where John Baptist saith: 'Behold the
Lamb of God, Which taketh away the sins of the
world.'　But it is the precious Blood wherewith we
are redeemed in the Passion of the Lord our Saviour: by Whose Flesh we are nourished, and
Whose Blood we drink."

"So[2] greatly did I love them, and so merciful a

---

[8] T. v. p. 523.　　　　　　[9] In Ezech. 44, 7, p. 542.
[1] In. Ezech. 45, 19, p. 571.
[2] L. iii. in Hos. Cap. xi. T. vi. p. 125.

shepherd was I, that I bare Myself the sick sheep upon My shoulders; but they knew not that by My Passion I healed them; and that I, Who am the lover of all men, with cords of love, was drawing them to believe, according to that which is written in the Gospel, 'No man cometh to Me, except My Father which hath sent Me, draw him.' And they thought My easy yoke to be very heavy; and I descended to them, leaving the kingdom of the heavens, that I might eat with them, having taken the form of man, or [3] I gave them of My own Body to eat, Myself both Meat and Guest."

"The [4] skirt of the Lord's garment and the slight touch sanctifieth none but him who hath eaten the Flesh of the Lamb, and drunk His Blood."

"We [5], by the corn of the elect or of the young men, and the wine that makes the maids to grow, or wine of good odour for the maids, understand the Lord the Saviour, Who saith in the Gospel, 'Except a corn of wheat fall into the ground and die, it abideth alone; but if it die, it bringeth forth much fruit [6].' Of this wheat is made that Bread which cometh down from Heaven, and 'which strengtheneth man's heart.' This bread they eat who are strong in Christ, and to whom John the Evangelist saith, 'I write unto you, young men, because the word of God abideth in you, and ye are strong, and have

---

[3] S. Jerome in commenting upon two renderings, "declinavi ad eum ut vesceretur," and Symmachus, "ad eum cibos."

[4] In Hagg. Cap. iii. p. 764.

[5] L. ii. in Zech. i. x. 17, pp. 869, 70.   [6] John xii. **24.**

overcome the wicked one [7].' He Who is the corn of the elect or the young men, is Himself too the wine which maketh glad the heart of man, and is drunk by those virgins who are holy both in body and soul, that, as it were inebriated and rejoicing, they may follow the Church, and of them it may be said, 'The virgins shall be brought after her to the king, her fellows shall be brought unto thee: with joy and gladness shall they be brought [8].'"

"The [9] Divine word upbraids negligent Bishops, Presbyters, and Deacons, or, since we are a priestly and a royal race, all who, having been baptized into Christ, are enrolled under the Name of Christ, 'why despise they the Name of God?' and when they ask, 'wherein have they despised His Name?' it shows the occasion of the offence. 'Ye offer,' it saith, 'upon Mine altar polluted bread.' We pollute Bread, that is, the Body of Christ, when, being unworthy, we approach the Altar, and being impure, drink pure Blood, and say, 'The Table of the Lord is contemptible.' Not that any man dares to speak this, and to utter in impious words what he impiously thinketh; but the deeds of sinners despise the Table of God."

"Jesus [1] willeth not to send them away fasting, lest they faint by the way. *He* then incurs peril, who without the celestial Bread hastens to arrive at the desired resting-place."

[7] 1 John ii. 14.　　　　[8] Ps. xliv. 15, 16, Vulg.
[9] In Mal. i. 7, pp. 948, 949.
[1] In Matt. xv. 32, L. 2, T. vii. p. 118.

"After [2] that the typical Passover was finished, and He had eaten the flesh of the lamb with the Apostles, He takes bread, which strengtheneth the heart of man, and passes to the true Paschal Sacrament; that as Melchisedec, Priest of the Most High God, offering bread and wine, had done in prefiguration of Him, He Himself might represent [to the Father] in the verity of His own Body and Blood."

"In fact [3], it was rather the operation of the wine than the creature of God that was condemned by us: and we took away liberty from the virgin glowing with the warmth natural to her age, lest upon occasion of drinking little, she should drink more and perish. On the other hand, we were aware, both that wine is consecrated into the Blood of Christ, and that Timothy was commanded to drink wine."

"But [4] in two ways are the Blood and Flesh of Christ understood, either that spiritual and Divine, whereof Himself said, 'My Flesh is Meat indeed, and My Blood is Drink indeed [5];' and 'Except ye eat My Flesh and drink My Blood, ye shall not have eternal life [6];' or the Flesh and Blood, the Flesh which was crucified, the Blood which was shed by the soldier's spear."

"There [7] is as great difference between the shew-

---

[2] Lib. iv. Cap. xxvi. p. 216.
[3] Lib. iii. in Gal. v. 19, p. 508.
[4] In Ephes. Lib. i. Cap. i. p. 553.
[5] John vi. 55.   [6] Ibid. 53.
[7] In Tit. Cap. i. p. 702.

bread and the Body of Christ, as between the shadow
and the substance, between the image and the
reality, between patterns of things to come, and
those things which were prefigured by the patterns.
Therefore even as gentleness, patience, temperance,
moderation, disregard of lucre, hospitality also and
kindness, ought to reside especially in the Bishop,
and eminence among all laymen, so also a special
chastity, and (so to speak) a priestly modesty, that he
may not only keep himself from an impure deed,
but that even the mind which is about to make the
Body of Christ may be free from roving gaze and
wandering thought."

53. S. Siricius.

Bishop of Rome A. D. 385—398; praised as "a good
shepherd " by S. Ambrose and a Council of Milan, A. D. 390.

" It * is even added, that certain Christians
(shocking to relate) going over to apostasy, have
been profaned both by worship of idols and defilement of sacrifices; whom we direct to be cut off
from the Body and Blood of Christ, by which they
were once redeemed by regeneration."

54. Theophilus of Alexandria.

Bishop A. D. 385—412. " A man of sound understanding and courage " (Theod. v. 22) ; freed Alexandria from
the remains of idolatry; in his later years, in his zeal against
Origenism, became the persecutor of S. Chrysostom.

He has been quoted already, as comparing the con-

* Ep. i. ad Himer. c. 3. Conc. ii. 1214.

secration of the elements of the two Sacraments by the coming of the Holy Spirit; and as speaking of the outward element "setting forth" the Body of the Lord, above, p. 277 (comp. p. 106).

" A [9] favourer of devils and not of men, he [Origen] with frequent calumnies persecutes the Son of God, and crucifies Him again, not understanding into what a deep and horrible whirlpool of impiety he is drawn down. For he who admits the premiss must admit also the inference; and he who says that Christ was crucified for devils, must admit that to them also it is to be said, 'Take, eat, this is My Body,' and 'Take, drink, this is My Blood.' For if He be crucified for devils, as this assertor of novel doctrines affirms, what special ground or reason will there be, that men alone should communicate of His Body and Blood, and not devils also, for whom in His Passion He shed His Blood? But neither shall devils hear, 'Take and eat,' or 'Take and drink,' nor will the Lord abolish His own commands, Who said to His disciples, 'Give not that which is holy unto the dogs, neither cast ye your pearls before swine, lest they trample them under their feet, and turn again and rend you.' For the Apostle too writing, 'I will not that ye shall be partakers with devils; ye cannot drink the Cup of the Lord and the cup of devils; ye cannot be partakers of the Lord's Table

---

[9] Epist. Pasch. A. 401, § 11, ap. S. Jerome, Ep. 96, i. 564, ed. Vall.

and of the table of devils,' shows thereby that it is impossible that devils should drink of the Cup of the Lord, and partake of His Table. By all which it is proved that Christ cannot be crucified for devils, lest devils should be partakers of His Body and Blood."

" Nor [1] do we call the bodily substance vanity, as he [Origen] thinketh (falling, in other words, into the doctrines of Manichæus), lest the Body of Christ also should be subject to vanity, through the eating whereof we, being satiated, daily ruminate on His words, ' Unless a man eat My Flesh and drink My Blood, he has no part in Me.'"

" That [2] we being raised above earthly deeds to the lofty house of virtue, may, like the disciples, eat the Passover in the upper room, having with us Christ Who was crucified for us; eating Him wholly, as Life."

55. JEROME.

Presbyter of Jerusalem (Damasc. de Imag. Or. 3, i. 385) about A.D. 386, wrote in the reign of Theodosius the Great. (See Gall. T. vii. Prolegom. c. 12, p. xviii.)

On his agreement with other Fathers in saying that the consecrated elements are not ' bare bread and wine,' see above, p. 93.

" Many [3] of those in the world often experience workings of such grace and of the Holy Spirit,

---

[1] Ib. § 17, p. 571.
[2] Id. Fragm. 1, ex Epist. i. Fest. Gall. vii. 640.
[3] Comm. Christiano util. Gall. vii. 529.

those, I mean, who assist at the Altar, and who approach to partake of the mysteries of Christ. For on a sudden they are filled with tears and joy and gladness. Whence also the Christian is fully convinced, that he doth not receive mere (ψιλὸν) bread and wine, but in truth the Body and Blood of the Son of God, sanctified by the Holy Ghost. For we do not experience any thing of this sort, or such grace or inworking, or sweetness, or compunction, when we eat the *bare* [ψιλὸν] bread and wine on our table, although that bread be purer than this bread, and the wine be older and better than that which is offered on the Altar."

"To enter the Church is not the sign of a true Christian. For many who are unworthy enter with us. Nor to make the sign of the Cross, nor to partake of the Body of Christ, are the signs of the true Christian. For perhaps unbelievers too and heretics partake of it, and all which we do, they do."

56. S. Gaudentius of Brescia.

Elected Bishop about A. D. 387, by S. Ambrose and the Bishops of Cisalpine Gaul, while he was absent in the East ; deputed, A. D. 405, by the Emperor Honorius and a Roman Synod to intercede with Arcadius in behalf of S. Chrysostom.

He has been quoted already as speaking of the Holy Eucharist as "a figure of our Lord's Body and Blood" (above, p. 110), a "pledge of His Presence" (p. 111). He says also that His "Blood is expressed by the 'kind' of wine." He calls the Holy Eucharist

" the figure of His Passion," and says that He appointed that the Sacrament of His Body and Blood should be offered in the "kind" of bread and wine. But by this word "kind" he means a real substantial thing.

"From ' the time that He came, of Whom that [Paschal] lamb was a type, He, the Lord Jesus, that true ' Lamb of God, Which taketh away the sins of the world,' and said, ' Except ye eat My Flesh and drink My Blood, ye have no life in you,' [from that time] vainly do the Jews practise carnally that which, except they perform spiritually with us, they have no life in them. For ' the law is spiritual,' as saith the Apostle, and 'Christ, our Passover, is sacrificed for us.' "

"In the shadow of that legal Passover not one lamb was slain, but many. For one was slain in every house, since one was not sufficient for all. But a figure is not the reality of the Lord's Passion. For a figure is not the truth, but an imitation of the truth. For man too was made in the image of God, but was not therefore God. Although indeed in the way in which they say he is the ' image of God,' he may be also called god ; since by nature there is one God ; by relation, many'. In this truth, then, in which we are, One died for all ; and the Same in each house of the Church, in the mystery of bread

' De Pasch. Tr. ii. B. P. v. p. 946.
' See S. Athanas. ag. Arians, ii. 21, p. 380, and note, O. T.

and wine, being sacrificed, refresheth; believed on,
quickeneth; consecrated, sanctifieth the consecrators.
This is the Flesh of the Lamb: this His Blood. For
'the Bread Which came down from Heaven' saith:
'The Bread Which I will give, is My Flesh for the
life of the world.' Rightly too is His Blood expressed[6] by the 'kind' of wine, in that He saith in
the Gospel, 'I am the true Vine.' He Himself
plainly declares all which is *offered in the figure of
His Passion* to be, in one, His Blood. Whence the
most blessed Patriarch Jacob prophesied of Christ,
saying, 'He shall wash His garments in wine, and
His raiment in the blood of the grape.' For the garment, the raiment of our body, He was about to
wash in His Own Blood. Himself then the Creator
and Lord of nature, Who 'bringeth forth bread
from the earth,' of bread again (for He both can,
and hath promised) makes His Own Body; and He
Who of water made wine, makes also of wine His
Own Blood."

"We'[7] ought, by the command of God, first to
mortify the lusts of the flesh, and so to receive the
Body of Christ, Who was slain for us, when slaves
in Egypt. 'Wherefore let a man examine himself,'
as saith the Apostle, 'and so let him eat of that
Bread and drink of that Cup.' But when he says,
we must 'eat it in haste,' he teaches that we receive

---

[6] "Vini specie sanguis ejus exprimitur."
[7] Ib. p. 947. col. 1, D.

not the Sacrament of the Lord's Body and Blood
with sluggish heart, and languid lips; but with all
eagerness of mind, as really 'hungering and thirsting
after righteousness.' For, 'Blessed,' saith the Lord
Jesus, 'are they which hunger and thirst after
righteousness, for they shall be filled.' But the
noble lesson set before you closes what it had said
with this most worthy end: 'For it is the Lord's
Passover.' 'O the depth of the riches both of the
wisdom and knowledge of God!' 'It is,' saith he,
'the Lord's Passover: that is, the passing over of
the Lord, that you may not think *that* to be earthly,
which has been made heavenly through Him who
passed into it, and made it His Body and Blood.
For what we have already explained generally, as to
eating the Flesh of the Lamb, we must observe
especially in tasting these same mysteries of the
Lord's Passion, that you think not, like the Jew,
that it is raw flesh, and raw blood, and reject it,
saying, 'How can This Man give us His Flesh to
eat?' nor, in the cauldron of a carnal heart, by
nature ever disposed to caprice, boil the Sacrament
itself down, deeming it a common earthly thing, but
that you believe that by the fire of the Holy Ghost
it is made That which it is declared; since what you
receive, is the Body of that heavenly Bread, and the
Blood of that sacred Vine. For when He reached
forth the consecrated Bread and Wine to His
disciples, He said, 'This is My Body; this is My
Blood.' Let us believe Him Whom we have be-

lieved. Truth cannot lie. Therefore when He
spake of eating His Flesh, and drinking His Blood
to the multitudes, amazed and muttering, 'This is a
hard saying, who can hear it?' He, that He might
by heavenly Fire do away those thoughts, which I
told you were to be avoided, added: 'It is the
Spirit that quickeneth; the flesh profiteth nothing.
The words that I speak unto you, they are Spirit
and they are life.' And therefore we are bidden to
eat, in the mysteries, the Head of His Divinity,
together with the feet of His Incarnation, and the
inward parts; that we may believe all things alike,
as they have been delivered, not breaking that most
solid bone of Him, 'This is My Body, This is My
Blood.' But if even now, aught remains over in any
one's mind, which he hath not received in that exposition, let it be burnt by the glow of faith. 'For
our God is a consuming fire,' purifying, teaching,
and enlightening our hearts to the understanding
of things divine; that, through His unspeakable
gift, we may know the cause and meaning of that
heavenly Sacrifice instituted by Christ; so shall we
give Him endless thanks. For truly this is the
hereditary gift of His New Testament, which He
left us in that night when He was betrayed to be
crucified, as a pledge of His Presence. This is that
food for our journey, whereby in this journey of life
we are fed and nourished, until, departing from this
world, we go forth unto Himself. Whence the
Lord Himself said, 'Except ye eat My Flesh, and

drink My Blood, ye have no life in you.' For He willed His benefits to abide with us. He willed our souls ever to be sanctified by His Precious Blood, through the image of His Own Passion. And therefore He commanded His faithful disciples, whom first He made Priests of His Church, unceasingly to put in use those mysteries of eternal life, which must needs be celebrated by all Priests throughout all Churches of the whole world, until Christ should come again from Heaven. And this He did, in order that the Priests themselves, and all we His faithful people alike, having daily before our eyes the pattern of Christ's Passion, and carrying it in our hands, and receiving it with mouth and heart, may hold it in indelible memory of our redemption, and may attain the sweet medicine of everlasting defence against the poisons of the devil. As the Holy Ghost exhorteth, ' Taste and see that the Lord is good.'

" But that He appointed the Sacraments of His Body and Blood to be offered in the form of Bread and Wine, there is a twofold reason. First, that the immaculate Lamb of God might deliver a pure Sacrifice to be celebrated by a purified people, without burning, without blood, without broth[5] of flesh, and which should be ready and easy to be offered by all. Then since bread must needs be made from many grains of wheat formed into dough by means of water, and completed by fire, reasonably is this

---

[5] Brodio, id est, jure.

taken as a figure of the Body of Christ, since we know that out of the whole multitude of the human race there is made one Body, perfected by the fire of the Holy Ghost. For He was born of the Holy Ghost, Who descended upon Him in the form of a Dove; thence He returns from Jordan, the Evangelist bearing witness: 'Jesus was full of the Holy Ghost.' And since it became Him 'to fulfil all righteousness,' He enters the waters of Baptism, to consecrate them, and then, full of the Holy Ghost, returned from Jordan. In like way too, the wine of His Blood, gathered from very many berries, that is, grapes of the vineyard which He had planted, is pressed out in the winefat of the Cross; and, in the large vessels of those who receive with faithful heart, ferments by its own virtue. This sacrifice of the Passover of the Saviour, do ye all, going forth from the power of Egypt and of Pharaoh the devil, receive with us with all eagerness of a religious heart, that by our Lord Jesus Christ, Whom we believe to be in His Sacraments, our inmost souls may be sanctified; Whose inestimable virtue abideth for ever."

"To [9] us Christ liveth; since for us He rose. For He was no more seen of the Jews: nor did He, after His Resurrection, enter the Synagogue of the Jews, but He came to His assembled Disciples. He entereth to us who are assembled in the house of the Church, and *showeth us the truth of His Venerable*

[9] De Lect. Ex. Tr. 4, p. 949.

Body: if indeed we have been or are meet to be His disciples."

57. S. ISAAC THE GREAT, or "The Teacher."

Presbyter of Antioch, and Archimandrite, a disciple of Zenobius (a distinguished disciple of S. Ephrem), A.D. 390; died (in extreme age) between A.D. 459—461. "He had much Divine wisdom and spiritual knowledge" (Abulberkat). "He wrote for a long period and much" (Gennad. c. 66). His date had better have been placed A.D. 412. Bar-Hebræus, Ebnarrahib, and Elmacin call him a contemporary of S. Cyril of Alexandria. Dates are assigned to extant works of his from A.D. 418—459. He wrote, chiefly in rhythm, many practical works, but also against Nestorianism and Eutychianism. One long and touching elegy on the earthquake of A.D. 459, which overthrew a fourth part of Antioch, he composed just before his death. (Assem. Bibl. Or. i. c. 16, pp. 207—234.)

" I beheld [1] that her cup was mingled, and instead of wine, it was full of Blood, and instead of bread, a Body was placed for her in the midst of her Table. I saw the Blood and trembled; and the Body, and fear seized me; and she [Faith] made a sign to me, ' Eat, and be silent; drink, child, and scrutinize not.' . . . She showed me a Body slain, and placed thereof between my lips, and cried to me sweetly, ' See what it is thou art eating.' She gave me the pen of the Spirit, and bade me subscribe; and I took, I wrote, and I confessed, ' This is the Body of God.' So again I took the Cup, and I drank in her feast, and from the Cup the scent of that Body, of which I had

---

[1] Serm. de Fide, ap. Assem. Bibl. Or. T. i. p. 220.

eaten, struck me, and what she said of the Body, that 'this is the Body of God,' that again I said of the Cup, that 'this is the Blood of our Redeemer."

As we have access to so little of him, I will add two more brief references to the Holy Eucharist.

"The[2] people of the Jews had a commandment that in Jerusalem only might it offer its offerings. And to the nations the Apostles command that in a church only they should offer the pure mysteries of Christ for propitiation to the receivers. Fools despise and reject things new and old; and by the walls and cross-ways they treat of the awful things."

"Faith[3] spake to me, and called to me, and said to me, that the Sacraments of the Church came forth from the opened Side of Christ."

58. S. Paulinus of Nola.

Born of Patrician parents A. D. 353; studied rhetoric and poetry under Ausonius; consul A. D. 375; converted and baptized A. D. 389; Monk, gave his large wealth to the poor, A. D. 392; Priest, Christmas Day, A. D. 393; probably Bishop of Nola A. D. 410; invited by the emperor to Ravenna, to heal the schism in the Roman Church, A. D. 419; died A. D. 431; the friend of S. Ambrose, S. Augustine, and S. Jerome. "From the richest opulence became voluntarily very poor, and in holiness most rich" (S. Aug. de Civ. Dei, i. 10). "Praised by the whole world" (Sulp. Sev. Dial. fin. See Eulogies and Life, Opp. T. 2, ed. Paris).

"'Therefore[4],' he saith, 'Moab is my washpot,'

<hr>

[2] Ib. p. 218.   [3] Ib. p. 243.
[4] Ep. 23, ad Sever. T. i. p. 125, ed. Par.

because not only of Judah, but of Moab, that is, not of the origin of the Saints only, but of sinners He took Flesh; for He, when the rawness of our flesh had been boiled away as it were in a pot, sanctified for ever His Flesh to be our Food. For His Flesh, as He Himself saith, is indeed the Flesh of Life. This is that pot in Jeremiah, burning our sins and consuming them in that fire, whereof He says, 'I am come to send a fire upon the earth;' which we desire may be enkindled in us also; that in the pot of the Lord's Body, that is, the Church, we may be thoroughly melted; and, being refined by the burning up of our vices, may be made 'silver, which from the earth is tried, and purified seven times in the fire,' that we may not be branches to be burned, but may abide fruitful vine-branches in the same Lord, that is, in the true Vine: and the same Lord, that sweet Cluster, may become our Food, Who, having hung for us upon the wood of the Cross, showed unto us the fruit of the land of promise."

"Because [5] she [Mary Magdalene] was an image of the Church, to be called out of the Gentiles, she bore about her all the tokens of the saving Mystery. She was anointed with the anointing of her gift; she had tears of penitence for her laver, bowels of love for sacrifice; and she took beforehand Himself, the living and life-giving Bread, in her hands and mouth: the Blood too of the Cup, before the Cup of

[5] Ib § 32, p. 142.

Blood yet was, she tasted with the lips which kissed. Blessed she who tasted Christ in the Flesh, and in His Very Body received the Body of Christ: deservedly preferred to the Pharisee, although he fed Christ; for she fasting, while the Jew was feasting, served; hungering, as I said, not for food, but for salvation."

" These⁶ venerable Altars veil Heaven's mysteries divine,
　Where, treasured with the holy Cross, the martyrs limbs recline ;
　There all the Saviour's witnesses together make abode,
　The Cross, the Body and the Blood, yea, e'en the Martyrs'
　　God.
　For God for us doth evermore store up His blessings true,
　And where is Christ, the Spirit is, and there the Father too.
　So, where the Cross, the Martyr ; where the Martyr, there the
　　Cross,
　To saints of holy martyrdom the sweet and sacred source.
　The food of immortality this hath to mortals given,
　This bore the crowns that give the Lord His worshippers in
　　Heaven.
　Upon the Cross was fix'd the Flesh I feed on, and the Blood
　Whence I drink life and cleanse my heart, 'twas from the
　　Cross it flowed.
　Lord, to Thine own Severus grant these Thine own gifts
　　combine !
　The bearer he and witness both of that dear Cross of Thine.
　Yea, make him through Thy Flesh to live ; Thy Blood his
　　cup afford,
　So may he live, and move, and have his being in Thy Word."

⁶ Written as an inscription for a Church, which Severus had built, for the consecration of which Paulinus had sent, in a gold tube, a piece of the true Cross which had been given by the Bishop of Jerusalem, and which was to be placed under the altar, together with relics of martyrs if obtained. Ep. 32, ad Sever. § 7, p. 204.   Comp. Ep. 31.

59. S. MARUTHAS.

Bishop of Tagrit, probably before A.D. 381; friend of
S. Chrysostom; wrought two miracles in the Court of Isde-
gerd, King of Persia, to whom he was sent by Theodosius
the Younger, to obtain toleration for the Christians; held
Council at Ctesiphon to restore discipline A.D. 414, and
caused the Nicene Canons to be observed there. He is said
to have been present at the Second General Council, A.D.
381, although his name does not appear. He *was* present
at a Council of Antioch, A.D. 383, held against the Messa-
lians (Conc. ii. 1209, ed. Col.).   Ass. B. O. i. 174—179.

"He'[1] saith to them, 'Do this continually in remembrance of Me.' It was needful and very right
that this should be. For if the perpetual participation
of the Mysteries had not been given, whence should
those who came afterwards, know the Redemption of
Christ? And who would be able to persuade them
or bring them to the knowledge? for it is difficult
oftentimes and to many to be believed. Besides,
the faithful afterwards would have been defrauded
of the Communion of the Body and Blood; but now
as often as we approach to the Body and Blood, and
take It in our hands, we believe that we embrace
the Body, and that we are of His Flesh and His
Bones, as it is written. For Christ did not call It a
type and a likeness, but that in truth 'This is My
Body, and This is My Blood.'"

60. S. AUGUSTINE.

Born A.D. 354; converted A.D. 386; baptized A.D. 387;

---

[1] Comm. Evang. apud Assem. l. c.

Presbyter A.D. 389; Assistant Bishop A.D. 395; died A.D. 430. His works were written between A.D. 387—429. See further, as to his life, his Confessions, Oxf. Tr.

He has been quoted already as using the words "figure," "sign," "signify," of the outward elements; "understood" of the inward part (above, pp. 107, 108); *as saying that we receive the Body and Blood of our Lord* in *or* under *the elements* (Sermon, p. 40, above, p. 132), *as interpreting our Lord's words "this fruit of the vine" of "the sacrament of wine," through which our "Lord commends to us His Blood"* (p. 139); *as using the words "spiritual eating, spiritual drinking"* (Sermon, p. 42).

I will prefix here one more passage in which he blends remarkably the significance of the Sacrament and the doctrine of the Real Presence, and will then give passages on the Real Presence as they occur in the order of his works.

In this first place S. Augustine is illustrating the manifestations of Almighty God under a bodily form in the Old Testament.

"If[8] then the Apostle Paul (although he still bare about him the burden of the body which is corrupted and weigheth down the soul, although as yet he saw in part and darkly, desiring to be dissolved and to be with Christ, and groaning in himself, looking for the adoption, to wit the redemption of his body) could yet preach the Lord Jesus Christ,

---

[8] De Trin. iii. 4, § 10, T. viii. p. 798.

signifying Him at one time by his tongue, at another
by letter, at another by the Sacrament of His Body
and Blood:—and yet neither his tongue, nor parch-
ment, nor ink, nor significant sounds uttered by the
tongue, nor marks of letters written upon skins, do
we call the Body and Blood of Christ, but That alone
which, taken of the fruits of the earth and consecrated with the mystic prayer, we receive solemnly,
to the salvation of our souls, in memory of our Lord's
Passion for us; and when this is, by the hands of
men, brought to that visible form, it is not sanctified
so as to become so great a Sacrament, save by the
Spirit of God working invisibly, since God works all
these things which in that work take place by bodily
acts, moving from the beginning His ministers within
(whether they be the souls of men or the obedience
of hidden spirits subdued to Himself): what wonder
is it, if in the creation of heaven and earth also,
of sea and air, God frameth things visible and tangible, as He willeth, to show and reveal Himself in
them as He sees right, not so that the very Substance should appear, whereby He Is, which is wholly
unchangeable, and more sublime in secret and within,
than all the spirits which He hath created?"

"She[9] [Monnica, his mother] had learned to
bring to the churches of the martyrs, a breast filled
with more purified petitions, and to give what she
could to the poor; that so the communication of the

[9] Conf. vi. 2, p. 87, Oxf. Tr.

K k 2

Lord's Body might be there rightly celebrated, where, after the example of His Passion, the martyrs had been sacrificed and crowned."

" Neither [1] in those prayers which we poured forth unto Thee, when the Sacrifice of our Ransom was offered for her, when now the corpse was by the grave's side, as the manner there is, previous to its being laid therein, did I weep even during those prayers."

" She [2], the day of her dissolution now at hand, took no thought to have her body sumptuously wound up, or embalmed with spices, nor desired she a choice monument, or to be buried in her own land. These things she enjoined us not; but desired only to have her name commemorated at Thy Altar, which she had served without intermission of one day: whence she knew that holy Sacrifice to be dispensed, by which the ' handwriting that was against us, is blotted out,' through which the enemy was triumphed over, who, summing up our offences, and seeking what to lay to our charge, ' found nothing in Him,' in Whom we conquer. Who shall restore to Him the innocent blood? Who repay Him the price wherewith He bought us, and so take us from Him? Unto the Sacrament of which our Ransom, Thy handmaid bound her soul by the bond of faith."

" He [3], Thine only Son, ' in Whom are hid all the

---

[1] Ib. ix. 32, p. 178.　　　　[2] Ib. § 36, p. 180.
[3] Ib. x. § 70, p. 223.

treasures of wisdom and knowledge,' hath redeemed me with His Blood. 'Let not the proud speak evil of me,' because I meditate on my Ransom, and eat It, and drink It, and dispense It: and 'poor,' desire to be 'satisfied' from Him, amongst those that 'eat and are satisfied, and they shall praise the Lord who seek Him.'"

"On[1] which ground that Word of God, by Whom all things were made, and Whom the whole Angelic bliss enjoyeth, reached forth ·His loving-kindness even to our misery, and 'the Word became flesh and dwelt among us.'   For so might man, while not as yet equalled to the Angels, eat Angels' Bread, if the Bread Itself of Angels vouchsafed to be made equal to men.   Nor doth He so come down to us, as to desert them; but at once entire to them, entire to us, feeding them inwardly through That Which God Is, admonishing us outwardly by that which we are, He maketh us, by faith, such whom He may feed equally 'by sight.'   For since the reasonable creature is fed by that Word, as its own best Food: but the human soul is reasonable, which was, in punishment, held in the mortal bands of sin, reduced to such low estate, as to strive, by comparisons of things visible, to understand invisible; the Food of the rational creature becomes visible, not by change of Its nature, but by putting on ours, that It might recall us following visible things, to Itself, the Invisible.   Thus the soul

[1] De lib. Arb. iii. § 30, p. 622.

finds Him lowly without, Whom in her pride she had inwardly left, that so she may imitate His visible lowliness, and return to His invisible loftiness."

"Whence [5] is it, that when the same Apostle had enumerated many vices, among which he placed the drunken, he concluded by saying, that ' with such we ought not even to eat?' But let us bear these things in our domestic luxury and corruption, and that of those feasts which are confined to private walls, and let us receive the Body of Christ with those with whom we ought not so much as to eat! But at least let so great a disgrace be kept off from the tombs of the bodies of saints, from the places of the Sacraments, from houses of prayer.

"I then [6] added, that the Jewish people itself, while as yet carnal, in that temple, where the Body and Blood of the Lord were not yet offered, never celebrated, I do not say drunken, but not even sober feasts."

"He [7] [one Urbicus] says that the sheep hath given place to the Bread; as though ignorant that both formerly Shewbread was wont to be placed on the Table of the Lord, and that now he himself receives a portion from the Body of the Lamb without spot. He says that ' the Blood hath given place to the

[5] Ep. 22, ad Aur. § 3, ii. 28.

[6] In allusion to a corruption of drunken feasts on the festivals of the Martyrs, which S. Augustine abolished. Ep. ad Alyp. xxix. 4, T. ii. p. 49.

[7] Epist. 36, ad Casulan. § 24, T. ii. p. 77.

Cup;' not reflecting that even now he receives the Blood in the Cup. How much better, then, and more fitly, might he in such wise say, that old things have passed away and become new in Christ, as that the Jewish Altar should give place to the Christian Altar (altare altari cederet), sword to Sword, fire to Fire, bread to Bread, sheep to Sheep, blood to Blood?"

"The [8] Lord Himself endureth Judas, a devil, a thief, and His betrayer: He allows him to receive, among the innocent disciples, What the faithful know to be our Ransom."

"First [9], therefore, I would have thee hold (which is the principal point in this argument) that our Lord Jesus Christ hath, as He says Himself in the Gospel, subjected us to His own easy yoke and light burden; and thence, by Sacraments, very few in number, very easy of observance, very mighty in significance, hath bound in one the community of a new people; such as are, Baptism hallowed by the name of the Trinity, the Communion of His own Body and Blood, and whatever else is prescribed in the Canonical Scriptures."

"Perhaps [1] some one will say that the Eucharist may not be received every day. Thou wilt ask, why? Because, saith he, those days are to be chosen, on which a man lives more chastely and continently,

---

[8] Ep. 43, ad Glor. Eleus. § 23, p. 99.
[9] Ep. 54, ad Januar. § 1, p. 124.
[1] Ib. § 4, p. 125.

that so he may come worthily to so great a Sacrament. 'For he that eateth unworthily, eateth and drinketh damnation to himself' (1 Cor. xi. 29).   'Nay,' saith another, on the contrary, 'if the wound of a man's sin and the violence of his disease be so great, that remedies such as these are to be put off, he ought, by the Bishop's authority, to be banished from the Altar, for a course of penitence, and by the same authority to be restored.   For this is unworthy receiving, if he receive at that time, in which he ought to be performing penance.   It is not that he is, of his own will, when he pleases, either to withdraw himself from Communion, or to return to it.   But if any man's sins are not so great, as that he should be deemed deserving of excommunication, he ought not to dissever himself from the daily medicine of the Lord's Body.'   More fitly, perhaps, does he adjust the difference of opinion between these, who exhorts that, first of all, they abide in the peace of Christ; but that each man do that which, according to his faith, he piously believes ought to be done.   For neither of them dishonours the Body and Blood of the Lord, but they eagerly vie in paying honour to that most healthful Sacrament.   Thus, neither did Zacchæus and that Centurion dispute one with another, nor did either of them advance himself before the other; when the one gladly received the Lord into his house, the other said, 'I am not worthy that Thou shouldest come under my roof' (Matt. viii. 8), both paying honour to the Saviour in a different, and, as it were, an opposite manner; both through sin miserable, both obtaining mercy."

"This[2] might rather raise a doubt in men's minds, whether, after having eaten, they should on that day either offer or receive the Eucharist, for that it is said in the Gospel, 'But as they were eating, Jesus took bread and blessed it' (Matt. xxvi. 26); and again, it had been said above, 'Now when the even was come, He sat down with the twelve, and as they did eat, He said, that one of you shall betray me' (Ibid. 20). For after this He delivered the Sacrament. And it clearly appears, that when first the disciples received the Body and Blood of the Lord, they did not receive it fasting. Is, then, for this reason, the Church Universal to be censured, because men always receive fasting? For on this account it seemed good to the Holy Spirit, namely, that for the honour of so great a Sacrament, the Lord's Body should enter the mouth of a Christian previously to other food. For on this account is that custom observed throughout the whole world. For neither ought the brethren, because the Lord gave that Sacrament after the meal, to assemble after dinner or supper for its reception; nor, as those did whom the Apostle reproves and corrects, to mingle that Sacrament with their own tables. For the Saviour, in order with more earnestness to commend the depth of that mystery, wished to fix it, as His last act, in the hearts and memory of the

[2] Ib. 7, 8, pp. 126, 127.

disciples, from whom He was about to depart to His Passion.   And for this reason He gave no command about the order in which it should be afterwards received, that He might reserve this point for the Apostles, through whom He was about to set in order the Churches.   For if He had prescribed this, that it should always be received after other food, I suppose that no one would have altered that custom."

"But [3] some have thought good, and that with show of reason, that on one fixed day in the year, on which the Lord gave the actual supper, it is lawful that the Body and Blood of the Lord should, as though for a more marked commemoration, be offered and received after eating.   But I deem that it would more fitly take place at such an hour, as that one who hath fasted, too, may be able to go to the oblation after the refection which takes place at the ninth hour.   Wherefore we compel no one to eat before that supper of the Lord, but neither dare we to forbid any one to do so."

"We [4] often so speak, as to say, when Passion-tide draws near, that to-morrow, or the day after, is the Lord's Passion; although He suffered so many years ago, and *that* Passion hath not actually taken place more than once.   Again, on the Lord's Day, we say, to-day hath Christ risen; whereas, so many years have passed by since He rose.   Why is it that no man is so foolish as to charge us with falsehood, in

---

[3] Ib. § 9, p. 127.   [4] Ep. 98, ad Bonifac. § 9, p. 267.

thus speaking, save that we name the days from their correspondence with those on which the events took place; and so that is called the actual day, which is not the actual day, but answers to it in the revolution of time; and that is said to be done on that day, because of the celebration of the Sacrament, which is not done on that day, but was done long ago? Was not Christ sacrificed once in His own Person, and yet in the Sacrament is sacrificed for the people, not only through all the festivals of Easter, but every day? And it is clear that he does not speak falsely, who, being asked, shall answer that He is sacrificed. For if Sacraments had not a certain resemblance to those things of which they are the Sacraments, they would not be Sacraments at all. But from this resemblance they receive, for the most part, the names even of the things themselves. As, therefore, after a certain manner, the Sacrament of the Body of Christ is the Body of Christ, the Sacrament of the Blood of Christ the Blood of Christ, so the Sacrament of Faith is Faith."

"The' 'rich upon earth,' in this place (Ps. xxii. 29) are to be understood as the proud. For it is not in vain that they have been so distinguished, that it should be said above concerning the poor, ' The poor shall eat, and be satisfied;' but in this place, ' All such as be rich upon earth have eaten and worshipped.' For they, too, have been brought to the Table of

---

' Ep. 140, ad Honorat. § 66, p. 447.

Christ, and receive of His Body and Blood: but they worship only; they are not satisfied because they do not imitate.   For, eating Him Who is poor, they disdain to be poor; since 'Christ suffered for us, leaving us an example that we should follow His steps.'"

"And[6] lest any should say that the way of salvation might consist of a good conversation and the worship of one God Almighty, without the Communion of the Body and Blood of Christ, he saith, 'There is one God and one Mediator between God and man, the Man Christ Jesus;' in order that what he had said, ' will have all men to be saved,' may be understood to be set forth in no other way, but through a mediator; not God, which the Word ever was, but the Man Christ Jesus, when 'the Word was made Flesh, and dwelt among us.'"

"But[7] what is to be done with them, if they fear to take out their [Heathenish] earrings, and fear not, with the mark of the devil, to receive the Body of Christ?"

"But[8] at this time, since, through the Resurrection of our Lord, there hath dawned the clearest manifestation of our freedom, we are no longer laden with the burdensome operation of those signs, whose meaning we now know; but the Lord Himself, and the Apostolic discipline, have handed down certain few instead of many, and those most easy to perform,

[6] Ep. 149, ad Paulin. § 17, p. 510.
[7] Ep. ad Poss. 24, § 2, p. 873.
[8] De Doct. Christ. iii. 13, T. iii. p. 49.

most majestic in meaning, most pure in the observance; such as are the Sacrament of Baptism, and the celebration of the Body and Blood of the Lord.".

"But [9] whereas the Lord says, 'Except ye eat My Flesh and drink My Blood, ye have no life in you;' why were the people so strictly forbidden the blood of the sacrifices which were offered for sins, if by those sacrifices this one Sacrifice was signified, wherein is the true remission of sins ; while yet the Blood of that Sacrifice itself, not only is no one forbidden to receive for nourishment, but rather all, who wish to have life, are exhorted to drink ?"

"The [1] lowliness of penitence hath been scattered wide and plentifully, for this purpose, that the Lord, Who resisteth the proud but giveth grace to the humble, might, as though with the glue of love, cleave to them, as a Man to men, so that He should be the Mediator between God and man, giving Himself to them as Food through the Sacrament of His own Body and Blood, choosing the foolish things of the world, as the stones, to bring to nought the wise.   For He is Food to the Angels, in that He is the Word of God with God : but that He might be Food to the stones, 'the Word was made Flesh, and dwelt among us.'"

"Ask [2] we him, 'Eatest thou the Flesh of the Son of Man, and drinkest the Blood of the Son of

[9] Quæstt. in Lev. qu. lvii. p. 516.
[1] In Job, p. 672.
[2] On S. Joh. iii. 3. Hom. xi. § 3, p. 167, Oxf. Tr.

Man?' he knows not what we say, because Jesus hath not trusted (or committed) Himself to him."

"We[3] too at this day do receive visible food; but the Sacrament is one, the virtue of the Sacrament another. How many receive from the Altar and die, yea by receiving die! Whence the Apostle saith, 'Eateth and drinketh judgment to himself.' It was not that the sop of the Lord was poison to Judas. And yet he received, and when he received, the enemy entered into him; not that he received an evil thing, but that he, being evil, did in evil wise receive what was good. Look to it then, brethren, eat ye spiritually the Heavenly Bread, bring innocence to the altar."

"'This[4] is the Bread which came down from Heaven.' This Bread the manna signified; this Bread the altar of God doth signify. Those were Sacraments: in signs they are diverse, in the thing signified they are alike. . . . 'This,' then, 'is the Bread that cometh down from Heaven, that whoso eateth thereof may not die.' But this, in regard of the virtue of the Sacrament, not in regard of the visible Sacrament: of him who eateth inwardly, not outwardly; who eateth in the heart, not who presseth with his teeth."

"'I[5] am the Living Bread, Who am come down from Heaven.' Therefore 'Living,' because I 'came

---

[3] Ib. Hom. xxvi. § 11, p. 407.
[4] Ib. Hom. xxvi. § 12, pp. 407—409.   [5] § 13, p. 409.

down from Heaven.' From Heaven came also the manna: yea, but the manna was a shadow, this is the verity. . . . The faithful know the Body of Christ, if they neglect not to be the body of Christ. Let them become the body of Christ, if they wish to live by the Spirit of Christ. By the Spirit of Christ liveth not any, but the body of Christ. . . . Wouldest thou also live by the Spirit of Christ? Be thou in the body of Christ. For, doth my body live by thy spirit? Mine liveth by my spirit, and thine by thine. The body of Christ cannot live but by the Spirit of Christ. Thence it is, that the Apostle Paul, expounding to us this Bread, saith, 'One Bread, one Body are we, being many.' O sacrament of piety! O sign of unity! O bond of charity! Whoso would live, hath where to live, hath whereof to live. Let him come, let him believe: let him be incorporated, that he may be quickened . . . let him cleave to the body, let him live to God by God; let him now labour on earth, that thereafter he may reign in heaven."

" 'He ' that eateth My Flesh, and drinketh My Blood, hath eternal life.' This, therefore, that man hath not, who eateth not this Bread, nor drinketh this Blood. For temporal life without Him men may have, but eternal they can in no wise have. Who then eateth not His Flesh, nor drinketh His Blood, hath not life in him: and who eateth His Flesh,

' § 15, p. 410.

and drinketh His Blood, hath life. It answereth, however, to both, that He said, 'Eternal.' Not so is it in this meat, which we take for sustenance of this temporal life. For if one take it not, he will not live; yet if one take it, he will not therefore live. For it may be, that, of old age, or some disease, or some casualty, very many who do take it shall die. But in this true meat and drink, that is, the Body and Blood of Christ, it is not so. For, both he that taketh It not, hath not life, and he that taketh it hath life, and that, of course, eternal. . . . The Sacrament of this thing, that is, of the unity of the Body and Blood of Christ, in some places every day, in some places at certain intervals of days, is on the Lord's Table prepared, and from the Lord's Table is taken: by some, to life; by some, to destruction: but the Reality of which it is the Sacrament, is for every man to life, for none to destruction, whoever shall be partaker thereof."

"'He' that eateth My Flesh and drinketh My Blood, dwelleth in Me, and I in him.' This, then, it is, to eat that meat and drink that drink; to dwell in Christ and to have Christ dwelling in him. And therefore, who dwelleth not in Christ and in whom Christ dwelleth not, without doubt doth neither [spiritually [8]] eat His Flesh nor drink His Blood

---

[7] § 18, p. 412.

[8] The words inclosed in brackets by the Benedictines are not S. Augustine's, but Bede's, to bring out what he believed to be the meaning of S. Augustine.

[albeit carnally and visibly he press with his teeth the Sacrament of the Body and Blood of Christ], but rather doth unto judgment to himself eat and drink the Sacrament of so great a thing."

"We [9] then live by Him, eating Him, that is, receiving Him as that eternal life which of ourselves we had not."

" 'This [1] is the Bread which cometh down from Heaven:' that by eating Him we may live, seeing we cannot have eternal life of ourselves. ' Not,' He saith, ' as your fathers ate manna and died: he that eateth this Bread shall live for ever.' That those died, He would have to be so understood, that they live not for ever. For temporally, even these without question shall die, who eat Christ: but they live for ever, because Christ is everlasting life."

" It [2] relates to the Body of the Lord, which He said that He giveth to be eaten for eternal life. He expounded the manner of this bestowing and of His gift, how He would give men His Flesh to eat, when He said, ' He that eateth My Flesh and drinketh My Blood, dwelleth in Me, and I in him.' The sign which shows that one hath eaten and drunk is this, if he dwelleth and is dwelt in, if he inhabiteth and is inhabited, if he cleaveth that he be not abandoned. This then it is, that He hath taught and admonished us in mystical words, that

[9] § 19, p. 413.   [1] § 28, p. 414.
[2] On vi. 57. Hom. xxvii. § 1, p. 416.

L l

we be in His Body, under Himself the Head in His members, eating His Flesh, not forsaking the unity of Him."

"Those [3] men saw Christ dying by their wickedness, yet believed in Christ forgiving their wickednesses.   Until they drank the Blood they had shed, they despaired of their own salvation."

"What [4] murderer should despair, if one was restored to hope, by whom even Christ was murdered?   There believed of them many: the Blood of Christ was given them, more to drink It for their deliverance, than to be held guilty for shedding It: who can despair?"

"The [5] Blood which in their raging they had shed, believing they drunk."

S. Augustine throughout his works [6] refers to this as a most signal instance of God's mercy.

"Did [7] *they* not believe the same things as we believe, they by whom these signs were ministered, they by whom the same things which we believe were prophetically foretold?   Of course they believed: only they believed that the things were to come; we, that they *are* come.   Accordingly he also saith thus: 'They drank the same spiritual drink;' spiritually the same; for bodily it was not the same.

---

[3] On vii. 34. Hom. xxxi. § 9, p. 459.
[4] On viii. 24. Hom. xxxviii. § 7, p. 527.
[5] On viii. 28. Hom. xl. § 2, p. 541.
[6] See e. g. on S. Joh. pp. 527. 541. 1104. 1200, Oxf. Tr.
[7] Hom. xlv. § 9, pp. 605, 606.

For what was it they drank? 'For they drank of that spiritual rock which followed them; and that rock was Christ.'   See then: the signs varied, while the faith is the same.   There the rock was Christ; to us That is Christ which is placed on the Altar of God.   And they, as a great Sacrament of the same Christ, drank water flowing from the rock; we drink, the faithful know What.   If thou look at the visible form, the thing is another; if at the intelligible signification, 'they drank the same spiritual drink.'"

" What [8] is 'the Table of the Mighty' ye know; upon it is the Body and Blood of Christ."

"Of [9] one bread hath Peter and Judas received: and yet what part hath a believer with an infidel? For Peter received unto life, Judas unto death. Thus as it was with that good odour, so with that good food.   As then the good odour, so also the good food, is life to the good, death to the bad. 'For whoso shall eat unworthily, eateth and drinketh judgment to himself:' 'judgment to himself,' not to thee."

" They [1] ate the Bread, the Lord; he, the bread of the Lord, against the Lord; they, Life; he, punishment.   'For he that eateth unworthily,' saith the Apostle, 'eateth judgment to himself.'"

" Why [2] marvellest thou then that there was given

[8] Hom. xlvii. § 2, p. 624.
[9] Hom. l. § 10, pp. 675, 676.
[1] Hom. lix. § 1, p. 737.   [2] Hom. lxii. p. 749.

L l 2

to Judas the Bread of Christ, that by it he should be made over to the devil, when thou seest, on the contrary, how there was given to Paul an angel of the devil, that by it he should be made perfect in Christ? Thus both to the evil man the good was a bane, and to the good the evil was a boon. Ye remember of What it is written, 'Whoso shall eat the bread or drink the Cup of the Lord unworthily, shall be guilty of the Body and Blood of the Lord.' And when the Apostle said this, the discourse was upon the subject of those who, treating the Lord's Body like any other food, took it in an undiscriminating and negligent way. If then this man is rebuked who does not discriminate, that is, see the difference of, the Lord's Body from other meats, how must he be damned, who, feigning himself a friend, comes to His Table a foe! If the touch of reproof is laid upon the negligence of the guest, with what punishment shall he be smitten through, who sells the Entertainer! And the sop given to the betrayer, what was it meant for, but to show to what a grace he had been ungrateful?"

"It[3] was not *then*, as some think who read negligently, that Judas received Christ's Body. For it is to be understood that the Lord had already distributed the Sacrament of His Body and Blood to them all, among whom was Judas also, as S. Luke most evidently relates the matter."

[3] Ib. § 3.

"For[4] what is the 'Table of the Mighty,' but that from which we receive the Body and Blood of Him Who laid down His Life for us?   And what is it to 'sit' thereat, but humbly to draw near thereto? And what to 'consider and understand the things that are set before thee,' but to think worthily of so great grace?"

"Many[5] of them believed, and the shedding of the Blood of Christ was forgiven them.   At first they shed It while they raged; now they drank It while they believed."

"The[6] rich of the earth too have eaten the Body of their Lord's humiliation, and though they have not, as the poor, been filled even to imitation, yet they have worshipped."

"'I[7] will offer my vows unto the Lord, in the sight of them that fear Him.'   The Sacrifice of peace, the Sacrifice of love, the Sacrifice of His Body the faithful know."

"In[8] His own Body and Blood He willed our health to be.   But whereby commended He His Body and Blood? By His own humility. For unless He were humble, neither could This be eaten nor That drunk.   Consider His Highness: 'In the beginning was the Word, and the Word was with God,

---

[4] On xv. 13. Hom. lxxxiv. § 1, p. 841.
[5] On S. Joh. ii. 5. Hom. i. p. 1104.
[6] In Ps. xxi. [xxii. Eng.] v. 29, p. 148.
[7] In Ps. xxii. Exp. 2, v. 28, p. 161.
[8] In Ps. xxxiii. [xxxiv.] Serm. i. n. 6, p. 346.

and the Word was God.' Behold the Food is from everlasting: but of It eat the Angels, of It eat the Hosts above, of It eat the Heavenly Spirits, and eating they are filled, and yet remaineth That whole Which satisfieth them and maketh them glad. But what man could be capable of that Food? How could his heart be made fit enough for that Food? Therefore behoved that table to become milk, and so to come even to babes. But how doth food become milk? How is food changed into milk, except it be passed through flesh? For the mother doth this: what the mother eateth, that eateth the infant; but because the infant is less fit to feed on bread, the same bread the mother incarnates, and through humility of her own breast and the juice of milk, of that very bread feeds the infant. How then did the Wisdom of God feed us with that same Bread? 'The Word was made flesh, and dwelt among us.' See then humility, in that man ate the bread of Angels, as it is written, 'He gave them of the bread of Heaven. Man did eat Angels' food;' that is, That Word by which the Angels live from everlasting, Which is equal to the Father, did man eat: because, 'being in the form of God, He thought it not robbery to be equal with God:' by that are the Angels filled. 'But He made Himself of no reputation,' that man might eat Angels' food, and 'took upon Him the form of a servant, and was made in the likeness of men; and being found in fashion as a man, He humbled Himself and became obedient unto death, even the death of the Cross:' that so from His Cross might be commended unto us the Body and the Blood of the Lord, for a new sacrifice."

"Recollect[3] the Gospel; when our Lord Jesus Christ spake concerning His Body, He said, 'Except a man eat My Flesh, and drink My Blood, he shall have no life in him. For My Flesh is meat indeed, and My Blood is drink indeed.' And His disciples who followed Him feared, and were shocked at His discourse; and understanding it not, they thought that our Lord Jesus Christ said some hard thing, as if they were to eat His Flesh, and to drink His Blood Which they saw; and could not endure it, saying as it were, How is it?"

"Doth[1] not this seem madness, 'Eat My Flesh and drink My Blood?' And He saying, 'Whoso eateth not My Flesh, and drinketh not My Blood, shall have no life in him,' seemeth to be mad. Therefore He quitted them, and departed; understanding fled from their heart, lest they should be able to comprehend Him."

"Christ[2] was carried in His Own Hands, when, commending His Own Body, He said, 'This is My Body.' For that Body He carried in His Own Hands. This is the humility of our Lord Jesus Christ; this is much commended unto men. According to this He exhorteth us, brethren, to live;

<hr>

[3] Ib. n. 8, p. 348.   [1] Ib. p. 349.
[2] Ib. n. 10, p. 350.

that is, that we should imitate His humility, that we should slay Goliath, and holding Christ, should conquer pride."

"How [3] 'carried in His Own Hands?' Because, when He commended His Own Body and Blood, He took into His Hands That which the faithful know; and in a manner carried Himself, when He said, 'This is My Body.'"

"Let [4] us approach to Him and be lightened; not as the Jews approached to Him, that they might be darkened; for they approached to Him that they might crucify Him; let us approach to Him that we may receive His Body and Blood. They by Him crucified were darkened; we, by eating and drinking the Crucified, are lightened."

"Those [5] sacrifices, then, as being but expressions of a promise, have been abrogated. What is that which has been given as its fulfilment? That *Body;* which ye know; which ye do not all of you know; which, of you who do know it, I pray God none may know it unto condemnation."

"The [6] fulfilment of the promise has done away with the words that express the promise. For if they still hold out a promise, that which was promised is not yet fulfilled. This was promised by certain signs. The signs that convey the promise are done away; because the substance that was promised is

---

[3] Ib. Serm. ii. n. 2, p. 353.

[5] In Ps. xl. n. 12, ii. p. 144.

[4] Ib. n. 10, p. 360.

[6] Id. p. 145.

come. We are in this *Body*. We are partakers of this *Body*. We know That which we ourselves receive; and ye who know not yet, will know it by and by; and when ye come to know it, I pray ye may not receive it unto condemnation. 'For he that eateth and drinketh unworthily, eateth and drinketh damnation unto himself.' 'A Body' hath been 'perfected' for us; let us be made perfect in the Body."

"Because[7] He walked here in very Flesh, and gave that very Flesh to us to eat, for our salvation; and no one eateth that Flesh, unless he hath first worshipped; we have found out in what sense such a footstool of our Lord's may be worshipped, and not only that we sin not in worshipping, but that we sin in not worshipping. But doth the flesh give life? Our Lord Himself, when He was speaking in praise of this same earth, said, 'It is the Spirit that quickeneth, the flesh profiteth nothing.' Therefore also when thou bowest thyself down prostrate before the 'earth,' look not as if unto earth, but unto that Holy One Whose footstool it is that thou dost worship; for on His account thou dost worship; wherefore he hath added here also, 'Fall down before His footstool, for He is holy.' Who is holy? He in Whose honour thou dost worship. 'His footstool.' And when thou worshippest Him, see that thou do not in thought remain in the flesh, unquickened by the Spirit;

[7] In Ps. [xcviii.] xcix. n. 9, T. iv. p. 454, O. T.

for He saith, 'It is the Spirit that quickeneth; the flesh profiteth nothing.' But when our Lord counselled this, He had been speaking of His own Flesh, and He had said, 'Except a man eat My Flesh, he shall have no life in him.' Some disciples of His, about seventy, were offended, and said, 'This is a hard saying, who can hear it?' And they went back, and walked no more with Him. It seemed unto them hard that He said, 'Except ye eat the flesh of the Son of Man, ye have no life in you.' They received it foolishly, they thought of it carnally, and imagined that the Lord would cut off parts from His Body, and give unto them; and they said, 'This is a hard saying.' *They* were hard, not the saying: for unless they had been hard, and not meek, they would have said unto themselves, 'He saith not this without reason, but there must be some latent mystery herein.' They would have remained with Him, softened, not hard; and would have learnt *that* from Him which they who remained, when the others departed, learnt. For when twelve disciples had remained with Him, on their departure, these remaining followers suggested to Him, as if in grief for the death of the former, that they were offended by His words, and turned back. But He instructed them, and saith unto them, 'It is the Spirit that quickeneth; the flesh profiteth nothing; the words that I have spoken unto you, they are Spirit, and they are life.' Understand spiritually what I have said; ye are not to eat this Body which ye see; nor to drink that Blood which they who will crucify Me shall pour forth. I have commended unto you a certain Mystery; spiritually understood, it will quicken. Although it is needful that this be visibly celebrated, yet it must be spiritually understood. 'O magnify the Lord our God, and fall down before His footstool, for He is holy.'"

"We[8] also feed on the Lord's Cross, since we eat His Body."

"Thou[9] hast thine own meat; the serpent also hath his own meat. If thou live well, thou wilt have Christ for thy Food; if thou depart from Christ, thou wilt be food for the serpent."

"In[1] the whole world our Ransom is received. Amen! it is answered."

"What[2] sweeter than Angels' Bread? How is not the Lord sweet, when man hath eaten Angels' Bread? Man does not live from One, the Angel from Another. It is Truth Itself, Wisdom Itself, the Might Itself of God. But thou canst not enjoy it in such sort as do the Angels. For how do they enjoy it? As It is, 'In the beginning was the Word, and the Word was with God, and the Word was God, by Whom all things were made.' And thou, how dost thou touch It? Because 'The Word was made Flesh, and dwelt among us.' For that 'man might

----

[8] In Ps. [c.] ci. n. 9, p. 491.
[9] In Ps. civ. 4, n. 11, T. v. p. 141.
[1] In Ps. cxxv. § 9.
[2] In Ps. cxxxiv. § 5, pp. 1495, 1496.

eat Angels' Bread,' the Creator of Angels became Man."

"How[3] many Judas' does Satan fill, unworthily receiving the morsel to their damnation? 'For he who eateth and drinketh unworthily, eateth and drinketh damnation to himself.' That which is given is not evil, but what is good is given to the evil to damnation."

"There[4] is a spiritual food also which the faithful know, which ye too will know, when ye shall receive It at the altar of God. This also is 'daily Bread,' necessary only for this life. For shall we receive the Eucharist when we shall have come to Christ Himself, and begun to reign with Him for ever? So then the Eucharist is our daily bread; but let us in such wise receive it, that we be not refreshed in our bodies only, but in our souls."

"When[5] this life shall have passed away, we shall neither seek that bread which hunger seeks, nor shall we have to receive the Sacrament of the Altar, because we shall be there with Christ, Whose Body we do now receive."

"Those[6] words also of His, 'He that eateth My Flesh, and drinketh My Blood, dwelleth in Me, and I in him,' how must we understand? Can we include in these words those too, of whom the Apostle says, 'that they eat and drink judgment to

---

[3] In Ps. cxlii. § 16.   [4] Serm. 57, n. 7, p. 85, Oxf. Tr.
[5] Serm. 59, n. 6, p. 101, O. T.
[6] Serm. 71 [21], n. 17, p. 178, Oxf. Tr.

themselves,' when they eat this Flesh and drink this Blood? What! did Judas the impious seller and betrayer of his Master (though as Luke the Evangelist declares more plainly, he eat and drank with the rest of His disciples this first Sacrament of His Body and Blood, consecrated by the Lord's hands), did he 'dwell in Christ and Christ in him?' Do so many, in fine, who either in hypocrisy eat that Flesh and drink that Blood, or who after they have eaten and drunk become apostate, do they 'dwell in Christ or Christ in them?' Yet assuredly there is a certain manner of eating that Flesh and drinking that Blood, in which whosoever eateth and drinketh, 'he dwelleth in Christ and Christ in him.' As then he doth not 'dwell in Christ and Christ in him,' who 'eateth the Flesh and drinketh the Blood of Christ' in any manner whatsoever, but only in some certain manner, to which He doubtless had regard when he spake these words; &c."

"Who[7] should despair of the forgiveness of his sins, when the crime of killing Christ was forgiven to those who were guilty of it? They were converted from among this people of the Jews; were converted and baptized. They came to the Lord's Table, and in faith drank that Blood, which in their fury they had shed."

"One[8] may say, Explain to me; what did that

---

[7] Serm. 77 [27], n. 4, p. 223. The same expression recurs, Serm. 80, n. 5. 87, n. 11. 89. 1.

[8] Serm. 89 [39], n. 7, p. 333.

signify, that 'He made a pretence of going further?'
For if it had no further meaning, it is a deceit, a lie.
We must then, according to our rules of exposition,
and distinctions, tell you what this 'pretence of
going further' signified. 'He made a pretence of
going further,' and is kept back from going further.
In so far then as the Lord Christ being, as they supposed, absent in respect of His Bodily Presence, was
thought to be really absent, He will as it were 'go
further.' But hold Him fast by faith, hold Him fast
at the breaking of bread. What shall I say more?
Have ye recognized Him? If so, then have ye
found Christ. I must not speak any longer on this
Sacrament."

"We ⁹ have heard the True Master, the Divine
Redeemer, the Human Saviour, commending to us
our Ransom, His Blood. For He spake to us of
His Body and Blood; He called His Body Meat,
His Blood Drink. The faithful recognize the Sacrament of the faithful. When therefore commending
such Meat and such Drink, He said, 'Except ye
shall eat My Flesh and drink My Blood, ye shall
have no life in you' (and this that He said concerning
life, Who else said it but the Life Itself? But that
man shall have death, not life, who shall think that
the Life is false), His disciples were offended, not all
of them indeed, but very many, saying within themselves, 'This is a hard saying, who can hear it?'"

⁹ Serm. 131, n. 1, p. 585.

"Assuredly [1], He Who could ascend Whole could not be consumed. So then He both gave us of His Body and Blood a healthful refreshment, and briefly solved so great a question as to His Own Entireness. Let them then who eat, eat on, and them that drink, drink; let them hunger and thirst; eat Life, drink Life. That eating is, to be refreshed; but thou art in such wise refreshed, as That whereby thou art refreshed, faileth not. That drinking, what is it but to live? Eat Life, drink Life; thou shalt have life, and the Life is Entire. But then this shall be, that is, the Body and Blood of Christ shall be, each man's Life; if what is taken in the Sacrament visibly is, in the truth itself, eaten spiritually, drunk spiritually."

"As [2] we heard when the Holy Gospel was being read, the Lord Jesus Christ exhorted us by the promise of eternal life to eat His Flesh and drink His Blood. Ye that heard these words have not all as yet understood them. For those of you who have been baptized, and the faithful, do know what He meant. But those among you who are yet called Catechumens, or hearers, could be hearers, when it was being read: could they be understanders too? Accordingly our discourse is directed to both. Let them who already eat the Flesh of the Lord and drink His Blood, think what it is they eat and drink, lest as the Apostle says, 'They eat and drink judgment to themselves.' But they who do not yet eat and drink,

[1] Ib. p. 586.   [2] Serm. lxxxii. [132], § 1, ii. p. 593.

let them hasten, when invited to such a banquet. Throughout these days the teachers feed you, Christ daily feedeth you, that His Table is ever ordered before you. What is the reason, O hearers, that ye see the Table, and come not to the banquet? And peradventure just now when the Gospel was being read, ye said in your hearts, 'We are thinking what it is that He saith, My Flesh is meat indeed, and My Blood is drink indeed. How is the Flesh of the Lord eaten, and the Blood of the Lord drunk? We are thinking what He saith.' Who hath closed it against thee, that thou dost not know this? There is a veil over it; but if thou wilt, the veil shall be taken away. Come to the profession, and thou hast resolved the difficulty. For what the Lord Jesus said, the faithful know well already."

"Keeping[3] your professions, approach ye to the Flesh of the Lord, approach to the Blood of the Lord."

"I[4] promised to you who have been baptized, a Sermon, in which I was to explain the Sacrament of the Lord's Table, which ye have even now seen, and whereof ye became partakers last night[5]. Ye ought to know what ye have received, what ye are about to receive, what ye ought daily to receive. That Bread which ye see on the Altar, sanctified by the Word of God, is the Body of Christ. That Cup,

---

[3] Ib. p. 596.   [4] Serm. 227, in die Pasch. iv. p. 973.
[5] Easter Eve.

rather what the Cup holds, sanctified by the Word of God, is the Blood of Christ. By these things the Lord Christ willed to commend His Body and Blood, which He shed for us for the remission of sins. If ye have well received, ye are what ye have received [6]."

"O remember [7], dearly beloved, how the Lord Jesus willed to be known, in the breaking of bread, by those whose eyes were holden, that they should not know Him! The faithful know what I mean: they know Christ in breaking of bread. For not all bread, but that which receives the blessing of Christ, becomes the Body of Christ."

"See [8], my brethren, where the Lord would be known. In 'breaking of bread.' We are safe; we break bread, and we know the Lord. He would not be known save there, for our sakes, who were not to see Him in the Flesh, and yet were to eat His Flesh. Whoever then of you is of the faithful, whoever art not idly called a Christian, who dost not enter a Church without cause, hearest the Word of God with fear and hope, let the breaking of bread comfort thee. The absence of the Lord is not absence: have faith, and He is with thee Whom thou seest not."

"Our [9] Lord Jesus Christ then, before the break-

---

[6] This is repeated, Serm. 229, p. 976.

[7] Serm. 234, Pasch. v. § 2, p. 987.

[8] Serm. 235, § 3, p. 990.

[9] Serm. 239, § 2, p. 998.

ing of bread, speaketh with men as one unknown; in breaking of bread He is known. For there He is found, where eternal life is received. He is received in our hospice, Who prepareth a home in Heaven."

" This [1] which ye see on the Altar of God, ye saw last night also; but what it was, what it meant, of how great a thing it contained the Sacrament, ye have not yet heard. What ye see, then, is bread and a cup; what your eyes also report to you; but what your faith requires to be taught, the bread is the Body of Christ, the Cup the Blood of Christ. But some such thoughts as this may arise in the mind of some one, 'Our Lord Jesus Christ, we know whence He took Flesh, of the Virgin Mary. He was nursed as an infant,' &c. (going briefly through His Life, Death, Resurrection.) 'He ascended into Heaven; thither He lifted aloft His Body; thence He is to come to judge the quick and dead; there He is now sitting at the Right Hand of the Father. How is the bread His Body? And the Cup, or what the Cup contains, how is it His Blood?' These things, Brethren, are therefore called Sacraments, because in them one thing is seen, another understood. What is seen, hath a bodily form [speciem]; what is understood, hath a spiritual fruit."

" In [2] that Church itself [Rome], as ye often hear, he [S. Laurence] bore the office of the Diaconate.

---

[1] Serm. 272, ad Infantes, incorporated also by S. Fulgentius, Ep. 12 ad Ferrand. de 2 quæstt., and Florus ad 1 Cor. x.

[2] Serm. 304, in Solemn. Laurent. M. iii. § 1, p. 1234.

There he administered the Sacred Blood of Christ: there for Christ he shed his own blood."

"In [3] that place, where he put off his mortal body, a savage multitude had then assembled, for hatred of Christ, to shed Cyprian's blood. There, to-day, a multitude flocks together in worship, which, on account of Cyprian's birthday, drinketh the Blood of Christ. And the more devotedly, then, for the Name of Christ, Cyprian's blood was shed, the more sweetly in that place, on account of Cyprian's birthday, is the Blood of Christ drunk."

"Lastly [4], let such a sentence issue from the mind itself, that a person judge himself unworthy to partake of the Body and Blood of the Lord, so that he who dreads lest, by the final sentence of the Supreme Judge, he be severed from the kingdom of heaven, be, by the ecclesiastical discipline, severed for the time from the Sacrament of the heavenly Bread."

"Many [5] receive the Sacrament of His Body: but not all who receive the Sacrament, will have the place promised to His members, with Him. Almost all indeed call the Sacrament His Body, for all feed together in His pastures: but He will come, Who shall divide, and place some on the Right Hand, some on the left."

"To [6] be made a partaker of that Table is to begin

---

[3] Serm. 310, in Nat. Cyprian. M. § 2, pp. 1249, 1250.
[4] Serm. 351, de util. pœn. § 7, p. 1356.
[5] Serm. 354, § 2, p. 1375.
[6] De Civ. Dei, xvii. 20, T. vii. p. 484.

to have life; for in Ecclesiastes, 'it is not good for a man save that he should eat and drink,' what can he be more probably thought to mean, than what appertains to the participation of this Table, which the Priest Himself, the Mediator of the New Testament, exhibits after the order of Melchizedec, of His own Body and Blood. For this Sacrifice succeeded all those sacrifices of the Old Testament, which were immolated as a shadow of That to come, of which we understand that Voice of the same Mediator speaking, through the prophecy in the 39th Psalm, 'Sacrifice and offering Thou wouldest not, but a Body hast Thou prepared for me;' because for all those sacrifices and oblations His Body is offered, and is ministered to the communicants."

" There ' are others, who promise deliverance from eternal punishment, not indeed to all men, but only to those washed by Christ's Baptism, who have become partakers of His Body, howsoever they may have lived, in whatsoever heresy or impiety, on account of what Jesus saith : 'This is the Bread Which came down from Heaven, that a man may eat of it, and not die. I am the Living Bread Which came down from Heaven ; if any man eat of this Bread, he shall live for ever.' They must then of necessity, say these, be freed from eternal death, and brought somehow to eternal life.

" There are also those who do not promise this,

' Ib. xxi. 19, 20, p. 639.

even to all who have the Sacrament of the Baptism
of Christ and of His Body, but to Catholics only,
because they have eaten the Body of Christ, not in
the Sacrament only, but in reality, being placed in
that very Body of His of which the Apostle saith,
' We, being many, are one bread, one body;' so that
although they should afterwards have lapsed into
some heresy, or even heathen idolatry, yet simply
because in the Body of Christ, *i.e.* in the Catholic
Church, they have received the Baptism of Christ
and have eaten the Body of Christ, they shall not
die for ever, but shall at length obtain eternal life,
and that all their impiety shall not avail to the
eternity, but, in proportion to its greatness, to the
duration and greatness of their punishments."

" He [8] who is in the unity of that Body, *i.e.* in
the compages of the members of Christ, of which
Body the faithful communicants are wont to receive
the Sacrament from the Altar, he is truly to be said
to eat the Body of Christ and drink the Blood of
Christ."

" They [9] [the wicked] are not to be said to eat
the Body of Christ, because neither are they to be
accounted among the members of Christ. For not
to mention other things, they cannot at the same
time be both the members of Christ and members
of a harlot. Lastly, He Himself when He saith,
' Whoso eateth My Flesh and drinketh My Blood,

---

[8] Ib. 25, p. 646.   [9] Ib. fin. pp. 646, 647.

abideth in Me and I in him,' showeth what it is to eat the Body of Christ and drink His Blood, not as to the Sacrament only, but in truth; that is, to abide in Christ, so that Christ also should abide in him. For He hath so said this, as though He said, 'Whoso abideth not in Me and in whom I abide not, let him not say or think that he eateth My Body or drinketh My Blood.' They then do not abide in Christ who are not His members; but they are not members of Christ who make themselves members of a harlot, unless through repentance they cease to be that evil thing, and by reconciliation return to this good thing."

After other miraculous cures through the Sacrament of Baptism, S. Augustine relates one where the domestics and animals had been infested by some disorder. "A [1] Priest went, offered there the Sacrifice of the Body of Christ, praying as earnestly as he could, that this harass might cease. Through the mercy of God, it presently ceased."

"For [2] the Blood of Christ hath a loud voice on earth, when, on receiving It, all nations answer, Amen. This is the loud voice of the Blood, which the Blood itself draws from the mouth of the faithful redeemed by that same Blood."

"This [3] signifies the end of the world, when the rest of the saints shall no longer be in the Sacrament

---

[1] Ib. xxii. 6, p. 666.
[2] Cont. Faust. xii. 10, T. viii. p. 231.
[3] Ib. c. 21, p. 237.

of hope, whereby the Church is, at this time, banded together, so long as That is drunk, which flowed from the Side of Christ; but [that rest] shall now be in the very perfection of eternal salvation, when the kingdom shall be delivered to God the Father, so that in that clear contemplation of the unchangeable verity, we shall need no corporeal mysteries."

"He [Faustus] would know that the heritage of God is to be shared with the few; its seals with the many: that he would have in common with the few holiness of life, and the gift of love 'shed abroad in our hearts by the Holy Ghost, Which is given unto us,' to Which inward Fount no alien approacheth; but with the many the holiness of the Sacrament, which whoso 'eateth and drinketh unworthily, eateth and drinketh judgment to himself;' which whoso neglecteth to eat, shall 'have no life in him, and therefore will not arrive at the life eternal.' And that those same few, compared with the multitude of the bad, are called few; but considered by themselves, are a great multitude, diffused throughout the world," &c.

"But our Bread and Cup is not any chance bread and cup, as those [the Manichees] aver, but by prescribed consecration is made to us mystical; it is not so by nature. Hence, what is not so made, bread and cup although it be, is food to refresh life, not a Sacrament of religion; though indeed we do

---

Ib. xiii. 16, p. 260.   Ib. xx. 13, p. 342.

bless and give thanks to the Lord, in all His gifts, not the spiritual only, but the bodily also."

"But [6] the Hebrews in the sacrifices from their flocks, which they offered to God, in many and various ways, (as was worthy of so great thing,) solemnized the prediction of that future Sacrifice, which Christ hath offered. Whence Christians now solemnize the memory of that completed Sacrifice, in the sacred Oblation and Communion of the Body and Blood of Christ."

"We [7] receive with faithful heart and mouth the Mediator between God and man, the Man Christ Jesus, Who gave us His Flesh to eat and His Blood to drink: although it may seem more dreadful to eat human flesh than to slay it, to drink human blood than to shed it."

"Infants [8] do not know as to that which is placed upon the Altar, and consumed, when the holy celebration is accomplished; whence or how it is made, whence it is adopted to the use of religion. And if they should never learn it by experience of their own or of others, and should never see that form of things, unless when it is offered and given at the celebrations of Sacraments, and it should be told them by very high authority Whose Body and Blood it is, they will have no other belief, but that the Lord altogether appeared to the eyes of men under that form, and

[6] Ib. 18, p. 345.
[7] Cont. Adv. Leg. et Proph. ii. 33, p. 599.
[8] De Trin. iii. 21, p. 804.

that such was the Side whence, when it was pierced, that liquor actually flowed."

" As[9] Judas, to whom our Lord offered the sop, not by receiving what was evil but by receiving evilly, made room in himself for the devil, so any one who unworthily receives the Sacrament of the Lord, does not, because he is evil himself, cause it to be evil; nor, because he receives not unto salvation, has he received nothing. For that was no less the Body and Blood of the Lord, to those also, to whom the Apostle said, 'He that eateth and drinketh unworthily, eateth and drinketh damnation to himself.'"

" As[1] the circumcision of the Jews in the flesh is one thing, but that of the baptized, which we celebrate on the eighth day, another; and one thing the Passover, which they to this day celebrate with a sheep, another that which we receive in the Body and Blood of Christ; so the Baptism of John was one Baptism, the Baptism of Christ another."

" None[2] say this, save they who with altered souls, receive the Cup of the Lord to eternal life, not they, who eat and drink judgment to themselves, as the Apostle says; and yet to both, not being one, that Cup is one."

" What[3] is more mad, than to communicate in the Sacraments of the Lord, and not to communicate in

---

[9] De Bapt. c. Donat. v. c. 8, § 9, T. ix. p. 146.
[1] Cont. lit. Petil. ii. 87, p. 246.
[2] Ib. § 110, p. 253.   [3] Ib. § 126, pp. 256, 257.

the words of the Lord ?   These will indeed say, ' In
Thy Name have we eaten and drunken ;' and will
hear, ' I know you not ;' for they eat and drink His
Body and Blood in the Sacrament; and His members,
spread abroad through the whole world in the Gospel,
they acknowledge not, and therefore they are not
accounted among them in the judgment."

" What [4] of the very Body and Blood of Christ,
the only Sacrifice for our salvation, although the
Lord Himself saith, ' Except a man eat My Flesh
and drink My Blood, he shall have no life in him ;'
doth not the same Apostle teach us, that this too
becomes harmful to those who use It ill?   For he
says, ' Whosoever shall eat this Bread or drink this
Cup of the Lord unworthily, shall be guilty of the
Body and Blood of the Lord."

" What [5] will you find to say here, save that Baptism must not be reckoned among those good things
pertaining to the law of God, which men may have,
and not be good; but that the law itself and knowledge and the Sacrifice of the Body and Blood of
Christ are good things of such kind, that men may
both have them and be bad; but Baptism a good of
such sort, that whosoever hath it, must needs be
good?   If ye choose to say this, ye will speak untruly."

" Of [6] the Bread itself and of the very Hand of the

---

[4] c. Crescon. i. § 30, p. 403.   [5] Ib. § 32.
[6] Ad Don. post Coll. c. 6, p. 586.

Lord, both Judas and Peter received; and yet what fellowship, what agreement, what portion hath Peter with Judas?"

"Since[7] then good and bad alike hear the same word of God, and alike receive the Sacraments of God, and yet their causes stand differently in regard to their acts; and through their diversity of will, their persons are held differently, the one eating worthily, the other unworthily, the same Holy Food; neither doth cause prejudice cause, nor person, person."

"He[8] had said, 'Bind him hand and foot, and cast him into outer darkness; there shall be weeping and gnashing of teeth.' He immediately added, 'For many are called, but few chosen[9].' How is this true, since rather one out of many was cast into outer darkness, unless in that one was prefigured the vast body of all wicked men, who before the judgment of the Lord shall be mingled together at the Feast of the Lord? From whom the good, meantime, separate themselves in heart and life, while together with them they eat and drink the Body and Blood of Christ, but with a great distinction. For *these*, in honour of the Bridegroom, are clad in the wedding garment, 'seeking not their own, but the things which are Jesus Christ's;' but *those* have not the wedding garment, that is, a most faithful love of

---

[7] Id. c. 7, p. 587.   [8] Id. c. 27, p. 597.

[9] Matt. xxii. 13, 14.

the Bridegroom, since they seek their own, not the things which are of Jesus Christ. And hereby, although at one and the same feast, these eat mercy, those judgment; for the psalm of the feast itself is, as also I have said above, 'I will sing to Thee of mercy and judgment, O Lord[1].' "

" Who[2] would offer the Body of Christ, save for those who are members of Christ ?"

I subjoin a fragment of a sermon of S. Augustine, published by Cardinal Mai. I do not add more, some of the sermons, apparently, not being S. Augustine's[3], others only repeat what has been often quoted already[4].

[1] Ps. ci. 11.

[2] De anim. et ejus orig. i. c. ix. § 10, T. x. p. 342.

[3] The volume requires the careful revision of such editors as the Benedictines, before it can be used with confidence. Parts of Serm. 143 are plainly taken from S. Chrysostome de Proditione Judae. In the same volume a sermon is published as S. Anselm's (pp. 505—531), the beginning of which is an expansion of Hugo de S. Victore. As to S. Augustine, I cannot doubt that Serm. 81, (p. 159, ed. Mai,) 93, (p. 178,) 118, (p. 247,) 120, (p. 264,) are not his, although some of them contain fragments of his. Card. Mai himself doubted as to Serm. 165, and gave up Serm. 195.

[4] Such are Serm. 26. 2, and 86. 2. On the other hand, Serm. 10, § 1, may probably relate only to the Incarnation ; Serm. 9, § 1, to the life to come only. This I will add, although doubting myself whether it refer to the Holy Eucharist.

" Hear the verse of this very psalm, ' And they shall delight themselves in the multitude of peace.' Thy silver and thy gold shall be peace to thee; thy possessions, thy life, thy God, shall be peace. Whatsoever thou desirest here, shall be peace, peace to thee; since here what is thy gold cannot be thy silver, what

" What [5] voice of the Lord have ye heard inviting us? Who invited? Whom did He invite? The Lord hath invited His slaves, and hath prepared for them Himself as their Food. Who would dare to eat his Lord? And yet He says, 'He that eateth Me, liveth by Me.' When Christ is eaten, Life is eaten. Nor is He slain that He may be eaten, but He quickeneth the dead. When He is eaten, He refresheth, and faileth not. Let us not then dread, Brethren, to eat that Bread, for fear that we should finish It, and afterwards should not find what to eat. Let Christ be eaten; when eaten, He lives; because when slain He rose again. And when we eat, we do not make it into parts. And indeed it so happens in the Sacrament, and the faithful know how they eat the Flesh of Christ. Each one receives his part, whence too the grace itself is called ' particles.' In parts He is eaten, and He the Whole remaineth entire. By parts He is eaten in the Sacrament, and He the Whole remaineth entire in Heaven, He the Whole remaineth entire in thy heart. For

is wine, cannot be thy bread : but thy God shall be all this to thee ; thou shalt eat Him, that thou hunger not ; thou shalt drink Him, that thou thirst not ; thine eyes shall be enlightened, that thou be not blind ; thou shalt be supported by Him, that thou fail not. Whole and Entire He shall possess thee whole and entire ; there thou shalt find no narrowness with Him with Whom thou shalt possess all ; for thou and He shall be one, which one whole He too shall have who possesseth you. These are what remain for the peacemaker." (T. i. p. 19.)

[5] Mai, Biblioth. Nov. Patr. T. i. Serm. 129, p. 303.

He was Whole with the Father, when He entered the Virgin. He filled her, and departed not from the Father. He came in the Flesh, that men might eat Him; and He remained entire with the Father, that He might feed Angels. For what ye may know, Brethren, both ye who know, and ye who know not, ought to know. When Christ was made Man, man did eat Angels' Food. Whence? How? In what way? By what merits? By right of what dignity would man eat Angels' Bread, unless the Creator of Angels had become Man? Let us eat then fearlessly. That which we eat is not consumed. And let us eat, lest we be consumed. What is to eat Christ? It is not only to receive His Body in the Sacrament. For many unworthy receive, of whom saith the Apostle, ' Whoso eateth the Bread and drinketh the Cup of the Lord unworthily, eateth and drinketh judgment to himself.'

"But how is Christ to be eaten? How, He Himself says: 'He that eateth My Flesh, and drinketh My Blood, abideth in Me, and I in him.' If he abideth in Me, and I in him, then he eateth, then he drinketh. But he that abideth not in Me, nor I in him, although he receive the Sacrament, he getteth great torment. What then ' he that abideth in Me ' means, Himself says in another place : ' He that keepeth My commandments, abideth in Me, and I in him.' See then, Brethren, that if ye who are faithful be separated from the Body of the Lord, it is to be feared that ye will die of hunger. For Himself hath said, 'He that eateth not My Flesh, and drinketh not My Blood, shall have no life in him.' If then ye be separated, so as not to eat the Body and Blood of the Lord, it is to be feared that ye will die. But if ye receive unworthily, and drink unworthily, it is to be feared that ye eat and drink judgment. Great is our strait. Live ye well, and the strait is widened. Do not promise life to yourselves, while living ill. When man promises what God doth not promise, he deceives himself. Thou art a bad witness to thyself. Thou promisest to thyself what Truth denies. Truth says, if ye live ill, ye shall die for ever; and dost thou say to thyself, I both live ill, and shall live for ever with Christ? How can it be, that the Truth should lie, and thou shouldest speak the truth? Every man is a liar. So then ye cannot live well, except He shall help you, except He shall give it you. Hence pray and eat. Pray, and ye shall be delivered from these straits. For He shall fill you, both in well doing and in well living. Let your conscience be looked into; your mouth shall be filled with the praise of God and with joy. And ye, freed from great straits, shall say to Him, 'Thou hast freed my goings under me, and my footsteps did not slide.'"

61. S. CHRYSOSTOM.

Born about A.D. 347: studied rhetoric under Libanius, A.D. 367; instructed in the faith for three years by Meletius, Bishop of Antioch; baptized; entered on Monastic life for four years, and studied under Diodorus (afterwards Bishop of Tarsus); lived as a solitary for two years; ordained Deacon about A.D. 380-1; Priest, A.D. 386; Bishop of Constantinople, A.D. 398; expelled, for the second time, A.D. 404; died, through severity of treatment, Sept. 14, A.D. 406, as had been foreshown him. (Pallad. Dial. c. xi. p. 40.)

S. Chrysostom has been quoted already, as stating that the nature of bread remains (pp. 83-5); as speaking of the Eucharistic elements as "symbols" (pp. 108-9); as regarding the coal of fire in Isaiah's vision, where there was both outward and inward substance, a type of the Holy Eucharist (pp. 124-6); as using the word in of the inward substance in the outward (pp. 137. 277); as interpreting our Lord's words, "this fruit of the vine," of the actual element of wine, which our Lord should, in proof of His Resurrection in the same Flesh, drink with His disciples (p. 138); as laying down as to both Sacraments that the senses could only report what is outward (pp. 276-7). The two words μετασκευάζω, μεταρρυθμίζω, each of which he uses in one place only, have been considered pp. 211— 225. I will add another of those appeals not to look to nature, but to the invisible grace. The very words imply that the visible nature had a real being, that as far as it was visible, it was what it seemed to be, though it contained what was above nature.

"When [c] he standeth by this holy Table, when he is about to offer that dread Sacrifice (the initiated

---

[c] De S. Pentec. Hom. i. § 4, ii. 463.

know what I mean), he does not touch the Elements
until he has first invoked on you the grace from the
Lord, and ye have responded to him, 'And with
thy Spirit,' reminding yourselves by this very
answer that he that is present doth nothing, nor are
the gifts that lie before us any doings of human
nature; but the grace of the Spirit being present,
and lighting upon all, accomplisheth that mystic Sacrifice.   For although it be man who is present, yet
it is God Who worketh through him.   Do not then
attend to the nature of what is seen, but consider the
invisible grace.   Nought is human of what is done
on this holy Altar."

The following passages, containing the doctrine of
the Real Presence, are given in the order in which
the works stand in the Benedictine edition:

" When ' thou seest the Lord sacrificed and lying,
and the Priest standing and praying over the Sacrifice, and all [the people] reddened with that Precious
Blood, thinkest thou that thou art yet among men and
standest upon the earth? or dost thou not straightway remove to Heaven, and casting forth from thy
soul every carnal thought, with bared soul and pure
mind, survey the things in Heaven?   O marvel!
O love of God for man!   He Who sitteth aloft with
the Father is at that hour held in the hands of all,
and giveth Himself to those who will, to enfold and
embrace.   But this they all do with the eye of faith."

' De Sacerdot. iii. 4, i. 382.

N n

"The [8] Priest standeth, not bringing down fire [as Elijah] but the Holy Spirit, and prayeth much, not that any torch sent down from above should consume what lieth there, but that the grace falling upon the Sacrifice, should, through it, kindle the souls of all, and make them brighter than silver purified in the fire. This most fearful Mystery then, who that is not exceeding mad or beside himself, can despise? Or art thou ignorant that never could soul of man endure that fire of the Sacrifice? but all would utterly perish, save for the great help of the grace of God. For [9] if one considers how great a thing it is, that a man, and one still clothed in flesh and blood, should be able to come near to that Blessed and Immortal Nature; then he will see well, how great honour the grace of the Spirit hath vouchsafed to Priests."

"But [1] when he [the Priest] calleth even the Holy Spirit, and completeth that most awful Sacrifice, and continually toucheth the common Lord of all, where shall we rank him? what purity and carefulness shall we demand of him? For consider what hands they should be, which minister such things, what a tongue which poureth forth those words [of consecration]? The soul which receiveth such a Spirit, what should be so pure and holy? Then, angels too do stand by the Priest, and the whole order of heavenly powers doth cry; and the place

<hr>

[8] Ib. p. 383.   [9] § 5.   [1] Ib. vi. 4, p. 424.

about the Altar is filled, in honour of That Which lieth thereon.   And this may be readily believed, even from the nature of the things there performed. But also I once heard one relate that a certain wonderful old man, accustomed to see visions, said that such a vision was once vouchsafed him, and that at that time [*i.e.* of the consecration] he suddenly saw, as man might see, a multitude of Angels, clothed in white robes, and encircling the Altar, and bowing down, as one might see soldiers standing in the presence of the king.   And I believe it.   And another, not having heard from any other, but having himself been accounted worthy to see and hear, that those who are about to depart hence, if they receive the Mysteries in a pure conscience, when they are about to give up the ghost, Angels, on account of That they have received, escort and carry them hence.   And dost thou not even now shudder, bringing to so holy a Mystery, such a soul, and presenting to that dignity of the priesthood, one clothed in filthy garments, whom Christ hath thrust out even from the common company of communicants?   For as a light which sheds its rays on the world, ought a priest's soul to shine."

"I [1] pray and beseech you all, to be present with all diligence and zeal, each emptying his own house; that we may see our Lord lying in the manger wrapped in swaddling clothes; that awful and wond-

[1] De B. Philogon. § 3, i. 497, 498.

rous sight! For what excuse have we, what pardon, when He Himself comes down from heaven for us, but we do not even come out of our house to Him? when the Magi, barbarians and foreigners, haste from Persia to see Him lying in the manger; but thou, O Christian, dost not even bear a little walk to enjoy this blessed sight? For if we come there with faith, we shall certainly see Him lying in a manger. For this Table occupies the place of the manger. For here too will the Lord's Body lie: not wrapped in swaddling clothes, as then, but encircled all round by the Holy Ghost. The initiated know what is meant. The Magi then only worshipped; but if thou approachest with a pure conscience, we will grant thee both to receive It, and to depart home. Do thou then approach too, bringing gifts, not such as they, but much holier. They brought gold; bring thou sobriety and virtue: they brought frankincense, bring thou pure prayers, spiritual incense: they brought myrrh, do thou bring lowliness of mind, and a humbled heart and alms. If thou approach with these gifts, with much fearlessness shalt thou enjoy this holy Table. And for this reason do I now use these words: because I know that in that day many will come and fall upon this spiritual Sacrifice. In order then that we do not do this to our hurt, nor to the condemnation of our soul, but to our salvation, I now testify beforehand and exhort, that ye, purifying yourselves in every way, would so approach the holy Mysteries."

" The ' Magi went forth from Persia: do thou go forth from cares of this life, and journey to Jesus. The interval is not long, if we will. For it is not necessary to cross the sea, nor to traverse mountain-tops: but sitting at home, displaying reverence and much compunction, thou canst see Him, thou canst destroy the whole partition-wall, remove the hindrance, shorten the length of the journey. For ' I am a God near at hand,' saith He, 'and not a God afar off:' and 'the Lord is nigh unto all that call on Him faithfully.' But now many of the faithful have reached such a height of folly and contempt, that they, though full of ten thousand ills, and absolutely taking no care at all of themselves, approach this Table on festivals at haphazard, not knowing that the time for Communion is not feast and solemn assembly, but a pure conscience and a life freed from sin. And as he who is conscious of no evil in himself, ought to approach daily, so for him who is involved in sin, and unrepentant, it is not safe to approach even on a festival. For not the coming once a year doth free us from our sins, if we approach unworthily, but this very thing doth the more condemn us: that, whereas we approach but once, not even then do we approach in purity. Wherefore I exhort you all, not simply for the necessity of the feast to receive the Divine Mysteries; but if ye mind to partake of this holy Offering, to purify your-

---

' pp. 499, 500.

selves thoroughly many days beforehand by penitence, and prayer, and alms, and spiritual exercises; and not to return 'as a dog to his vomit.'"

"Know[4] ye not that this Table is full of spiritual fire: and as fountains gush forth with the nature of water, so this too hath a certain ineffable fire. Approach not then with stubble, or wood, or hay, lest thou increase the conflagration, and consume the soul which partaketh; but with precious stones, gold, silver, that thou mayest make the substance purer, that thou mayest depart, having received great gain." . . . . "Thou art about to receive the King within (ὑποδέχεσθαι) by communion. When the King entereth the soul, there ought to be a great calm, great quietness, a deep peace of thoughts."

"Elias[5] left a mantle to his disciple, but the Son of God ascending left to us His own Flesh! Elias indeed, casting off his mantle, went up, but Christ left it behind for our sakes, and yet ascended retaining it! Let us not then be cast down, let us not lament, nor fear the difficulty of the times; for He Who did not refuse to pour out His Blood for all, and again gives us to partake of His Flesh and of His Blood, what will He refuse to do for our safety?"

"What[6] dost thou, O man? At the sacred Table

---

[4] Ib. p. 500.

[5] Ad Pop. Ant. Hom. 2, fin., on the Statues, p. 52, Oxf. Tr.

[6] Ib. xv. 14, p. 259.

thou **exactest** an oath, and where Christ lies slain, there thou slayest thine own brother."

"Think [7] with thyself, O man, what Sacrifice thou art about to touch, what Table to approach! Lay to heart that, being earth and ashes, thou partakest of the Body and Blood of Christ. If a King call you to a feast, you sit down with fear, and partake of the food which lies before you with modesty and quiet; but when God invites thee to His own Table, and setteth before thee His Own Son, when the Angelic powers stand by with fear and trembling, and the Cherubim vail their faces, and the Seraphim cry trembling, 'Holy, Holy, Holy Lord,' tell me, dost thou come brawling and disturbing to the Spiritual Feast? Let us draw near, as approaching to the King of Heaven."

"That [8] ark [of Noah] when the tempest was assuaged, remained on earth; but this Ark [our Lord's Body], the wrath being assuaged, was taken up into heaven; and now that spotless and undefiled Body is at the Right Hand of the Father. But since I have mentioned the Lord's Body, I must needs say something to you thereupon. I know that many among you, on account of the wont of the feast, crowd to this sacred Table. For as I have often said before, when one would communicate, one should

[7] In Diem Nat. J. C. § 7, T. ii. p. 365.
[8] De Bapt. Christi, fin. ii. pp. 373—375.

not watch for feasts, but cleanse the conscience and so touch that holy Sacrifice. For he who is guilty and unclean would not be meet, even in a feast, to partake of that holy and awful Flesh. But he who is pure, and who has, through careful repentance, wiped away his offences, would, at the Feast alike and at all times, be meet to partake of the Divine Mysteries, and to enjoy the gifts of God. But since some, I know not how, neglect this, and many, laden with countless ills, when they are aware of the approach of the Feast, as if driven by the day, touch the sacred Mysteries, which, so disposed, they ought not even to see; those who are manifest to us, we will altogether repel; but those whom we know not, we will leave to God, Who knoweth the secrets of each man's conscience. What, however, is an open sin of all, we will correct this day. What then is this sin? That men approach, not with awe, but kicking, beating, full of wrath, crying out, abusing, shoving their neighbours, full of disturbance. This I have often said, and will not cease to say. See ye not at the Olympian games, when the president of the games walketh through the market-place, having the crown on his head, clad in the robe, with the rod in his hand, what order there is, when the herald proclaimeth, that there is to be peace and decorum? How then is it not monstrous, that when the devil leads the procession, there should be so great quietness; but when Christ calleth to Himself, there should be much confusion? In the market-place, stillness; in the Church, outcry! in open sea, a calm, and in the harbour, breakers! Tell me, men, why this tumult? why this press? doth urgency of business quite summon thee? knowest thou then indeed, that thou hast business at that hour? rememberest thou indeed, that thou art upon earth? thinkest thou, that thou art among men? How were it not a heart of stone to think at that time that thou standest on the earth, and not to join the choirs of angels with whom thou hast sent up that mystical Hymn; with whom thou hast lifted up aloft that song of victory to God? Wherefore also Christ called us eagles, saying, ' Where the Body is, thither shall the eagles be gathered together,' that we might mount up to Heaven, that borne lightly by the wings of the Spirit, we might fly on high. But we, like the serpents, creep on the ground and eat the dust. What dost thou, O man, when Christ is present, when the Angels stand by, when this awful Table is before you, when your brethren are yet being made partakers of the mysteries, dost thou leave them and spring away? . . . He Himself giveth thee to partake of His Flesh, but thou dost not requite Him even with words. When thou enjoyest bodily nourishment, after the table thou turnest to prayer; but when thou partakest of the Spiritual Food surpassing all creation visible or invisible, thou being a man, and of a mean nature, thou dost not wait to give thanks either in word or deed."

"That[9] feast [the Passover] was a continual memorial of their deliverance. Nay, this was not their only gain, that it reminded them of former benefits; another and greater gain was it, that it prefigured what was to come. For that lamb was a figure of another spiritual Lamb; and that sheep, of a Sheep. The one was a shadow, the other, Truth. But when the Sun of righteousness dawned, the shadow ceased. For when the sun arises, the shadow vanishes. Wherefore on that Table also there was either Passover, both that in the figure, and That in the truth. For as painters on the same tablet both trace the outlines, and mark the shadows, and then place thereon the truth of the colours, so also did Christ. For on the same Table, He both gave the outline of the figurative Passover, and added the true. 'Where willest Thou, that we should make ready for Thee to eat the Passover?' This was the Jewish Passover. But when the sun is come, away with the lantern; when the Truth has come, let the shadow cease."

"Aforetime[1] was the Jewish Passover, but now it hath been abolished, and there hath come in its stead the Spiritual Passover which Christ then delivered. For when they were eating and drinking He took bread, brake it and said, 'This is my Body which is broken for you for the remission of sins.' The initiated know what I mean: and again, the

---

[9] De Prodit. Jud. § 4, ii. 382.
[1] Ib. § 5, p. 383.

Cup, saying, 'This is My Blood which is shed for many for the remission of sins.' And Judas was present when Christ said this. This is the Body which thou didst sell, O Judas, for thirty pieces of silver; this is the Blood for which a little before thou madest that shameless compact with the reckless Pharisees. O the love of Christ for man! O the phrenzy, the madness of Judas! for Judas sold Him for thirty pieces of silver; but Christ even after this refused not to give the very Blood which was sold, for the remission of sins, to him who sold it, if he willed."

"But[2] it is now time to approach the awful Table; let us all then approach with a becoming soberness and carefulness; let there be no Judas any more, no bad man, none harbouring poison, none having one thing in his mouth, another in his mind. Christ is present now too. The same Who adorned that Table, adorneth this too now. For it is not man who maketh what lieth there to become the Body and Blood of Christ, but Christ Himself Who was crucified for us. The priest standeth, filling up a figure, speaking those words; the power and the grace are of God. 'This is My Body,' He saith. This word re-ordereth what lieth there, and as that Voice, 'increase and multiply and replenish the earth,' was spoken once, but throughout all time in

[2] Ib. § 6, p. 384.

effect giveth power to our race to the procreation of children, so also that Voice once spoken doth on every Table in the Churches from that time even till now and unto His Coming, complete the Sacrifice."

"Since [3] then we too shall this evening [4] see Him Who was nailed on the Cross, as it were a Lamb slain and sacrificed, let us approach with trembling, I beseech you, and much reverence and godly fear. Know ye not how the Angels stood at the tomb which had not the Body, the empty tomb? But yet since it had once received the Body of the Lord, they show much honour even to the place. The Angels, who surpass our nature, stood at the tomb with so great reverence and godly fear; and *we*, who are about to stand, not before an empty tomb, but at the very Table which containeth the Lamb, do we approach with tumult and distraction? and how shall we then be pardoned? I do not say these things at hazard; but seeing many this evening tumultuous, shouting, justling one another, jumping, abusing one another, and bringing on themselves punishment rather than salvation; for this cause I admonish you. Man! what dost thou? When the Priest stands before the Table, stretching forth his hands to Heaven, calling the Holy Ghost to

[3] De Coem. et Cruce, T. ii. p. 401.
[4] Easter Eve.

be present, and touch the offerings, great is the stillness, great the silence. When the Spirit gives the grace, when He comes down, when He touches the offerings, when thou seest the Lamb sacrificed and made ready, then dost thou introduce tumult, confusion, strife, railing? And how canst thou enjoy this Sacrifice, coming to this table with so great confusion? Is it not enough for us, that we approach with our sins? Cannot we even bear that the very time of our approach should be without transgression? For when we wrangle, when we are disorderly, when we devour one another, how shall we be without sin? Why in a hurry? Tell me, why press forward, when, as it is, thou beholdest the Lamb slain? For if, the whole night through, thou couldest look on this Sacrifice, tell me, shouldest thou have too much of it? The whole day thou hast persevered; thou hast gone through the greater part of the night; and dost thou give up and lose so great labour in a brief moment of time? Consider What it is that lieth before thee, and what caused it. He was slain for thy sake, and thou neglectest to see Him sacrificed. 'Where the Body is,' saith He, 'there the eagles.' But we approach not as eagles, but as dogs. So great is our shamelessness. Consider What it is that is shed. It is Blood, Blood Which hath washed away the handwriting of sins; Blood, Which hath purified thy soul, Which hath washed away thy stain, Which hath triumphed over principalities and powers."

"We [5] have lately read to you Paul's law concerning the participation in the mysteries, laid down for all the initiated. The law was this, (for there is no reason that I should not now read it to you again,) ' let each examine himself, so let him eat of that Bread and drink of that Cup.' They who are initiated in the mysteries know what we say, and what that Bread is, what that Cup. For he saith, ' Whoso eateth and drinketh unworthily of the Lord, he shall be guilty of the Body and Blood of the Lord.' This law we have rehearsed to you ; and we have explained the meaning of the words. I have said what it means, ' He shall be guilty of the Body and Blood of the Lord.' It is, that he shall undergo the same punishment as they shall endure who crucified Christ. For he says, ' as they, the murderers, were guilty of the Blood, so those also who partake unworthily of the mysteries.' For this is, ' He shall be guilty of the Body and Blood of the Lord.' What I said seemed to be excessive, and the threat unendurable. I add a ground from an instance, which has much analogy. For, as I said, if any tear the Royal Purple, or defile it with mire, he in like way insults the King who is clad with it; so also here. They who slew the Lord's Body, and they who received with an unclean mind, equally insult the royal raiment. The Jews rent it by the Cross, but he who receiveth It in an impure soul defileth It.

[5] Non esse ad Grat. concionand. § 1, p. 659.

So that though the transgression is different, the insult is the same."

"As[6] thou hast a marvellous draught, the Saviour's Blood, so they too had a marvellous nature of drink, not finding fountains or running streams, but receiving from the hard and dry rock a large abundance of waters. Wherefore also he called it 'spiritual,' not as though it were so by nature, but because it became such by the mode of supply. For it was not given to them after the course of nature, but according to the working of God Who led them. And this was what he meant, explaining himself. For having said, 'And they all drank the same spiritual drink, whereas it was water which was drunk, wishing to show that he therefore called it spiritual, not on account of the nature of the water, but of the mode of the supply, he added, 'For they drank of that spiritual rock which followed them, and that rock was Christ.' Not, he would say, the nature of the stone, but the power of God operating, sent forth those streams."

"As in the Church the rich partaketh not of one Body, and the poor of another, nor the one, of one Blood, the other, of another; so then also the rich did not receive one manna, and the poor another, nor did the one partake of one fountain, the other of a poorer. But as now the same Table, the same Cup, the same Food is set before all who come

---

[6] In ill. nolo vos ignorare. §§ 4, 5, T. iii. p. 236.

in hither, so also the same manna, the same fountain was placed before all."

" Having [7] spoken much concerning those who communicate of the Mysteries unworthily, and having vehemently upbraided and rebuked them, and having shown that they who receive the Body and Blood of Christ lightly and carelessly, shall undergo the same punishment as those who slew Him, he returneth to his former subject."

" I [8] will tell thee another ground. Let those listen who are admitted to the Mysteries. He Himself, when He would nourish thee, spareth not even His Own Flesh; when He would give thee to drink, spareth not, nor grudgeth His Blood; and wilt thou give neither bread nor cup, and how wilt thou obtain pardon, who receivest things so great and precious, and sparest things so cheap?"

" Why [9] is He [Christ] called a Robe? Because I am clad with Him in Baptism. Why is He called a Table? Because I eat Him, when I partake of the Mysteries. Why is He called a house? Because I dwell in Him. Why an inhabitant? Because we become His temple, &c."

" The [1] soldiers entering in, where the Holy Things were laid up, saw all which was there (some of them being, as we know, non-communicants), and the

---

[7] In ill. oportet hæreses esse, § 5, T. iii. 247.

[8] In ill. Vidua eligatur, fin. iii. 327.

[9] Hom. de capt. Eutrop. § 8, iii. 393.

[1] Ep. 1, ad Innocent. § 3, iii. 519.

most holy Blood of Christ (as would happen in such a tumult), was poured out on the garments of the aforesaid soldiers."

In a later part of the Epistle to Cæsarius, already quoted, S. Chrysostom introduces an argument of the Apollinarians.

"They [2] are wont to plead this also : ' Do we not receive the Body and Blood of God faithfully and devoutly ?' ' Yea,' we must say, ' not that the Divine Nature had Body and Blood before the Incarnation, but because He appropriated the things of the Flesh to Himself, it is so said.' Oh, monstrousness ! Oh, the ungodly thought ! The honour of the Divinity is in danger from them. And again they endure not, to confess the Lord's Body to be a true Body. For they put their meanings on words, and so imagine that This was converted into Godhead, thence making one Nature, and yet unable to say Whose this very nature is ! "

" Consider [3], O man, how wine became useful, and stand in awe. For through this the substance of the good things of our salvation is celebrated."

"But [4] our [song of victory] is much greater; not the Egyptians but the demons, being overwhelmed ; not Pharaoh, but the Devil, being conquered ; not visible armour being taken, but wickedness destroyed ; not on the Red Sea, but in the laver of regeneration ;

---

[2] P. 745.   [3] Hom. 29, in Gen. n. 3.
[4] In Ps. xlvi. § 2, v. 189.

not on going forth to the land of promise, but jour-
neying to Heaven; not eating manna, but fed with
the Body of the Lord; not drinking water from the
rock, but Blood from His Side. Wherefore, he
saith, 'Clap your hands;' because freed from stocks
and stones, ye have mounted above the heavens and
the heaven of heavens, and have stood before the
royal throne itself."

"He [5] has made the flesh well-reined unto thee;
He has given to thee as arms, the breastplate of
righteousness, the girdle of truth, the helmet of salvation, the shield of faith, the sword of the Spirit.
He hath given thee the earnest; He nourisheth thee
with His Body; He gives thee to drink of His Blood;
He hath placed the Cross as a spear in thy hands, a
spear never bent; He hath bound thine enemy; He
hath cast him to the ground; so that thy defeat would
be without excuse, and if overthrown, thou wert un-
pardonable, for thou hast countless means of victory."

"Think [6] how much holiness thou oughtest to
have, who hast received far greater symbols than
those which the Holy of Holies then received. For
thou hast not Cherubim, but thou hast the Lord
Himself of the Cherubim indwelling; not pot and
manna and tables of stone and the rod of Aaron, but
the Body and Blood of the Lord; and Spirit instead
of the letter, and grace surpassing human thought,

---

[5] In Ps. cxxiii. § 2, v. 347.
[6] In Ps. cxxxiii. v. 382.

and gift unutterable. For the higher the symbols which have been vouchsafed to thee, and the more awful the mysteries, the greater holiness is required of thee, and the greater the punishment, if thou transgress what is enjoined."

"Think[7] that this is the member wherewith we converse with God, through which we send up our praise; this is the member through which we receive the awful Sacrifice, (the faithful know what I mean;) wherefore also it ought to be pure from all accusing and reviling and shameful talking and calumny."

"Thou[8] hast become a son, and enjoyest the spiritual Table, fed with the Flesh and the Blood Which regenerated thee."

"The[9] spiritual things again are common, even the Holy Table itself; the Lord's Body, the Precious Blood, the Promise of the Kingdom, the Laver of Regeneration, the cleansing of sins, Righteousness, Sanctification, Redemption, the unspeakable good things, 'which eye hath not seen, nor ear heard, neither hath entered into the heart of man.' How is it not monstrous, that they who communicate with one another in such things, and in nature, and in grace, and promises, and laws, that these should be so covetous of money, and not maintain an uniform equity?"

A passage from S. Chrysostom's comment on

[7] In Ps. cxlviii. § 4, v. 433.
[8] In Ps. cxliv. init. v. 467.
[9] In Ps. xlviii. p. 524.

Isaiah's vision has been already given [1]. There
follows :

" Wherefore [2] I too now cry with a loud voice,
and protest, and entreat, and implore, that you
would not approach this Holy Table with an evil
conscience ; for this would not be approach or
Communion, though we were countless times to
touch that Holy Body, but condemnation and chastisement, and increase of punishment. Let no
sinner then approach, nay, rather I say not, no sinner,
since then I should first exclude myself from the
Holy Table, but let no one approach who persevereth
in sin."

" Shall [3] we then provoke Him ? How were not
this more bitter than Hell itself, and the deathless
worm, and the unextinguishable fire ? When then
thou art about to approach to the Holy Table, think
that there the King of all is present ; for He is
present indeed, observing the mind of all, and seeth
who approacheth with befitting holiness, and who,
with an evil conscience, with unclean and foul
thoughts and wicked deeds."

" Then [4] God will say to thee, ' When thou sawest,
not silver nor golden vessel stolen from My house,
but soberness despoiled, and him who had received
the Precious Body, and had partaken of so great a

---

[1] Above, pp. 125, 126.
[2] In ill. Vidi Dom. Hom. 5, § 3, vi. 142.
[3] Ib. § 4, p. 143.
[4] Contra ludos and theatra, § 4, p. 277.

Sacrifice, departing to the place of the Devil, and doing such lawless deeds, how wert thou silent? How didst thou endure it? How didst thou not tell the Priest, that thou mightest not have to give an awful account?"

"Hasten[5] to Bethlehem, where is the house of the Spiritual Bread. For though thou be a shepherd, and come hither, thou wilt behold the young Child in an inn: though thou be a king, and approach not here, thy purple robe will profit thee nothing: though thou be one of the wise men, this will be no hindrance to thee. Only let thy coming be to honour and adore, not to spurn the Son of God; only do this with trembling and joy: for it is possible for both of these to concur in one."

"But take heed that thou be not like Herod, and say, 'that I may come and worship Him,' and when thou art come, be minded to slay Him. For him do they resemble, who partake of the Mysteries unworthily; it being said, that such an one 'shall be guilty of the Body and Blood of the Lord.' . . . Many of our women are so delicate that they go not over so much as one crossing of the streets to behold Him on the Spiritual Manger, unless they can have mules to draw them."

"Whereas the Barbarians accomplished so great a journey for His sake, before seeing Him; thou, not even after thou hast seen Him, dost emulate them,

---

[5] In S. Matt. Hom. vii. § 6, pp. 101, 102, Oxf. Tr.

but forsakest Him after seeing Him, and runnest to see the stage-player. And seeing Christ lying in the manger, thou leavest Him, that thou mayest see women on the stage."

" A [6] spiritual well of fire gushes up out of this Table. And thou leavest this, and runnest down to the theatre, to see women swimming, and nature put to open dishonour, leaving Christ sitting by the well! Yes: for now, as of old, He sits down by the well, not discoursing to a Samaritan woman, but to a whole city. Or perchance now too with a Samaritan woman only. For neither now is any one with Him; but some with their bodies only, and some not even with these. But nevertheless, He retires not, but remains, and asks of us to drink, not water, but holiness. For 'His Holy Things He gives unto the Holy.' For it is not water that He gives us from this fountain, but living Blood; and it is indeed a symbol of death, but it is become the cause of life. But thou, leaving the fountain, the awful Cup, goest thy way unto the fountain of the devil."

" For [7] this cause, even the awful Mysteries, so full of that great salvation, which are celebrated at every Communion, are called a Sacrifice of Thanksgiving, because they are the commemoration of many benefits, and they signify the very sum of God's care for us, and by all means they work upon us to be thankful. For if His being born of a Virgin was a

[6] § 7, p. 103.   [7] Hom. xxv. § 4, p. 381.

great miracle, and the Evangelist said in amaze, 'Now all this was done;' His being also slain— what place shall we find for that? tell me.   I mean, if to be born is called 'all this;' to be crucified, and to pour forth His Blood, and to give Himself to us for a spiritual Feast and Banquet,—what can that be called?   Let us therefore give Him thanks continually, and let this precede both our words and our works."

" Dost[8] thou not call to mind the water that dashed over thy countenance, the Sacrifice that adorns thy lips, the Blood that hath reddened thy tongue?"

" What[9] excuse shall we have, who are continually partaking of the Lord's Body?"

" Let[1] us recollect ourselves, as many of us as partake unworthily of the Mysteries; such men being guilty of the Body and Blood of Christ.   Wherefore, when thou art talking of the murderer, take account of thyself also. For he indeed hath murdered a man, but thou art under the guilt of slaying the Lord; and he, not having partaken of Mysteries, but we, while enjoying the benefit of the sacred Table."

" Seest[2] thou not that for the Priest alone is it lawful to give the Cup of His Blood?"

" Let[3] us also then touch the hem of His garment, or rather, if we be willing, we have Him

[8] Hom. xxx. § 6, p. 446.   [9] Hom. xxxii. § 10, p. 476.
[1] Hom. xxxvi. § 4, p. 530.   [2] Hom. xlv. § 3, p. 626.
[3] Id. Hom. l. § 3, pp. 683, 684.

entire. For indeed His Body is set before us now; not His garment only, but even His Body; not for us to touch It only, but also to eat, and be filled. Let us now then draw near with faith, every one that hath an infirmity. For if they that touched the hem of His garment drew from Him so much virtue, how much more they that possess Him entire? Now to draw near with faith is not only to receive the Offering, but also with a pure heart to touch It; to be so minded, as approaching Christ Himself. For what, if thou hear no voice? Yet thou seest Him laid out; or rather thou dost also hear His Voice, while He is speaking by the Evangelists. Believe, therefore, that even now it is that Supper, at which He Himself sat down. For *This* is in no respect different from *That*. For neither doth man make This and Himself the Other; but both This and That is His own work. When therefore thou seest the Priest delivering It unto thee, account not that it is the Priest that doeth so, but that it is Christ's Hand that is stretched out. . . . For He that hath given the greater, *i. e.* hath set Himself before thee, much more will He not think scorn to distribute unto thee of His Body. Let us hear, therefore, both priests and subjects, what we have had vouchsafed to us; let us hear and tremble. Of His Own Flesh He hath granted us our fill; He hath set before us Himself sacrificed. What excuse shall we have then, if, when feeding on such Food, we commit such sins? when eating a Lamb, we become wolves?

when feeding on a Sheep, we spoil by violence like the lions? . . . For if He spared not Himself for us, what must we deserve, sparing our wealth, and lavish of a soul, in behalf of which He spared not Himself? . . . Be not therefore ashamed of the Cross: for these are our venerable things, these our Mysteries; with this Gift do we adorn ourselves, with this we are beautified.

"That ⁴ Table at that time was not of silver, nor that Cup of gold, out of which Christ gave His disciples His own Blood; but precious was every thing there, and awful, for that they were full of the Spirit! Wouldest thou do honour to Christ's Body? neglect Him not when naked; do not, while here thou honourest Him with silken garments, neglect Him perishing without of cold and nakedness. For He that said, 'This is My Body,' and by His word confirmed the fact, This Same said, 'Ye saw Me an hungered, and fed Me not;' and, 'Inasmuch as ye did it not to one of the least of these, ye did it not to Me.'"

"After ⁵ this, Satan entered into him [Judas], not as despising the Lord's Body, but thenceforth laughing to scorn the traitor's shamelessness. . . . Like as the Old Testament had sheep and bullocks, so this has the Lord's Blood. . . . That was shed for the preservation of the first-born, this for the re-

---

⁴ Ib. § 4, p. 685.
⁵ Hom. lxxxii. § 1, pp. 1082—1084.

mission of the sins of the whole world. For, 'This,' saith He, 'is My Blood, Which is shed for the remission of sins' . . . And He Himself drank of It. For lest on hearing this, they should say, 'What then? do we drink Blood and eat Flesh?' and then be perplexed, (for when He began to discourse concerning these things, even at the very sayings many were offended,) therefore lest they should be troubled then likewise, He first did this Himself, leading them on to the calm participation of the Mysteries. Therefore He Himself drank His own Blood."

"Let [6] us then in every thing believe God, and gainsay Him in nothing, though what is said seems to be contrary to our thoughts and senses, but let His Word be of higher authority than both reasonings and sight. Thus let us do in the Mysteries also, not looking at the things set before us, but keeping in mind His sayings. For His Word cannot deceive, but our senses are easily beguiled. That hath never failed, but this in most things goeth wrong. Since then the Word saith, 'This is My Body,' let us both be persuaded and believe, and look at it with the eyes of the mind. For Christ hath given us nothing sensible, but, though *in* things sensible, yet all to be perceived by the mind . . . How many now say, I would wish to see His Form, the mark, His clothes, His shoes. Lo! Him thou

----

[6] Hom. lxxxii. § 4, p. 1090.

[7] ἐν αἰσθητοῖς μὲν πράγμασι, πάντα δὲ νοητά.

seest, Him thou touchest, Him thou eatest.   And
thou indeed desirest to see His clothes, but He
giveth Himself to thee not to see only, but also to
touch and eat, and receive within thee. . . . Consider* how indignant thou art against the traitor,
against them that crucified Him.   Look therefore,
lest thou also thyself become guilty of the Body and
Blood of Christ.   They slaughtered the All-Holy
Body, but thou, after such great benefits, receivest It
in a filthy soul.   For neither was it enough for Him
to be made Man, to be smitten and slaughtered, but
He also commingleth Himself with us, and not by
faith only, but also in very deed maketh us His
Body.   What then ought not he to exceed in purity,
that hath the benefit of this sacrifice?   Purer than
what sunbeam should not that hand be, which is to
sever this Flesh, the mouth that is filled with spiritual fire, the tongue that is reddened by that most
awful Blood?   Consider with what sort of honour
thou wast honoured, of what sort of Table thou art
partaking!   That which when Angels behold, they
tremble, and dare not so much as look up at It without awe, on account of the Brightness that cometh
thence; with This we are fed, with This we are commingled, and we are made one body and one flesh
with Christ.   ' Who shall declare the mighty works
of the Lord, and cause all His praises to be heard?'
What shepherd feeds his sheep with his own limbs?

* § 5, p. 1091.

And why do I say, shepherd? There are often mothers that, after the travail of birth, send out their children to other women as nurses; but He endureth not to do this, but Himself feeds us with His own Blood, and by all means entwines us with Himself . . . With each one of the faithful doth He mingle Himself in the Mysteries, and whom He begat He nourishes by Himself, and putteth not out to another; by this also persuading thee again, that He had taken thy flesh. . . . The works set before us are not of man's power. He that then did these things at that Supper, this Same now also works them. We occupy the place of servants. He Who sanctifieth and changeth them is the Same. Let then no Judas be present, no covetous man. If any one be not a disciple, let him withdraw. The Table receives not such. For 'I keep the passover,' He saith, 'with My disciples.' This Table is the same as That, and hath nothing less. For it is not so that Christ wrought that, and man this, but He doth this too. This is that upper chamber, where they were then."

"Let[9] no one communicate who is not of the disciples. Let no Judas receive, lest he suffer the fate of Judas. This multitude also is Christ's body. Take heed, therefore, thou that ministerest at the Mysteries, lest thou provoke the Lord, not purging this body. Give not a sword instead of meat."

"But if thou darest not do it thyself, bring him to

[9] § 6, p. 1094.

me; I will not allow any to dare to do these things. I would give up my life rather than impart of the Lord's Blood to the unworthy; and will shed my own blood rather than impart of such awful Blood contrary to what is meet."

" By [1] 'bread' He meaneth here either His saving doctrines and the faith which is in Him, or His own Body; for both nerve the soul."

" It [2] is necessary to understand the marvel of the Mysteries, what it is, why it was given, and what is the profit of the action, We become one body, and ' members of His Flesh and of His Bones.' Let the initiated follow what I say. In order then that we may become this, not by love only, but in very deed, let us be blended into that Flesh. This is effected by the Food which He hath freely given us, desiring to show the love which He hath for us. On this account He hath mixed up Himself with us; He hath kneaded up His Body with our's, that we might be a certain One Thing, like a body joined to a head. . . . This also Christ hath done, to lead us to a closer friendship, and to show His love for us; He hath given to those who desire Him, not only to see Him, but even to touch and eat Him, and fix their teeth in His Flesh, and to embrace Him and satisfy all their love. Let us then return from that Table like lions breathing fire, having become terrible to

---

[1] On S. John vi. Hom. xlvi. § 1, p. 396.
[2] Ib. pp. 399, 400.

the devil; thinking on our Head, and on the love which He hath shown for us. Parents often entrust their offspring to others to feed; 'but I,' saith He, 'do not so, I feed you with Mine own Flesh, desiring that you all be nobly born, and holding forth to you good hopes for the future. For He Who giveth out Himself to you here, much more will He do so hereafter. I have willed to become your Brother; for your sake I shared in flesh and blood; and in turn I give out to you the Flesh and the Blood by which I became your kinsman.' This Blood causeth the image of our King to be fresh within us, produceth beauty unspeakable, permitteth not the nobleness of our souls to waste away, watering it continually, and nourishing it. The blood derived from our food becomes not at once blood, but something else; while this doth not so, but straightway watereth our souls, and worketh in them some mighty power. This Blood, if rightly taken, driveth away devils, and keepeth them afar off from us, while it calleth to us Angels and the Lord of Angels. For wherever they see the Lord's Blood, devils flee, and Angels run together. This Blood, poured forth, washed clean all the world. Many wise sayings did the blessed Paul utter concerning It in the Epistle to the Hebrews. This Blood cleansed the secret place and the Holy of Holies. And if the type of It had such great power in the temple of the Hebrews, and in the midst of Egypt, when smeared on the door-posts, much more the reality. This Blood sanctified the golden altar; without it the High Priest dared not enter into the secret place. This Blood consecrated priests, This in types cleansed sins. But if it had such power in the types, if death so shuddered at the shadow, tell me how would it not have dreaded the very reality? This Blood is the salvation of our souls, by This the soul is washed, by This is beautified, by This is inflamed. This causeth our understanding to be more bright than fire, and our soul more beaming than gold; this Blood was poured forth, and made heaven accessible. Awful in truth are the Mysteries of the Church, awful in truth is the Altar."

"This[3] Blood was ever typified of old in the altars and sacrifices of righteous men. This is the price of the world; by This Christ purchased to Himself the Church; by This He hath adorned Her all. For as a man buying servants giveth gold for them, and again when he desireth to deck them out, doth this also with gold; so Christ hath purchased us with His Blood, and adorned us with His Blood. They who share this Blood stand with Angels and Archangels and the Powers that are above, clothed in Christ's own Kingly robe, and having the armour of the Spirit. Nay, I have not as yet said any great thing; they are clothed with the King Himself. . . . 'For,' It saith, 'he that eateth and drinketh unworthily' of the Lord, 'eateth and drinketh damna-

---

[3] Ib. §§ 4, 5, p. 401.

tion to himself;' since if they who defile the Kingly purple are punished equally with those who rend it, it is not unreasonable that they who receive the Body with unclean thoughts, should suffer the same punishment as those who rent it with the nails."

"' For ⁴ My Flesh is true meat, and My Body is true drink?'

"What is it that He saith? He either desireth to declare that this is the true meat which saveth the soul, or to assure them concerning what had been said, that they might not suppose the words to be a mere enigma or parable, but might know that it is by all means needful to eat the Body. Then He saith, 'He that eateth My Flesh dwelleth in Me.' This He said, showing that such an one is mingled in Him."

"'What ⁵ then, is not His Flesh, flesh?' Most certainly. 'How then saith He, that the flesh profiteth nothing?' He speaketh not of His Own Flesh (God forbid!), but of those who received His words in a carnal manner. But what is 'understanding carnally?' It is looking merely to what is before our eyes, without imagining any thing beyond. This is understanding carnally. But we must not judge thus by sight, but must look into all mysteries with the eyes within. This is seeing spiritually. He that eateth not His Flesh, and drinketh not His

----

⁴ Ib. vi. 55, 6. Hom. xlvii. § 1, p. 404.
⁵ Ib. § 2, p. 408.

Blood, hath no life in him. How then doth 'the flesh profit nothing,' if without It we cannot live? Seest thou that the words, 'the flesh profiteth nothing,' are spoken, not of His Own Flesh, but of carnal hearing?"

"'There[6] came forth water and blood.' Not without a purpose, or by chance, did those founts come forth, but because by means of these two together the Church consisteth. And the initiated know it, being by water indeed regenerate, and nourished by the Blood and the Flesh. Hence the Mysteries take their beginning; that when thou approachest to that awful Cup, thou mayest so approach, as drinking from the very Side."

"It[7] is not for nothing that the Deacon cries, 'For them that are fallen asleep in Christ, and for them that make the memorials for them.' It is not the Deacon that utters this voice, but the Holy Ghost; I speak of the Gift. What sayest thou? There is the Sacrifice in hand, and all things laid out duly ordered. Angels are there present, Archangels, the Son of God is there; all stand with such awe, and in the general silence those stand by, crying aloud. And thinkest thou that what is done, is done in vain? Then is not the rest also all in vain, both the oblations made for the Church, and those for the Priests, and for the whole body? God forbid! but all is done with faith."

[6] On S. John xix. 34.   Hom. lxxxv. § 3, p. 761.
[7] On Acts ix.   Hom. xxi. § 4, p. 310.

"Reverence[8] now, oh, reverence this Table whereof we all are partakers! Christ, Who was slain for us, the Victim that is placed thereon!"

"As[9] this was a symbol of the Font, so that which follows, of the Holy Table. For as thou eatest the Lord's Body, so they the manna; and as thou drinkest the Blood, so they water from a rock.

"Perceivest thou the wisdom of Paul, how in both cases he points Him out as the Giver, and thereby brings the type nigh to the Truth? 'For He who set those things before them,' saith he, 'the Same also hath prepared this our Table; and the same Person both brought them through the sea, and thee through Baptism; and before them set manna, but before thee His Body and Blood.'"

"'The[1] cup of blessing which we bless, is it not the Communion of the Blood of Christ?' What sayest thou, O blessed Paul? When thou wouldest appeal to the hearer's reverence, when thou art making mention of awful Mysteries, dost thou give the title of 'Cup of blessing' to that fearful and most tremendous Cup? 'Yea,' saith he, 'and no mean title is that which is spoken. For when I call it "blessing," I unfold all the treasures of God's goodness, and call to mind those mighty gifts.' Very persuasively spake he, and awfully. For what he

---

[8] On Romans iv. 21.   Hom. viii. p. 131.
[9] In 1 Cor. x. 1—5.   Hom. xxiii. § 3, pp. 312, 313.
[1] Ib. 16.   Hom. xxiv. § 3, pp. 326, 327.

says is this: 'This which is in the Cup, is that which flowed from His Side, and of that do we partake.' But He called it the Cup of blessing, because holding it in our hands, we so proceed to exalt Him in our hymn, wondering, astonished at His unspeakable gift, blessing Him, among other things, for the pouring out of this selfsame draught, that we might not abide in error; and not only for the pouring it out, but also for the imparting thereof to us all. 'Wherefore if thou desire blood,' saith He, 'redden not the altar of idols with the slaughter of brute beasts, but My Altar with My Blood.' Tell me, what can be more tremendous than this? What more tenderly kind? This also lovers do. When they see those whom they love desiring what belongs to strangers, and despising their own, they give what belongs to themselves, and so persuade them to withdraw themselves from the gifts of those others. Lovers, however, display this liberality in goods, and money, and garments, but in blood none ever did so. Whereas Christ even herein exhibited His care and fervent love for us. And in the old covenant, because they were in an imperfect state, the blood which they used to offer to idols, He Himself submitted to receive, that He might separate them from those idols; which very thing again was a proof of His unspeakable affection; but here He hath transferred the sacred office to that which is far more awful and glorious, changing the very Sacrifice itself, and instead of the slaughter of irrational creatures, commanding to offer up Himself."

"'The' bread which we break, is it not the communion of the Body of Christ?' Wherefore said he not, the participation? Because he intended to express something more, and to point out how close was the union; in that we communicate, not only by participating and partaking, but also by being united. For as that body is united to Christ, so also are we united to Him by this bread. But why adds He also, 'which we break?' For although in the Eucharist one may see this done, yet on the Cross not so, but the very contrary. For 'a bone of Him,' saith one, 'shall not be broken.' But that which He suffered not on the Cross, this He suffers in the Oblation for thy sake, and submits to be broken, that He may fill all men. . . . 'For why speak I of Communion?' saith he, 'we are that self-same body.' For what is the bread? The Body of Christ. And what do they become who partake of It? The body of Christ; not many bodies, but one body. For as the bread consisting of many grains is made one, so that the grains no where appear; they exist indeed, but their difference is not seen, by reason of their conjunction; so are we conjoined both with each other and with Christ; there not being one Body for thee, and another for thy neigh-

¹ § 4, p. 327.

bour to be nourished by, but the very Same for all.
. . . He gave not simply even His Own Body, but
because the former nature of the flesh, which was
framed out of earth, had first become deadened by
sin, and destitute of life ; He brought in, as one may
say, another sort of dough and leaven, His Own
Flesh, by nature indeed the same, but free from sin,
and full of life ; and gave to all to partake thereof,
that being nourished by this, and laying aside the
old dead material, we might be blended together
unto the eternal life, by means of this Table."

"But[3] do thou, I pray, consider how with regard
to the Jews he said not, 'they are partakers with
God,' but they are partakers of the Altar; for what
was placed thereon was burnt ; but in respect to the
Body of Christ not so.   But how?   It is the Communion of the Lord's Body.   For not of the Altar,
but of Christ Himself, are we made partakers."

"To[4] this that fearful and tremendous Sacrifice
leads us, warning us above all things to approach it
with one mind and fervent love, and thereby becoming eagles, so to mount up to the very Heaven.
'For wheresoever the carcase is,' saith He, 'there
also will be the eagles,' calling His Body a carcase
by reason of His death.   For unless He had fallen,
we should not have risen again.   But He calls us
eagles, implying that he who draws nigh to this Body
must be on high, and have nothing common with

[3] § 5, p. 329.   [4] § 7, p. 332.

the earth, nor wind himself downwards and creep along; but must ever be soaring heavenwards, and look on the Sun of Righteousness, and have the eye of his mind quick-sighted. For eagles, not daws, have a right to this table. Those also shall then meet Him descending from Heaven, who now worthily have this privilege, even as they who do so unworthily, shall suffer the extremest torments. For if one would not inconsiderately receive a king (why say I a king? nay, were it but a royal robe, one would not inconsiderately touch it with unclean hands, though he should be in solitude, though alone, though no man were at hand; and yet the robe is nought but certain threads spun by worms; and if thou admirest the dye, this too is the blood of a dead fish; nevertheless one would not choose to venture on it with polluted hands;) I say now, if even a man's garment be what one would not venture inconsiderately to touch, what shall we say of the Body of Him Who is God over all, spotless, pure, associate with that Divine Nature, the Body whereby we are, and live; whereby the gates of hell were broken down, and the sanctuaries of Heaven opened? How shall we receive this with so great insolence? Let us not, I pray you, let us not slay ourselves by our irreverence, but with all awfulness and purity let us draw nigh to It; and when thou seest It set before thee, say thou to thyself, 'Because of this Body am I no longer earth and ashes, no longer a prisoner, but free; because of this I hope for

Heaven, and to receive the good things therein, immortal life, the portion of Angels, converse with Christ; this Body, nailed and scourged, was more than death could stand against; this Body the very sun saw crucified, and turned aside his beams; for this, both the veil was rent in that moment, and rocks were burst asunder, and all the earth was shaken. This is even that Body, the blood-stained, the smitten, out of which gushed the saving fountains, the one of blood, the other of water, for all the world.'

" Wouldest thou from another source also learn Its power? Ask of her, diseased with an issue of blood, who laid hold not of Itself, but of the garment with which It was clad; nay, not of the whole of this, but of the hem; ask of the sea, which bare It on its back; ask even of the Devil himself, and say, ' Whence hast thou that incurable stroke? Whence hast thou no longer any power? Whence art thou captive? By whom hast thou been seized in thy flight?' And he will give no other answer than this, ' The Body that was crucified.' By this were his stings broken in pieces; by this was his head crushed; by this were the powers and the principalities made a show of. ' For,' saith he, ' having spoiled principalities and powers, He made a show of them openly, triumphing over them in it.'

" Ask also Death, and say, ' whence is it that thy sting hath been taken away? thy victory abolished? thy sinews cut out? and thou become the laughing-stock of girls and children, who wast before a terror even to kings, and to all righteous men?' And he will ascribe it to this Body. For when this was crucified, then were the dead raised up, then was that prison burst, and the gates of brass were broken, and the dead were loosed, and the keepers of hell-gate all quaked for fear. And yet, had He been one of the many, death on the contrary should have become more mighty; but it was not so. For He was not one of the many. Therefore was death dissolved. That Body, which he could not work upon, he received; and therefore had to cast forth those also which he had within him. Yea, he travailed, whilst he held Him, and was straitened, until he vomited Him up. Wherefore saith the Apostle, 'Having loosed the pains of death.' For Christ came not forth again by the mouth of death, but having burst asunder, and ripped up in the very midst the belly of the dragon, thus from His secret chambers right gloriously He issued forth, and flung abroad His beams not to this heaven alone, but to the very throne most high. For even thither did He carry It up.

"This Body hath He given to us both to hold and to . eat; a thing appropriate to intense love. For those whom we kiss vehemently, we ofttimes even bite with our teeth. Wherefore also Job, indicating the love of his servants towards him, said, that they ofttimes out of their great affection towards him, said, 'O that we . were filled . with his flesh!' Even so

Christ hath given to us to be filled with His Flesh, drawing us on to greater love."

" This [5] Body even lying in a manger, the Magi reverenced. And men profane and barbarous, leaving their country and their home, both set out on a long journey, and when they came, with fear and great trembling worshipped Him.   Behold now, let us at least imitate those barbarians, we who are citizens of Heaven.   For they indeed, when they saw Him but in a manger, and in a shed, and no such thing was in sight as thou beholdest now, drew nigh with great awe; but thou beholdest Him not in the manger but on the Altar; not a woman holding Him in her arms, but the Priest standing by, and the Spirit with exceeding bounty hovering over the gifts set before us.   Thou dost not see merely this Body Itself, as they did, but thou knowest also Its power, and the whole economy, and art ignorant of none of the holy things which are brought to pass by It, having been exactly initiated into all.

" Let us therefore wake ourselves up, and be filled with horror, and let us show forth a reverence far beyond that of those Barbarians; that we may not, by random and careless approaches, heap fire upon our own heads.   But these things I say, not to keep us from approaching, but to keep us from approaching without consideration.   For as the approaching at random is dangerous, so the not communicating

[5] § 8, p. 334.

in those mystical suppers is famine and death. For this Table is the sinews of our soul, the bond of our mind, the foundation of our confidence, our hope, our salvation, our light, our life. When with this Sacrifice we depart into the other world, with much confidence we shall tread the sacred threshold, fenced round on every side as with a kind of golden armour. And why speak I of the world to come? Since here this mystery makes earth become to thee a heaven. Open only for once the gates of heaven, and look in; nay, rather not of heaven, but of the heaven of heavens, and then thou wilt behold what I have been speaking of. For what is there most precious of all, this will I show thee lying upon the earth. For as in royal palaces, what is most glorious of all, is not walls, nor golden roofs, but the person of the king sitting on the throne; so likewise in heaven the Body of the King. But this thou art now permitted to see upon earth. For it is not angels, nor archangels, nor heavens, and heavens of heavens, that I show thee, but the very Lord and Owner of these. Perceivest thou how that which is more precious than all things is seen by thee on earth; and not seen only, but also touched; and not only touched, but likewise eaten; and after receiving It thou goest home?

" Make thy soul clean then, prepare thy mind for the reception of these mysteries. For if thou wert entrusted to carry a king's child with the robes, the purple, and the diadem, thou wouldest cast away all things which are upon the earth.   But now that it is no child of man, how royal soever, but the Only-begotten Son of God Himself, Whom thou receivedst; dost thou not thrill with awe, tell me, and cast away all the love of all worldly things, and have no bravery but That, wherewith to adorn thyself? or dost thou still look towards earth, and love money, and flutter after gold?"

"But⁶ how saith he, that he 'received it from the Lord?' since certainly he was not present then, but was one of the persecutors. That thou mayest know that the first table had no advantage above that which cometh after it. For even to-day also it is He Who doeth all, and delivereth It even as then. . . . Since⁷ Christ for His part gave Himself equally to all, saying, 'Take, eat.' He gave His Body equally, but thou dost not give so much as the common bread equally. Yea, It was indeed broken for all alike, and became the Body equally for all.

"What is it which He saith, 'This Cup is the New Testament?' Because there was also a cup of the Old Testament; the libations and the blood of the brute creatures. For so, after sacrificing, they used to receive the blood in a chalice and bowl, and so pour it out. Since then instead of the blood of beasts, He brought in His own Blood; lest any should be troubled on hearing this, He reminds them of that ancient sacrifice."

⁶ Hom. xxvii. § 5, p. 377.   ⁷ p. 378.

" Next, having spoken concerning that Supper, he connects the things present with the things of that time, that even as on that very evening, and reclining on that very couch, and receiving from Christ Himself this Sacrifice, so also now might men be affected.

" ' Whosoever [8] shall eat this bread and drink this Cup of the Lord unworthily, shall be guilty of the Body and Blood of the Lord.' Why so? Because he poured it out, and makes the thing appear a slaughter, and no longer a sacrifice. Much therefore as they who then pierced Him, pierced Him not that they might drink, but that they might shed His Blood; so likewise doth he that cometh for It unworthily, and reaps no profit thereby. . . . Thou hast tasted the Blood of the Lord, and not even thereupon dost thou acknowledge thy brother. Of what indulgence then art thou worthy? . . . Doth it not come into thy mind, what thou wert, and what thou hast become?"

" Is [9] it not so, that at such times, immediately after the Communion, drunkenness succeeds, and contempt of the poor? And having partaken of the Blood, when it were a time for thee to fast and watch, thou givest thyself up to wine and revelling."

" And [1] these things thou doest when thou hast enjoyed the Table of Christ, on that day on which thou hast been counted worthy to touch His Flesh

[8] § 6, p. 379.   [9] § 7, p. 380.   [1] p. 381.

with thy tongue. Whosoever thou art then, that those things be not so, do thou purify thy right hand, thy tongue, thy lips, which have become a threshold for Christ to tread upon. . . . Wherefore I beseech you, that we do not this to condemnation; let us nourish Christ, let us give Him to drink, let us clothe Him. These things are worthy of that Table. Hast thou heard holy hymns? Hast thou seen a spiritual marriage? Hast thou enjoyed a royal Table? Hast thou been filled with the Holy Ghost? Hast thou joined in the quire of the Seraphim? Hast thou become partaker of the powers above? Cast not away so great a joy, waste not the treasure, bring not in drunkenness, the mother of dejection, the joy of the devil, the parent of ten thousand evils. If thou wouldest not choose to meet with a friend when intoxicated, tell me, durst thou, when thou hast Christ within, to thrust in upon Him so great excess?"

" But ' why doth he eat condemnation to himself? ' Not discerning the Lord's Body;' not searching, not bearing in mind, as he ought, the greatness of the things set before him; not estimating the weight of the gift. For if thou shouldest come to know accurately, Who it is that lies before thee, and Who He is that gives Himself, and to whom, thou wilt need no other argument, but this is enough for thee to use all vigilance; unless thou shouldest be altogether fallen."

' Hom. xxviii. § 2, p. 384.

" Through[3] these gates and doors Christ both hath entered into us, and doth enter, whensoever we communicate. Ye who partake of the mysteries, understand what I say. For it is in no common manner that our lips are honoured, when they receive the Lord's Body."

" Since[4] our discourse is concerning this Body [of Christ crucified], as many of us as partake of that Body and taste of that Blood, consider that we are partaking of that which is in no wise different from that Body, nor separate, as regards participation; that we taste of that Body that sitteth above, that is adored by Angels, that is next to the Power that is incorruptible. Alas! how many ways to salvation are open to us! He hath made us His own Body, He hath imparted to us His own Body, and yet not one of these things turns us away from what is evil."

" I observe[5] many partaking of Christ's Body lightly and heedlessly, and rather from custom and form, than consideration and understanding. When, saith a man, the holy season of Lent sets in, whatever a man may be, he partakes of the Mysteries, or, when the day of the Lord's Epiphany comes. And yet this does not make a fit time for approaching. For it is not the Epiphany, nor is it Lent that makes people fit to approach, but it is sincerity and purity

---

[3] Hom. xxx. 2 Cor. xiii. 12, (2,) p. 335.
[4] On Ephes. i. Hom. iii. p. 130.   [5] p. 131.

of soul.   With this, approach at all times; without
it, never.   'For as often,' saith he, 'as ye do this, ye
do show the Lord's Death,' *i. e.* 'Ye make a remembrance of the salvation that has been wrought for
you, and of the benefits which I have bestowed.'
Consider those who partook of the sacrifices under
the old Covenant, how great abstinence did they
practise?   How did they not conduct themselves?
What did they not perform?   They were always
purifying themselves.   And dost thou, when thou
drawest nigh to a Sacrifice, at which the very Angels
tremble, dost thou measure the matter by the revo-
lutions of seasons? and how shalt thou present
thyself before the judgment-seat of Christ, thou who
presumest upon His Body with polluted hands and
lips?   Thou wouldest not presume to kiss a king
with an unclean mouth, and dost thou kiss the King
of Heaven with an unclean soul?   It is an outrage.
Tell me, wouldest thou choose to come to the Sacrifice with unwashen hands?   No, I suppose not.
But thou wouldest rather choose not to come at all,
than come with soiled hands.   And then, thus scrupulous as thou art in this little matter, dost thou
come with soiled soul, and thus dare to touch It?
And yet the hands hold It but for a time, whereas
into the soul It is received entirely.   What! do ye
not see the holy vessels so thoroughly cleansed all
over, so resplendent?   Our souls ought to be purer
than they, more holy, more brilliant than they.   And
why so?   Because those vessels are made so for our

sakes. They partake not of Him that is in them, they perceive Him not. But we do;—yes, verily. Now then, thou wouldest not choose to make use of a soiled vessel, and dost thou approach with a soiled soul? . . . Look, I entreat: a royal table is set before you, Angels minister at that Table, the King Himself is there, and dost thou stand still and gape? Are thy garments defiled, and yet dost thou make no account of it? or are they clean? Then fall down, and partake. Every day He cometh in to see the guests, and converseth with them all. Yes, at this moment is He speaking to your conscience: ' Friends, why stand ye here, not having on a wedding garment?' He said not, ' Why didst thou sit down?' No; before he sat down, He declared him to be unworthy, so much as to come in. He saith not, ' Why didst thou sit down to meat?' but, ' Why camest thou in?' And these are the words that He is at this very moment addressing to one and all of us, that stand here with such shameless effrontery. For every one that partaketh not of the Mysteries, is standing here in shameless effrontery. It is for this reason, that they which are in sin are first of all put forth. For just as when a master is present at his table, it is not right that those servants who have offended him should be present, but they are sent out of the way, just so also here when the Sacrifice is brought forth, and Christ, the Lord's Sheep, is sacrificed. When thou hearest the words, ' Let us pray together,' when thou beholdest the curtains drawn up, then imagine that the Heavens are let down from above, and that the Angels are descending!"

" Think " what words thy mouth utters, to what a Table do they belong! Think What it touches, What it tastes, of what manner of Food it partakes! Dost thou deem thyself to be doing nothing grievous in railing at thy brother? And yet if he be not a brother, how sayest thou, 'Our Father?' For the word *our* is indicative of many persons. Think with whom thou standest at the time of the Mysteries! With the Cherubim, with the Seraphim! The Seraphim revile not: no, their mouth fulfils this one only duty, to sing the Hymn of glory, to glorify God. And how then shalt thou be able to say with them, 'Holy, Holy, Holy,' if thou use thy mouth for reviling?"—" Why ', if a servant, even here with us, beats his fellow-servant or assaults him, even though he do it justly, yet we at once rebuke him, and deem the act an outrage; and yet dost thou, who art standing with the Cherubim beside the King's throne, revile thy brother? Seest thou not these holy vessels? Are they not used continually for one only purpose? Does any one ever venture to use them for any other? Yet art thou holier than these vessels; yea, far holier. Why then defile, why contaminate thyself? Art thou standing in Heaven, and dost thou revile? Hast thou thy citizenship with

---

 ' In Ephes. iv. 30. Hom. xiv. p. 260.   ' p. 261.

Q q

Angels, and dost thou revile? Art thou counted worthy the Lord's kiss, and dost thou revile? Hath God graced thy mouth with so many and great things, with hymns angelic, with food, not angelic, no, but more than angelic, with His own kiss[8], with His own embrace, and dost thou revile?"

"How[9] 'of His Flesh?' Ye know, as many as partake of the Mysteries. For from Him are we at once created anew. And how? Hear again this blessed saint, where he saith, 'Forasmuch then as the children are partakers of flesh and blood, He also Himself likewise took part of the same.' Only here He imparts to us, not we to Him."

"The[1] plain falleth not on thy sight [as in Paradise], thou seest not tree, nor fountain, but straightway thou takest into thee the Lord Himself; thou art mingled with His Body; thou art intermixed with that Body that lieth above, whither the Devil cannot approach."

"Many[2] such instances still occur. For since the Priests cannot know who are sinners, and unworthy partakers of the Holy Mysteries, God often in this way delivers them to Satan. For when diseases, and attacks, and sorrows, and calamities, and the like occur, it is on this account that they are inflicted. This is shown by Paul. 'For this cause many are

---

[8] See S. Cyprian's Ep. vi. p. 15, n.
[9] On Eph. v. 30. Hom. xx. p. 319.
[1] On Col. i. Hom. vi. fin. p. 254.
[2] On 1 Tim. i. 20. Hom. v. § 2, pp. 44, 45.

weak and sickly among you, and many sleep.' But how, saith one, when we approach but once a year? But this is indeed the evil, that you determine the worthiness of your approach, not by the purity of your minds, but by the interval of time. You think it a proper caution, not to communicate often ; not considering that you are scared by partaking unworthily, though only once ; but to receive worthily, though often, is salutary. It is not presumptuous to receive often, but to receive unworthily, though but once in a whole life. But we are so miserably foolish, that, though we commit numberless offences in the course of a year, we are not anxious to be absolved from them, but are satisfied that we do not often make bold, impudently to insult the Body of Christ, not remembering that those who crucified Christ, crucified Him but once ? Is the offence then the less because committed but once ? Judas betrayed his Master but once. What then, did that exempt him from punishment ? Why indeed is time to be considered in this matter ? Let our time of coming be, when our conscience is pure. The Mystery at Easter is not of more efficacy than that which is now celebrated. It is One and the Same. There is the same grace of the Spirit; it is always a Passover. You who are initiated know this. On the Preparation, on the Sabbath, on the Lord's Day, and on the day of Martyrs, it is the same Sacrifice that is performed. 'For as often,' he saith, 'as ye eat this Bread and drink this Cup, ye do show the Lord's Death.'"

Q q 2

"I am³ about to say what may appear strange, but be not astonished nor startled at it. The Offering is the same, whether a common man, or Paul or Peter offer it. It is the Same which Christ gave to His disciples, and which the Priests now minister. This is no wise inferior to that; because it is not men that sanctify even this, but the Same who sanctified the one, sanctifies the other also. For as the words which God spake are the same which the Priest now utters, so is the Offering the same, and the Baptism, that which He gave. Thus the whole is of faith. The Spirit immediately fell upon Cornelius, because he had previously fulfilled his part, and contributed his faith. And this is His Body, as well as that. And he who thinks the one inferior to the other, knows not that Christ even now is present, even now operates."

"What⁴ then? Do not we [Christians] daily offer? We do offer, but making a memorial of His Death. And this is one and not many. How one and not many? Because it was once offered, as was that which was brought into the Holy of Holies. This is a type of that, and this itself of That. For we always offer the Same (τὸν αὐτόν); not now one animal, to-morrow another, but always the same thing. So then the Sacrifice is one. Else since it is offered in many places, there were many Christs.

---

³ On 2 Tim. i. 12. Hom. ii. fin. pp. 184, 185.
⁴ On Heb. ix. 28. Hom. xvii. § 3, xii. 169, Ben.

But no. There is but One Christ every where, here fully and there fully, One Body. As then He, being offered in many places, is One Body, and not many bodies, so also there is One Sacrifice. Our High Priest is He Who offered the Sacrifice which cleanseth us. That same Sacrifice which was then also offered, we offer now too; That, the inexhaustible. For this is for a Memorial of That Which took place then. For He saith, 'This do, as a memorial of Me.' We do not make a different, but always the same Sacrifice; or rather we make a memorial of that Sacrifice."

" They [5] shed the Righteous Blood, who drink the Blood of the Lord, and are defiled with foul deeds."

62. Council of Carthage III. (under Aurelius ii.), A.D. 397.

"That [6] in the Sacraments of the Body and Blood of the Lord, nothing more should be offered, than the Lord Himself delivered, *i. e.* bread and wine mingled with water. [But let the first fruits, or milk and honey, which are wont to be offered on one most solemn day for the mystery of the new-baptized, although offered on the Altar, have their own benediction, that they may be distinguished from the Sacrament of the Body and Blood of the

---

[5] S. Chrys. in Prov. vi. 17. Mai, Biblioth. Nov. Pat. iv. p. 163, App.

[6] Can. 24, T. ii. p. 1403, ed. Col. The part in brackets " is in old MSS." (Ib.) The can. is quoted de Consecr. D. 2, c. 5.

Lord.]   Nor let more be offered in the Sacrifices [from the first fruits] than from grapes and corn."

COUNCIL OF CARTHAGE (under Aurelius ii.), A.D. 398, or A.D. 401.

"That', if need compel, the Deacon may, in the presence of the Presbyter, at his bidding, deliver to the people the Eucharist of the Body of Christ."

63. PHILO CARPASIUS.

Bishop of Carpasia in Cyprus, A.D. 401.   "A holy man," said to have been ordained Bishop by S. Epiphanius upon revelation (Vit. S. Epiph. c. 49), who mentions him as "of blessed memory." (Ep. ad Joh. Hieros. in S. Jerome, Ep. 51, § 2, i. 542, ed. Vall.)   The following extracts are preserved by Cosmas, who wrote A.D. 535—547.

"'As' the apple tree among the trees of the wood, so is my Beloved among the sons.'   The apple hath in itself both meat and drink, that it may express the mystic joy which the Bridegroom hath given to her, saying, 'Take, eat, This is My Body,' and 'Take, drink, This is My Blood, Which is shed for you for the remission of sins.'   Wherefore, I ween, he says, 'As an apple.'   For the apple containeth three good things ; meat, whereby he covertly signifieth the Body of Christ ; drink, whereby he signifieth the Saving Blood ; and sweet savour, which expresseth faith."

' c. 38, p. 1440, quoted Dist. 97, c. 18.
' In Cant, c, 37, p. 52, ed. Giacom.

" The [9] 'neck,' I suppose, signifies the most pure order of Deacons, since 'the Head of the Church is Christ.' These bear the Body of Christ and His Blood, the Head of the Church."

" The [1] apples have two things in themselves, meat and drink; as also the good savour of faith hath both the mystical Meat and Drink of the Body and Blood of Christ."

" These [2] spiritual provisions, then, of the Body and Blood of Christ, the Church having tasted, hath the 'roof of her mouth' like 'the best wine.' For wine, when it is drunk, endeth sorrow, and changeth the heart to joy.   So too this sorrow-resting Name of life is given 'for the remission of sins.' For it rests our sorrow for these, since Christ says, 'Take, drink, this is My Blood, Which is shed for you for the remission of sins.' And wonderfully says he, 'that goeth in uprightness to My beloved.' For this Drink is given to the upright, as the Apostle saith, 'Let a man examine himself, and so let him eat of that Bread, and drink of that Cup;' to wit, having the uprightness befitting the Mysteries."

" For [3] her sake did He also drink wine; and that, through the Apostles, He drank before of the 'spiced wine,' *i.e.* that mingled by the Holy Ghost, which He also drank of before, saying, 'Take ye, drink, This is My Blood, Which is shed for you.'

[9] Ib. c. 198, p. 164.
[1] c. 209, p. 174.
[2] c. 210, p. 176.
[3] c. 228, p. 191.

How then doth she [the Church], drinking through the Apostles, promise in turn to give Him to drink, save, that (as hath been said before) when Christ is formed in the newly enlightened, He, in the new born themselves, receiveth of the 'spiced wine' to drink, *i.e.* of the wine of the Mysteries, which the Church has received from Him?"

64. VICTOR OF ANTIOCH, placed A.D. 401, but later.

This date was probably given to the Epitomator so entitled in MSS., because he himself says in the beginning of his Commentary, that " no one at all, I think, had explained the Gospel according to Mark." Since then Cassiodorus mentions S. Chrysostom as one who was said (ferunt) to have commented on all the Divine Scriptures of the Old and New Testament from the beginning to the end (de Inst. Div. Litt. Præf. ii. 538), it was inferred that this writer must have lived before S. Chrysostom wrote on S. Mark (Fabr. v. 17, T. 7, p. 769, note).   But this compiler quotes by name S. Chrysostom [" John, Bishop of the royal city, who is among the saints," p. 408], Apollinarius, and Theodorus of Mopsuestia; he cites also (without naming him) S. Cyril of Alexandria, and transcribes largely S. Chrysostom.   This would require that he should be placed somewhat later.   But beyond this, the Compiler of the Catena speaks of the commentators from whom he compiled, in the character of older authorities.   He must then, probably, have lived some time afterwards ; and so I set him down here, rather as embodying those authorities, than as a witness of this age.   His words are, " Whereas many have composed commentaries on the [Gospel] according to Matthew, and that according to John the son of thunder, but few on that according to Luke, and no one at all, as I think, having explained that according to Mark (for I have heard of none up to this day, and that having diligently inquired as to this, of those who take pains to bring together the labours *of the more ancient*), I have decided to bring together, what has been said upon it by *the teachers of the Church*, in detached places, up and down [in their works], and to make a compendious comment, in order that it alone of the books of the New Testament may not seem to have been overlooked, either as though it needed no attention, or as though we could, from the interpretation of the rest, discover the meaning of this Gospel also." (Cramer, Catena, T. 2, p. 263.)

This writer interpreted our Lord's words " This fruit of the Vine," of our Lord's drinking wine in proof of His Resurrection, above, p. 139.

" The one [4] saith, that the [5] traitor himself remained partaking of the Mysteries, and after he had been admitted to that most awful Table, was not changed : as Luke too showeth, saying, that 'after this Satan entered into him, not despising the Body, but mocking the shamelessness of the traitor. But Christ forbad him not, though knowing all things, that thou mayest learn, that He leaveth nothing undone which may conduce to amendment.' Another says that Judas went out first, as John hath shown. For he that was to be the instrument of the death of Christ, could not have received the *type* of the saving Communion. The Lord bore all the rest; but this He permitted not. I suppose no one would deny, that He thus delivered to His disciples, how they should celebrate the Mystery of the New Testament. For

[4] In Cramer's Catena, i. 422.
[5] S. Chrysostom, Hom. lxxxii. in S. Matt. p. 460, ed. Field.

therefore He both blessed, and when He gave it to them, bade them to partake of what was meet, that they, through the blessing and Eucharist, might learn how truly great and worthy of all thanksgiving are those things which are dispensed through the Passion of Christ, of which He delivered to them these *symbols* to celebrate. But when He said 'This is My Body, and this is My Blood,' [He taught] that they who set forth the bread ought, after the Eucharistic Thanksgiving, to think that they partake of the Body, and to consider the Cup in the place of the Blood, as to which the Passion took place for the common salvation of all, and for forgiveness of their sins. For the faith herein at once contains a confession of the things fulfilled, and bestows on those who believe, the participation of forgiveness. Another saith, 'He teacheth us not to look to the nature of the elements, but to believe that through the Eucharistic blessing *these* things are *Those*. For the life-giving Word of God, having united Himself with His own Flesh, &c.'"

Thereupon follow two passages from S. Cyril of Alexandria's Commentary on S. Luke, which will be given in their context under that Father. The first short passage, although quoted as though from the same writer, is not in S. Cyril.

64 b. MARK THE HERMIT.

Palladius (Hist. Laus. c. 21) and Sozomen (H. E. vi. 29). Sozomen mentions a celebrated Ascetic of this name, who, from his youth, knew the Holy Scriptures by heart. Palladius says, that he was told by S. Macarius of Alexandria, that Mark received the Holy Eucharist at the hands of an Angel. It is not mentioned that this Mark left writings, but neither is any other writer named, to whom the writings can belong."

"Then [*] Melchizedec brought forth bread and wine for the refreshment of those returning from war ; so too Christ, the great High Priest, to those who returned to Him from the spiritual war, giveth sanctified bread and wine, saying, 'Take, eat ye all of this.' "

64 c. APOLLO.

Ascetic contemporary with Palladius (Hist. Laus. c. 52), quoted by Rufinus (Hist. Mon. c. 7, p. 155).

"But he [Apollo] gives this advice too, that if possible, the monks should communicate daily in the Mysteries of Christ, lest, perchance, he who keeps far from these, should become far from God : whereas he who received them more frequently, seems more frequently to receive the Saviour Himself, since the Saviour Himself thus says, 'Whoso eateth My Flesh and drinketh My Blood, dwelleth in Me, and I in Him.' But also the very commemoration of the Lord's Passion, when diligently made by the monks, is of great benefit to them, as an example of patience. Also each is thereby admouished to study ever to be found so prepared, that he be not thought unworthy of the Lord's Mysteries. To this he added, that remission of sins is hereby given to the faithful."

[*] Opusc. x. Gall. 8. 97.

65. S. Chromatius, Bishop of Aquileia.

Succeeded to Valerian, A.D. 388; consecrated probably by S. Ambrose; friend of S. Ambrose, S. Jerome, S. Chrysostom, and Rufinus; prominent among those who induced S. Jerome to translate the Old Testament from the Hebrew; laboured for the restoration of S. Chrysostom; his letter, together with that of Innocent I., was sent by the Emperor Honorius to Arcadius, A.D. 405; died about A.D. 408. (Gall. T. viii. c. 15.) S. Jerome calls him "the most learned and holy Bishop of his time." (Præf. in Paralip.) We have of his only fourteen short sermons, which (except one) are on the Sermon on the Mount.

"This[1] we ought to observe is spiritually enjoined us, that we should ask our daily bread, *i. e.* that heavenly and spiritual Bread which we receive daily to the healing of our soul and the hope of everlasting salvation; of which the Lord says in the Gospel, 'The Heavenly Bread is My Flesh which I will give for the life of the world.' For this Bread we are enjoined daily to ask, *i. e.* that through the vouchsafement of the mercy of the Lord we may be made meet daily to receive the Bread of the Lord's Body. For the holy Apostle says, 'Let a man examine himself, and so let him eat of the Bread of the Lord, and drink of that Cup.' And again, 'Whoso eateth the Bread and drinketh the Cup of the Lord unworthily, shall be guilty of the Body and Blood of the Lord.' Whence with good reason we ought ever to pray that we may be made meet to receive

[1] Tract. xiii. in S. Matt. § 5. Gall. viii. 348.

daily the heavenly Bread, lest through the intervention of any sin, we should be separated from the Body of the Lord."

65 b. PALLADIUS, friend and biographer of S. Chrysostom.

If, as seems probable, the same is the author of the Historia Lausiaca, he was born about A.D. 368; lived among the Ascetics of Egypt, A.D. 388—397, in Palestine, A.D. 397—400; was consecrated Bishop of Helenopolis, and was sent by S. Chrysostom to Ephesus, with two others, to try the Bishop Antoninus; banished with S. Chrysostom, A.D. 404; wrote the Hist. Laus. about A.D. 421.

Three instances have been given above, p. 109, *in which Palladius calls the consecrated elements by the name "symbols." A fourth occurs in the same Dialogue.*

" Having[s] communicated of the Lord's *symbols,* he [S. Chrysostom] makes the last prayer, while the rest were present, using his wonted words, ' Glory to God for all things.' And having set the seal of the last Amen, he lifted up his feet, which ran beautifully for the salvation of those who willed to repent, and for the reproof of those who cultivated sin in abundance."

65 c. *Apostolical Constitutions.*

The difficulty about this work is, that, while containing much which is good, it is, in its present form, a forgery. Perhaps the right solution may be, that the body of the work was not written by the author of the passages which

---

[s] Vit. S. Chrys. c. xi. p. 40.

claim for it Apostolic authority.   These passages are often
very easily detached from the rest; sometimes they consist
in what may have been very slight interpolations.

The claim is put forward, in very different degrees, in
different parts of the work.   Thus in the first book, there
is nothing except the four lines prefixed; which need form
no part of it.   In the second, which is by far the longest,
there are but three places, and those very subordinate[*].   In
the third book, there are two places in chapters which in-
terrupt the context[1].   In the fourth book, there is but one
place, in which the words "to me" may have been interpolated[2] (iv. 7).   There is none in the twelve last chapters
of the sixth book (19—30); and, with the exception of one
chapter (46), only one very trifling passage in the forty-nine
chapters of Book vii.

There is also, in these very places, something stiff, even

[*] In ii. 39, Matthew, who is alleged together with Zacchæus
and others, as an instance of repentance is made to speak in the
first person, "For I Matthew one of the twelve who are speaking to you in this teaching, am an Apostle."   In ii. 55, in the
enumeration of those through whom, from the beginning, God
had called men to repentance, the Apostles are introduced as
speaking in the first person.   In ii. 57, p. 262, ed. Cot., in the
direction for reading Holy Scripture, the Gospels are quoted,
"which I, Matthew and John, we delivered unto you, and which
the helpers of Paul, Luke, and Mark, having received, left
you."

[1] The subject of the third book of the Constitutions (c. 1—8,
12—15) is the order of widows.   This is twice broken.   1) At
the beginning of c. 6 there is a direction about *women's* not
teaching.   The rest of the chapter is on widows   2) Chap. 9, 10,
11, contain directions restricting women, laity, and inferior clergy
from certain offices.   Chap. 12 returns to the subject of widows.
In c. 6 and 9 is the only mention of the Apostles.

[2] The chapter is "on the offerings of the unworthy," the
words "But Simon Magus too offering money to [us] Peter and
John."

to pedantry, in the way in which the Authorship of the Apostles is most often claimed for the Constitutions. Whenever any fact of the Holy Scriptures is alluded to, which related to any of the Apostles, the word " I," " me," is thrust in before the name, " I, Matthew " (ii. 39, p. 248) ; " I, Matthew and John " (ii. 57, p. 262) ; " to me, Peter " (iv. 7 ; vi. 8) ; " through me, Peter " (v. 7) ; " to me, Thomas " (v. 19).   Now, this is not the way in which the sacred writers speak of themselves, nor in which it is natural for a body (in which character the Apostles were here supposed to be writing) to speak of individuals of their number. It is simply a stupid way of bringing before the eyes the supposed authorship.

But with this great stiffness, there is combined the opposite carelessness.   The inspired writers of the New Testament could not, even after the Canon was completed, quote themselves as *authority*.   They quote the Old Testament, in order to show the harmony of the law and the Gospel.   But they do not quote *themselves* as *authority*, because what they wrote in one Epistle, had the same authority as what they had written before.   It is *to us* one of the proofs that the Constitutions are not Apostolic, that they do quote the New Testament.   S. Matthew and S. John would not have quoted " the Gospels."   But a writer, who had intellect enough to write the Constitutions, would have seen this as clearly as we.   The same writer would not have guarded so stiffly every instance in which an Apostle's name was mentioned, by the insertion of " I," " me," in order to make it apparent that the Apostles were the writers, and at the same time have quoted their writings in a way in which it is obvious that the Apostles would not have quoted them. Amid the stiffness on the one side, there is a fearless quoting of the New Testament, as it would be quoted by one who was simply considering his subject, with nothing to guard, nothing to hide.

In Book viii. the two sets of passages are strangely out

of keeping.   The greatest part of it (as is well known) consists of prayers for ordinations, including the Liturgy for Catechumens, Energumens, those to be baptized, the faithful, before and after communion, &c.   These are dovetailed in, with (mostly) little dry injunctions [s], ascribed to eleven of the Apostles, including James, brother of John, who elsewhere in the Constitutions is spoken of as martyred. Without them, the greater part of the eighth book would be a collection of prayers.

It is now also admitted, on all hands, that the (so-called) " Apostolical Canons," appended to the Constitutions, are older than the time of their collection, being, in fact, the Ante-Nicene Canons, at least in the East.

Since, then, on the one hand, the passages which claim the Apostles for the authors of the book are no essential part of it, but might easily have been introduced into a pre-existing collection, and the main body of the work presents no characteristics of forgery ; and on the other hand, the anomalies of the book itself in its present state, are more easily accounted for, by supposing the forger to have altered a part than to have composed the whole (of which he would probably have been incapable), it seems to me most probable, that the Apostolic Constitutions are also, in their substance, older than the date of the forger, who affixed to them the authority of the Apostles, and thereby destroyed their own.

Some of them are quoted by S. Epiphanius, yet the pre-

---

[s] I too James brother of John, son of Zebedee, say, " Let the deacon say at once " (c. 12).   " Of the ordination of Presbyters, I, beloved of the Lord, enjoin you, the Bishops, when you ordain a Presbyter, O Bishop, thyself lay thy hand on his head, together with the presbytery and deacons " (c. 16).   Those ascribed to S. Philip (c. 17), S. Bartholomew (c. 19), S. Thomas (c. 21), S. Matthew (c. 22), are all cast in the same mould, and still drier.

sent collection cannot have been in his hands; since he quotes others which are not found in it. But the author of the "imperfect work on S. Matthew" in Latin, who does quote them in their present division into books, can have been very little later than Theodosius the Great. The substance of the Constitutions must have been much older.

"How[4] much more does the word exhort you to honour your spiritual parents, and to love, as benefactors and ambassadors to God, those who regenerate you through water, fill you with the Holy Spirit, feed you with the milk of the word, bring you up in the doctrine, stablish you with the exhortations, bestow upon you the Saving Body and the Precious Blood, loose you from your sins, make you partakers of the holy and sacred Eucharist, and partakers and fellow-heirs of the promises of God."

"Let[5] the Deacons after the prayer, some attend exclusively to the offering of the Eucharist, ministering to the Lord's Body with fear; others carefully look through the crowd, and keep them quiet."

"After[6] these things let the Offering take place, all the people standing, and praying in silence; and when It hath been offered, let each order by itself partake of the Lord's Body and the Precious Blood, in order, with reverence and godly fear, as though approaching to the Body of the King."

"Instead[7] of sacrifices of blood, He instituted a reasonable, unbloody and Mystic Sacrifice, which perfects the grace of the symbols in respect of which

---

[4] ii. 33. [5] L. ii. c. 57, p. 264.
[6] Ib. p. 265. [7] L. vi. c. 23, p. 353.

is celebrated there the Death of the Lord, [the Sacrifice] of His Body and Blood."

"We[8] entreat Thee graciously to look upon these gifts that lie before Thee, O God Who needest nothing, and look favourably upon them for the honour of Thy Christ, and send down Thy Holy Spirit upon this Sacrifice, the witness of the Sufferings of the Lord Jesus, that He may declare this bread the Body of Thy Christ, and this Cup the Blood of Thy Christ, that the partakers thereof may be confirmed unto godliness, may obtain remission of sins, may be freed from the devil and his deceit, may be fulfilled with the Holy Ghost, may become worthy of Thy Christ, may obtain everlasting life, Thou being reconciled to them, O Almighty Lord."

" Having[9] partaken of the Precious Body, and the Precious Blood of Christ, let us give thanks to Him Who hath accounted us worthy to partake of His holy Mysteries, and let us beseech Him that it be not to condemnation, but to our salvation, to the good of soul and body, to perseverance in holiness, to the remission of sins, to the life of the world to come."

65 d. PSEUDO-DIONYSIUS.

The author called Pseudo-Dionysius can hardly be later than this date, since Andreas of Cæsarea, A.D. 500, quoted him as "the Divine Dionysius;" Ephrem, Patriarch of Antioch, about A.D. 526, quoted him as " Dionysius the Areopagite." (Ap. Phot. Cod. 229. See Pearson, Vind. Ignat. i. 10.)

[8] L. viii. c. 12, p. 403.　　　[9] viii. c. 14, p. 405.

He has been cited (p. 110) *as using the word "symbols" of the consecrated elements. Again, " The venerable symbol* through which Christ is signified and partaken of, *having been placed on the Divine Altar."*

Of the effect of Communion, he says, in his obscure and involved language;

"The [1] all-holy consecrators of the All-Holy things, who love to gaze thereon, contemplating holily, as is meet, the most holy consecration, celebrate, with a general hymn of praise, the Principle Who is the Worker and Giver of good, through Which the saving consecrations have been exhibited to us, consecrating the holy deifying of communicants. But this hymn some call ‘ hymnology,’ others, ‘ a symbol of worship,’ others, as I think, a ‘ Divine and Hierarchical Eucharist,’ as comprising all the Divine gifts which come to us from God. For the account of all the Divine operations towards us, for which thanks are given, seems to me, that it beneficially supports our substance and our life, and forms what is Deiform in us in its beauty from its Original, makes us partakers of a more Divine habit, and lifts us up; and, regarding our dearth of Heavenly gifts inherent in us through our negligence, recals us to our ancient estate by the good which it heaps upon us, and wholly taking what is ours imparts to us most perfectly what is Its own, and thus bestows upon us communion with God and things Divine."

[1] § 7.

R r 2

That which wholly takes into Itself what is ours, can only be our Lord's Divinity taking to Itself our Manhood perfectly; and it is This, Dionysius says, which He, in turn, in Holy Communion, imparts perfectly to us.

Again;

"The[2] approach to the Divine things, in a sincere habit of mind, bestoweth upon those who approach, communion, so as to become like unto them [the Divine things]."

He also calls the Holy Eucharist "the[3] consecration of consecrations." He says, that "scarce any Hierarchic consecration can be perfected, unless the most Divine Eucharist, at the head of whatsoever is, in detail, celebrated, by its sacred operation gathereth into one that which is consecrated, and through the God-delivered gift of the perfective mysteries, worketh the communion with God." The consecration itself he speaks of in this veiled language:

"The Hierarch, having celebrated the holy operations of God, consecrates the most Divine things, and brings under sight those things which are celebrated through the symbols which are sacredly set forth, and having exhibited the gifts of the Divine Operations, he himself goeth to the holy Communion of these things, and exhorts others [to partake]."

A Divine Presence in the elements seems to me also implied in this comparison[4];

<hr>

[2] § 1.   [3] iii. 1.   [4] § 3, p. 286.

"The [5] Divine Blessedness, which is above all things, although, in Divine Goodness, It comes forth to the Communion of those who partake of Its Holy Things, yet doth not depart from its Essential Immoveable Stability and fixedness; and shineth, in their proportion, upon all who have the Divine likeness, while abiding ever in Itself, and not removed any way from Its own Sameness of Being; so the Divine Sacrament of the Communion, although having one, simple, compact Principle, is, out of love for man, multiplied into the holy variety of the symbols, and reacheth to whatsoever beareth the traces of the Divine Image, yet from all these gathereth Itself together again into Its own proper Unity, and [gathereth] in one those who are sacredly led to It."

He speaks also of " the supernatural consecration of Divine things," of " the [6] sight and communion of the All-Holy Things," being " most reasonably withdrawn from the Energumens." The doctrine of the Real Presence is implied throughout ; although it is difficult to draw out in proof what is purposely veiled.

65 e. PRUDENTIUS.

A Spanish layman, born at Saragossa, A.D. 348; first lawyer, then in the army, twice " Prætor of noble cities ;" made Præfectus Militiæ, and so next to the Emperor; retired in his 57th year. Like S. Augustine, he led an early life of which he repented ; but does not say when he was converted. He began a *more* religious life, and to

[5] § 7, p. 292.   [6] p. 291.

write Christian poetry, A.D. 404. (Præf. to his Cathemerinon.)

A few words in Prudentius' hymn on the Martyr Eulalia, are commonly quoted as containing the doctrine of the Real Presence. Her bones, as was usual, were placed under the Altar. Prudentius says, "She, placed beneath the Feet of God, looks forth on these things," "Illa, Dei sita sub pedibus, Prospicit hæc." It is supposed that in like way as God says, "Heaven is My throne, and earth is My footstool," and "Fall down before His footstool, for it " or "He is Holy;" so here, the Martyr was said to be under the Feet of God, because the Body of Christ was, at times, sacramentally on the Altar. But Prudentius himself speaks in another hymn, of the *souls* beneath the heavenly Altar (Rev. vi. 10). This agrees better with the word "prospicit;" and in this very place, the martyr herself is spoken of, rather in contrast with the bones there buried.

66. S. Cyril of Alexandria.

Succeeded his uncle Theophilus as Archbishop, A.D. 412; restored the name of S. Chrysostom to the diptychs, A.D. 419; began writing against Nestorius, A.D. 429; President of the third General Council, at Ephesus, A.D. 431; died A.D. 444. His Epistle against Nestorius was adopted as a statement of faith by the Council of Ephesus. (P. ii. Act. i. T. iii. p. 991 sqq. ed. Col.) The Bishops at Ephesus exclaimed, " to Cyril, a new Paul." (Ib. Act. ii. p. 1147.) The celebrated Epistle of S. Leo was accepted by many of the Bishops at the Council of Chalcedon, as " agreeing with the faith set forth by the fathers at Nice and Constantinople, and the Epistle of the most blessed and holy Cyril ' our most holy Father Cyril' confirmed at Ephesus. (Act. iv. T. iv. p. 1385 sqq. ed. Col.)

"For [7] the last sign to the world was the Death of Christ, and the purification by water and Blood, the Holy Body also being joined thereto. . . . Not dumb is the Mystery of Christ, but it calls all men throughout the whole world, with loud and piercing cry, to the purification through water and Blood, and indeed to quickening too, after the participation of the holy Flesh."

"They [8] anointed the door-posts with the blood, according to the law ordained them by Moses; but the Mystery of Christ they made, as it were, an armour and fortification of their souls. For the Death of Christ is the medicine which dissolveth death; and the partakers of the mystic Eucharist are mightier than destruction, according to that, 'Verily, verily, I say unto you, he that eateth My Flesh, and drinketh My Blood, hath everlasting life.'"

"*We* [9] live in the time of the Holy Table, *i. e.* the mystical Table of Christ, whereon we eat the life-giving Bread from Heaven; and so death, aforetime dreadful and irresistible, hath been destroyed, God having been entreated. And the destroyer was hardly put to shame. For when he would fain have put forth his destroying hand against those too who

[7] De Adorat. in Sp. et Ver. L. ii. p. 73.   [8] p. 79.
[9] iii. p. 97.

inhabit the holy city, the spiritual Jerusalem, God being entreated, then at length was he hardly restrained. 'It is enough,' saith He, 'stay now thine hand.' But the holy city is the Church, whose inhabitants they are, who are perfected unto holiness through the living Bread."

"Hath [1] it not been clearly pointed out [through the shewbread] that our Bread from Heaven should lie at due seasons upon the holy Tables of the Churches, giving life to the world? Pallad. Yea, very clearly."

"The [2] Flesh is holy Food for them who have been chosen to the service of God. It is given together with unleavened bread, no stranger partaking of it, or, if he did so, he was to be put to death. For the partaking of the holy Food, that is, of the Body of Christ, befitteth holy souls, and the blessing is unapproachable by an alien. But by the alien is meant the yet infidel and unbaptized generation, and, further, those perverted to an alien mind, inconsistent with the mind of the saints, and as it were severed off by wickedness of doctrine. All that remains of this sacrifice is consumed in the fire; the Law not suffering to eat it on the morrow. For I suppose we shall have another kind of sanctification in the life to come, no longer corporeally, but spiritually inwrought, as God knoweth who transfashioneth all things, and transposeth them as He wills."

[1] L. ix. p. 297.　　　　　　　[2] L. xi. p. 398.

" They [3] who are still liable to secret infirmities in the mind within, will partake of the Blessing [Eucharist] of Christ, and yet not, as it were, in the rank of the saints, for increase of holiness, and stablishment of mind, and patience rooted in all excellence, but, as it were, in a manner suited to the sick, for the putting away of evil, and ceasing of sin, and mortification of pleasures, and recovery of spiritual health. For since Christ is a new creation, according to the Scriptures, we too thus receive Him in ourselves through His holy Body and Blood, that being transelemented to newness of life through Him and in Him, we might 'put off the old man, which is corrupt according to the deceitful lusts,' as it is written."

" The [4] Table having the shewbread signifieth the Unbloody Sacrifice, through which we consecrate, when we eat the Bread from Heaven, that is, Christ, Who was born among us, yet, thus also, was and is God, both coming from above and from the Father, and being above all, as being King and Lord of all."

" These [5] will be types of Christ, Who was sacrificed for us, and endured death that He might take away the sin of the world. But the sin-offerings were to be eaten by the priests only. For not for unhallowed souls is it fit to partake of the holy Body of Christ, but for the chosen and pure, to whom one

---

[3] L. xii. p. 419. [4] L. xiii. p. 457.

[5] p. 464.

might say, 'Ye are a chosen generation, a royal priesthood, an holy nation, a peculiar people.'"

"That[6] he who has been made partaker of Christ, through partaking of His Holy Flesh and Blood, ought also to have His Mind, and follow His inward acts, clearly understanding what is incumbent upon him, he straightway showed, saying, 'that the head must be eaten with the feet, and with the inwards.' For have we not said, that the 'head' is clearly a type of understanding; that the 'feet' every where signify progress as in action; and again, the 'inwards' of the sacrifice are the things within and hidden?"

"It[7] is senseless to suppose, that Adam, being earth-born and a man, should transmit the power of the curse which came upon him, as a sort of inheritance, extending by way of nature to his whole race: but that He Who is from above and from Heaven, and is God by Nature, Emmanuel, and Who hath a likeness to us, and was born the second Adam for us, should not make those who should choose by faith to partake of fellowship with Him, to share richly of His own Life. For we have become of one body with Him through the Mystic Eucharist."

"After[8] slaying it, He orders to anoint with the blood the posts of the dwellings and the jamb, will-

---

[6] L. xvi. p. 596.

[7] Glaph. in Gen. L. i. p. 11. Some lines just preceding have been given above, p. 203.

[8] In Ex. L. ii. pp. 270, 271.

ing, as seems to me, to signify nought else, than that by the holy and precious Blood of Christ, we make our earthly habitation, *i.e.* our body, secure, driving out thence the deadness from transgression through partaking of life. For the partaking of Christ, is life and holiness. And troubling the destroyer himself, as, through the anointing, driving very far from us the devil who plots against us, we mortify the passions arising from carnal motions. You will understand the doors of our aforesaid house, to wit our senses."—"The Prophet Joel mentions these doors, saying, 'They shall enter in at our doors as thieves.' For they were not anointed with the Blood of Christ. He commands the Flesh to be eaten in that night, *i.e.* in the present life. For so Paul too calls it, saying, 'The night is far spent, the day is at hand.' Here plainly calling the life to come, 'day,' whereof Christ Himself is the Light. They 'eat' then 'the Flesh' in this life. For while we are in this world, we shall, in a more sensible way, through the holy Flesh and Blood, partake of Christ. But when we arrive at 'the day of His Power,' as it is written, and mount up to the brightness of the saints, we shall again be sanctified after another sort, and as the Dispenser and Giver of the good things to come knoweth. In another way also the participation of the holy Flesh, and the Drink likewise, which is of the Saving Blood, confesseth the Passion and the Death of Christ, which He underwent according to the Dispensation. For so He saith to His friends, when laying down rules for the Mystery; 'For as oft as ye eat this Bread, and drink this Cup, ye show forth My Death.' In the present life then, through participation of what I have just named, we do, as is meet, show forth His Death."

" Perhaps⁹ this (Ps. xxiii. 5) is said by believers that thou hast prepared for us a spiritual Table, that we, eating and receiving strength, may be able to meet those who at any time trouble us. For the Spiritual Food, strengthening the soul, makes it resist both unclean spirits, and teachers of error; yea, the mystical Table, the Flesh of the Lord, makes us strong against passions and devils. For Satan fears those who reverently partake of the mysteries."

" The ¹ tongue of the dogs, again the unclean heathen, tasted the Undefiled Blood, when they turned to Him from the devil."

" 'If² any man thirst,' saith He, 'let him come to Christ, and drink,' receiving the plenteous consolation through the Holy Ghost, and grace, and most pure sacraments. And he shall receive, not buying with money, but delighting in the most unbounded munificence of Him Who invites him. Approaching, he saith, or coming, and, as it were, bounding from one place to another, that is, from the deceit of old to the knowledge of the truth. 'Buy and drink

---

⁹ Id. in Ps. xxii. 5 [LXX.]. Mai Bibl. Nov. ii. 213.
¹ Id. in Ps. lxvii. 24. Ib. p. 386.
² In Is. L. v. T. ii. p. 773.

without money and without price.' How then do they buy at once, and receive freely and without money? We receive grace from Christ, as a requital of our faith, paying down nought of things temporal and perishable. For one saith, 'I said to my Lord, Thou art my God: my goods are nothing unto Thee.' But in place of gifts and prizes, we offer to Christ the confession of our faith in Him. 'Without money therefore, and without price,' is this drink, and the most abundant largess of graces from Him. But what do we pay, and what kind of drink do we buy? 'Wine,' he saith, and besides, 'food of fat and of wheat.' And doubtless, the plenteous gift of the graces from Christ rejoiceth the soul, and becometh to her spiritual wine. And indeed the fat too, that is the food. For it strengtheneth her, and maketh her most strong. Not incredible is it that the force of these verses before us glances at the Mystery of Christ. For they who have drunk of the living water, *i.e.* have been enriched with the grace of the Spirit, through participation of Him, and who have bought this through faith, will become partakers both of wine and fat, that is, of the Holy Body, and the Blood of Christ."

"The [3] wild feed with the tame. Christ 'the Living Bread Which came down from Heaven, and giveth life to the world,' is their Food. He feedeth us both with His own Flesh, reforming us to in-

[3] L. v. T. vi. p. 907.

corruption and life, and, with His own, *i.e.* the Evangelic, preaching. 'For not by bread alone,' saith He, 'shall man live, but by every word that proceedeth out of the Mouth of God.'"

" Not[4] in the Roman world alone has the Gospel been preached. It traverses even the barbarous nations. Every where are Churches, pastors and teachers, guides and teachers of the Mysteries, and Divine Altars. Spiritually the Lamb is sacrificed by the holy priests even among the Indians, and Æthiopians."

" He[5] found man reduced to the level of the beasts. Therefore was He laid in a manger, as it were Food; that we men, having changed our brutish life, might recover the understanding befitting a man: and that we, brutish in soul, coming to the manger, His Table, might find no longer fodder, but the Bread from Heaven, the Body of Life."—" Since Bethlehem is interpreted the 'house of bread,' where should the shepherds, after the preaching of peace, be assembled, rather than at the spiritual house of the heavenly Bread, that is, the Church? wherein mystically, 'the Bread Which came down from Heaven and giveth Life to the world,' is daily sacrificed."

" One[6] may see, the Truth Itself witnessing thereto, that not to man, born of a woman, being

[4] In Zeph. T. iii. p. 617.
[5] In Luke ii. 7.   Mai Bibl. Patr. Nov. ii. 124.
[6] Ib. iv. 38, p. 167.

considered apart by himself, did the Only Begotten give His Glory, but, as being One Son, together with the Holy Body united to Him, He wrought the miracles; and is worshipped by the creation as God. He entered accordingly into Peter's house, where his wife was laid on a bed, consumed by a severe fever; and He, being able to speak as God, 'Lay aside thy fever and rise,' did not do this: but showing that His own Flesh had power to healing, (since it was the Flesh of God,) He took her by the hand, and 'immediately,' saith he, 'the fever left her.' But let us also receive Jesus. For when He cometh into us too, and we receive Him into our mind and heart, then will He quench the fever of strange pleasures, will raise us up, and make us spiritually strong, so as to minister to Him, *i. e.* to fulfil those things which please Him.

" Consider again how great profit the touch of His holy Flesh hath. For It driveth away even divers diseases, and many devils, and overthroweth the power of the devil, and healeth such a multitude in one moment of time. And though He could by word and will accomplish the miracles, yet that He may teach us needful lessons, He layeth His Hands also upon the sick. For we needed to learn, that the holy Flesh bore the efficacy of the power of the Word, Which [Flesh] He made His own, having implanted a Divine power therein. Let It then touch us also, yea rather, we It, through the Mystic Eucharist, that It may deliver us too from sickness

of our souls, and from the inroad and lawless might
of the devils."

" ' I will ' not taste,' saith He, ' of such a passover,'
i. e. that which was typically signified by food, ' until
it be fulfilled in the kingdom of God :' pointing out
the time when the kingdom of Heaven is preached.
For it is fulfilled in us, who reverence a worship
above the law, the true Passover.   And not a lamb
out of the flock sanctifies those who are in Christ,
but rather Himself holily sanctified through the
Mystic Eucharist, wherein we are blessed and quickened: for He hath become to us ' the Living Bread,
Which came down from Heaven, and giveth Life
unto the world.' "

" He[7] gives thanks, *i.e.* in the form of prayer,
He converseth with God the Father, showing that
He, as it were, joined in and co-approved of the
Life-giving Eucharist which was to be given to us.
For every grace and every perfect gift cometh down
to us from the Father through the Son in the Holy
Spirit.   But what He did then was a pattern to our-
selves of that prayer which must be sent up, if the
grace of the mystical and Life-giving Offering was to
be set forth by us, which also we are wont to do.
For sending up the thanksgiving, and praising the
Son with the Holy Spirit together with God the
Father, we approach to the Holy Table, believing
that thus we are quickened and blest both in body

[7] Ib. c. xxii. 14, p. 413.   [8] Ib. xix. p. 414.

and soul. For we receive in ourselves the Word of God the Father, Who for us became Incarnate, Who is Life and Life-giving. Then let us inquire, as we can, what is the meaning of the Mystery given us. The God of the universe created all things to be immortal, and the generations of the world are healthful, but by envy of the Devil death entered into the world; for he led the first man into transgression and disobedience, and for this cause under the Divine curse. For it was said to him, 'Dust thou art and unto dust shalt thou return.' But the tender love of the Creator transcended the mischief of his waywardness; for He came to the succour of those on the earth. For God the Father, Who is Life by Nature, sent forth as His Brightness, Christ being Himself also Life. For the Word, Who goeth forth essentially from Life, could not be otherwise. God the Father begetteth then to life all things through the Son in the Holy Spirit. How then was man upon earth, mastered by death, to return to incorruption? it needed that the dead flesh should become partaker of the Life-giving power from God. But the Life-giving power of God the Father is the Only Begotten Word. Him He sent to us as a Saviour and Redeemer, and He became Flesh, not undergoing change or conversion into that which He is not, nor again departing from being the Word; but rather, born after the flesh of a woman, and making His own the body from her, that He might insert Himself into us by an indissoluble union, and might make us superior to death and destruction. For He clad Himself with our flesh, that, raising it from the dead, He might make a way for the flesh which was brought back from death to a return to Immortality: as Paul saith, 'For since by man came death, by Man came also the resurrection of the dead. For as in Adam all die, even so in Christ shall all be made alive.' He then, having united with Himself the flesh subject to death, being God the Word and Life, expelled from it corruption, and made It Life-giving also. Doubt not of what I say, but rather receive the Word in faith: from little examples gathering a full assurance in this matter. For when you put a little bread into wine or oil, or any liquid, you will find it full of its quality. When iron meeteth fire, then it is filled with its efficacy, and being iron in its own nature, conceives the power of fire. So then the Life-giving Word of God, having united Himself with His own Flesh, in what way He Himself knoweth, made It Life-giving. For He Himself saith, 'Verily, verily, I say unto you, he that believeth on Me hath everlasting life.' And again, 'I am the Living Bread Which came down from Heaven. If any man eat of this Bread, he shall live for ever. And the Bread which I will give is My Flesh. Verily I say unto you, unless ye eat the Flesh of the Son of man, and drink His Blood, ye have no life in you.' So then, eating the Flesh of Christ, the Saviour of us all, and drinking His Precious Blood, we have life in us, being made one thing with Him and abiding in Him, and having Him also in ourselves. He must needs then be in us through the Holy Ghost after a divine sort; and also be mingled, as it were, with our bodies, through His holy Flesh and His Precious Blood; Which we also had for a Life-giving Blessing, as in bread and wine. For in order that we should not be horrified, seeing flesh and blood set out on the holy tables of our churches, God condescending to our infirmities, sendeth [9] forth the power of life into the elements, and transfers them into the efficacy of His own Flesh: that we might have them for life-giving participation, and that the Body of life might be found in us a life-giving seed. And doubt not that this is true, since He clearly saith, 'This is My Body and This is My Blood;' but rather receive in faith the Word of the Saviour; for being Truth, He doth not lie."

"Believe [1] not, that that bread [the Manna] was the bread from Heaven. For 'I am that Bread of life,' Who of old was fore-announced to you, as in promise, and shown, as in type, but now am present, fulfilling the promise to which I am a debtor. 'I am the Bread of life,' not bodily bread which cutteth off the suffering from hunger only, and freeth the body from the destruction therefrom, but re-moulding the

---

[9] ἐνίησι τοῖς προκειμένοις δύναμιν ζωῆς, καὶ μεθίστησιν αὐτὰ πρὸς ἐνέργειαν τῆς ἑαυτοῦ σαρκός.

[1] On the words, 'I am the Bread of life,' S. John vi. 34, T. iv. p. 322, ed. Aub.

s s 2

whole living being wholly to eternal life, and making man who was formed to *be*, superior to death.   By these words he points to the life and grace through the Holy Flesh, through which this property of the Only-Begotten, *i.e.* life, is introduced into us. Since [2] then we have been called to the kingdom of Heaven by Christ (for this and nought else, I deem, it pointeth to, that some entered into the land of promise), then that typical manna no longer belongeth to us (for we are no longer nourished by the letter of Moses), but the Bread from Heaven, *i.e.* Christ nourishing us unto eternal life, both through the supply of the Holy Spirit, and the participation of His Own Flesh, which infuseth into us the participation of God, and effaceth the deadness which cometh from the ancient curse."

"What [3] then doth Christ promise?   Nothing corruptible, but rather that Eucharist in the participation of His Holy Flesh and Blood, which restoreth man wholly to incorruption, so that he should need none of the things which drive off the death of the flesh, food and drink.   The Holy Body of Christ then, giveth life to those in whom It is, and holdeth them together unto incorruption, being commingled with our bodies.   For we know it to be the Body of no other, but of Him which is by nature life, having in itself the whole virtue of the united Word, and inqualitied ($\pi\epsilon\pi o\iota\omega\mu\acute{\epsilon}\nu o\nu$) yea or rather, filled with

---

[2] Ib. 323.   [3] p. 324.

His effectuating Might, through which all things are quickened, and retained in being. But since these things are so, let those who have been baptized and have tasted the Divine Grace, know, that if they go sluggishly or hardly at all into the Churches, and for a long time keep away from the Eucharistic gift through Christ, feigning a pernicious reverence, in that they will not partake of Him sacramentally, they exclude themselves from eternal life, in that they decline to be vivified. For rather ought they urgently to gather up the implanted power and purpose, and so to be resolute [γοργοὶ] to clear away sin, and essay to lead a pure life, and so to hasten with all boldness to the participation of Life. Breaking off then the bond of Satan, and shaking off the yoke of covetousness cast upon us, let us serve the Lord with fear, and approach to that Divine and Heavenly Grace, and ascend unto the holy participation of Christ; for thus, then, shall we overcome the deceit of the Devil, and, having become partakers of the Divine Nature, shall mount up to life and incorruption."

"Christ [*] then gave His Own Body for the life of all; but again through It He maketh life to dwell in us; and how, I will say as I am able. For when the life-giving Word of God dwelt in the flesh, He transformed it (μετεσκεύασεν) into His own proper good, *i.e.* life, and by the unspeakable character of

[*] Ib. 51, l. iv. c. 2, p. 354.

this union, coming wholly together with It, made It life-giving, as Himself is by nature. Wherefore the Body of Christ giveth life to all who partake of It. For It expels death, when It cometh to be in those subject to death, and removeth corruption, producing by Itself perfectly (ὠδίνον ἐν ἑαυτῷ) that Word which abolisheth corruption."

"If[5] thou persisteth, O Jew, saying 'How?' I too will imitate thine ignorance, and say to thee, 'How' camest thou out of Egypt? or 'How,' tell me, was the rod of Moses changed into a serpent? 'How' became the hand leprous and was again restored, as it is written? 'How' was the water changed (μετέστη) into the nature of blood? 'How' passedst thou through the Red Sea, as through the dry land? 'How' was the bitter water of Mara changed (μετεσκευάζετο) into sweet? or 'how' was water supplied to thee from the breasts of the rock? 'How' was the manna brought down to thee? or 'how' stood the Jordan in one place? or 'how' through a shout alone was the impregnable wall of Jericho shattered? And will that '*how?*' never fail thee? For thou art detected, already amazed at many mighty works, to which if thou appliest that '*how,*' thou wilt wholly disbelieve all Divine Scripture, and wilt overthrow all the words of the Holy Prophets, and, above all, the holy writings of Moses himself. It were meeter far, that, believing in Christ and

---

[5] Ib. 53, pp. 359, 360.

assenting unhesitatingly to His words, ye should zealously learn the mode of that blessing, and not say inconsiderately, like men stupified with wine, ' How can *this* Man give us His Flesh to eat ?' The very word 'this Man,' they say in disdain."

" Wholly [6] destitute of all share and taste of that life which is in sanctification and bliss, are they who do not through the mystical Eucharist receive the Son. For He is Life by Nature, inasmuch as He was begotten of the Living Father. But no less vivifying also is His Holy Body, being in a manner brought together (συνενηνεγμένον) and ineffably united with the all-vivifying Word. Wherefore It is accounted His, and is conceived as one with Him. For, since the Incarnation, It is inseparable; save that we know that the Word which came from God the Father, and the Temple from the Virgin, are not indeed the same in nature; for the Body is not consubstantial with the Word from God. Yet It is one by that ineffable coming-together and concurrence. And since the Flesh of the Saviour became life-giving, (as being united to That which is by nature Life, the Word from God,) then, when we taste It, we have life in ourselves, we too being united with It, as It to the indwelling Word. For this cause also, when He raised the dead, the Saviour is found to have operated, not by word only, or God-befitting commands, but He laid a stress on employing His

[6] Ib. 54, p. 361.

Holy Flesh as a sort of co-operator, for this especial end, that He might show that It had the power to give life; and was, as it were, already made one with Him. For it was indeed His Own Body and not another's. When, for instance, He raised the little daughter of the chief of the Synagogue, saying, ' Maid, arise,' He laid hold of her hand, as it is written. For giving life, as God, by His All-Powerful command, and, again, giving life through the touch of His Holy Flesh, He showed that there was one kindred operation through both. When He went into the city called Nain, and one was being carried out dead, the only son of his mother, again He touched the bier, saying, ' Young man, I say unto thee, arise.' Thus He gave not to His Word only power to give life to the dead, but that He might show that His Own Body was life-giving (as I have said already), He touched the dead, thereby also infusing life into those already decayed. But if by the touch alone of His Holy Flesh, He giveth life to that which is decayed, how shall we not profit yet more richly by the life-giving Eucharist, when we taste It? For It will transform altogether into Its own good, *i. e.* immortality, those who partake of It. Marvel not hereat, nor inquire in Jewish manner, ' how ? ' "

" In ' an unspeakable manner then, and passing human understanding, the Word, united to His Own

' On 55, p. 363.

Flesh, and having, as it were, transformed It all into Himself (according to the operation which lieth in His power of quickening things lacking life), hath cast out the corruption of our nature, and hath driven forth too death which of old prevailed by means of sin. He therefore that 'eateth the Holy Flesh of Christ, hath eternal life.' For the Flesh hath in Itself the Word Which is by Nature Life. Wherefore He saith, 'I will raise him up at the last day.' Instead of saying, 'My Body shall raise him up,' *i.e.* him that eateth It, He hath put 'I'; not as though He were other than His Own Flesh, and not altogether [One] by Nature. For after the Union He cannot be severed into a duality of Sons. 'I, then,' He saith, 'being in Him will by Mine Own Flesh raise up him who eateth thereof, in the last day.' For since Christ is in us by His Own Flesh, we must altogether rise. For it were incredible, yea rather, impossible, that Life should not make alive those in whom It is. For as if one buried a spark amid much stubble, in order to keep alive the seed of fire, so also our Lord Jesus Christ hideth in us life through His Own Flesh, or inserts it as a seed of immortality, abolishing all corruption in us."

"For [5] as if one joineth wax with wax, he will see the one in the other, in like manner, I deem, he who receiveth the Flesh of our Saviour Christ, and drinketh His Precious Blood, as He saith, is found

<hr>

[5] Ib. 57, pp. 364, 365.

as one substance with Him (ἓν ὡς πρὸς αὐτὸν), commingled as it were and immingled with Him (συνανακιρνάμενος ὥσπερ καὶ ἀναμιγνύμενος αὐτῷ) through the participation, so that he is found in Christ, and Christ again in him.   As then Paul saith that a little leaven leaveneth the whole lump, so the least portion of the consecrated elements blendeth (ἀναφύρει) our whole body with itself, and filleth it with its own mighty working, and thus Christ cometh to be in us, and we in Him.   Decide then to lead a holier life, in harmony with Christ's law, and so receive the Eucharist, believing that it hath power to expel, not death only, but the diseases in us [*i.e.* in the soul].   For Christ *thus coming to be in us* (ἐν ἡμῖν γεγονὼς) lulleth the law which rageth in the members of the flesh, and kindleth carefulness to Godward and deadeneth passions."

" *That* " was not the true Food and Bread from Heaven, that *is;* but the Holy Body of Christ, Which nourishes to immortality and life everlasting, will be the true Food.   'But they drank also water from the rock.'   'And what then,' he says, 'or what profit to them who drank? for they are dead.'   That too then was not true drink; but true Drink in truth is found to be the Precious Blood of Christ, which uproots utterly all corruption, and dislodges death which dwelt in the flesh of man.   For it is not merely the blood of a chance man, but of That

* On 56, p. 364.

Which is by Nature Life.   Wherefore we are entitled both 'the body' and 'the members of Christ,' as receiving through the Eucharist the Son Himself in ourselves."

"When [1] the Son saith that He was sent, He signifieth His Incarnation and nothing else.   But by Incarnation we mean, that He became wholly Man. 'As then the Father,' He saith, 'made the Man, and since I was begotten of that which is, by nature, Life, I, being God the Word, live, and, having become Man, filled My Temple, that is, My Body, with Mine Own Nature, so then, in like manner, shall he also who eateth My Flesh, live by me.   For I took mortal Flesh : but, having dwelt in it, being by nature Life, because I am of the living Father, I have re-elemented (ἀνεστοιχείωσα) it wholly into My Own Life.   The corruption of the flesh conquered not Me, but I conquered it, as God.   As then (for again I say it, unwearied, since it is to profit), although I was made flesh (for the 'being sent' meaneth this), again I live through the living Father, that is, retaining in Myself the natural excellence (εὐφυΐαν) of Him who begat Me, so also he, who, by the participation of My Flesh, receiveth Me in himself shall live, being wholly and altogether transelemented (μεταστοιχειούμενος) into Me, Who am able to give life, because I am, as it were, of the life-giving Root, that is, God the Father.' "

[1] Ib. 58, iv. 3 init. p. 366.

"From [2] utter ignorance, certain of those who were being taught by Christ the Saviour, were offended at His Words. For when they heard Him saying, 'Verily, verily, I say unto you, except ye eat the Flesh of the Son of Man, and drink His Blood, ye have no life in you,' they supposed that they were invited to some brutish savageness, as though they were enjoined inhumanly to eat flesh, and to swallow blood, and were constrained to do things, which are dreadful even to hear. For somehow they understood not the beauty of the Mystery, and that most beautiful dispensation, devised for it. Besides this, they reasoned thus with themselves: 'How can the human body implant in us everlasting life, and what can a thing of nature like with ourselves avail to immortality? Christ therefore, understanding their thoughts, (for all things are naked and bared in His Eyes,) heals them again, leading them by the hand manifoldly to the understanding of those things of which they were ignorant. 'Very foolishly,' saith He, 'are ye offended at My Words. For if ye cannot yet believe, albeit oftentimes instructed in the Mystery, that My Body will infuse life into you, how will ye feel,' He saith, 'when ye shall see It ascend even into Heaven? For I do not only promise, that I will ascend even into Heaven itself, that ye may not again say, How? The sight shall be in your eyes, shaming every gainsayer. If then ye shall see,'

---

[2] On 62, p. 374.

saith He, 'the Son of Man ascending into Heaven, what will ye then say? For ye will be convicted of no slight folly. For if ye suppose that My Flesh cannot put life into you, how can It ascend into Heaven like a bird? For if It cannot quicken, because It was not formed to quicken, how will It soar in air, how will It ascend into the heavens? For this too is equally impossible for flesh. But if It ascends contrary to nature, what hinders It from quickening also, even if It was not formed to quicken, in Its own Nature? For He Who hath made That heavenly which is from earth, will also render It Life-giving, according to His Word, even if It was formed to perish."

"It[1] is the Spirit which quickeneth; the flesh profiteth nothing. 'It is not so unreasonable,' He would say, 'that ye supposed the flesh incapable of giving life.' For when the nature of the flesh is considered alone by itself, plainly it is not life-giving. For no created thing can give life. Rather itself is in need of Him Who can produce life. But when the mystery of the Incarnation is carefully considered, and ye then learn Who it is who dwelleth in this Flesh, ye will then be disposed [to receive it] unless you would impute to the Divine Spirit also, that He cannot impart life, although of itself the flesh altogether profiteth nothing. For since it is united to the Life-giving Word, it hath become wholly Life-

---

[1] On 64, p. 376.

giving, rising up to the power of the higher Nature, not itself forcing even unto its own nature Him Who cannot be in any wise subjected. Although then the nature of the flesh is in itself powerless to give life, yet it will inwork this, when it has the life-working Word, and will produce the whole operations of that Word. For it is the Body of That which is by nature life, not of any earthly being, as to whom *that* might rightly hold, 'the flesh profiteth nothing.' For not the flesh of Paul, as it might be, or Peter or any other, would alone work this in us; but only and specially that of our Saviour Christ, in Whom dwelt all the fulness of the Godhead bodily. For it would be most absurd that honey should infuse its own quality into things which naturally have no sweetness, and to transfer into itself (εἰς ἑαυτὸ μετα-σκευάζειν) that wherewith it is mingled, and that the life-giving Nature of the Word of God should not be able to elevate to Its own good that Body in which it dwells. Wherefore as to all other things that will be true, that the flesh profiteth nothing ; but as to Christ alone it holdeth not."

"The[4] true Passover was not that of the Jews, but that of the Christians, who eat the Flesh of Christ, the true Lamb. But those who sinned wilfully or involuntarily were, according to the old rite, previously purified, so no heathen, no uncircumcised, no stranger, no hireling, no defiled person, celebrated

[4] Ib. Fragm. Libb. vii. viii. p. 693.

the typical passover; all which takes place spiritually through Christ."

" What[5] is the cause and efficacy of the mystical Eucharist? Why do we receive It within us? Is it not that It may make Christ to dwell in us corporeally also[6] by participation and communion of His Holy Flesh? Rightly would he answer, I deem. For Paul writes that the Gentiles are embodied (σύσσωμα) with, and co-heirs, and co-partakers of Christ. How are they shown to be 'embodied?' Because, being admitted to share the Holy Eucharist, they become one body with Him, just as each one of the holy Apostles. For why did he (S. Paul) call his own, yea, the members of all, as well as his own, the members of Christ (1 Cor. vi. 15). And the Saviour Himself saith, ' Whoso eateth My Flesh and drinketh My Blood, dwelleth in Me, and I in him.' For here it is especially to be observed, that Christ saith that He shall be in us, not by a certain relation only, as entertained through the affections, but also by a natural participation. For as, if one entwineth wax with other wax, and melteth them by the fire, there resulteth of both one (ἕν τι), so through the participation of the Body of Christ and of His precious Blood, He in us, and we again in Him, are co-united. For in no other way could that which is by nature corruptible be made alive, unless

<hr>

[5] Ib. in xv. 1, L. x. c. 2, p. 862.
[6] ἆρ᾽ οὐχὶ καὶ σωματικῶς ἡμῖν ἐνοικίζουσα τὸν Χριστόν;

it were bodily entwined with the Body of That
Which is by nature Life, the Only Begotten[7]. And
if any be not persuaded by my words, give credence
to Christ Himself, crying aloud, 'Verily, verily, I say
unto you, Except ye eat, &c.' (S. Joh. vi. 53, 54).
Thou hearest now Himself plainly declaring, that,
unless we 'eat His Flesh and drink His Blood,' we
'have not in ourselves,' that is, in our flesh, 'Eternal
Life.' But Eternal Life may be conceived to be, and
most justly, the Flesh of That Which is Life, that is,
the Only Begotten."

"Above[8], we have said, that the union of believers through likeness of mind and soul, ought to
imitate the manner of the Divine Unity, and the
essential identity of the Holy Trinity. But on these
words [as Thou, Father, art in Me and I in Thee,
that they also may be one in Us] we will essay to
show that the oneness, according to which we are
bound to one another and all to God, is in a manner
one of nature; and, may be, not lacking in a bodily
oneness with one another, although our bodies are
different from one another, and each has his own
personal being. There being confessedly a natural
oneness of Father, Son, and Holy Ghost (for one
Godhead in the Holy Trinity is believed and glorified), let us consider in what way we too are found
one, both bodily and spiritually, both towards each

---

[7] εἰ μὴ συνεπλάκη σωματικῶς τῷ σώματι τῆς κατὰ φύσιν ζωῆς,
τοῦτ' ἔστι, τοῦ Μονογενοῦς.

[8] Ib. in xvii. 21, L. xi. c. 11, p. 997.

other and towards God. The Only Begotten, having shone upon us from the very Essence of God the Father, and having in His Own Nature all which the Father is, became Flesh according to the Scriptures, having, as it were, mingled Himself with our nature, through the ineffable concurrence and union with the body which is from the earth. Thus, He, by Nature God, was truly called and became a heavenly Man, not bearing God (as some say who do not accurately understand the depth of the mystery) but being in one, God and Man, having that in a manner, co-united in Himself what by nature was far apart and alien from all sameness of nature, He might make man to communicate in and partake of the Divine Nature. For the communication and abiding of the Spirit passed through to us also, having taken its beginning through Christ and in Christ first, being, as Man, anointed and sanctified, although, being by nature God, (as He appeared from the Father,) He Himself with His Own Spirit hallowed His Own temple and the whole creation made by Him, and whatsoever admits of being hallowed. The mystery of Christ then was made a sort of beginning and way whereby we too might partake of the Holy Spirit, and of oneness with God. For in Christ are we all hallowed in the way afore spoken. In order, then, that we ourselves too, although differing both in souls and bodies through that which is personal to each, might come together and be commingled into an unity with God and one another,

T t

the Only Begotten contrived a way, devised through the Wisdom befitting Him and through the counsel of the Father. For by One Body, His Own, blessing through the Mystical Communion [the Eucharist] those who believe in Him, He makes us incorporate with Himself and with one another. For who should separate and remove from a natural oneness with one another, those who through the One Holy Body are bound up into oneness with Christ? For if we all 'partake of the One Bread,' we are all made 'one Body.' For Christ cannot be divided. Wherefore the Church is called also 'the body of Christ,' and we too 'are members in particular,' according to the mind of Paul. For we all, being united by One Christ through the Holy Body, in that we have received in our own bodies Him, the One and Indivisible, owe our members more to Him than to ourselves. But that, by partaking of the Holy Flesh, we obtain that union with Christ which is in a manner bodily, Paul will testify, speaking of 'the mystery of godliness which in other ages was not made known unto the sons of men, that the Gentiles should be co-heirs, and con-corporate, and co-partakers of His promise in Christ.' But if we are all concorporate with one another in Christ, and not only with one another, but with Himself, in that He is in us through His Own Flesh, how are we not all clearly one, both with each other and with Christ? For Christ is the Bond of Oneness, being in One, God and Man.

" But as to His Oneness in Spirit, we all, having received One and the same Holy Spirit, are in a manner mingled with each other and with God. For although in us, being many, Christ giveth the Father's and His Own Spirit to dwell in each of us, yet is He One and Indivisible, holding together in oneness, through Himself, the spirits, which, in their several existences are severed from oneness, and making all to appear as one in Himself. For as the power of the Holy Flesh maketh those concorporate in whom It is, in like way, I deem, the One Indivisible Spirit of God, dwelling in all, bringeth all together to the Spiritual unity."

" We[9] are united [not only with each other but] with God also. And how, the Lord Himself hath explained. 'I in them, and Thou in Me, that they may be perfected in one' (εἰς ἕν). For the Son cometh to be in us corporeally as Man, commingled and co-united with us by the Mystical Eucharist; but spiritually again as God, by the energy and grace of His Own Spirit re-creating the spirit which is in us, to newness of life and making us partakers of the Divine Nature. Christ then is shown to be the Bond of unity between us and the Divine Nature, binding us to Himself as Man, but, as God, being by nature in God His Own Father. For in no other way could the nature, subject to corruption, rise aloft to incorruption, unless the Nature,

---

[9] Ib. v. 23, xii. 12, p. 1001.

superior to all corruption and change, had descended to it, lightening in a manner that which ever sunk downwards, and raising it to Its own excellences, and, by communion and commingling with Itself, all but uplifting it from the conditions conformable to created nature, and re-forming according to Itself that which is not so of itself. We are perfected into unity with God the Father, through Christ the Mediator. For having received into ourselves, bodily and spiritually, Him Who is by Nature and truly the Son, Who hath an essential Oneness with Him, we, becoming partakers of the Nature Which is above all, are glorified."

"They [1] then who are yet uncircumcised, *i.e.* unclean, ought not to touch the Holy Body, but rather when they have been made clean through the spiritual circumcision. For the circumcision of the heart is in the Spirit, according to the words of Paul. But the circumcision in the Spirit cannot take place in us, if the Holy Spirit doth not dwell in us, through faith and Holy Baptism."

"Most [2] reasonably then [since Christ appeared to His disciples on the eighth day] do we in the Churches make holy assemblies on the Octaves; and if I may speak in a more mystical manner, the thought constraining us uncontrollably, we shut to the doors and Christ appeareth to us all visibly and

[1] Ib. L. xii. pp. 1083, 1086.
[2] Ib. on xx. 16, xxii. pp. 1104, 1105.

invisibly, invisibly as God, and visibly again in the Body, and He permitteth and giveth us to touch His Holy Flesh. For according to the grace of God, we approach to the participation of the mystical Eucharist, receiving Christ in our hands, that we too may firmly believe that He hath truly raised His Own Temple. For that the Communion of the mystical Eucharist is a sort of confession of the Resurrection of Christ, will very readily become clear to any one, by what He Himself said when He accomplished in His Own Person the type of the mystery. For having broken the bread, as it is written, He distributed it, saying, 'This is My Body which is given for you, for the remission of sins. Do this in remembrance of Me.' The participation then of the Holy Mysteries, is a true confession and memorial of His dying and rising again for us and on our account, in addition to our being therefore filled with the Divine Blessing."

"The [3] Word of God, according to the good pleasure of God the Father, took the likeness of sinful flesh, that He might condemn sin in the flesh. For He became man, having condescended to empty Himself; and who can doubt that His Body is like in form and nature to ours? Save that the bodies of all others might be called sinful flesh, on account of the diseases of lawful pleasures, arising by nature

[3] In Ep. ad Rom. viii. 3, ap. Mai Patr. Bibl. Nov. iii. pp. 26, 27.

in us.   But the Body of Christ, one must say, is not sinful flesh (God forbid!), but 'the likeness of sinful flesh;' that is, it was like to our bodies, but knew not the sickness of bodily defilement.   For that Divine Temple was holy from the womb.   As far as relates to conceptions and thoughts of nature, no one would shrink from saying, that since it were flesh, it would have had in itself its own implanted motion. But since the Word which sanctifieth all creation dwelt in it, the power of sin was condemned, that the victory might pass over to us also.   For we partake of Him both spiritually and bodily.   For when *Christ indwelleth in us also, through the Holy Spirit and the mystical Eucharist*, then altogether the law of sin is condemned in us also."

"How[1] should our members be members of Christ?   We have Him in ourselves, sensibly and spiritually.   For He dwelleth in our hearts through the Spirit; and we have partaken also of His Holy Flesh, and we have been hallowed in a twofold way; and He hath dwelt in us as living and life-giving, that He might destroy through Himself the death which had stricken our members.   Since then He is the Head of the body of the Church, we then are severally members of Him.   When then we fall into disgraceful pleasures, then we offend against Him Whose members we are."

"Come[2] as many as delight in the Mysteries, and

---

[1] Id. in 1 Cor. vi. 14.   Mai Bibl. Nov. iii. 56.
[2] Hom. de Myst. Cœna, v. 2, p. 371, ed. Aub.

are partakers of the heavenly calling, having clad
ourselves all-eagerly with the wedding garment,
faith undefiled, let us hasten together to the mystic
Supper. Christ to-day banquets us; Christ to-day
ministers to us; Christ, the lover of mankind, refreshes us. Awful is it to say, awful what is wrought.
The fatted Calf is sacrificed; the Lamb of God
which taketh away the sin of the world is slain.
The Father is gladdened; the Son is willingly
immolated; not now by God's enemies, but by Himself, that He may show, that of His Own free will
was His saving Passion. Ready is the bounteous
Giver of great things; before you are the Divine
Gifts; the mystical Table is prepared; the Life-
Giving Cup is mingled. The King of Glory sends
for you; the Son of God receives you; the Incarnate Word of God exhorts you; the In-existing
Wisdom of God the Father, who built herself a
temple not made with hands, distributes her own
Body as bread, and bestows her life-giving Blood as
drink. O awful mystery! O ineffable dispensation!
O condescension inconceivable! O tenderness un-
searchable! The Creator sets Himself before His
creatures to enjoy; Life Itself gives Himself to
mortals for Food and Drink. 'Come eat ye My
Bread,' He exhorts you, 'and drink ye Wine which
I have mingled for you. I have prepared Myself
for Food; I have mingled Myself for them who
long for Me. Of Mine own will, being Life, I
became Flesh; of Mine own choice I, being the

Word and the In-existing Image of My Father, partook of Flesh and Blood, to save you. Taste and see that the Lord is gracious. Ye have tasted and seen that bitter is the food of a bitter counsellor. Taste now the evil-expelling fruit of obedience, and ye shall know that it is better and more advantageous to obey God. Ye tasted unseasonably and died; taste seasonably and ye shall live. Taste and see that I the Lord am most true. It is not possible from truth to obtain offspring of falsehood, nor from life the blossom of death. For contraries are incompatible. Eat Me, Life, and ye shall live; for this is My Will; eat Life unfailing. For this cause I came, that ye might have life and have it more abundantly. Eat ye My Bread. For I am that Life-giving grain of wheat, and I am the Bread of Life. Drink ye the wine which I have mingled; for I am the draught of immortality. . . . I am Life and the Resurrection. I am the Bread of Life Who came down from Heaven and gave life to men. Receive Me as leaven in your lump, that ye may partake of the life indestructible which is from Me. I am the true Vine. Drink ye My gladness which I have mingled for you. . . . Eat the Bread which reneweth your nature. Drink wine, the delight of immortality. Eat Bread which cleanseth away the ancient bitterness, and drink wine which dulleth the anguish of the wound. This is the medicine of nature; this the chastisement of him who wounded us. For, for you I became as you, not changing My Own Nature, that ye may become, through Me, partakers of the Divine Nature. Be ye changed then with that beauteous change, that ye may be lovely, turning from the world to God, and from flesh to Spirit. I am the true Vine in your race, that ye may in Me yield fragrant fruit. Suck the richness of My Food of immortality, and be ye well-favoured. I, the Lord, am He Who giveth food to all Flesh, but especially to those that fear Me, as David fore-announced, saying, 'Gracious is the Lord and merciful; He giveth food to them that fear Him. . . . Not as they [Israel] eating manna, died in the wilderness, so give I you My Body. For he that eateth this Bread shall live for ever.'"

"Let us go together to the far-famed Zion, and contemplate that citadel, how He Who holdeth the high places of the earth prepareth Himself for that mystical feast; how He who sitteth above the Cherubim, lay down at the supper; how He Who was typically eaten in Egypt, there of His Own Will sacrificeth Himself, and eating the types, as the Fulfiller of the thing typical, manifested the truth, forthwith Himself setting Himself before them, as Food of life, that, to the end of the things prophesied of Him, He, conjoining the beginning of what He had in perfect Wisdom decreed, might bestow the Divine gift of His loving-kindness, to extend by one common appointment for ever to the race of man."

"Hear the holy Gospels. 'As they did eat, Jesus

took bread and brake it,' &c. O marvel, O holy consecration, O Divine Mystery! He led the way by the letter; He perfected them by the Spirit; He taught them by types; He gave grace by deeds." "Again [6] I say, see, beloved, how great the honour of this glorious day! Besides this clear knowledge, ye have the feast, the presence of God, the celebration of the dread Sacrifice, the gift of Immortality, and pledges of endless life. Therefore, my longed for, and ' partakers of the heavenly calling, let us imitate,' as far as possible, ' the Captain and Perfecter of our salvation, Jesus.' Let us long for the lowliness which bears us up on high, the love which unites to God, and the pure faith in these Divine Mysteries."

" Let those praters [who denied our Lord's Divinity], of all the most foolish, tell us, on Whose Body the nurselings of the Church are fed, or by what streams her foster-children are refreshed. If indeed the Body of God is given them, here is Very God, Christ the Lord, and not mere man, nor an angel, as they say, to minister, nor some incorporeal being. And if the Drink be the Blood of God, the Son of God, One of the Adorable Trinity, is not bare God, but God the Word Incarnate. But if the food be the Body of Christ, and the drink the Blood of Christ, and thus mere man according to them, how is it preached that it is eternal life to those who approach the holy Table? How, again, is it divided here

[6] p. 377.

and every where, and is not diminished? For *mere* (ψιλὸν) body never gushes forth with life to them that partake of it." "Therefore let us partake of the Body of Very Life, Which tabernacled for our sakes in our body (as saith the Divine John) 'For the life was manifested.' And again, 'And the Word was made Flesh, and tabernacled among us,' Who is Christ the Son of the Living God, One of the Holy Trinity. And let us drink His Holy Blood for the propitiation of our transgressions, and participation of the immortality in Him, believing at the same time, that He abideth a Priest and Sacrifice, Himself the Offerer and Offered, Receiver and Imparter, not dividing into two persons the Divine and Undivided and Unconfused Unity of the all-honoured Trinity, to Whom be glory and worship with the Father and the Holy Ghost, for ever and ever. Amen."

"There' is One Son, and Lord, the Word, Who took not man by conjunction, so making him partaker of his own dignities and imparting to him of His Sonship and Lordship (as certain babblers say and write); but Himself the Word of God, Light of Light, becoming Man, and being Incarnate. Into His Death are we baptized; He having suffered, as Man, in His Own Flesh, but, as God, remaining Impassible, and Ever Living. For He is Life of Life, God the Father. Thus was death overcome which had dared

---

' Ep. ad Monach. in S. Symbol. v. 2. Epp. p. 189.

to attack the Body of Life. Thus is corruption brought to nought even in us; and the power of death itself is weakened.   Accordingly Christ said, ' Verily, verily, I say unto you, Except ye eat the Flesh of the Son of Man, and drink His Blood, ye have no life in you.'   Life-giving then is the Holy Body and Blood of Christ.   For It is, as I said, the Body not of some man, who is a partaker of life, but rather the Very Body of Him Who is by Nature Life, the Only Begotten.   In these things the whole body of the holy Christ-loving Fathers agree with us, and our most holy and devout brother and co-bishop Proclus himself, who now adorns the Chair of the Holy Church of Constantinople."

"He', being the Life of all, through His unspeakable Birth of the Living Father, is said to receive life among us.   It is nevertheless easy to see that He bestowed on His Own Flesh the glory of His Divine Operation, and again made what belonged to the appropriated Flesh His Own, by an union according to this dispensation, and clothed it with His Own Nature.   But some one will say: Is it not rather befitting to Him Who is really by Nature the Word of God the Father, to come from above, and to be able to quicken from Heaven, those things to which He willeth to give life.   But what? tell me, will any one grant that creation after a Divine sort belongs to human nature?   By no means.

' De Rectâ Fide, pp. 34—36.

What then? He quickeneth us as God: yet not alone by the partaking of the Holy Ghost, but also by setting before us Food, the Flesh of the Son of Man Which He hath taken. For He said, 'Verily, verily, I say unto you, Except ye eat the Flesh of the Son of Man, and drink His Blood, ye have no life in you.' But when the Jews once reviled Him, and undertook, I know not how, to give the preference to the blessed Moses, and said openly, ' Our fathers did eat manna; what sign givest Thou, that we may believe Thee? What dost Thou work, Who hast [Thou sayest] brought down Thy Body to us from above and from Heaven?' He says, ' Verily, I say unto you, Moses gave you not,' &c. ' For the Bread of God is He Who came down from Heaven, and giveth life to the world;' and, in addition, all but pointing with His Finger to Himself as Incarnate, 'I ⁹ am the Living Bread.' &c. Yet how is it not true to say, that the Flesh did not come down from Heaven, but was born of a Virgin, according to the Scriptures? as also it is not the Word that is to be eaten, but He gathereth into one, according to the arrangement of the dispensation, the properties of both Natures. Of this we have countless proofs. For to Nicodemus, when he understood not the Mystery, and ignorantly exclaimed, ' How can these things be?' He said, 'If I have told you earthly things, and ye believe not,

⁹ S. Joh. vi. 51. 56, 57.

how shall ye believe, if I tell you of heavenly
things? And no man hath ascended up into Heaven, but He that came down from Heaven, the Son
of Man, which is in Heaven.' To the Jews, again,
who had the same disease of gross ignorance as
Nicodemus, and who chose to deride Him, I understand not how, because He said that His Own Body
was life-giving, and from Heaven, He said, 'Doth
this offend you? What, and if ye shall see the Son
of Man ascend up, where He was before?' Do we
not say that Immanuel was born of a woman?
Where then was He before? or how did He ascend
up, where, He saith, that He *is*, although the Body
born of the holy Virgin was united to Him? Shall
I not confess that the Flesh from the earth had in
its own nature no power to quicken? How then,
tell me, is the Flesh quickening? or how can that
of earth be understood to be of Heaven too? I say,
by union, the union with the Living Word from
Heaven. For thus shall we think what is very
right, and agreeable to the holy words. For one
and the same is Creator, whether thought of as God,
or as not apart from Flesh."

"*Nest.* Yea ', I will speak those words of offence :
The Lord Christ was speaking with them of His
Own Flesh, 'Except ye eat,' He saith, 'the Flesh
of the Son of Man, and drink His Blood, ye have
no life in you ;' they who heard could not bear the

' Adv. Nest. iv. 5, T. vi. p. 109.

loftiness of the saying, they thought, in their folly, that He was bringing in cannibalism."

" *S. Cyr.* And how is the thing not plain cannibalism, and in what way is the mystery still lofty, unless we say that the Word of God the Father was sent, and confess that the mode of that sending was the Incarnation? For then we shall see clearly that the Flesh being united with Him, and not that of another, can give life, but that it is His Very Own Who can quicken all things. For if this visible fire infuses the force of its natural inherent power into those substances which come in contact with it; and changes water itself, although cold by nature, into that which is contrary to its nature, and makes it hot; what wonder, or how can one disbelieve that the Word of God the Father, Who is Life by Nature, makes the Flesh, Which is united to Him, Life-giving? For it is His Very Own, and not that of another, considered apart from Him and one of us. But if you separate the Life-giving Word of God from the true and mystical union with His Body, and entirely disjoin them, how canst thou show that it is still Life-giving? For Who was He Who said, ' He that eateth My Flesh, and drinketh My Blood, abideth in Me, and I in him?' If it were a mere man, and not rather the Word of God had come among us, the deed were cannibalism, and the participation wholly unprofitable. For I hear Christ Himself saying, 'The flesh profiteth nothing: it is the Spirit that quickeneth.' For as far as pertaineth to its own nature, the flesh is corruptible. In no wise then will it quicken others, having itself the disease of corruption. But if you say it is the Own Body of the Word Himself, why these portentous and vain fables? Why contend, that not the Word of God the Father was Himself sent, but some other instead of Him, that is, a visible being, or His Flesh, albeit the divinely-inspired Scripture every where proclaimeth One Christ, strongly asserting that the Word became Man with us, and defining herein the tradition of the true faith?"

"He[2] [Nestorius] twists, as it seems, my words, to a seeming absurdity and ignorance. 'Let us see,' saith he, 'who it is that misinterprets: As the Living Father hath sent Me; I too live (according to him), God the Word by the Father: and, He that eateth Me, he shall live by Me; Which do we eat, the Godhead or the Flesh?' Seest thou not now, how your mind is gone? For the Word of God Who says that He is sent, says also, 'He that eateth Me, even he shall live by Me.' But we eat, not consuming the Godhead (away with the folly), but the very Flesh of the Word, Which is become Life-giving, because He liveth by the Father: and we do not say that by outward and adventitious participa-

<hr>

[2] p. 110.

tion, the Word quickeneth by the Father, but rather we maintain throughout that He is Life by Nature. For He is begotten of the Father, being Life."

" As[3] the Body of the Word Himself is quickening, He having made It His Own by a true union passing understanding and language; so we too, who partake of His holy Flesh and Blood, are quickened in all respects and wholly, the Word dwelling in us Divinely, through the Holy Ghost, and again, after a human sort, through His holy Body and Precious Blood. The most holy Paul will confirm the truth of what I have said, writing thus to those in Corinth, who believed in our Lord Jesus Christ: 'I speak as to wise men, judge ye what I say: the Cup of blessing which we bless, is it not the Communion of the Blood of Christ? the Bread which we break, is it not the Communion of the Body of Christ? for we, being many, are one Bread and one Body: for we all are partakers of that one Bread.' For having been partakers of the Holy Ghost, we are made one both with Christ Himself the Saviour of all, and with one another: but we are of the same body in this way, that ' we, being many, are one bread, one body, for we all are partakers of the One Bread.' For the Body of Christ which is in us binds us together into unity, and is in no way divided. But that through the Body of Christ we have been brought together into unity with Him and with one another, the

---

[3] Ibid.

blessed Paul will confirm, writing that the 'Gentiles should be fellow-heirs, and of the same body (σύσ-σωμα), and partakers of the promises in Christ.' "

"That[‘] the Mystery is Divine, and the participation quickening, and the might of this unbloody Sacrifice far better than the worship under the law, is easy to see, even from his saying that those things ordained by Moses to them of old time were a shadow, but that Christ is the fulness, and the things of Christ the truth. The most wise Paul too will help us herein, who writes, 'He that despised Moses' law died without mercy under two or three witnesses: of how much sorer punishment, suppose ye, shall he be thought worthy, who hath trodden under foot the Son of God, and hath counted the Blood of the covenant, wherewith he was sanctified, an unholy thing, and hath done despite unto the Spirit of grace?' For they that of old did sacrifice the lamb ate thereof; but the force of the eating was not simply the satisfying of the belly, nor was it for this that the sacrifices were performed under the law; but that, when death fell on the others [the Egyptians] they might overcome it, and might escape the destroyer. And indeed in one night the first-born of the Egyptians were destroyed; but these, guarded in a bare type, alone were saved by it, having the shadow for their shield, and prevailed gloriously over death itself. The types then saved

‘ Ib. p. 112.

those before us. How then is it as to our things,
on whom the Truth itself hath shined, that is, Christ,
Who setteth before us His Own quickening Flesh
to partake of? is it not clear to all? Very wonderfully
better, and with exceedingly superior advantages!
And our Lord Jesus Christ maketh clear the power
of the Mystery (S. John vi. 46—51). For since the
children of Israel marvelled at Moses for the supply
of manna, sent down to those there in the desert,
furnishing a type of the mystic Eucharist (for the
law is a shadow), therefore with exceeding wisdom
doth our Lord Jesus Christ dissipate and diminish the
type to the truth. For He does not say, ' *That* was
the Bread of life,' but rather, ' I from Heaven,' Who
both quicken all things, and infuse Myself into them
that eat Me, through My Flesh united to Me;
Which indeed He made clearer, saying, ' Verily I
say unto you, except ye eat the Flesh of the Son of
Man, and drink His Blood, ye have no life in you,'
&c. (vv. 53—57.) Consider then how He abideth
in us, and maketh us superior to corruption, infusing
Himself into our bodies, as I said, even by His Own
Flesh, Which is the true meat, whereas the shadow
in the law, and the worship under it had no truth
[*i. e.* substance]. And the plan of the Mystery is
simple and true, not overwrought with varied devices of imaginations unto unholiness, but simple, as
I said. For we believe that to the Body born of the
Holy Virgin, having a reasonable soul, the Word of
God the Father united Himself. The union is

unspeakable and altogether a mystery. He made it quickening, being, as God, Life by nature, that, making us partakers of Himself, both spiritually and bodily, He might both make us superior to corruption, and might through Himself destroy the law of sin which is in our members."

" He[5] [Nestorius] by no means understandeth, that we, setting forth the Death of Christ, confessing His Resurrection, and thereby being perfected in our faith, then becoming partakers of His Divine Nature, in that we partake of unity with Him, are sanctified both spiritually and bodily, and are quickened."

" You[6] seem to me to forget that it is by no means the Nature of the Divinity that lieth upon the holy Tables of the Churches, but the Own Body of the Word Begotten of God the Father. But the Word by Nature and in truth, is God. Why then do you confound all things, and jumble them without understanding, all but mocking at our Bread which is from Heaven and giveth life unto the world, because it is not called the Godhead by the voice of Divines, but rather the Body of Him Who became Man for us, that is, of the Word of God the Father? But why, (tell me,) do you call It at all the Lord's Body, save because you know it to be Divine and of God : for all things serve their Maker'[7]?"

[5] Ib. p. 115.

[6] Ib. p. 116.

[7] And so it would not be called " the Lord's Body " as belonging to Him merely, as the Creator. For this would be nothing

"If[8] any one should dare to say that the Word of God was transformed into the Nature of the Body, one might very reasonably object to him, that He, on giving His Body did not rather say, 'Take, eat, this is My Divinity which was broken for you,' and 'This is—not My Blood, but rather—My Divinity which is shed for you.' But since the Word, being God, hath made the Body, born of a woman, His Own, without undergoing any alteration or change, how was it not right and true that He said to us, 'Take, eat, this is My Body?' For being Life, as God, He made It both Life and Life-giving."

"If[9] any one confess not that the Flesh of the Lord is Life-giving, and that it is the Own Flesh of the Word of God the Father, but say that it is of some other than He, joined to Him in dignity, (*i. e.* having, as it were, an indwelling only,) and that it is not rather Life-giving, as we have said, because it is become the Own Flesh of the Word which can quicken all things, let him be Anathema."

Eleventh Explanation.

"We celebrate the holy, and life-giving and un-bloody Sacrifice in the Churches, not believing the Offering to be the Body of one of us, and of a common Man: likewise also the precious Blood; receiving them

distinctive. Since in this sense all bodies belong to Him and might be called His.

[8] Ib. fin. pp. 118, 119.

[9] Expl. xii. Cap. xi. p. 156.

rather as being the Own Body and also Blood of the Word Who quickeneth all things. For common flesh cannot quicken : and the Saviour Himself witnesseth this, saying, 'The flesh profiteth nothing ; it is the Spirit that quickeneth.' For since it became the Own Flesh of the Word, it is so understood, and is quickening, according as the Saviour Himself saith : 'As the Living Father hath sent Me, and I live by the Father, he that eateth Me, even he shall live by Me.' Since Nestorius, and they who agree with him do ignorantly destroy the power of the Mystery, therefore and reasonably is this Anathema."

"We[1] say that it became the Own Body of the Word, and not of some man, conceived of as Christ and Son, separate and distinct from Him. As then the own body of each one of us is said to be the body of himself individually, so too must we understand of the One Christ For albeit it is of like nature with our bodies, that is to say, consubstantial, (for it was born of a woman,) it is, as I said, understood and said to be His Own. But since the Word of God the Father is Life by Nature, He hath made His Own Flesh quickening. Thus He hath become to us a life-giving Blessing [Eucharist]. And indeed Christ saith, 'Verily, verily, I say unto you, I am the Living Bread, Which came down from Heaven, and giveth life to the world.' And again, 'And the Bread, which I will give, is My Flesh for the life of

---

[1] Apol. adv. Or. p. 192.

the world.'   And again, 'He that eateth My Flesh and drinketh My Blood, dwelleth in Me, and I in him.'   Consider then how He every where calls the Body born of a woman His own Body, through the highest degree of union."

"No [2] one, on the ground that the Nature of the Godhead is not eaten, would therefore call the holy Body of Christ common.   Ye should know, that, as we have said already, it is the own Body of the All-quickening Word.   Since It is the Body of Life, It is life-giving.   For therefore It infuseth life into our mortal bodies: as also It destroyeth the power of death."

"He [3] gave us not the sensible manna, but rather Himself as a Holy, Life-giving, and in very deed, all-Holy Food."

"I hear [4] that they say that the mystic Eucharist is unavailing for blessing, if a portion of it remain to the next day.   They are mad who say this.   For Christ is not altered, nor shall His Holy Body be changed: but the power of the Eucharist and the life-giving grace is abiding in it."

I will close these extracts by giving, more fully than the limits of the sermon admitted, the extract from his Synodical letter, approved by the Council of Ephesus.

[2] Ib. p. 193.

[3] c. Julian. viii. P. 2, p. 258.

[4] Ep. ad Calosir. p. 365, also in Maii Auctt. Class. x. 373, note.

"Showing[5] forth the Death according to the Flesh of the Only Begotten Son of God, *i. e.* Jesus Christ, and confessing His Resurrection from the dead and Ascension into the Heavens, we celebrate the unbloody Sacrifice in the Churches; we approach to the Mystic Eucharists, and are sanctified, having become partakers of the Holy Flesh, and the Precious Blood of Christ, the Saviour of us all. And receiving It,—not as common Flesh, God forbid! nor as that of a man sanctified and joined to the Word in unity of dignity, or having a Divine Indwelling; but—as truly Life-giving, and the Flesh of the Word Himself. For He, as God, being, by Nature, Life, when He became one with His Flesh, made It life-giving. So that though He say to us, 'Verily, verily, I say unto you, except ye eat the Flesh of the Son of Man, and drink His Blood,' we shall not account It as the flesh of one of us; (for how shall the flesh of a man be, by its own nature, life-giving?) but as having become truly the own Flesh of Him, Who, for us, became, and was called, the Son of Man."

67. S. Isidore of Pelusium.

So called from the Monastery of Pelusium, where he was Priest and Archimandrite; a disciple and defender of S. Chrysostom. He survived the Council of Ephesus, A.D. 431, which he besought Theodosius the Younger to visit in person, in order to prevent the interference of his Count in sacred things. (L. i. Ep. 311.) "Far-famed among all for deed and word, he so wasted away his flesh by toils, so

[5] S. Cyril. et Synod. Alex. ad Nest. c. 7, T. v. 2, pp. 72, 73.

enriched his soul by elevating doctrines, that he passed an angel's life on earth, and was throughout a living pillar, both of the monastic life, and of the contemplation of God." (Evagr. Schol. i. 15.)

" If [6] our God and Saviour, being made Man, gave the Holy Ghost to be the completion of the Divine Trinity, and as being, in the invocation of Holy Baptism, numbered together with the Father and the Son, as freeing from sins, and as, upon the mystical Table, making the common bread, the Very Body of His Own Incarnation, how dost thou teach, thou senseless one, that the Holy Ghost is made or created, or of servile nature, and not rather akin to, and consubstantial with, the Lordly, Creative, Royal Substance ? "

To Count Dorotheus.   Explanation of the Eucharistic service.

" The [7] fine linen that is spread out underneath the ministry of the Divine gifts, is the ministration of Joseph of Arimathea. For as he, having wrapped the Body of the Lord in fine linen, committed to the tomb that Body, through which our whole race has gained the fruit of the resurrection, so we, consecrating the shewbread upon fine linen, find undoubtedly the Body of Christ, gushing forth for us with that incorruptibility, which He Whom Joseph attended to the tomb, the Saviour Jesus, rising from the dead, bestowed."

[6] Ep. L. i. 109, ad Marathon. p. 34.
[7] L. i. Ep. 123, p. 38.

To Nilus.   Why he commanded to eat the flesh of the lamb roast with fire.

"The[8] Hebrews used to eat the flesh roast with fire, shadowing forth in a type by that eating the great mystery of the Divine dispensation, and learning beforehand of the Lamb of God, Who in an unspeakable manner unites the fire of the Divine Essence with that Flesh which is now eaten by us, and worketh the remission of our sins."

To Count Soranus.   On the Holy Communion.

"The[9] participation of the Divine Mysteries is called Communion, because it gives us oneness with Christ, and admits us to the community of His Kingdom."

"Melchisedech[1], performing the Priest's office with bread and wine, whereby he showed before the type of the Divine Mysteries."

"Through[2] this (the priesthood) we are both born again, and are partakers of the Divine Mysteries, without which we could not be partakers of the heavenly Gifts, according to the unerring oracles of the Truth, which say, at one time, 'Except a man be born of water and of the Spirit, he cannot enter into the kingdom of heaven;' and again, 'Except ye eat My Flesh and drink My Blood, ye have no part with Me.'"

To Nilammon, a deacon.

---

[8] L. i. Ep. 219, p. 64.   [9] L. i. Ep. 228, p. 65.
[1] L. i. Ep. 431, ad Pallad. p. 110.
[2] L. ii. Ep. 52, ad Theodos. Episc. p. 144.

"They[3] who fall, and dare not to approach to the holy mysteries, are right-minded, and will quickly come round to abstain from sin. But they who transgress, and dare to touch the pure mysteries with defiled hands (of whom Zosimus is, as you have written, one), are worthy of manifold punishment. For (according to the true saying of S. Paul), they make themselves guilty of the Body and Blood of the Lord. Wherefore the devil doth not strongly attack those former, knowing that, although they stumble, they are conscious of it, and maintain reverence for the Divine Mysteries. But the latter, who transgress, and know it not, or, knowing, despise, and dare to touch the holy mysteries, he assaults furiously with all his might, with reason thinking this a proof of insensibility and utter corruption. So too he acted to the traitor. For he did not, as you suppose, enter into him, despising the Lord's Body, but having discovered his wickedness, that he was incurably sick. For Judas, with fixed purpose to betray, and yet not declining to receive, went his way. For if Satan had seen Judas reverential towards the Divine Mystery, and declining it, he might perchance have passed him by, as still in his sound mind. But when he saw him dizzied by love of money, and no longer having his right reason, but maddened by unsatiable drunkenness of desire, and not only so,

[3] Lib. iii. Ep. 364, p. 308.

but daring to touch, What he, being such, ought not to have touched, he having discovered that he was 'past all feeling,' entered wholly into him."

" I must ' speak what I would not. Why so mad against thyself? Why hold wickedness with so strong a grasp? Why insult virtue, as far as in thee lies? Why pollute the temples? Why tremble not to burlesque the Divine consecration? Why prepare men, looking at your life, to suppose that even the saving *symbols* are injured thereby? . . . Either cease from doing such things, or sever thyself from the holy Table; that the nurslings of the Church may henceforth come securely to those Divine Mysteries, without which they cannot be saved."

67 b. Theodotus, Bishop of Antioch.
Died a. d. 427.

Theodoret calls him " the pearl of sobriety " [or " chastity "], and says that he was " remarkable for gentleness, and adorned with exactness of life." He succeeded Alexander in the see of Antioch.—(H. E. v. 38, and Ep. 83.)

The following passage was quoted by Bullinger, a Roman Catholic, in his work against Casaubon, from a Greek MS. Aubertin (p. 744) thanks him for it.

" As the king himself and his image are not two kings, neither are the very Personal Body of Christ, which is in heaven (αὐτὸ τὸ Χριστοῦ σῶμα τὸ ἐνυπό-

---

' L. v. Ep. 569, ad Zosim. Presbyt. pp. 722, 723.

στατον) and the bread, the antitype thereof, distributed to the faithful by the priests in the Churches, two bodies."

68. PAULINUS, THE DEACON.

So called, as having been Deacon and notary of S. Ambrose, afterwards Priest; Procurator and defender of the Church of Milan.—(Prædestin. Hær. 88.) Appeared before Council of Carthage, A.D. 412, against Cœlestius, accomplice of Pelagius, wrote the life of S. Ambrose at the desire of S. Augustin.

"Honoratus[5], also priest of the Church at Vercellæ, when he had laid himself down to rest in the upper part of the house, heard three times the voice of one calling him, and saying to him: 'Arise, make haste, for he is now about to depart.' He, going down stairs, offered to the Saint the Body of the Lord: which when he had received and swallowed, he yielded up his spirit, bearing with him good Food for the way: so that his soul, refreshed in the strength of that Food, might now rejoice in the company of the angels, whose life he lived on earth, and in the society of Elias; for as Elias, so he, through fear of God, never feared to speak to kings or any powers."

69. S. MAXIMUS, OF TURIN.

Had seen Martyrs who were put to death A.D. 397. Bishop (it is supposed) about A.D. 412; present at the Council of Milan A.D. 451, to accept S. Leo's tome against

---

[5] Vita S. Ambros. n. 47, ap. S. Ambros. Opp. T. ii. App. p. xii.

Eutyches; at Roman Council A. D. 465; subscribed, on account of his great age, next to Hilary, Bishop of Rome. "Well versed in Holy Scripture" (Gennad.), eminent for practical zeal, and for the conversion of heathen and heretics.

"Yet [6] I should rather call Mary herself the manna, for she is delicate, glorious, sweet, and a virgin: who coming as it were from heaven, poured out a Food sweeter than honey to all people of the Churches, which whosoever shall neglect to eat and drink, cannot have life in himself, as the Lord Himself saith: 'Except ye eat the Flesh of the Son of man, and drink His Blood, ye have no life in you,' but rather that very Food shall turn to condemnation, as the Apostle saith: 'He that eateth and drinketh unworthily, eateth and drinketh damnation to himself.' As was prophesied to the Children of Israel mysteriously in their covenant. For to those who handled the manna contrary to the Divine commands, it bred worms, that is, avengers and punishers of their rebellion; Which setteth forth in a figure Christ the Lord: Whom, the sweet Food and delicious Drink, whoso shall neglect to drink, shall endure as a Judge, as Himself saith: 'For the Father judgeth no man, but hath committed all judgment to the Son.'"

"What [7] can be said more reverent, what more honourable, than that they rest under that Altar, whereon Sacrifice is offered unto God, where the

[6] Hom. Hiem. xlv. in Ps. 21, pp. 138, 139, ed. Rom.
[7] Serm. 73, de Sanctis præcip. S. Cyprian. pp. 599, 600.

Lord is Priest, according as it is written: 'Thou art a Priest for ever, after the order of Melchisedech?' Rightly therefore are the Martyrs under the Altar, since Christ is placed upon the Altar. Rightly do the souls of the righteous rest under the Altar, since on the Altar the Body of the Lord is offered. Nor unfitly is inquisition for blood there required in behalf of the righteous, where even for sinners the Blood of Christ is shed. Fitly then, and as though for a sort of fellowship, was it appointed that the Martyrs should be buried *there*, where the Lord's Death is daily celebrated, as He Himself saith: 'As often as ye do this, ye do show forth My Death, till I come.' So should they who died for His Death, rest under the mystery of His Sacrament. Fitly I say, and as though for a sort of fellowship, is the tomb of him who was slain placed *there*, where the Lord's slain Body is placed, that they whom the cause of one Suffering had bound with Christ, the sanctity of one place might unite. We read that many of the righteous are cherished in Abraham's bosom, and some enjoy the delights of Paradise, yet none obtained more than the Martyrs: that is, to rest, where Christ is both Sacrifice and Priest. So should they obtain propitiation, by the offering of the Sacrifice, and receive the blessing and office of a Priest."

"May[s] they see the spiritual pasture; may they

---

[s] Tract v. contra Judæos, p. 745.

see, if they are worthy, the heavenly Feast, may they see the Lord's Table, and sing with us with the most holy Prophet David, saying: 'The Lord is my Shepherd, therefore can I lack nothing: He shall feed me in a green pasture.'"

70. THEODORET.

Born, it is supposed, about A.D. 386, educated in a monastery near Antioch with Nestorius, and John of Antioch: taught by Theodorus of Mopsuestia and S. Chrysostom; Bishop of Cyrus in Syria A.D. 420; converted and brought to Baptism above 10,000 Marcionites (Ep. 145, ad Monach. Const. iv. 1251); wrote against S. Cyril A.D. 429; formed a Conciliabulum with John of Antioch at Ephesus A.D. 451; and wrote against the Council; reconciled with S. Cyril; deposed at the Conciliabulum of Ephesus; satisfied S. Leo as to his faith; formally restored at Chalcedon after anathematizing Nestorius A.D. 451; died A.D. 457.

Theodoret, while affirming the doctrine of the Real Presence, says distinctly that the Eucharistic elements after consecration do not depart from their own nature, for they remain in their former substance (above pp. 85, 86), and are NOT *changed (pp. 87, 88). He repeatedly calls them "symbols," and also "types, antitypes," and at the same time "the Lord's Body" (pp. 111—113). He regards the Coal in Isaiah's vision as a type of the Holy Eucharist (p. 127). He uses the word "symbol" again, in speaking of Melchisedech's sacrifice, as a type of the Holy Eucharist.*

"Melchisedech [1] was priest, not of the Jews, but

---

[1] In Ps. 109, pp. 1396, 1397.

of the Gentiles: so too the Lord Christ offered Himself to God, not for the Jews only, but also for all men. But He enters on His Priesthood in that night, after which He suffered: when 'He took bread, and, having given thanks, He brake it, and said, Take, eat of it: this is My Body. Likewise also having mingled the Cup, He gave it to His disciples, saying, Drink ye all of this: for this is My Blood, of the New Testament, Which is shed for many for the remission of sins.' But we find that Melchisedech was both priest and king: (for he was a type of the true Priest and King:) and that he offered to God no sacrifices of beasts, but bread and wine. For these also he offered to Abraham, spiritually foreseeing the archetype of his own high priesthood, in the loins of the Patriarch. If then Christ be from David according to the Flesh, and David from Judah: Christ received this Priesthood 'after the order of Melchisedech.' The Levitical priesthood ceased, and the blessing of the greater Priesthood passed into the tribe of Judah. But now Christ is Priest, Who hath sprung from Judah according to the Flesh, not offering ought Himself, but the Head of them who offer. For He calls the Church His Body, and through it, as Man, He exercises the Priest's office; as God, He receiveth the offerings. But the Church offereth the *symbols* of His Body and Blood, hallowing the whole lump through the first-fruits."

And again:

"Having[2] called for a sponge, and having therewith moistened and washed his mouth, he placed upon it the *symbols* of the divine mysteries."

Again, in the context, more than once, after the passage already cited from his first dialogue[3]:

"*Orth.* Knowest[4] thou that the Lord called Himself a Vine? *Eran.* I know that He said, 'I am the true Vine.' *Orth.* What name hath the fruit of the vine when pressed out? *Eran.* It is called wine. *Orth.* When the soldiers with a spear pierced the Side of the Saviour, what do the Evangelists say was shed therefrom? *Eran.* Blood and water. *Orth.* He then called the Blood of the Saviour the blood of the grape. For if the Lord was called a Vine, and the fruit of the vine is called wine, and streams of Blood and water, shed forth from the Lord's Side, poured down over the rest of His Body, reasonably then and meetly did the Patriarch say, 'He washed His Raiment in Blood, and His Clothes in the blood of the grape.' For as we call the mystic fruit of the Vine, after the consecration, the Blood of the Lord, so did Jacob call the Blood of the true Vine blood of the grape. *Eran.* Mystically at once and clearly hath the present argument been proved."

"*Orth.* Since[5] it is agreed that the Lord's Body was called by the Patriarch both 'raiment' and 'clothes,' and we have come to the argument about

---

[2] Rel. Hist. iii. 1269.

[3] Above, p. 87.

[4] Immut. T. iv. pp. 24, 25.

[5] Ib. pp. 26, 27.

the Divine Mysteries, tell me, by the Truth, 'whereof thinkest thou the all-holy Food is a *symbol* and *type ?*' Of the Godhead of the Lord Christ, or of His Body and Blood? *Eran.* Plainly of those things, whose names they have received. *Orth.* Do you mean the Body and Blood? *Eran.* I do. *Orth.* You have spoken as a lover of truth. For the Lord also, when He took the *symbol* did not say, 'This is My Divinity;' but 'This is My Body.' And again, 'This is My Blood.' And in another place, 'The Bread which I will give, is My Flesh, which I will give for the life of the world.' *Eran.* These things are true, for they are Divine Oracles. *Orth.* If then they are true, the Lord indeed had a Body."

Again :

"The [6] Lord Himself promised to give, not His Invisible Nature, but His Body for the life of the world. For, He saith, 'the Bread, which I will give, is My Flesh, Which I will give for the life of the world.' And when delivering the Divine Mysteries, He took the *Symbol* and said, 'This is My Body Which is given,' or 'broken,' according to the Apostle, 'for you.' And no where, in discoursing of His Passion, did He mention the Impassible Godhead."

"His [7] Body He calls 'a garment,' and the Blood 'wine,' since the Lord too has called the mystic [Sacramental] wine ' Blood.' "

[6] Ep. 130, ad Timoth. p. 1218.
[7] In Gen. c. xlix. T. i. p. 115.

x x 2

"He[8] bade them take a bunch of hyssop, and, having dipped it in the blood of the lamb that was sacrificed, to anoint the lintel, and door-posts, that, when the destroyer came in to smite the first-born of Egypt, he, seeing the blood, might pass over the dwellings of the Hebrews. Not that the Incorporeal Nature required such signs, but that through the signs, they might learn the care of God's Providence, and that we, who sacrifice the Spotless Lamb, might know that the type had been described beforehand."

"*Qu.* How[9] is that of the Apostle to be understood, 'They were all baptized unto Moses,—they did all eat the same spiritual meat? (1 Cor. x. 2—4).'

"Old things were the type of new, and the law of Moses was the shadow, but Grace is the body ... Pharaoh is the type of the devil; the Egyptians, of dæmons; the manna, of the Divine Food; the water from the rock, of the saving Blood. For as they, after crossing the Red Sea, enjoyed the strange food and miraculous water, so we after the saving Baptism partake of the Divine Mysteries."

"The[1] crossing took place before the Passover. For they crossed on the tenth day, and celebrated the feast of the Passover on the fourteenth. Since, in truth, after saving Baptism, cometh the partaking of the Lamb without spot."

[8] Qu. 24, in Ex. c. xii. p. 139.
[9] Qu. 27, in Exod. p. 144.
[1] Qu. 2, in Jos. fin. p. 305.

"He[2] [David], by partaking of the things assigned to the Priests alone, prefigures the mystical [sacramental] Table which should be set before all the devout. For not those who are consecrated Priests alone partake of the Lord's Body and Blood, but all who have obtained holy Baptism."

"We[3] know the Divine Food, and the spiritual teaching, and the sacramental and immortal Feast, which the initiated are acquainted with."

"They[4] who have eaten and been filled, giving thanks for the immortal Food, will worship as God Him Who supplieth these things: and since in the verse before he mentioned 'the fat' only, as having been made such by that Divine Word, with reason did he say, 'All they that go down into the dust shall kneel before Him.'"

"The[5] mysteries of Grace were foreshadowed, and the door of the Divine Munificence opened beforehand to believers. For the heavenly Food is no longer confined to the Priests alone, but the partaking of heavenly things is offered to all who will."

"The[6] meaning which lies hid in the depth of the letter hints at the Grace of the Divine Mysteries. For through All-holy Baptism the true illumination is bestowed on those who approach it, and the tasting of the Life-giving Food plainly

---

[2] Qu. 52, in 1 Reg. i. 388. [3] In Ps. xxi. p. 744.
[4] On v. 30, p. 745. [5] In Ps. xxxiii. p. 813.
[6] Ib. p. 815.

shows the goodness of the Saviour. For what so clearly exhibits His love for man as the Cross, and the Passion, and the Death undergone for our sakes, and His being at once the Food and the Well of His own sheep ? "

" 'That ' I might behold Thy Power and Thy glory.' I stand by Thee, meditating on Thy unspeakable Power. For since Thy Nature cannot be attained unto, from Thy acts do I take the occasion of praise. The people which, from the Gentiles, hath believed on Thee will ever say, 'Thus have I appeared before Thee in Thy Sanctuary,' that is, in Thy Temple, where Thou art sacrificed unsacrificed, and divided undivided, and expended remaining unspent."

" Let [8] not any of those who grovel on the ground and cleave to the earth be amazed at the mention of kisses. But let him consider how at the sacramental time when we receive the members of the Bridegroom, we kiss and embrace Him, and by our eyes place them in our hearts, and represent as it were a nuptial embrace, and think ourselves to be with Him, and to embrace Him, and to kiss Him, ' love casting out fear,' according to Holy Scripture."

" Now [9] I know in part; but then I shall know even as I am known. Therefore he saith, 'I delighted and sat under His shadow, and His fruit was

---

[7] In Ps. lxii. 3, p. 1019.   [8] In Cant. c. i. init. ii. 25.
[9] Ib. c. ii. 3 ; ii. 56.

sweet in my throat.' For sitting under the shade I pluck the fruit, and partake of it.   And the initiated bear witness, who delight in the members of the Bridegroom."

"He[1] called that 'the day of espousals, and the day of the gladness of the heart.' For on that day was the communion of the marriage. 'For after supper,' he says, 'He took bread, and when He had given thanks, He brake it, and gave it to His disciples, saying, Take, eat ye all of it, for This is My Body, Which is broken for you unto remission of sins. Do this in remembrance of me.' They therefore that eat the members of the Bridegroom, and drink His Blood, obtain the nuptial Communion with Him."

"To[2] us the Life-giving Cross hath become the tree of life. For it hath received as a kind of fruit the Life-giving Body, to which those who stretch forth their hands, and partake of the Fruit, live eternal life."

"If[3] in company with such, we ought not to partake of common food, much less of the Mystic and Divine."

"Do[4] not we, enjoying the holy mysteries, communicate with the Lord Himself, Whose Body and Blood we say they are? For we all are partakers of that one Bread."

[1] Ib. c. iii. fin. ii. 89.   [2] In Esai. lxv. 22 ; ii. 397.
[3] In 1 Cor. v. 11 ; iii. 194.   [4] In 1 Cor. x. 16 ; iii. 228.

"How[5] can we communicate with the Lord through His Precious Body and Blood, and again with devils through meat offered to idols?"

"He[6] called to their remembrance that sacred and all-holy night, in which He both put an end to the typical Passover, and showed the Archetype of the type, and opened the doors of the saving mystery, and not to the eleven Apostles only, but to the traitor also, He imparted His Precious Body and Blood. He teacheth them how they may ever enjoy the good things of that night. 'For as oft as ye do eat this Bread and drink this Cup, ye do show the Lord's death till He come.' For after His coming, there will be no more need of the *symbols* of His Body, since His Body Itself will appear."

"'Whosoever'[7] therefore shall eat this Bread, or drink this Blood of the Lord unworthily, shall be guilty of the Body and Blood of the Lord.' Here he pricketh the ambitious, he pricketh the fornicator, and with these he pricketh those who without distinction were partakers of things offered to idols. In addition to these, us also, who with an evil conscience dare to partake the holy Mysteries. But 'he shall be guilty of the Body and Blood,' showeth this, that like as Judas betrayed Him, and the Jews insulted Him, so they dishonour Him, who receive His All-holy Body with impure hands, and bear It to their defiled mouth."

[5] On v. 21, p. 229.   [6] Ib. xi. 23, pp. 237, 238.
[7] Ib. v. 27, p. 238.

"But [8] let us who have received the benefit here-from, flee whatever injureth faith; let us diligently consider the poor, and purifying our consciences beforehand, let us so partake of the Divine Mysteries, that we may receive the Good Lord as our Indweller, to whom with the Father and Holy Ghost, be glory and honour, now and ever, and to endless ages. Amen."

"Things [9] present, he says, are shadows of the things to come. For in All-holy Baptism, we see the type of the Resurrection, but then we shall see the Resurrection itself. Here we behold the *symbols* of the Lord's Body; there we shall see the Lord Himself. For this is ' Face to face.' But we see, not His invisible nature, which is invisible to all, but that which was taken of us."

"' Even [1] as Christ the Church.' Nourishing it and cherishing it and giving it His Own Body and Blood. ' For we are members of His Body, of His Flesh, and of His Bones.' For as Eve was formed from Adam, so we from the Lord Christ; for we are buried with Him in Baptism, and rise again with Him, and eat His Body and drink His Blood."

"He [2] calls the Lord's Flesh the veil. For through This do we attain an entrance into the Holy of Holies. For as the high-priest according to the law used to enter into the Holy of Holies, and he could

[8] Vers. Ult. pp. 239, 240.   [9] Ib. xiii. 12, p. 255.
[1] In Eph. v. 25, pp. 434, 435.
[2] Epist. ad Heb. c. x. p. 608.

not enter in any other way; so they who have believed in the Lord shall, through the participation of His All-holy Body, enjoy the citizenship of Heaven."

"The [3] chiefs of this heresy [the Messalian] were Dadoes, &c., who did not withdraw from the Communion of the Church, saying that neither profit nor harm came from the Divine Food. Whereof the Lord Christ said, 'Whoso eateth My Flesh, and drinketh My Blood, shall live for ever.'"

Theodoret also quotes *Eusebius Emesenus*, who explains S. John vi. of the Holy Eucharist, in connexion with the words of the Institution. Eusebius is showing that what belongs to the Human Nature of our Lord may be said of His Divine, on account of their Union (the 'communicatio idiomatum'). In proving this, Eusebius argues that the word "Bread" in S. John vi. meant His Flesh, because it is so used in the institution of the Holy Eucharist.

"The [4] Lord saith, 'the Bread of God came down from Heaven;' and, interpreting, (although I cannot speak more clearly on account of the Mysteries,) says as much as that 'it is My Flesh.' Did the Flesh of the Son come down from Heaven? It did not come down from Heaven. How then does He say, 'The Bread of God liveth, and hath come down from Heaven;' and that, when interpreting? Since the

[3] E. H. iv. 10, p. 965.
[4] Impat. as quoted in App. pp. 259, 260.

Power having taken it came down from Heaven, that which the Power hath, is reckoned to the Flesh."

71. Theodotus, Bishop of Ancyra.

In the Council of Ephesus, A.D. 431, he took a prominent part against Nestorius, against whom he also wrote.

" He [5] Who then drew the Magi with unspeakable might to holiness, hath now also to-day gathered together this joyous assembly; He, no longer laid in the manger, but lying on this saving Table. For that manger was the mother of this Table. For that cause did He lie in that [manger], that on this [Table] He might be eaten, and might to the faithful become saving Food.

72. S. Peter Chrysologus.

Educated holily by a holy Bishop Cornelius, who was a father to him; consecrated by him to the priesthood (Serm. 165); led still an ascetic life (Serm. 107, see Tillemont, H. E. Art. S. Pierre Chrysol. note 2); Bishop of Ravenna some time before Council of Ephesus, A.D. 431 (Ib. note 4); appealed to by the heretic Eutyches against judgment of Flavian, as one of the chief bishops of the West, A.D. 449; died before A.D. 457. People flocked from all quarters to learn of him (see Tillemont).

" Christ [6] ever speaketh what concerneth ourselves, our own selves, yea, what will profit all of us. To correct *us*, doth the Lord multiply mystic examples in parables; for He would be the Father of His ser-

---

[5] Hom. in Nativ. Dom. in Conc. Eph. p. 3, c. 9, iii. 1526, ed. Col.

[6] Serm. 2, de Prodig. Filio, B. P. vii. 847.

vants; He would be loved rather than feared; He Himself is the Bread of life, and hath poured out His own Blood into the Cup of salvation."

"The[7] woman touched His Raiment, and was healed, and was freed from her long weakness. Wretched we, who daily handle and receive the Body of the Lord, and are not healed of our wounds. Not Christ is lacking to us sick, but faith. For much more could He, now abiding[8] in us, heal the wounded, Who thus passing by healed the woman concealing herself."

"O[9] what did that woman see dwelling in the Christ, within, who saw the whole virtue of Divinity indwelling in the hem of Christ! O how did the woman teach, how great is the Body of Christ, who showed that there is so much in the hem of Christ! Let Christians, who daily touch the Body of Christ, hear how much medicine they can take from the Body Itself, when the woman seized all her health from the hem only of Christ. But, (which we must bewail,) the woman bore away medicine from her very wound; to *us* the medicine itself is distorted into a wound. Hence it is that the Apostle in such wise admonishes and bewails those who touch unworthily the Body of Christ, saying, 'Whoso touches unworthily the Body of Christ, receives to himself judg-

---

[7] Serm. 33, p. 871.

[8] I have corrected "in nobis manens" for "manentes," as required by the antithesis with "præteriens."

[9] Serm. 34, p. 872.

ment.' And that such boldness derives weakness thence, whence faith should receive strength, he again urged, 'For this cause many are weak and sickly among you, and many sleep.'"

"Let [1] no one suppose that Zacchæus, by offering half his goods, did not attain the height of perfection: who afterwards so gave himself and his all to the Lord, that, supported by the honour of the Episcopate, he passed from the Table of publican gain to the Table of the Lord's Body; and, leaving the deceitful wealth of the world, he found the true riches of the world in the poverty of Christ."

"He [2] bids us seek this, which He forbids us to take thought for, inasmuch as the heavenly Father encourages us, His heavenly children, to ask for heavenly bread, He Himself said, 'I am the Bread, Which came down from Heaven.' Himself is the Bread, Which sown in the Virgin, leavened in the Flesh, kneaded in His Passion, baked in the furnace of the sepulchre, laid up in Churches, placed on the Altars, provides heavenly Food daily for the faithful."

"'Give [3] us this day our daily bread.' After the kingdom of heaven, who would ask for temporal bread? But daily and every day He would have us ask for bread for our journey in the Sacrament of His Body; that by it we may attain unto endless

[1] Serm. 54, fin. p. 887.   [2] Serm. 67, p. 899.
[3] Serm. 68, ib.

day, and to the table of Christ Himself, that from Him, from Whom we have here received a taste, we may there receive fulness and perfect satiety."

"'Give' us this day our daily bread.' After the kingdom of heaven, we are not bidden to ask for earthly bread. Himself forbids it, when He says, 'Take no thought what ye shall eat or what ye shall drink.' But since Himself is 'the Bread which came down from Heaven,' we seek and pray that the very Bread whereby we shall daily, *i. e.* continuously live in eternity, we may this day, *i. e.* in the present life, receive from the Feast of the Holy Altar for the strengthening of body and mind."

"He [5] added, 'Give us this day our daily bread. After the Fatherhood of God, after the hallowing of the Divine Name, after the kingdom of heaven, we are bidden to ask for ' daily bread.' Christ forgetteth not ; Christ commandeth not the contrary to His Own commands ; Himself said, 'Take no thought for your life, what ye shall eat, or what ye shall drink.' But because He is Himself the Bread Which cometh down from Heaven, Which through the millstone of the law and grace was formed into flour, Which was kneaded by the Passion of the Cross, Which was leavened in the Sacrament of great goodness, Which bore from the tomb the light dough, to lighten [our sorrows] [6]; Which, that It might be baked in the heat

---

[4] Serm. 70, p. 901.   [5] Serm. 71, p. 902.

[6] " Levamentum levis conspersionis." The word " conspersio " is from 1 Cor. v. 7.

of Its Divinity, Itself burnt away the oven of hell; Which is daily brought to the Table of the Church for heavenly Food; Which is broken for the forgiveness of sins, Which feeds and nourishes them Who eat It to life everlasting: this Bread we daily ask to be given to us, until we enjoy It wholly in that endless day."

"We[7] call 'daily' constant; for our constant Bread is He, Who came down from Heaven. 'I am the Bread, Which came down from Heaven.' The perfection then of bliss, 'this day,' *i.e.* in the present life, is to live already on the Food of that Bread, of that Bread, by Whose endless store, because It is 'daily,' we shall be satisfied for ever."

"He[8] asked the Lord, 'to eat bread with him.' Thou askest, Pharisee, to eat with Him; believe, be a Christian, and thou eatest of Him. 'I,' He says, 'am the Bread Which came down from Heaven.' God ever giveth more than He is asked. For if He gave Himself to be eaten, Who was asked to permit that one might have boldness to eat with Him, and yet so gave this, as not to refuse what He was asked, doth He not promise this, and of His own accord to His Disciples: 'Ye who have continued with Me, shall eat and drink at My Table in My Kingdom?' Christian, He Who has given Himself to thee to eat here, what of His can He deny thee hereafter? And He Who has prepared

[7] Serm. 73, p. 903.   [8] Serm. 95, p. 920.

for thee so great Food for the way, what will He not prepare for thee in that endless home? 'Ye shall eat at My Table in My Kingdom.' Thou hast heard, it is the Feast of God; be not anxious as to the quality of that Feast. He who is admitted to a King's Table, will eat whatsoever the dominion and power of the realm possesseth! So he who shall have come to the Feast of the Creator, will have for his enjoyment whatever is contained in creation. But to return. And 'He went into the Pharisee's house.' What house? He went into the Synagogue and sat down. In the Synagogue, Brethren, Christ then sat down, when He set[9]. But He transmitted His Body to the Table of the Church, that It might be heavenly Flesh for the nations to eat unto salvation. 'Except ye eat the Flesh of the Son of Man, and drink His Blood, ye have no life in you.' But how the Flesh of Christ is eaten, how too His Blood is drunk, they know who have been admitted to the heavenly sacraments."

"I grieve[1], truly do I grieve, when I see that the Magi poured gold around the cradle of Christ, and I see that Christians have left empty the Altar of the Body of Christ."

"The[2] Baptism of Christ so regenerates, so changes, so makes a man new from being old, that he knows not things past, recollects not former things;

---

[9] "Accubuit, quando occubuit."   [1] Serm. 103, p. 927.
[2] Serm. 137, p. 951.

being for earthly, heavenly, he already possesseth things heavenly and divine. Hence is it, that to the son returning from 'riotous living' the Father restores the 'first robe' of Immortality, He puts on him the ring of liberty, He kills the 'fatted Calf,' He turns the waters of penitence into the wine of grace, that now cups of pure wine may satisfy the Feast of grace; so that the sober inebriation of the Lord's Cup may efface the pangs of conscience, the groans of penitence, the lamentations of sinners. As the Prophet saith, 'Thine inebriating Cup, how excellent it is!' "

73. S. Proclus, Bishop of Constantinople.

"A Reader when very young, frequented the schools, studied rhetoric. When grown up, secretary to Atticus, much with him, transcribed his discourses; imitated his goodness, but was more tolerant" (Socr. vii. 41); nominated Bishop by Theodosius, A.D. 434 (Ib. c. 40); died A.D. 447. "A holy man, diligent in opposing those who taught error; habitually successful in maintaining the truth." (S. Cyril. Ep. ad Joann. Ant. et Syn. in Conc. Eph. P. 3, c. 44, T. iii. p. 1728, ed. Col.) Quintianus, Bishop of Askelon, A.D. 484, relates the celebrated revelation to S. Proclus, that he should pray the Trisagion, during the earthquake at Constantinople, and how on their so praying the earthquake ceased. (Ep. ad Pet. Full. in Conc. Rom. i. A.D. 483, Conc. v. 225.)

"The ³ Festival of the Sacred Mysteries is at

³ Orat. x. init. 655. In the Orat. viii. in Dom. Transf. § 2 (Ib. p. 650), there is the expression, " If Christ were to leave us here, [as S. Peter said, 'Lord, it is good for us to be here,'] why did He ἐκοινώνησεν ἡμῖν αἵματος καὶ σαρκός ?" But I believe this is best rendered, "Why did He share with us in Flesh and

hand; the evening, brighter than any day, hath dawned. For in this present evening what took not place, of wonder and of awe? The Lord supped with the servants; He opened to them the paradise of the mysteries; He gave as food the sinless Flesh; as the sponge of sins He gave the Cup."

"Let [4] us all shun covetousness; let us cast forth, with avarice, hypocrisy also; let us embrace one another heartily, now that we are about to approach the Divine Mysteries; let us cast away all anger, let us cleanse ourselves from all malice; that our Lord, when He entereth our souls, may not find any full of hypocrisy, like Judas; but may find all pure, like John, declaring with faith the Mystery of the Bosom of the Father; like Paul, crucified to the world; like Peter, piously proclaiming, 'Thou art the Christ the Son of the Living God;' that so we may attain the blessing of the Lord."

"Of [5] old, my brethren, by the law the Mystery of the Passover was mystically celebrated in Egypt; but symbolically represented, through the slaughter of the lamb. But now through the Gospel, we spiritually celebrate the Paschal Feast of the Resurrection. For there a lamb of the flock was sacrificed according to the law; here, Christ Himself, the Lamb of God, is offered. There a sheep of the fold; here, instead of a sheep, 'the Good Shepherd Him-

Blood?" *i.e.* why should He become incarnate? This Gallandi prefers, supposing S. Proclus to refer to Heb. ii. 14.

    [4] Ib. § 4, p. 657.   [5] Or. xiv. § 2, pp. 663, 664.

self, Who layeth down His Life for His sheep.' There, the sign of the sprinkling of the blood of a brute beast became a preservative of all the people; here, the precious Blood of Christ is poured forth for the salvation of the world, that we may obtain remission of our sins. There he slew the first-born of Egypt; here, the manifold brood of our sins are destroyed through confession[6]. There Pharaoh with his fearful army was drowned; here the spiritual Pharaoh with all his force is drowned through Baptism. There the children of the Hebrews, after they passed the Red Sea, sang a hymn of victory to their Benefactor, saying, 'Sing unto the Lord, for He hath triumphed gloriously;' here they that have been accounted worthy of Baptism, sing the song of victory, saying in the Mysteries, 'One[7] Holy; one Lord Jesus Christ, in the Glory of God the Father. Amen.' But the Prophet crieth aloud, saying, 'The Lord is King, and hath put on glorious apparel.' The Hebrews after passing the Red Sea, did eat manna in the wilderness; now, they who come from the Laver eat ' the Bread Which came down from Heaven.' For His is the Voice Which saith, ' I am the Bread, Which came down from Heaven.' "

"Painters[8] represent him [the sun] riding in a

---

[6] ἐξομολογήσεως. The whole course of public penitence. (See Note L, on Tertullian, p. 370, Oxf. Tr.)

[7] The Choir in the Liturgy of S. Chrysostom p. ξθ. ed. Ven.

[8] Or. 17, §§ 1, 2, p. 669.

chariot, Divines herald him [the Sun of righteous-
ness] reclining in a manger, a manger representing
Heaven; a manger, likened to the Cherubim; a
manger, compared to the ineffable Throne; a manger,
enfolding the spiritual Food; a manger, which received
the Life of the universe; a manger, bearing Him
Who beareth all things; a manger, wider than all
creation together. For Him Whom creation containeth not, the manger, through grace, contained.
A manger, pointed out by a star whose course was all
day long; a manger, pourtraying in itself the Altar;
a manger, which made the cave a Church.

"Come then, let us too rival these devout Magi,
and consider the Church in the place of Bethlehem;
instead of the cave, let us embrace the Sacerdotal
Sanctuary; instead of the manger, let us fall down
before the Altar; instead of the Babe, let us embrace
the Bread blessed through the Babe."

· "After [9] our Saviour's Ascension into Heaven, the
Apostles, before they were dispersed through the
whole world, being assembled with one accord, gave
themselves all day to prayer; and finding the Mystical
consecration of the Lord's Body a comfort to them,
they sang it at very great length. For this, and the
office of teaching, they considered the most important
of all things. Much more with gladness of heart
and greatest joy did they continue stedfastly in so
divine a Sacrifice, ever mindful of the word of the

---

[9] Tract de tradit. Liturg. Div. pp. 680, 681.

Lord, 'This is My Body,' and, 'Do this in remembrance of Me.'   And, 'He that eateth My Flesh and drinketh My Blood, dwelleth in Me, and I in him.' Wherefore also with contrite spirit they chanted many prayers, entreating earnestly the Deity.   Nay, further, accustoming the newly-enlightened, both of the Jews and Gentiles, to the Mysteries of grace, and teaching them to leave off the things before grace, being but a shadow of grace, they instructed them holily.   By such prayers then they looked for the descent of the Holy Ghost, that by His Divine Presence, He might make and declare the Bread offered for Sacrifice, and the wine mingled with water, that very Body and Blood of our Saviour Jesus Christ; Which takes place no less even until now, and shall take place unto the end of the world."

74. SEDULIUS.

Studied philosophy, as a layman, in Italy; afterwards a Presbyter, lived under Valentinian and Theodosius.   "The Opus Paschale of the venerable man Sedulius, which he wrote in heroic verse, we extol with great praise." (Roman Council of seventy Bishops, A.D. 494.   Conc. v. 388, ed. Col.)   See further, Galland. Art. Sedulius, T. ix. c. 20, p. xxxv.

" Who [1], by a better sweetness of Food, restorest man perishing through sweetness of the forbidden apple, and with the Drink of consecrated [2] Blood expellest the poison infused by the serpent."

[1] Op. Pasch. L. i. B. P. vi. p. 460, D.
[2] " Immaculate" prose version. (c. 2. Ib. p. 473.)

" Nor [3] did his plots escape the Lord, Who showed him to be the author of the yet future guilt; to whom Himself gave bread, He the Bread Who was to be betrayed. For after He had consecrated the two gifts of His Body and Blood, and gave them as Food and Drink, through Whose perpetual supply faithful souls without spot might never hunger or thirst, forthwith into Judas, where envy had its abode, that foulest spirit entered."

75. S. Leo the Great.

Perhaps Acolyte at Rome, A.D. 418; Deacon under Pope Celestin; induced Cassian to write on the Incarnation against Nestorius, A.D. 430; was employed to pacify divisions in Roman army in Gaul, A.D. 439, and so elected Bishop of Rome while absent, A. D. 440; coincided, on fuller knowledge, in S. Flavian's condemnation of Eutyches, to which he had, on report, demurred; in Roman Synod, annulled the Robber-Council of Ephesus; his Epistle to S. Flavian was accepted as exposition of faith by Council of Chalcedon, A.D. 451, as agreeing with that of the three General Councils before it; went, at Valentinian's desire, to intercede with Attila, A.D. 452, induced him to spare Italy; mitigated Genseric, when Rome was taken, A.D. 455; laboured with others to uphold the faith in Alexandria against Timothy the Cat.; died, A.D. 461.

" Our [4] Lord Jesus Christ, most beloved, is present

---

[3] Ib. L. iv. init. p. 469. In Sedulius' prose, Ib. p. 489. " After the Lord Jesus Christ had consecrated the gifts of life of His Body and Blood, and had given to His disciples the spiritual food and drink, whereby, enriched with the Heavenly Feast, souls, now faithful, could not again feel hunger and thirst, there entered into the heart of Judas, &c."

[4] Serm. 5 (de Nat. Ips. v.), c. 3, p. 21, ed. Ball.

(as we confess not rashly, but faithfully) in the midst of the faithful; and although He sitteth at the Right Hand of God the Father, 'until He make His enemies His footstool,' yet is not the great High Priest absent from the assembly of His Priests, and rightly is it sung to Him by the mouth of all His Priests, and the whole Church, 'The Lord sware, and will not repent: Thou art a Priest for ever after the order of Melchisedec.'   For Himself is the true and eternal Bishop, Whose office can have neither change nor end.   Himself it is, Whose likeness Melchisedec set forth, offering to God not Jewish sacrifices, but the Sacrifice of that Sacrament, Which our Redeemer consecrated in His Body and Blood."

"They[5] [the Manichees] shrink from the Sacrament of man's salvation, and believe not that Christ our Lord was in true flesh of our nature truly born, that He truly suffered, was truly buried, and truly raised again.   And for this reason they condemn, by the sadness of their fast, the day of our rejoicing. And when, in order to conceal their infidelity, they venture to be present at our assemblies, they so compromise with themselves in the Communion of the Sacrament, as sometimes, lest they should not be able entirely to escape notice, to receive with unworthy mouth the Body of Christ, but the Blood of our Redemption they altogether refuse to drink."

"Hence[6] thou wast of all men, O Judas, the most

---

[5] Scrm. 42 [Quadr. 4], c. 5, p. 161, ed. Ball.
[6] Serm. 54 [de Pass. 3], p. 205.

wicked and the most miserable. For repentance did
not call thee back to the Lord, but despair dragged
thee to the halter. Thou shouldst have awaited the
consummation of thy crime, deferred that foul death
of hanging, until the Blood of Christ should be shed
for all sinners. And while so many miracles of the
Lord, so many gifts, were torturing thy conscience,
those Sacraments at least should have called thee
back from casting thyself headlong, which, in the
Paschal Supper, thou, already detected in thy per-
fidy by the token of Divine Knowledge, hadst still
received. Why distrust His goodness, Who repelled
thee not from the Communion of His own Body and
Blood ?"

" That[7] the shadows then might give place to the
Body, and images cease under the presence of the
truth, the old observance is taken away by the new
Sacrament, sacrifice passes into Sacrifice, blood is
taken away by Blood, and the legal festivity is at
once changed and completed."

" Jesus[8], stedfast in His design, and unshaken in
the work appointed by the Father, consummated the
Old Testament, and founded the new Passover. For
when His disciples sat down with Him to eat the
Mystic Passover, while those in the hall of Caiaphas
were debating how Christ might be put to death,
He, ordaining the Sacrament of His Body and Blood,

---

[7] Serm. 58 [de Pass. 7], § 1, fin. p. 219.
[8] Ib. § 4, p. 220.

was teaching, what sort of Sacrifice should be offered to God, nor did He remove even the traitor from this Mystery; that so it might appear that *he* was not exasperated by any injury, whose impiety was foreknown."

"Through [9] this translation, from circumcision to uncircumcision, from carnal sons to spiritual sons, the propitiation of the Immaculate Lamb, and the fulness of all Sacraments, hath passed over [to us]. ' For Christ, our Passover,' as saith the Apostle, ' is sacrificed for us :' Who, offering Himself to the Father a new and true Sacrifice of Reconciliation, not in the temple, whose reverence was now at an end, nor within the bounds of the city which in reward of its guilt was to be destroyed, but without and out of the camp was crucified, that so, the mystery of the old victims ceasing, a new Sacrifice might be laid upon a new Altar, and the Cross of Christ be the Altar, not of the temple, but of the world."

"This [10] it is [the mercy of God in Christ], whereby the Passover of the Lord is lawfully celebrated in the unleavened bread of sincerity and truth: when, the leaven of the old malice being cast away, the new creature is inebriated and fed from the Lord Himself.   For nought else doth the participation of the Body and Blood of Christ effect, save that we pass over into That which we receive; and Him in

[9] Serm. 59 [de Pass. 8], c. 5, p. 227.
[10] Serm. 63 [de Pass. 12], fin. p. 247.

Whom we died, and were buried and rose again, Himself we bear through all things both in Flesh and Spirit, as the Apostle saith: 'For ye are dead, and your life is hid with Christ in God. When Christ, Who is your Life, shall appear, then shall ye also appear with Him in glory.'"

In the three following passages, S. Leo argues against the Eutychians, (as others [1] before him,) from the truth of the Real Presence in the Holy Eucharist to the truth of the Incarnation.

"Since [2] the Lord says, 'Except ye eat the Flesh of the Son of Man, and drink His Blood, ye have no life in you,' ye ought so to communicate of the holy Table, as to doubt nothing of the truth of the Body [3] and Blood of Christ. For by the mouth is received what by faith is believed; and vainly is Amen answered by them, who dispute against what they receive."

"If [4] he receives the Christian faith, and does not turn away his ear from the preaching of the Gospel; let him see what Nature, transfixed with nails, hung on the wood of the Cross, and the Side of the Crucified having been laid open by the soldier's lance, let him understand Whence flowed the Blood and Water, that the Church of God might be bedewed both by the Laver and the Cup."

[1] See above, p. 85, and the whole of Note G.
[2] Serm. 91 [de Jejun. 7 mens. 6], fin. pp. 355, 356.
[3] *i. e.* of the Incarnation, as the Eutychians did.
[4] Ep. 28 ad Flavian. c. 5, pp. 829—831. This is the celebrated Tome which was received by the Council of Chalcedon.

"Out [5] of the gift of Divine grace, and out of the Sacrament of man's Salvation, are they to be considered, who, denying the Nature of our flesh in Christ, both contradict the Gospel, and fight against the Creed. Nor do they perceive that they are borne by their blindness to this precipice, so as to stand fast in the truth neither of the Lord's Passion, nor of His Resurrection. For both are made void in the Saviour, if He is not believed to have in Him Flesh of our race. In what darkness of ignorance, in what torpor of sloth have those men hitherto lain! So that they neither learn by hearing, nor understand by reading, what in the Church of God is so concordantly in the mouth of all, that not even by tongues of babes is the truth of the Body and Blood of Christ in the Sacrament of the Communion passed over in silence. For in that Mystic distribution of spiritual nourishment, This is imparted, This is taken ; that we, receiving the virtue of the heavenly Food, may pass into His Flesh, Who was made Flesh of us."

"In [6] the Church of God, which is the Body of Christ, neither are the priestly offices valid, nor the Sacrifices true, except the true High Priest in our own proper nature reconcile us, the true Blood of the Immaculate Lamb cleanse us. Who, though He is set at the Right Hand of the Father, yet in the same Flesh, Which He took of the Virgin, is

---

[5] Ep. 59 ad Cler. et Pleb. Const. § 2, pp. 6, 7.
[6] Ep. 80 ad Anatol. § 2, p. 1040.

the Sacrament of Propitiation wrought, as saith the Apostle, 'Christ Jesus, Who died, yea rather, Who is risen, Who is set on the Right Hand of God, Who also maketh intercession for us.'"

76. SALVIAN.

"A Presbyter of the Church of Marseilles, well furnished with Divine and human literature, a teacher of Bishops. He wrote many homilies for Bishops, and several on the Sacraments" [which are lost]. (Gennad. de Virr. Ill.) He finished his work, de Gubernat. Dei, A.D. 440, when Genseric took Carthage; and was yet alive "in a good old age" when Gennadius finished his de Virr. Ill. between A.D. 492—496. Praised by Hilary of Arles, and for "holiness, eloquence, and knowledge," by Eucherius.

"The' Jews of old had a shadow of things, we the truth; the Jews were slaves, we, adopted sons; the Jews received a yoke, we, freedom; the Jews, curses, we, grace; the Jews, the letter that killeth, we, the Spirit that giveth life; to the Jews a servant was sent to be their master, to us, the Son; the Jews passed through the sea to the wilderness, we by Baptism enter the kingdom; the Jews did eat manna, we, Christ; the Jews, the flesh of birds, we the Body of God; the Jews, 'hoar-frost' from heaven, we, the God of heaven: Who, being, as the Apostle saith, in the form of God, humbled Himself even unto death, even the death of the Cross; not content merely to suffer death for us,

' Adv. Avarit. L. ii. p. 246, ed. Baluz.

without adding to that voluntary undertaking of death, the endurance of the extremest tortures."

77. S. Nilus.

A disciple of S. Chrysostom; of noble birth, so that he was made Prefect of Constantinople, his native city, under Theodosius the younger. "Being in great affluence and power, he exchanged them for an ascetic life" (Niceph. Call. H. E. xiv. 54); wrote to the Emperor Arcadius to expostulate with him as to the banishment of S. Chrysostom.

"A leaf of paper [8] made of papyrus and size, is called mere [ψιλὸς] paper: but when it receives the signature of the Emperor, it is (as is well known) called Sacra. So conceive with me also of the Divine Mysteries, that before the intercession of the Priest and the descent of the Holy Ghost, the oblations are *mere* (ψιλὸν) bread and *common* (κοινὸν) wine: but that, after those dread invocations and the coming of the Adorable, Good, and Life-giving Spirit, the Oblations, laid on the holy Table, are no more *mere* (ψιλὸν) bread and *common* (κοινὸν) wine, but the Precious and Immaculate Body and Blood of Christ, the God of all, 'purifying from all iniquity' those who communicate with fear and great longing."

"The [9] faithful, winged by understanding and knowledge, fly upon the immaculate and saving patins, and eat the Bread Which came down from Heaven and giveth us eternal life."

[8] Ep. i. 44, ad Phil. Schol. p. 21, ed. Rom.
[9] L. i. Ep. 78, ad Ruffin. p. 34.

"They[1] who are diligent to in purifying their own souls, will not only abound in spiritual 'bread and water,' but will also attain to Flesh. For 'strong meat is for the perfect,' as the Apostle saith. And Moses proclaims to the people, 'Sanctify yourselves against to-morrow, and eat flesh;' meaning by the flesh the Divine Body, (as, accordingly, the faithful in the Church eat It,) and the most blessed knowledge of Christians, which passeth all knowledge."

"Well[2] did the great Moses say this also, 'Not to-day, but to-morrow ye shall eat flesh:' that he might point out the times after the Coming of Christ, God and Lord of all. For that flesh of quails fell out to the Hebrews for wrath, and colic, and destruction, and cholera; but our most blessed Flesh giveth strength, and power and growth, and joy and life everlasting, to all who are accounted worthy to partake thereof."

"Why[3] dost thou marvel if the good servants of Christ, purifying themselves by fear of God and faith and good works, obtain Flesh eternal and incorruptible? For they shall also have the Divine Wine plenteously.—For having overpassed the 'flood' of unbelief, they drink sobering wine, and are inebriated, as David saith, 'My Cup runneth over.'"

"Thou[4] sayest that that is an obscure saying,

---

[1] L. i. Ep. 99, ad Silv. Ep. pp. 42, 43.
[2] Ib. Ep. 100, ad eundem, p. 43.
[3] Ep. 101, ad eundem, ib.
[4] L. ii. Ep. 144, ad Pamphil. p. 186.

'Give not to the ungodly the food of the just.' The letter hath then another interpretation also; this do thou now receive. The Food and Nourishment and Clothing of all the faithful, is the Saviour Christ. For in Him we were created, and 'live and move and are.' Since then the Lord's Body, and the Blood of God the Word is, through the dispensation, the Food of all Christians, and by this Mystery are they fed and It they drink, it would be misplaced for an ungodly and deceitful man (as Simon Magus, who pretended to believe), to partake of that Mystery."—"Again you asked me how one should understand the saying of Solomon, ' Be not deceived by the fulness of the belly.' For, we should not partake, thou Christ-loving soul, as though of *common* (κοινοῦ) bread and wine to the filling of the belly, of that dread and desired Table in the Church; but a small portion is given to us by those who minister to God, and we, gazing stedfastly on high with the eyes of our soul, receive, to the cleansing of transgressions, and the obtaining of holiness and salvation."

"Unless [5] Christ the God of all, and God our Benefactor, having truly died, truly rose from the dead, vain is our faith, vainly do we eat the Mystic Body and drink the Blood to our own cleansing, that we may declare not only the Death, and Burial, but also the Resurrection, and Glory, and Unending Kingdom of Christ."

[5] Ib. Ep. 233, ad Dometian. p. 239.

"The[6] luminary of the great Church in Byzantium, or rather of the whole world, John[7], that wondrous priest, having a clear gift of sight, often saw the Lord's House, at almost every hour, not lacking the guardianship of Angels, nor wholly deserted by them; but chiefly at the time of the Divine and Unbloody Sacrifice. Filled therefore with amazement and joy, he related the matter privately to the truest of his spiritual friends. 'When,' he said, 'the Priest began to make the sacred Oblation, suddenly very many of the blessed Powers, coming down from Heaven, clothed in raiment of exceeding brightness, with bare foot, stedfast gaze, and face bent down, compassing the Altar with reverence and great quiet and silence, stand by until the consummation of the dread Mystery. Then dispersed hither and thither over the whole holy House, co-operating, each of them, with the Bishops, Priests, and all the Deacons there present, who were administering the Body and venerable Blood, they aided and strengthened them. These things I write that ye, learning the awfulness of the Divine Liturgy, may neither yourselves be relaxed, regardless of the fear of God, nor suffer any others to converse, or to whisper during the Oblation; nor nod in a bold way, or restlessly to shift from that grave posture, nor to look about hither and thither, nor roll about, relaxedly and vulgarly. For the Lord saith to Moses,

---

[6] Ib. Ep. 294, ad Anast. p. 266.   [7] S. Chrysostom.

and by him to Priests: 'Sanctify the sons of Israel, and make them not despisers.' "

" Let[8] us not approach to that Mystic Bread, as to *mere bread* (ψιλῷ ἄρτῳ). For It is the Flesh of God ; Flesh Venerable, and Adorable, and Life-giving. For It quickens men dead in sins. But *common Flesh* (σάρξ κοινὴ) could not give life to the soul. This has Christ the Lord said in the Gospel, 'The flesh,' *i. e. common* and *mere* flesh (κοινὴ καὶ ψιλὴ), 'profiteth nothing.' We then participating in the Blood and Flesh of God the Word, with blessing and longing, inherit eternal life. For he who eats and drinks with upright heart is pronounced blessed."

" It is[9] impossible for the faithful to be saved and to obtain remission of his sins, and to attain the heavenly kingdom, save by partaking with fear and longing of the Mystic and Immaculate Body and Blood of Christ God."

" Abstain[10] from all corruption, and become daily a partaker of the Mystic Supper; for so the Body of Christ begins to become ours."

The following extract from a Commentary on the Canticles, compiled out of S. Gregory of Nyssa, S. Nilus, and S. Maximus, is probably S. Nilus'. It is not S. Gregory's.

---

[8] L. iii. Ep. 39, ad Cyr. Mon. pp. 322, 323.

[9] L. Ep. iii. 280, ad Orig. p. 435.

[10] Paraenesis 120, Bibl. Pat. T. vii. p. 1149. This is only in Latin, as far as I know ; but I have found the Latin translation in the Bibl. Pat. correct, when I have compared it with the Greek.

"For[1] he calleth God the Word 'wine which gladdeneth the hearts' of those who partake of it, and translateth them to Divinity. 'The house of wine' [Cant. ii. 4] is the Flesh taken by Him, into which house the Church is brought, to be one flesh with Christ; as the Apostle saith, 'they twain shall be one flesh; I say it of Christ and the Church.' For the Church of the faithful, partaking of the Body and Blood of Christ, and becoming concorporate with Him, and as to knowledge, learning through the Angels the doctrine of the Incarnation, and in holy life displaying their conversation, entereth into 'the house of wine,' 'being made an habitation of God in the Holy Spirit.'"

78. S. Prosper.

A layman of Aquitaine; a disciple of S. Augustine, through his writings, although unknown to him by face; wrote (A.D. 428) to inform him of the objections raised to his teaching by the Semi-Pelagian Presbyters at Marseilles; defended S. Augustine in his Carmen de Ingratis, Resp. ad Capit. Gall., Resp. ad Capit. Obj., Vincent, &c.; wrote against Cassian, A.D. 432; went with S. Leo to Rome, A.D. 440. Gennadius, although siding with Cassian against S. Prosper, says, " The Epistles of S. Leo on the Incarnation of Christ, written against Eutyches to divers persons, are said to have been dictated by him" (de Virr. Ill. c. 84). This seems utterly incredible. The style is so wholly S. Leo's. Yet S. Leo may have consulted S. Prosper, as Pope

---

[1] Comment. in Cant. e S. Greg. Nyss., S. Nil., and S. Maxim. in Gall. vi. p. 661.

Damasus did S. Jerome. S. Prosper was spoken of as alive A.D. 463. See further his life prefixed to his works.

"The[2] first man had received the bread of the Word in the law of the Commandment, but taking the forbidden food, he forgot that Bread from Whom he lived; and thence, 'his heart was withered like grass.' Let him then now revive, and eat the Bread which he had forgotten, which is now in the Body of Him Who says, 'I am the Living Bread, Which came down from Heaven.'"

"The[3] merciful Lord will give the Food of virtue and of life, that is, that incorruptible 'Bread, Which came down from Heaven,' that the Word of God might be the Food of men, as It is the Bread of Angels."

"By[4] the 'poor' are meant those of whom it is said, 'Blessed are the poor in spirit,' and, 'Blessed are they that hunger and thirst after righteousness; for they shall be filled:' that is, with the Food of grace and bread of righteousness, that they may eat Him, Who says, 'I am the Bread, Which came down from Heaven.'"

"He Himself[5] as 'the Word made Flesh,' is the Bread of men; Who, by descending to us, made for us, through us, an ascent to Himself through Himself; and by drinking the Cup of our infirmity, made us taste the Cup of His might, that we might know and confess, 'how sweet the Lord is.'"

[2] In Ps. 101, 5, p. 202.   [3] In Ps. 110, 4, p. 224.
[4] In Ps. 131, 15, p. 254.   [5] In Ps. 134, 1, p. 255.

" ' Who [6] giveth food to all Flesh?' This is the Food, whereof the Lord saith, ' My Flesh is true Meat,' Which is given to all nations. For no one of the faithful regenerate is debarred from eating It."

" A [7] great safeguard is it to be fed with the sacred Food, if no crimes weigh down the heart of the receiver; for he doubles to himself the burden of his sins, who receives what is good, shuns not what is evil."

79. *African author of the work "On the Promises and Predictions of God," among S. Prosper's works.*

The writer says of himself, that, as a young man, he was present when Aurelius consecrated, as a Christian Church, the great temple of the Goddess Cœlestis. This was in consequence of an Edict, A.D. 399, giving the idol-temples to the Church. The writer speaks, in that place, of Aurelius, as " *now* a citizen of his heavenly country." (P. 3. Prom. 38.) Aurelius is said to have died A.D. 426. Another event he dates, " in our times, Asper being Consul," *i.e.* 434. (Dim. temp. c. 6.) He wrote the close of the third part of his work under Valentinian III. after the death of Placidia, and so between A.D. 450—455. The work has been ascribed to S. Prosper, and even to S. Leo.

" To [8] us in this famine, our Joseph, Christ the Lord, ministers, out of His garners, the Divine Provision of His Body, which we tasting, see how good the Lord is."

---

[6] In Ps. 135, 25, p. 259.   [7] Epigr. 72, p. 354.
[8] On the type of Joseph. de Prom. et Præd. Dei, 1, 29, App. S. Prosper. p. 77, ed. Bass.

" When [9] all the bread was spent which they had taken with them out of Egypt, the people murmuring, required of Moses bread, longing also for the flesh pots of Egypt. But Moses, that mediator, quickly obtained for them of the Lord bread and flesh. The people is bidden to receive bread in the morning, flesh in the evening. But these things were figures of us. For first the people received that holy bread to eat which came down from Heaven; afterwards, the Flesh of Christ, prepared in His Passion, whereof the Lord Himself saith, 'Except ye eat the Flesh of the Son of Man, ye have no life in you.'—But this same people again murmured against Moses in the wilderness for water to drink. When Moses asked, the Lord said unto him, 'I will stand before thee upon the rock in Horeb, and thou shalt smite the rock, and there shall come water out of it, that the people may drink.' And so it came to pass. And David testifieth, 'He clave the rocks in the wilderness, and gave them drink as out of the great depths.' What this rock was, the Apostle Paul explaineth, attributing to Christ the Lord all that was then done in a mystery; he says, 'All our fathers were under the cloud, &c. For they drank of the Spiritual Rock that followed them, and that Rock was Christ.' This Rock also satisfying us, saith, ' Whoso drinketh of the water that I shall give Him shall never thirst;

[9] Ib. c. 39, p. 83.

but it shall be in him a well of water welling up into everlasting life.' This rock smitten on the Cross, shed forth Blood and Water, whereby we are in soberness inebriated."

"The[1] Table and Altar placed, to receive the holy Flesh and that of the Sacrificer; what else do we understand by these, than the Cross whereon our Lamb was sacrificed? Himself Priest and Victim, affirming the Sanctified Bread [to be] His Consecrated Body, on His Own Table."

"He[2] took this from the mouth of the dead lion, Who, when casting aside the Jews, ministered the law itself even to the Gentiles. And eating that Body of our most mighty Judge Christ the Lord, he says, 'How sweet are Thy Words unto my throat, yea, sweeter than honey to my mouth!'"

"For[3] His thirsty body there flowed Blood and Water from His Side, as from a cleft, whereby every Christian soul being satisfied says, 'He leadeth me beside the waters of comfort; He restoreth my soul.'"

"That[4] to the same Elias, settled in the desert, the ravens by Divine command brought bread in the morning, and flesh in the evening, has been shown to be a figure of the whole Body of the Lord, when the Jews, as ravens, ministered to the Gentiles first bread in the law, afterwards the Flesh of the Lord's

---

[1] L. ii. c. 2, fin. p. 88.
[2] On the type of Samson, ib. c. 21, p. 100.
[3] On the water gushing out at Lehi, ib. 22, p. 101.
[4] Ib. c. 28, p. 107.

Passion. . . . Like these birds then, the Jews, preparing for the Gentiles the flesh from the wood of the Cross, cried out to Pilate, like ravens, with one hoarse voice, 'Crucify, crucify.' This Flesh *they* eat, who hear him say, 'Except ye eat the Flesh of the Son of Man and drink IIis Blood, ye have no life in you.' Yet here too 'for the three times and half a time' designated by the three years and six months (as we have mentioned above), the heavenly rain is, by the deep judgment of God, denied to those who, not eating His Flesh, nor redeemed by drinking His Blood, are found aliens from His Body.   .

This writer also relates a history, "which," he says, "what inhabitant of that country knows not of?" in which one possessed was delivered through reception of the Holy Eucharist. He mentions the sin, for which a young Arab girl, who had the garb of a consecrated virgin, was seized. For seventy nights and days she took no food, and being brought to the priest, and inclosed in a monastery, yet still for fourteen days took no food. This writer thus relates the issue, which, he says, took place at Carthage, and was known to all in that country.

"The⁵ Sacrifice being completed, when she, with the other women, received of the priest a small particle of the Lord's Body dipped [in the consecrated wine], after chewing It for half an hour, she could

---

⁵ Dimid. Temp. c. 6, p. 135.

not swallow It, since *he* was not as yet put to flight, of whom the Apostle saith, 'What fellowship hath Christ with Belial?' And again, 'Ye cannot drink the Cup of the Lord, and the cup of devils. Ye cannot be partakers of the Lord's Table, and of the table of devils.' The priest therefore holding her head with his hand, that she might not cast out the holy Thing, it was suggested by a certain deacon, that the Bishop should put the Saving Cup to her mouth. When this was done, the Devil, at the command of the Saviour, immediately left that place which he had held, and the girl cried out, praising the Redeemer, that she had swallowed the Sacrament which she had in her mouth."

80. Basil of Seleucia.

He was present at the Council of Constantinople, A.D. 448, and joined in condemning Eutyches; was induced by Dioscorus in the Latrocinium of Ephesus to condemn S. Flavian, and anathematize those who believed the two Natures in Christ; was deposed on that ground in the first session of the Council of Chalcedon; restored in the fourth; lived A.D. 458, when he wrote to the Emperor Leo from his synod in Isauria (Cave).

" What[6] kind of vessel was the Mother of God? who contained, not manna like the golden pot, but contained in her womb the heavenly Bread, Which is given for Food and strengthening to the faithful."

81. Zacchæus, *i. e.* probably Evagrius, and if so,

---

[6] Orat. 39, p. 218.

about A.D. 420 or 423; in any case early in the fifth century.

The writer of the work Consultationes Zacchæi Christiani et Apollonii Philosophi has been identified with the writer of the Altercatio inter Theophilum Christianum et Simonem Judæum, on the ground of the similarity of form and style. The Dialogue with the Jew has been supposed to be a fourth book, appended to the three books of the Dialogue with the Philosopher. The title *Altercatio* is in several MSS. given to the Consultatio also. But Gennadius (de Virr. Ill. c. 50) ascribes the Dialogue with the Jew to a second Evagrius, not Evagrius Monachus; and adds, the work "is known to almost all."

The absence of any mention of the later heresies has been alleged as a proof that the author lived early in the fifth century. He refers to the great writers before him as authorities (ii. 1). The style is supposed to be African. See further, D'Achery Spicil. i. p. 2, and De la Barre's additions, in Gallandi, T. i. x. Proleg. c. vi.

" If' any one, O Zacchæus, can either by words render worthy thanks to God for the benefits conferred on him by His mercy, or understand it in His mind,—I, most of all, ought to discharge this duty of confession and understanding, who, by His Inspiration and thy teaching, extricated from so great meshes of errors, have laid aside the chains of death; and 'having put off the earthly man,' have, by adoption, passed into the hope of the heavenly joys of God: having moreover been made partaker of the eternal Sacrifice, yea, by receiving God, made a part of Him, I ought, with the whole power of my mind,

' Consult. L. ii. Præf. in Gall. T. ix. p. 223.

both to seek out what is healthful and to destroy what is amiss."

82. *The Author of the work entitled Prædestinatus, a Pelagian.*

Sirmondi, who edited the work under this name, ascribed it to Arnobius Junior, whom Cave placed A.D. 461. The writer seems to have lived just before the heresy of Eutyches, since he speaks of the condemnation of Nestorius (A.D. 431) as past history, and does not mention that of Eutyches, but proceeds to that of the Prædestinati, which was his chief object. His idea of preventing grace is altogether Pelagian. See further in Gallandi Bibl. P., T. x. Proleg. c. ix.

"Of[8] our own will we sacrifice to God, and of our own will we confess. Sacrifice, whereby we are redeemed by the Blood of Christ, and are bedewed by the water from His Side; confession, whereby we, confessing our error, again obtain pardon of our sins."

"Ye[9] say of this which we have already received, 'Hope, which is seen, is not hope.' Our whole hope seems to consist in the sanctification of baptism. Therefore 'hope that is seen, is not hope.' In the anointing of the chrism of Christ, we see the foundation of our hope. Therefore 'hope that is seen is not hope.' We see the Body of Christ, our hope. Therefore 'hope that is seen is not hope.' We look to the Blood of Christ, our Redemption. Therefore 'hope that is seen is not hope.' Ye have made

---

[8] Cont. Hæres. Prædest. L. iii. c. 7, T. x. p. 388, Gall.

[9] Ib. c. 25, p. 398.

void the Sacraments, ye have emptied out the Mysteries."

" Look [1] for another Body of Christ, another Blood of Christ. For ye idly say, that that [Baptism] is not in deed but in hope."

" Suppose [2] one, before the enlightening of Baptism, to have presumed upon the Body of the Lord : will not that man be damned for presuming upon that which is good? For that which, bestowed in due order, confers salvation upon some, that causes damnation to others, when received out of order, out of time."

I have now, as I could in the space of time which seemed open to me, before this fundamental doctrine might be disputed before a legal tribunal, gone through every writer who in his extant works speaks of the Holy Eucharist, from the time when S. John the Evangelist was translated to his Lord, to the date of the Fourth General Council, A.D. 451, a period of three centuries and a half. I have suppressed nothing; I have not knowingly omitted any thing; I have given every passage, as far as in me lay, with so much of the context, as was necessary for the clear exhibition of its meaning. Of course, in writers of whom we have such large remains, as S. Augustine and S. Chrysostom, or in some with whom I am less familiar, I may have

[1] Ib. c. 26. [2] Ib. c. 31, p. 399.

overlooked particular passages. Yet the extracts
are already so large, so clear, and so certain, that
any additional evidence could only have coincided
with what has been already produced. Albertinus
did his utmost on the Calvinistic side. His strength
lies in his arguments against a physical doctrine of
Transubstantiation ; his weakness, in the paradox
which he strangely maintains, that the Fathers did
not believe a real Objective Presence. In so doing,
he treats the Fathers, as others of his school have
treated Holy Scripture on the other Sacrament.
When his school would disparage the doctrine of
Baptism, they select passages from Holy Scripture,
in which it is not speaking of that Sacrament. In
like way, Albertinus gains the appearance of citing
the Fathers on the orthodox side (as he calls it), *i.e.*
the disbelief of the Real Presence, by quoting them
when they are not speaking of the Holy Eucharist,
but, *e. g.*, of the Presence of our Lord's Human
Nature in Heaven, or the absence of His Visible
Presence upon earth ; of the natural properties of
bodies ; or of spiritual, as distinct from sacramental
Communion ; or of the Eucharistic and outward Symbols, under which the Sacramental Presence is conveyed. Supported, as he thinks, by these, he proceeds
to explain away, as he best may, the clear and distinct
passages which had hitherto been alleged from the
Fathers, in proof of the Doctrine of the Real
Presence. Yet the very diligence of Albertinus on
the one side, or of Roman Catholic controversialists

on the other, obviously gives the more security, that nothing can have been overlooked, which could seem to support either side.

In the present collection, I have adduced the Fathers, not as original authorities, but as witnesses to the meaning of Holy Scripture. I have alleged them on the old, although now, on both sides, neglected rule, that what was taught "every where, at all times, by all," must have been taught to the whole Church by the inspired Apostles themselves. The Apostles planted; they watered; they appointed others to take their ministry, to teach as they had themselves taught from God. An universal suppression of the truths which the Apostles taught, and the unmarked substitution of falsehood, is a theory which contradicts human reason, no less than it does our Lord's promise to His Church. There is no room here for any alleged corruption. The earliest Fathers, S. Ignatius, S. Justin Martyr, S. Irenæus, S. Clement of Alexandria, Tertullian, or S. Hippolytus, state the doctrine of the Real Presence as distinctly as any later father.

And now, reader, if you have got thus far, review for a moment, from what variety of minds, as of countries, this evidence is collected. Minds, the most simple or the most philosophical; the female martyrs of Persia, or what are known as the philosophic fathers; minds wholly practical, as Tertullian or S. Cyprian, S. Firmilian, S. Pacian or S. Julius, or those boldly imaginative, as Origen, or poetic minds, as S. Ephrem, or S. Isaac, or S. Paulinus; fathers who most use a figurative and typical interpretation of the Old Testament, as S. Ambrose, or such as, like S. Chrysostom, from their practical character and the exigencies of the Churches in which they preached, confined themselves the most scrupulously to the letter; mystical writers, as S. Macarius, or ascetics, as Mark the Hermit, or Apollo, or the Abbot Esaias; writers in other respects opposed to each other; the friends of Origen, as S. Didymus, or his opponents, as Theophilus of Alexandria and S. Epiphanius; or again, S. Cyril of Alexandria or Theodoret; heretics or defenders of the faith, as Eusebius and Theodorus Heracleotes, Arians, or S. Athanasius; Apollinarius or S. Chrysostom, who wrote against him, Nestorius or S. Cyril of Alexandria,—all agree in one consentient exposition of our Lord's words, "This is My Body, This is My Blood." Whence this harmony, but that One Spirit attuned all the various minds in the one body into one; so that the very heretics were slow herein to depart from it?

There is a difference ofttimes in the setting, so to speak, of the one jewel of truth. We may meet with that truth, where *we* should not have expected it; some may even be deterred here and there, by the mystical interpretations of Holy Scripture, amid which he finds it. That mystical interpretation is no matter of faith. But, a mode of interpretation, which presupposes any object of belief to be alluded to, when scarce any thing is mentioned which may recall it to the mind, shows at least how deeply that belief is stamped upon the soul. It is a common saying, how " Bishop Horne found our Lord Jesus Christ every where in the Psalms, Grotius no where." Certainly our Lord must have been much in Bishop Horne's heart, that every thing in the Psalms spoke to his soul of Him. So much the more, then, must our Lord's Gift of His Body and Blood have been in the hearts of the early Fathers, that words which would not suggest the thought of them to others, spoke of It to them.

But, however different the occasions may be, upon which the truth is spoken of, in whatever variety of ways it may be mentioned, the truth itself is one and the same, one uniform, simple, consentient truth; that what is consecrated upon the Altars for us to receive, what, under the outward elements is there present for us to receive, is the Body and Blood of Christ; by receiving which, the faithful in the Lord's Supper do verily and indeed take and receive the Body and Blood of Christ; by presuming to approach which, the wicked (*i.e.* those who with impenitent hearts wilfully purpose to persevere in deadly sin, and yet venture to "take that Holy Sacrament [3]") become guilty of the Body and Blood

[3] " Therefore if any of you be a blasphemer of God, an hinderer or slanderer of His Word, an adulterer, or be in malice, or envy, or in any other grievous crime, repent you of your sins, or else come not to that holy Table, lest, after the taking of that

of the Lord ; *i.e.* become guilty of a guilt like theirs who laid hands on His Divine Person, while yet in the Flesh among us, or who shed His All-Holy Blood [*].

Now, we have been accustomed to value Ante-Nicene Testimonies to the Divinity of our Lord; we are struck when S. Cyprian (while deciding as to the Baptism of infants on the eighth day) lays down the doctrine of the transmission of original sin, as clearly as S. Augustine amid the Pelagian controversy.

Yet the principle of these quotations is one and the same. The argument is valid for all or for none. Either it is of no use to show that Christians, before the Council of Nice, did uniformly believe in the Divinity of our Lord, as the Church has since ; or it *is* a confirmation of the Faith, that they did receive unhesitatingly in their literal sense our Blessed Lord's words, "This is My Body."

This argument from the consent of those who had handed down the truth before them, was employed as soon as there were authorities which could be alleged. So rooted was the persuasion, that the certain truth must have been known to those who received the faith from the first, that even heretics

holy Sacrament, the devil enter into you, as he entered into Judas, and fill you full of all iniquities, and bring you to destruction both of body and soul." (First Exhortation in the Prayer Book.)

[*] See S. Chrysostom above, pp. 558. 560. 588, and elsewhere.

resorted to the argument, and garbled or misrepresented the fathers before them, in order to bring them to some seeming agreement with themselves. The argument was used by minds in other respects of a different mould. Theodoret and S. Leo appended to works on controversial points of faith, citations from the fathers before them. S. Augustine vindicated against Pelagius, and S. Athanasius against Arius, authorities which they had misrepresented. Even the fathers, assembled from the whole world in General Councils, have, in proof of their decisions wherein all were agreed, alleged the authorities of yet older fathers, who were known, in previous ages, to have handed down the Apostolic truth.

Yes! along the whole course of time, throughout the whole circuit of the Christian world, from East and West, from North and South, there floated up to Christ our Lord one harmony of praise. Unbroken as yet, lived on the miracle of the Day of Pentecost, when the Holy Spirit from on high swept over the discordant strings of human tongues and thoughts, of hearts and creeds, and blended all their varying notes into one holy unison of truth. From Syria and Palestine and Armenia; from Asia Minor and Greece; from Thrace and Italy; from Gaul and Spain; from Africa Proper, and Egypt, and Arabia, and the Isles of the Sea; wherever any Apostle had taught, wherever any Martyr had sealed with his blood the testimony of Jesus; from the polished cities, or the Anchorites of the desert, one Eucharistic voice ascended; "Righteous art Thou, O Lord, and all Thy words are truth." Thou hast said, "This is My Body," "This is My Blood." Hast Thou said, and shalt not Thou do it? As Thou hast said, so we believe.

Truly, O Lord, "Thy holy Church throughout all the world doth acknowledge Thee."

Thursday in
Holy Week, 1855.

Thanks be to God.

GILBERT AND RIVINGTON, PRINTERS, ST. JOHN'S SQUARE, LONDON.